Ibn Khallikan

Ibn Khallikan's Biographical Dictionary

Translated from the Arabic by Bn. Mac Guckin De Slane

Ibn Khallikan

Ibn Khallikan's Biographical Dictionary
Translated from the Arabic by Bn. Mac Guckin De Slane

ISBN/EAN: 9783741176401

Manufactured in Europe, USA, Canada, Australia, Japa

Cover: Foto ©Andreas Hilbeck / pixelio.de

Manufactured and distributed by brebook publishing software
(www.brebook.com)

Ibn Khallikan

Ibn Khallikan's Biographical Dictionary

IBN KHALLIKAN'S

BIOGRAPHICAL DICTIONARY.

VOL. IV

PARIS. — PRINTED BY ÉDOUARD BLOT,
7, Rue Biot, 7.

* كـــتــاب وفـــيـــات لأعـــيــان *

IBN KHALLIKAN'S

BIOGRAPHICAL DICTIONARY

TRANSLATED FROM THE ARABIC

BY

D* MAC GUCKIN DE SLANE,

MEMBER OF THE FRENCH INSTITUTE, ACADÉMIE DES INSCRIPTIONS ET BELLES-LETTRES, ETC.

VOL. IV.

PARIS,

PRINTED FOR THE

ORIENTAL TRANSLATION FUND OF GREAT BRITAIN AND IRELAND.

MDCCCLXXI.

LIFE OF IBN KHALLIKAN

On the left bank of the Tigris, opposite to the southern part of the province of Mosul, lies an extensive territory, bounded, on the north, by the greater Zab, on the east by the chain of mountains which separates that part of the Ottoman empire from Persia, on the south by a line which may be supposed to have extended from the town of Kefri to the Tigris, and, on the west, by the waters of that river. Arbela, the capital of this region, lies at the distance of twenty hours, or leagues, to the N. N. E. of Mosul.

During upwards of forty years, from A. H. 587 (A. D. 1191) to A. H. 630 (A. D. 1233), the principality of Arbela was governed by a brother-in-law of the sultan Saláh ad-Dín (Saladin), and enjoyed, under that chieftain's sway, a period of continual prosperity (a). His name was *Kükubúri*, an alteration of the words *Ghúik-Búri*, which, in the Jaghatái dialect of the Turkish language, mean *the blue wolf*. The titles by which he was generally designated, in conformity to the custom of the age, were *al-Malek al-Moazzam Muzaffar ad-Dín* (the exalted prince, the triumphant in religion). His father, Ali Ibn Bektikín (*the valorous boy*), was a feudatory prince who had faithfully served the celebrated Núr ad-Dín, and whose

---

(a) See Ibn Khallikan's *Biographical Dictionary*, vol. II, page 536 of my.

usual titles were *Ali Kutchek Zain ad-Din* (little Ali, the ornament of religion). Kô-kubôri took an active share in the wars carried on by the sultan Salâh ad-Din against the Crusaders, and Arabic historians remark that, in every battle with the enemy, his standard always came off victorious. Appointed by Salâh ad-Din to the government of the city and province of Arbela, he reigned over that little state in the character of an independant sovereign, and consecrated the revenues of the country to the foundation of mosques, schools, hospitals, asylums for the blind, for widows, for orphans and for foundlings. The second volume of the present work, page 535 *et seq.* contains a long and interesting description of the institutions and practices by which Kûkubôri displayed the ardour of his zeal for the Moslim faith. Doctors of the law, literary men and students found in him a generous protector; to his well-directed patronage it was that Ibn Khallikân, the author of this biographical dictionary, was indebted for his education.

It is worthy of remark that the province of Mosul, on the opposite side of the Tigris, was governed, nearly at the same time, by a prince who rivalled in talent and beneficence with the sovereign of Arbela. *Badr ad-Din Lâlâ al-Malik ar-Rahim* (Lâlû, the full moon of religion, the clement prince), such were his name and titles, was the patron and friend of Izz ad-Din Ibn al-Athir, and to his encouragement we owe that historian's excellent book of annals bearing the title of the *Kâmil*.

The family called the Bani Khallikân drew its descent from Jaafar Ibn Yahya Ibn Khâlid the Barmekide, and held a distinguished place in Arbela. It derived its name from the father of the great grand-father of our historian. M. de Sacy in the third volume of his *Chrestomathie Arabe*, 2nd edition, page 538, says that the name of *Khallikân* does not occur in the genealogy of the family, but the list to which he himself refers, that given by Tydeman in his *Conspectus*, and another furnished by Abû'l-Mahâsin, in his *Manhal*, life of Ibn Khallikân, do really contain it. The *Tabakât al-Fukahâ*, MS. of the Bib. Nat. ancien fonds, no 755, fol. 144 *verso*, and the *Tabakât ash-Shafiyin*, ancien fonds, no 861, fol. 72, insert also the name of *Khallikân* in the genealogy of our author.

Great uncertainty prevails respecting the prononciation of the word here transcribed *Khallikân*, it being written in Arabic *Khlkân* (خلكان), with the omission of the short vowels and of the sign which redoubles the letters; but the form adopted throughout this work is probably the true one.

Our biographer bore the ethnic surname of *al-Barmaki* (the descendant of Barmek). Effectively, the family of which he was a member drew its origin from the celebrated Yahya, the son of Khálid, and the grand son of Barmek. That genealogy has come down to us in three complete copies, one of them by the anonymous author of the biographical notice inserted by Tydeman in his *Conspectus*, another by the manuscrit of the Bib. Nat. *fonds Saint-Germain*, no 83, and the third, by Abû'l-Mahâsin in his *Manhal* (b).

The Khallikân family were greatly favoured and protected by Kûkubûri and by Ibn Bektikin, that prince's father. " Our family," says the author of this biographical dictionary (c), " was under such obligations to Muzaffar ad-Dîn Kûkubûri " that, to repay even a part of them, our utmost efforts would be vain. The " benefits and favours conferred by him on us, and by his forefathers on ours, " were boundless." In another place he mentions that his father, Muhammad Ibn Ibrahîm, was professor in the college founded at Arbela by al-Malik al-Moazzam Muzaffar ad-Dîn, meaning Kûkubûri, and that he continued to teach till the hour of his death. That event took place on the 21st of Shaabân, A. H. 610 (5th January, A. D. 1214) (d). The author was then in the second year of his age, for he informs us that he was born at Arbela, in the college founded by Kûkubûri, on the 11th of the latter Rabî, A. H. 608 (22nd September, A. D. 1211) (e). This indication proves that his father was lodged in the college, probably by special favour. His mother, whose name we are unable to give, was a descendant of Khalaf Ibn Aiyûb, one of the imâm Abû Hanîfa's disciples (f). Of his brother, named Dîn ad-Dîn Isa, we only know that, towards A. H. 626 (A. D. 1228-9), he went to study at Aleppo under Bahâ ad-Dîn Ibn Shaddâd, the au-

(b) This biographical notice we have given in vol. I, page VIII of the Introduction.

(c) *Biog. Dict.*, vol. II, page 541.

(d) *Ibid.*, vol. I, page 91.

(e) *Ibid.*, vol. I, page 681.

(f) So says Abû 'l-Mahâsin in his *al-Manhal as-Safi*. See the Introduction to the first volume of this translation, page IX. An article on Ibn Aiyûb will be found in the *Tabakât el-Fakahâ*, MS. of the Bibliothèque nationale, supplément arabe, n° 889, fol. 97, verso. — Some of the indications given here and further on are taken from notes collected by the translator in former years and may, perhaps, not be precisely exact. To verify them now, May, 1871, is impossible, the manuscripts from which they were borrowed and which belong to the Bib. nat., having been removed to a place of safety, where they are to lie as long as Paris remains in its present unsettled state.

thor of the life of Salâh ad-Dîn (g), and that he was probably the elder son. We
may suppose he was about sixteen years of age.

Before our author had completed his second year, he received the first ele-
ments of instruction from his father; even in that year, he obtained from
a very learned lady, Zainab, the daughter of as-Shari and one of the celebrated
Zamakhshari's pupils, a licence certifying that he had learned perfectly well some
texts which she had taught him (h). It would be of little importance were we to
insert here the names of the teachers from whom he took lessons in his early
youth; one of these professors may, however, be noticed. His surname was
Sharaf ad-Dîn; his family was that of the Banû Manâ, a distinguished house which
produced a number of learned men (i). "When a boy," says Ibn Khallikân (j), "I attended his lessons. — He was the best of men, and when I think
" of him, the world is of little value in my eyes."

He continued to reside at Arbela for some years. He was there in A. H. 618
(A. D. 1221-2), when an attempt was made on the life of Ibn al-Mostauû (k).
At the age of thirteen, he heard al-Bokhari's Sahîh explained by the sheikh Mo-
hammad Ibn Hibat Allah as-Sûfi (l). In the year 623 (A. D. 1226), he saw
Ibn Onain at Arbela, whither that poet had been sent on a political mission (m).
Between the years 618 and 626 (A. D. 1221-1228), he went more than ten times
from Arbela to Mosul, where Dîâ ad-Dîn Ibn al-Athîr, the brother of the historian, was residing: " I tried" said he, " to get introduced to him (n), because
" I knew that he had been the intimate friend of my father, and I wished to
" study something under his tuition. I did not, however, succeed in my pro-
" ject." In A. H. 625 (A. D. 1227-8), he left his native place, with the intention of continuing his studies at Aleppo.

(g) Biog. Dict., vol. II, page 445, vol. IV, p. 489. — For the life of Bahâ ad Dîn Ibn Shaddâd, consult
vol. IV, page 417 et seq.; a very interesting article but, as usual with our author, badly drawn up.

(h) Biog. Dict., vol. I, page 381.

(i) Ibid., vol. IV, pages 397, 398.

(j) Ibid., vol. I, page 91.

(k) Ibid., vol. II, page 549.

(l) Ibid., vol. II, page 171.

(m) Ibid., vol. III, page 177.

(n) Ibid., vol. III, page 348.

The north of Syria formed, at that time, a principality the capital of which was Aleppo. The sovereign, al-Malik az-Zâhir (الملك الظاهر), who was one of Salâh ad-Dîn's sons, had taken for vizir and privy-counsellor the kadi Abû 'l-Mahâsin Yûsuf, surnamed familiarly Ibn Shaddâd and generally known by the title of Bahâ ad-Dîn (*splendor of religion*). This statesman had been one of Salâh ad-Dîn's ministers and secretaries; at a later period he wrote the life of that sultan, the same work of which Albert Schultens has given us an edition under the title of *Vita et res gestæ Saladini, auctore Bohadino Ibn Sjeddad*: " There were but few " colleges (or *high schools*) in Aleppo till Bahâ ad-Dîn went there (o), and lear- " ned men were very rare. Abû 'l-Mahâsin (*Bahâ ad-Dîn*) was therefore induced " to reorganize these institutions and provide them with teachers learned in the " law." During his life a great number of colleges were thus established." He founded also a college at his own expense and a school for the teaching of the Traditions concerning the Prophet (p). " When Aleppo, " says our au- thor (q), " was brought into this (prosperous) state, legists arrived there from " all quarters, studies became active and the number of persons who went to " the city was very great. A close intimacy, a sincere and friendly attachment, " subsisted between my deceased father and the kâdi Abû 'l-Mahâsin (*Bahâ ad-* " *Dîn*), from the time in which they were fellow-students at Mosul. My brother " went to study under him, a very short time before my arrival there, and a letter " of recommendation, drawn up in the strongest terms, was sent to him (*Bahâ* " *ad-Dîn*) by (*Âkubâri*,) the sovereign of our city. In this missive he said: " ' You know what is necessary to be done with these boys; they are the sons " ' of one who was to me as a brother and who was also as a brother to you. I " ' need not add any stronger recommendation.' "

It was towards the end of the month of Ramadân, 626 (about the 20th of Au- gust, A. D. 1229) that Ibn Khallikân left Arbela. On reaching Mosul, he went to visit one of the most learned men of the age, the celebrated legist, divine and mathematician, Kamâl ad-Dîn Ibn Mani, of whom he afterwards wrote a biogra- phical notice. " I went frequently to see him, " said he (r) " on account of the

(o) *Ibid.*, vol. IV, page 448.
(p) *Ibid.*, vol. IV, page 421.
(q) *Ibid.*, loco laudato.
(r) *Ibid.*, vol. III, page 467.

" close and intimate friendship which existed between him and my deceased
" father; but I had not an opportunity of receiving lessons from him, because
" I could not make any stay (in *Mosul*) and was obliged to hurry off to Syria."
In the month of Shauwál, 625 (August-September, A. D. 1229), Ibn Khallikán
passed into the province which, at that time, was called *as-Sharkiya* (the oriental,*),
and then proceded from Harrán (t) to Aleppo, where he arrived on the first of Zú
'l-Kaada (21st September) of the same year (u).

" The kádi Abú 'l-Mahásin, being very obliging (v), received us most hono-
" rably and treated us as well as he possibly could, just in a manner worthy of
" himself.   He lodged us in his college, inscribed us on the list of those who
" received commons and placed us in the class of the elder boys, though we
" were still very young and merely beginners.   I and my brother remained
" with him till the day of his death (14 Safar, A. H. 632, 8th November, A. D.
" 1234).   During all that time there was not a general course of lectures in the
" college, because the professor, Abú 'l-Mahásin himself, was much advanced in
" years and so very weak that he could hardly move, much less commit his les-
" sons to memory and deliver them.   He therefore confided to four legists of
" merit the duty of going over the lessons with the students, and it was under
" the tuition of these masters that all the school pursued their studies.   I and
" my brother read our lessons under the *shaikh* Jamál ad-Dín Abú Bakr al-
" Mábáni, because he was our townsman and had been a fellow-student of my
" father's.   I then attended the lectures given by the *shaikh* Najm ad-Dín Ibn
" al-Khabbáz in the Saifiya college and read, under his direction, al-Ghazzáli's
" (*law treatise, the*) *Wajíz* from the beginning of the work to the chapter on
" affirmations."

" Aleppo was then filled with learned men and with students.   The gramma-
" rian Muwaffak ad-Dín Ibn as-Sáigh was at that time the chief of the literary
" community and stood in it without a rival.   I began to study under

(s) In some passages of our translation the word *Sharkiya* has b'en erroneously explained by *Irak* and *Mesopotamia*. It designated northern Mesopotamia and Diár Bakr.

(f) *Biog. Dict.*, vol. III, pages 241, 490.

(u) *Ibid.*, vol. IV, pages 29, 844.

(v) *Ibid.*, vol. IV, page 419.

" him; he taught in the great mosque and held his class in the northern *mak-*
" *sûra*. In the interval between the *maghreb* and the *asha* prayers he taught
" in the *Rawdhiya* college. I commenced by Ibn Jinni's *Luma* (اللمع) and read
" to him the greater part of that work, besides which I listened to the lec-
" tures which he addressed to the assembly. This was towards the close
" of the year 627 (Oct.-Nov., A. D. 1230) (*w*)." Ibn Khallikân then bestows
great commendation on this professor. He informs us elsewhere (*x*) that, on
his arrival at Aleppo, he met the historian Ibn al-Athîr, who was residing as
a guest with the *atâbek*, or guardian, of the reigning prince. I was." says
" he, " his constant visitor and, as a close intimacy had subsisted between
" him and my lamented father, he (*Ibn al-Athîr*) received me with the utmost
" regard and kindness. I continued to cultivate his society with unceasing as-
" siduity till he removed to Mosul."

The only information furnished by Ibn Khallikân respecting his early education is that contained in the preceding paragraphs. A manual of jurisprudence
by al-Ghazzâli, a grammatical treatise by Ibn Jinni and the Traditions of al-Bokhâri are the only works which he mentions. But he certainly must have learned by heart the contents of many other books treating of dogmatical and scholastic theology, of the shafeite system of law, of grammar and of philology; such
works or text-books as were then employed in the schools.

In the beginning of the month of Shauwâl, A. H. 632 (10th of June, A. D. 1235),
about seven months after Bahâ ad-Dîn's death, he went to see the professor Ibn
as-Salâh (*y*) at Damascus, and resided with him for a year, which time he passed
in close study. In A. H. 633 he was still in that city (*s*), and two years later,
in the month of Rajab (March, A. D. 1238) he was present in the great mosque
of Damas when the death of the sultan al-Malik al-Kâmil was announced to the
congregation (*a*).

After residing about ten years in Syria, he proceeded to Egypt in the year

(*w*) *Ibid.*, vol. IV, page 160.
(*s*) *Ibid.*, vol. II, page 189.
(*y*) *Biog. Dict.*, vol. II, page 189.
(*s*) *Ibid.*, vol. III, pages 67, 243, and vol. IV, page 571.
(*a*) *Ibid.*, vol. III, page 246.

636 (A. D. 1238-9) (b), five months of which he passed in Alexandria (c). Towards the end of the following year we find him dwelling in Cairo, where he had made the acquaintance of Bahá ad-Dín az-Zubair (d), an eminent literary scholar and secretary of the sultan al-Malik as-Sálih Aiyûb.

We now lose sight of Ibn Khallikân till the year 645 (1247-8), when we find him occupying a seat in the imperial tribunal at Cairo (e). He was then acting as deputy of the kâdi Sinjar, who was chief judge and magistrate of all Egypt (f). There is no need of reproducing here the anecdote related by him, concerning a townsman of his, named Jamál ad-Dín Ibn Abd, as he gives it in the first volume, page 393, of the present work. A short biographical article on Ibn Khallikân, inscribed on the first leaf of the manuscrit n° 83 of the *fonds Saint-Germain*, informs us that he passed from the place of deputy-kadi to that of the kadiship in al-Mahalla (for المحل, read المحلة), probably the Mahalla of Dakla, situated between Cairo and Damietta. Our author states, in his article on Kamál ad-Dín Ibn Maná (g), that, after undergoing many vicissitudes of fortune, he got married and that Mûsa, his eldest son, was born at Cairo, in the month of Safar, 651 (April, A. D. 1253). Three years later he had the pleasure of terminating the first copy of his Biographical Dictionary, which, however, was retouched by him later (h). In the month of Zû 'l-Kaada, 659 (Sept.-Oct., A. D. 1261), he was appointed to act as chief kâdi over all the provinces of Syria. His tribunal was at Damascus, to which city he had accompanied the mamlûk sultan Baibars (i) al-Bondukdâri, who had been raised to the throne of Egypt and Syria the year before. It was to this sovereign that he owed his nomination.

(b) *Ibid.*, vol. III, page 471. The date given in the translation is false, the Arabic cypher ٦ having been taken for ٥.

(c) *Ibid.*, vol. III, page 52.

(d) *Ibid.*, vol. I, page 548.

(e) *Ibid.*, vol. I, page 388. The words مجلس الحكم العزيز are there incorrectly rendered by the council of state.

(f) *Ibid.*, vol. IV, page 149.

(g) *Ibid.*, vol. III, page 478.

(h) *Ibid.*, vol. I, page 5; see also page xviii of the present notice.

(i) In this translation the name of Baibars has been incorrectly transcribed Bîbars. The true pronunciation is indicated in the manuscript of al-Makrîzi's *Sulûk*, where we always find the first letter of this word surmounted with a fatha. That should be, for Bai-bars signifies *the lord*, or *boy*, *leopard*.

Three years later, he ceased to hold under his jurisdiction the followers of the Hanifite, Malikite and Hanbalite sects; each of these communities having received from the same sultan a kâdi of its own class. The Shafites alone remained under our author's judicial authority.

During ten years Ibn Khallikân filled with general approbation the duties of the office conferred upon him, but, towards the end of the year 669 (A. D. 1270-1), he was replaced by Ibn as-Saigh (j). Having no further inducement to remain in the capital of Syria, he returned to Egypt and obtained a professorship in the Fakhriya college; one of those literary institutions which abounded in Cairo (k). He remained in that city during seven years, teaching, giving legal consultations and making biographical researches; but so narrow were the circumstances to which he was reduced that the high treasurer, Badr ad-Din, ordered him an ample donation in money and (a yearly gift of) one hundred bushels of wheat. This generous offer he did not accept (l). Reading of poetry and philological studies seem to have then engaged a considerable portion of his time. None was better acquainted than he with the poems of al-Mutunabbi (m), and if we are to believe a passage extracted from a historical work composed by the shaikh Tâj ad-Dîn al-Fazâri, which passage is inserted in a short notice on Ibn Khallikân given in the List of shafeite doctors, man. n° 861, fol. 72, ancien fonds of the Bib. nat., he could recite from memory the contents of seventeen dîwâns of poetry. In the year 672 (A. D. 1273) we find him discussing a literary question with one of his friends (n). Towards the end of the year 676 he was again nominated chief kâdi of Syria for the shafeite sect, and, in the first month of the following year (May-June, A. D. 1278) he arrived at Damascus. Izz ad-Dîn Aidmor, the governor of that city, accompanied by all the military chiefs and the directors of the civil administration, went out in state to receive him; the principal inhabitants having already gone to meet him at the distance of some days' journey (o).

(j) Al-Makrizi's Soluk, translated in part by Mr Quatremère and published under the title of Histoire des sultans mamlouks, vol. 1, part 8, page 40.

(k) Tydeman's Conspectus, page 11.

(l) Biog. Dict., page XI of the Introduction.

(m) See the anonymous life given by Tydeman in his Conspectus operis Ibn Challicani, page 89, and the Menhal of Abû 'l-Mahâsin, vol. 1 of this translation, page XI of the Introduction.

(n) Ibid., vol. IV, page 135.

(o) Ibid., vol. 1, page 2 of the Introduction; Soluk, vol. 1, 2nd part, page 161.

A few years later, Ibn Khallikân was arrested, and cast into prison. He was accused of having declared by a formal decision that Sonkor al-Ashkar, the emir and governor of Syria, had as good a right to be sultan of that country as Kalavûn had to the throne of Egypt. After the defeat of Sonkor's troops and the occupation of Damascus by the Egyptian army, a number of that emir's partisans were imprisoned by order of the sultan Kalavûn. After a short of time, a letter of amnesty was sent to Damascus by the sultan, and Ibn Khallikân was present at the public reading of that document. The emir Alam ad-Dîn al-Halebi then undertook to plead in his favour: ' A letter, said he, sent by the sultan ' has arrived at Damascus and guarantees the safety of all those who bear it read. ' Ibn Khallikân is one of those persons and therefore cannot incur the penalty of ' death.' The deposition of Ibn Khallikân from the kadiship of Damascus took place on the 21st of Safar (A. H. 679, 22 June, A. D. 1280). On the 24th of the same month he was taken to the Najîbiya Khongah (a dervish monastery) and placed in confinement; but, on the 9th of the first Rabi (9th of July), he was set at liberty in pursuance to a written order sent by the sultan His successor, Ibn Sani ad-Dawla then declared against him and summoned him to leave the Aâdiliya college. On Wednesday, the 19th of the same month, he set a guard over him and treated him rigorously, in order to oblige him to quit that residence. Ibn Khallikân consented to obey and, on the fourth hour of the same day, he commenced removing his books and furniture. Whilst he was thus engaged, a police-guard came in, and he, thinking that the man had been sent for the purpose of hastening his departure, said he was getting ready as quick as he possibly could. Being then informed by the guard that a messenger, sent in post-haste from Egypt, had just arrived, he went to see the governor of the city, thinking that some untoward circumstance had taken place. To his great relief of mind the governor told him that he had received a letter from the sultan, disapproving of Ibn Sani ad-Daula's nomination, in as much as he was deaf, and then containing the following passage : ' We have granted a general pardon to all, from the highest to the lowest, ' and it is not therefore fitting that any single subject of ours should suffer from ' our anger. We know well the high merit of the kadi Shams ad-Dîn Ibn Khal-' likân; we were formerly on terms of intimacy with him, and he has always ' shewn us great respect. Moreover, he is one of those persons who filled public ' offices under the reign of (the ex-sultan) al-Malik as-Sâlih. We have therefore

' decided that he be reinstated in his place.' Ibn Khallikán being then arrayed in a robe of honour by order of the emir Alam ad-Din al-Halabi, proceeded, on horseback, to the Aádiliya College, where he took up his residence at mid-day and resumed his judicial occupations (p).

Ten months later (22nd Moharram, 680, 13th May A. D. 1281), he was again dismissed from office by the sultan Kalavûn and, from that time, he remained in his lodgings at the Najîbiya College, in Damascus (q), and never again went out of doors. He died there on the 16th, or the 26th, of Rajab, A. H. 681 (20th October, or 30th Oct., A. D. 1282), at the age of seventy-three lunar years, and was buried in the cemetery of as-Sâlihiya, a well-known village situated on the declivity of mount Kasiûn, at a very short distance to the north of Damascus (r).

Arabic biographers are profuse in his commendation. They describe him as a pious man, virtuous, and learned; amiable in temper, in conversation serious and instructive. According to them, he possessed every merit which could give illustration to a doctor of the law, to a magistrate and to a man of letters. His exterior was highly prepossessing, his countenance handsome and his manners engaging. We may, perhaps, form a clearer idea of his character and cast of mind by the perusal of his work, the only one he ever produced. There we remark a noble sentiment of humanity, a taste for literature and a great fondness for poetry, particularly that of Moslim times. Pieces composed by the Arabs anteriorly to Mahomet he seems not to have cared for; the more a piece of verse was modern and affected, the more he admired it. As a philologer and a grammarian he certainly displayed extensive acquirements and, as a collector of dates, anecdotes and biographical information, he held a rank to which the ablest of his numerous predecessors never attained. His extensive sphere of literary pursuits furnished him with extracts of great historical interest, and we must feel grateful to him for having preserved and transmitted to us a quantity of passages taken from works now lost, but which were undoubtedly replete with historical and literary information. He

(p) Solîtá, vol. II, first part, page 21. Not having means of consulting the original text, we follow the translation given by Mr Quatremère.

(q) Biog. Dict., vol. I, page X of the Introduction.

(r) Ibid., vol. I, page X of the Introduction; Tydeman's Conspectus, page 65; Tabakât al-Fokahâ, nº 155, fol. 144 verso; Fod. as-Shafyia, nº 881, fol. 73.

was a kind and honorable man, sincerely attached to his friends and a lover of justice; the joy with which the inhabitants of Damascus received him on his restoration to the kadiship of Syria proves in favour of his integrity as a magistrate. Like many of his contemporaries among the learned, he used to compose verses, some of which have come down to us (s). They are not remarkable for merit, the ideas being trite and the style deficient in elevation. One or two of those pieces are, besides, tainted with a sentiment which though openly avowed in the Moslim world, is repugnant even to the Moslim religion. It is true that poems of this description were generally explained as being euphemistic; delicacy requiring that no direct allusion should be made to the female sex. Those verses do not deserve being transcribed or translated; yet some of them have been published, little to the honour of the author (t).

His motives for collecting information respecting eminent men and his reasons for drawing up the Biographical Dictionary in alphabetical order being indicated in his own preface (u), we need not repeat here what he has already said. We shall merely remark that the arrangement adopted by him is of little use to readers who wish to find out the article which concerns any particular individual. It is not every person who whould think of searching for the notice on Abû Hanîfa under the word Nomân, that of al-Ghazzâli amongst the Muhammads and that of Abû Tammâm under Habîb. This defective system prevails in all biographical dictionaries composed by Musulmans and could hardly be replaced by any other; with that people indexes were very seldom thought of (r), and indeed they could be applicable only to the single manuscripts for which they were compiled. Though acknowledging that the author could not have adopted, under the circumstances, a better mode of arrangement for his work, we must declare that his idea was most unfortunate when he decided on omitting the biographical notices of many persons highy eminent, because he was unable

---

(s) See Tydeman's Conspectus, pages 47, 83, 87 et seq.; Biog. Dict., vol. I, page XII; MS. of the Bib. nat., ancien fonds, n° 649, fol. 58 verso; the edition of Bâlâk, vol. II, pages 429 et seq.

(t) Tydeman's Conspectus, pages 79 et seq.

(u) Biog. Dict., vol. I, page 8.

(r) The most remarkable exception which we know of is the Tabakât as-Shâfiyîn or chronological list of eminent Shâfite doctors. This manuscript contains four indexes, one for the names, one for the surnames, one for the patronymics and one for the ethnics.

to ascertain the precise dates of their death. It is true that he considered his work
to be an obituary; but he might have perceived, on further reflection, how much
more useful it would have been, had it contained some information respecting
those persons. The translator has endeavoured to remedy the silence of his
author by giving in the notes such indications as might be requisite, but he
regrets to say that he has not always been successful.

Ibn Khallikán informs us, in his preface (w) that, in the year 654 (A. D. 1256),
being at Cairo, he put his work in order, though taken up by other avocations
and living under circumstances by no means favorable to such a task. In his
first copy he terminated with the life of Yahya Ibn Khálid the Barmekide (x),
preserving a number of articles for another and a more extensive dictionary.
This projected work was to contain ten times as much matter as the preceding
one and furnish ample details relative to certain events which he had slightly
touched on before (y). He perceived however, that it was impossible for him to
fulfil this plan (z); being obliged to pass into Syria and accept the kadiship of Damascus, he was overwhelmed with business to such a degree that no leisure remained for the accomplishment of that task. Ten years later, he returned to
Cairo and, finding there some books requisite for his purpose, he decided on
completing his first work by the addition of about fifty articles, those perhaps
which he had reserved for the second. They belong to the Y, the last letter of
the Arabic alphabet. The articles of this letter which he had already given in
the first edition of his work seem to have received their actual development
for the sole reason that they might obtain a place in the greater work, the execution of which he always hoped to accomplish.

In the preface to the first volume, page VI, we mentioned our intention of giving
here a notice on the *Times of Ibn Khallikán.* Were we however to retrace the
events which occurred in the lifetime of that biographer and give an account of the
state in which the Moslim empire was then placed by a series of revolutions, we
should have to draw up a history of the Crusades and relate the rise and fall of

(w) Biog. Dict., vol. I, page 1.
(x) Ibid., vol. IV, page 158.
(y) Ibid., vol. IV, page 211.
(z) Ibid., vol. IV, page 113.

the dynasty founded by Salâh ad-Dîn. But a subject so extensive would lead us very far and occupy too many pages for a simple introduction. The subject will, however, be treated elsewhere; a work containing all the passages in which upwards of fifty Arabic historians speak of the Crusades being now in the press. The first volume of this publication, undertaken by the Academy of Inscriptions and Belles-Lettres, and placed under the direction of the author of the present notice, will soon appear.

The Arabic text of which these four volumes contain the translation, is represented, for nearly one half, by the first and only volume hitherto published of the edition drawn up by us, after a number of manuscripts, most of them belonging to the *Bibliothèque nationale*(a). For the other half we have followed the typographical edition of Dûlâk and the lithographied edition published at Goettingen by Dr Wuestenfeld; both of them carefully collated by us with the manuscrits just indicated. The Dûlâk edition is merely tolerable; whole phrases are often omitted by the inattention of the compositor or of the corrector, and the proper names, both of men and of places, are frequently inexact. Of geography and history the editor had little or no knowledge. The literary portion of the work is more satisfactory and justifies to a certain degree the high reputation of the editor, Nasr al-Hôrini, as an Arabic scholar; but neither he, nor any another musulman of the present day, is capable of giving a truly *critical* edition of a historical text. The edition of Goettingen offers a number of false readings and omissions resulting from the incorrectness of the manuscrips on the authority of which it was drawn up. When the true readings were not given by these two editions, we followed the text of our manuscripts and inserted the corrections in our translation, enclosing them between crochets.

The first half of the third volume was printed on or about the year 1844. The translator, being then sent, by the French government, to explore the libraries of Constantinople, was under the necessity of suspending the impression of his work. After a residence of eighteen months in that city, he was appointed *interprète principal de l'armée d'Afrique*, and obliged to join his post. Twelve years later, circumstances allowed him to return to Paris, and, at the request

(a) This Edition, bearing the title of *Vie des Hommes illustres de l'Islamisme par Ibn Khallikân, texte arabe*, was published at Paris in the year 1842.

of his lamented friend, the Rev. D' Cureton, dean of Westminster, he undertook
to reprint the first half of the third volume, which had been destroyed by accident, to translate the rest of the work and to get it through the press. Much
delay occurred, but, fortunately, the task is now achieved. Critical readers will
certainly discover in these volumes a great number of faults, some attributable to
the printer, many more to the translator; but, when they consider the difficulty of
rendering into English a work so various in its contents and in its style, so ill
drawn up in some places, so obscure in others, they will treat with indulgence
the conscientious efforts of him who first undertook the rendering of Ibn
Khallikan's Biographical Dictionary into a European language.

IBN KHALLIKAN'S

BIOGRAPHICAL DICTIONARY.

YARUK AT-TURKOMANI

Yàrûk Ibn Arslân at-Turkománi was a chief who had great influence over his people. It was after him that the horde of Turkomans called the Yàrûkiya was thus named. He was of a colossal stature, a formidable aspect, and resided outside of Aleppo, in the country to the south of the city. He, his family and followers built for themselves, on a lofty hill bordering the river Kuwaik, a great number of houses and large edifices which are known by the appellation of al-Yàrûkiya and bear the appearance of a village. He and his people resided there. It is yet inhabited by a numerous population and is frequently visited by the people of Aleppo in the spring season, for the purpose of amusing themselves in its green fields and looking down on the Kuwaik. It is a place of amusement and diversion. Yàrûk died in the month of Muharram, 564 (Oct.-Nov. A.D. 1168); so says Bahâ ad-Dîn Ibn Shaddâd, in the Life of the sultan Salâh ad-Dîn.—The word بارق is to be pronounced Yàrûk. —Kuwaik is the name of a little river which passes near Aleppo; its waters flow abundantly in winter and in spring, but cease to run in summer. Poets have often mentioned it in their verses, Abû Obâda al-Bohtori (vol. III. p. 657) particularly, who has repeatedly spoken of it in his kasîdas. He says, for instance, in one of his pieces :

O ye lightnings! disclose (to my sight) the Kuwaik and the two outskirts of Aleppo! flash over the castle of Batyta! Show me the land of roses tinged with yellow, the land where the myrtle is gathered (*majna*). When I went to that country, it assembled around me (*its delights*) and greatly tranquillised my heart.

Batyda is the name of a village which lay outside of Aleppo, but is now so completely ruined that not a trace of it remains. Sâlih Ibn Ali Ibn Abd Allah Ibn al-Abbâs Ibn Abd al-Muttalib (1) built there a castle which he inhabited and his sons (*after him*). It was situated between an-Nireb and es-Sâlihiya, villages lying near each other and to the east of Aleppo. The castle was built on a hill which commands an-Nireb, but nothing now remains of it except some mouldering ruins. So I find it written in the handwriting of a well-informed native of Aleppo.

(1) This was the father of Abd al-Malik, the Abbaside prince of whom we have spoken in the first volume, page 111.

YAKUT AL-MAUSILI, *THE PENMAN*

The *kâtib* (*secretary or writer*) Abû 'd-Durr (*the father of pearls*) Yâkût (*hyacinth*) al-Mausili (*an inhabitant of Mosul, was*) the son of a Musulman (*abd Allah*). He obtained the title of Amîn ad-Dîn (*trustworthy in religion*) and was surnamed al-Malaki (*the Malakian*) after (*his patron*) the sultan Abû 'l-Fath Malak Shâh II, the son of Saljûk, the son of Muhammad, the son of Malak Shâh I. Having settled at Mosul, he studied with great assiduity under Abû Muhammad Said Ibn al-Mubârak, an Egyptian grammarian who is more generally known by the surname of Ibn ad-Dahhân (*vol. I. p. 574*). He read over, under the tuition of this master, all the works composed by him, as also al-Mutanbbei's *Diwân*, al-Hariri's *Makâmât* and some other treatises. He wrote a great deal and specimens of his penmanship, which was extremely beautiful, spread abroad into (*distant*) countries. In the latter part of his life he remained without a rival in the art of calligraphy. The style of writing employed by) Ibn al-Bawwâb (*vol. II. p. 282*) in the transcription (*of books*), excellent and renowned as it is, does not come up to his. He had a passion for transcribing the *Sahâh* of al-Jauhari (vol. *I. p.* 29) and wrote a great number of them, each copy forming one volume. Some of them, which I have seen, are now sold for one hundred dinars (1) a piece. Numbers of students received from him lessons in writing and profited greatly under his direction. During his lifetime, he enjoyed a high reputation, and people came to study under him from all quarters. An-Najîb Abû Abd Allah al-Husain Ibn Ali Ibn Abi Bakr al-Wâsiti (*of the town of Wâsit*) sent him a *kasîda* which he had composed in his praise; he had never seen him, but only heard of his (*eminent talent*). In this poem, which is a good one of its kind, the author extols, in the highest terms, the beauty of Yâkût's handwriting. Here is the piece :

Where are the gazelles (*maidens*) of Adjî and al-Musalla? those fawns that dwelt near the stream of al-Musalla? Do the branches of the willow (*slender-wristed girls*) still flourish on the sandhills? do full moons (*handsome faces*) still shine in that horizon? Have those gazelles still got faces so beautiful that their aspect would alleviate (*a lover's*) sadness? Compared with these nymphs, what is the tender narcissus which, after sustaining the attacks of the zephyr, erects again its stem? Compared with those cheeks, what is the tint of the rose when the cloud sheds upon it copiously its waters and its dews? Do those hands offer (*to our sight*) starlike oranges, borne on branches which are bent down and brought near (*the hand*)? How could you think that any water could match that of the Tigris? they who judged so uttered a falsehood! it is by no means true; God forbid! Does any city on earth resemble the Abode of Welfare (2)? to find the like of Baghdad would be a miracle. It shows us, each day, faces different from those of yesterday and seemingly pregnant (*with mischief*); (*it shows us*) maidens of whom a sage would become enamoured, were he to see their mincing and coquettish gait. They bind their hair with Nîsirîan ribbons (3) and thus reduce you to bondage (4). They pay no regard to your saying : " Were it not (*that I fear*) .."; they only know (*how to say*) these words: " (*we must have*) the entire (*heart*) or else (*none at all*)." That is a pasture-ground for the hearts (*of lovers*); on the retreat of spring it is always watered by successive showers. That is a city where a man acquires new ideas and gains the summits of learning, of gravity and of gaiety. (*Baghdad,*) to be perfect, requires only the possession of a bracelet (*yelkât*); O that she had it already to adorn her! Who will come to her aid, so that the perfume of Amla ad-Dîn's presence may float around her? that alone would suffice for her pre-eminence. Had she a reason to hope for Yâkût's visit, even speechless things would (*find a tongue and*) exclaim: " A hearty welcome ! " Relators of anecdotes may tell her of the perfume (*which his talent spreads around*), but she would feel much more pleasure at his sight. (*He is*) an ocean of generosity; the noblest of men follow in his steps; for the generous man, when noble deeds are done, has always followers. He unites in himself every scattered portion of knowledge; were he not living, the mother of all talents would be childless. He possesses a reed (*pen*) whose attacks inspire terror to the lions (*powerful chiefs*), and to which squadrons of horse submit with humility. When its mouth (*nib*) opens to let flow black (*ink*) upon white (*paper*), the white and the yellow (*the swords and spears*) are suspended. (*He is*) vigilant in guarding the kingdom, yet be neither aims an arrow nor bares a blade. Eloquence is sent (by him) on messages where sheets of paper can fulfil the duties of ambassadors. The arrogant there recoil, filled with terror at what he dictates and prescribes. Sometimes you see him mix with his hand the lots (of the game) of science, phrase by phrase; (so as to form a picture) like meadows enamelled with flowers, or like strings of pearls; (producing thus a piece) elegant in penmanship, brilliant in expressions and in the thoughts which they convey. O you who aspire to proficiency! prepare (for your work) like Amín ad-Dín; take your time, and fatigue your mind but greatly. You, my lord! the (sworn) brother of generosity and the nurturer of glory! you, the son of high renown! you who bear off the prize! you are the full moon of which the penman, the son of a crescent (5), was the father. He that retreats (before obstacles) is good for nothing. Though he was the first (in point of time), you are more worthy of preference, for you outran him and he came in the second. Amín ad-Dín! you in whom God shews how he can smile, as in one sheaf, liberality and every merit! I am one of those who bear eulogiums to your tribe (your dwelling), so that it (my poem) may ever continue to roam about and be recited (6). When your eulogium is indited by a kádi (by a competent judge), an adl (competent witness) (7) can bear testimony (to its truth). Accept this virgin (piece) from a father who never troubled his mind about seeking a husband for his daughter. I desire neither reward nor recompense; but I really see that you are worthy of praise. The impulse of friendship bears this (poem) towards you, and it goes, wishing to obtain a kind reception from your good opinion. Since it is difficult for me to reach you, let my heart answer for my sincerity; (that you can appreciate,) for you are a man of an excellent judgment. Continue to enjoy good health as long as the syndrome of darkness hovers round the horizon! as long as the morning unsheathes the blade (of its light)!

Amín ad-Dín (Yákút) died at Mosul in the year 618 (A. D. 1231-2), at an advanced age. When he grew old, his penmanship changed (for the worse).

(1) Between forty and fifty pounds.

(2) The abode of welfare (Dár as-Salám) was the poetical name of Baghdad.

(3) This fashionable ribbon was perhaps named Násiria in honour of the sultan Saladin, whose official title was Al-Malik an-Násir (the victorious king).

(4) Literally: and thus undo your knotting and untying. The expression, " to knot and untie, " signifies " to possess sovereign authority, to have the power of nominating and deposing governors. "

(5) The son of a crescent, in Arabic: Ibn Hilál. This was the patronymic appellation of the famous penman Ibn al-Bawwáb. (See vol. II, p. 282.)

(6) I read with one of my manuscripts, and the edition of Búlák يظل تيها ويتلي. The other reading لعل لا يتلا means: " has remained incomparable," and is evidently not to be accepted.

(7) The adl is an officer in the kádi's court; he writes out his judgements, signs them as a witness and draws up deeds. He must be a man of approved integrity and veracity.

YAKUT AR-RUMI *THE POET*

Abú 'd-Durr Yákút Ibn Abd Allah (1) ar-Rúmi *(the Greek)*, surnamed Muhaddab ad-Dìn *(pure in religion)*, was the *mawla* of a merchant named Abú Mansûr al-Jìli. This celebrated poet, having studied the science *(of law)* and acquired extensive literary information, directed his genius to the composition of verses and attained proficiency in that art. When his talent raised him to distinction, he assumed the name of Abd ar-Rahmân. His place of residence, at Baghdad, was the Nizâmiya college. In the *Zail* (or supplement to as-Samâni's *historical continuation*), the author, Ibn ad-Dubaithi (vol. III. p. 102), mentions him among the Abd ar-Rahmâns, and says: "He passed his early youth in Baghdad, where he "learned by heart the sacred text of the Korán, got some acquaintance with general "literature and learned to write a good hand. He used to recite verses of his own "composition, most of which consisted in blandishments addressed to his mistress "and in the expression of his passion. All these pieces are on love-matters and are "full of tenderness; many people know them by heart." He (Ibn ad-Dubaithi) then gives some passages of his poetry and mentions that one of them was recited to him by the author himself. It begins thus:

O my two friends! I swear that the night never got dark without inspiring the lover with desire or with folly.

The rest of the piece may be found in the *Majmúa 's-Saghîr* (*the lesser compilation*) (2). Ar-Rúmi's verses have got into general circulation and are sung to music. They are full of grace and tenderness. Here is one of his poems:

If your tears cease to flow after the departure of those whom you love, all (*the passion*) that you affect to feel is false and counterfeit. How can you admit consolation or forget their images (*even in your dreams*), now that their dwellings and native soil are deprived of their presence? May God never afflict (*us*) with the departure of a tribe by whose removal full moons (*handsome forms*) and pliant branches (*slender waists*) disappeared from our eyes! They set out and my heart followed in the track of their caravan; all my provision of firmness was exhausted when they went away. Since they are gone, the earth never discloses its smiles (*its flowers*); the willow and the lotus-tree agitate their branches no more. On the morning of our separation, rare and sadness caused my tears to flow and lighted up a fire in my heart. All the waters of Noah's flood were (poured forth) from my eyes, and the flames which the Friend of God encountered (3) raged within my bosom. If solid rocks could feel such sorrow as I endure for my beloved, (the mountains of) Ohod and Lubnân (Lebanon) would shrink (4) before it; Yazbul would melt away under such pain as mine; Radwa would be shattered to pieces, and Thahlân would sink under the weight (5). O thou whose splendid beauty holds me captive! thou sovereignty of thy charms has showed me no kindness. Be, however, as thou wilt! no one shall ever replace thee in my affection. Thou art for me a limpid fountain, and my heart is parched with thirst.

Here is another of his poems :

Who will bear to Baghdad the news of what I suffer for that maid and of the love I feel for her? Who will bear my salutation to the Abode of Welfare (6)? Breath of the zephyr! carry the salutation of an ill-starred wretch to her who has harassed me and who heeds not the promises she made me. Describe to her a part only of the love which she inspired me; perhaps she may have pity on one who is borne down by passion and delirium. Declare in the public place of az-Zaurâ (Baghdad) that I have there a fawn (a maiden) whose absence has driven sleep from my eye-lids and whose beauty is marvellous; when she departed, my firmness of mind departed also and, when she turned away, she turned me over to death. When she repelled me, sleep was repelled from my eyes, and, when she shunned me, the wine which I drank was mingled with tears. My life and death are in her hands; she is for me paradise or hell; she is the only fountain where I can calm my longing and allay my thirst. Her absence is my death; her presence is, for me, life, happiness and the obtainment of my wishes. From her cheeks proceed the fires which consume me; her slender waist is the cause of my emaciation, and her languishing eyes make me languish to sickness. You who blame me cannot but excuse me : the grace of her movements indicates sufficiently that I was forced to love her and adore her.

I heard many jurisconsults in Syria and Irâk recite a piece of his which they knew by heart and which began thus :

O thou who enchest troubles in my bosom! since thy departure, my body is emaciated through the love I bear thee and will never be restored to health until thou givest consent to my wishes by saying : " Yes. " O thou who, as often as censors have blamed my love, hast offered them my justification in (letting them see) thy flowing ringlets! Tell me if my tyrant is authorized by the Hâjis to slay me! Jaïl said so in the Tahdib or the Shâmil? Does the Muhaddab (7) say that a lover whose eyes are moist and whose tears flow in torrents deserves to be tormented? Have your seductive eyes told you it was lawful to take away our lives with glances whose magic is like that of Babel (8)?

The piece contains more verses than these, but I have here given all that I am able to recollect. A literary man recited to me, at Aleppo, some verses of Yâkût ar-Hûmî's, one of which was as follows :

Art thou not sweeter in qualities than (all other) maids? Why then dost thou dwell in a heart which is a hell (9)?

He mentioned also that some of the Baghdad critics objected to this verse. I reflected on the matter and then said to him : " Fault was found with it perhaps in this
" particular that her being sweeter in qualities than the other maidens did not ne-
" cessarily imply that she should not be in hell; for she, being sweeter in qualities than
" they were, was not (to be counted as) one of them ; and what is denied is merely
" that the maidens should be in hell." To this he replied : " You are in the right !
" that is the very point in which they found fault with him. (10)".—In the year
625 (A.D. 1227-8), I met at Arbela a man of eminent merit who related to me as
follows : " I was in Baghdad, at the Nizâmiya college, in the year 620, and, one day,
" I found this Abû 'd-Durr (Ydhâl) sitting at the door of that institution. I sat
" down beside him, and engaged in a conversation on literary matters. Whilst
" we were thus occupied, an elderly man, weak in body and in a very sorry plight,
" came up, leaning on a staff, and sat down near us. Abû 'd-Durr asked me if I
" knew who he was and, on my answering that I did not, he said : ' That is the
" ' mamlûk (white slave) on whom his master, (the poet) Dais Bais (vol. I. p. 559)
" ' composed these lines :

Put on what cap (11), what gown, what veil you please; you cannot add to the love which I
bear you. Less love than that which you are worthy of possesses already the totality of my
heart; if you wish to augment that (love), give (me) another heart (the one I have is insufficient
to contain it).

" I turned to look at the man, observing his appearance and reflecting on the
" state to which he was reduced." I searched for these two verses in the diwân of
Hais Bais's poems, but was unable to find them. God best knows (if they be his) !—
Abû 'd-Durr left a diwân of poems which, as I am told, forms a small volume. I
have never seen it, but have met with numerous pieces taken from it. His verses
are currently known in Irâk, in the province of the East (Mesopotamia) and in
Syria ; so, what we have given may suffice. In the life of al-Khidr Ibn Akîl al-Irbali
(vol. I. p. 488) we have inserted three verses of ar-Rûmi's.—Since the above was
written, two copies of his diwân came into my possession : this was at Damascus, in
the year 667 (A.D. 1268-9); the book is a small one, containing only ten quires
(two hundred pages).—I read in a historical work of those latter times, that Abû 'd-
Durr (Ydhâl) was found dead in his lodgings at Baghdad, on the 19th of the
first Jumâda, 622 (22nd May, A. D. 1225); but the people said that he had been

dead for some days. Ibn an-Najjár (*vol. I. p. 11*) mentions, in his History of Baghdad,
that Abû 'd-Durr was found dead in his room, on Wednesday, the 13th of the first
Jumâda of that year. He had left the Nizâmiya and gone to reside in a house situated in the Darb Dinâr as-Saghir (*Lesser Dînar-street*). It is not known at what age
he expired but I am inclined to think that he was advanced in years (12).—
Rúmi means *belonging to the country of the Rûm (Greeks)*, which is a vast and celebrated region, filled with cities.—This is a fit place for introducing a piece of
curious information which is often needed and frequently asked for: The people of
Rûm (*the Greeks and the Romans*) are designated also as the *Banú 'l-Asfar* (*sons of
the tawny one*), and poets often employ this expression in their verses. Adî Ibn
Zaid al-Ibâdi (*vol. I. p. 189*) says, in one of his *kasîdas*:

> The noble sons of al-Asfar, kings of ar-Rûm, have left no remembrance of their deeds.

I frequently sought for the origin of this denomination, but could find no one
capable of allaying the thirst I had (*for that piece of information*): till I at length met,
by chance, with an old book entitled *Al-Lataif (the miscellany)* [13], but, on which the
name of the person who dictated its contents (i.e. *the author*) was not inscribed. I
copy here a passage of it in which the narrator says: "Al-Abbâs informed me that
"he heard his father make the following statement: In the first period (*of the
"empire*), the king of the Rûm died [14], leaving a wife. Rival chiefs aspired to
"the empire and great mischief was done between them. It was then agreed
"upon to take for their king the first person who would appear to them, and they ·
"held an assembly for that object. Now, a man had set out from Yemen for ar-
"Rûm, taking with him an Abyssinian slave. He (*the slave*) ran away and appeared
"before them. "See,' said they, 'into what we have fallen!' They married
"him to that woman, and she bore a son whom they named *al-Asfar* (*the
"Tawny*). The master (*of the slave*) remonstrated with them and the boy (*the
"slave*) said: 'He has spoken the truth! I am his slave.' They tried to appease
"him (*the master*) and made him gifts till he was satisfied. The Rûm were there-
"fore called *the Sons of the Tawny*, on account of the yellowness of the child, who
"was the son of an Abyssinian and a white woman."—God knows best (15)!

----

(1) The meaning of these names is explained at the beginning of the preceding article.

(2) This work is not known.

(3) According to the Koran, *sûrat* 91, Abraham, the Friend of God (*Khalil Allah*), was cast by Nimrod into a fiery furnace and miraculously saved.

(4) The true reading is evidently لَحْم.

(5) These are mountains of Arabia.

(6) The Abode of Welfare (*Dâr as-Salâm*) was one of the names by which Baghdad was designated.

(7) These are well-known treatises on law.

(8) The inhabitants of Babel were well-skilled in magic, as they had for teachers the fallen angels, Hârût and Mârût. (Koran, sur. 2, verse 96.)

(9) The poet's idea is: my heart is filled with the flames of love and yet I bear you in it.

(10) It is difficult to understand the objection and the author's explanation of it.

(11) For the meaning of the word شرف see Mr. Dozy's *Dictionnaire des noms des vêtements des Arabes*.

(12) خطأ is evidently the equivalent of طامن.

(13) This work is no longer known.

(14) Or, according to other readings, *tore into pieces, was burned.*

(15) The learned among the Mussulmans and some of our European orientalists have offered various solutions of this problem, but none of their explanations is satisfactory. I am inclined to believe that the denomination *Banû 'l-Asfar* signified *the sons of the emperor*, and that it was given to the Greeks of the Eastern empire because their sovereign bore, amongst his other titles, that of *Flavius*, which had been transmitted by Vespasian to his successors. An interpreter, confounding *Flavius* with *flavus*, may have told the Mussulmans that this name signified *yellow (asfar)*.

YAKUT AL-HAMAWI

Abû Abd Allah Yâkût Ibn Abd Allah, a Greek (*of Asia*) by origin and by birth, received the surname of al-Hamawi because he was enfranchised at Hamât, and obtained that of al-Baghdâdi because he made a residence in the city of Baghdad. He bore the honorary title of Shihâb ad-Dîn (*flambeau of religion*). When a child, he was carried off a captive from his native place and sold at Baghdad to a merchant named Askar Ibn Abi Nasr Ibn Ibrâhim al-Hamawi. His master sent him to school, with the intention of deriving profit from him later, in making him keep the accounts of his commercial transactions. This Askar could not write correctly and knew nothing except commerce. He inhabited Baghdad, got married there and had

a number of children. When Yákùt was grown up and had acquired some knowledge of grammar and literature, he was employed by his patron as a travelling clerk
and, in that capacity, he went back and forward from Syria to Kis(1), Omàn and the
neighbouring countries. His master was then under the necessity of enfranchising
him and turning him away, in consequence of a disagreement which took place
between them. This happened in the year 596 (A.D. 1199-1200). Yákùt then commenced copying books for a salary and, by their perusal, he acquired considerable
information. At a later period, he received some (money) from his patron, who had
taken pity on him, and was sent off by him on a voyage to Kis. Finding, on his
return, that his benefactor was dead, he realized part of what was in his hands and
gave to the widow and orphans wherewithal to satisfy them. The remainder served
him as a trading capital with which he travelled to different countries, and part of it
he employed in the book-trade. The lecture of some kharijite books impressed on his
mind a considerable portion of the doctrines (professed by these sectarians) and he conceived a strong prejudice against Ali, the son of Abù Tàlib. In the year 613
(A.D. 1216-7) he went to Damascus, and, as he was sitting in one of the bazars, he
got into a discussion with a partisan of Ali. In the course of the dispute, he was
led to speak of Ali in a manner not to be borne and was assaulted so violently by the
people that he had like to be killed. Having got out of their hands, he fled from
Damascus, but not before the governor of that city had received intelligence of what
took place and given orders to arrest him. Search was made for him, but without
success. He reached Aleppo where he stopped, full of apprehension and waiting to
see how things would end. On the first third or, by another account, on the second
third of the latter Jumáda, 613 (Sep.-Oct. A.D. 1216), he left that city and went to
Mosul, whence he proceeded to Arbela and from that to Khorásàn. He avoided
entering Baghdad, knowing that the person with whom he had the discussion was a
native of that place and fearing to lose his life if his adversary mentioned what he had
said. On arriving in Khorásàn, he stopped there for the purpose of trading to the
towns in that country, and fixed his residence at Marw (Meru). From that he proceeded to Nasa and then entered into the province of Khuwárezm where he encountered the invading army of the Tartars. This was in the year 616 (A.D. 1219-20).
Having barely escaped with his life, he fled as naked as when he shall be raised
from the dust of the grave on the day of the resurrection, and arrived at Mosul, after
suffering on the way such hardships and fatigue as would even tire a narrator before he

could describe them all. Deprived of every resource, in want of even the vilest food and the coursest clothing, he remained for some time at Mosul and then went to Sinjár. From that he removed to Aleppo and, having taken lodgings in the caravanserail outside the city, he continued to reside there till his death. The date of this event we shall give farther on.—I copied the following notes from the work compiled by Abû 'l-Barakât Ibn al-Mustaufi (vol. II. p. 556) and treating of the history of Arbela : Yâkût arrived in that city, A. H. 617, in the month of Rajab (September, A. D. 1220). He had been residing in Khuwârezm, but left it after the battle which took place between the Tartars and Muhammad Ibn Tukush Khuwârezm Shâh, the sovereign of that country. As he had previously been occupied in making historical researches, he composed a work in four large volumes and entitled : *Irshâd al-Alibbâ ila marifa til-Udabâ* (*Guide of the intelligent to an acquaintance with the learned*). In the beginning of the work he says : " I have given in this work " all the information I could obtain respecting the grammarians, the philologers, " the genealogists, the eminent Koran-readers, the relators of historical facts, the " annalists, the booksellers of note, the writers of renown, the authors of such " epistles as have been collected into volumes, the persons distinguished for the " beauty of their *manrúb* (2) handwriting, and all those who composed or compiled " works on literature. In this task, I aimed at concision, though unable to remain " within the limits of brevity, and I spared no pains in determining the dates of the " deaths and fixing the days and the hours of the births. I mention the works composed " by them, the more interesting of the anecdotes concerning them, their origin, their " genealogy and some of their poetry. (*I compiled this work*) during my travels in " various countries and my intercourse with the inhabitants. The *imâds* (3) I have " suppressed except those which contain but a few names and which are easy to be " learned ; and, moreover, I did all in my power to have the exactness of these tra- " ditions certified by oral declaration and by the licences given to teach them. As " it was my object to produce a small but useful work, I have indicated in it the " sources whence I derived my information and the places where I found it: the " books, for instance, composed by such of the learned as were considered sure " authorities in these matters and on whose declarations all relied for the genuineness " of these traditions." He (Ibn al-Mustaufi) then states that Yâkût composed a work on the history of the poets both ancient and modern. Other works were written by Yâkût, such as the *Mojam al-Buldân* (*gazetteer or alphabetical list of places*)(4).

the *Mojam ash-Shuward* (*biographical dictionary of poets*), the *Mojam al-Udabá* (*biographical dictionary of literary men*), the *Mushtarik waddn wa 'l-Mukhtalif sakán* (*a dictionary of geographical synonyms*) which is a useful book, the *Kitáb al-Mabdd wa 'l-Mádl* (*the Commencement and the End*), treating of history, the *Kitáb al-Dual* (*book of Empires*), the collected sayings of Abû Ali 'l-Fárisi (*vol. I. p. 379*), an *Onwán* (*title or preface*) to the *Kitáb al-Aghdni* (*vol. II. p. 249*), the *Muktadib fi 'n-Nisab* (*selection of genealogies*) containing those of the Arabian tribes, an account of al-Mutanahhi (*vol. I. p. 102*) and a treatise entitled *Kitáb man lahu himma etc.* (*book for him whose high aspirations are directed towards the acquisition of knowledge*) (5). — Al-Kádi 'l-Akram (*the honorable kádi*) Jamâl ad-Dîn Abû 'l-Hasan Ali Ibn Yûsuf Ibn Abd al-Wáhid as-Shaibáni at-Kiftí (*vol. II. p. 491*), who was vizir to the sovereign of Aleppo, states, in his *Anbá 'r-Ruwdt fi Abná 'n-Nuhát*, that Yákút, on arriving at Mosul, whither he had fled on escaping from the Tartars, wrote to him a letter in which he describes his situation and relates what passed between him and these invaders. It begins by the invocation of the divine name and the praises of God, after which, it continues in these terms : "Your mamlûk (*humble servant*) Yákút Ibn
" Abd Allah al-Hamawi, wrote this letter from Mosul, in the year 617 (A. D. 1220-1),
" on his arrival from Khuwârezm whence he was driven by the Tartars whom God
" exterminate ! (*He sent it*) to the presence of his sovereign lord (6), the vizir Jamâl
" ad-Dîn al-Kádi 'l-Akram Abû 'l-Hasan Ali Ibn Yûsuf Ibn Ibráhîm Ibn Abd al-
" Wáhid as-Shaibáni at-Taimi (*member of the tribe of Shaibân and descended from*)
" Taim Allah, who was the son of Shaibân, the son of Thalaba, the son of Okába
" May God cast his shelter around him and exalt his rank in the scale of domination (7).
" (*To him*), who is, at the present day, vizir to the sovereign of Aleppo and al-
" Awâsim (8) (*is addressed*) this account of what has passed in Khuwârezm and of what
" has happened to the writer. (*It offers*) a slight indication of the manner in which
" he began and ended (*his career*) on taking leave of your (*excellence*). He shrank
" from the idea of submitting it to your appreciation ; such was his respect and ve-
" neration for your dignity and such his repugnance to offer you a document so un-
" worthy of your exalted merit. But now, that a number of practitioners in the
" art of prose and verse have been informed of these (*events*) and have hastened, as
" I well know, to set them down in writing and to hurry in active competition to-
" wards the task of transmitting the knowledge of them (*to future ages*) ; now, that
" the generosity of him who holds me enslaved has, no doubt, unsealed these (*epistles*)

" and assigned to their (*authors*) a high rank in his favour, I feel encouraged to pre-
" sent this (*notice*) to my (*honored*) master and to a judgment which will shew how
" exalted it is by perusing it and treating its imperfections with indulgence.   For
" (*I am not a professed writer ;*) every person who fingers dirhems should not be
" taken for a money-changer, neither is the man who acquires a pearl to be con-
" sidered as a jeweller.   Here follows my statement :

     " In the name of God, the Merciful, the Clement !   may God render durable, for
" the advantage of science and of those who cultivate it, for the prosperity of Islamism
" and its sons, the gift which he has conferred, bestowed and granted to enjoy ;
" namely, the ample (*and beneficent*) shade of the lord vizir, whose partisans may
" God exalt, whose glory and power may He redouble !   whose ensigns and standards
" may He maintain victorious !   whose pen may He long allow to run (*on the sur-*
" *face of paper*), so that it may direct towards all lands the flow of his donations !
" May He prolong his life and exalt his glory to the heavens, whilst He surrounds
" him with favours of which the freshness shall never fade and of which the num-
" ber and the multitude shall never be restrained by limits.   May his vigour and
" his sword never be broken !   may the love which all bear him and the number of
" those who love him be never diminished !   God prolong his rule for the advantage
" of the world and of our religion !   so that he may repair their disorder ,
" drive away their affliction, elevate their beacon and, by his salutary influence,
" enable them to leave a lasting impression.   May his light shine forth, his blos-
" soms open, his flowers brighten and his lustre be augmented !   May God extend
" the shade of his (*the vizir's patronage*) over the sciences and those who profess them ;
" over literature and those who cultivate it ;   over meritorious acts and those who
" practise them ;   so that, by his well established bounty, he may exalt these (*fair*)
" structures, adorn their diadems with the finest jewels of his glory, embellish their
" duration with the mature (*honours*) of his exalted dignity, give them great im-
" portance for mankind by the loftiness of his views, and establish in the highest
" degree of merit their utility and their rank.   By the efficiency of his orders he has
" exalted the influence of the Moslim states; he presides as a guardian over the
" foundations which support the dogmas of the faith, he exalts those who defend
" them and abases those who attack them.   By the excellence of his government
" he strengthens the arms (9) (*of the true doctrine*) and, by his well-directed efforts,
" he has smoothed for it the way to the attainment of its purposes. Thus, by the ex-

" cellence of his administration, hath he become a brilliant star on the forehead of
" the age, and a model to be imitated by every man whom nature has formed for
" (the exercise of) justice and benevolence.   Therefore shall he enjoy a fitting re-
" compense as long as the two companions (light and darkness) shall subsist, as long
" as days and nights shall be renewed, as long as there shall be a sun to shine in
" the east, and a soul to rejoice at the prospect of conversing with his Excel-
" lence (10)!

" After (these preliminaries), the humble slave (who writes this) exposes to (your)
" high and seigniorial dignity, to (your) right honorable and exalted station, which
" God favour with happiness long to endure, brilliant with lustre, satisfying all our
" wishes and embellished with every mark of excellance (11),—a state of things the
" relation of which is rendered unnecessary by your lordship's quick intelligence,
" and for the elucidation and description of which, the clear judgment you are
" gifted with might dispense me from employing (inda) the pen.   But, let it be
" sufficient for him (the vizir) to recollect in what terms our blessed Prophet de-
" scribed the true believers : " Certainly," said he, " my people are fond of talk-
" ing (12)."   This (letter) is (merely) a disclosure of the writer's sincere devotion
" (to you) as a client, of the pride he feels in being an humble servant to (your)
" seigniorial presence and in being considered as such ; for your quick genius suf-
" fices to prevent him from manifesting, out of what is laid up in his mind, senti-
" ments which might have the appearance of adulation.   Indeed, the proofs of your
" humble servant's zeal in the religious duty of clientship are evident to all the
" world, and the mark impressed on him by the stamp indicating the sincerity of
" his love for your honorable name is still apparent on the pages of time.   So also
" is his faith in the sacred laws (of gratitude) imposed by that bounty (of yours) which,
" covering all the land, has rendered clearly visible, by its splendor, the edifice of
" noble deeds (which you created).   Your servant's repeating, in your praise, the
" recitals whose authenticity has been verified by personal experience, is well justi-
" fied (13).   He summoned the people of all lands to assert with zeal their faith in
" the supremacy of your (generosity, proofs of) which he has (often) received in his
" hand.   Your friend, sincerely devoted to the belief in your superiority, and es-
" pecially distinguished by the intention of collecting all the scattered (recollections),
" all the (accounts) wide-spread (of your bounty), was accustomed to toil in the sweat
" of his brow ; so that, at length, he rendered you a knoba of generosity towards

" which it was not necessary to prescribe the obligation of pilgrimage for those who
" were able to undertake the journey, neither was that duty incumbent on those
" who possessed means, to the exclusion of the indigent and the way-worn travel-
" ler.   All of them obtain (*from you*) a meed sufficient to fortify them, a portion
" adequate to their wants and on which they counted.   The grandees have drawn
" from your source an abundant supply of noble deeds ; the learned have found
" examples of merit in those persons who are attached to your service ; the poor
" have received from you letters of protection against the vicissitudes of time and
" the frowns of fortune ; therefore have they prescribed as a sacred rite towards you,
" the saluting and the glorifying of your noble and illustrious character, the touch
" ing with their lips and the kissing of your generous hand.   God is a witness that
" your humble servant, in his journeyings and sojournings, in private and in public,
" in conduct and in reputation, had always for his distinctive mark the custom of
" perfuming the assemblies of the worthy and the meetings of the learned with
" (*the account of*) the services which your Excellence has rendered and which were
" obtained from your generosity.   He made it his pride (*to speak of them*) be-
" fore all people, and thus prepare an embroidery for the discourse he was about to
" utter :

   " When I through cupidity, gave lustre to other men by my poems, I gave my verses lustre
   " by the mention of your name.

   " *They upbraid thee that they have embraced Islamism.   Answer : Upbraid me*
   " *not with your having embraced Islamism ; rather God upbraideth you, that he hath*
   " *directed you to the faith.   Avow the fact if you can speak sincerely* (14).   May God
   " never debar us, (*the visir's*) trusty friends, from the ample stock of his continual
   " favours, nor preclude us all, who are his servants, from the constant flow of his
   " gifts ! O God ! Lord of the expanded earth, of the exalted heavens, of the swollen
   " seas and of the winds compelled to work (*thy will*) (15) ! hearken to my invocation
   " and listen to my prayer !   Help us up to that height in his favour which we desire
   " to reach and which we hope to attain, through the merits of Muhammad the pro-
   " phet and of his companions and of his kindred !
   " When your humble servant left your noble presence and departed from the
   " abode of unsullied glory and exalted merit, he intended to conciliate frowning
   " Fortune and draw milk from the udder of this age, wicked and unruly as it is.

" For he was seduced by the idea that changing place — brings grace, — that pas-
" sing into a foreign land — brings wealth to hand, — that dwelling with one's
" friends — disgrace and pain upon us sends, — and that the lover of home who
" stirs not space, — is distanced in the race (17.)

> " After stopping for a time in hesitation, I felt assured that death was preferable to poverty.
> " So, I bade farewell to my family, whilst my heart was filled (*with grief*), and left my native
> " land in the pursuit of wealth. My wife wept on our separation, and I said to her : ' Bear
> " ' it with patience! death is surely better than a life of misery. I shall gain a fortune or die
> " ' in a town where few tears will be shed over my grave '.

" Mounted on the steed (18) of hope, your servant rode off to a distant land, and
" placed his foot in the stirrup of peregrination with every company (*that offered*);
" he crossed the valleys and the hills till he nearly reached the Sudd (19); but per-
" fidious Fortune did not befriend him, neither did the times, now run mad, treat
" him with kindness :

> " Ask the nights and the days to acknowledge their fault; they will not conceal that news.

" I was like a mote in the eye of fortune or a bone in her throat ; so, to get rid of
" me, she deluded me in promising to fulfil my wishes and finished by casting me
" into the snares of death :

> " He stopped not long in any land before he set out for another ; his person was with
> " (*his fellow-travellers*) but his mind was far distant. One day, he was at Hazwa; another,
> " at al-Akik ; another, at al-Ozaib, and another, at al-Kholaisa. Now he went towards Najd
> " and Awena, (*near*) the valleys of al-Tinaa, and then to the castle of Taima (20).

" But, alas ! after all these lessons of adversity, how far was I from the accom-
" plishment of my wishes and the attainment of my desire ! The frowns of ill-luck
" drew smiles from cruel time, and I ceased not to blame Fortune and reproach her
" with her errors, till, instead of getting wealth, I was satisfied in reaching home (21).
" And, during all that, your humble servant tried to pass away those days and
" to get over them ; deluding himself with the hopes of sustenance, covering his
" head with the veil of endurance and self-denial, arrayed in abstinence and in
" scanty fare, but not resigned to the wearing of such clothing ; *your brother was*
" *forced and had not strength to resist (22)*. He remained there, consoling himself
" in the society of his fellow-merchants whose humours he could support and from

" whom he had no affronts to fear ; he treated them with politeness and was happy
" to receive from them a pittance.   Otherwise, no advantage could be expected from
" them and no harm could be feared :

   " If I must absolutely have a family and a home, let it be in a place where I can have nothing
   " to fear from those whom I meet, and they, nothing to fear from me.

" My mind had once formed the thought of assuming high airs, of riding on a
" spirited horse, of seeing my ambitious desires come forth from the egg, fledged
" and winged, and of striking fire (drawing profit) from every steel, whether lavish
" or sparing of its sparks ; (but now) :

   " Instructed by experience, I care not if people shun me and if I never receive nor make
   " a visit.   Never, whilst I live, shall I ask if the army has marched or if the general has de-
   " parted.

" The place where I stopped was called Marw ash-Sháhján, which (latter) word, ac-
" cording to the explanation given by them, means the soul of the sultan.   I found
" there some works treating of the sciences and of literature, volumes composed by
" men of intelligence, and, whilst I studied them, I forgot family and country, and
" thought no longer of sincere friends nor of my home.   Amongst them I discovered
" some stray volumes which I had long sought for, and some works which I had ar-
" dently desired.   To them I applied with the avidity of a glutton and, having assi-
" gned to them a place from which they could not easily depart, I began to browse in
" these gardens, to admire the beauty of their form and of their contents, to let my
" eyes rove freely over these pasture grounds, to enjoy these detailed accounts, these
" compendiums, and to think that I should remain in that quarter till I became a
" neighbour of (those who repose under) the earth :

   " When adversity attacks me with troops having sadness and expatriation in the van, I lay for
   " them an ambuscade of which the two chiefs are a lamp and a book; and I pass the night in
   " relating, of Fortune's character, things so wonderful that their truth would excite doubt.   I
   " dispel my cares by quiet, as the cares of others are dispelled by wine.

" (So things continued) till the catastrophy arrived by which Khorásán was over-
" whelmed with ruin, with evil all-destroying and with desolation.   Now, I declare

" on my life and by Allah ! that it was a country beautiful in all its parts, charming
" in all its regions : a fertile garden enjoying an air pure and languishing (mild),
" and in which the trees inclined their branches with delight at the singing of the
" birds. In it the rivulets shed tears whilst each flower smiled at the other; the
" breath of the zephyr was sweet and the temperature of the climate healthy. Never
" shall I forget those delightful arbours and those trees sinking under (*the weight of*)
" their foliage. The southern gales bore thither its wine-skins filled with the
" liquor of the clouds ; the meadows drank the wine of the dew, and on the flowers
" were formed drops like pearls fallen from the string. When the thirst of its groves
" was quenched with that liquor, their odour was the intoxicating breath of the
" zephyr ; they drew near to each other, even closer than friend to friend, and em-
" braced even more tenderly than lovers. In the intervals were seen anemonies
" whose colours were mixed with that of the love-sick wooer (23) and which re-
" sembled the lips of two maidens who draw near, one to the other, for the purpose
" of giving and receiving an affectionate kiss. Their aspect sometimes deceived the
" most intelligent (*nakrir*), so that he took them for burning coals (*jimr*) on which
" drops of water were poured successively in order to extinguish them (*intilàf*) (24).
" There you saw the ox-eye flourish so brilliantly that the eye of the spectator is
" cheered at the sight, whilst its blossoms glittered like little cymbals of gold or like
" dinars of that metal. Among them appeared the (*white flowers of the*) anthemis,
" shining like the teeth of the beloved when she bites the cheek of the lover. How
" rich (*that land*) in prospects which delight the eye and of which the colours are
" charming (*râik*). It is, in a word, and without exaggeration, a copy of Paradise :
" there was to be found all the heart could wish for, all that could enchant the sight.
" Encircled with its noble endowments, it offered, throughout all its tracts, a pro-
" fusion of rich products to the world. How numerous were its holy men pre-emi-
" nent for virtue (*râkat khiaruha*) ! how many its doctors whose conduct had for
" motive the conservation of Islamism ! The monuments of its science are in-
" scribed on the rolls of time ; the merits of its authors have redounded to the ad-
" vantage of religion and of the world, and their productions have been carried into
" every country. Not a man of solid science and sound judgment but emerged
" like the sun, from that part of the East ; not a man of extraordinary merit but
" took that country for his setting-place or longed to go and join its inhabitants.
" Every quality truly honorable and not factitious was to be found among them and,

" in [*the garden of*] their sayings, I was enabled to cull the roots of every generous
" impulse. Their children were men, their youths heroes, and their old men saints;
" the testimonies of their merit are clear; the proofs of their glory are manifest;
" yet, strange to say! the sultan who reigned over these provinces abandoned them
" them with unconcern and said to himself: ' Take to the open country (25), or
" else you will encounter perdition.' So, he hastened off as a young ostrich runs
" away and, when he began to look about, where nothing was to be seen, he
" thought that he perceived a man or many men (*in pursuit of him*) (26). *How*
" *many gardens, springs of water, fields of corn, honourable stations and advantages*
" *which they enjoyed, did they leave behind!* But Almighty God *did not give the*
" *same unto another people* (27), because he averted those saints from the station of
" the wicked. But he put them to the proof, and found them grateful; he afflicted
" them, and found them patient; so he caused them to join the company of the
" holy martyrs and raised them to the lofty stations of the virtuous elect. *Yet per-*
" *chance ye hate a thing which is better for you, and perchance ye like a thing which*
" *is worse for you; but God knoweth and ye know not* (28). The people of infidelity
" and impiety roamed through those abodes; that erring and contumacious race
" dominated over the inhabitants; so that those palaces were effaced off the earth
" as lines of writing are effaced from paper, and those abodes became a dwelling
" for the owl and the raven: in those places, the screech-owls answer each other's
" cry, and in those halls, the winds moan responsive to the simoom. Old friends
" who enter there are filled with sadness; Iblis himself would bewail the great
" catastrophy:

   " (*It is woe*) as if no charming companion, handsome as a statue, had ever been there; as
   " if princely chiefs, born in bravery (*had never resided there*). Yet, in generosity, they were
   " Hátims and sons of Máma (29); if prudence were taken into count, they were Ahnafs (30) and
   " Saads (31). But time, in its vicissitudes, hath hurled them to destruction, so that their fate is
   " now a moral lesson, fitted to make our hearts bleed and those of our posterity.

" We belong to God and to God we shall return! It was an event sufficient to break
" the back, to destroy life, to fracture the arm, to weaken the strength, to redouble
" sadness, to turn grey the hair of children, to dishearten the brave, to blacken
" the heart and to stupify the intelligence. Then did your humble servant turn
" back and retrace his steps. Filled with grief, he sought a friendly retreat where his
" mind might repose in security; (*he fled,*) his heart beating, his tears flowing, his

" reason lost and his intelligence absent. It was with difficulty that he accomplished
" his purpose and arrived at Mosul, where he stopped, after encountering dangers,
" undergoing sufferings, supporting misfortunes with resignation, diminishing
" his baggage and, more than once, running the risk of his life. For he passed
" through drawn swords, troops flying in disorder, ranks broken, blood spilt with
" impunity. Every time he got on a camel's saddle or crossed a desert, he had these
" words in his mouth (38) : ' In this journey we have met with misfortune, but,
" ' praise be to God who has left to us the power of praising him, and who has
" ' conferred on us favours which surpass enumeration ! ' In a word, if the term of
" my life had not been appointed for a later period, it would have been difficult for
" my friends to have said : ' The unfortunate man has escaped or is arrived ! ' and
" ' they would have struck their hands like people whose hopes have been disap-
" ' pointed; and he would have been joined to the millions of millions, or even
" ' more, who perished by the hands of the infidels. Then he would have left his
" ' dearest treasure, her who derives subsistence from his life :

        " Fortune does not appreciate my worth; she knows not that I have strength of mind and
        " can make light of the events brought about by time. Adversity passes the night in shewing
        " how she can transgress against me, and I pass it in letting her see what patience is.

" Your humble servant now declares that he has no means of tranquillising his
" mind, no promise by which to flatter his heart or his eyes, except in beguiling them
" with the hope that his afflictions shall disappear, once he stands in your noble presence.

        " Enjoy good health, continue (to do so) and pass your days in pleasure; for your existence
        " will console (us all) for what is past and gone. You are the soul of glory; mankind is its
        " body; you are a pearl, and we (possessing it) regret not the shell.

" Your humble servant is now residing at Mosul and endeavouring to repair the
" harm done to him by this grave and disquieting event. He passes his time in the
" exercise of his profession, but Fortune is ready to say to him, in plain and intel-
" ligible language : ' By Allah! you have fallen into your old mistake!' For now,
" one object occupies his thoughts and, on my life and by Allah! that is nothing more
" than procuring a provision of books which he may transcribe and of (written) leaves
" which may serve him as companions;—in that occupation, his toil is great and
" his profit small ; — then (he thinks of) travelling and resolves that, after accom-

" plishing his task and attaining in some degree the object on which he has set
" his mind (*karûna*). he will invoke divine assistance and journey forth (33) in
" the hope of accomplishing his wish; namely, to appear in your presence, regale
" his sight, even for a single moment, with the aspect of your greatness, and then,
" casting away the staff of travel in your spacious hall, repose under the shelter of
" your wing till he attain the hour which is to give him (*everlasting*) repose. He
" will take his place among your Excellency's servants, for such he always professed
" himself to be, even when far from your presence; and if your Excellency take him
" by the hand, Fortune, becoming indulgent, may exalt him after having cast
" him down. For, with his diminished strength, he is unable to accomplish his
" projects and incapable of entering the lists and encountering new hazards (34).
" Besides, the earth has now enclosed his brethern in its bosom and the succession
" of days and nights has removed (*most of*) his contemporaries out of sight; grayness
" has settled on his beard; his means are insufficient for (*the satisfying of*) his
" wants; the falcon of hoary age has swooped at and seized on the raven (*the black
" hair*) of his youth; the daylight of prudence has invaded and repelled the night
" of ignorance; the services he rendered to his friends have been repaid with evil (35),
" and the brilliant garment of youth he has exchanged for the tattered cloak of
" hoary age :

" My youth departed and was ended before I enjoyed it; since it left me I can only expect death.
" Old age precludes me from attaining what I seek for.

" Your humble servant composed the following elegy in verse on the loss of his
" youth; but how little does it avail (*ghand*) a man to weep for those who are depo-
" sited in the earth, amongst mouldering bones!

" Since my hair has turned gray, Fortune knows me no more, and the marks by which she
" is distinguished can no longer be recognised by me (36). When my soul thinks of it (my
" youth), it yearns for it with longing desire and my eyes pour forth tears; till a time comes to
" embellish what has passed away and recollection supplies me with abundant sighs. Why
" not? since nought (*leaunnd*) remains in the bottom of my drinking-cup but a mere mouthful,
" filled with grounds. The contents of every goblet are clear at first, but in the bottom are
" found only a few drops (*mazjá hum-bi*) and some sediment.

" Your humble servant hopes that the above example of senile garrulity will
" obtain from you a glance of benevolence; for, assuredly, the judgment of our

" lord and master, the vizir, of him who is the asylum of the human race, from
" east to west, procures, when he applies it, according to his glorious custom, an
" increase of rank and honour *(for him who is the object of it. Receive my)*
" salutation."

I have lengthened greatly this article by the insertion of Yákút's epistle, but
it was impossible to give it by extracts. My friend (adhib) al-Kamál Ibn as-Shiâr al-
Maosili (37) writes as follows, in his work entitled *Okûd al-Jumân (clusters of
pearls)* : " Abû Abd Allah Muhammad Ibn Mahmûd, generally known by the sur-
" name of Ibn an-Najjâr *(vol. I. p. 11)* and the author of a history of Baghdad,
" spoke to me in these terms : ' The above mentioned Yákút recited to me the fol-
" ' lowing three lines and told me that he had composed them on a young Turkish
" ' slave who, having inflamed eyes, wore a black veil to protect them :

" ' That Turkish youth whose face might be taken for a full moon shining in all its refulgence,
" ' shades his eyes with the border of a veil *(lit. of a protector)* to prevent their brightness from
" ' fascinating his admirers. But, by Allah! since these eyes have wounded hearts through
" ' coats of mail, what is there to protect the protector!

" Yákút was born in the country of the Greeks *(Asia Minor)*, in the year 574 (A.
" D. 1178-9), or 575." So says the author just cited. He died on the 21st of the
month of Ramadân, 626 (13th August, A. D. 1229), in a khân situated outside the
city of Aleppo, as we have already mentioned towards the beginning of this article.
He left his books as a *wakf* (38) to the mausoleum *(mash-hed)* of az-Zaidi (?), which
establishment is situated in Dinâr street *(Darb dînâr)*, Baghdad. He delivered
them to Izz ad-Dîn Abû'l-Hasan Ali Ibn al-Athîr *(vol. II. p. 288)*, the author of the
great historical work, and this *shaikh* carried them to their destination. When
Yákút rose to distinction and got into reputation, he changed his name into Yákûb.
In the beginning of the month of Zû 'l-Kaada, 626 (in the latter part of September,
A. D. 1229), I arrived at Aleppo for the purpose of pursuing my studies. This was
subsequent to Yákút's death ; and I found every one speaking in his praise, extolling
his merit and his great literary acquirements. It was not therefore in my destiny to
meet with him.

(1) The island of Kis is situated at the entrance of the Persian Gulf, opposite to Ormus.

(2) See vol. II, p. 381.

(3) See Introduction to vol. I, p. xlii.

(4) This and the *Mushtarik* are the only works of Yákút which I have met with. The *Mojam al-Buldán* forms five or six folio volumes and contains much curious information. I understand that Mr. Wüstenfeld has prepared an edition of it which is now (1865) in the press.

(5) The loss of these compilations is much to be regretted.

(6) Literally : the master of his thraldom.

(7) This long letter contains very little information and was evidently composed with the intention of displaying the great command of language possessed by the author. Its style, though laboured and excessively affected, is by no means remarkable for elegance, though the vizir Ibn al-Kifti and Ibn Khallikán have inserted it in their respective works. Nothing can be conceived more verbose and more jejune than this pompous epistle. It is almost needless to say that the copyists did not always understand it and have committed numerous faults in its transcription. Some of these errors I have rectified, but a few passages remain of which the last cannot be amended though the meaning be tolerably clear.

(8) *Al-Awásim (the fortresses)* was the name given to that part of ancient Cilicia which borders on the north of Syria.

(9) The Arabic word signifies : the part of the arm on which the bracelet is worn.

(10) Literally : his illustrious presence.

(11) Literally : with a white forehead and white pasterns. These were considered by the bedwin Arabs as marks of a good horse.

(12) Literally : my people are speakers.

(13) Literally : his recital of the traditions of glory, the truth of which are most (easy to be verified), is established by his personal observation.

(14) Koran, surat 49, verse 17. The application of this verse is by no means clear.

(15) and (16). The epithets here employed are taken from the Koran.

(17) These are rhyming proverbs.

(18) Literally : the camel's hump.

(19) The rault or barrier of Gog and Magog was supposed to exist on the west side of the Caspian sea.

(20) All these places are mentioned in the poems composed by the bedwin Arabs and were situated in Arabia.

(21) Literally : instead of booty I was content to return. A well known proverb.

(22) For the explanation of this proverb, see Freytag's *Meidáni*, vol. 1, p. 144.

(23) The text is corrupt but the meaning appears to be that which is given here. I read *shíddeh* with one of the manuscripts.

(24) That means : the colour of these flowers was red with dark spots.

(25) Literally : to the air.

(26) For an account of Khowárezm-Sháh's flight before the troops of Jenguiz-Khán, see Abú 'l-Fedá's Annals, A. H. 617.

(27) Koran, surat 44, verses 24, 25. These verses apply to the Egyptians who went forth in pursuit of the Children of Israel. God gave their possessions to another people; so says the Koran; but our author remarks that God did not leave those of the Khárezmites to the invaders, because he would not class the mansûbs like the people of Pharaoh.

(28) Koran, sur. 2, verse 212.

(59) The generosity of Hátim at-Táï is well known; Kaab Ibn Máma, one of the principal chiefs of the tribe of Iyád, was also noted for his liberality. See Freytag's *Meidâni*, t. 2. p. 815, and Mr. Casimin de Perceval's *Essai*, t. II, p. 113.

(60) See vol. I, p. 635, and Freytag's *Meidâni*, t. I, p. 894.

(61) Saad Ibn Rustam ﺳﻌﺪ died some years before the introduction of Islamism. He was so celebrated for his wisdom that the bedwin Arabs used to take him for judge in their contestations. (D'Herselin, *Biblioth. orientale.*)

(62) Lit: al'y : this was his distinctive mark.

(63) Literally : ride on the direction of the road.

(64) Literally : theirs; i. e. viciniludes of fortune.

(65) The word ﻣﻌﻨﻪ, which is not rendered in the translation, may perhaps signify : which is a case particular to him alone.

(66) Or else : her favours are denials. The two words are also technical terms of Arabic grammar and, in that case, they signify : her definite (*nouns*, i. e. ﻣﻌﺮﻓﻪ) are, for me, indefinite; which may mean : I obtain them not.

(67) Abû 'l-Barakât al-Mubârak Ibn Hamdin Ibn ash-Shâir ﺍﻟﺸﺎﻋﺮ surnamed Kamâl ad-Din al-Mosuli (*belonging to Mosul*), composed a voluminous work on the poets of the seventh century of the Hijra. He died A. H. 684 (A. D. 1285-7). — (Hajji Khalifa; *Ghirbâl at-Zemân.*)

(68) See vol. I, p. 49, and vol. III, p. 547.

YAHYA IBN MAIN

Abû Zakariya Yahya Ibn Main Ibn Aûn Ibn Ziâd Ibn Bestâm Ibn Abd ar-Rahmân al-Murri, a native of Baghdad and a celebrated *háfiz*, was a doctor of the highest authority, deeply learned and noted for the exactitude of his (*traditional*) information. He came, it is said, from a village situated near al-Anbâr and called Nakiya. His father was secretary to Abd Allah Ibn Malik (1) or, according to another statement, he was chief of the *kharâj* (or *land-tax*) offices at Rai. He left, on his death, a sum of one million and fifty thousand dirhems (2) to his son Yahya. All this sum was spent by the latter in (*collecting*) Traditions, so that, at length, he had not a shoe to put on. Being asked how many traditions he had written down, he answered: " I wrote " down with my own hand six hundred thousand Traditions." Ahmad Ibn Okba,

the person who related this anecdote, said: "And I believe that the relaters of Tra-
" ditions had also written out for him six hundred thousand and as much more."
(*When Ibn Main died*) he left one hundred and thirty cases filled with books and
four water-jar stands filled with them also. He was the great master in the art of improbation and justification [3]. The most eminent doctors learned Traditions from
him and taught them on his authority. Amongst them were Abù Abd Allah Muhammad Ibn Ismail al-Bukhári (*vol. II. p. 594*), Muslim Ibn al-Hajjàj al-Kushairi (*vol. III.
p. 348*), Abù Dàwùd as-Sijistàni (*vol. I. p. 589*), and other hàfizes. A close fellowship
and intimacy subsisted between him and Ahmad Ibn Hanbal (*vol. I. p. 44*), and they
studied together all the sciences connected with the Traditions. This is a fact so
well known that we need not expatiate on the subject. He (*Ibn Hanbal*) and Abù
Khaithama [4] related Traditions on his (*Ibn Main's*) authority, and were his contemporaries. Ali Ibn al-Madini [5] said: "In Basra, the science (*of the law and the
" Traditions*) passed down to Yahya Ibn Abi Kathir [6] and Katàda [*vol. II. p. 513*);
" in Kùfa, it reached Abù Ishàk (*vol. II. p. 392*) and al-Aàmash (*vol. I. p. 587*);
" the science of Hijàz passed to Ibn Shihàb (*vol. II. p. 581*) and Amr Ibn Dinàr
" (*vol. I. p. 580*). All these six were at Basra, and what they knew was transmitted
" to Saïd Ibn Abi Arùba [7], Shoba (*vol. I. p. 493*), Mamar [8], Hammad Ibn Salama
" (*vol. I. p. 261*) and Abù Awàna [9]. At Kufa the heads of the science were
" Sofyàn ath-Thauri (*vol. I. p. 576*) and Sofyàn Ibn Oyaina (*vol. I. p. 578*); in
" Hijàz its head was Màlik Ibn Anas (*vol. II. p. 545*); in Syria, its head was al-
" Aùzài (*vol. II. p. 84*). The knowledge possessed by these passed to Muhammad
" Ibn Ishàk (*vol. II. p. 677*), Hushaim (*vol. I. p. 187*), Yahya Ibn Saïd (*vol. II.
" p. 679*). Ibn Abi Zàida, Waki (*vol. I. p. 374*), Ibn al-Mubàrak (*vol. II. p. 12*),
" who was the most learned of them all, Ibn Mahdi [10] and Yahya Ibn Aadam [11].
" The united knowledge of them all passed to Yahya Ibn Main." Ahmad Ibn Hanbal
declared that every tradition which was not known to Yahya Ibn Main was not a
(true) tradition. He said also: "There is in this place a man whom God created
" for the purpose of exposing the falsehoods of lying traditionists;" and the person
whom he meant was Ibn Main. "Never", said Ibn ar-Rùmi [12] did I hear any
" one except Ibn Main speak equitably of the shaikhs (*the Traditionists*); others
" fall upon them in their discourse, but Yahya (*Ibn Main*) would say: 'I never
" ' saw a man make a mistake without my casting a veil over his fault or trying to
" ' excuse him; and I never reproached a man, to his face, with anything that might

" · displease him; I preferred pointing out to him, in a private conference, the
" · mistake into which he had fallen and, if he did not take my observations
" · well, I left him there'." He used also to say : " I wrote down (quantities of
" Traditions) under the dictation of liars, and made use of the paper for heating
" my oven ; I thus obtained (at least one advantage,) bread well baked." He sometimes recited these lines :

> Wrath gained by lawful or unlawful means will all disappear, leaving nothing behind but the
> iniquities it wrought. The devout man does not really fear God unless he gains honestly what
> he eats and drinks. (His heart) concealed within him should be pure, as also the work of his
> hands, and his words should be employed only in virtuous discourse (13). Thus hath the Pro-
> phet spoken in the name of the Lord ; so, the blessing of the Lord and his salutation be on the
> Prophet.

Ad-Dárakutni (vol. II. p. 239) mentions Yahya Ibn Main as one of those who
delivered Traditions received by orally from as-Sháfi (vol. II. p. 569). In our
article on the latter, we have spoken of Ibn Main's conduct towards him and of what
passed, on that occasion, between Ibn Main and the imám Ahmad (Ibn Hanbal).
Ibn Main heard also Traditions delivered by Abd Allah Ibn al-Mubárak, Sofyán Ibn
Oyaina and others of the same class. When he made the pilgrimage, which he
frequently did, he used to go to Mekka in passing through Medina. The last time
he went, he visited Medina on going and, on his return, he staid there three days.
Having then set out with his fellow-travellers, he stopped with them at the first
halting-place in order to pass the night, and he had a dream in which he heard a
voice call out to him, saying : "O Abû Zakariya! dost thou then dislike my neigh-
" bourhood (14) ?" When the morning came, he said to his companions : " Con-
" tinue your journey ; as for me, I return to Medina." They did so, and he went
back to that city where he passed three days and then died. His corpse was borne
to the grave on the bier which had been made use of at the Prophet's burial. The
Khatib (vol. I. p. 75) says, in his History of Baghdad, that Ibn Main's death took
place on the 23rd of Zû 'l-Kaada, 233, but he is certainly mistaken, as I shall here
prove : Ibn Main went to Mekka and made the pilgrimage, after which, he returned
to Medina and there died. But how is it possible that a man who has made the
pilgrimage could die, the same year, in the month of Zû 'l-Kaada (15)? Had the
Khatib said that he died in Zû 'l-Hijja, the thing had been possible. Some persons
suppose that the mistake was committed by the transcriber of the work, but I found,

in two copies of it, that the passage is the same as we have just given. It is therefore difficult to admit that the error proceeded from the copyist. Further on, the same author says that he died before accomplishing the pilgrimage. In that case, the date which he gives might pass for correct; but I since met with a historical work entitled: *Kitáb el-Irshád fi marifat Ulamá il-Bilád* (*the directory, containing information respecting the learned men of all countries*), and compiled by the *háfiz* Abú Yala 'l-Khalil Ibn Abd Allah Ibn Ahmad Ibn Ibráhim Ibn al-Khalil al-Khalili (16), and, in it I read that Yahya Ibn Main died on the 22nd of Zú 'l-Hijja, in the year above mentioned (28th July, A. D. 848). From this, it appears that he did make the pilgrimage. The Khatib states also that he was born in the latter part of the year 158 and then adds : " He died at the age of seventy-seven years, wanting ten " days." This cannot be, as will be found of the calculation be made. In another historical work I read that he lived to the age of seventy-five years. God knows best! The funeral prayer was said over the body by the governor of Medina and was afterwards repeated several times. Ibn Main was buried in the Bakl cemetery. When they were carrying him to the grave, a man preceeded them, crying out : " This is he who expelled falsehoods from the Traditions left by the Prophet of God." A Traditionist composed on his death an elegy in which he said :

He is departed, that learned man who corrected the faults of every Traditionist, cleared up the contradictions in the *isnáds*, and dissipated the doubts and ambiguities which perplexed the learned of all countries.

The word ﻣﻴﻦ must be pronounced *Main.*—*Bistámi* has an *i* after the *b ;* remarks on the other letters are needless.—I read in a historical work that Yahya Ibn Main was the grandson of Ghiáth, the son of Ziád, the son of Aún, the son of Bistám, who was a *mawla* of al-Junaid Ibn Abd ar-Rahmán al-Ghatafáni al-Murri, the same who governed Khorásán in the name of the Omaiyide Khalif Hisbám Ibn Abd al-Malik. The genealogy given at the beginning of this article is that which is generally accepted as the more correct.—*Murri* means *belonging to the tribe of Murra,* who was a descendant of Ghatafán, being the son of Aúf Ibn Saad Ibn Dubyán Ibn Baghíd Ibn Raith Ibn Ghatafán. It is a large and famous tribe. A great number of Arabian tribes bear this name.—As-Samáni (*vol. II. p.* 156) says, in his *Ansáb :* " ﻧﻜﺎ may " be pronounced *Nakiyd* or *Nakayd.* It is the name of a village near al-Anbár. From

" it came Yahya Ibn Main an-Nakyai." The Khatib says that Pharaoh was a native
of this village ; God knows best !

(1) " In the year 162 (A.D. 867-8), Abd Allah Ibn Mâlik marched with a body of ten thousand men against
" the Khurramiya (*the partisans of Bâbek*) who were stirring up troubles in Adarbaijân. After killing and
" taking prisoners (*many of the insurgents*), he returned victorious. " — (*Nujûm*.)

(2) Upwards of twenty thousand pounds sterling.

(3) The science called *Tajrîh wa tadîl* (*improbation and justification*) had for object to determine the degree
of credibility to which every witness in a court of law and every reporter of Traditions were entitled. For
that purpose, it was necessary to study the life of the individual. The requisite points in a Traditionist were
good conduct, piety, veracity, exactness and a retentive memory.

(4) Abû Khaithama Zuhair Ibn Harb an-Nasâi, an eminent Traditionist, was distinguished for learning and
piety. Nasâ was his native place, but he travelled to many countries and afterwards settled at Baghdad. He
died in the month of Shaabân, 234 (March, A.D. 849). — (*Nujûm* ; *Huffâz*.)

(5) Ali Ibn Abd Allah, surnamed Ibn al-Madîni, was a Traditionist of the highest authority. He died at Medina in the month of Zû 'l-Kaada, 234 (May-June, A.D. 849). — (*Nujûm; Huffâz*.)

(6) Yahya Ibn Abi Kathîr al-Yamâni, named also Sâlih Ibn al-Motawakkil, was a Traditionist of considerable reputation. He died A. H. 110 (A.D. 748-9), according to the author of the *Nujûm*; in the *Tabakât al-
Huffâz*, his death is placed a year later.

(7) Abû 'n-Nasr Saîd Ibn Abi Arûba, a Traditionist of Basra, died A. H. 156 (A.D. 772-3), or 157. — (*Kitâb
el-Madrif; Huffâz*.)

(8) Mamar Ibn Râshid al-Harrâni al-Basri, a Traditionist of good authority, died A. H. 168 (A.D. 769), or
153. — (*Huffâz*.)

(9) The Hâfiz Abû Awâna al-Waddâh Ibn Abd Allah, was a member, by enfranchisement, of the tribe of
Yashkur. He died at Basra in the month of the 1st Rabi, 176 (June-July, A.D. 792). — (*Nujûm; Huffâz*.)

(10) Abû Saîd Abd ar-Rahmân Ibn Mahdi, an inhabitant of Basra and a Hâfiz of the highest authority, died
in that city, A. H. 198 (A.D. 613-4), at the age of sixty-three years. — (*Nujûm ; Huffâz*.)

(11) The Hâfiz Abû Zakariya Yahya Ibn Amâm أدم was a Traditionist of the highest authority. He died
A. H. 208 (A.D. 823-4). — (*Huffâz*.)

(12) The Ibn ar-Rûmi here mentioned speaks of Ibn Main as if he had conversed with him and could appreciate his merit. He cannot therefore be the poet of that name (see vol. II, p. 297), who was only twelve
years of age when Ibn Main died.

(13) This hemistich may also be rendered thus : his discourse should consist in Traditions only.

(14) Muhammad's tomb is at Medina.

(15) The pilgrimage takes place in Zû 'l-Hijja, the month which immediately follows Zû 'l-Kaada.

(16) Abû Yala 'l-Khalîli's work treated of the persons who transmitted tradition. He composed another
work bearing also the title of *Irshâd* and containing a history of Kazwin, his native place. As a Hâfiz, he
held a high reputation. He died in the latter half of the fifth century of the Hijra (A.D. 1062-1108). —
(*Hajji Khalifa; Huffâz*.)

YAHYA IBN YAHYA

Abû Muhammad Yahya al-Laithi was the son of Yahya, the son of Kathír, the son of Wislásen or Wislás, the son of Shammál, the son of Manghàyà. He drew his origin from the Masmûda, a berber tribe which had contracted clientship with the (Arabian) tribe of Laith. He, for that reason, bore the appellation of al-Laithi. His grand-father, Abû Isa Kathír, the first of the family who passed into Spain, fixed his residence in Cordova. It was there that he (Yahya) heard (the lessons) of Ziàd Ibn Abd ar-Rahmán Ibn Ziàd al-Lakhmi, surnamed Shabatûn (1), who was a native of that city and the person who (there) knew best by heart and could dictate the contents of the Muwatta composed by Málik Ibn Anas (vol. II. p. 545). He heard also traditional information delivered by Yahya Ibn Modar al-Kaisi, a native of Spain. At the age of twenty eight years he travelled to the East and learned perfectly the Muwatta under the dictation of Málik, with the exception of some paragraphs belonging to the chapter which treats of the spiritual retreat (2). Not being sure of having heard these passages well, he learned to repeat them correctly under the direction of Ziàd. At Mekka he heard (traditional information delivered by) Sofyàn Ibn Oyaina (vol. I. p. 578) and, in Misr (Old Cairo), he received lessons from al-Laith Ibn Saad (vol. II. p. 543), Abd Allah Ibn Wahb (vol. II. p. 15) and Abd ar-Rahmán Ibn al-Kásim (vol. II, p. 86). After attending assiduously the lessons of Málik and profiting greatly by his tuition, he studied the law under the principal disciples of that imám, both those of Medina and those of Misr. Málik used to call him the adkil (or intel-ligent man) of Spain. His motif for doing so is thus related : Yahya was, one day, at Málik's lecture with a number of fellow-students, when some one said : " Here " comes the elephant !" All of them ran out to see the animal, but Yahya did not stir : " Why," said Málik, " do you not go out and look at it? such animals are not " to be seen in Spain." To this Yahya replied : " I left my country for the purpose " of seeing you and obtaining knowledge under your guidance; I did not come " here for the purpose seeing the elephant." Málik was so highly pleased with this answer that he called him the adkil of the people of Spain. Some time after, Yahya returned to Spain and, having become chief (of the island), he propagated through-

out all that country the system of law draw up by Málik. It was accepted by immense multitudes, and the number of persons who taught the doctrines which they
had learned from him was very great. The best edition (3) of the *Muwatta* and
that which has the greatest reputation was given (*orally*) by Yahya Ibn Yahya. By
his rectitude and piety he obtained the highest respect from the emirs (*the men in
power*) and acquired great influence over them; such was his self-denial, that he
scrupulously avoided accepting any office under government. The elevated rank
which he held (*in public estimation*) was much superior to that of a kádi, and his refusal, through religious motives, to accept such an office gave him more influence
over men in power than any *kádi* could possess. The Spanish writer, Abù Muhammad Ali Ibn Ahmad, generally known by the surname of Ibn Hazm (*vol. II. p. 267*),
says: " Two systems of law were at first promulgated by persons in power and high
" station : that of Abù Hanífa (*vol. III. p. 555*) and that of Málik. Abù Yùsuf Ya-
" kùb, the disciple of Abù Hanífa,"—we shall give his life,—" being appointed
" (*chief*) kádi, acquired the right of nominating all the others, and there was not a
" city, from the far East to the most distant of the African provinces, in which he
" did not establish, as a kádi, one of his own disciples or one of those who professed
" his doctrines. Here, in Spain, we adopted the system of Málik for the following
" reason : Yahya Ibn Yahya was in high favour with the sultan, and his advice in
" whatever concerned (*the nomination of*) kádis was always followed. So, no kádi
" was ever appointed to act in any part of the Spanish provinces till Yahya had gi-
" ven his opinion and pointed out the person whom he preferred. He never desi-
" gnated any person for that office except one of his own disciples or of those who
" followed his doctrines. Now, as all men hasten towards that which is advanta-
" geous for them in the world, they adopted willingly what they hoped would con-
" duce to their interest. I must add that Yahya Ibn Yahya never filled the duties
" of a kádi and would never consent to accept such a place. This line of conduct
" served to augment his influence with the men in power and disposed them to
" follow more readily his advice. " The following anecdote is related by Ahmad
Ibn Abi 'l-Faiyàd (4) in the work composed by him : " The emir Abd ar-Rahmàn
" Ibn al-Hakam, surnamed al-Murtada (5) and the (*fourth*) Omaiyide sovereign of
" Spain, convoked, by letter, the jurisconsults into his presence, and they all went
" to the palace. It was in Ramadán (*the month of strict abstinence*), and he,
" happening to look at one of his concubines whom he loved passionately,

"was so much excited (*by her beauty*) that he lost all self-command and had "commerce with her. He then regretted deeply what he had done and con-"sulted these doctors respecting the mode of manifesting his repentance and "expiating his sin. Yahya Ibn Yahya replied : ' A sin of that kind can be expiated "by a fast of two consecutive months'. As he had hastened to give this opinion "(*fetwa*) before the others had time to speak, they kept silent, but, on leaving Abd "ar-Rahmān's presence, they spoke to each other of what had passed and then said "to Yahya : ' What prevented you from giving a *fetwa* conformable to the doctrine "' of Mālik?' That *imām* said : ' He who sins thus has the choice of manumitting "' (a slave), of giving food (*to the poor*), or of keeping a fast.' To this he answer-"ed : ' Had we opened to him such a door as that, he would satisfy his passion "' every day and repair his fault by freeing a slave. So I imposed on him the se-"' verest penalty in order to prevent him from relapsing.' "—When Yahya left Mālik, with the intention of returning to his native country, he went to Misr and found there Abd ar-Rahmān Ibn al-Kāsim, who was occupied in making a written compilation of the doctrines which he had learned from Mālik. (*On seeing this collection*) he resolved on hastening back and hear Mālik himself treat the questions which Ibn al-Kāsim had enregistered. He therefore travelled (*to Medina*) a second time and, finding, on his arrival, that Mālik was very ill, he abid with him till he expired. After attending the funeral, he returned to Ibn al-Kāsim, who recited to him the doctrines such as he heard them from Mālik's own lips. Abū 'l-Walid Ibn al-Faradi (*vol. II. p. 68*) mentions that fact in his historical work, with some other particulars of the same kind.—When Yahya Ibn Yahya returned to Spain, he became the paragon of the age and had none to equal him in that country. He was a man of great intelligence. Muhammad Ibn Omar Ibn Lubāba (6) said : " The (*great*) ju-"risconsult of Spain is Isa Ibn Dīnār (7); its most learned man is Abd al-Mālik Ibn "Habib (8), and its most intelligent man is Yahya Ibn Yahya."—Yahya, being suspected of having had a share in the (*great*) revolt (9), fled to Toledo and then sollicited a letter of protection, which was granted to him by the emir al-Hakam. He then returned to Cordova.—" Never," said Ahmad Ibn Khālid (10), " since the time of "the introduction of Islamism, did any of the learned in Spain enjoy such good "fortune, such influence and such a reputation as Yahya Ibn Yahya."—Ibn Bashkuwāl (*vol. I. p. 491*) says, in his historical work : " The prayers which Yahya Ibn "Yahya addressed to God were always fulfilled. In his appearance, dress and man-

" ner of sitting he greatly resembled Mâlik.   It is related that he said : ' I (one day)
" ' went to take hold of the stirrup of al-Laith Ibn Saad (vol. II. p. 543), and his
" ' servant boy tried to prevent me, on which he addressed to me these words : ' You
" ' shall have all the learned men for servants ;' and that I have lived long enough
" to witness."   The same author adds : " Yahya Ibn Yahya died in the month of
" Rajab, 234 (Feb. A. D. 849).   His tomb is situated in the cemetery of the
" Abbasides, and prayers are offered up at it in times of drought."   This cemetery
lies outside Cordova.   Abû Abd Allah al-Humaidi (vol. III. p. 1) informs us, moreover, that he died on the 22nd of that month.   Abû 'l-Walid Ibn al-Faradi states that
his death took place in 233, or, by another account, in 234 and in the month of
Rajab.   God knows best.— *Wildi* or *Wildsen* is a Berber word which signifies *he
hears them* (11).— *Shammdl* is pronounced with an *a* after the *sh* and a double *m*.—
Manghâyd signifies *a killer* in Berber (12).   We have already spoken of the words
Laithi (vol. II. p. 409), *Berber* (vol. I. p. 35) and *Masmâda* (vol. III. p. 215).

---

(1) I follow the orthography of one ms. and of the printed text of Makkari's Spanish History. — Abû Abd
Allah Ziâd Ibn Abd ar-Rahmân al-Lakhmi, generally known by the name of Shabtûn, was a native of Cordova and a doctor of the rite of Mâlik. It was he who first introduced into Spain the system of jurisprudence
drawn up by that imâm and who taught there the Muwatta (vol. II, p. 110). Hishâm Ibn Abd er-Rahmân, the
second Omaiyide sovereign of Spain wished to have him for a kâdi at Cordova, but could never obtain his consent. The Ziâd died A. H. 904 (A. D. 619-20), or 198, according to another statement. It was by his advice that Yahya Ibn Yahya travelled to the East for the purpose of studying under Mâlik. — (Gayangos's Makkari, vol. II, p. 500 et seq.)

(2) The spiritual retreat (itikâf) consists in remaining some days and nights successively in a mosque and
passing that time in prayer, fasting and meditation.

(3) Literally a recital. The contents of these classical works were taught orally, the professor knowing
them by heart.

(4) This author is not mentioned by Hajji Khalîfa, and al-Makkari merely informs us that the subject of his
work was historical. According to an indication given by Ibn al-Athîr in his Kâmil, it contained information respecting the Abbaside dynasty. See Mr. Dozy's Historia Abbadidarum, IInd part, p. 94.

(5) This is a mistake; his surname was al-Muzaffar.

(6) Muhammad Ibn Omar Ibn Lahâba (لهابة), a native of Spain, a teacher of Mâlikite jurisprudence and
a Traditionist, died A. H. 314 (A. D. 916-7).—(Gayangos's Makkari, and the arabic edition of the same work.)

(7) According to al-Makkari, this Ibn Ibn Dinâr was a jurisconsult and composed a work entitled al-Hidhya
(the guide). He left Cordova during the reign of Hishâm Ibn Abd ar-Rahmân, the second Omaiyide sovereign,
and travelled to the East, where he studied the law under Mâlik.

(8) Abû Marwân Abd al-Malik Ibn Habîb was a native of Cordova and one of the Spanish doctors who travelled to the East for the purpose of studying under Mâlik. He contributed to the introduction of that imâm's doc-

crimes into Spain. Ad-Dabbi places his death in the month of Zú 'l Hijja, 319 (May, A. D. 934). See Casiri's *Bibliotheca Arabica Hispanica*, t. II, p. 111. According to the authority followed by Mr. de Gayangos (*Makkari*, vol. I, p. 911), he died at Cordova, A. H. 329, after composing not less than one thousand works or treatises on various subjects.

(9) This is the famous revolt of the suburb (*rabad*) of Cordova which took place A. H. 198 (A. D. 814), under the reign of al-Hakam Ibn Hishâm. A full and exact account of this event, which led to the conquest of Crete by these suburbians (Rabadis), is contained in Mr. Dozy's *Histoire des Musulmans d'Espagne*, t. II, p. 68 et seq.

(10) Ahmad Ibn Khâlid, a doctor of the law and a traditionist, was a contemporary of Ibn Labîba (see note 8). The Omaiyide sovereign Abd ar-Rahmân an-Nâsir esteemed him so highly that he had him brought to Cordova and lodged in one of the houses belonging to the mosque near the palace. He allowed him a daily ration of provisions and made him considerable presents. The enemies of Ibn Khâlid reproached him for accepting them favours, and he composed a work in vindication of his conduct. — (*Makkari*, arabic text, vol. II, p. 10A.)

(11) The word *tlamm* is berber and signifies *he heard them*.

(12) In Berber, the root *engh* or *negh* (نغ) signifies *to kill*. A *killer* or *murderer* is designated by the words *inngh* or *inghân*. The same root appears in the name of *Manghâyd*, which, however, has not a Berber form.

YAHYA IBN AKTHAM

Abû Muhammad Yahya Ibn Aktham Ibn Muhammad Ibn Katan Ibn Samân Ibn Mushannaj at-Tamîmi al-Usaiyidi al-Marwazi (*a member of the tribe of Usaigid, which was a branch of that of Tamîm, and a native of Marw*) drew his descent from Aktham Ibn as-Saifi, the judge of the Arabs (1). He was learned in the law and sagacious in his judgments. Ad-Dârakutni (vol. II. p. 239) mentions him as having been one of as-Shâfi's (vol. II. p. 569) disciples, and the Khatîb (vol. I. p. 75) says, in his History of Baghdad : " Yahya Ibn Aktham was untainted with heresy and followed the doc-
" trine professed by the people of the Sunna (*the orthodox*). He heard (*Traditions*)
" from Abd Allah Ibn al-Mubârak (vol. II. p. 12), Sofyân Ibn Oyaina (vol. I. p. 578)
" and others."—We have already related, in our article on Sofyân, what passed between Yahya and that doctor. — " Traditions were delivered on his authority by
" Abû Isa at-Tirmidi (vol. II. p. 679) and others."—Talha Ibn Muhammad Ibn

VOL. IV.   5

Jaafar (2) said of him : '' Yahya Ibn Aktham was a man of note in the world; his
'' proceedings and his history are well known; neither great nor small are ignorant
'' of his merit, his learning, the high authority which he held and the skill with
'' which he minded his own interests and those of the khalifs and sovereigns who
'' were his contemporaries. He possessed an extensive knowledge of jurisprudence,
'' great literary acquirements, singular skill in the conduct of affairs (3) and the ta-
'' lent of surmounting difficulties.'' He obtained such influence over al-Mâmûn's
mind that no one could surpass him in that khalif's favour. Al-Mâmûn himself was
versed in the sciences; so, when he knew the character of Yahya Ibn Aktham and
perceived that he held the highest station in learning, he set his whole heart on him
and went so far as to appoint him to the office of kâdi 'l-kudât (4) and confide to him
the administration of his subjects. The vizirs charged with the direction of public
affairs took no decision without submitting it to Yahya for his approval. We know
of no person's having ever obtained such complete influence over the mind of his
sovereign except Yahya Ibn Yahya (p. 29 of this vol.) and Ahmad Ibn Abi Dûwâd (vol.
I. p. 61). A person, noted for speaking with great elegance, being asked which of the
two, Yahya Ibn Aktham or Ahmad Ibn Abi Dûwâd, was the better man, he answered in
these terms : '' Ahmad was grave with his concubine and with his daughter; Yahya was
'' gay with his adversaries and his enemies; Yahya was untained with heresy and
'' followed the orthodox doctrine, whilst Ahmad was quite the contrary.''—In our article on Ahmad we have said some words of his religious belief and of his partiality
for the Motazelites. Yahya was heard to say : '' The Korân is the word of God, and
'' whoever says that it is created should be invited to abandon that opinion; and if
'' he do not, his head should be struck off.'' The jurisconsult Abû 'l-Fadl Abd al-
Azîz Ibn Ali Ibn Abd ar-Rahmân al-Usbaubi (5), surnamed Zain ad-Dîn, mentions,
in his treatise on the partition of hereditaments (fardid), the problems designated by
surnames (6), and, amongst them, that one which is called the Mâmûnian (al-Mâmû-
niya) and which is the fourteenth in order. It runs thus : (A person died, leaving)
father and mother and two daughters. Before the inheritance was shared (between them), one of the daughters died, leaving (as survivors) the other persons spe-
cified in the problem (7). It was called the Mâmûnian for the following reason :
(The khalif) al-Mâmûn wished to find a man fit to act as a kâdi and, hearing of Yahya
Ibn Aktham's talents, he had him sent for. Yahya, being introduced, saw clearly
that the khalif disdained him on account of his low stature; on which he said :

" Commander of the faithful ! if it is for my learning that you require me and not
" for my stature, ask me a question." Al-Mâmûn proposed to him the one above
mentioned and Yahya answered : " Commander of the faithful ! was the person who
" died first a male or a female?" The khalif perceived immediately that he was
acquainted with the problem and appointed him kâdi. In this problem, if the first
who died was a male, the two questions (to which it gives rise) can be resolved by (di-
viding the inheritance into) fifty-four (equal parts); and if the first who died was a
female, the grandfather (of the daughters) could not inherit in the second case (that
is, on the death of the daughter), because he is a father of a mother (the maternal
grandfather); and the questions (involved in the problem) can both be resolved by (di-
viding the inheritance into) eighteen parts (8). — The Khatîb says in his History of
Baghdad : " Yahya Ibn Aktham was nominated as kâdi of Basra at the age of
" twenty years, or thereabouts. The people of that city found him look so young that
" they asked each other of what age he might be. Yahya, being informed of this,
" spoke (to them) as follows : ' I am older than Attâb Ibn Asîd (9) whom the Prophet
" ' sent to act as a kâdi in Mekka; I am older than Moâd Ibn Jabal (10), whom the
" ' Prophet sent to act as a kâdi for the people of Yemen; and I am older than Kaab
" ' Ibn Sûr (11), who was sent by Omar Ibn al-Khattâb to act as a kâdi for the people
" ' of Basra.' In making this answer, he produced his own justification."—The
Prophet nominated Attâb Ibn Asîd kâdi of Mekka, on the taking of that city, and he
(Attâb) was then twenty-one years of age, or twenty-three, according to another statement. He became a Moslim on the day in which Mekka was taken, and addressed
these words to the Prophet : " I shall be your companion and never quit you ;" on
which the Prophet said to him : " Would you not consent to my appointing you over
" the family of God?" Attâb continued to act as their kâdi till he died. (The Khatîb)
adds : " Yahya remained a year without receiving any one as a (competent) witness (12.)
" One of the amîns (syndics of corporations) then went to him and said : " O kâdi !
" ' you have put a stop to all proceedings and made too long a delay (13).'—' How
" ' so ?' said Yahya.—' Because,' said the amîn, ' you who are the kâdi will receive
" ' no one as a witness.' In consequence of this remonstrance, he authorised, that
" very day, seventy persons of the city to act as witnesses." Another author states
that Yahya Ibn Aktham was appointed kâdi of Basra in the year 202 (A. D. 817-8).
We have already mentioned, in the life of Hammâd Ibn Abî Hanîfa (vol. I. p. 469),
that Yahya succeeded Ismaîl, the son of that Hammâd, in the kâdiship of Basra.

Omar Ibn Shabba (vol. *II. p.* 375) relates in his *Kitáb Akhbár il-Basra* (*History of Basra*) that the Ládiship of Basra was taken from Yahya in the year 210. Muhammad Ibn Mansúr (14) relates as follows: " We were with al-Mámún, on our way to " Syria, when he ordered a proclamation to made declaring *metd* (*temporary*) mar- " riages to be lawful. On this Yahya Ibn Akthem said to me and Abú 'l-Ainá (vo- " *lume III. p.* 56) : ' Tomorrow morning, early, go both of you (15) to him and, if you " ' find an opportunity of speaking (*to him on the subject*) do so; if not, remain silent " ' till I go in.' We went there and found him with a toothpick in his hand and " exclaiming, in a violent passion : ' Two *metds* occurred in the time of the Prophet " ' of God and in that of Abú Bakr; and shall I forbid the practise? Who are you, " ' vile scarabee! to dare forbid me to follow what was practised by the Prophet of " ' God and by Abú Dakr?' On this, Abú 'l-Ainá made me a sign and said : " ' Muhammad Ibn Mansúr! that is a man who is capable of attributing to Omar " ' Ibn al-Khattáb what he has just said; how can we speak to him (16)?' So we " held our peace. Yahya Ibn Akthem then came in and sat down. We sat down " also, and al-Mámún said to him : ' Why do I see you look so troubled?' Yahya " answered : ' Commander of the faithful! it is with grief for a novelty introduced " ' into Islamism.'—' What novelty?' said the khalif.—' Yahya replied : ' A pro- " ' clamation has been made declaring *metd* marriages lawful, declaring fornication " ' lawful.'—' Fornication?' exclaimed al-Mámún.—' Yes; *metd* is fornication!'— " ' On what authority do you say so?'—'On that of the book of Almighty God and of " ' a declaration made by his Prophet. God said : *Now are the true believers happy,* " ' *and so forth to the words: and those who keep themselves from carnal knowledge* " ' *of any except their wives or the* (*slaves*) *whom their right hands possess; and who-* " ' *so coveteth any* (*woman*) *beyond these, they are transgressors* (17). Commander of " ' the faithful! a *metd* wife is she a woman possessed by the right hand (a *slave*)?' " The khalif answered : ' No!'—' Is she a wife who can inherit and be inherited of " ' lawfully in the sight of God? a wife bearing legitimate children? one whose mar- " ' riage is regulated by lawful conditions?'— ' The khalif answered : ' No.'— " ' Then,' replied Yahya, ' whoever passes these two limits is a transgressor. Com- " ' mander of the faithful! there is az-Zuhri (vol. *II. p.* 581) who related on the au- " ' thority of Abd Allah and al-Hasan, the sons of Muhammad Ibn al-Hanafiya " ' (vol. *II. p.* 573), that they heard their father declare that he heard Ali Ibn Abi " ' Tálib say: *The Prophet ordered me to proclaim that metd marriages were forbid-*

" ' den and unlawful, after he had authorised them.'—Al-Mámún then turned towards
" us and said : ' Is it well ascertained that this tradition came from az-Zuhri?'—
" We replied : ' It is, Commander of the faithful! a number of Traditionists have
" ' related it, such as Málik (vol. II. p. 545), to whom God be gracious!'—On hea-
" ring this, he exclaimed : ' God forgive me! proclaim that wed marriages are for-
" ' bidden!' and a proclamation to that effect was immediately made."—The kádi
Abú Ishák Ismaïl Ibn Ishák Ibn Ismaïl Ibn Hammád Ibn Zaïd Ibn Dirhim al-Azdi (18),
who was a doctor of Malikite jurisprudence and an inhabitant of Basra, said, in
speaking of Yahya Ibn Aktham and extolling his merit : " He one day did to Isla-
" mism a service the like of which no man ever rendered to it before."—Yahya's
works on jurisprudence are excellent, but so voluminous that they are neglected by
readers. He composed some treatises on the fundamentals of jurisprudence and published a work against the people of Irák (the Hanefites), to which he gave the title of
at-Tanbih (the warning). He had frequent discussions with Dáwûd Ibn Ali (vol. I.
p. 501). When he was a kádi, a man went up to him and the following dialogue ensued :
" May God preserve you! how much should I eat?"—Yahya replied : " Enough to
" get over hunger and not enough to attain satiety."—" How long may I laugh?"
—" Till your face brightens, but without raising your voice."—" How long should
" I weep?"—" Weeping should never fatigue you, if it be through fear of God."
—" What actions of mine should I conceal?"—" As many as you can."—" What
" are the actions which I should do openly?"—" Those which may serve as exam-
" ples to good and virtuous men whilst they secure you from public reprobation."
— On this, the man exclaimed : " May God preserve us from words which abide
" when deeds have passed away! (19)."—Yahya was the most acute of men
and the most skilful in the management of affairs. I read in a miscellany that
Ahmad Ibn Abi Khálid al-Ahwal (vol. I. p. 20), al-Mámún's vizir, was standing,
one day, in the presence of his sovereign when Yahya came forth from a closet to
which he had retired and stood (also in the khalif's presence). " Come up," said
al-Mámún. He went up and sat with him on the sofa, but at the farthest end of
it. Ahmad then said : " Commander of the faithful! the kádi Yahya is for me a
" friend to whom I confide all that concerns me, but he is changed from what
" he used to be for me." On this, al-Mámún said : " O Yahya! the ruin
" of a sovereign's prosperity is caused by the misintelligence which arises be-
" tween his ministers. No one can equal you or Ahmad in my esteem; what

" then is the motive of this mutual distrust?" Yahya replied : " Commander
" of the faithful! I declare, by Allah! that my feelings towards Ahmad are even more
" friendly than what he said; but he, seeing the rank which I hold in your favour,
" fears that, one day or other, I may turn against him and disserve him in your
" mind. I prefer telling this to you openly, so that he may be relieved from his
" apprehensions, and I declare that, even if he injured me to the very utmost,
" I should never speak ill of him in your presence."—" Is that the fact?" said
the khalif to Ahmad. He replied : " It is so." Al-Mâmûn then exclaimed :
" God protect me from you both! I never met with men more shrewd and more in-
" telligent than you.'—No vice could be reproached to Yahya except a certain inclination which was attributed to him and of which he had the reputation (20); but God
best knows how he may have been in that respect. The Khatib (vol. I. p. 75) states,
in his History of Baghdad, that Ahmad Ibn Hanbal (vol. I. p. 44), being informed
of the imputations cast on Yahya Ibn Aktham's character, exclaimed: 'Good God!
" who can say such a thing?" and denied the fact in the most positive manner. It is
related, moreover, that the jealousy borne to Ahmad was excessive.—He was acquainted with a great number of sciences and, when he had a conversation with any one
and found him skilled in jurisprudence, he questioned him on points relative to the
Traditions and, if he discovered that he knew traditions by heart, he would propose to
him some grammatical difficulty; then, if he found that he was acquainted with
grammar, he would question him on scholastic theology; and all that for the purpose
of confounding the man and bringing him to a stand. A very intelligent native of
Khorâsân, who knew by heart many Traditions, went to see him one day and was
drawn by him into a discussion. When Yahya discovered that he was versed in a
variety of sciences, he asked him if he knew any Tradition which had served as a
fundamental principle of jurisprudence. The other replied : " I learned from Sha-
" rîk (vol. I. p. 622) that Abû Ishâk (vol. II. p. 392) told him that al-Hârith (21) rela-
" ted to him that Ali caused a pederast to be lapidated." Yahya, on hearing this,
stopped short and addressed not another word to the man. The Khatib then relates
that Yahya received a visit from the two sons of Masada (22), who were extremely handsome. Whe he saw them walking across the court of his house, he recited extem-
pore these lines :

    O you who have left your tents to visit me! may God grant you both long life with his blessing! Why have you come to me when I am unable to do either the lawful deed or the deed forbidden. It saddens me to see you stand before me and to have nothing to offer you except fair words.

He then made them sit down before him and kept them in amusing chat till they went away. It is said that he was dismissed from the kádiship on account of these verses (23). I read in a miscellany that Yahya Ibn Aktham was jesting, one day, with al-Hasan Ibn Wahb, the same person of whom we have spoken in the life of his brother Suleimán (vol. I. p. 596), and who was then a boy. In playing with him, he tapped him on the cheek and, perceiving that he was displeased, he recited these lines:

O full moon, whose cheek I tapped and who, highly offended, turned away from me in anger! If a scratch displease you or a bite, wear always, my master! a veil (to conceal your face). Let not those locks appear as a temptation, nor let their ringlets cover your cheeks, lest you slay the wretched, or tempt the anchorites, or leave the kádi of the Moslims in torment.

Ahmad Ibn Yúnus ad-Dabbi related as follows: " The kátib Ibn Zaidún, who was an " extremely handsome youth, was writing under the dictation of the kádi Yahya Ibn " Aktham, when the latter pinched his cheek. He felt much confused, blushed and " threw away the pen. ' Take up your pen,' said Yahya, ' and write down what I am " going to say to you.' He then dictated to him " — the above mentioned verses.—The following anecdote was related by Ismaïl Ibn Muhammad Ibn Ismaïl as-Saffár (24): " I heard Abú 'l-Ainá say, at one of Abú 'l-Abbás al-Mubarrad's " (vol. III. page 31) sittings (or conferences): ' I was at one of Abú Aásim an-" ' Nabíl's (25) sittings, and Abú Bakr, the son of Yahya Ibn Aktham, began to pull " ' about a young slave who was there. The boy cried out; Abú Aásim asked who " ' was that man ? and, being informed that it was Abú Bakr, the son of Yahya Ibn " ' Aktham, he said : If he be guilty of theft, his father hath been also guilty of " ' theft heretofore (26). " This anecdote is given by the Khatib, in his History of Baghdad. The same author relates, in that work, that al-Mámún asked Yahya " who was the author of this verse :

A kádi who considers fornication as meriting corporal chastisement, and thinks a worse crime no ,

Yahya replied : " Does the Commander of the faithful not know whom it is ? "—

"I do not ", said the khalif. "Well ", said Yahya, " it was uttered by that pro-
"fligate, Ahmad Ibn Abi Noaim, the same who said :

> "I think that tyranny will never cease so long as the nation is governed by an Abbaside.

The narrator says that al-Mámún was confounded, and that, after a moment's
silence, he gave orders to have Ahmad Ibn Abi Noaim banished to Sind. These two
verses belong to a piece which I shall give here :

> Fortune, which reduced me to silence, now permits me to speak of the afflictions which have
> kept me so long astounded. Cursed be Fortune for crushing some men and depressing others !
> May that nation never prosper, —that nation which deserves to suffer lengthened adversity and
> lasting perdition ! —if it consent to undergo the administration of Yahya, of a man who is
> incapable of ruling it ; a kádi who considers fornication as meriting corporal chastisement and
> thinks a worse crime no harm. He would judge in favour of his smooth-faced fondling and give
> sentence against Jarir and Abbás (27). God protect us ! justice hath disappeared and little
> honesty is to be found with mankind. Our emir takes bribes ; our judge acts like the people
> of Lot, and our breed (the khalif) is the worst of rulers. Did religion prosper and flourish,
> every just measure would be taken for (the welfare of) the people ; but I am sure that tyranny
> will never cease, as long as the nation is governed by an Abbaside.

I am inclined to think that this piece contained more verses than what are inserted
here, but these are all which the Khatíb gives.—The Amáli (or dictations) drawn up
by Abú Bakr Muhammad Ibn al-Kásim al-Anbári (vol. III. page 53) contains an
anecdote which I shall now insert : "The kádi Yahya Ibn Aktham said to a person
"whom he admitted into his familiarity and with whom he was accustomed to jest :
" ' Tell me what you heard the people say of me.'—The other replied : ' They say
" ' nothing of you but what is good.'—Nay', said the kádi, ' I do not make you this
" ' question for the purpose of obtaining from you a certificate of morality.' The
" man then answered : ' I never heard them accuse the kádi of any thing except
" ' an irregular inclination.' Yahya laughed and said : ' I ask God's pardon for
" ' all the sins of which I am accused except that which you have mentioned (28),
" ' (for I never committed it).' "—Abú 'l-Faraj al-Ispaháni (vol. II. page 249)
relates, in his Kitáb al-Aghání, a number of similar anecdotes concerning Yahya.
He says also : " Al-Mámún, having frequently heard imputations of this
" nature cast upon Yahya, resolved on putting him to the test and invited
" him to a private interview. He then said to a young mamlúk (white slave) who
" was a Khazarian by nation and remarkably handsome : ' You alone shalt

" ' attend us, and, when I go out, do not leave the room.' When they met in
" the sitting-room and had conversed together for some time, al-Mámûn retired as
" if on some necessary occasion and, having left the slave with Yahya, he concealed
" himself in a place whence he could see what would happen. The slave, whom
" he had told to jest and make sport with Yahya, did what he was ordered, and the
" khalif well knew that Yahya would not dare to take liberties with the boy.
" ' Having then heard Yahya say : ' *Were it not for you (who seduced us), we*
" ' *should have been true believers!* ' (*Korán*, sur. 34, verse 30), he came into the
" room and recited these verses :

" ' We hoped to see justice made manifest, but that hope was followed by disappointment.
" ' How can the world and its inhabitants prosper, if the chief (*kádi*) of the Moslims acts like the
" ' people of Lot?' "

The *kátib* Abû Hakîma Râshid Ibn Ishâk Ibn Râshid, who was the author of these
verses, composed a great number of pieces on Yahya.—In the article on al-Mâmûn which al-Masûdi has given in his *Murûj ad-Dahab*, will be found some anecdotes concerning Yahya ; we abstain from inserting them here because they are of
the same kind as those just mentioned.—A story is told of Moawia Ibn Abi Sofyân
which greatly resembles the one we have just related of al-Mámûn's asking who was
the author of a certain verse and of Yahya's replying by another verse taken from
the same poem. When Moawia Ibn Abi Sofyân the Omaiyide was laid up with the
malady of which he died, he suffered so greatly that his life was dispaired of, and
one of Ali Ibn Abi Tâlib's sons, whose name I do not recollect, went to make him
a visit. Moawia rallied all his strength and sat up in his bed, in order to receive
him and not give him the gratification of seeing how ill he was. Being too weak
to hold himself up, he at length leaned back upon a pile of cushions and recited
this verse :

I rally all my strength, so that those who are ready to rejoice at my sufferings may see that I
am a man whom misfortune cannot overcome.

The son of Ali immediately rose from his seat and went out, reciting this line :

When death grasps you in its clutches, you will find all your amulets of no avail.

The persons present admired greatly this repartee. The verses here mentioned are taken from a long *kasida* which was composed by Abù Duwaib Khuwailid Ibn Khàlid al-Hudali (*the Hudailite*) (29) on the death of his sons, five of whom were carried off, in one and the same year, by the plague. They had fled from their native place with their father and were going to Egypt. Abù Duwaib died on his way to that country, or, by another account, on his way to Ifrîkiya (*North Africa*), whither he was accompanying Abd Allah Ibn az-Zubair.—I have since read, in the ninth chapter of Ibn al-Habbâriya's (*vol. III. p.* 150) *Falak al-Madni*, that al-Husain, the son of Ali Ibn Abi Tàlib, went to visit Moawia during his illness, and that the latter said to his attendants : " Prop me up (*with cushions*) " and then recited the verse of Abù Duwaib's, applying it to his own case. Al-Husain saluted (*on entering*) and then repeated the other verse. God knows if this be exact. Abù Bakr Ibn Dàwûd az-Zàhiri (*vol. II. page* 662) relates the same anecdote in his *Kitâb az-Zuhara*, and attributes the reply to al-Hasan, the son of Ali. I must here observe that neither Ibn al-Habbâriya nor az-Zàhiri mention that Moawia was in his last illness when this happened, and such could not possibly have been the case, because al-Hasan died before Moawia, neither could al-Husain have been present at Moawia's death, for he was then in Hijàz and Moawia breathed his last in Damascus.—I since found, towards the beginning of the work entitled *Kitâb at-Tadzi* (*book of consolations*) and composed by Abù 'l-Abbàs al-Muharrad (*vol. III. page* 31), that this scene passed between al-Husain and Moawia. It was probably from this work that Ibn al-Habbâriya took his account of it.—An anecdote of a similar kind is related of Akîl, the son of Ali Ibn Abi Tàlib : Having abandoned his father, he joined the party of Moawia, who received him with great kindness and treated him with the highest honour ; but that was merely for the purpose of annoying Ali. After the murder of Ali, Moawia remained sole possessor of the supreme authority and, finding Akîl's presence becoming irksome, he began to say in his presence things that might offend him and oblige him to go away. One day, at a levee where all the most eminent of the Syrian (*Arabs*) were assembled, Moawia said to them : " Do you know who was the Abù " Lahab of whom God (*in his Koran, surat* 111) spoke in these terms : *The hands* " *of Abû Lahab shall perish?*" The Syrians answered that they did not. "Well," said he, " Abù Lahab was the paternal uncle of that man, " pointing to Akîl. He had no sooner pronounced these words that Akîl said : " Do you know who was Abù Lahab's wife, of whom God said : *And his wife also, the bearer of faggots, having on her neck a rope made of palm-tree fibres ?*" They answered that they did not :

" Well ", said he, " she was the paternal aunt of that man ", pointing to Moawia.
The fact was that Omm Jamil, Moawia's aunt and the daughter of Harb Ibn Omaiya
Ibn Abd Shams Ibn Abd Manâf, was the wife of Abû Lahab Abd al-Ozza and the
person who is indicated in this sûrat of the Koran. It was really a silencing answer.
—An anecdote similar to the foregoing is told of a certain king who laid siege to a
city. He had with him an immense army of cavalry and infantry, with provisions
in abundance. He sent a letter to the lord of the city, advising him to surrender
the place or else he should be attacked. In this letter he spoke of his numerous
troops and the great quantity of munitions which he had brought with him, and in
it he inserted this passage of the Koran : *Until they came to the valley of the ants;
and an ant said :* " *O ants! enter into your dwellings lest Solomon and his*
" *forces tread you under foot and perceive it not* (30)." The lord of the city, having received this epistle, pondered over it for some time and then read it to his
officers. " Who ", said he, " can return to that a proper answer? " One of the
secretaries replied : " Let these words be written to him : *And he smiled, laughing at*
" *its words* " (31). This answer was approved of by all present.—An anecdote of a
similar kind is thus related by Ibn Rashîk al-Kairawâni (*vol. I. page* 384), in his
Anmûdaj : Abd Allah Ibn Ibrahîm Ibn al-Muthanna at-Tûsi, generally known by the
surname of Ibn al-Muwaddib, belonged to a family of al-Mahdiya (32) and was
a native of Kairawân. He had some reputation as a poet but led a wandering
life, being always in search of minerals and the philosopher's stone. His manner
of living was very miserable and parcimonious, as he spent (*in chemical operations*)
whatever he was able to gain. Having left his country with the intention of going to
Sicily, he was taken prisoner, at sea, by the Christians (*Rûm*) and remained a long
time in captivity. Thika tad-Dawla Yûsuf Ibn Abd Allah Ibn Muhammad Ibn al-Husain al-Kudâi, the prince of Sicily, having concluded a truce with the Christians,
obtained that all the captives should be sent to him. Ibn al-Muwaddib, who was one
of the number, recited to Thika-tad-Dawla a poem in which he extolled his merit
and thanked him for what he had done. Not receiving, in return, a gift adequate to
his expectations and being inordinately desirous (*of obtaining money*), he spoke (*to
that emir on the subject*) and was most importunate (*in his demands*) (33). At that
time, he was living concealed in the house of an alchimist with whom he was
acquainted, and remained there a long while. Having then gone out (*one night*) in
a state of intoxication, with the intention of purchasing sugar-plums (*to eat with his*

wine), he was arrested before he was aware and carried before the chief of the *shurta* (*police guards*), by whom he was conducted to the governor. "You good-for-nothing " fellow!" said the latter, "what is this I hear of you?' The poet replied : "A pack " of lies! may God protect our lord the emir!" The prince then asked him who it was that said in one his poems :

> The man nobly born is always plagued by scoundrels (34).

The poet replied : "It was the same person who said :

> " The enmity of poets is the worst of acquisitions."

The prince remained silent for some time and then ordered him a sum of one hundred *rubdis* (35); but, fearing that he might again be irritated against him and punish after pardoning, he expelled him from the city.—The lines cited here are the second hemistichs of two verses belonging to that *kasida* of al-Mutanabbi's (*vol. I.* p. 102) which rhymes in *na* and which he composed in praise of Badr Ibn Ammár. It begins thus :

> Love takes away from the tongue the faculty of speech, and the complaints which give most solace to a lover are those which he utters aloud.

It is a well-known poem. The verse to which the first hemistich belongs is as follows :

> Impose silence on that adviser who, in accusing me, leads you into error. The man nobly born is always plagued by scoundrels.

The second verse is this :

> The complots of fools turn against themselves, and the enmity of poets is the worst of acquisitions.

Having mentioned the name of Thika-tad-Dawla, we shall give here a poem composed in his praise by Abù Muhammad Abd Allah Ibn Muhammad at-Tanùkhi, generally known by the appellation of Ibn Kàdi Mìla (*the son of the kàdi of Mìla*). The poet recited it to him on the festival of the Sacrifice. This *kasida*, which is so remarkable for its originality, was not to be found complete, but I at length discovered a copy of it written on the cover of a book. Till then, I knew only a part of it and never heard of any person's knowing more. As it is so fine a poem and so rare, I have decided on giving it here :

Love and my afflicted heart cause my tears to flow, whilst my eyes gather (*a harvest of*) that passionate desire which is imposed (*on every hour*). True it is that I am called towards that object which I wished to avoid and from whose abode I had departed; it is a soft-voiced gazelle (*maiden*) adorned with ear-rings who lurk me. Hers are the large, dark eyes, the languishing glances, (*the waist so slender that it leaves*) the girdle empty, and the bracelet holding firmly (*to the arm*). The brackish water flowing from her country is (*for me*) sweet-tasted, and its cold winds shed genial mildness. What makes me despair of our meeting are the dangerous grounds which intervene and in which (*even*) the nocturnal breeze (*loses its force and*) dies. The jealous spy abstains from sleep lest he should see, in a dream, (*my*) union effected (*with her whom I love*). He passes the day regretting that, though our dwelling-place was near (*to him*), his inattention prevented him from seeing what had passed. The atmosphere gives us to expect a thunder-cloud, pouring down its showers and whose lightnings, like yellow serpents, glance around. When it appeared and the thunder howled, and the eyelids of the black cloud shed their waters, I was like a man stung by a scorpion : the thunder was the incantation of the serpent-charmer, and the mizzling rain was the saliva which he blew from his mouth; so great were the sufferings I endured. By that was recalled to my mind the recollection of (*my beloved*) Raiya and of what I had forgotten; I now remember (*all*), but that redoubles my affliction. When we met in the sacred territory (*of Mekka*), Raiya rejoiced our hearts by the cry of *labbaika* (*here I am at your call*) our camels then roamed freely; I looked at her, whilst the humps of the camels were dropping blood (36), and she said (*to her female companions*) :
" Does any of you know that young man? his gazing at me so long makes me uneasy. When
" we are in march, he walks on a line with us, and when the camels' feet cease to move, he
" also stops. " I then said to her two companions : " Tell her that I am smitten with love
" for her; " and they replied : " We shall manage (*to do so*) cautiously." — " Say also to her :
" ' O Omm Amr! is not this (*the valley of*) Mina? whilst made in the vale of Mina are
" ' never disappointed (*tokhtofu*). It was for me an omen (*tofaletto*) of your fulfilling your
" ' latest promise, when you let me see, as if by accident, the tips of your fingers dyed with
" ' henna. In Arafat, I find what informs (*me*) of a favour I shall obtain; that of your heart's
" ' inclining towards me. The (*traces left by the*) blood of the victims will always serve to
" ' guide us, even when my reason is absorbed in converse with love. The kissing of the sacred
" ' stone will announce to me the approach of good fortune and of a time favorable to our love.' "
They bore (*her*) my message and she said, in smiling : " The words of augury are deceptive.
" On my life I did I not tell you both that he arrays his discourse in the embroidered robe of
" ' eloquence? Trust as little as you can to his insidious words and say (*to him*) : ' Thou shalt
" ' know, to-day, which of us is the better augur. You hoped, in (*the valley of*) Mina, to
" ' obtain your wish, and, when to that vale, you injured my reputation. Our pilgrim's
" ' sacred garment has announced that we are forbidden to meet and that I shall refuse to grant
" ' what you desire. There (*is my answer*). And, when I cast the pebbles, that should have
" ' informed you of my removal, by a distant journey, from the dwellings where you reside.
" ' Take care lest I disdain you, on the night of the departure; it will be quickly done, but
" ' the persons skilled in augury are few. ' " Never did I see two such devoted lovers as we

are; but tongues are sharp and have a double edge. Were it not for a sweet-voiced and slender-waisted maiden, for the brilliant whiteness of her teeth, for her large, dark eyes and her long eyelashes, the passionate lover would recover (*his senses*), be that could not close his eyes would enjoy sleep, he that despaired would hope, and he that was sick would cease (*to suffer*). Censorious females sometimes reproach me for lavishing my wealth on those who awaited my gifts in silent expectation, and not on my companions who asked (*them*) with importunity. They said : " When you have spent all your money and are in want, who will give you more? " And my answer was: " Yusuf! that illustrious descendant of Kodaa, whose generosity hastens to " grant in abundance that which calls forth gratitude. " Whenever a cloud (*of beneficence*) which promised abundant showers, frustrated our hopes, we found that the rains of his bounty never disappointed us. When he and other princes toil to acquire glory, he succeeds easily, but they must labour hard and only obtain the gleanings. Always vigilant, he combines mildness with energy ; his hands procure him what he wants and protect him against what he fears. He is a sword drawn to strike the enemies of the faith, and a protecting curtain lowered down over those who fear God. When in march, two armies accompany him : his prudence and his troops ; he has for companions two swords : firm resolution and the sharp-edged steel. Always ready to chastise those who offend him, he regulates the actions of fate by his decisions. His foresight discovers that which no other can perceive, and arranges matters which could not be settled by the spear. May God protect him who guards, by his vigilance, religion's sacred ground and who protects the hills of Islamism even in the darkest night! (*God protect*) him who gives full career to his promises in the arena of glory and who regulates his threats conformably to the obligations of justice I him who cuts his enemies to pieces whilst their chiefs take to flight before the swords which fall upon their heads! He directed against them an army which levelled the earth by the very sound of its march; and the hills were unable to sustain the weight of all the arrows which oppressed them. His lances, in the brightness of the morning, were like serpents gliding through the thick vapours of the mirage ; the brightness of his swords lighted up the darkness, and clouds of dust obscured the day. The light of the sun was hidden by the dust, but the action of his swords in striking foemen's necks was not interrupted. Every year you send against them an army, charged to claim from them (*what you exact*), and it obtains satisfaction at the point of the spear. When they concealed the wound which one year had inflicted and were recovered from their sufferings, you began again to open that wound (ﻛﻠﻢ). How many (*chiefs*), with faces covered by the twisted braids of their hair, whom you left (*on the field of battle*), with their necks no longer covered (*akshafu*) by the beard of the chin (ﺍﳊﻨﻚ). (*Each of them*) was a sword which cut deeply into the object on which it fell ; yet they fled, and you may now see shortened those (*bodies*) which were so long. By my life! you transgressed against God by imploring his favour (*for you possessed it already*), and you rendered services of which God (alone) knows the number. You pursued them for the sake of your people, till they were scattered far and wide; you invited them to the faith until they became orthodox believers (*takannuft*). O Thika al-Mulk I you whose empire is an arrow fledged and pointed for piercing the hearts of the enemy I may you enjoy this festival of which you are the ornament and which borrows from your brilliant qualities its noblest epithets. The (*victim with*) its sides marked, appeared in brilliant array, as if its back was covered with the variegated quote of Irák. After a year's absence, it (*this festival*) comes to visit you, because it longed to see you and looked anxiously forward to this day of meeting. You gave to it your glory to serve it for a collar and for ear-rings; and it thus appears before us decked in rings and jewels. The presence of your son Jaafar renders this day doubly fortunate ; how admirable the festival which enjoys the presence of two kings! May you never come to be asked for favors and to grant them, to inspire hopes and to fulfil them, to be called on when misfortunes are impending and to avert them (37).

Here ends the kasîda.—Thika tad-Dawla had a son named Tâj ad-Dawla Jaafar, who was versed in literature and had a talent for poetry. A well known piece of verse was composed by him on two pages, one of whom was dressed in red silk and the other in black. Here it is :

> I see two rising moons (ferrs), each borne on a branch (a slender body) and in just proportion ; they are arrayed in robes one of which is tinted like the cheek and the other like the pupil of the eye. Here, behold the sun in the red sky of evening, and there, the moon in the shades of nightfall.

These verses were composed by him in the year 527 (38).—On the tenth of Muharram, 215 (9th March, A. D. 830), al-Mámûn arrived in Misr (Old Cairo) and set out again, towards the end of the month of Safar (April). The kâdi Yahya Ibn Aktham, whom he had taken with him and appointed to the kâdiship of Misr, held that place during three days and then departed with his sovereign. It was for this reason that Ibn Zûlâk (vol. I, p. 388) has inserted his name in the History of the kâdis of Egypt. It has been handed down that Yahya related the following extraordinary fact : " When " I was in ar-Rusâfa (vol. I. p. 46), said he, a man, who was a grandfather in the " fifth degree, claimed, at my tribunal, the inheritance of the grandson of his great " grandson (39)."—Abd as-Semad Ibn Abi Amr al-Muaddal Ibn Ghailân Ibn al-Muhârib Ibn al-Dohtori al-Abdi (vol. I. p. 354), the celebrated poet, went frequently to visit the kâdi Yahya and used to drop in at his levees. One day, having found great difficulty in approaching him and undergone some humiliation, he ceased his visits. Being then pressed by his wife to renew them, he answered her in these terms :

> She would oblige me to disgrace myself, thinking my dishonour a trifle in comparison with her advantage. " Ask favours," said she, " from Yahya Ibn Aktham;" and I replied : " Ask them " from the lord of Yahya Ibn Aktham."

This kâdi continued to pass through many vicissitudes of fortune till the reign of al-Mutawakkil ala-Allah. When the kâdi Muhammad, the son of the kâdi Ahmed Ibn Abi Duwâd (vol. I. p. 66) was dismissed from office, Yahya was appointed to suc-

ceed him and, on that occasion, the khalif invested him with five robes of honour.
In the year 240 (A. D. 854), al-Mutawakkil deposed him, seized on his riches and
nominated, in his place, a member of the Abbaside family named Jaafar Ibn Abd al-
Wâhid Ibn Jaafar Ibn Sulaimân Ibn Ali Ibn Abd Allah Ibn al-Abbâs al-Hâshimi.
Jaafar's secretary then went to Yahya and said : " Surrender up to me the adminis-
" tration with which you are charged." Yahya replied : " Not till two creditable
" witnesses shall declare that the Commander of the faithful sent me orders to do so."
The administration was taken from him by force, and al-Mutawakkil, who was greatly
incensed against him, seized on all his estates and ordered him to remain a prisoner in his own house. Some time after, he (Yahya) set out to make the pilgrimage
and took his sister with him, as he intended making a residence in the holy city.
Having then learned that al-Mutawakkil had forgiven him, he renounced the project
of settling (at Mekka) and departed for Irâk but, on reaching ar-Rahada, he breathed
his last. This took place on Friday, the 15th of Zû 'l-Hijja, 242 (14 April, A. D.
857), or, according to another statement, on the first day of the following year
(30th April, A. D. 857). He was interred at that place, having then attained the age of
eighty-three years.—Abû Abd Allah al-Husain Ibn Abd Allah Ibn Said related as follows :
" The kâdi Yahya Ibn Aktham was, for me, a sincere friend; he loved me and I loved
" him. When he died, I wished that I might see him in a dream, so that I might
" ask him how God had treated him. And, one night, I had a dream in which I
" saw him and asked him that question. He replied : ' God has forgiven me, but
" ' he reprimanded me and said : ' O Yahya! thy mind was alloyed (and turned) from
" ' me during thy dwelling in the world.' I answered : ' Lord! I place my reliance
" ' on a Tradition which was related to me by Abû Moawîa ad-Darîr (vol. I. p. 187),
" ' who had learned it from al-Aamash (vol. I. p. 587), who had heard it from Abû
" ' Sâlih (40) who had heard Abû Huraira (vol. I. p. 570) say that the Prophet of
" ' God pronounced these words : ' God said : I should be ashamed to punish in the
" ' fire a grey-headed man.' On this, God said to me : ' Yahya! I pardon thee; my Pro-
" ' phet said the truth, but yet thy mind was turned from me during thy abode in
" ' the world.' " This relation is given by Abû 'l-Kâsim al-Kushairi in his Risâla (41).
—" Aktham means a corpulent man or sated with food. This name is sometimes
" written Aklam, but, in both cases, the signification is the same." So says the
author of the Muhkam (vol. II. p. 272).—Katan and Samân take the vowels here indicated.—I consulted a great number of books and of persons versed in this art (ety-

mology] respecting the word *Mushannaj* but could obtain no certain information about it. I then met with a correct copy of the Khatib's History of Baghdad, which had been written out under the dictation of a master who knew the work by heart, and I read there that *Mushannaj* should be written as here indicated. I since found the same pronunciation given in Abd al-Ghâni Ibn Saîd's *al-Mukhtalif wa 'l-Mûtalif* [*vol. II. p.* 169).—*Usaiyidi* means *belonging to the tribe of Usaiyid*, a branch of that of Tamîm. Usaiyid, the son of Amr, the son of Tamîm, was the progenitor of this family.—We have already spoken of the relative adjectives *Tamîmi* and *Marwazi* [*vol. I. p.* 7].—The village of ar-Rabada is a dependancy of Medina. It lies on the great pilgrim road and is a regular halting-place for their caravans. It was to this place that Abû Durr al-Ghifâri was banished by Othmân Ibn Affân (42). He remained there till his death; his tomb is still to be seen and is often visited (by pious pilgrims).—*Mîla* is a small town in one of the districts of Ifrîkiya; but God knows best (43).]—The kâdi Jaafar Ibn Abd al-Wâhid bore the surname of Abû Abd Allah and died in the year 258 (A. D. 871-2), or, by another account, in 266 or 269.

---

(1) Aktham Ibn as-Saifi, a chief of the Tamîm tribe, was so highly renowned for his wisdom, that the Arabs of all the tribes used to take him for judge, in their contestations. He died towards the fifth year of Muhammed's preaching, having then attained a very advanced age. — (See Mr. Caussin de Perceval's *Essai sur l'histoire des Arabes*, t. II, p. 579; Ibn al-Jawzi; Ibn Duraid.)

(2) Talha Ibn Muhammad Ibn Jaafar was one of the witnesses who signed the Khalif al-Mufi's (المطيع) abdication. This took place A. H. 363 (A. D. 974). — (Najdm.)

(3) The Arabic word is الفُرَيِّا, but one of the MSS. has الفاضي. If this reading be adopted, the meaning is *speaking with elegance*.

(4) The kâdi 'l-kudât (kadi of kadis or lord chief justice), resided in the capital and had all the other kâdis under his jurisdiction.

(5) Abû 'l-Fadl Abd al-Aziz Ibn Ali al-Tabandi, a doctor of Shafite jurisprudence, was a native of Ushnah, a village near Arbela, in Adarbaijan. He studied the law at Baghdad and composed, on the *faraïd*, or partition of inheritances, a work of great repute. He afterwards returned to Ushnah where he died in the first fifth of the sixth century (A. H. 491-590; A. D. 1097-1196). — (Tabakât as-Shâfiiîn; one of the Bibl. imp. ancien fonds, n° 561.)

(6) In the science which treats of the partition of inheritances, some problems occur which are so remarkable that each of them is distinguished by a particular name; such, for instance, as the Akdariîn, the Gharawîn, the Malikîya, the Hindrîya, etc. On this subject the reader may consult the 6th volume of Dr. Perron's translation of Sidi Khalîl's treatise on Malikite jurisprudence. This work is included in the collection entitled *Exploration scientifique de l'Algérie*.

(7) The parents and the two daughters were, each of them, entitled to a certain portion of the inheritance.

but, as one of the daughters died before the partition, her share was to be divided among the survivors. In this case, two separate calculations must be made.

(8) For the rules of inheritance partitions, see Dr. Perron's *Sidi Khalil*, vol. VI; D'Ohsson's *Tableau général de l'Empire Ottoman*, V, p. 200, and the *Note sur les successions musulmanes*, which was drawn up by Mr. Solvet and inserted in Mr. Bresnier's *Chrestomathie arabe*.

(9) Abâb Ibn Asid, a member of the Omaiyide family, was appointed governor of Mekka by Muhammad. He died A. H. 12 (A. D. 634), the same day as Abû Bakr. — (*Kitâb al-Maârif.*)

(10) Muâd Ibn Jabal, of the tribe of Khazraj, was a native of Medina and one of Muhammad's companions. He died A. H. 18 (A. D. 639), aged thirty-eight years. — (*Madrif.*)

(11) Kaab Ibn Sûr belonged to the tribe of Azd. He joined the party of Aäisha and lost his life at the battle of the Camel, A. H. 36 (A. D. 656). — (*Madrif.*)

(12) According to the Moslim law of testimony, none but persons noted for integrity and piety can be received either as witnesses in a court of justice or as witnesses to bonds and deeds.

(13) I read تربّبت.

(14) This person is not known to the translator.

(15) The vulgar and incorrect form هذا, employed here instead of أغذرُا, is worthy of remark.

(16) The text of this passage is corrupt. The edition of Bûlâk inserts وقل before رجل and two manuscripts read بكلمة instead of تكلمه. I believe the right reading to be فدوني ابو الغيثاه الّي وقال يهد and, as such, I adopt it. The reading با جمل instead of راجعتك is given by the edition of Bûlâk and one of the manuscripts.

(17) These verses are to be found in the beginning of the twenty-third sûrat of the Korân.

(18) Ismaîl Ibn Ishâk was appointed kâdi of Baghdad A. H. 260 (A. D. 873-4). — (*Nujûm.*)

(19) The reading followed here is قول قطن وعمل طاعن, which phrase signifies: "Word abiding "and deed transitory."

(20) This innuendo is more than sufficiently explained, a little farther on.

(21) Al-Hârith Ibn Kaîs was one of the *Tâbis*, or disciples of Muhammad's companions.

(22) One of these brothers was perhaps the Amr Ibn Maslik whose life is given in this work, vol. II, p. 416.

(23) These verses have most certainly a double meaning; the expressions employed in them being very equivocal.

(24) Abû Alî Ismaîl Ibn Muhammad as-Saffâr, the same traditionist of whom mention is made in the life of Abû Salaimân al-Khattâbi (vol. I, p. 478), died A. H. 341 (A. D. 952). — (*Nujûm.*)

(25) Abû Aäsim ad-Dahhâk as-Shaibâni, surnamed an-Nabîl (*the genius*), was a traditionist of the best authority and a native of Basra. He died A. H. 212 (A. D. 827-8), or 213, at the age of ninety-one years. — (*Nujûm; Tabakât al-Huffâs.*)

(26) This is an application of the seventy-seventh verse of the twelfth sûrat of the Korân, which refers to Joseph and Benjamin. Abû Aäsim substituted in it the words *his father* in place of one of *his brothers*. For the thrust committed by Joseph, see Sale's note on this verse.

(27) This verse seems to mean that the kâdi would prefer the society of a vile minion to that of poets such as Jarir (vol. I, p. 294) and al-Abbâs Ibn al-Ahnaf (vol. II, p. 7). The whole piece is very obscure, as it contains expressions and allusions which can only be explained by conjecture.

(28) The true reading is: المشهور هنا غير.

(20) Abû Duwaib Khuwailid Ibn Khâlid was a member of the tribe of Hudail. He went to Mekka, with the intention of seeing Muhammad but, on arriving, he found him dead. In the khalifate of Omar he accompanied an expedition sent against the Greeks and died in that campaign. According to another statement, he died on his way to Mekka, when Othmân was khalif. He was said to have been the best poet of the tribe of Hudail, which was also the most poetical of all the Arabian tribes.—(Suyûti's *Shardhid li-Nogim*.)

(30) *Korân*, sûr. 37, verse 10.

(31) This is the continuation of the foregoing verse.

(32) Al-Mahdiya is a seaport town in the province of Tunis.

(33) This passage may also signify: He discovered (in alchimy) and searched with great ardour (*the philosopher's stone*).

(34) Literally : by sons of fornication.

(35) I can discover nothing precise respecting the value of the coin called *radd*, which word, in Arabic, means a quadruple.

(36) Literally : were like tears dropping blood.—The camels intended to be sacrificed were marked with an arrow stuck into the hump.

(37) We do not possess another text of this very obscure poem; so that in many passages, I have been obliged to correct and translate by conjecture. It has been published, with a great number of various readings, by Mr. Amari, in his *Biblioteca Arabo-Sicula*, p. ٣٣٣ et seq.

(38) This date is false. The emir Tâj ad-Dawla succeeded to his father Thika ad-Dawla, A. H. 385 (A. D. 995), and abdicated on 419 (A. D. 1019-20). It is not probable that he could have composed this madrigal even in the year 497.

(39) By the Moslim law, the nearest surviving male ascendant has a right to a certain share in the property left by his descendant.

(40) Abû Sâlih as-Sammân, named also Dhakwân and surnamed as-Zaiyât, was a mawla of the tribe of Ghatafân and an eminent Traditionist. He died at Medina, R. H. 101 (A. D. 719-20).—(*Nujûm, Nuffâ.*)

(41) See vol. II, p. 155 and, for an account of the *Risâla*, my translation of Ibn Khaldûn's *Prolegomena*, 1st part, p. 453.

(42) Abû Darr Jundab Ibn as-Sakan al-Ghifâri, one of the earliest converts to islamism, died at ar-Rabada, A. H. 32 (A. D. 652-3.)—(*Nujûm, Nadîrî.*)

(43) The town of Mîla lies 18 or 90 miles N. W. of Constantina.

YAHYA IBN MOAD

Abû Zakariya Yahya Ibn Moâd ar-Râzi (a *native of Rai and*) a celebrated preacher, was one of the *men of the path* (vol. *I*. p. 259). Abû 'l-Kâsim al-Kushairi (vol. *II*. p. 152) mentions him in his (*celebrated treatise, the*) *Risâla* and includes him in the

number of the Shaikhs [the most eminent súfi doctors]. "He was," says he, "the
"only man, in his day, who had no model but himself; he was most eloquent
"on the subject of hope (in God's mercy); particularly when he discoursed on
"the knowing (of God)." He went to Balkh where he resided for some time
and then returned to Naisápûr, where he died. One of Yahya's sayings was:
"How can he be abstemious (from worldly enjoyments) who is without the fear
"of God? respect that which is not thine and use with great moderation that
"which is thine." He used sometimes to say : "Hunger is a spiritual exercise
"for those who aspire (to the knowledge of God), a trial for those who are turning
"(unto God), a regular practise for those who abstain (from the enjoyments of this
"world) and a favour granted to those who have acquired the knowledge (of God's
"perfection). Solitude is the fit companion for the sincerely devout; missing
"the opportunity (of obtaining salvation) is worse than death; for missing (such
"a thing) is the being cut away from the truth, whereas death is only the being
"cut away from the living. Abstinence consists in three things : poverty, soli-
"tude and hunger. If a man thinks to deceive God by trying to cast a veil
"over his sins, God will tear off that veil and expose them to the public."
He learned traditions from Ishák Ibn Sulaimán ar-Rázi [1], Makki Ibn Ibráhím
al-Balkhi [2] and Ali Ibn Muhammad at-Tanáfisi [3]. A number of strangers
belonging to Rai, Hamadán and Khorásán taught, on his authority, a few well-
supported Traditions. The Khatib (vol. I. p. 75) says of him, in the History of
Baghdad : "When he came to Baghdad, the shaikhs of the Súfis and the devotees
"gathered round him and, having set up a throne, they placed him on it, sat
"down before him and entered into a conference. Al-Junaid (vol. I. p. 338) then
"uttered some words, on which Yahya said : ' Be silent, my lamb! what have
"' you to do with speaking when all the people are talking?'" The allusions and
expressions which he employed were remarkably elegant. One of his sayings was :
"A pious discourse is a fine thing, but its meaning is finer; its use is finer than its
"meaning; the recompense which it merits is finer than its use and, finer than its
"recompense is the favour of Him for whose sake that discourse was made." He
said also : "True friendship cannot be augmented by kindness nor diminished
"by unkindness." Another of his sayings was : "He whose aspect is not as silver
"for the vulgar, as gold for the aspirants (to the knowledge of God), as pearls and ru-
"bies for those who know God and are advanced in his favour, that man is not one

" of God's sages who aspire to know Him." He said also : " The finest thing in
" the world is a correct discourse uttered by an eloquent tongue and proceeding
" from a handsome face; a shrewd discourse, drawn from a profound ocean (the
" heart) by the tongue of an ingenious man." He said also : " My God! how can
" I forget Thee, I who have no other lord but Thee? my God! never shall I utter
" the words : Never again shall I return (to sin), for I feel that my heart is liable to
" break its promises; yet shall I utter them, provided that I die before I relapse."
One of his prayers was as follows : " Almighty God! though my sins cause me to fear,
" my hopes in Thy mercy assure me against danger. Almighty God! Thy kindness
" has concealed my sins from this world, but is for me more necessary that they
" should be concealed from view on the day of the resurrection. Thou hast been
" bountiful towards me in preventing them from appearing before the company of
" true believers; do not, therefore, bring me to shame on that day, in the presence
" of all Thy creatures, O Thou most merciful of the merciful!"—A descendant of
Ali who resided at Balkh and to whom he went to pay his respects, said to him :
" Tell me, Master! and may God assist you! what is your opinion of us who are
" the people of the house (the members of Muhammad's family)!" Yahya replied :
" It is that which I would say of clay kneaded with the water of (divine) revelation and
" sprinkled (?) with the water of the (heavenly) mission : can it give out any other odour
" than the musk of true direction and the ambergris of piety?" The Alide (was so
highly pleased with this answer that he) filled Yahya's mouth with pearls. The next
morning, Yahya received a visit from the Alide and said to him : " Your coming to
" see us is an effect of your goodness, and our going to see you was on account of your
" goodness; so, you, in visiting and being visited, are doubly good." Another of
Yahya's sayings was: "To him who is going to see a true friend the way never appears
" long; he who goes to visit his beloved never feels lonely on the road." He said also:
" How miserable are the sons of Adam! if they feared hell as much as they fear po-
" verty, they would all enter into Paradise."—"No man," said he, " obtained his
" utmost wish without longing for death as ardently as the hungry man longs for
" food. He sees causes of ruin approach, is uneasy about his family and his brethern
" and is just falling into a state which would trouble the soundest reason." He said
again: " He who neglects the minor duties of piety will not obtain the greater gifts
" (which God bestows)." Another of his sayings was : " Of the things which fall to
" the lot of those among you who are truly believers, the best are three, namely,

" that which, if it profits them not, will not harm them; that which, if it rejoices
" them not, will not madden them, and that which, if it does not gain them praise,
" will not bring upon them blame." He said again : (" *A man's*) acts are like the
" mirage; (his) heart is devastated (and deprived) of piety; (his) sins are equal in
" number to the sands and the grains of dust; yet he desires to possess the high-
" bosomed maidens of his time. Woe be to you! you are drunk, but not with
" wine. How perfect would you be had you striven against (تقتل) your hopes!
" how great, had you hastened in fulfilling your appointed duty! how strong,
" had you resisted your passions!" On such subjects he uttered many fine
maxims. He died at Naisâpûr in the year 258. Muhammad Ibn Abd Allah said :
" I read these words on the tomb-stone of Yahya Ibn Moâd ar-Râzi : ' The sage of
" ' the epoch, may God whiten his face and unite him with the blessed Prophet!
" ' died on Monday, the sixteenth of the first Jumâda, 258 (30th March, A. D.
" ' 872), at Naisâpûr.' "

(1) According to the author of the *Tobakât el-Huffâz*, Abû Yahya Ishâk Ibn Soleimân ar-Râzi was a sure
and exact Traditionist, and a native of Kûfa. He settled at Rai and taught Traditions on the authority of
Mâlik and others. His piety and the holiness of his life led the people to consider him as one of those mysterious personages who were designated by the title of *abdâls* and of whom Mr. Lane has given a very good
account in his translation of the *Thousand and one Nights*, chap. III, note 61. This ascetic died A. H. 200
(A. D. 615-6), or 199, according to the compiler of the *Nujûm*.

(2) Mekhi Ibn Ibrâhim al-Balkhi (a native of Balkh) taught Traditions on the authority of Jaafar as-Sâdik,
Abû Hanîfa, Mâlik and others. He died A. H. 214 (A. D. 829-30), or 215.—(*Huffâz.*)

(3) Ali Ibn Muhammad al-Tanâfisi, a Traditionist whose authority was cited by Ibn Mâja and other eminent doctors, died A. H. 203 (A. D. 814-5).—(*Huffâz, Nujûm.*)

YAHYA IBN MANDA

Abû Zakariyâ Yahya al-Abdi was the son of Abd al-Wahhâb, the son of the imâm
Abû Abd Allah Muhammad, the son of Ishâk, the son of Muhammad, the son of
Yahya, the son of Manda, the son of al-Walîd, the son of Manda, the son of Batta,

the son of Islandâr, the son of Jibârbakht, the son of Firuzân. *Manda* is a surname; he who bore it was called Ibrâhîm. It is said that Islandâr's real name was al-Firuzân; God knows! Yahya Ibn Manda was a most distinguished *hâfiz* and one of the most eminent among the Traditionists. We have already spoken of his grandfather (vol. *III. p. 7*). Yahya was designated by the surname of Abû Zakariya, his father by that of Abû Amr, his grandfather by that of Abû Abd Allah, his great-grandfather by that of Abû Muhammad and his great-great-grandfather by that of Abû Yakûb. He was a native of Ispahân and a Traditionist, as were his father, his grandfather, his great-grandfather and his great-great-grandfather before him. Highly distinguished for his merit, his talents and his vast knowledge in traditional lore, he was also a trustworthy relator of Traditions, an accomplished *hâfiz* and one of those who were noted for the copiousness of their information and for their veracity. The works composed by him were numerous, his conduct exemplary and the duties he imposed on himself arduous. At that epoch, the family to which he belonged had not a member worthy of being compared to him. He published, for the first time, some collections of Traditions, part of which he drew from his own stock and the rest from the lips of the numerous *shaikhs* and teachers who resided at Ispahân. He heard Traditions delivered by Abû Bakr Muhammad Ibn Abd Allah Ibn Zaid ad-Dabbi, Abû Tâhir Muhammad Ibn Ahmad Ibn Muhammad Ibn Abd ar-Rahîm al-Kâtib, Abû Mansûr Muhammad Ibn Abd Allah Ibn Fadlawaih al-Ispahâni, his own father and his two paternal uncles, Abû 'l-Hasan Obaid Allah and Abû 'l-Kâsim Abd ar-Rahmân. His other teachers were Abû 'l-Abbâs Ahmad Ibn Muhammad Ibn Ahmad Ibn an-Nomân al-Kamâl, Abû Abd Allah Muhammad Ibn Ali Ibn Muhammad al-Jassâs, Abû Bakr Muhammad Ibn Ali Ibn al-Husain al-Haurdâni and Abû Tâhir Ahmad Ibn Muhammad ath-Thakafi. Having gone to Naisâpûr, he there heard Traditions taught by Abû Bakr Ahmad Ibn Mansûr Ibn Khalaf al-Mukri and Abû Bakr Ahmad Ibn al-Husain al-Baihaki (vol. *I. p. 57*). At Hamadân he learned Traditions from Abû Bakr Muhammad Ibn Abd ar-Rahmân Ibn Muhammad an-Nubâwandi; at Basra he studied them under Abû 'l-Kâsim Ibrâhim Ibn Muhammad Ibn Ahmad as-Shâbid, Abd Allah Ibn al-Husain as-Saadâni and at great number of other professors. One of the works compiled by him was a (*biographical*) History of Ispahân. Having gone to Baghdad, on his way to the pilgrimage, he taught Traditions in that city and made dictations in the mosque of al-Mansûr. So great was his reputation and so high the rank which he held (*as a Traditionist*), that a crowd of *shaikhs* went to note down his observations, and amongst them were Abû 'l-Fadl Muhammad Ibn Nâsir, Abd al-Kâdir Ibn Abi Sâlih al-Jîli, and the grammarian Abû Muhammad Abd Allah Ibn Ahmad Ibn Ahmad Ibn Ahmad al-Khashbâb. Traditions were delivered on his authority by the *hâfiz* Abû 'l-Barakât Abd al-Wahhâb Ibn al-Mubârak al-Anmâti, Abû 'l-Hasan Ali Ibn Abi Turâb az-Zankawi al-Khaiyât, both of them natives of Baghdad, Abû Tâhir Yahya Ibn Abd al-Ghaffâr Ibn as-Sabbâgh, the *hâfiz* Abû 'l-Fadl Muhammad Ibn Hibât Allah Ibn al-Alâ, and a great number of others. The *hâfiz* Ibn as-Samâni (*vol. II.* p. 156) mentions him in the *Kitâb az-Zail* and says : " He wrote out for me a licence to teach all the Traditions which he " himself had learned." He then adds : " The *hâfiz* Abû 'l-Kâsim Ismail Ibn " Muhammad, whom I asked what he thought of him, extolled him highly and " praised his good memory, his knowledge and his learning." Farther on he says : " I heard the *hâfiz* Abû Bakr Muhammad Ibn Abi Nasr Mansûr Ibn Muhammad al-" Laftawâni say : ' The family of Ibn Manda began by a Yahya and ended by a " ' Yahya;' meaning in the knowledge of the Traditions, in science and in merit." —Abd al-Ghâfir Ibn Ismail Ibn Abd al-Ghâfir al-Fârisi, the *hâfiz* of whom we have already spoken (*vol. II.* p. 170) mentions him in the *Siâk* (*or continuation*) of the History of Naisâpûr and says : " Abû Zakarîya Yahya Ibn Manda was a man of great " merit and came of a family noted thoughout the world for learning and for the " knowledge of Traditions. He travelled [*to many cities*], met there the great doc-" tors, and learned Traditions from their lips. He composed a work on the two *Sahîhs* (*that of Muslim and that of al-Bukhâri*]."— It is related on the best authority that one of the learned gave the following saying as Ibn Manda's : " Excessive " laughter is a mark of folly; folly and precipitation result from weakness of mind ; " weakness of mind proceeds from want of judgment; want of judgment comes from " a bad education, and a bad education draws down contempt. Heedlessness is a " sort of madness; envy is a malady for which there is no cure, and detraction en-" genders hatred."—It has been handed down from al-Asmâi (*vol. II.* p. 123), through a series of creditable narrators, that the following anecdote was related by Ibn Manda : " I was in the desert and went into a mosque. The imâm stood up to " direct the prayer and then recited the passage of the Korân (*sûr.* 71, *verse* 1) in " which God says : *We sent Noah unto his people.* Here he got embarrassed and " continued to repeat the same words, on which a bedouin Arab, who was standing " behind him and accompanying the prayer, exclaimed : ' Well. man! if Nûh

" ' has not gone there, send some one else.' "—Yahya Ibn Manda used often to repeat these lines of a poet :

> I wondered how a man could purchase error at the price of true direction; but he who purchases worldly goods at the price of his religion is more to be wondered at . But still more wonderful is the man who sacrifices his religion to obtain the worldly advantages possessed by another : he is yet a greater loser than the two former.

He was born at Ispahán on tuesday morning, the 19th of Shawwál, 434 (1st of June, A. D. 1043), and he died there on the feast of the Sacrifice, 512 (24th March, A. D. 1119). After his death, the Manda family never produced a man like him. —Ibn Nukta (vol. III. p. 101) says, in the Ikmál al-Ikmál, that his death took place on Saturday, the 12th of Zú 'l-Hijja, 511, and that his father Abd al-Wahháb was born in the year 386 (A. D. 996) and died in the mont hof the latter Jumáda, 475 (Oct.-Nov. A. D. 1082).—We have marked the orthography of his ancestors' names in our article on his grandfather Abû Abd Allah Muhammad (1).

(1) The passage here indicated is not to be found in our manuscripts.

IBN SAADUN AL-KORTUBI

Abù Bakr Yahya Ibn Saadûn Ibn Tammám Ibn Muhammad al-Azdi al-Kortubi (a *member of the Arabian tribe of Azd and a native of Cordova*), bore the title of Sáin ad-Dîn (*preserver of the faith*) and was one of the imáms (or *great masters*), who, in latter times, were well versed in the Koranic readings, the sciences connected with the koranic text, the Traditions, grammar, philology, etc. He left Cordova in the flower of his youth and proceeded to Egypt. In Alexandria, he heard the lessons of Abû Abd Allah Muhammad Ibn Ahmad Ibn Ibráhim ar-Rázi and, in Misr (*Old Cairo*), those of Abû Sádik Murshid Ibn Yahya Ibn al-Kásim al-Madani al-Misri (a *native of Medina who had settled in Egypt*). There also he studied under Abû Táhir Ahmad

Ibn Muhammad al-Ispaháni, generally known by the appellation of as-Silafi (col. I.
p. 86) and other matters.   In the year 517 (A. D. 1123-4), he arrived in Baghdad
and read the Korán under the direction of the shaikh Abù Muhammad Abd Allah
Ibn Ali al-Mukri (*teacher of the Korán-readings*), who was generally known by the
designation of Ibn Bint as-shaikh Abi Mansùr al-Khaiyát (*the son of the daughter of the
shaikh Abd Mansùr the tailor*).   He heard from the lips of that professor the contents of a great number of books, one of which was Sibawaih's *Kitáb* (col. II. p. 396).
He read Traditions under Abù Bakr Muhammad Ibn Abd al-Báki al-Bazzár, surnamed Kádi 'l-Máristán (*the kádi of the infirmary*), Abù 'l-Kásim Ibn al-Hoçain (الحسين),
Abù 'l-Izz Ibn Kádis and other masters.   He was religious and devout, remarkable
for such gravity and dignity of bearing as inspired respect.   As a Traditionist he was
a sure authority, veracious and trustworthy ; his talents were great, his words few, his
good actions numerous and his discourse instructive.   He resided at Damascus for
some time and then went to inhabit Mosul, whence he removed to Ispahán.   From
that he returned to Mosul and all the shaikhs (*or eminent doctors*) of the time went to
hear his lessons.   The háfiz Ibn as-Samáni (col. II. p. 156) mentions him in the
Zail and says : " I met him in Damascus, where he gave lessons which (*even*) the
" shaikhs under whom Abù Abd Allah ar-Rázi had studied, went to hear.   I myself
" selected some choice passages out of his lectures.   Having asked him the date
" and place of his birth, he replied that he was born in the year 486 (A. D. 1093-4)
" at Cordova, a city in Spain."—I read in a book that his birth took place in the
year 487, but the former date is the true one.   Our shaikh the kádi Bahá ad-Dìn
Abù 'l-Mahàsin Yùsuf Ibn Ráfi Ibn Tamìm generally known by the surname of Ibn
Shaddàd and kádi of Aleppo, took pride in stating that he had learned Traditions and
Korán-readings from Abù Bakr al-Kortubi.   To this we shall recur in our article on
Ibn Shaddàd.   " We used," said he, " to read (*the Korán*) under him at Mosul,
" and, every day, we saw a man come in, salute him without sitting down, hand
" him a packet the contents of which were unknown to us and then retire.   We
" tried to discover what was in it, and at length found out that it was a fowl ready
" plucked which the shaikh purchased, every day, from that man, for his own use,
" and which, on returning to his house, he cooked with his own hands."   The
same kádi states, in his *Dalaïl al-Ahkám*, that he read (*the Korán*) under him during
the space of eleven years and finished in the year 567 (A. D. 1171-2).   The shaikh
Abù Bakr al-Kortubi often repeated the following verses, tracing them, through a

regular series of transmitters, up to the author, the *kâtib* Abû 'l-Khair al-Wâsiti :

The pen of fate writes out what is to happen; so, whether we move or remain quiet, it is just the same. How foolish is time to toil for continuance! is not continuance granted even to the embryo in the womb?

He said also : " The following verses were repeated to us by Abû 'l-Wafâ Abd ar-
" Razzâk Ibn Wahb Ibn Hassân, who stated that they were recited to him in Old Cairo
" by Abû Abd Allah Muhammad Ibn Manî (منيع), who gave them as having been
" composed by himself :

" I have a device by which calamity may be averted, but no device can serve against a liar.
" No stratagem of mine can avail against him who says things of his own invention."

The shaikh Abû Bakr al-Kortubi died at Mosul, on the day of the festival of the Sacrifice, 567 (4th August, A. D. 1172).

YAHYA IBN YAMAR

Abû Sulaimân, or, as some say, Abû Saîd, Yahya, the son of Yamar al-Adwâï al-Wabki, was a grammarian of Basra and a *Tâbi (one of those who had received lessons from a companion of Muhammad)*. He met (and knew) Abd Allah Ibn Omar (vol. I. p. 567), Abd Allah Ibn al-Abbâs (vol. I. p. 89), and others (of the Companions). Katâda Ibn Diâma as-Sadûsi (vol. II. p. 513) and Ishâk Ibn Suwaid al-Adawi handed down Traditions on his authority. He was one of the chief Korân-readers(1) of Basra, and it was from him that Abd Allah Ibn Abi Ishâk learned the manner of reading (that book). He removed to Khorâsân and was appointed kâdi at Marw. The text of the Korân, the rules of grammar and the various dialects of the Arabs were equally familiar to him. He acquired his knowledge of grammar from Abû 'l-Aswad ad-Duwali (vol. I. p. 662). It is related that, when Abû 'l-Aswad drew up the chapter on the agent and patient (the subject and object of the verb), a man of the tribe of Laith added thereto some chapters and, having found, on examination, that there existed, in the language of the (desert) Arabs, some expressions which could not be made to enter into that (section), he stopped short and abandoned the work. It is possible that this person was Yahya Ibn Yamar who, having contracted an alliance, by oath, with the tribe of Laith, was considered as one of its members. He was a Shiite of the primitive class, one of those who, in asserting the superior merit of the *People of the house* (2), abstained from depreciating the merit of those (Companions) who did not belong to that family. Aasim Ibn Abi 'n-Najûd (vol. II. p. 1) the Korân-reader, related as follows : " Al-Hajjâj Ibn Yûsuf (vol. I. " p. 356), being informed that Yahya Ibn Yamar declared al-Hasan and al-Husain " to be of the posterity of the Apostle of God, and that he was then in Khorâsân, " wrote to Kutaiba Ibn Muslim (vol. II. p. 514), the governor of that province, " ordering him to send Yahya to him. This was done and, when Yahya stood in his " presence, he said to him : ' Do you pretend that al-Hasan and al-Husain were of " ' the posterity of the Apostle of God? by Allah! I shall cast (to the ground) that " ' part of you which has the most hair on it (3), unless you exculpate your- " ' self. ' — ' If I do so ', said Yahya, ' shall I have an amnesty? ' — 'You shall '. " ' replied al-Hajjâj. — ' Well ', said Yahya, God, may his praise be exalted! said : " ' *And we gave unto him (Abraham) Isaac and Jacob; we directed them all; and Noah* " ' *had we before directed, and, of his posterity, David and Solomon, and Job, and* " ' *Joseph, and Moses, and Aaron; thus do we reward the virtuous; and Zakarias,* " ' *and John, and Jesus, and Elias; all of them were righteous.* (Korân, sur. 6, " ' verse 84.) Now, the space of time between Jesus and Abraham is greater that which " ' separated al-Hasan and al-Husain from Muhammad, on all of whom be the bless- " ' ing of God and his salvation ! ' — Al-Hajjâj answered : ' I must admit that you " ' have got out of the difficulty; I read that before but did not understand it. ' "— This quotation was most appropriate; how admirable the talent displayed by Yahya in adducing that passage! How finely he applied it! —" Then, " said Aasim, " al-Hajjâj " said ot him : ' Where were you born?' — Yahya answered : ' At Basra.' — ' Where " ' were you brought up?' —' In Khorâsân.'—' And this pure Arabic (which you speak), " ' how did you come by it (4)? '—' It was God's gift.' — 'Tell me if I commit faults " ' in speaking. '— Yahya remained silent, but as al-Hajjâj insisted on having an " ' answer, he at length said: ' O Emir! since you ask me, I must say that you exalt " ' what should be depressed and depress what should be exalted (5). '—' That, by

"' Allah! is a grave fault.' He then wrote these words to Kutaiba : 'When this,
"' my letter, reaches you, take Yahya Ibn Yamar for your kádi. Salutation!"—Ibn
Sallám (vol. II. p. 486) stated that he heard Yúnus Ibn Habíb (6) relate as follows :
"Al-Hajjáj said to Yahya Ibn Yamar : 'Do you remark any incorrection in my
"' speech?'—'Yes;' replied Yahya, 'in one point.'—'What is that?'—'In
"' reading the Korán.'—'That were shameful indeed! what is it?'—' In reci-
"' ting this verse: Say, if your fathers and your sons, and so forth to the words be
"' more dear (ahabba) to you than God (Korán. súr.9, verse 24), you pronounce ahabbo."
"' Ibn Sallám here observed : "It would appear from this that, as the phrase was
"' long, al-Hajjáj forgot how it commenced. Al-Hajjáj then said : 'be assured that
"' you shall never hear me commit such a fault again.' Then," said Yúnus, "he
"sent him to Khorásán which, at that time, was governed by Yazid, the son of al-
"Muhallab Ibn Abi Sufra."—God best knows which of these statements is exact.—
Ibn al-Jauzi (vol II. p. 96) says, in his Shuzúr al-Okúd (7) : "In the year eighty-
"four of the Hijra (A. D. 703), al-Hajjáj banished Yahya Ibn Yamar because, on
"saying to him : 'Do I speak incorrectly,' he received this answer : 'You do;
"but the fault is scarcely perceptible.'—'I give you three days,' said al-Hajjáj,
"'and, if I find you, after that, in the land of Irák, I shall put you to death.' In
"consequence of this, Yahya left the country."—Abú Amr Nasr Ibn Ali Ibn Núh
Ibn Kais stated that the following relation was made to him by Othmán Ibn Mih-
san : "The Commander of the faithful prononced a khotba at Basra and, in
"this discourse, he said : 'Fear God! he that fears God incurs no huscdra.' The
"congregation did not understand what he said and asked its meaning from Yahya
"Ibn Yamar. He answered that the word huscdra signified loss and that the khalif
"meant to say : He who fears God shall sustain no loss."—Al-Kazzás (vol. III.
p. 85) says, in his Kitáb al-Jámi : Hawdrdt means dangers; its singular is hawdra.
—Ar-Rázi said : "I related this to al-Asmái (vol. II p. 123) and he answered : 'I
"' never heard that till this very moment, now that you have told it to me. The
"' rare expressions of the language are really very numerous, but that one I never
"' heard.'"—Al-Asmái related as follows : "My father told me that Yazid, the
"son of al-Muhallab, wrote, when in Khorásán, a letter to al-Hajjáj Ibn Yúsuf in
"which he said : 'We met the enemy and forced him to take refuge on the summit
"' (orora) of the hill, and we are at the foot of it (al-hadhídh).'—'How,' said
"al-Hajjáj, 'did the son of al-Muhallab come by such words as these?' and,

" being told that Yahya Ibn Yamar was with him, he said : ' Ah! that explains it. '
—Yahya composed poetry and was the author of this verse :

People concur only in hating any family; but, from the oldest times, people hate those who
are good (8).

, Khálid al-Haddá (vol. II. p. 588) stated that Ibn Sirin (vol. II. p. 586) possessed
a copy of the Korân in which Yahya Ibn Yamar had marked the vowel points. He
spoke the purest Arabic, using the most elegant terms without effort and quite natu-
rally. His adventures and remarkable sayings are well known. He died in the year
129 (A. D. 746-7(9).—Yamar, or Yamur,— but this latter form is neither current
nor correct,— is the present tense of the verb amira, which signifies to live long.
This name, like that of Yahya (he lives), was given to him as a presage of long life.
—Adwáni means descended from Adwân, whose true name was al-Hârith and who
was the son of Amr Ibn Kais Ailân. He received the surname of Adwân (hostility)
because he attacked his brother with the intention of killing him.—Waahhi means
descended from Waahh, who was the son of Aûf, the son of Bakr, the son of Yashkur,
the son of that same Adwân.

(1) See vol. I, p. 158.
(2) See page 58 of this volume.
(3) That is : I shall strike off your head.
(4) The true reading is amma bis lata.
(5) This passage signifies also : you put in the nominative what should be put in the accusative and vice
versa. I suspect that Yahya employed this equivocal expression designedly.
(6) The life of Ibn Habib is given in this volume.
(7) This was a historical work. Its title signifies : Golden bands for necklaces.
(8) Literally : the fat. — This verse is by no means clear, and its application is not evident unless we
suppose it to have been uttered by one of the Adwân.
(9) Hahahá, cited by the author of the Nujûm, places the death of Yahya Ibn Yamar in the year 89 of the
Hijra.

AL-FARRA THE GRAMMARIAN

Abù Zakariya Yahya Ibn Ziàd Ibn Abd Allah Ibn Manzûr al-Aslami ad-Dailami
al-Kûfi (*a Dailamite by origin and a native of Kufa by birth*), was generally known
by the surname of al-Farrà. He was a member, by enfranchisement, of the tribe of
Asad, or, according to another statement, of the tribe of Minkar. Al-Farrà was
the most eminent of all the doctors of Kûfa and also the most distinguished by his
knowledge of grammar, philology and the various branches of literature. Abù
'l-Abbàs Thalab (*vol. I. p. 83*) is stated to have said : " Were it not for al-Farrà,
" pure Arabic would no longer exist; it was he who disengaged it (*from the ordinary
" language*) and fixed it (*by writing*). Were it not for al-Farrà, good Arabic had gone
" to the ground ; (*before his time,*) it was a matter of discussion ; every one who
" pleased had the pretention of knowing it and discoursed on it as well as his intelli-
" gence and his genius would permit, so that it had nearly disappeared." He and al-
Ahmar (1) learned grammar from Abù 'l-Hasan al-Kisàï (*vol. II. p. 237*); they were
the most eminent of his disciples and also the most attached to him. Al-Farrà,
having resolved on entering into the service of (*the khalif*) al-Màmòn, went a great
number of times to the door of the palace (*with the hope of obtaining admittance*),
and, one day, whilst he was waiting there, Abù Bishr Thumàma Ibn al-Ashras an-
Numairi (*vol. II. p. 473*), a Motazelite doctor who was intimate with (*the khalif*)
al-Màmùn, went up to him. " I saw,' said Thumàma, ' a person in the attire of
" a literary man ; so, I sat down beside him and commenced putting to the test his
" knowledge of philosophy. Finding that he was (*in that branch*), an ocean (*of learn-
" ing*), I tried him in grammar and discovered that he had not his parallel ; I then
" examined him in jurisprudence and perceived that he was a good legist and well
" acquainted with the conflicting opinions of those people (*the jurisconsults*) ; I ascer-
" tained also that he was an able astronomer, a learned physician, and well-versed
" in the history of the (*desert*) Arabs, their battle-days and their poetry. On this,
" I said to him : ' Who are you? you must be al-Farrà ! ' He replied : ' I am he.'
" I immediately went in to the Commander of the faithful, al-Màmùn, informed him
" of the circumstance and got the order to have al-Farrà introduced without delay.

" It was thus that he became acquainted with al-Mâmûn."—Kutrub (vol. III. p. 29)
related as follows : " Al-Farrâ entered into the presence of (the khalif) ar-Rashîd and
" made a discourse in which he committed solecisms. On this, Jaafar Ibn Yahya
" the Barmekide (vol. I. p. 301) said : ' Commander of the faithful ! he speaks in-
" ' correctly.' The khalif said to al-Farrâ : ' You commit solecisms ?' and received
" this answer : ' Commander of the faithful ! it is in the nature of the (desert) Arabs
" ' to employ correctly the final inflexions, and in the nature of those who inhabit
" ' fixed abodes to employ them incorrectly ; when I am on my guard, I do not
" ' commit faults but, when I return to my natural habit, I commit them.' The
" khalif was satisfied with this answer.—The Khatîb (vol. I. p. 75) says, in his
history of Baghdad : " When al-Farrâ got acquainted with al-Mâmûn, the latter bid
" him draw up a work which should contain the principles of grammar and all the
" pure Arabic expressions which he had heard. He then ordered him to be confi-
" ned in a chamber of the palace, and appointed male and female servants to attend
" him and furnish him with every thing which he required ; hoping, by this means,
" to deliver his heart from all preoccupations and to leave him nothing to wish for.
" They were even to inform him of the hours of prayer by chaunting the adan (or
" call) at the proper times. He sent to him also a number of copyists and attached
" to his service confidential men and agents charged to pay the expenses. Al-Farrâ
" then dictated, and the copyists wrote down his observations ; and this continued
" during two years, until they had finished the work. It was entitled al-Hudûd
" (the limits or chapters (2). Al-Mamûn ordered this book to be transcribed (and
" placed) in his libraries. When al-Farrâ had finished his task, he went out in
" public and began the composition of the Kitâb al-Madni (rhetorical figures
" employed in the Koran (?)). The narrator (of these facts) says : ' We tried to
" ' count the member of persons who assembled for the purpose of hearing him dic-
" ' tate (and publish) the text of the Kitâb al-Madni, but, not being able to do so
" ' (they were so many,) we counted the kâdis only and found that there were
" ' eighty.' He continued to dictate the work till he finished it. The copyists
" then withheld it from the public, so that they might make money of it, and
" declared that they would not communicate it to any person unless he consented to
" have it copied by them at the rate of one dirhem for five leaves (3). Al-Farrâ, to
" whom complaints were made on this subject, sent for the copyists and remonstrated
" with them. Their answer was : ' We attended your lessons in order to profit by

" ' your learning; of all your works this is the most essential; so, allow us to
" ' gain a livelihood by means of it.' He replied : ' Be more compliant with
" ' them; it will be for your advantage as well as theirs.' Finding that they would
" not follow his advice, he said to them : ' I shall let you see (*what you do not*
" ' *expect*),' and then announced to the public that he would dictate the *Madni* and
" join to it a complete commentary, with fuller remarks than those already given.
" He therefore held sittings and dictated one hundred leaves on the word *al-hamd* (4)
" alone. The copyists then went to him and said : ' We shall concede to the
" ' public what they demand and copy for them at the rate of one dirhem for ten
" ' leaves.'" What induced him to (*compose and*) dictate the *Madni* was, that one of
his disciples, who was then in the service of al-Hasan Ibn Sahl (*vol. I. p. 408*)
and whose name was Omar Ibn Bukair, wrote to him in these terms : " The emir
" al-Hasan is always asking me questions relative to the Korân, and I cannot readily
" call to mind the proper answers. Would you be pleased to lay down for me cer-
" tain fundamental principles and compile, on that subject, a work to which I may
" refer." On reading this note, he invited his disciples to assemble and hear him
dictate a work on the Korân. On the appointed day, when all were present, he
came in to them and told a man who acted as a muwazzin in the mosque and who
knew well the Korân, to commence reciting (*the text of that book*). The man began
by the *Fâtiha* (5) and al-Farrâ explained it, and this continued till they went over
the whole book; the muwazzin reciting and the professor explaining. This commentary fills about one thousand leaves; nothing like it had ever been composed
before, and no person can possibly add to it.—Al-Mâmûn placed his two sons
under al-Farrâ's tuition, so that they might be instructed in grammar. One day,
al-Farrâ rose from his place, on some necessary occasion, and the two young princes
hastened to bring him his slippers. They struggled between themselves for the
honour of offering them to him, and they finally agreed that each of them
should present him with one slipper. As al-Mâmûn had secret agents who informed him of every thing that passed, he learned what had taken place and
caused al-Farrâ to be brought before him. When he entered, the khalif said to
him : " Who is the most honoured of men ?" Al-Farrâ answered : " I know not
" any one more honoured than the Commander of the faithful."—" Nay;" replied
" al-Mâmûn, " it is he who arose to go out and the two designated successors of the
" Commander of the faithful contented for the honour of presenting him his slippers,

" and at length agreed that each of them should offer him one." To this al-Farrà
answered : " Commander of the faithful! I should have prevented them from doing
" so had I not been apprehensive of turning them away from some honourable exam-
" ple which they had already received or discouraging their minds in the pursuit of
" that high estimation to which they ardently aspire. We know by tradition that
" Ibn Abbàs held the stirrups of al-Hasan and al-Husain, when they were getting
" on horseback after paying him a visit. One of those who were present said to
" him : ' How is it that you hold the stirrups of these striplings, you who are their
" ' elder?' To which he replied : " Ignorant man! no one can appreciate the
" merit of people of merit except a man of merit.' Al-Màmùn then said to him :
" Had you prevented them, I should have inflicted on you the penalty of censure
" and reproach, and should have declared you in fault. That which they have done
" is no debasement of their dignity ; on the contrary, it exalts their merit,
" renders manifest their excellent nature and inspires me with a favorable opinion
" of their character. No man, thought great in rank, can be dispensed, by his
" high position, from three obligations : he must respect his sovereign, venerate
" his father, and honour his preceptor. As a reward for their conduct, I bestow
" on them twenty thousand dinars (£. 10,000), and on you, for the good education
" which you give them, ten thousand dirhems (£. 500)."—The following anecdote is
related also by the Khatìb : " One day, al-Farrà was sitting in the house of the legist
" Muhammad Ibn al-Hasan, who was the son of his aunt, and happened to say that
" few men ever mastered one branch of science without finding the others quite
" easy. On this, Muhammad said : ' You, Abù Zakariya! have studied pure Ara-
" ' bic; so, I shall question you on a point of (canon) law.'— Let us heard your
" ' question,' said al-Farrà, ' (and I shall answer) with the blessing of God.' Muham-
" mad then said to him : ' What do you say of a man who, in making the two satis-
" ' factory prostrations that some neglect in the accomplishement of the prescribed
" ' prayer rendered necessary, neglects, again, in these prostrations, something
" ' important?' Al-Farrà reflected for some time and then replied that the man
" ' incurred no obligation. ' Why so?' said his cousin. ' Because,' said he,
" ' according to us grammarians, a diminutive noun cannot be diminished again ;
" ' and besides, the two prostrations are the completion of the prayer, and that which
" ' is complete requires no further completion.' On hearing this, Muhammad
" exclaimed : ' Now, I am sure that a descendant of Adam never engendered a son

" ' like you ! ' " I already mentioned this anecdote in the life of al-Kisâi (vol. II.
p. 236) and there referred to the account which I give of it here. —Al-Farrâ had a leaning towards the doctrine of the Motazelites. Salama, the son of Aâsim, related as
follows : " Al-Farrâ told me that he and Bishr al-Marisi (vol. I. p. 260), lived together,
" in the same house, for twenty-one years and that neither of them learned any
" thing from the other."—Al-Jâhiz (vol. II. p. 405) said : " I arrived at Baghdad,
" in the year 204 (A. D. 819-20), at the time of al-Mâmûn's entry into that city.
" Al-Farrâ used then to come to see me, and I wished him to learn scholastic theo-
" logy (kalâm), but he had no desire of doing so."—Abû 'l-Abbâs Thalab said :
" Al-Farrâ used to hold public sittings in the mosque adjoining his own house.
" He philosophized (employed the philosophical style) in his works to such a degree
" that he introduced philosophical terms into his discourse."—Salama, the son of
" Ahmad and the grandson of Aâsim said : " I wondered at al-Farrâ's esteem for
" al-Kisâi whom he much excelled in grammatical knowledge."—" One of al-Farrâ's
" sayings was : " When I am dying, my soul shall undergo in some measure, the
" influence exerted by (the conjunction) hatta : it will be depressed, elevated and
" afflicted (6)."—No verses have been handed down as his excepting the following,
which were given by Abu-Hanifa ad-Dinauri (vol. I. p. 455) on the authority of Abû
Bakr at-Tuwâl :

> Lord of a single acre of ground, you have also chamberlains ! You sit in an old ruin and
> have door-keepers to exclude visitors ! Never did I hear of a door keeper in a ruined dwelling !
> Never shall the eyes (of men) see me at a door of yours ; a man like me is not made to support
> repulses from door-keepers.

I since discovered that these verses are attributed to Ibn Mûsa 'l-Makfôf ; God
knows best !—Al-Farrâ was born at Kûfa, whence he removed to Baghdad, which
continued to be his usual place of residence. He was so ardent in the pursuit of
gain that he could not remain quietly at home and, when he had passed a whole year
in hoarding up money, he would go to Kûfa and pass there forty days with his people
to whom he generously distributed the sum which he had collected. He composed
a number of works, such as the Hudâd and the Madni, of which treatises we have
already spoken ; two works, one much larger than the other, on the mushkil (or expressions of doubtful import) which occur in the Korân (7); the Kitâb al-Bahî (7), a
small volume, of which I met a copy after drawing up the present article. It con-

tains the greater part of the terms which Abù 'l-Abbàs Thalab inserted in his *Fasih* (vol. I. p. 84); it is of the same size as that book, and the only difference between them is, that the latter offers the same matters in another order; al-Farrà merely remodeled the work and made thereto a few additions. I may add that the *Baht* contains a few terms which are not to be found in the *Fasih*, but there is very little difference between the two books. His other works are the *Kitáb al-Loghát* (on dialectical expressions), the *Kitáb al-Masddir*, etc. (on the nouns of action which are found in the Korán), the *Jamá wat-Tathniya*, etc. (on the plurals and duals which occur in the Korán), the *Kitáb al-Wákf wa 'l-Ibtidà* (on the full stop and the commencement of phrases, the *Kitáb al-Fákhir*; var. *al-Mufakhir*), the *Kitáb Ala tal-Kátib* (the tool for secretaries), the *Kitáb an-Nawàdir* (on rare expressions), the *Kitáb al-Wàw* (on the copulative conjunction), etc.—Salama, the son of Aàsim, states that al-Farrà dictated (most of) his works from memory; those dictated by him from copies which he held in his hand were the *Kitáb Muldzim*(?) and the *Kitáb yafl wa yafàa* (7). According to Abù Bakr al-Anbàri (vol. III. p. 53), those two books contained about fifty leaves, and all his works filled three thousand leaves.—Muhammad Ibn al-Jahm (8) composed a poem in honour of al-Farrà; its rhymes are formed by an u followed the syllable *hi*; but I abstain from inserting it here, to avoid lengthening this article.—Al-Farrà died A. H. 207 (A. D. 822-3) on the road to Mekka, and at the age of sixty-three years. He was surnamed *al-Farrà* (the furrier), not because he manufactured or dealt in furs, but because he was a *farrá* (skinner or sifter) of words. So says as-Samàni in his *Ansáb*, and he cites for his authority the *Kitáb al-Alkáb* (9).—Abù Abd Allah al-Marzubàni (vol. III. p. 67) says, in his work (10) that Ziàd, the father of al-Farrà, was maimed of his hand, it having been cut off in the war with al-Husain, the son of Ali. This assertion requires to be examined : al-Farrà lived sixty-three years and was therefore born in the year 144; the war with al-Husain took place in A. H. 61 ; so, between that event and al-Farrà's birth, eighty-four years must have elapsed ; to what age then did his father live? If the person who lost his hand was al-Farrà's grandfather, the thing had been possible.— خنذر must be pronounced *Manzár.*—We have already spoken of the word *Dailami*, and of the *Banù Asad.*—*Minhar* was the son of Obaid, the son of Mukàla, whose real name was al-Hàrith, the son of Amr, the son of Kaab, the son of Saad, the son of Zaid Manàt, the son of Tamim, the son of Murra. The tribe named after him is very numerous and has produced a great number of remarkable men, some of whom were companions of the Prophet. They were all surnamed al-Minkari. Such were Khálid, the son of Safwán, and Shabíb, the son of Shabba (11). Safwán and Shabba were the sons of Abd Allah Ibn Omar Ibn al-Ahtam al-Minkari. Khálid and Shabíb were noted as good orators, speaking with elegance and precision. Khálid had frequent sittings with the Commander of the faithful, as-Saffáh, as is well-known, and Shabíb was often in the society of (the khalifs) al-Mansúr, al-Mahdi and others. Mention has been made of them both in our article on al-Bohtori (vol. III. p. 657).

(1) Ali al-Ahmar (the red) was a soldier in ar-Rashíd's guild, or body-guard. His knowledge of pure Arabic was so extensive that al-Kisái got him appointed as tutor to that khalíf's children. He died on his way to Mekka, A. H. 194 (A. D. 809-10).—(Flügel's Grammatische Schulen der Araber, 1st part, p. 184.)

(2) For the contents of this grammatical work, see Flügel's Grammatische Schulen, p. 184.

(3) It is worthy of remark that a dirhem, or six grace, for ten pages of copy, was considered as an exorbitant price, at Baghdad, towards the beginning of the ninth century of our era.

(4) Al-Hamd is the first word of the expression which, in Arabic, means: " Praise be to God " and by which most Moslim books commence.

(5) The Fátiha, or Opening, is the name given to the first súrat of the Korán.

(6) These terms, in the language of the grammarians, signify: govern the genitive case, the nominative and the accusative.

(7) It is said that, in the whole Arabic language, no root furnishes two adjectives having the same signification and exactly similar in their form to the adjectives páff (يَفّ) i. e. adult, and yafás (يَفَاس) which come from the root yafá (يَفَا).

(8) An interesting anecdote of this member of the Barmekíde family is given in the first volume, p. 68.

(9) In the bibliographical dictionary of Hajji Khalífa, four works are mentioned which bear this title.

(10) Hajji Khalífa gives the titles of five works composed by Abú Abd Allah al-Marzubáni.

(11) See vol. II, p. 4.—Two mss. and the lithographied text of Ibn Kutaiba's Kitáb al-Maârif read Shaíba.

ABÚ MUHAMMAD AL-YAZÍDI

Abú Muhammad Yahya Ibn al-Mubárak Ibn al-Mughíra al-Adawi, surnamed al-Yazídi, was a teacher of the koranic readings, a grammarian and a philologer. He studied under Abú Amr Ibn al-Alá al-Basri (vol. II. p .399), the great teacher of the readings, and succeeded him in that occupation. He inhabited Baghdad and there taught Traditions which he had learned from Abû Amr, Ibn Juraij (*vol. II. p. 116*) and others. Traditions were received from him and transmitted down by his son Muhammad, by Abû Obaid al-Kâsim Ibn Sallâm (*vol. II. p. 486*), by Ishak Ibn Ibrahim al-Mausili (*vol. I. p. 183*), by a number of his own sons and grandsons, by Abû Omar ad-Dûri (*vol. I. p.* 401)(1), Abû Hamdûn at-Taiyib Ibn Ismail (2), Abû Shoaib as-Sûsi (3), Aîmir Ibn Omar al-Mausili (4), Abû Khallâd Sulaimân Ibn Khallâd and others. He differed from Abû Amr respecting the manner of reading a few words in the Korân, having adopted for them a manner of his own. As he had been preceptor to the children of Yazid Ibn Mansûr Ibn Abd Allah Ibn Yazid al-Himyari (5) (*the khalif*) al-Mahdi's maternal uncle, he was surnamed al-Yazîdi (*the Yazîdian*). Hârûn ar-Rashîd, to whose service he was subsequently attached, confided to him the education of his son al-Mâmûn, who was still a child (6). Abû Muhammad al-Yazîdi was considered as a trustworthy Traditionist, a learned Korân-reader and an elegant speaker; he was well acquainted with the idioms of the (*desert*) Arabs, skilled in grammar and veracious (*as a Traditionist*). A number fine works were composed by him. His views were just and his poetry (*so good that it*) was collected into a dîwân. The philological work entitled *Kitâb an-Nawâdir* (*book of rarities*) was drawn up by him on the plan of the *Nawâdir* which al-Asmâi (*vol. II. p.* 123) composed for Jaafar the Barmekide (*vol. I. p.* 301), and contains, designedly, the same number of leaves as that treatise. He obtained his knowledge of pure Arabic and of the history of the people (*the adventures and quarrels of the Arabic tribes*) from Abû Amr (*Ibn al-Alâ*), al-Khalil Ibn Ahmad (*vol. I. p.* 493) and other learned men of that age. Abû Hamdûn at-Taiyib related as follows : " I met the son of Abû 'l- " Atâhiya (*vol. I. p.* 202) who had just taken down in writing a mass of information " which had been dictated to him by Abû Muhammad al-Yazîdi and all of which " the latter declared to have received from Abû Amr Ibn al-Alâ. It filled nearly " one thousand *jilds* (or *skins*), each *jild* forming about ten leaves; so there were " ten thousand leaves in all." Al-Yazîdi obtained an immense quantity of philological information from al-Khalil Ibn Ahmad, and wrote down under his dictation the rules of prosody, which science that master had just began to discover; he placed, however, his principal reliance on Abû Amr, whose extensive acquaintance with pure Arabic he highly appreciated. At one time, he kept a school for boys, opposite to the house in which Abû Amr resided, and was then admitted into the familiarity of that doctor, who became very partial to him on account of his quick intelligence. The information transmitted down by him is considered as perfectly genuine. His works are the : *Nawddir* of which we have just spoken, the *Maksur wa 'l-Mamdud (on the short and the long alif)*, a compendium of grammar and a treatise on the vowels *(nukat)* and diacritical points *(shakl)*. Ibn al-Munàdi (7) related as follows : " I frequently asked about *(the moral character of)* of Abù Muhammad al-Yazîdi, " his veracity and his credibility as a relater of traditional knowledge. These " questions I addressed to a number of our *shaikhs*, some of them professors of " Arabic, others of Korân-reading and others of Traditions; and they all declared " that he was trustworthy and veracious, and that he never felt fatigue nor dislike " in the pursuit even of the slightest information which could be obtained from oral " tradition. 'But,' ' said they, 'he was suspected of being inclined towards the doc- " ' trines of the Motazelites.' " Abû Obaid al-Kàsim Ibn Sallàm taught the text of the *Gharîb (unusual and obscure expressions of the Korân and the Traditions)* on the sole authority of Abû Muhammad al-Yazîdi, because he well knew the eminent merit of that doctor. In the reign of ar-Rashîd, al-Yazîdi and al-Kisài (vol. II. p. 237) held sittings together and taught Korân-reading to the public. Al-Kisài was preceptor to al-Amîn *(the son of ar-Rashîd)*, and al-Yazîdi to al-Màmûn *(the other son)*. By the order of that khalif, al-Kisài taught his pupil the system of reading *(harf)* adopted by Hamza (vol. I. p. 478) and al-Yazîdi taught his the system of Abû Amr *(Ibn al-Alâ)*. " Al-Yazîdi," said al-Athram (vol. II. p. 568), " entered one day into " the house of al-Khalîl Ibn Ahmad and found him seated on a cushion. Al-Khalîl " made room for him and invited him to sit down beside him. Al-Yazîdi did so " and then said : ' I am sure that I inconvenience you.'—' Nay,' replied al-Khalîl, " ' no place is too narrow for two friends or too wide for two enemies.' "—Al-Mà- mûn, having asked al-Yazîdi about something, received from him this answer : " No; and may God accept my life as a ransom for yours, Commander of the faith- " ful !"—" Well said !" exclaimed the khalif, " never was the word and better " placed than in the phrase which you have just uttered (8)." He then made him " a present."—" One day," said al-Yazîdi, " I went to see al-Màmûn; all nature " was smiling (9), and his female musician Nuem, who was one of the handsomest " women of the age, was singing to him an air of which these were the words :

"' You pretended that I had wronged (you) and, fled from me, but in flying, you shot an " arrow which pierced me to the heart. You did well to fly; but be indulgent and pardon me:

" this is the spot where the proscript finds a refuge ; this is the place to which he whom love has
" afflicted may retreat, to which he whose eyes have been wounded by your beauty may run for
" protection. You have robbed my heart of its ease, yet, may God never paralyse the hand
" which committed that theft !

" Al-Mámûn made her sing the same piece three times and then said : ' Tell me,
" ' Yazídí ! can there be any thing (in *life*) better than what who are now engaged
" ' in?' I answered : ' There is, Commander of the faithful ! '—'What is it?' said
" he.—I replied : ' The giving of thanks to Him who has granted to you this great
" ' and signal favour.'—He answered : ' You are in the right and have said the
" ' truth.' He then, after making me a present, ordered one hundred thousand
" dirhems (£. 2,500) to be brought in, so that he might give it away in alms. I
" have still before my eyes the sight of the purses as they were brought in and of
" the money as it was distributed."—Al-Yazídí complained, one day, to al-Mámûn
of being in great need, by reason of debts which he had incurred. The khalif answered : " We have not, at present, means of giving you wherewithal you may ob-
" tain (*the deliverance*) you desire."—" Commander of the faithful," said al-Yazídí,
" I am reduced to great straits and my creditors are hard upon me. Think of
" some expedient for me." Al-Mámûn reflected a little, and it was then agreed upon
between them that al-Yazídí should come to the door of the palace, when the khalif
was holding one of his familiar parties, and there write a note in which he would
request to be admitted or to have one of the sovereign's boon companions sent out to
him. When the company were assembled, al-Yazídí came to the door and gave the
servant a sealed letter. Al-Mámûn, to whom it was brought in, opened it and found
that it contained these lines :

Worthiest of brethren and of friends ! I am here, as a parasite, waiting at your door. Let
me make one of the society or send out to me one of my companions (*to keep me company*).

Al-Mámûn read the letter to those who were present and said : " It is not fit that
" such a parasite should enter here, in such a state (as we are)." He then sent out
to him this message : " Your entrance here, at this hour, is impossible; chose for
" yourself the person whom you wish for a boon companion." When al-Yazídí received this missive, he answered : " I can make for myself no better choice than Abd
" Allah Ibn Táhir (*vol. II. p. 49*)." Al-Mámûn then said to Abd Allah : " His
" choice has fallen on you, so you must go out to him." The other replied :

" Commander of the faithful! must I become the associate of a parasite?" The khalif answered : " I cannot possibly turn him from his intention ; but you have the " choice of going out to him or of avoiding that obligation by paying a fine."— " I shall give him ten thousand dirhems (£ 500)," exclaimed Abd Allah.—" I " do not think," said al-Mámûn that, for so small a sum, he will forego the pleasure " of your company." Abd Allah then offered ten thousand more, and then another ten, whilst the khalif continued to say : " I do not think that enough for him."— When the offer mounted up to one hundred thousand dirhems, al-Mámûn said : " Send them to him quickly." Abd Allah wrote a draught on his intendant for the sum and sent it off by a messenger. Al-Mámûn then said (to al-Yazîdi) : " In " the present case, it is better for you to accept this sum than to carouse with Abd " Allah Ibn Táhir whilst he is in his present state."—Al-Yazîdi consented to receive the money. He (al-Mámûn?) was very adroit in every thing he did.—Abû Ahmad Jaafar al-Balkhi (10) relates, in his book (11), that al-Yazîdi asked al-Kisâi's opinion respecting the following verses :

I do not think that a kharab can be hatched from its egg by a falcon. The air is not a horse's foal (, it) is not ; the foal (u bat) a foal.

—The word kharab signifies a male bustard (12), and aîr means the male of the ona- ger.—Al-Kisâi answered that (the last of the words) foal ought to be in the accu- sative, because it is the object of the verb to be (which, in Arabic, governs the accusative) (13) ; so, that being admitted, there is, in the rhyme, a fault of the kind called ikwâd (14).—" Nay," replied al-Yazîdi, " the verse is correct, for the phrase " finishes with the second is not, which merely serves to corroborate the first. Af- " ter these words, the poet enonces a new proposition and says : The foal (is but) a " foal." He then (bowed so low that he) struck the floor with his bonnet and ex- claimed : " (It is) I, Abû Muhammad (who say so!)." Yahya Ibn Khâlid the Barme- kide (who was there present, felt scandalized at this conduct and) said to him : " How " dare you (be so familiar as to) pronounce your surname in the presence of the " Commander of the faithful? By Allah! al-Kisâi's mistake joined to his good breed- " ing, is better than your right answer, joined to your unpoliteness." To this, al-Yazîdi answered : " The sweetness of my triumph put me off my guard."—I must here observe that al-Kisâi was wrong in saying that the verse contained an ikwâd, for, in the technical language of the prosodians, the term ikwâd designates specially a change in the grammatical inflexion (or *raaab* which accompanies the letter (or consonant) forming the rhyme, and this change consists in nothing more that the substitution of an *o* (*the sign of the nominative*) for an *i* (*the sign of the genitive*) or *vice versa*; that is, one of the rhyme-consonants takes an *o* and the other an *i*; but if the discordance exist between two verses, so that one rhyme-consonant takes an *a* (*the sign of the accusative*) and the other an *o* or an *i*, that irregularity is not called an *ikwd* but an *irdf*. — Abû 'l-Alâ al-Maarri (*vol. I*. p. 94) alludes to these irregularities in one of his longer poems containing a lament on the death of the *sharîf* at-Tâhir, the father of ar-Rida (*vol. III. p. 116*) and of al-Murtada (*vol. II. p. 256*); he thus describes the croaking of the raven :

     It is modelled on the *itd* and is devoid of *ikwd*, of *ikfl* and of *iwdf* (15).

This verse being connected (by its meaning) with those which precede, cannot be rendered intelligible unless the others be cited, and that we think unnecessary to do here. I merely quote it as an example; that is all. Some say that the *irdf* is a variety of the *ikwd*; if that be so, al-Kisâi was right in what he said.— This paragraph is a superfluity, but contains some useful information.—The greater part of al-Yazîdi's poetry is good. Hârûn Ibn al-Munajjim (*vol. III. p.* 604) speaks of him in the *Kitâb al-Bârî* and gives some fragments of his composition ; such, for instance, are the following satirical lines, directed against al-Asmâi al-Bâhili (*vol. II. p.* 123):

     You who pretend to draw your origin from Asmâ, tell me how you are connected with that noble race ? Are you not a man whose genealogy, if verified, proves that you descend from Bâbila (16) ?

" This last verse," says Ibn al-Munajjim, " is one of the most satirical which have " been composed by the later poets." I may add that the idea contained in it is borrowed from the following verse in which Hammâd Ajrad (*vol. I. p.* 474) attacked Bashshâr, the son of Burd (*vol. I. p.* 254) :

     You call yourself the son of Burd, though you are the son of another man ; or, grant that Burd married your mother ; who was Burd !

Here is another of his (*al-Yazîdi's*) satirical pieces :

     Be careful not to lose the friendship of Abû 'l-Mukâtil, when you approach (*to partake of*) his meal. Breaking his crumpet, is, for him, as bad as breaking one of his limbs. His guests has against their will and without meaning to obtain the (spiritual) reward which is granted to fasting.

In our article on al-Mubarrad, we have given (vol. III. p. 36) a passage taken from one of al-Yazidi's poems and directed against Shaiba Ibn al-Walid. Amongst the numerous anecdotes and stories which he handed down, we may notice the following ; " A man, pretending to be a Prophet, was arrested and taken before (the " khalif) al-Mahdi : ' Are you a Prophet?' said al-Mahdi.—' I am,' said the priso- " ner.—' To whom were you sent (on a mission)?'—The man replied : ' Did you " ' allow me to go to any person? why, the very moment I received my mission, you " ' cast me into prison!' The khalif laughed and said : 'Go and be converted unto " ' God.' " —Al-Yazidi had five sons who became distingued as men of learning, philologers, poets and narrators of historical anecdotes. Their names were Abû Abd Allah Muhammad, Ibrâhîm, Abû 'l-Kâsim Ismaïl, Abû Abd ar-Rahmân Obaid Allah and Abû Yakûb Ishâk. All of them composed works on philology and genuine Arabic. Muhammad, who was the eldest, was also the best poet among them (17). According to Dibil al-Khuzâi (vol. I, p. 507), he was the author of these lines :

> Why should you travel about when the person whom you love (and pursue) dwells in a fixed abode? That, assuredly, is an enormous fault. As long as you resist Fortune and Care against yourself, whom can you have to blame? (The lover answered :) I am miserable, yet shall I ne- ver think of her with indifference, neither will she be clement, though, by her, I am miserable.

He composed also these lines :

> O thou whose dwelling is so far off I thou whose name is always on my tongue and whose image is in my heart (18). The vicissitudes of Fortune may remove thee to a distant land, yet still shall my desires bring near to me thy image.

He composed a great quantity of good poetry and assisted his father in the educa- tion of al-Mâmûn. In the latter part of his life he became dull of hearing. When al-Mâmûn set out for Khorâsân, he (Muhammad al-Yazîdi) went with him, and re- mained in his service after their arrival in the city of Marw. He continued to re- side there till the accession of al-Motasim, whom he then accompained to Egypt, where he died. His father, Abû Muhammad, died A. H. 202 (A. D. 817-8) in Kho- râsân, and probably at Marw, whither he had accompanied al-Mâmûn from Baghdad and where the latter had established his residence.—I since found in Abû 'Amr ad- Dâni's (19) Tabakât al-Kurrâ (chronological list of Koran-readers), that he died at Marw

in the year just mentioned, but the author then adds these words : " Ibn al-Munddi
" related that, according to what he had heard, he lived to within a few years of a
" century and died at Basra ; but the first statement is the truest."   God knows best!
—We have already spoken of his grandson Abû Abd Allah Muhammad Ibn al-Abbâs
Ibn Muhammad Ibn Abi Muhammad al-Yazîdi (vol. *III*. p. 50), and given the date
of his death with some account of him and of his merit.—*Adawi* means *belonging to
the family of Adi*, who was the son of Abd-Manât, the son of Odod, the son of Tâ-
bikha, the son of al-Yâs, the son of Modar, the son of Nizâr, the son of Maadd, the
son of Adnân.   The descendants of Adi formed a numerous and celebrated tribe.
Abû Muhammad al-Yazîdi belonged to it in the quality of a *mawla;* his grandfather,
al-Moghîra, having been the enfranchised slave of an Adawide woman and having
therefore been surnamed *al-Adawi*.—At the beginning of this article we have explained the meaning of the surname *al-Yazîdi* and mentioned who Yazîd was ; I need
not repeat that account here.   Many of al-Yazîdi's descendants were men of eminent
talent and renown, authors of books and composers of charming and celebrated poems.
Some of these pieces I should give here, were I not apprehensive of lengthening this
article too much.—The posterity of al-Yazîdi were highly proud of the work composed
by his son Ibrâhîm and entitled *Mâ 'ttafak lafzuh*, etc. (*list of homonyms*).   This
treatise contains every term which has different significations.   I saw a copy of it in
four volumes.   It is a most valuable work and affords an evident proof of the vast
learning and extensive information possessed by the author.   Other good and useful
works were composed by the same person.   This also may be said of the other members of his family : they composed works which are in great repute.—Yazîd the
Himyarite, who was the maternal uncle of (*the khalif*) al-Mahdi, held a high rank
under the Abbasides and acted as governor of Basra and of Yemen in the name of
al-Mansûr.   He died at Basra, A. H. 165 (A. D. 781-2).   It was of him that Bashshâr Ibn Burd said :

> Abû Khâlid ! you who, when young, were an able swimmer in the ocean (*of generosity*), are en-
> camped on its border, now that you are grown old.   You were formerly beneficent, but you
> fell back from that habit, till you went treading in the beaten path of ordinary men.   The rank
> to which you attained is exalted to an extreme degree and, to an extreme also, has your fair
> renown declined ; you are like Abd Allah's cat which, when young, was sold for a dirhem and,
> when old, for a *kirât* (20).

After searching uselessly for the anecdote of Abd Allah's cat in the works which I imagined would have contained it, I consulted the persons who were versed in those matters, but could obtain no information on the subject. I then met with the following verses, the author of which was al-Farazdak (*vol. III. p. 612*) :

> I saw other people increase in honour, day by day, whilst your honour gradually declined.
> (*You are*) like the cat which, when young, bears a high value and, when old, is cheap.

It was from these verses that Bashshár borrowed his idea; he did not mean a particular cat, but meant to say that every cat which, when young, was sold dear, lost its value when it grew old.

(1) The manuscripts and the printed editions read *Abú Amr*, but I follow the excellent copy of the *Tabakát al-Kurrá* which is in the Bibl. imp., ancien fonds, n° 749 ; see fol. 52.

(2) Abú Hamdún al-Taiyib Ibn Ismaíl ad-Dahhî, a native of Baghdad and a teacher of the Korán-readings was noted for the sanctity of his life. The date of his death is not given.—(*Tab. al-Kurrá*, f. 52.)

(3) Abú Shuaib Sálih Ibn Ziád as-Súsí, a Korán-reader of great authority, died A. H. 261 (A. D. 874-5), aged upwards of ninety years.—(*Tab. al-Kurrá*, f. 53.)

(4) Abú 'l-Fath Aámir Ibn Omar, a native of Mosul, a teacher of the Korán-readings and a Traditionist, died A. H. 230 (A. D. 844-5).—(*Tab. al-Kurrá*, f. 80.)

(5) Our author speaks of this chief at the end of the present article.

(6) The Arabic merely says : He placed al-Mámún in his lap.

(7) Abú 'l-Husain Ahmad Ibn Jaafar al-Muntabî, a celebrated Traditionist and Korán-reader, was highly esteemed for the exactitude of his information, his knowledge of history and his acquaintance with pure Arabic. He died in the month of Muharram, 336 (July-August, A. D. 947).—(*Tab. al-Kurrá*, f. 78.)

(8) Had the word *and* not been inserted, the phrase would have signified : May God and accept my life, etc.

(9) Such appears to be the meaning of the expression *ad-dunyá ghámida*, which signifies literally : the world was flourishing.

(10) Abú Ahmad Jaafar Ibn Abd Allah al-Balkhî was a doctor of the hanafite sect and the author of some controversial works, the titles of which are given by Hajji Khalîfa, in his Bibliographical Dictionary. The year of his death is not mentioned.

(11) I am unable to indicate the title of this book, the author having composed more works than one.

(12) In Arabic, *Anádra*. Dr. Shaw has given a description of it in his Travels.

(13) Al-Khali means to say that *madra*, which is the last word of the verse and in the nominative case, should have been put in the accusative and pronounced *madra*.—He was mistaken.

(14) For the meaning of this technical term and those which occur farther on, see de Sacy's *Traité de prosodie arabe*, and Freytag's *Darstellung der Arabischen Verskunst*.

(15) These terms of prosody have probably other significations in the ordinary language, but it is not necessary to indicate them.

(16) "More despicable than a Bahila" was a common proverb among the Arabs.

(17) For an account of the members of the Yazîd family, most of whom were distinguished literary men, see professor Flügel's *Grammatische Schulen der Araber*, p. 90.

(18) Literally : who are joined to my heart and to my tongue.

(19) See vol. III, p. 443.—One of ad-Dâni's works is a manual for the control of the Korânic readings and is entitled the Muâni. Its contents have been made known to us by Mr. de Sacy, in the Notices et Extraits, t. VIII. See also t. XX, p. 464 of the same work, in the second part of my translation of the Khaldûn's Prolegomena.

(20) By the term khidr, the poet probably meant to designate the twenty-fourth part of the dirhem.

AT-TIBRIZI

Abû Zakariya Yahya Ibn Ali Ibn Muhammad Ibn al-Hasan Ibn Bistâm as-Shaibâni at-Tibrîzi (*a member of the tribe of Shaibân and native of Tauris*), generally known by the title of al-Khatîb (*the preacher*), was one of the great masters in (*the science of Arabic*) philology, and possessed a perfect knowledge of polite literature, such as grammar and philology. He made his studies under Abû 'l-Alâ al-Maarri (*vol. I. p. 94*), Abû 'l-Kâsim Obaid Allah Ibn Ali ar-Rakki (1), Abû Muhammad ad-Dahhân the philologer (2), and other literary men. He heard Traditions delivered, in the town of Sûr (*Tyre*), by the legist Abû 'l-Fath Sulaim Ibn Aiyûb ar-Râsi (*vol. I. p. 584*), Abû 'l-Kâsim Abd al-Karîm Ibn Muhammad Ibn Abd Allah Ibn Yusûf ad-Dallâl as Sâwi (3), Abû 'l-Kâsim Obaid Allah Ibn Ali Ibn Obaid Allah ar-Rakki and others. Traditions were delivered on his authority by the khatîb and hâfiz Abû Bakr Ahmad Ibn Ali Ibn Thâbit (*vol. I. p. 75*), the author of the History of Baghdad, by the hâfiz Abû 'l-Fadl Muhammad Ibn Nâsir (4), Abû Mansûr Mauhûb Ibn Ahmad al-Jawâliki (*vol. III. p. 498*). Abû 'l-Hasan Saad al-Khair Ibn Muhammad Ibn Sahl al-Andalusi (5) and other distinguished men. A great number of students commenced and finished their education under him. The hâfiz Abû Saad as-Samâni (*vol. II. p. 156*) speaks of him in the Zail and in the Ansâb; he enumerates his merits and says: " I heard Abû Mansûr Muhammad Ibn Abd al-" Malik Ibn al-Hasan Ibn Khairûn (6), the teacher of the Korân-readings, state that " Abû Zakariya Yahya Ibn Ali at-Tibrîzi did not hold a satisfactory conduct; he then " related some things respecting him and said : ' I asked the hâfiz Abû 'l-Fadl Mu-

" ' hammad Ibn Nàsir his opinion of what Ibn Khairûn had said (*concerning al-*
" ' *Tabrizi's character*), but he kept silent as if he would not contradict what had
" ' been said [7], but he at length declared that al-Tibrizi, as a philologer, was a
" ' sure authority and that the information which he handed down was worthy of
" ' credit.' "—Al-Tibrîsi composed some instructive works on literature, such as a
commentary on the *Hamdsa* (*vol. I. p. 318*), a commentary on al-Mutanabbi's
(*vol. I. p. 102*) poems, a commentary on Abù 'l-Alà el-Maarri's (*vol. I. p. 95*)
Diwân entitled *Sikt az-Zand* (8), a commentary on the seven *Moallakas*, a commentary on the *Mufaddaliyât* (9), a *Tahdîb* (or *remodeling*) of the *Gharîb al-Hadîth* (10),
a *Tahdîb* of the *Islâh al-Mantik* (11). He is the author of a good introduction to
grammar, having for object the elucidation of the secrets of that art; this work is
very rare. He composed also a treatise on prosody and rhyme, entitled *al-Kâfi*
(*the sufficient*), a treatise on the parsing of the Korân, to which he give the title of
al-Mulakhkhas (*the summary*), and a copy of which I saw in four volumes. His
commentary on the *Hamdsa* forms three works, the greater commentary, the
middle and the less (12). Other works also were composed by him. We have
related in our article on the Khatîb Abù Bakr Ahmad Ibn Ali what passed between
that historian and al-Tabrizi, when the latter was studying under him at Damascus
and to that article we refer the reader (13). He (*al-Tibrizi*) studied polite literature
at the Nizàmiya college in Damascus. The motive which induced him to go to
Abù 'l-Alà al-Maarri was, that, having procured a copy of Abù Mansùr al-Azhari's
(*vol. III. p. 48*) *Kitâb at-Tahdîb*, in four small volumes, he wished to verify the
correctness of its text under the direction of some person well versed in philology,
and Abù 'l-Alà was indicated to him as the fit man. He put the volumes into a
bag and carried them on his back from Tauris to al-Maarra, not having the means
of hiring whereon to ride. The transpiration penetrated from his back into the
books and left on them marks of humidity. They are now in a *wakf* (14) at
Baghdad and, when a person not acquainted with what happened, sees them, he
thinks that they must have remained for some time under water; these stains are,
however, nothing else that the sweat of al-Tibrizi. So I find it related in the history of the grammarians composed by al-Kâdi al-Akram Ibn al-Kifti, the vizir of
Aleppo (*vol. II. p. 494*). God knows if his account be true! Al-Tibrizi went to
Egypt when a young man and had there for a pupil the *shaikh* Abù 'l-Hasan Tàhir
Ibn Bâbshâd, the grammarian (*vol. I. p. 647*), to whom he communicated some

philological information. He then returned to Baghdad and continued to reside
there till the day of his death. He taught from memory a great number of poems
which he had learned from the author, Abù 'l-Hasan Muhammad Ibn al-Mozaffar
Ibn Mutairis (15) al-Baghdâdi; such, for instance as the following piece, given by
as-Samâni in that article of the *Zail* which treats of the Khatib at-Tabrizi. It is
the best known of that poet's productions:

> O my two friends! how sweet were the morning draughts which I took on the bank of the
> Tigris and yet sweeter were those of evening at as-Sartt (16). Near these two streams I drank
> the liquor of a vine; it was like melted carnelian, and they were like liquid pearls. Two
> moons were then present; one, that the heavens and the other a moon (a young beauty) of the
> earth; one inspiring desire for the sweets of love, the other enamoured. I kept filling the cup
> (for that earthly moon) and sipping nectar from her lips whilst she kept filling for me and drink-
> ing from my lips. I said to the fair moon (of heaven): " Do you know who is this? " and
> she answered: " I do; it is my twin sister (17). "

These verses are the finest and the most elegant which poetry can offer. The
idea expressed in the second verse is borrowed from Abù Bakr ad-Dâni Ibn Labbâna
(vol. *III.* p. 192), who said, in a long *kasîda* which he composed in praise of al-
Motamid Ibn Abbâd (vol. *III.* p. 182), the sovereign of Seville:

> I asked his brother, the (beautiful) ocean, what he thought of al-Motamid, and he answered:
> He is my brother; but he is always tranquil and sweet.

It was not sufficient for the poet to represent that prince as the brother of the
ocean, but he must add that he was tranquil and sweet, whereas, the ocean is
agitated and salt. This is an example of pure and original eulogium. The
kasîda itself begins thus:

> She wept on bidding me farewell, and her fellow-travellers knew not whether those tears
> were drops of dew or pearls fresh (from the shell). She was followed by a band (of maidens).—
> Nay! I am wrong;—the word band cannot be said of stars shining through the darkness of night.

This poem is of considerable length, and I therefore abstain from giving it all,
lest I should be drawn away from my subject.—The Khatib (at-Tabrizi) related that
the following lines were recited to him by the author, who was the Ibn Mutairis
above mentioned:

> Maidens of the tribe of Modar! (your companions) Salma is sister to the moon (in beauty).
> O may Salma never afflict me (with her disdain)! she has abandoned my eyes to unceasing

wakefulness. Whether she turn away from me or towards me, my heart's blood is equally in peril. I have lodged the whiteness of her teeth in the black (core) of my heart and (the pupil) of my eye.

He himself composed some poetry, such, for instance, as the following lines:

Some persons are surfeited with a day's travelling, but I am surfeited with dwelling in the same place. I have resided in Irâk amongst the vilest of men, descendants of the vile.

He related also that al-Imâd al-Faiyâd wrote to him as follows:

Say to Yahya, the son of Ali, — though discourse assumes various characters, yet, mine contains neither falsehood nor deception; — (say to him): You are merit in person, when the eyes of men are turned towards merit; true merit has obtained, through you, its real value. All those who once existed are surpassed by you, and those who now exist are fatigued in following your footsteps. You were born under one of those conjunctions which occur after a lapse of many centuries. Other men, compared with you, are as cloudy weather compared to a clear sky. When inquiries are made respecting them, the accounts received are various; from what we have heard and seen, (some are like) level plains and (others like) rugged ground. If we weighed against you all who ever existed, (we would find you to be) a king (and them serfs) artisans. What are now (the tribes of) Shaibân and Asd? all said respecting them is mere conjecture. You are the stem of (the tree of) learning and other men are only its branches. You are the ocean, and the men most distinguished for their merit are mere springs of water. The sword, if put (جم) to the test, is far superior to scabbards. The scrolls is not equal to the faulá, neither is Bajda to be compared with Mekka's temple (18). Mirth and levity may amuse, but serious affability is far above them. White females and brown are not on an equality in beauty. A married female may please, but nothing is so charming as a young virgin. I said to the envious: "Be whatever you wish to be; he who shoots farthest obtains the prize, "whether you be proud or humble." May your life endure as long as the definition of motion differs from that of rest! May your wishes be accomplished as long as birds dwell in nests! My affection for you has been carefully preserved from all admixtures which alter affection; in me its exterior manifestation is not in discord with the interior; nay, the love which my heart bears towards you is formed of sincerity. Make a wager (about it), for wagers are sometimes made on love-matters; if one man be deceitful, another is sincere.

Ibn al-Jawâlîki (vol. III. p. 498) relates that his shaikh the Khatib Abû Zakariya (al-Tibrîzi) said to him: I then wrote to al-Imâd al-Faiyâd these verses:

Say to al-Imâd, the brother of high eminence: I am but a drop of water from your overflowing ocean. You have raised me to honour and gained me high renown, in bestowing on me so ample a recompense of eulogium. Oo! your gracious bounty you have clothed me in a raiment of poetry, and I, proud of that attire, have marched about in the bright (of glory) and in the gardens (of delight). I here give you a pebble in return for a pearl which was the produce of a cultivated mind. My genius would be at a stop, did it attempt any thing similar;

it could hardly produce a fraction (of such excellence as yours). How could a streamlet compete with the vast ocean? how could a pebble be compared with a pearl? You, the able horseman in (the career of) that jewel-adorned poetry and that prose which dissipate even the pains of sickness! you who, by your abilities, aim at the highest point (of perfection and attain it) I know that my talent cannot reach so far. Impose not on me the task of giving you fitting praise; such a duty I am unable to fulfil. My talent has been always too feeble for poetry; I have often turned away from making verses, and even with great aversion. Be then so kind as to excuse me; I avow that, compared with your abundance, talent like mine is in poverty.

Al-Tibrîzi was born in the year 421 (A. D. 1030); he died suddenly at Baghdad, on Tuesday, the 27th of the latter Jumâda, 502 (1st Feb., A. D. 1109), and was interred in the cemetery at the Abrez gate.—In *Bisîâm*, the letter *b* is followed by an *i*.—We have already spoken of *Shaibâni* (col. I. p. 85) and of *Tibrîzi* (col. II. p. 644): so, we need not repeat our observations.

(1) Abû 'l-Kâsim Obaid Allah Ibn Ali Ibn Obaid Allah Ibn Zumais (زُبيْز) ar-Rakki (a native of Rakra, in Mesopotamia) and an inhabitant of Baghdad, was highly distinguished for his talents. He was versed in grammar, arabic philology, polite literature and the art of calculating inheritance shares. He composed also a work on the theory of the rhyme, in prosody. One of his masters was Abû 'l-Alâ al-Maarri. His death took place in the year 450 (A. D. 1058-9).—Soyûti's *Biographical Dictionary of grammarians and literary men*; ms. of the Bibl. imp., supplement n. 688.

(2) Our author has already noticed an Abû Muhammad Said Ibn al-Mubârak ad-Dahhân (vol. I, p. 371), a grammarian of great celebrity; but the Abû Muhammad ad-Dahhân of whom he speaks here, lived in the preceding century, and was the son of Muhammad Ibn Ali. He was an able grammarian, versed in arabic philology, jurisprudence and the Korân-readings. In his lectures on jurisprudence, he adhered to the system followed in Irâk (the doctrine of Abû Hanîfa), and, in dogmatic theology, he followed the system of the Motazelites. He taught also the Traditions and had at-Tibrîzi for a pupil. He was very negligent in his dress. Died A. H. 447 (A. D. 1055).—(Soyûti's *Grammarians*).

(3) Various readings : as-Saydri, as-Sarghti.

(4) Abû 'l-Fadl Muhammad Ibn Nâsir, one of the great Traditionists of Irâk, was born A. H. 467 (A. D. 1074-5). He became eminent as a grammarian, philologer, jurist and historian. He died in the month of Shaabân, A. H. 550 (October, A. D. 1155).—(*Tabakât al-Huffâz*.)

(5) Abû 'l-Hasan Said al-Khair Ibn Muhammad al-Anaâri, a native of Valencia in Spain, received also the surname of as-Sini (the Chinese), because he had gone to China in search of traditional information. After encountering many dangers in his travels, he fixed his residence in Baghdad, where he studied jurisprudence under the celebrated doctor Abû Hâmid al-Ghazâli. Subsequently to a journey made to Ispahân, where he heard Traditions taught by the doctors of that city, he returned to Baghdad, studied the belles-lettres under Yahya at-Tibrîzi and died there, in the month of Muharram, 541 (June-July, A. D. 1146).—(Al-Makhari, arabic text, vol. I, p. 695.)

(6) Abû Mansûr Muhammad Ibn Abd al-Malik Ibn Khairûn, a native of Baghdad and teacher of the Korân-

readings, was noted for the merity of his information and the sanctity of his life. He composed a work on the readings, entitled al-Hifdá (the key) and died in the month of Rajab, A. H. 546 (January, A. D. 1143), at an advanced age.—(Fahadát al-Aarvá, n. 742, fol. 142.)

(7) Tabrisí's moral character does not appear in the best light, if we may judge after a piece of verse composed by him and given farther on. Ibn Khairún must have been often scandalised by facts of this nature, as the most eminent doctors and many of the sovereigns who patronized poets and literary men, took the greatest pleasure in composing and listening to poems which cannot be transferred, undisguised, into any European language. The Khalilán himself cites, with complacency, verses which do not admit of a literal translation. Amongst the Moslim princes, wirand, káldis and poets, there were probably but few who could say, with Ovid : *donera posterorum longer avivos.*

(8) See de Sacy's *Chrestomathie arabe,* t. III, p. 98.

(9) The *Mufaddaliyát* is a collection of ancient poems. An edition of this rare and precious compilation with al-Marzúkí's commentary, is to be published at Berlin by Mr. Gosche.

(10) Ghárib al-Hadíth means rare and obscure expressions occurring in the Traditions. A number of works were composed on this subject, but the most noted was that of Abú Obaid al-Kásim Ibn Sallám (vol. II, p. 487).

(11) The work entitled *Islah al-Mantik* (correction of discourse) was composed by Ibn as-Sikkít, a philologer whose life will be found in this volume.

(12) Tabrisí's middle commentary on the Hamása is that which has been published by Freytag. It is frequently diffuse and unsatisfactory. The information borrowed by the author from his predecessors is often very useful, but his own communications are generally philological futilities. In explaining the verses of the text, he dilates on what is simple and evident, but seldom attempts to clear up a real difficulty.

(13) The passage to which our author refers is not to be found in any of the manuscripts. It is absent also in the printed editions.

(14) See vol. III, p. 607.

(15) According to some MSS. *Nakib.* The person who bore this name is not noticed in the works consulted by the translator.

(16) See vol. I, p. 616.

(17) In this translation the word *sister* is placed for *brother* and the gender of certain pronouns has been changed. For the reason, see note (9).

(18) The Arabs of the desert made use of ten arrows in casting lots; each arrow had a particular mark and a particular name. That which gained the entire pool was called the *moálla;* that which entitled the drawer to one seventh of the pool was called the *fadd.*—Mejés was the name of a valley near Mekka.

IBN MOTI AZ-ZAWAWI

Abù l'-Husain Yahya Ibn Abd al-Moti [1] Ibn Abd an-Nùr az-Zawàwi, surnamed Zain ad-Din (*the ornament of religion*), was a member of the Hanefite sect and one of the great masters of the age as a grammarian and a philologer. He resided at Damascus for a long time and had a great number of pupils to whom his tuition was highly profitable. Some useful works were composed by him [2]. Having removed to Misr(*Old Cairo*), on the invitation of al-Malik al-Kàmil (vol. *III.* p. 240), he opened a course of literature in the mosque called *al-Jâmi' 'l-Atik*, and received, for his pains, a fixed salary. He remained there till his death : he died in New Cairo, towards the end of the month of Zù 'l-Kaada, 628 (September, A. D. 1231), and was buried, the next day, on the border of the Khandak (*fosse*) which is in the vicinity of the imàm as-Shàfi's mausoleum. His tomb is still to be seen. He was born in the year 564 (A. D. 1168-9).—*Zawâwi* means *belonging to the Zawâwa (Zoaves)*, a great tribe which, with its numerous branches and subdivisions, inhabits the country outside of Bejàiya (*Bugia*), a government (*town*) in the province of Ifrikiya.

(1) It is probably by error that this surname is here written *Ibn Abd al-Moti*. In the grammar of Ibn Malik, verse 5, and in the first verse of the author's own grammar (see Hâji Khalifa's *Bibliographical Dictionary*, vol. I, p. 115) we read *Ibn Moti*, and such is the appellation by which he is generally known. In the *Biographical Dictionary of the grammarians* by as-Suyûti, the surname given to him is also *Ibn Moti*.

(2) His grammatical treatise entitled the *Alfya*, because it consisted of about one thousand verses, was in great repute till cast down by the treatise of Ibn Malik which bears the same title. The *Fusûl* or *aphorisms*, another of Ibn Moti's grammatical works, had a great number of commentators.

YAHYA IBN AL-MUNAJJIM

Abù Ahmad Yahya was the son of Ali, the son of Yahya, the son of Abù Man-sûr, surnamed al-*Munajjim* (*the astrologer*), and whose real name was Abbàn

Hasis, the son of Urid, the son of Kád, the son of Mihánidád Hasis, the son of Far-rúkhdád, the son of Asád, the son of Mihr Hasis, the son of Yezdegird (the last of the Sásánide kings of Persia). He commenced his career as a boon companion of al-Muwaffak Abú Ahmad Talha, the son of the khalif al-Mutawakkil and the father of the khalif al-Motadid Billah. Al-Muwaffak never became khalif, but acted as the lieutenant of his brother, al-Motamid ala-Allah, and was constantly engaged in fighting against the Karmats. As his achievements in this war are well known and would furnish matter for a long narration, this is not a fit place for relating them. After (the death of) al-Muwaffak, Yahya (Ibn al-Munajjim) became the boon companion of the succeeding khalifs and, more particularly, of al-Muktafi Billah, the son of al-Motadid. He attained to a high rank in that prince's favour and was preferred by him to all the other courtiers and table-companions. He professed those doctrines of scholastic theology which were received by the Motazelites and wrote a number of treatises on that subject. Sittings were held by him in the presence of al-Muktafi, and many schoolmen attended them. Amongst the numerous works composed by him, we may notice the Báhir (eminent), containing the history of such poets as had flourished under the two dynasties (that of the Omaiyides and that of the Abbásides). It begins by an article on Bashshár Ibn Burd (vol. I. p. 254) and ends with another on Marwán Ibn Abi Hafsa (vol. III. p. 343). His son Abú 'l-Hasan Ahmad Ibn Yahya terminated this work, which had been left unfinished, and had the intention of adding to it an account of all the modern poets. He, in consequence, gave in it notices on Abú Dulâma (vol. I. p. 534), Wâliba Ibn al-Hubâb (vol. I. p. 395), Yahya Ibn Ziâd (vol. II. p. 403), Muti Ibn Iyâs (vol. I. p. 438) and Abú Ali al-Basîr. Abú 'l-Hasan was a scholastic theologian and, as a legist, he adhered to the system of jurisprudence drawn up by Abú Jaafar at-Tabari (vol. II. p. 597). The (other) works composed by him were, a history of his own family, in which he traced its origin up to the Persians, the Ijmâa (general agreement) treating of at-Tabari's system of jurisprudence, a Mudkhil (or introduction) to the study of that system and a vindication of its principles, a Kitâb al-Aukât (treatise on the hours of prayer (?), etc. His father, Yahya, had many curious and amusing encounters with al-Motadid; such, for instance as that which Abú 'l-Hasan Ali Ibn al-Husain Ibn Ali al-Masûdi (vol. II. p. 618) gives in his Murûj ad-Dahab: "Yahya Ibn al-Munajjim," says he, "related as follows : I was one day in the pre-"sence of al-Motadid, who was then in an angry mood. His mawla, Badr, of

" whom he was very fond, came in, and the khalif, having distinguished him at a
" considerable distance, laughed aloud and asked me who was the poet that said :

" ' In her face is so intercessor which obliterates the wounds she inflicted on our hearts;
" ' whenever she intercedes, she is heard with deference?'

" I replied : ' It was al-Hakam Ibn Amr as-Sâri (1) who said so.' On this, he
" exclaimed : ' He has expressed the thought admirably well! let us hear the whole
" piece.'—I, in consequence, recited to him these lines :

" O! how I suffer from a person who has driven away my sleep, so that it will return no
" more, and who has added fresh torments to those which afflicted my heart! The sun seems
" to be rising out of her shoulders, so handsome is her face; or rather, the moon is rising out
" of her buttoned vest. She is looked on with kindness by her lover, despite the wrongs he
" suffered from her (cruelty), and whatever she does is forgiven. In her face is an intercessor
" which obliterates the wounds she inflicted on our hearts; whenever she intercedes, she is
" heard with deference. "

Abû 'l-Fath Ibn Kushâjim (vol. I. p. 301). the celebrated poet, says, in that chapter of his work entitled al-Masâid wa 'l-Matârid which treats of hunting lions with
arrows, that Abû Ahmad Yahya Ibn Ali Ibn Yahya al-Munajjim, who was the boon
companion of (the khalif) al-Muktafi Bil'ah, related as follows : " The Commander of
" the faithful, al-Muktafi Billah, was displeased with me because, when he was about
" returning from ar-Rakka, I set out before him and made the first stage of the jour-
" ney by water. This I had been induced to do by Abû 'l-Abbâs Ahmad, the son
" of Abd as-Samad (vol. II. p. 143) who asked me go in the same boat with him.
" I did not think that the khalif would be displeased by my doing so or offended at
" my leaving him and staying away. When we arrived at (the town of) ad-Dâlia,
" he gave orders that I should be taken back to Karkisiya and remain there till I had
" killed a lion and sent it to him. I was therefore obliged to return, and a
" number of the vocal musicians, who had taken the water-conveyance, were sent
" back with me. I then wrote to the khalif some verses, but could not induce him
" to relent; so, I returned to ar-Rahaba, and there went to lodge with Abû Muham-
" mad Abd Allah Ibn al-Hasan Ibn Said al-Kutrubulli. I passed the time with
" him in the enjoyments of life; and we had drinking parties, morning, noon and
" night. He was highly pleased with my society. One of our companions was
" Abû Jaafar Muhammad Ibn Sulaimân, the grandson of (the vizir) Muhammad Ibn

" Abd al-Malik az-Zaiyât (vol. *III.* p. 249). I then wrote from ar-Rahaba to the
" vizir Abû 'l-Husain al-Kâsim Ibn Obaid Allah (vol. *II.* p. 299-300) and, in my let-
" ter, I enclosed a piece of verse which I requested him to read to al-Muktafi. It
" ran as follows :

" Fortune would rather perish than procure us pleasure and unite us with our friends. She
" struck me and my brethren with an arrow which reared our souls and left them quite appaled.
" We were sent back when the rest of the company went forward on their way, and then our
" affliction was extreme. Were we told of such a misfortune as ours happening to any other,
" the recital would fill us with terror. We were ordered to hunt lions and, for my part, I
" should think it fortunate if the lion did not hunt us. Were we to disobey, then, you would
" find this (proverb) justified : *What people can obey if tasked above their force?*
" Every task may be imposed on a man except that which is impossible. Princes are
" always fond of jesting, but their jests are accompanied with speedy favours. The vizir neglect-
" ed us, and we were ruined : a man's deserts (even) in serving the cause of God, are (some-
" times) unrequited. We stretched forth our hands to him, and our hopes took refuge in
" his bounty. He is an intercessor whose prayer is never rejected, even when the request of
" the ablest intercessor is not granted. The sports of kings bring on familiarity and fructify
" into gifts of real value (2). You, the director of the khalif's empire render us a service
" and speak to him in our favour : the best of men is he who is the most obliging.

" This letter was put into the government letter-bag and sent off with Muhammad
" Ibn Sulaimân, the dispatch-bearer. When (the vizir) al-Kâsim received it, he
" did not lay it out of his hand till he went in to al-Muktafi and read to him both it
" and the poem. (The khalif) found the verses very good and gave orders that a
" letter should be immediately sent off, authorizing me to depart from the place
" where I was and to have myself provided with a conveyance, so that I might proceed
" to the (khalif's) court. In a very short time, the messenger brought me the letter and
" I started off. On arriving in Baghdad, I recited to al-Muktafi the following
" verses :

" The nights which appeared to me so short in the Karkh (a suburb) of Baghdad, seemed
" very long when I was in Karkisiya. Was it well done to depart and leave me there, like a
" pledge, me a stranger and unwell ! I was the only one punished, yet I had accomplices in
" my fault; but patience! God is the only protector I require. If God grant that I return safe
" to Baghdad, before grief kills me, and, if he let me see that the khalif al-Muktafi, the descendant
" of the khalifs, be on whom our hopes are fixed, is still for me as he was, neither shewing me
" aversion nor disapprobation nor altered sentiments, then indeed, all the pains I suffered will
" appear light because they were inflicted with a good intention.

" The khalif admired this piece and was much touched with its contents ; I percei-

" ved even from his looks and tone of voice that he pitied me."—The anecdotes told
of him are numerous and many of his productions are beautiful. He was born in
the year 241 (A. D. 855-6), and he died on the eve of Monday, the 13th of the first
Rabi, A. H. 300 (28th October, A. D. 912).—We have already spoken of his father
Ali (vol. II. p. 312), of his brother Hārūn (vol. III. p. 604) and of his nephew Ali
(vol. II. p. 313). I did not then trace up their genealogy, not having discovered it
till I was drawing up the present article. I give it here as I found it written in the
Fihrist (vol. I. p. 630) of Abû 'l-Futûh Muhammad Ibn Ishak an-Nadîm, but I do
not attempt fixing the orthography of the proper names, not having the means of
verifying them; so I transcribe them here as I found them.

(1) In some of the manuscripts this name is written an-Sâder.

(9) Literally : miserable.

ABU BAKR IBN BAKI

Abû Bakr Yahya Ibn Muhammad Ibn Abd ar-Rahmân Ibn Baki, a celebrated poet
and a native of Cordova in Spain, was the author of the muwashshahas (stanzas,
sonnets) which are so much admired. Al-Fath Ibn Muhammad Ibn Obaid Allah al-
Kaisi (vol. II. p. 455), speaks of him in these terms, in his Matmah al-Anfus (1) :
" He was expert in verse and prose, firm and regular in the texture of his style (2);
" he possessed (great) qualities and, by the beauties of his (productions), he embel-
" lished the morning (assemblies and those of) the evening. In the career of per-
" fection, he sped on and reached the goal, and he built (edifices) of information on
" the most solid columns. But Fortune refused him her favours, cut and severed
" the cord of his pasturing (in the enjoyments of life); she accomplished none of
" his projects, neither did she shed on him one drop of prosperity. She granted not
" to him (عيشة) a just share of respect, and established him not in the fertility of a
" (rich) pasture-ground. He therefore became a rider (a courser) of mountains, a
" traverser of deserts; never halting for a single day and never finding people with

" whom he had a right to be pleased. And moreover, his mistrustful imagination was
" not to be overcome by (the assurance of) safety; his mind was (fickle and) unstable,
" like the pearls of a broken necklace. (This continued) till Yahya Ibn Ali Ibn al-
" Kásim (3) snatched him out of that vacillation, granted to him the means of sub-
" sistence, raised him to the heaven in which he himself stationed, watered him
" with the stream of his bounty, furnished to him a retreat under the shelter of his
" (patronage) and prepared for him a path of comfort in which he might expatiate
" (as he liked). He (Ibn Bakî) lavished on him therefore (the finest of) his sayings,
" and, in return for many gifts, ennobled him in his rhymes, bestowed on him
" exclusively the most precious pearls (of poetry) and adorned his breast with the
" collars of brilliant kasîdas." The same author speaks of him again in the Kaldîd
al-Ikiyân and says : " It was he who bore aloft the standard of poetry, who pos-
" sessed the talent (4) of open declaration and indirect allusion; it was he who esta-
" blished the rules of that (art) and revealed its beauties; the (expressions the most)
" untractable became obedient to his will. When he drew up verses, he put to shame
" the row of pearls on a necklace, and produced (a poem) more beautiful than robes of
" flowered silk; and (yet) his evil fortune domineered ('اغ') over him, and the
" days of his (existence) never brightened up." —The following piece is attributed to Abû Bakr (Ibn Bakî), but I do not find it given by al-Fath in either of the
above mentioned works. It is, however, a very fine poem, one of the best composed
by the author and the most generally known :

> Dearer to me than the life of my father is that gazelle (maiden) whom my eyes saw with admi-
> ration, (as she roamed) between al-Ozaib and the banks of the (river) Bárik. I asked her to let
> me gaze yet longer and thus allay the thirst of my passion, and she answered by a promise soon
> to be fulfilled. We passed the night in darkness, under a canopy adorned with brilliant stars,
> and, whilst the night swept on, I bended to her a (liquor,) dark as musk and, like it, fragrant
> to the smell. I held her to me (as closely) as the warrior grasps his sword; and her two long
> ringlets hung, like the sword-belt, round my neck. At length, drowsiness overcame her and I
> removed her (a little) from me whilst she clasped me to her arms. I placed her at a distance
> from the heart which loved her, so that she might not have under her head a palpitating pillow.
> When I saw the night drawing towards its end and perceived that its (dark) locks and the crown
> of its head were turning grey, I bade adieu to my beloved and said, with a sigh : " Give me
> the pain of seeing you depart. "

The hâfiz Abû 'l-Khattâb Ibn Dihya (vol. II. p. 384) has inserted some of these
verses in the work which he entitled : Al-Mutrib min Ashâr ahl il-Maghrib (volume of
amusements, extracted from poems composed by natives of the West). Another of Ibn

Baki's poems is a long *kasîda* in which he praises Yahya Ibn Ali Ibn al-Kâsim, the same person who has been already mentioned in this article. Here is an extract from the eulogistic part :

> There are two lights which cannot be hidden from mortals : nobleness of character and beauty of aspect. Both are united in Yahya; so, let him renounce *(attempt of)* concealing that superiority which is evident to all. In every land, his praises spread a perfume which surpasses that of the penetrating vapours arising from the censer. Add to his qualities; add to his generosity; you might as well add leaves to the forest, water to the rain-cloud (5). On that generous man rests the calm of gravity joined to such courage as is displayed by the lion in his den. He is like the sword which, even when hidden in the scabbard, appals the hearts of those who inhabit towns. He surpasses *(in bounty)* the dark cloud, shedding its rains without interruption; he bestows as it does, but prayers are never offered up to obtain his beneficent showers. He puts to shame the copious ocean; for, in each of his hands, are five seas. I am come to obtain a share of your beneficence, which is as the pouring forth of the rain, or rather, the pure water of paradise. I saw that the concurrence of prosperity, near you, was *(smiling and)* white, and therefore, to reach you, I rode across the green waters of every sea. Towards you speeded the ship which bore an able poet (باتـع عامر); it was *(obedient)*, as the camel which is guided by a halter fastened to his nose. The daughters of Awaj (6) were fatigued with bearing me company; so many were the solitary deserts which they had to cross.

The author of the *Kalâid al-Ikiyân* gives the following fragment of a piece by the same author :

> O thou who, of all mankind, art the most killing in glances and the sweetest in kisses! since when are aloes and honey combined in thee? Thy cheek is like the rising sun and, on its surface, is a rose to which wine and modest shame add fresh colours. Love for thee is, for my heart, an article of belief, and is confirmed by the letters which issue from thy cheeks and by the messengers coming from thy glances. If you know not that I have lately lost my liberty, command me what thou wilt : I shall do it and obey. Consider thou now my heart, thou wouldst perceive therein a wound not yet healed up and inflicted by thy glances.

The Kâtib Imad ad-Din (*vol. III. p.* 300) mentions him in the *Khorida* and inserts there some extracts from his poems; then, at the end of the book, he speaks of him again and gives, as his, the following verses :

> In a goblet was a cool *(wine)* which *(in aspect,)* resembled a cornelian sky, studded with stars. *(That liquor)* has built a *knoba (temple)* for pleasure in the *harim (sacred ground)* of youth, and, to it, sports hasten on their pilgrimage from every side.

The poetry of Ibn Baki offers numerous beauties. He died A. H. 540 (A. D. 1145).—The word *Baki* (بكى) takes an a and a double i.

(1) Abú 'l-Fath, better known by the surname of Ibn Khákán, wrote in a style so affected, so full of obscure expressions and so extravagant in its metaphors, that the reader is very often in doubt respecting the true meaning of those turgid and pompous phrases. The extracts taken by the Khalíkán from his works have not been always reproduced correctly by the copyists, who evidently understood very imperfectly what they were writing. This may be seen in comparing the text of the passage here cited with that which al-Makkari, in his *History of Spain*, vol. II, p. 84, of the Arabic edition, gives of the same passage. The translation here offered is probably not always exact.

(2) Literally : numerous in the handling of his threads and in the irregularity.

(3) I can find no information respecting this Yahya Ibn Ali Ibn al-Kásim, but, from his name, I am almost inclined to suppose that he descended from the Hamamdáite branch of the Mricide family.

(4) Literally : the sign; which probably means the distinguishing mark.

(5) The last hemistich, rendered literally, signifies : between the grove and the rain-cloud.

(6) Awaj was the name of a horse celebrated for his good qualities and the excellence of his breed.

MUIN AD-DIN AL-HASKAFI

Abú 'l-Fadl Yahya Ibn Salama Ibn al-Husain Ibn Muhammad, surnamed Muin ad-Dín (*aider of the religion*) and generally known by the title of al-Khatíb al-Haskafi (*the preacher of Hisn Kaifa*), is the author of a *diwán* containing poems, exhortations and epistles. Born at Tanza, he was brought up at Hisn Kaifa, whence he removed to Baghdad. In that city, he studied literature under the Khatib Abú Zakariya al-Tibrizi (*page 78 of this vol.*) and, by the solid information which he thus acquired, he rose to distinction. He studied also, with success, the Sháfite system of jurisprudence. Having left Baghdad with the intention of returning to his native place, he stopped at Maiyáfárikin, where he fixed his residence and filled the office of a khatíb. He acted also as a mufti (*expounder of the law*) and gave public lessons which were highly profitable to those who attended them. The Kátib Imád ad-Dín (*vol. III, p. 300*) mentions him in the Kharída and says : "In science, the most learn-
" ed man of the time ; in talent for poetry and prose, the Maarri (*vol. I, p. 94*) of the
" epoch ; his were the elegant assonances and the admirable paranomasias, the paral-
" lelisms and (their) exactitude, the style firm and delicate, the thoughts simple and
" profound, the perfect tajnís (*the expression of different ideas in the same verse*) and

"the talent (of which the renown was) widely spread and lasting." The same
writer then says, after making a long eulogium of the poet and enumerating his
merits : " I wished to meet with him, and flattered myself that, on my arrival at
" Mosul, I should see him: for I was ardently desirous of instruction and most
" assiduous in frequenting men of talent, for the purpose of augmenting my acqui-
" rements. But the length of the journey and my inability of supporting fatigue
" were obstacles which prevented our meeting." He then gives a number of passages extracted from the poems of this author and, amongst them, the following :

> I passed the evening in reprimanding a dissolute fellow, but he took my reproaches as a jest :
> "Wine," said I," is a bad thing."—He replied : " God preserve it from turning bad! "—"It
> brings on obscene discourse," said I.— " The pleasure of life is in such discourse," said
> he.— "It excites vomiting; " said I.— " I honour it, " said he, " too well to discharge it
> " by the ordinary passage; but, after all, I shall give it up, "—" When? " said I.— " When
> " I am laid in the tomb. "

I may here observe that the Khatib borrowed the expression : *discharging by the
ordinary passage,* from another poet with whose name I am unacquainted, but who
composed the following (*five*) verses which are currently known :

> A censor reproached me for loving wine, and I answered : " I shall drink it whilst I live
> " and even in my grave. Arise! pour me out a liquor, red, clear and pure; though it is for-
> " bidden, I care not. Casuists declare that it is lawful when boiled down; but I have in my
> " stomach a fire which will reduce it to one third (1). If they ask me why I cast it up, my
> " answer is : I respect it too much to discharge it by the ordinary passage. "

Imád ad-Din al-Ispaháni adds : " A person of merit recited to me, at Baghdad,
" some verses similar to the five which are so currently known. They are much ad-
" mired for their natural turn and the art with which they are composed. Here
they are :

> " I complain to God of two fires (*which consume me*) ; one proceeding from the cheeks of
> " my beloved, and the other lighted up by her in my heart. (*I complain*) of two maladies; one
> " which her glances have excited in my blood, the other which is settled in my body. (*I com-
> " plain*) of two debtors ; one is my tears which, when I think of her, betray my secret; the
> " other, the spy who always watches over her. (*I complain*) of a double weakness; one is
> " that of my patience, when I think of her and of my love ; the other, that of people who think
> " her obedient to my will. She is so thin and slender that I exclaim, in admiration : Is that
> " her waist or my little finger? Is that her skin or my own? "

One of his good pieces is that in which he satirises a vocal musician and which we here give :

A musician whose singing reduced him from riches to poverty; such a one I met with in an assembly of persons whom I liked to have for companions. When I saw him, my talent in physiognomy did not deceive me, and I said : " What is that I can such " a countenance ever become pleasing ? " To remain no longer in doubt respecting him, I spoke from amidst the company, saying : " Come, my man! sing us the air " of : O for the days passed at Said (2); the days passed at Said are not to be " despised." On this, he raised up one of his eyebrows, lowered the other, and emitted from his mouth a foul gale which filled the room and which, whilst he marked the mea- sure, was, for every one of us, a cause of annoyance. When he began to speak (sing), a person who was listening in a dark corner of the hall (قاعة) said : " He is not satisfied with " modulating and confounding (notes), but must also sing false! There he is for you! will " he never have done calling his servant scoundrel and drawing near to us (3)? He pretends " to scan (to accent well the words of) the air and only gets more embroiled!" His into- nation was a cry frightful beyond the bounds of description (4); he who had sent for him did not forsee the annoyance which the fellow would give to the company. Some of the assembly stopped their noses; others, their ears, and the rest covered their eyes, to avoid seeing him. I was so provoked that I could not refrain from expressing my indignation, and exclaimed : " Listen, sirs ! I or the singer must be heard! Now I declare that I shall not sit " down unless this man be sent away! drag the dog out by the heels! be it (for us) a " cause of sickness and malady ! " They answered : " You have pitied our sufferings and " delivered (خلّص) us from torture." Then, in sending him out, I secured my own tran- quillity and obtained the thanks (of the company). When his face was turned from us, I re- cited this prayer at the head of the assembly : " Praise be to God who has delivered us from " affliction."

In our article on the shaikh as-Shátibi (vol. II. p. 500) we have given a piece of his, forming an enigma the word of which is bter. The idea of it is very good. Most of al-Haskafi's poetry is remarkable for this kind of wit and for the neat man- ner in which the thoughts are expressed. He was attached to the Shiite doctrines, as may be easily perceived in his poems.—In the town of Aámid, were two youths who had a great fondness for each other and were almost always together (5). One of them rode out to the country, set off at a gallop, the horse fell and he was killed. The other immediately sat down to drink wine, was choked by the liquor and died the same day. A literary man spoke of their fate in the following lines :

They shared between themselves the clear draught of life and the troubled draught of death. We never before saw two equal partakers in the same destiny. They continued in mutual love till the last moment of their existence, and seldom does fidelity in love last till the hour of death.

When the Khatib (al-Haskafi) heard these lines, he said : " The poet did not
" work out the idea, not having mentioned the cause of their death: but I did so in
" a piece composed on the same occurrence and said :

" (*I should have given*) my life to save the two brothers who lived in Aâmid and who re-
" ceived the stroke (*of death*) on a day unlucky and frowning (*obûs*).   One was killed by a
" horse and the other by wine (*henderris*).

" Had he said : One was killed by a horse (*sâfinât*) and the other by liquor (*sâfiyât*),
" it would have been much better, on account of the assonance.   The poet (*adopt-
" ed this correction and, to preserve the rhyme*,) altered the first verse somewhat in
" this manner :

" My life etc..... who received the stroke of death on a day severe in its evils (*ndads*)."

I since found the two first mentioned verses in the *Kitâb al-Jinân*, a work composed by al-Kâdi ar-Rashîd Ibn az-Zubair (vol. *I. p.* 143), who there attributes them
to the eminent legist and teacher of the Korân-readings, Abû Ali al-Husain Ibn
Ahmad al-Moallim; but I met with the account above given in the handwriting of a
contemporary (6).— The Khatib al-Haskafi left some fine moral exhortations and
some choice epistles.   He continued to hold a high rank (*in public estimation*) and
to teach up to the day of his death.   This occurred A. H. 551 (A. D. 1156-7), or
in 553, according to another statement.   He was born in or towards the year 400
(A. D. 1067-8).   — *Haskafi* means *belonging to Hisn Kaifa*, a strong and lofty castle
situated between Jazîrat Ibn Omar and Maiyâfârikîn.   Had this adjective been formed regularly, it would have been al-*Hisni*, which term is even sometimes employed; but, when a relative adjective is formed from two nouns one of which governs the other in the genitive, the two are (*generally*) combined together so as to
make one word and from that word the relative is derived, and so it was in the present case.   It is thus that from *Râs Aîn* has been formed *Rasani*; from *Abd Allah*,
Abdali, from *Abd Shams*, *Abshami*, and from *Abd ad-Dâr*, *Abdari*; the same rule
applies to all other names of a similar kind. — *Tanza* (طنزة) is the name of village
in Diâr Bakr, situated higher up than Djazîrat Ibn Omar.   It has produced some
eminent traditionists and other learned men, all of whom bore the surname of at-
Tanzi.   The *Kâtib* Imâd ad-Din says, in the *Kharîda :* " From this village came
" Ibrahim Ibn Abd Allah Ibn Ibrahim at-Tanzi, the same who composed these verses :

" I still love the land of Tanza, though my townsmen, since I left them, deceived my expec-
" tations. May God bless that land I could I again see its soil, I should take it as a collyrium
" for my eyes, so dearly do I love it."

The same author adds : " This poet was still alive in the month of Ramadán,
" 568 (April-May, A. D. 1173).

(1) The Hanefite doctors declared that the juice of the grape, boiled down to one third of its of primitive
volume, was a lawful drink.

(2) According to the author of the *Merásid*, Sall was the name of a place in the neighbourhood of Medina.

(3) The text is here corrupt, the manuscripts offering a number of various readings. The translation is
probably not exact.

(4) The right reading appears to be الِيَا.

(5) This passage, in parenthesis, is omitted in most manuscripts.

(6) According to another reading : of a Maghribin.

YAHYA IBN TAMIM AS-SANHAJI

Abû Tâhir Yahya Ibn Tamîm Ibn al-Moizz Ibn Bâdis al-Himyari as-Sanhâji (*vol. I.
p. 282*), was a sovereign of Ifrîkiya and the neighbouring countries. We have already spoken of his father(*vol. I. p. 281*) and traced up their genealogy; some of
his ancestors also have been mentioned in this work. He was appointed to act as his
father's lieutenant at al-Mahdiya, on Friday, the 25th of Zû 'l-Hijja, 497 (19th September, A. D. 1104), at the moment in which the seventh degree of Capricorn was
the ascendant. On the day of his father's death, when the supreme authority devolved on him, he was aged forty three years, six months and twenty days. He then
rode out (*in state*), according to custom, with all the officers of the empire around
him, and, on returning to the palace, he gave to every person connected with government, such as the courtiers and the (*chiefs of the*) troops, magnificent robes of honour to replace the (*mourning*) dresses which they had put on in consequence of the
death of Tamîm. He distributed also to the soldiers (*jund*) and (*armed*)negro slaves

large sums of money, and made them most flattering promises. In the *Kitâb el-Jamd wa 'l-Baiyân* (*collection and exposition*) a work treating of the history of Kairawân and composed by Izz ad-Dîn (*the glory of religion*) Abd al-Azîz Ibn Shaddâd Ibn Tamîm Ibn al-Moizz Ibn Bâdis, who was the son of Yahya's brother, I found the following passage : " The emir Tamîm, a very short time before his death, sent for " his son Yahya, who was then in the government palace (*dâr al-imâra*) with his " officers and companions Yahya entered with them all, and they found Tamîm in " the treasury room. He told them to sit down and said to one of the company : " ' Arise! go into that closet and look for a book of such and such an appearance ; " ' it is in such and such a place ; go and bring it here.' The man went and " brought the book which, on examination, proved to be a collection of predictions " relative to the fate of empires (1). ' That is it ;' said he. ' count off from the be- " ' ginning so many leaves and read the page to which you come.' There, the fol- " lowing words were found written : *The king against whom treason shall be wrought* " (*al-malik al-maghdûr*) *will be of a lofty stature, have a mole on the right thigh and a* " *black spot on the left side*. The emir Tamîm then told him to shut the book and put " it back into its place. When that was done, he said ; ' Two of those marks I have " ' already seen, but the third remains to be discovered. Rise up, you, Sharîf! and " ' you, such a one, and procure me certain information respecting the third.' " They rose up and went with Yahya into a place where they could not be seen by " Tamîm. Yahya them uncovered his body and showed them, on his left side, a spot " shaped like a crescent. They returned to Tamîm and informed him of the cir- " cumstance, on which he said : ' It is not I but God that has given him (*the* " ' *power*)!' He then spoke to them in these terms : ' I shall relate to you an ex- " ' traordinary occurrence ; a slave-merchant offered me for sale the girl who " ' became that man's (*Yahya's*) mother. I found her handsome and, my mind " ' being inclined towards her, I purchased her and placed her in the hands of the " ' attendants of the palace. I then told the merchant to come to me another " ' time for payment, and I began to consider where I could find money pure (*in* " ' *the sight of God*) and acquired by lawful means, with which I might pay the price. " ' Whilst I was reflecting on the matter, I heard as-Sâmiki (2) calling out in a loud " ' voice and requesting permission to speak with me. I passed my head out of the " ' window and asked him what he wanted. He replied : ' I was just this moment " ' digging in the (*ruined*) palace of al-Mahdi and found there a trunk closed with

" ' a padlock; so I left it as it was and am come to inform you of the fact.' I sent
" ' with him a person in whom I could confide, and they found in the trunk a quan-
" ' tity of robes embroidered with gold fringes and rotten with age. I ordered the
" ' fringes to be melted down and thus obtained neither more nor less than the
" ' price of the young girl.' The persons present were filled with admiration on
" hearing this recital and invoked on Tamim the favour of God. Money and robes
" were then distributed to them by his orders; after which, they retired."—Abd al-
Aziz the historian just mentioned, says also: " As to the book of which we have
" spoken, I met with it since, in the possession of the sultan al-Hasan, now decea-
" sed."—He meant al-Hasan the son of Ali and the grandson of Yahya.—He
then gives, from that book, a number of predictions which received their accomplishment. Let us return to our account of Yahya: Once seated on the throne,
he took the direction of affairs, governed his subjects with justice and reduced a
number of fortresses which his father had been unable to take. Abd al-Aziz says,
in his History : " Under his reign,"—that is, the reign of Yahya,—"the Mahdi Muhammad Ibn Tûmart (vol. III. p. 205) arrived from Tripoli at al-Mahdiya, on his
" return from the pilgrimage. He stopped at a mosque situated to the south of the
" Masjid as-Sabt (the mosque of Saturday), and there a number of people from al-
" Mahdiya gathered round him for the purpose of studying, under his direction,
" some works treating of the fundamentals of the faith. He then took on himself
" the task of putting a stop to the many scandalous acts which were publicly com-
" mitted, and Yahya, to whom his conduct was reported, assembled a number of the
" legists and had him brought before them. The humble appearance of Ibn Tû-
" mart, his squalid dress and his profound learning made such an impression on the
" emir that he asked the man for his blessing. The other replied : ' May God pro-
" ' sper thee for the welfare of thy subjects and render their happiness profitable to
" ' thy offspring." Ibn Tûmart remained but a short time at al-Mahdiya and then
" went to al-Monastir where he stopped for a while, and, from that, he proceeded
" to Bugia."—In the life of Tamim, the father of Yahya, we mentioned that Muhammad Ibn Tûmart passed at Bugia whilst that prince was reigning; God knows if
that be true!— Farther on, Abd al-Aziz says : " In the year 507 (A. D. 1113-4),
" some strangers arrived at al-Mahdiya and asked for an interview with Yahya;
" pretending that they were practitioners of the great art (alchimy) and that they had
" attained the end for which that art was instituted.—He allowed them to enter and,

" when they appeared before him, he asked to see a specimen of their talent. To
" this they replied : ' We can deprive tin of its dimness and its particular sound, so
" ' that it is not to be distinguished from silver. Your Lordship has saddles,
" ' swords, standards, tents and vases worth many quintals of silver; in place of
" ' these we shall give you as much as you wish, as much as you can employ in
" ' the important affairs which engage your attention (3); but you must allow us to
" ' operate (before you) in private.' To this he consented and admitted them to a
" place where they might work in his presence. The emir had no person with him
" except the Sharíf Abú 'l-Hasan Ali and the general Ibráhím, commander of the
" cavalry (4). The operators, who were also three in number, had agreed upon a
" private signal; and as soon as they found a fair opportunity, one of them called
" out : Dárat al-bútaka ! (the crucible is upset !). Each of them then sprung forward,
" with a dagger in his hand, and rushed upon the person opposite to him. The
" emir was sitting on a sofa; he who attacked him exclaimed : ' I am a saddler,"
" and struck him on the top of the head. The blow cut through some folds of the
" turban but inflicted no wound. A second stroke, directed by an unsteady hand
" against his breast, merely scratched the skin. The emir them struck the assassin
" with his foot and threw him on his back. The servants, hearing the noise, open-
" ed the door which gave on the room in which they were, and Yahya, having
" gone in to them, bolted that door against his assailant. He who attacked the Sharíf
" did not leave off till he killed him. The Káid Ibráhím, having drawn his sword,
" continued to fight against the three till the guards broke in the door which was at
" their side, entered into the room and slew the assassins. As they wore the Spanish
" (Moslim) dress, a number of persons thus attired were massacred in the city. The
" emir Yahya went out immediately and walked through the streets till the tumult
" was calmed."—Yahya governed with justice; he was particulary watchful over the
interests of his people and knew exactly what were the receipts and the expenditure
of the administration; following thus the line of conduct which is marked out by an
intelligent mind and a sound judgment. In the books of predictions he is designated by the title of al-Maghdúr, and how justly it was applied to him is demonstra-
ted by the occurrence of which mention has been just made. He was well acquainted with history and biography, having read many books treating of these
matters; he was a protector of the weak, kind and charitable to the poor, whom he
always provided with food in times of distress; he admitted into his familiarity the

men of learning and of merit, and kept in such order the (nomadic) Arabs who inhabited his territories, that they stood in awe of him and abstained from giving career to their avidity. He was well-skilled in the practise of astrology and the art of drawing judgments from the stars. His countenance was handsome; over one of his eyebrows was a black spot; his eyes were dark blue, his stature somewhat lofty and his legs thin. He had always at his court a number of poets, who went there to sing his praises and immortalize his renown in their dîwáns. One of them was Abù 's-Salt Omaiya Ibn Abd al-Azîz Ibn Abi 's-Salt, the same of whom we have already spoken (vol. I. p. 228). This poet obtained Yahya's protection after having travelled over many countries and been tost by fortune from one place to another. He is the author of the well-known epistle which treats of Egypt, its wonders, its poets, etc., and he composed a great number of fine eulogiums on Yahya, on Abù 'l-Hasan Ali, the son of Yahya, and on al-Hasan Ibn Ali, his grandson. Here is an extract from one of these poems :

Restrain your mind from every passion except that of bestowing and that of fighting : true glory is composed of bravery joined to liberality. Such is the conduct of Yahya, whose gifts revived our expiring hopes, by the fulfilment of his promises. He bestows a whole flock of camels at a time, camels slender-limbed and smooth, or horses sleek and strong, full-grown and robust. His are the lofty mind and the eye proudly glancing : his the tents pitched on a mountain (of glory), on the keystone of the vault in which culminate the Pleiades. When he appears seated (in state) on the imperial throne, you have before your eyes a Joseph (in beauty) stationing in the sanctuary erected by David. The race from which he sprung were, for their usual clothing, coats of plated mail, and had for dwelling-place the backs of well-trained steeds, obedient to the rein. (They were) envied because they had none to equal them ; and where shall we find a great man who is not exposed to envy ! One common origin unites you all, but every sort of wood does not give out the perfume of the lignum aloes. I say to the rider who hurries on his camel, traversing the earth, from one desert to another : " Pass " not by a source of which the waters are pure ; expect not, from the solid rock, a spring to " quench your thirst. Here are the fountains of Yahya which never run dry ; this is the " way which leads to them ; it is always open. Let your sword decide your claims ; the " decision of the sword is not to be rejected (3)."

He composed other poems besides those.—Yahya died on Wednesday, the festival of the Sacrifice, 509 (25th April, A. D. 1116). His astrologer said to him (that) day : " The casting of your nativity to-day announces for you evil fortune; " so, do not ride out." Yahya followed his advice, and his sons proceeded (without him) to the Musalla (vol. I. p. 605), accompanied by the great officers of the empire. When the prayer was over, they all entered into the presence of the sovereign for the purpose of offering him their salutations, according to the established custom. Chanters then recited passages of the Koran and poets repeated their verses; after which, the company proceeded to the great saloon and partook of a repast. Yahya stood up with the intention of going there but, on reaching the door, he made a sign to one of his slave-girls and leant upon her for support; he had then scarcely made three steps into the room when he fell down dead. His son Ali, whom he had appointed to act as his lieutenant at Sfax, a small town in Ifríkiya, was sent for and, on his arrival, received (from the people) the oath of fidelity. Yahya was buried in the palace (or citadel, kasr), according to custom; but, a year after, his remains were transported to Kasr as-Sída, one of the castles within the walls of al-Monastir. This town is also in Ifríkiya. He left thirty male children. His son and lieutenant, Ali (Ibn Yahya) was born at al-Mahdiya on Sunday morning, the 15th of Safar, 479 (1st June, A. D. 1086). On the death of his father, who had given him the government of Sfax, the principal officers of the empire assembled and drew up a dispatch in his father's name, ordering him to come to him in all haste. He received this message at night and set out immediately, escorted by some of the chiefs who commanded the (nomadic) Arabs. He travelled with the utmost diligence and arrived on the noon of Thursday, the day after the festival of the Sacrifice. The first thing he did was to hasten the interment of his father and to say over him the funeral prayer. Yahya was buried on Friday morning, the 13th of Zú 'l-Hijja. The new sovereign then held a sitting for the reception of the people; and they all entered and saluted him with the title of emir (imára). He then rode out at the head of his troops and bands, after which, he returned to the palace. —It was under his reign that his brother Abú 'l-Futúh, the son of Yahya, went to Egypt, taking with him his wife Bullára, who was the daughter of al-Kásim (Ibn Tamím), and his son al-Abbás, who was then a child at the breast. On his arrival at Alexandria, he was lodged in a palace and treated with great honour, by the order of al-Aámir who, at that time, was the sovereign of Egypt. He died in that city after a very short residence, and Bullára married al-Aádil Ibn as-Sallár, whose true name was Ali and of whose we have spoken in this work (vol. II. p. 350). When al-Abbás grew up, he was gradually advanced in dignity by al-Háfiz, the sovereign of Egypt, and succeeded to al-Aádil as vizir. Our professor, Ibn al-Athír (vol. II. p. 288), has an article in his history, under the head of various events of the year 502, in which he speaks of the three men who went to Yahya under the pretext of conversing with him on alchimy. According to him, they attacked Yahya, that year, and then occurred what we have related. This event coincided with the coming of Abû 'l-Fatûh and his companions fully armed, to the door of the palace; but they were refused admission. " Yahya," says Ibn al-Athîr, " was " therefore convinced that they were all in the plot, and ordered Abû 'l-Fatûh to " be sent with his wife Bullâra to Kasr Ziâd (a fortress situated between al-Mahdiya " and Sfax), and there kept in confinement. Bullâra was his (Abû 'l-Fatûh's) cousin. " On the death of Yahya, his son and successor (Ali) dispatched them by sea to Egypt " and they landed at Alexandria." End of the extract.—Things continued to go on prosperously till the death of Ali, who expired on Tuesday, the 22nd of the latter Rabî, 515 (10th July, A. D. 1121). He was buried in the Kasr. Before dying, he designated his son Abû Yahya al-Hasan Ibn Ali Ibn Yahya as his successor in the supreme authority. Al-Hasan was born in the town of Sûsa and in the month of Rajab, 502 (February, A. D. 1109). On the day of his accession, he had attained the age of twelve years and nine months. The day after his father's death, he appeared in public and, having received the salutations and good wishes of the people, he rode out in the midst of his troops. The events which occurred during his reign are too numerous to be related and we shall only notice one of them. Roger the Frank, sovereign of Sicily, took Tripoli of Africa by assault, on Tuesday, the 6th of Muharram, 541 (18th of June, A D. 1146), massacred all the (male) inhabitants, reduced to slavery the women and children, and seized on all their wealth. He then began to repeople it and filled it with men and military stores. On Monday, the 12th of Safar, 543 (1st of July, A D. 1148), he occupied al-Mahdiya, which had been evacuated by al-Hasan Ibn Ali. This prince, feeling his inability to resist an attack, had departed from the city, carrying off with him whatever objects of value could be easily transported. All the inhabitants fled with the exception of such as were too feeble to depart. The Franks took possession of the city and found there an immense quantity of money and treasure.—This family produced nine kings; the first, Ziri Ibn Manâd (vol. I. p. 550), and the last, al-Hasan Ibn Ali, with whom fell the dynasty of the Bâdisides, which had subsisted two hundred and sixty-eight years. Al-Hasan retired to al-Malga, a strong castle in the neighbourhood of Tunis (and near Carthage), which was then held by Abû Mahfûd Mahriz Ibn Ziâd, one of the Arab chiefs (6). He underwent there such vexation and annoyance from Mahriz that he did not make a long stay and resolved on going to Egypt and putting himself under the protection of al-Hâfiz, the Fatimide sovereign of that country. When the officer whom Roger had left in al-Mahdiya as his lieutenant heard of al-Hasan's intention, he set spies to watch his proceedings and fitted out twenty galleys for the purpose of seizing him if he retired by sea. Al-Hasan, being informed of this, gave up his project and resolved on going to Abd al-Mûmin Ibn Ali (vol. II. p. 182), in the city of Morocco. He therefore sent three of his sons to Bugia, a city lying at the extreme limit of Ifrikiya, with directions to ask from (Yahya Ibn Azîz) the sovereign of that city, the permission to set out from thence for Morocco. This prince, fearing that, if al-Hasan reached Abd al-Mûmin, they would both concert some plan detrimental to himself, dissimulated his real intentions and sent back the messengers with a letter filled with a profusion of fair promises and containing these words : " There is no necessity for your going to Abd al-Mûmin ; I shall do for " you everything you can desire." Al-Hasan set out, in consequence, for Bugia ; but, on arriving near that city, he found that the sovereign, instead of coming out to meet to him, had given orders to transport him to Algiers, a town situated beyond Bugia. Al-Hasan was taken to Algiers and lodged in a place by no means suitable to a person of his rank. The daily allowance of provisions assigned to him was quite insufficient for the number of his followers, and he was prevented from going about. It was in the month of Muharram, 544 (May-June, A. D. 1149) that he arrived in Algiers. In the year 547, Abd al-Mûmin took Bugia, and the sovereign of that city fled to Constantine (7). Roger, the sovereign of Sicily, died in the first third of the month of Zû 'l-Hijja, 548 (February, A D. 1154), and had for successor his son William I (8). It was to the prince (William II) that Abû 'l-Fath Nasr Allah Ibn Kalâkis, the poet of whom we have spoken (vol. III. p 537), went to recite laudatory verses. This was in the year 563 (A. D. 1107-8). On the death of William, the authority passed to his daughter, who became the mother of the emperor of Germany (al-anberûr malik al-Lâmânîa), the same who is still living. When she died, her son, who was then a child, obtained the supreme power. He has reigned a long time, is clever and intelligent, and keeps up a regular intercourse by letters and otherwise with al-Malik al-Kâmil (vol. III. p. 240), the sovereign of Egypt. God knows how far these indications may be true !—Abd al-Mûmin arrived before al-Mahdiya (which was then in the hands of the Franks) and took it after a most obstinate resistance. He made his entry into the city on the festival day of Aâshûra, A. H. 555, (21st of January, A. D. 1160) and established there a lieutenant (9). Al-

Hasan Ibn Ali (*whom he had found at Algiers*) accompanied him in this expedition and, being well acquainted with the resources of the country, was now left with that lieutenant for the purpose of assisting him in the direction of affairs. Two farms in the neighbourhood of the city were assigned to him for his support, and a house was given to him in which he might reside with his sons and followers. I have not been able to discover the date of his death (10). — Mahriz Ibn Ziad, the chief above mentioned, was killed at the combat of Svtlf (11), on a Thursday, in the second third of the latter Rabi, 555 (April, A. D. 1160) (12). — It was for this al-Hasan Ibn Ali that Abû's-Salt Omaiya Ibn Abd al-Aziz composed the work entitled al-*Hadika* (vol. I. p. 228).

(1) In Arabic, *mulhems*. See my translation of Ibn Khaldûn's *Prolegomena*, vol. II, p. 216.

(2) I suppose that the word السامكي is a proper name.

(3) وتسهيل ذلك في مهماتك is the reading of the manuscripts and is here followed.

(4) Literally : *Adid al-Aimma (leader of the imrûns*).

(5) This last verse has no connexion with those which precede and must be out of its place.

(6) For a fuller account of these events and of the persons here named, see the second volume of my translation of the *History of the Berbers*, by Ibn Khaldûn.

(7) Ibn Khaldûn has written, by mistake, *al-Kustantîna (Constantinople)* instead of *Kostantîna (Constantine)*. See the *Histoire des Berbers*, t. II, p. 16.

(8) In the Arabic text this name is written قَصْرة (*Gârnia*). The same name is written قَلْبَرة (*Galirim*) in the inscription traced on the parapet of the old Norman palace called La Cuba, near Palermo. See Mr. Amari's article in the *Revue archéologique* of 1849, p. 649.

(9) See *Histoire des Berbers*, t. II, p. 499.

(10) Al-Hasan Ibn Ali died A. H. 563 (A. D. 1167-8).

(11) The combat of Setif, in which the Almohades, commanded by Abd Allah, the son of Abd al-Mûmin, defeated the Arabs of Rîfâiya, took place in the year 546 (A. D. 1151-2). [*Histoire des Berbers*, t. II, p 195.]

(12) According to the author of the same work, t. II, p. 194, Mahriz was killed at the battle of Kairawân, A. H. 555 (A. D. 1160).

YAHYA THE BARMEKIDE

Abû Ali Yahya, the vizir of Hârûn er-Rashîd, was the son of Khâlid and the grandson of Barmek. We have already spoken of his sons, Jaafar (vol. I. p. 301) and al-Fadl (vol. II. p. 459). Their ancestor Barmek was a Magian of Balkh and

the servant (*officiating minister*) of the Nûbehâr, a place of worship which the Ma-
gians had in that city. It was he who lighted therein the (*sacred*) fires. Barmek
and his sons were generally designated as the *sâddins* (or *guardians*) of that temple.
He was a man of great authority among those of his religion. I do not know
whether he became a Muslim or not. His son Khâlid rose to power under the
Abbasides and succeeded to Abû Salama Hafs al-Khallâl(*vol. I. p.* 467) as vizir to Abû
'l-Abbâs as-Saffâh. We have spoken of him in the article on Jaafar and mentioned
there the date of his death. Abû 'l-Hasan al-Masûdi says, in his *Murûj ad-Dahab*:
" The height to which Khâlid Ibn Barmek attained in prudence, bravery, learning,
" generosity, and other noble qualities was never reached by any of his sons : Yahya
" did not equal him in judgment and intelligence, nor al-Fadl, the son of Yahya,
" in liberality and disinterestedness, nor Jaafar, the son of Yahya, in epistolary
" writing and elegance of language, nor Muhammad, the son of Yahya, in nobleness
" and elevation of mind, nor Mûsa, the son of Yahya, in bravery and energy. When
" Abû Muslim al-Khorâsâni (*vol. II. p.* 100) sent Kahtaba Ibn Shabîb at-Tâi against
" Yazid Ibn Omar Ibn Hubaira al-Fazâri, who was governing the two Irâks in the
" name of the (*Omaiyide khalif*) Marwân Ibn Muhammad, Khâlid was one of those
" who accompanied him. They halted, on the way, at a village and, whilst they were
" breakfasting on the terrace of one of the houses, they saw several flocks of gazelles
" and other wild animals coming from the desert and approaching so near that they
" got (*into the camp*) among the soldiers. ' Emir ! ' said Khâlid, ' order the men to
" saddle and bridle!' Kahtaba stood up in amazement and, seeing nothing to alarm
" him, said : ' What do you mean, Khâlid ! by this advice? ' The other replied :
" The enemy are in march against you ; do you not see that, if these flocks of wild
" animals draw so near to us, they must be flying before a numerous body of men ? '
" The troops were scarcely on horseback when the dust (*raised by the approaching*
" *army*) was perfectly visible. Had it not been for Khâlid, they would all have
" perished."— As for Yahya, he was perfect in talent, judgment and noble qualities. Al-Mahdi, the son of Abû Jaafar al-Mansûr, placed his child, Hârûn ar-Rashîd,
under his care and confided to him the boy's education. When Hârûn became
khalif, he acknowledged his obligations to Yahya and said to him : " My dear father !
" it is through the blessings and the good fortune which attend you and through
" your excellent management that I am now seated on this throne ; so, I confide
" to you the direction of affairs." He then handed to him his signet-ring. Allu-

sion to this is made in the following lines, composed by al-Mausili, a poet whom
I suppose to be the same person as Ibrahîm an-Nadîm (vol. I. p. 20), or else his
son, Ishak (vol. I. p. 183) :

> Did you not see that the light of the sun, once languishing (and dim), brightened up on the
> accession of Hârûn ? (That happened) through the good fortune which attends God's trusty
> servant, Hârûn the beneficent; Hârûn is now chief of the state and Yahya is his vizir.

Ar-Rashîd had so deep a respect for Yahya that, in speaking of him, he always called him my father, and authorised him to take the initiative in every affair and bring
it to a conclusion. This lasted till he overthrew the Barmekides. Being then irritated against Yahya, he imprisoned him for life and put to death his son Jaafar, as
we have already related. Yahya was highly distinguished for wisdom, nobleness of
mind and elegance of language. One of his sayings was : " Three things indicate
" the degree of intelligence possessed by him who does them ; the bestowing of
" gifts, the drawing up of letters and the acting as ambassador." He used to say to
his sons : " Write down the best things which you hear; learn by heart the best
" things which you write down ; and, in speaking, utter the best things which you
" have learned by heart." He said also : " This life is a series of vicissitudes, and
" wealth is (given to us as) only a loan ; let us follow the models (of virtue) offered
" by our predecessors and leave a good example to those who come after us." —
Al-Fadl Ibn Marwân (vol. II. p. 476) states that he heard Yahya Ibn Khâlid say :
" As for the man to whom I have done no good, I have always before me the choice
" (of doing so or not), and as for him to whom I have done good, I am engaged to
" serve him (for the future)." The Kâdi Yahya Ibn Aktham (page 33 of this
vol.) related as follows: " I heard al-Mâmûn say : ' Yahya Ibn Khâlid and his sons
" ' had none (to equal them) in ability, in elegance of language, in liberality and
" ' in bravery; it was well said by a poet that :

> " ' The sons of Yahya are four in number, like the elements ; when put to the test, they
> " ' are found to be the elements of (which) beneficence (is formed) !

" I said to him : ' Commander of the faithful ! their ability, their elegance of
" ' language and their liberality we all acknowledge ; but in which of them was
" ' courage ?' He replied : ' In Mûsa, the son of Yahya ; I had even the intention
" ' of establishing him as governor in the frontier province of Sind.' "—Ishak

al-Mausili, the son of Ibráhím an-Nadím, states that his father made to him the following relation : " I went to Yahya, the son of Khálid Ibn Barmek, and com-
" plained to him of a (pecuniary) embarrassment. He answered : ' Alas ! what I
" ' can I do for you ? I have nothing at the present moment. However, I shall point
" ' out to you a thing which I hope you will be the man to execute : The agent of
" ' the governor of Egypt came to see me and requested me to ask a gift from his
" ' master for myself. I refused, but he still insists. Now, I am told that such a
" ' one, your slave girl, cost you three thousand (dinars); so here is what I may
" ' do : I shall ask him to make me a present of that girl and tell him that she
" ' pleases me very much ; but do not you consent to sell her for less than thirty
" ' thousand dinars. You will then see what will happen.' Well, by Allah ! I had
" scarcely time to look about me when in came the agent. He asked me how much
" I would take for the girl ; I replied that I would not dispose of her for less than
" thirty thousand dinars ; he continued bargaining with me and finished by offer-
" ing twenty thousand. When I heard this sum mentioned, I had not the heart
" to refuse it and I sold her. Having received the money, I went to see Yahya,
" the son of Khálid. He asked me what I done in the sale of the girl, and I re-
" plied : ' By Allah ! I could not refrain from accepting twenty thousand dinars, as
" ' soon as I heard the offer.' He answered : ' That was mean-spirited on your part ;
" ' but the agent of the governor of Persia has come to me on a similar mission ; so,
" ' here is your girl ; take her back and do not sell her for less than fifty thousand
" ' dinars when he goes to bargain with you for her. He will certainly give you
" ' that price.' This man came to me, and I asked fifty thousand dinars. He began
" to bargain and, when he offered me thirty thousand, I had not the heart to refuse
" that sum and could scarcely believe my ears. I accepted his offer and them went
" to Yahya, the son of Khálid. ' For how much did you sell the girl ?' said he.
" I told him, and he exclaimed : ' You unfortunate fellow ! was your first (fault)
" ' not sufficient to prevent you from committing a second ?' I replied : ' My
" ' heart was too weak to refuse a sum for which I could have never hoped ! Here,'
" said Yahya, ' is your girl; take her and keep her !' ' I replied : I have gained by
" ' her fifty thousand dinars and am again become her owner. Bear witness that I
" ' declare her free and that I promise to marry her.' " — It is thus I found the
anecdote related, but I since met with the history of the vizirs composed by al-Jihshiári (vol. II. p. 137), and there I read that Ibráhím al-Mausili was told by Yahya

not to accept less than one hundred thousand dinars and that he sold her for fifty
thousand, and that, the second time, he was told not to accept less than fifty thousand and that he sold her for twenty thousand. — Al-Asmâi (vol. *II.* p. 123) related
as follows : " I went, one day, to visit Yahya and he said to me : ' Tell me, As-
" ' mâi ! are you married?' I replied that I was not. ' Have you a slave-girl?'
" ' said he. I answered : ' I should willingly be indebted to you for one.' He
" then ordered a young girl to be brought in : she was in the height of beauty, of
" grace and of elegance ; and he said to her : ' I give you to this man ;' and then
" he told me to take her. I thanked him and was wishing him every happiness
" when she burst into tears and exclaimed : ' O my lord ! how can you give me
" ' away to such a man as that ? do you not see how deformed and ugly he is ?' He
" ' said to me : ' I will give you in exchange for her two thousand dinars.' I an-
" ' swered : ' I have no objection to that.' The money was given to me and the
" girl was taken back to Yahya's house. ' That girl,' said he, ' did something to
" ' displease me, and I meant to punish her in giving her to you, but then I had
" ' pity on her.'—' Why did you not inform me of that previously ?' said I, ' so
" ' that I might have reassumed my pristine form ; you should at least have allow-
" ' ed me to comb my beard, wipe my eyes, perfume my person and make myself
" ' handsome.' He laughed (*at this sally*) and ordered another thousand dinars to
" be given to me." — The following anecdote was related by Ishak an-Nadîm :
" When Yahya, the son of Khâlid rode out, the usual gift which he bestowed on
" those who went up to him with an application was two hundred dirhems (1).
" One day, as he was riding out, a literary man, who was also a poet, drew near to
" him and said :

> " ' O thou who art the namesake of Yahya the chaste (*saint John the Baptist*) ! the
> " ' bounty of the Lord hath assigned to thee a double paradise (*one on earth and the other in
> " ' heaven*). Two hundred (*dirhems*) is the gift of every one who cometh thy path ; but
> " ' that sum is too little for a man like me ; 'tis what he receiveth from thee who runneth the
> " ' quickest !

" Yahya replied : You say true ; let this man be taken to my house." When he
returned from the khalif's residence, he asked the man what was his business and
received this answer : " ' I have contracted marriage and am under the necessity of
" ' fulfilling one of three obligations : either to pay the dowry (*which I have settled
" ' on my wife and*) which amounts to four thousand dirhems (E. 100), or to divorce

" ' (her), or to pay (her) a pension till such time as I shall have the means of procu-
" ' ring the bride's outfit.' Yahya gave orders that he should receive four
" thousand dirhems for the dowry, four thousand for the purchase of a dwelling,
" four thousand for the requisite furniture of a house, four thousand for the recep-
" tion of the bride and four thousand for future maintenance. He received the
" twenty thousand and departed." — Muhammad Ibn Munádir (vol. I. p. 299),
the celebrated poet, related as follows : " Ar-Rashid made the pilgrimage with his
" two sons, al-Amín Muhammad and al-Mámún Abd Allah. Yahya Ibn Khálid ac-
" companied him with his two sons, al-Fadl and Jaafar. When they arrived at Me-
" dína, ar-Rashid held a public sitting with Yahya Ibn Khálid, and distributed to
" the inhabitants the customary donations. Al-Amín then held a sitting with al-
" Fadl and distributed donations ; after which al-Mámún, accompanied by Jaafar,
" did the same. For this reason, the people of Medína named that year *the year*
" *of the three donations.* Never had they seen the like before. I composed, on
" this subject, the following verses (2) :

        " They are come to us, the descendants of the kings belonging to the family of Barmek.
        " What good news ! what a beautiful sight ! Their rule is, to make, every year, an expedi-
        " tion against the enemy and a journey to the Temple ancient and pure. When they halt in
        " al-Bat'ha, (*the valley*) of Mekka, that *city* is illuminated by their presence. Baghdad is
        " then in darkness and, whilst they perform the pilgrimage, three moons dispel the shades
        " which covers us in Mekka. Their hands were created for nothing else but deeds of libera-
        " lity, and their feet were made for (*treading*) the boards of the pulpit. "

The Khatíb (vol. I. p. 75) says, in the article on Abú Abd Allah Muhammad Ibn
Omar al-Wákidi (vol. III. p. 61) which he inserted in his History of Baghdad, that
he (al-Wákidi) related as follows : " I traded in corn at Medína and had in my hands
" one hundred thousand dirhems which has been lent to me in order that I might
" make them productive. This money I lost and then I went to Irák for the pur-
" pose of seeing Yahya, the son of Khálid. Having sat down in his antechamber,
" I entered into conversation with the servants and door-keepers, and asked how
" I could get to see him. They answered : ' When his dinner is taken in to him,
" ' no one is prevented from entering ; we shall then admit you.' When the
" dinner was brought, they let me in and seated me with him at the same table."
" ' Who are you ? ' said he,' and what do require ?' I told him and, when the dishes
. " were removed, we washed our hands; after which I went over to him with the in-

" tention of kissing him on the head, but he drew back from me.   When I (retired
" and) reached the place where the guests mount their horses on departing, a ser-
" vant came to me with a purse containing one thousand dinars and said : ' The
" ' visir wishes you a good evening; he bids you help yourself out of your diffi-
" culty with this and requests you to come to see him to-morrow morning.'   I re-
" turned to see him (the next morning) and sat down to table with him, and he
" began to question me as he had done the day before.   When the dishes were re-
" moved, I went up to him for the purpose of kissing him on the head, but he
" drew back from me.   On my going to the mounting-place, a servant brought me
" a purse containing one thousand dinars and said : ' The visir wishes you a good
" ' day, bids you help yourself out of your difficulties with this and requests you to
" ' return to morrow.'   I took the money, retired, and, the next day, went again
" to see him.   He then gave me as much as I had received the two days previously.
" On the fourth day, I went to visit him as I had done before, and he then allowed
" me to kiss him on the head.   ' I did not at first permit you to do so,' said he, ' be-
" ' cause I had not rendered you a service which intitled me to that mark of re-
" ' spect.   But now, I have been of some use to you.'   (He then called his servants
" and said :) ' Boy ! let such and such a house be given to this man ; Boy ! fit it up
" ' with such and such a set of furniture ; Boy ! give him two hundred thousand dir-
" ' hems, the half to pay his debts and the other half to put him in better circum-
" ' stance.'   He then said to me : ' Become my companion and reside in my house.'
" I replied : ' May God exalt the visir ! I hope you will allow me to return to Medina
" ' that I may repay there what I owe ; after that, I shall reappear in your presence ;
" ' that, for me, would be more befitting.'   He gave his consent and furnished me
" with every requisite for travelling.   I went to Medina, paid my debts and, ha-
" ving returned, I never quitted him since."—Abû Kâbûs al-Himyari went, one
" day, to see him and recited to him the following verses :

> May the plenitude of God's favour descend on Yahya, who bestows such gifts as not a man
> before him ever gave.   He forgets the services which he renders, but never forgets his promise.

Yahya granted to the poet what he came to apply for and bestowed on him also a
sum of money.   I may here observe that the (idea expressed in the) second verse was
afterwards (borrowed and) applied by Sharaf ad-Dawla Muslim Ibn Koraish (vol. III.
p. 143) : A man said to him : " Emir ! I do not forget my demand," and he replied :

"Not till I have fulfilled it." Muslim Ibn al-Walid al-Ansári (3) makes (honourable)
mention of Yahya, the son of Khálid in the following passage :

Mayest thou (fair world) be ever fortunate ! knowest thou not that during those nights which
had borrowed their darkness from the colour of thy hair, I used to wait with patience till their
obscurity was dispelled by the brightness of a face which shone like the face of Yahya, when
(his son) Jaafar was mentioned (with commendation).

Yahya used to say : "Spend when Fortune turns towards you, for her bounty
"cannot then be exhausted; spend when she turns away, for she will not remain
"with you." He said also : " The benefactor who reminds (a person) of a service
"rendered alloys the value of that service ; and he who forgets a favour received
"is guilty of ingratitude and neglect of duty." Another of his sayings was : "The
"sincere intention (of doing a good action) and a legitimate excuse (for not doing it)
"are equivalent to its accomplishment." He said again : " In adverse fortune;
"wiles (and stratagems) lead to perdition." Al-Hasan Ibn Sahl (vol. I. p. 408) was
heard to say : " When a man's conduct towards his brethren is changed on obtaining
"authority, we know that he is not fitted for that place (4); so said the president of
"the board of generous actions, Abù Ali Yahya, the son of Khálid Ibn Barmek."—
Yahya had a private secretary whom he admitted into his familiarity. This secretary
resolved on having his son circumcised, and people of all classes made preparations
for being present at the ceremony. The great officers of the empire, the chiefs of
the civil administration and the government-writers offered, all of them, presents
suitable to their respective ranks. A friend of the secretary, being in reduced circumstances and unable to satisfy his desire of doing like the others, took two large and
clean bags, filled one of them with salt, the other with perfumed potash, and
sent them to him with a letter of which we give here a copy: " Could I fulfil my
"will, I should conform to the custom and, if my means permitted me to accom-
"plish my ardent desire, I should outdo even the foremost in this race of genero-
"sity and surpass those who make the greatest efforts to shew you honour. But
"my means preclude me from doing what I wish and the narrowness of my for-
"tune prevents me from engaging in a rivality with the wealthy. Fearing, how-
"ever, that the register of our gifts should be closed before the inscribing of my
"name therein, I send you some of that which, at the beginning (of a repast), brings
"good luck and a blessing, and of that which concludes (the repast) by its perfume

" and cleansing quality. (*In so doing*) I bear with patience the pain which my in-
" ability gives me, and support the anguish of not having the power to execute
" (*my intentions*).   But, as long as I find not the means of filling my duty towards
" you, I shall offer, for my excuse, this word of almighty God : *No blame*
" *shall be incurred by those who are weak, or by the sick, or by those who find*
" *not wherewithal to contribute.* (*Coran, sur. 9, verse 92*). Receive my salu-
" tations." When Yahya Ibn Khálid arrived at the place where the festival was
held, his secretary shewed him all the presents which he had received and even the
two bags with the accompanying letter.   The idea of sending these two objects appeared to Yahya very good, and he ordered them to be filled with money and taken
back to the person who had sent them. The sum thus given was four thousand
dinars (£ 2,000).—A man said to Yahya : " By Allah! thou art milder in temper
" than al-Ahnaf Ibn Kais (*vol. I. p.* 635)," and received this answer : " Those who
" offer me more than I deserve shall not have a place in my favour."—Ishak Ibn
Ibrahim al-Mausili called on one of his servant-boys and, not getting an answer
from him, he said : " I heard Yahya, the son of Khálid, observe that a man's mild-
" ness of temper is indicated by the ill-breeding of his servants."—Yahya was one
day riding out with ar-Rashid when a man stopped before the khalif and said :
" My mule is dead."   Ar-Rashid replied : " Let five hundred dirhems (£ 10) be
" given."   On this, Yahya made him a sign and, when they dismounted, ar-Rashid said to him : " Father! you made me a sign about something and I do not under-
" stand what it meant."   Yahya replied : " The mention of so small a sum as that
" should never proceed from your lips; a person of your rank should say : five thou-
" sand, or ten thousand."—" Well," said ar-Rashid, " and when a demand such as
" that is made to me, what shall I answer ?"   " You must then say :" said Yahya,
" buy him a mule."—To conclude, we may observe that the anecdotes related of
the Barmekide family are very numerous, and that an abridgment such as this will
not admit the insertion of any more.—When Harûn ar-Rashid put to death Jaafar,
the son of Yahya the Barmekide, he reduced to ruin all that family and cast into
prison Yahya and al-Fadl, the son of Yahya.   The place of their confinement was
ar-Ráfika, called also Old Rakka and situated near the town of New Rakka, which
is a well-known place on the bank of the Euphrates.   To designate both towns, they
say *the two Rakkas*, giving thus to one name a predominance over the other.   Examples of a similar licence are offered by the names al-Omardni (5), al-Kamardni (6)

and some others.—Al-Jihshiári relates, in his History of the Vizirs, that, when Yahya, the son of Khálid, was in prison, where they kept him closely confined, he had one day a longing to eat some *sikbája* (7). Having obtained, with great difficulty, the permission to prepare some, he cooked it, but, when he had finished, the skillet in which he had made it fell from his hand and was broken to pieces. On this, he recited some verses, upbraiding Fortune and expressing his loss of every hope and every desire. He remained in the prison of ar-Ráfika till his death, which event took place on the 3rd of Muharram, 190 (29th November, A. D. 805). He died suddenly, without any previous illness, being then seventy years of age, or seventy-four, according to another account. His son al-Fadl said over him the funeral service. He was buried on the border of the Euphrates, in the suburb called Rabad Harthama. In his pocket was found a paper on which was written in his own hand : " The accuser has gone forward (*to the tribunal*) and the accused " will soon follow; the *kádi* will be that equitable judge who is never unjust and who has no need of taking evidence." Ar-Rashíd, to whom this paper was sent, wept, the remainder of that day, and his countenance, for some days after, bore striking marks of sorrow (8).—Yahya settled a monthly pension of one thousand dirhems (£ 25) on Sofyán ath-Thauri (*vol. I. p. 576*), and the latter used to say, when prostrated in prayer : " O Lord! Yahya has delivered me from the cares of this life; " deliver him from the pains of the next." When Yahya died, one of his brothers saw him in a dream and asked him how God had treated him ? To this he replied : " He forgave me in consideration of Sofyán's prayers." Some say that the Sofyán of this anecdote was Sofyán Ibn Oyaina (*vol. I. p. 578*). God knows best !—"Ar-Rashíd," says al-Jihshiári, " repented of his conduct towards the Barmekides and deeply " regretted the manner in which he had treated (*the prisoners*). He said, before some " of his brothers that, if he could be assured of their fidelity, he would reinstate them " in their places. He used also to say:—' Some people impelled us to punish our ablest " ' and most faithful advisers, and they made us believe that they themselves were " ' capable of replacing them ; but, when we did what they wanted, they were not " ' of the least use to us.' He then recited this line :

" Infamous wretches (9) ! spare us your calumnies, or fill (*with ability*) the place which
" they filled (so evil) (10)."

I may observe that this verse has for its author al-Hutaiya (*vol. I. p. 209*), and that, after it, comes the following :

They were persons who, if they built, built well; if they took an engagement, they fulfilled it, and if they imposed an obligation, they rendered it binding.

Az-Zamakhshari (*vol. III. p.* 321) says, somewhat to this effect, in his *Rabî al-Abrâr* : " Under the bed of Yahya, the son of Khâlid, was found a paper on which " was inscribed :

" By the reality of God ! injustice is disgraceful ; an unhealthy pasture ground is that of " injustice. We must go before Him who shall retribute every action on the day of judgment ; " all adverse parties must appear before God.

I must now say (11) that I have inserted in this compendium the quantity (*of information*) which it was possible for a person to give who had but little leisure. I have omitted under this letter, which is the Y, a considerable number of articles which I intended to have inserted, but had not time enough (*ittasâ*) to do so. I have kept them back, with a great deal of rough draughts, so that they may serve (••••[1]) for another (*akhar*) and a more extensive work which I mean to compile on the same plan, if God grant me time and if he aid me in my undertaking [*wa waffak lil-ami*]. It shall contain (*mahtawian*) a mass (*jumma*) of that information which is required by persons who occupy themselves with these matters, and will dispense the reader from the necessity of recurring to a great number of books [*wa yastaghni man yutalidhu ân murajâât kutub kathîra*] ; for I have selected my notes from standard works of history and from the (*authentic*) accounts given of those who lived in ancient and in modern times. To the best of my belief [*fî ma yaghlib ala dhanni*], I have not neglected to consult any of the noted works which are in the hands of the public or any of those which are less known (*al-khâmila*), whether they were voluminous or concise ; and I have always taken care to select therefrom whatever seemed fit to enter into [*fî*] this work. It is my intention, with the will and the help of God, that it shall form more than ten (*akhar min ashara*) volumes ; but assistance must be demanded from the Almighty and his aid must be implored to direct me (12).

(1) About five pounds sterling.

(2) Mr. de Sacy has given three verses in his *Chrestomathie arabe*, t. I, p. 13.

(3) This Muslim died A. H. 998 (A. D. 522-3). We have spoken of him in vol. I, p. 95.

(4) Literally : We knew that authority is greater than he.

(5) *Al-Omardân* (the two Omars) was a term employed to designate the two first khalifs, Abû Bakr and Omar.

(6) The term al-Azmaráin (the two moons) was employed to designate the sun and the moon.

(7) The méléja was a dish prepared with barley-meal, minced meat and vinegar.

(8) In some of the manuscripts, this biographical notice ends here.

(9) The arabic imprecation is : no father to your father, and seems to signify : may God's curse be on your ancestors.

(10) The manuscript belonging to Mr. Caussin de Perceval has او شدوا الخيار, and the edition of Bûlâk او شدوا البياد, which readings I do not understand.

(11) The following paragraph is to be found in professor Wüstenfeld's edition, but none of our manuscripts gives it except that which belongs to Mr. Caussin de Perceval. It is omitted in the edition of Bûlâk. I follow the text of Mr. Caussin's manuscript, that of the lithographed edition being very incorrect.

(12) The work which our author here promised never appeared. The articles which follow were added to the present work by Ibn Khallikân himself, some years after the appearance of the autograph copy. See the note by which he concludes this volume.

THE VIZIR IBN HUBAIRA

Abû 'l-Muzaffar Yahya Ibn Muhammad Ibn Hubaira Ibn Saîd Ibn al-Hasan Ibn Ahmad Ibn al-Hasan Ibn Jahm Ibn Amr Ibn Hubaira was surnamed Aûn ad-Dîn (aid of the religion) and drew his descent from Shaibân (the progenitor of the Arabic tribe which bears this name). His ancestor Hubaira was the son of Alwân, the son of al-Haufazân, whose real name was al-Hârith, the son of Sharîk, the son of Amr, (or Motar) the son of Kais, the son of Shurahbîl, the son of Morra, the son of Hamnâm, the son of Dhuhl, the son of Shaibân. Thalaba, Shaibân's father, was the son of Okâba, the son of Saab, the son of Ali, the son of Bakr, the son of Wâil, the son of Kâsit, the son of Himb, the son of Afsa, the son of Domi, the son of Jadîla, the son of Asad, the son of Rabîa, the son of Nizâr, the son of Maadd, the son of Adnân.—It is thus that his genealogy has been given by a number of authors, such as Ibn ad-Dubaithi (vol. III. p. 102) in his historical work and Ibn al-Kâdisi (vol. I. p. 290) in his Kitâb al-Wuzará (book of visirs). It was not made public till some years after his accession to the vizirate, when it was mentioned by the poets in their eulogies. He was a native of Kirya Bani Aukar, a village situated in that part of Irâk which is called Dujail. It is the same place which bore the name of Dâr

Armánya, and which is now named, after him, *Dár al-Wazír* (*the monastery or village of the vizir*). His father belonged to the *jund* (or *military colony* (*vol. II. p. 132*) established there. Yahya professed the doctrine taught by Ahmad Ibn Hanbal. He learned Traditions, acquired considerable information in each branch of knowledge, learned the *readings* of the noble book (*the Korán*) and concluded that study by going over all the systems of Koran-reading and the different lessons which have been handed down. He studied grammar, became acquainted with the history of the desert Arabs and of their battle-days, cultivated assiduously the art of penmanship, got by heart the locutions employed by elegant speakers and applied himself to the acquisition of a good epistolary style. His master in polite literature was Abû Mansûr al-Jawâlîki (*vol. III. p. 498*) and, in law, Abû 'l-Husain Muhammad Ibn Muhammad al-Farrâ. He was also a pupil of the preacher Abû Abd Allah Muhammad Ibn Yahya Ibn Ali Ibn Muslim Ibn Mûsa Ibn Imrân az-Zabîdi (1). He learned the Traditions respecting the Prophet from Abû Othmân Ismail Ibn Muhammad Ibn Kaila al-Ispahâni, Abû 'l-Kâsim Hibat Allah Ibn Muhammad Ibn al-Husain (ٱلحسين) the *kâtib*, and from those who came after them. He himself taught Traditions, some of which he had learned from the *imâm* al-Muktafi li-Amr Illah, the Commander of the faithful. A great number of persons received Traditions from him and, amongst them, the *háfiz* Abû 'l-Faraj Ibn al-Jauzi (*vol. II. p. 96*). The first office which he filled (*under government*) was the inspectorship of the plantations (*ishráf al-akriha*) (2) situated on the west (*bank of the Tigris*); he then passed to the inspectorship of the taxes paid in kind (*al-ikámát al-Makhzamiya*), and was afterwards appointed inspector of the *Makhzen* or government stores (*al-ishráf bil-makhzan*). This place he did not long fill, having been nominated, in the year 542 (A. D. 1147-8), clerk of the khalif's household (*kitâba dîwán az-simdân*), from which post he was raised to the vizirate. The author who compiled the biography of Ibn Hubaira relates, in these terms, the motives which led to his nomination : " Amongst " the things which increased his influence and raised him to the vizirship was the " conduct held by Masûd al-Hilâli, the *shihna* (or *resident agent*) whom the sultan " Masûd Ibn Muhammad Ibn Malek Shâh the Seljôkide had established at Baghdad " as his lieutenant. Al-Bilâli was one of those Abyssinian slaves and eunuchs who " held so high a rank in the (*seljûk*) empire. He used to behave with great impolite- " ness in the presence of the khalif, transgressing the rules of etiquette which were " always to be observed, and permitting his licentious followers to spread disorder

" [through the city]. Kauwâm ad-Dîn Abû 'l-Kâsim Ali Ibn Sadaka, who was, at
" that time, the khalif's vizir, wrote a number of letters to the sultan Masûd, re-
" questing him to reprimand al-Bilâli for his conduct, but could never obtain an
" answer. When Aûn ad-Dîn was appointed clerk of the household, the khalif
" spoke to him on the subject and bade him write to the sultan. Aûn ad-Dîn,
" knowing that the vizir had already written a number of letters and that they had
" remained unanswered, sent off request after request till he obtained a reply.
" The letter (which had this effect) was drawn up by himself, and I should insert it
" here, were it not so long; but I may mention, in a summary manner, that it con-
" tained good wishes for the sultan's welfare, reminded him of the exemplary con-
" duct held by his predecessors towards the khalifs, of their sincere obedience, the
" respect which they always shewed them and the protection which they afforded
" them against those who dared to thwart them. He then complained of Masûd al-
" Bilâli, mentioned that he written a number of times on that subject without re-
" ceiving an answer and spoke to a great length on this matter. It was in the mouth
" of the latter Rabî, 512 (september, A. D. 1147) that he wrote this letter. Very
" soon after, he received an answer containing the sultan's excuses with a formal
" disapproval of al-Bilâli's conduct. The khalif al-Muktafi was highly pleased to
" have followed the advice of Aûn ad-Dîn and felt deeply obliged to him; so, Aûn ad-
" Dîn continued to enjoy his favour and was raised to the vizirate." The same
author says : " Another motive which conduced to Aûn ad-Dîn's nomination
" was, that, in the year 543 (A. D. 1148-9), two of the sultan's emirs, one of
" whom was al-Baksh al-Masûdi, lord of al-Lihf, which is a place in Irâk, and
" the other, Ildeglz as-Sultâni, came to Baghdad with a numerous body of troops
" and committed in it the greatest disorders. This will be found related in the
" books of annals (3). The visir Kauwâm ad-Dîn Ibn Sadaka undertook to bring
" about an arrangement, but without success. Aûn ad-Dîn then asked and obtain-
" ed the khalif's authorisation to treat with the invaders who had attacked him
" and, by his skilful management, he succeeded in putting a stop to their evil
" doings till such time as he had assembled sufficient forces to resist them, and
" enabled the people to seize on their riches. This event was a means em-
" ployed by destiny for the elevation of Ibn Hubaira and the dismissal of Ibn Sa-
" daka from the vizirate. Effectively, when this serious affair was terminated, the
" khalif al-Muktafi summoned Ibn Hubaira to his presence by a notification (mund-

" *lea*), which was carried to him by two emirs of the empire. When Ibn Hubaira
" read it, all his family made great demonstrations of joy (4) and, as he rode with
" his followers to the khalif's palace, the public learned that he had been appointed
" vizir. On his arrival at the door of the *hujra* (the *khalif's cabinet*), he was called in
" and found al-Muktafi seated, to receive him, on the right side of the *Táj* (5). He
" kissed the ground, saluted and had then, during an hour, a conversation with
" the khalif which no other person could overhear. On retiring, he found a robe
" of honour (*tashríf*) prepared for him, according to the custom followed towards
" vizirs. He put it on and, being called in a second time, he kissed the ground and
" invoked blessings on the khalif in a style which excited that prince's admiration.
" He then pronounced these words :

> " As long as my life endures, I shall thank Aun for services of which he never vaunted,
> " great though they were. He saw my indigence even there where it was concealed, and kept
> " it in sight until it disappeared."

I may observe that these are two verses of three which were composed by Ibráhim
Ibn al-Abbás as-Sóli (6). The verse which should have come after the first was :

> A generous man whose wealth is never withheld from his friend, and who never manifests a
> complaint if the alms (*fortune*) slips from under him.

Aûn ad-Dîn, in reciting the two verses, altered the last half of the second, which
originally ran thus :

> and it was like a mote in his eye, till removed.

Having thought fit to address the khalif in this style, he altered the expression,
through respect. When he retired, they brought him a bay horse, with white
pasterns, a white spot reaching from the forehead to the nose, and a rich capari-
son; such being their custom with respect to vizirs. The details of this ceremony I have abridged. He then rode forth, preceded by the great functionaries,
the officers of the empire, the emirs attached to the court, all the khalif's servants
and all the chamberlains of the divan ; with drums beating before him and the *mas-
nad* (cushion) borne after him, according to the usual practise on such occasions.
He entered into the divan, dismounted apart and took his seat on the *dest* (*sopha*, cush-

ion). The shaikh Sadid ad-Dawla Abû Abd Allah Muhammad Ibn Abd al-Karîm Ibn al-Anbâri then stood forward to read the diploma (of the visir's nomination). It was a remarkable piece of its kind and, were it not so long, I should insert it here; besides, it is well known and copies of it are in the hands of the public. When he finished, the Korân-readers chanted (passages of the Korân) and the poets recited pieces of their composition. Ibn Hubaira was installed in the visirship on Wednesday, the 3rd of the latter Rabi. 544 (10th August, A. D. 1149). He bore at first the title of Jalâl ad-Dîn (grandeur of religion), but, on being appointed visir, he received that of Aûn ad-Dîn. Eminent for learning and for merit, he displayed also an unerring judgment and a virtuous disposition; during his visirship he conducted matters in a manner which attested the greatness of his abilities and the excellence of his counsels. This assured him (the khalif's) gratitude, entitled him to high consideration and contributed largely to his good fortune. As he had a great respect for the learned, his receptions were attended by all men distinguished for talent, no matter in what line. Traditions were repeated in his presence and controlled by him and the shaikhs (professors) who were there; discussions were carried on and useful information was communicated to an extent which cannot be described. He composed some works such as the Ifsâh fi madni 's-Sahâh (elucidation of passages in [Jauhari's Arabic dictionary,] the Sahâh), forming nineteen books (volumes?); a commentary on the Jamâ bain as-Sahîhain (see vol. I. p. 420), with an exposition of the maxims uttered by the Prophet and contained in that work; the Kitâb al-Muktid (which hits the mark) — this word takes an i after the s; a complete commentary on it, in four volumes, was drawn up by the celebrated grammarian Abû Muhammad Ibn al-Khashshâb (vol. II. p. 66); an abridgment of the Islâh al-Mantik (?); the Kitâb al-Ibâdât, etc. (treatise on devotional rites), according to the system of canon law taught by the imâm as-Shâfi; an Arjûza etc. (technical verses) on the long and the short final a; an Arjûza on the art of penmanship (or orthography (الخط).—Our professor Izz ad-Dîn Abû 'l-Hasan Ali, generally known by the surname of Ibn al-Athîr (vol. II. p. 288) gives, in his lesser historical work, that which treats of the Atâbeks, a chapter concerning the siege of Baghdad in the month of Zû 'l-Kaada, 553 (Nov.—Dec. A. D. 1158) by al-Malik Muhammad and Zain ad-Dîn. He says there that al-Muktafi li-Amr Illah made every effort to put that city in a good state of defence and that his visir, Aûn ad-Dîn Ibn Hubaira, helped him in a manner of which no other person could have been capable. He adds : " By al-Muktafi's

" order, a proclamation was made in Baghdad, promising five dinars (2 l. 10s.) to
" every person who should be wounded during the hostilities, and, effectively, that
" sum was given to every one who received a wound. A man of the people got
" wounded and went to the vizir, who said : ' That is a mere scratch, not worth
" ' a penny.' The man returned to the fight and got a stroke across his belly,
" so the entrails were falling out; he then came back the vizir and said : ' My Lord !
" will that satisfy you ?' The vizir laughed, ordered him a donation and sent for a
" doctor to dress his wound." End of the extract. I must here make an observation : the Muhammad of whom Ibn al-Athir speaks was the son of Mahmûd Ibn
Muhammad Ibn Malek Shâh, the Seljûkide, and the Zain ad-Dîn was Abû 'l-Hasan Ali
Ibn Dektikin, generally known by the (Turkish) appellation of Kutchek (the little) and
the father of Musaffar ad-Dîn, lord of Arbela [vol. II. p. 535]. According to another
author, this Malik Muhammad was Muhammad Shâh, and the event took place in the
year 552. God knows which of the two is in the right ! It is Ibn al-Jauzi who says
so in his Shuzûr al-Okûd, and he must have been better acquainted with what passed
than any other, for Baghdad was his native place and he was there all the time. I have
spoken of Muhammad Shâh (8) in the article on his father. The imâm (khalif) al-
Muktafi li-Amr Illah Muhammad bore the surname of Abû Abd Allah and was the son
of al-Mustazhir; he died on the eve of Sunday, the 2nd of the first Rabi, 555 (12th
March, A. D. 1160). His son al-Mustanjid Billah Abû 'l-Musaffar Yûsuf was then
proclaimed khalif. Ibn Hubaira went in to him, took the oath of fealty, was received honorably and confirmed in the vizirship. Fearing to be dismissed from office,
he never attempted to contradict his sovereign, and he continued in place till the
hour of his death. His praises were celebrated by the most distinguished poets of
the age, and one of them, Abû 'l-Fawâris Saad, surnamed Hais Bais (vol. I. p. 559)
and generally known by the appellation of Ibn Saifi, composed on him some exquisite
eulogiums. In one of these pieces he says :

> Anecdotes of generosity excite him, even in his calmest mood, as the red intoxicating liquor
> excites the drinkers of the nomadic village. He stands firm when other people spring from
> their seats in dismay, and when the loftiest pinnacles (chiefs?) tremble before the storms of
> calamity. He interrupts vile discourse, avoids opprobrious language and is always taken up
> with the love of glory. He is incapable of committing the slightest act of meanness, and his
> bosom is annoyed by the dangers incurred in those deeds which lead to glory. When the
> name of Ain-ad-Dîn Yahya is pronounced, the clouds flash forth their lightnings (sharkingvrr
> of rain), and the strong lances wave proudly (9).

It was the custom at Baghdad that, in the month of Ramadán, the great officers of the empire partook of a repast (*simát*) given by the khalif at the house of the vizir, and this repast was called the *tabak*. Hais Bais, who was a high-minded man and had all the noble pride of a true Arab, was one of the guests. Seeing that a number of persons, having no other merit than that of being paid functionaries, passed before him to a higher place, he was so highly offended that he wrote to the vizir Aûn ad-Dîn a letter in which he requested that (*for the future*) his absence might be pardoned. (*It ran thus :*)

Thou who, in wealth and in poverty, wert always lavish of thy money ! than who, morning and night, furnishest provisions to (needy) travellers ! Thou who convokest the persons enriched by thee to partake of an augmentation from thy bounty ! In every house there is a table supplied with provisions by thy generosity, and yet thou invitest its master to the *tabak*. Thy gifts are poured forth like a torrent and, were those on whom they light not afraid of thy just severity, they would cry out : " Save us from drowning ! " Thy noble qualities cover the land with a constant shower ; even in the day of battle, thou drenchest the soil with the blood and the sweat of the horsemen. Spare my shoulders from being pressed in a manner which, if I resented, would expose my reputation and my character to sarcasm. If thou permittest it, such a humiliation will degrade me ; and how often hast thou loaded me with a burden (of gifts) which I could hardly bear ! I am sick of the fortune (which pursues me) and of her attacks ; my noble pride alone preserves my life. Grant me the favour which I ask ; (grant it as readily) as thou bestowest thy numerous gifts. To be liberal in granting honour is far above being liberal with money. The disk of the sun, exalted though he be, turneth yellow from grief, when obliged to descend towards the horizon. People consider as folly such (amiability as mine) ; but often hath innate dignity been confounded with folly.

The vizir Aûn ad-Dîn received the present of an inkstand made of rock-crystal and inlaid with coral. Seeing at his levee a number of poets and, amongst them, Hais Bais, he observed that it would be well to compose a piece of verse on that object. One of the persons present, a blind man whose name I have not met with, then recited these lines :

Iron was, by divine favour, rendered soft for David, so that he wrought it at will into coats of mail (10). The crystal, though a stone, has been softened for you, yet bending it to one's wish is hard and difficult.

Hais Bais here observed that the poet had spoken, not of the inkstand but of the maker ; on which the vizir said : " Let him who finds fault change (it for the better)." Hais Bais did so in these lines :

Your inkstand was made of your two days (11), and these have been mistaken for crystal and for coral. One is your day of peace, which is white and pours forth abundance; the other is your day of war which is red, like red blood.

I since found the two first verses in the *Kitáb al-Jinán*, a work composed by the shaikh al-Kádi ar-Rashíd Ahmad Ibn az-Zubair al-Ghassáni, the same of whom mention has been made towards the beginning of this work (vol. I. p. 143). He attributes them to al-Kádi ar-Rashíd Ahmad Ibn al-Kásim as-Sakalli (12), kadi of Misr, who, as he relates, went to the levee of al-Afdal Sháhansháh Amír al-Juyúsh (vol. I. p. 612) and, seeing before him an inkstand of ivory inlaid with coral, extemporized these lines :

Iron was, by divine favour, rendered soft for David, so that he wrought it, at will, into coats of mail. Coral, though a stone, has been softened for you, yet it is hard and disobedient to the will.

Abù Abd Allah Muhammad Ibn Bakhtyár, generally known by the name of al-Ablah (vol. III. p. 159) composed, in this … 's praise, a number of kasídas, one of which I insert here because it is the finest :

The zephyr and the (pliant) willow (bán) of the sandhill have committed a falsehood : they offered themselves as the likeness (13) (of my beloved), but they forgot the ornaments (of her person) and her (graceful) neck. O thou who art a statue (in beauty) I thou whose anklets are too wide (14) for the instep and whom I am unable not to love I I once had tears and strength of mind; but now, neither tears nor strength of mind remain. Thou hast rendered my body a dwelling-place for sickness, since you dwelleth in al-Jarn, after having departed from Tabála (15). O (my friend I) thou who seest those gazelles (maidens) cross our way I know that my heart, and not the winding valley, is their pasture-ground. Her waist is pliant like a wand, and she polishes date-tree blossoms (her teeth) with a piece of árák wood. When she holds discourse with you, she fails not to bring back (to you) the days of passionate love. Often have I passed the wine-cup to my companions, whose eyes shewed inebriation and who staggered in their gait. (We were then) in an arbour embellished with flowers, whose raiment was not (made of the silks) from Yemen or from Sanáa. In the morning, I hastened with ardour to visit the soil of that spot (where I met my beloved; I was there) before the turtle-doves had mounted to the top of the bán-tree. The lightning-clouds shook over it their flashing swords, and the lake, through fear of them, put on a coat of mail (16). O thou who blamest me! load me, as you please, with reproaches sufficient to rend even the solid rock; but know that I was formed by nature for loving, just as the rain was formed by nature for deeds of liberality.

The poet then makes his transition to the eulogium which, to avoid prolixity, I suppress. Abû 'l-Fath Sibt Ibn at-Taâwîri (*vol. III. p. 162*) composed also in his honour a single *kasîda* which I here give :

May the rains descend on these vernal shades and on three hills which, since the departure of their inhabitants, look sickly and emaciated The one. For her (*who is absent*) I have engaged that my eyelids shall be a fountain and pour from their angles an abundant flood of tears. Though her dwelling-place be much changed from the state in which I saw it, the love which is in my heart shall never be known to change. O my two friends! the aspect of that cloud whose lightnings gleam dimly over al-Ajraân has renewed my affection for her and awakened my passion. My eyes and my sight have been delivered over to constant waking by the slowness of that procrastinating maid in the fulfilment of her engagement. When I said to her : " My body is emaciated by " love!" she would reply : " Where is the lover who is not emaciated!" When I said : " Let " my tears bear witness to the sadness which you cause me;" she would answer : " Tears are " not witnesses whose evidence can be accepted." Blame me not, my two friends ! if I weep in my foolish passion for one who always breaks her promise and always procrastinates. The heaviest affliction which a lover can undergo is the irksome indifference of his beloved and the fatiguing remonstrances of censorious friends. At the foot of you insulated sandhill are (*the maidens*) fair and incomparable, who played with those hearts of ours and with our reason, as the morning in which their glances and our hearts met together and which was not free from the blood of wounded (*lovers*). O I how admirable is the valley of al-Arâk, where the perfume of your presence is revealed by the northern and the southern breezes. In that cool valley, morning and evening, as often as blew the zephyr, a love-sick heart found alleviation. I invoked indifference, but it would not aid me; I attempted to use patience (*and to bear with her*), but it was of no avail. Then (*my beloved*) knewest all the causes of love and you heaped them on a back which was already loaded with misfortunes. The only profit I derived from the loving of fair maidens was watching the nights of longing desire, how slowly they passed over. How often did those nights inspire me with the hope of meeting a man renowned, dignified in manners, grave, prudent and not precipitate; in the enjoyment of whose favour I might proudly swing my body from side to side, and, in whose court, I might sweep haughtily along in trailing robes. Now I have been long accustomed to his gifts and only desire to kiss that beneficent hand ; the generous character of Yahya the vizir gives me the assurance of that favour's being granted, and Abu ad-Dîn is the very best of sureties.

This vizir frequently recited the following verses :

The secrets of love can be explained to you by no man, till it has procured for thee the vexation of being reproved. The love which I bear her will not consent that she should ever permit me to see in her even the slightest imperfection.

The *shaikh* Shams ad-Dîn Abû 'l-Muzaffar Yûsuf Ibn Kizoghli Ibn Abd Allah (*vol. I. p. 439*), who was a daughter's son of the *shaikh* Jamâl ad-Dîn Abû 'l-Faraj Ibn al-Jauzi (*vol. II. p. 90*) states, in his *Mirât az-Zamân*, a historical work of which - I saw, in Damascus, a copy composed of forty volumes, all of them in the author's own handwriting, that his father, Kizoghli, was a white slave (mamlûk) belonging to Aûn ad-Dîn and that his mother was the daughter of the shaikh Jamâl ad-Dîn Abû 'l-Faraj just mentioned. Their son was therefore a mawla (17) to him (Aûn ad-Dîn). He states also that he heard his preceptors at Baghdad relate that Aûn ad-Dîn gave the following account of his elevation : " I was in such straitened circumstances that, " for some days, I remained without food. One of my family then advised me to " visit the tomb of Marûf al-Karkhi (vol. III. p. 384), and there ask God's assis- " tance, because all prayers offered up at that tomb were fulfilled. So I went to " the tomb of Marûf, prayed there and invoked (the help of God). I then retired, " with the intention of returning to the town (beled)," — by the word town he meant Baghdad, — " and I passed through Katufa,"—a place near Baghdad, — " and " there I saw a deserted mosque. I went into it for the purpose of saying a prayer " of two rakas, and saw there a sick man lying on a mat. I sat down by his head " and asked him if he desired anything. He replied : ' A quince.' I went to a " fruiterer's, and got from him two quinces and an apple, for which I left my cloak " (mizar) in pledge. The man eat part of a quince and bade me shut the door. " When I had done so, he got off the mat and told me to dig there. I dug and " found a jar. ' Take it,' said he, ' for you are more deserving of it than any other.' " I asked him if he had not an heir, and he answered : ' No; I had a brother whom " ' I have not seen this long time and who, as I am told, is dead. We were na- " ' tives of ar-Rusâfa.' He was still talking to me when he died. I washed his " body, put it into a shroud and buried it. Having taken the jar, which con- " tained five hundred dinars (£. 250), I went to the Tigris with the intention " of crossing over, when a waterman, dressed in rags and having an old boat, call- " ed out : ' Come with me ! come with me !' I dropped down the river with him, " and never did I see a man so like to the one that had just died. ' Where do you " ' belong to ?' said I. He answered : ' To ar-Rusâfa. I have some daughters and " am very poor.'—' Have you any relatives ?' said I. ' No,' said he, ' I had a bro- " ' ther, but it is very long since I saw him, and I know not what God has done with " ' him.'—' Hold your lap ;' said I. He did so, and I poured all the money into " it. Seeing him greatly astonished, I related to him what had passed. He then " bade me take the half of it, but I replied : ' I shall not take even a single piece.' " I then went up to the residence of the khalif, wrote a supplication (and sent it in.) " It came out endorsed thus : " The inspectorship of the makhzen." From that

" post I mounted to the vizirate."—Ibn Kisoghli continues thus : " My grandfa-
" ther, Abû 'l-Faraj, relates, in his *Muntazim*, that the vizir begged of God to die a
" martyr and, every time he found an opportunity of risking his life for the faith,
" he encountered the danger. On Saturday, the 12th of the first Jumâda, 560 (27th
" March, A. D. 1165), he was in good health. That night, he went to bed per-
" fectly well, but, at day-break, he had a fit of vomiting and sent for a doctor. This
" man attended him and gave him a draught which, some say, was poisonous,
" and he died. About six months afterwards, this doctor drank poison and
" then said repeatedly : 'That which I gave to drink has been given to me !' till
" he died."—(Ibn al-Jauzi) says, in the *Muntazim* : " On the night of the vizir's
" death, I was sleeping, with my companions, on the roof of the house, and I had a
" dream in which, methought, I was in the palace of the vizir and that he was there
" seated. A man came in with a javelin in his hand and struck him with it between
" the *unthian* (18), so that the blood gushed out like a fountain and struck the (op-
" posite) wall. I then turned round and, seeing a gold ring lying on the ground,
" I took it up and said : ' To whom must I give it?' (*The answer was :*) ' Wait till a
" ' servant come forth and to him give it.' On awaking, I related the dream to
" my companions and had scarcely finished when a man came up and said : 'The
" ' vizir is dead.' One of those who were present exclaimed : ' That is impossible ! I
" ' left him, yesterday evening, in the very best health.' Another man then came
" and confirmed the news. The son of the vizir ordered me to wash the corpse. I
" began to do so and, on lifting up the arm in order to wash the *maghâbin*,"—by this
word are designated the folds made by certain parts of the body, the armpits, for instance; its singular is *maghbin*; —" the ring fell from the hand to the ground and,
" on seeing it, I marvelled greatly, by reason of my dream. Whilst washing the
" corpse, I remarked on the face and on the body spots which denoted that he had
" been poisoned. When the bier was brought out, all the shops in Baghdad were
" closed and not a single inhabitant but accompanied the funeral. The prayer was
" said over the corpse in the Mosque of the Citadel (*Jâmé 'l-Kasr*) and interred in
" the college (*madrasa*) founded by the vizir himself, but of which even the ruins
" have now disappeared. A number of poets composed elegies on his death."
End of Ibn al-Jauzi's recital.—The author of the history of this vizir states that the
cause of his death was a sudden predominance of phlegm over his natural tempera-
ment. Having gone out to hunt with (*the khalif*) al Mustanjid, he took a laxative

draught which was not sufficient to operate the evacuation of the phlegm. On
Friday, the 6th of the first Jumáda, he rode back to Baghdad, supported on the saddle (by servants), and went to his pew in the mosque, where he attended the public
prayer. After that, he returned to his house and, at the hour of the morning prayer,
he had a recurrence of the attack and swooned away. The waiting-maids screamed
out, but he recovered and told them to be silent. His son, Izz ad-Dín Abú Abd
Allah Muhammad, who was his lieutenant in the vizirship, being informed of what
had passed, hastened to see him and said, on entering into the room : " The ustád
" ad-dár (mayor of the palace) has sent different persons to know the cause of the
outcry."—This ustád bore the names of Abú 'l-Faraj Muhammad and the surname
of Ibn Maslama ; he was the son of Abd Allah, the son of Hibat Allah, the son of al-
Muzaffar, (the son of the Ráis ar-Ruwasá (vol. III. p. 48).—" The vizir smiled (on
" hearing these words), notwithstanding his state of suffering, and pronounced
these lines :

" How many are those who, in their folly, will rejoice at my death and wield the sword with
" tyranny after my decease. If they, poor fellows ! were aware of the evils which shall befal them
" when I am gone, they would die before me.

" He then swallowed a draught which brought on an evacuation, after which, he
" called for water to make the ablution preparatory to prayer. He said the prayer
" in a sitting posture and made the prostration, but, as he continued for a conside-
" rable time without sitting up, the attendants shook him and perceived that he was
" dead. The imam (khalif) al-Mustanjid, being informed of this event, gave orders
" for his burial." Aún ad-Dín left two sons, Izz ad-Dín Muhammad, him of whom
mention has been just made, and Sharaf ad-Dín Abú 'l-Walîd al-Muzaffar. As for
his birth, Abú Abd Allah Ibn al-Kádisi (vol. I. p. 290) states, in his History of the
Vizirs, that this vizir, according to his own declaration, was born in the year
487 (A. D. 1103-4). One (of his contemporaries) said : " I saw him in a dream,
" subsequently to his death, and asked him in what state he was? He replied :

" We are asked concerning our state, after undergoing a change of state and being for ever
" concealed from sight. We have obtained a double reward for what we wrought in view of
" our own salvation, and we found that the good we did to others was selected (and put aside
" as the best)."

When the news of his death reached the mayor of the palace, Adud ad-Dín Ibn al-

Muzaffar, the poet Sibt Ibn al-Taáwisi was present. He was a mawla to the Muzaffar family, his father Nushtikin having been a mamlúk (white slave) to one of its members. It was the son who changed the name of Nushtikin into that of Abd Allah. Ibn al-Taáwisi, wishing to ingratiate himself with Adud ad-Dín who, to his knowledge, was not on good terms with the vizir, extemporized these lines :

> People told me that the vizir was dead : " Come." said they, " let us weep for Abú 'l-Muzaffar Yahya." I replied : " That is for me the slightest of misfortunes and afflictions, since Ibn al-Muzaffar (Adud ad-Dín) is alive (yahya)."

Another individual, whose name I do not now recollect, but who was a poet of some celebrity, pronounced these verses (on the same event) :

> O Lord! the noble (Yahya) Ibn Hubaira is dead and Yahya Ibn Jaafar (19) is alive ! With one Yahya have disappeared all meritorious and princely qualities, but, with the other Yahya lives (yahya) every folly and every vice.

My intention (in relating these anecdotes) is to show how numerous were the merits of Ibn Hubaira, and I have prolonged this article for the purpose of attaining that object.—I remarked in Abú 'l-Khattáb Ibn Dihya's (vol. II. p. 384) work, the *Kitáb an-Nibrás fi táríkh khulafá bani 'l-Abbás (the book of the lamp, on the history of the Abbaside khalifs)*, an error which I am anxious to point out, lest those who read that book may suppose the author's statement to be correct. In speaking of the khalif al-Muktafi Lillah, he has something to this effect : " That khalif was highly fortu-" nate in possessing such a vizir as Abú 'l-Muzaffar Aún ad-Dín Yahya Ibn Muham-" mad Ibn Hubaira, who was a descendant of the great emir Abú Hafs Omar Ibn " Hubaira, whose transcendent merit, loudly celebrated by all historians, was trans-" mitted to his grandson Aún ad-Dín." He then relates something highly honorable for Omar Ibn Hubaira, who was governor of the two Iráks under the Omaiyides. Ibn Dihya thought that the vizir of whom we have here spoken was a descendant of that emir. I was greatly surprised at his making such a mistake : the vizir drew his origin from the progenitor of the tribe of Shaibán, as we have already shewn at the beginning of this article, and the emir belonged to the tribe of Fazára, as will be seen in our article on his son Yazíd; and wide is the difference between Shaibán and Fazára. The author was, no doubt, led into this error by finding in the genealogy of the vizir an Omar Ibn Hubaira, which person he took for the emir. Such a fault, coming from a man like Ibn Dihya, is not to be pardoned; for he was a háfiz (*knowing by heart traditional information*) and should have been well acquainted with general biography. The mistake is evident, but, to err is in the lot of humanity. —Most of the persons whose names occur in this article have been already mentioned in this (*biographical*) history and have, each of them, a separate article, but we have not spoken of as-Zabdi. This *shaikh* was a man of great influence, an active reformer of manners (20) and a person whose society was always profitable to the vizir. As I have not mentioned him in this work, I feel it my duty to direct towards him the reader's attention, for a man like him should not be passed over. He arrived in Baghdad A. H. 509 (A. D. 1115-6) and died in the month of the first Rabi 555 (March-April, A. D. 1160). Abû Abd Allah Ibn an-Najjár (*vol. I. p. 11*) says, in his History of Baghdad: "He was born at Zabid (*in Yemen*), on the eve of Wed-" nesday, the 22nd of Muharram, 460 (3rd December, A. D. 1067); he died on " Monday, the 1st of the first Rabi, 555 (11th March, A. D. 1160), and was buried " in the cemetery adjoining the Djemé (*or mosque*) of al-Mansûr at Baghdad."—As for the verse of the poet: " O lord ! the noble (*Yahya*) Ibn Hubaira is dead and Yahya " Ibn Jaafar is alive;" the last words refer to Abû 'l-Fadl Yahya Ibn Abi 'l-Kâsim Obaid Allah Ibn Muhammad Ibn al-Moaromar Ibn Jaafar, surnamed Ziim ad-Dîn (*the champion of the faith*). He was appointed inspector of the *Makhzen* in the month of the latter Jumâda, 542 (Oct.-Nov. A. D. 1147), and remained in office till the year 567 (A. D. 1171). He was appointed vizir on the dismissal of Abû 'l-Faraj Ibn al-Muzaffar (21) and occupied that post till his death. His conduct entitled him to praise and gratitude, and he was a friend to men of learning. His birth took place at Baghdad after the last evening prayer of Thursday, the 29th Safar, 511 (2nd July, A. D. 1117). He died in Baghdad on the 20th of the first Rabi, 570 (19th October, A. D. 1174), and was interred in a mausoleum (*turba*) which he had erected for himself in the Harbiya cemetery.

(1) See towards the end of this article.

(2) The names of the offices mentioned in this paragraph are here rendered by their probable signification; as we do not yet possess any precise information respecting the internal administration of the khalifate in its latter days.

(3) Ildegiz was governor of Arrân and Adarbaijân. He and a number of other emirs revolted against the sultan Masûd, marched towards Baghdad, defeated the khalif's troops and committed all sorts of atrocities. They then asked and obtained the khalif's pardon, retired and spread ravage and devastation over all the countries through which they passed.—(Ibn al-Athîr's Kâmil; Mirkhond.)

(5) The meaning of the text is doubtful.

(6) The *Táj*, or crown, was a pavilion adjoining the palace of the khalifs at Baghdad. — See M. de Sacy's *Chrestomathie Arabe*, tome I, page 74. It was in it that the khalif appeared in state, on the days of solemn audience.

(6) These verses are given in the *Hamása*, page ٦١٧. The commentator, at-Tibrizi, says that they were composed by a native of Medina in honour of Amr Ibn Saïd Ibn al-Aāsi, who, as we learn by the *Nujûm*, was put to death, in the year 69 (A. D. 688-9) by the Omaiyide khalif, Abd al-Malik Ibn Marwân. Ibrahim as-Sâbi could not have composed this piece, for he died A. H. 240 (A. D. 857) and was not a native of Medina.

(7) The life of Ibn as-Sikkit, the author of the *Islâh al-Mantîk*, is given in this volume.

(8) I read : Mahmúd Shâh; see vol. III, p. 284.

(9) The copyists and editors, not having well understood this piece, have given it very incorrectly. In the third line, I read : الدنيا and, in the fourth, but with doubt, يَبْنَى .

(10) Korán, sur. 34, verse 10.

(11) The meaning of this is explained in the next verse.

(12) Ahmad Ibn al-Kâsim, surnamed al-Kâdi ar-Rashid, was a native of Sicily, from which country he removed to Egypt. He died A. H. 484 (A. D. 1091-2).—(*History of the kâdis of Misr*; ms. of the Bibl. imp., ancien fonds, n° 691.)

(13) Literally : they described them.

(14) I suppose that the poet wrote وسعت " are wide," instead of ضيقت " are tight," as thick ankles were probably not considered to be a point of beauty. — By the word *aukâis* are meant the bracelets worn on the ankles by Moslim ladies. These ornaments are of a crescent shape and as thick as the thumb. They are hollow inside and contain a little ball of metal which, as it rolls about, makes a clinking sound.

(15) Tabâla was a village on the road leading from Mekka to Yamen; al-Jara lay probably at a great distance from that place.

(16) That is : the surface of the water was wrinkled with waves. " The breeze has changed the water into " a coat of mail," said al-Motamid Ibn Abbâd to Ibn Ammâr, in one of his sportive rambles. See Dozy's *Histoire des Musulmans d'Espagne*, t. IV, p. 119.

(17) See introduction to the second volume.

(18) L'arkâin (*the two fanticles*). It is difficult to conceive how such a wound could be inflicted. Did the author mean to write thiêdin (*the two nipples*)?

(19) The author speaks of this person at the end of the present article.

(20) See vol. III, p. 216, note (3). The arabic expression is : to command what is laudable and forbid what is reprehensible.

(21) The same who was mayor of the palace. See page 185.

IBN ZABADA

Abù Tàlib Yahya Ibn Abi 'l-Faraj Said Ibn Abi 'l-Kàsim Hibat Allah Ibn Ali Ibn Zabàda tan-Shaihàni (*belonging to the Arabic tribe of Shaibàn*) was a *kàtib* (*writer in a government office*) and a *munshi* (*a drawer up of official dispatches*). His family belonged to Wàsit, but Baghdad was the place of his birth, of his residence and of his death. He bore the surname of Kiwàm ad-Dìn (*support of religion*) or, according to another statement, Amìd ad-Dìn (*column of religion*). Eminent in rank and in talent, he obtained the highest reputation as a *kàtib*, a *munshi* and an arithmetician; besides which, he possessed some skill in jurisprudence, dogmatical theology, the fundamentals (*of law*) and other sciences. As a versifier, he displayed great talent. When a student, he attended the lessons of Abù Mansùr al-Jawàlìki (*vol. III. p. 498*) and studied Koran-reading under the tuition of that professor and of his successors. He learned Traditions under some of the teachers and, from his early youth till the time of his death, he filled (*successively*) a number of places in the service of the Diwàn (*the government of the khalif*). His epistles are remarkable for the graces of their style, the elegance of their thoughts, the beauty of their ornaments and the delicacy of their allusions. In drawing up dispatches, he paid more attention to the ideas than to the cadence; his letters are elegant, his thoughts just, his poetry good and his merits are so conspicuous that they need not be described. Being nominated director of the office which administered (*the cities of*) Basra, Wàsit and al-Hilla, he continued to fill that post till the month of Muharram, 575 (June-July, A. D. 1179), when he was recalled from Wàsit and appointed to act as *hàjib* (*chamberlain*) at the Nùba door (1) and to render justice in all cases of appeal to the sovereign (2). In the month of the first Rabi, 577 (July-August, A. D. 1181), he was dismissed from all these offices and, in the month of the first Jumàda, 582 (July-Aug. 1186), he was restored to them again. When the mayor of the palace (*Ostàd ad-Dàr*) Majd ad-Din Abù 'l-Fadl Hibat Allah Ibn Ali Ibn Hibat Allah Ibn Muhammad Ibn al-Hasan, generally designated by the surname of Ibn as-Sàhib, was put to death (*by order of khalif en-Nàsir*), which event occurred on Saturday, the 19th of the first Rabi, 583 (29th May, A. D. 1187), Ibn Zabàda was appointed to succeed him. In the year 585 (A. D. 1189-90), he was dismissed from office and sent back to Wāsit where he remained till the month of Ramadān, 592 (August, A. D. 1196), and was then recalled (to Baghdad). On Monday, the 22nd of Ramadān, he was appointed director of the official correspondance and obtained again the inspectorship of the board of government grants (mukātadt), which places he held till his death. His conduct was exemplary and the line of life which he followed most praiseworthy. He was particularly careful in fulfilling his religious duties, and transmitted down a few Traditions. A great quantity of his prose writings and poetical compositions has been written down under his dictation by different persons. One of these pieces is as follows :

> In times of trouble, the worthless are raised to such eminence that the affliction is general. When tranquil water is agitated, the dregs rise from the bottom.

By the same :

> People never find one more firm than when I am in the power of sudden misfortunes. It is then that the sun does not display all his force till he enters into the mane (3) of the Lion.

In the following verses, written by him to al-Mustanjid, he compliments that khalif on the arrival of the festival day (the 10th Zú 'l-Hijja) :

> Glorious prince! thy elevation is so great that our felicitations cannot reach thee; it is we who should obtain felicitations, reposing, as we do, under the shelter of thy favour. Thou art time (good fortune) itself; the day of the festival is a part of time, and it is not the custom to compliment time on the arrival of the festival.

By the same :

> If you aspire to command, act uprightly; then, even if you wish to reach the heavens, you will succeed. The alif (l), one of the written letters of the alphabet, is placed at the head of the others because it is upright.

By the same :

> Envy not those who are vizirs, even though they obtain from their sovereigns, by the favour of fortune, more than they expected. Know that a day will come when the solid earth shall sink from under them as it used to sink before them through awe. Aaron, the brother and partner of Moses, would not have been seized by the beard (1), had he not been (his brother's) vizir.

To Ibn Zabáda belonged every sort of elegant ideas. He left a diwán (or collection) of epistles; I saw a copy of it in my native place, but am unable to insert here any of its contents, as I cannot call them to mind. Abù Abd Allah Muhammad Ibn Saìd ad-Dubaithi (vol. III. p. 102) says, in his History : " Abù Tálib Yahya Ibn Saìd " Ibn Hibat Allah,"— meaning Ibn Zabáda, — " recited to me from memory the " following lines which, as he told me, had been repeated to him by Abù Bakr " Ahmad Ibn Muhammad al-Arrajáni (vol. I. p. 134) :

The eyes of that maiden had their attention divided (between two objects), whilst she was bewildered at departing and afflicted by the coming of the camels, which was announced to her by the burden of the driver's song. With one eye, she answered my salutation and, with the other, she watched the looks of the jealous spies. Seeing around her persons ready to denounce her, she suppressed her tears and withdrew into the asylum of her tent. On the morning in which I bade them farewell, whilst tears flowed from my eyes and my mind was troubled at being separated from my companions, the reflection of those tears appeared on her cheeks, and (our fears) were jealous, thinking that she wept at my weeping.

When Ibn Zabáda was dismissed from the inspectorship of Wásit, the poet, Abù 'l-Ghanáim Muhammad Ibn Ali, generally known by the appellation of Ibn al-Muallim (vol. III. p. 168), wrote to him these lines :

When the rains refused to moisten the earth, you poured upon mankind the showers of your liberality. You were not removed from the province for a motive which might expose you to depreciation and neglect ; but, when the torrents of your generosity seemed ready to overwhelm the land, they sent you away, in order to save the country from a deluge.

Al-Wajíh Abù Abd Allah Muhammad Ibn Ali Ibn Abi Tálib, generally known by the name of Ibn Suwaid, and who was a merchant of Takrít, related to me the following anecdote : " The shaikh Muhi ad-Dín Abù 'l-Muzaffar Yûsuf, who was the " son of Jamál ad-Dín Abù 'l-Faraj Ibn al-Jauzi (vol. II. p. 96), the celebrated háfiz and preacher, was sent from Baghdad on an embassy to the court of al-Malik " al-Aádil Ibn al-Malik al-Kámil Ibn Aiyúb (vol. III. p. 235), who was then reigning " in Egypt. Al-Malik as-Sálih Najm ad-Dín Aiyub, the brother of al-Malik al-Aá- " dil, was at that time detained as a prisoner in the fortress of al-Karak."—I have already spoken of this in the article on al-Kámil (vol. III. p. 256).—" When Muhi " ad-Dín passed through Damascus, on his return to Bagdad, I happened to be " there and went to visit him with the shaikh Aúl ad-Dín Abù 'l-Fadl Abbás Ibn " Othmán Ibn Nahhán al-Irbili (a native of Arbela), who was then chief of the

" (corporation of) merchants. We sat down and, in the conversation which en-
" sued, he (Muhî ad-Dîn) said : ' I prevailed on al-Malik an-Nâsir Dâwûd, the lord
" ' of al-Karak, to swear that he would not allow al-Malik as-Sâlih to leave the pri-
" ' son, unless an order came to that effect from al-Malik al-Aâdil.' On this,
" al-Asil said to him :' Tell me, master! did you do so by the order of the August
" ' Dîvân (the khalif's government)?' Muhî ad-Dîn answered : ' Was any authorisa-
" ' tion necessary for making such a demand? The welfare of the public required
" ' me to do so; but you, Asil! are an old fellow (5).' To this, our master (al-Asil)
" replied :' It is true; I am an old fellow, and know not what I say; but I shall re-
" ' late to your Worship an event which has some analogy to this and which I know
" ' to be very curious.'—' Let us hear it' ; said Muhî ad-Dîn. Al-Asil then spoke
" as follows :' Ibn Râis ar'Ruwasâ (6), being director of the administration at Wâ-
" ' sit, was bound to send (to Baghdad), every month, the sum of thirty thousand
" ' dinars (£. 15,000), as the contribution of Wâsit, and the custom was that no de-
" ' lay, not even of a single day, should be allowed. On one of these months, he
" ' was unable to make up the sum and, feeling uneasy on the subject, he consulted
" ' his nâibs (lieutenants). They replied :' There, my Lord! is Ibn Zabâda who is
" ' indebted (to the administration) for many times that sum ; call him to an account
" ' and he will make up to you over and above what you have to send off.' He, in
" ' consequence, sent for Ibn Zabâda and said to him :' Why do you not pay (your
" ' taxes) like the others?' Ibn Zabâda answered that he had a note in the khalif al-
" ' Mustanjid's handwriting, dispensing him from paying. ' Have you a note in
" ' the khalif an-Nâsir's handwriting?' said the other.' I have not,' replied Ibn
" ' Zabâda. ' Be off!' said Ibn Râis ar-Ruwasâ, ' and bring here what you owe.'
" ' Ibn Zabâda answered : ' I care for nobody and shall bring nothing!' He then
" ' stood up and walked out of the room. The nâibs then said to their master :
" ' You possess the two cushions (emblems of civil and military authority (7)) and
" ' have the right of control over all the government intendants; no one has the
" ' high hand over you, and who is this man that he should return you such an an-
" ' swer? You would do well to enter by force into his house and seize on all that
" ' it contains; no one will dare to make any observation.' In pursuance of their
" ' advice, he ordered boats to be got ready for himself and his soldiers. Ibn Za-
" ' bada resided at that time on the other side of the river, opposite to Wâsit. When
" ' the boats were brought for Ibn Râis ar-Ruwasâ and his men, a sebzeb (or yawl)

" ' was seen coming, as if from Baghdad. When he perceived it, he said : ' This
" ' sebzeb must be coming on an affair of importance; let us see what it may be;
" ' after that we shall resume what we are about. As the boat drew near, some of
" ' the khalif's servants who were in it cried out : ' Kiss the ground! kiss the
" ' ground!' He obeyed, and they handed to him a notification (muklaa) contain-
" ' ing this order : ' We send you a robe of honour and an inkstand for Ibn Zabâda;
" ' place the robe on your head, hold the inkstand to your breast, and go on foot
" ' to him; clothe him in the robe and send him off to us, in order that he may be
" ' our vizir.' He put the robe on his head, held the inkstand against his bosom and
" ' went off on foot. When he met Ibn Zabâda, he recited to him this verse :

" ' Whilst a great man is living, people hope in him and fear him; but no one knows what is
" ' concealed in futurity.

" ' He then began to make excuses and received this answer: ' No blame on you
" ' for to-day.' Ibn Zabâda then embarked in the yawl and set off for Baghdad. No
" ' other example is known of a person's having had the vizirate sent to him. When
" ' he arrived, the first thing he did was to dismiss Ibn Râis ar-Ruwasâ from the
" ' inspectorship of Wâsit, saying that he was not fit for such an office. Now,' said
" ' al-Asil, ' who can assure your Worship that al-Malik as-Sâlih will not get out
" ' of prison and obtain the throne? You may then be sent to him as an ambassa-
" ' dor, and how will you be able to look him in the face without blushing?' Muhl
" ad-Din answered him by this line :

" (That will happen) when the two gatherers of acacia-berries shall return, and when Ko-
" laib shall be raised from the dead for the tribe of Wâil (7).

" Very soon after, al-Malik as-Sâlih got out of the prison of al-Karak, obtained
" the government of Egypt, and then happened what happened. I was in Misr, "
said al-Wajih, " when Muhl ad-Din came there as ambassador to al-Malik al-Aâdil,
" but this prince having been arrested (by his officers), was replaced by al-Malik as-
" Sâlih. Muhl ad-Din went forth to compliment the latter; of that I was an eye-
" witness."—It was in these terms that al-Wajih related to me the anecdote, but it
contains a mistake, committed either by him or by al-Asil : Ibn Zabâda was never
appointed vizir; he filled no other places than those which I mentioned at the beginning of this article; so, if the narration be true, the thing happened when he was

sent for to act as *munshi*. God knows the truth! Ibn ad-Dubaithi says : " I asked
" Abû Tâlib Ibn Zabâda when he was born, and he answered : On Tuesday, the
" 25th of Safar, 522 (1st March, A. D. 1128). He died on the eve of Friday, the
" 27th of Zû 'l-Hijja, 594 (30th October, A. D. 1198). The funeral service was
" said over him in the mosque of the Castle, at Baghdad, and he was interred near
" the mausoleum of Musa Ibn Jaafar (*vol. III. p. 463*)."—*Zabdda* means *a bit of
sabdd (curd)*, which is a perfume made use of by women.

YAHYA IBN NIZAR

Abû 'l-Fadl Yahya Ibn Nizâr Ibn Said al-Manbeji (*a native of Manbej*), is mentioned, in these terms, by the *hâfiz* Abû Saad Abd al-Karim Ibn as-Samâni (*vol. II.
p. 156*), in the *Zail*, a work which was composed as a supplement to the Khatîb's
History of Baghdad (*vol. I. p. 75*) : " He composed poetry in a natural and unaffect-
" ed style, and wrote down for me some of his verses. When I asked him the date
" of his birth, he answered : ' In the month of Muharram, 486 (February, A. D.
" ' 1093), at Manbej." The same author then gives some of his pieces, one of which
is as follows :

     There was a clear-complexioned youth, the line of whose *izâr* (1) augmented the trouble and the cares of his admirers. Oceans of beauty undulate in his cheeks and cast ambergris (2) upon their shores. Youth lets its waters flow over his cheeks, so that the borders of those streamlets produce myrtle (3).

It has come into my mind that there are things to be criticized in this piece : The poet says, in the second verse, that oceans of beauty undulate in his cheeks; why then does he say, in the third verse, that youth lets its waters flow over them? What congruity is there between the water of youth and oceans of beauty? Not content with committing that fault, he represents the water as flowing in streamlets, that is to say, in rivulets; but rivulets are not to be placed on a line with oceans. In the same verse, he compares the *izâr* to ambergris; why then, in the third, does he assimilate it to myrtle? It is true that poets, when they seek for objects to which the *izâr* may be compared, have the custom of designating it as ambergris or as myrtle, but they never bring both together in the same piece. At the time in which I studied polite literature, I heard two verses recited which pleased me much; they are by an author whose name I could not learn, and run thus :

O thou who reproachest me with admiring one whose cheeks are encircled with an *izâr* ! know that the fertile and the sterile soils are not to be compared. A sea of beauty undulates on those cheeks and casts ambergris upon its shores.

In the beginning of the year 672 (July-August, A. D. 1273), a volume of the work entitled *as-Sail wa 'z-Zail* and composed by the *kâtib* Imâd ad-Dîn al-Ispahâni as a supplement to his *Kharîda tal-Kasr* (vol. III. p. 303), fell into my hands. In it I found an article on Yahya Ibn Nizâr al-Manbeji in which is introduced a piece of ten verses composed by him in praise of the sultan Nûr ad-Dîn Mahmûd Ibn Zinki (vol. III. p. 338). As that piece contains the second of the two verses just mentioned, I perceived that the person who versified the idea contained in the second of the three verses above given was the author of those which are inserted in the Sail. Soon after, I received a visit from my friend Jamâl ad-Dîn Abû 'l-Mahâsin Yûsuf Ibn Ahmad, generally known by the surname of al-Hâfis al-Taghmûri, and, in the course of our conversation, mention was made of the two verses. On this, he observed that the author of them was Imâd ad-Dîn Abû 'l-Manâkib Husâm Ibn Ghossi Ibn Yûnus al-Mahalli (a native of al-Mahalla in Egypt) who had settled in Damascus. " I heard him recite them," said he, " and he mentioned that they were of his own " composing."—" Nay," said I, " the verse containing the idea (which we have re-

" *marked*; was composed by Yahya Ibn Nizâr 'al-Manbeji; Imâd ad-Din al-Mahalli
" may have made the first verse for the purpose of introducing the other as a cita-
" tion, as is customary in some cases; but he should have indicated that it was a
" citation, lest those who read them both might suppose it to be his. Observe that
" the first verse is not in the piece which Yahya al-Manbeji composed in honour of
" Nûr ad-Din."—At a later period, it struck me that al-Mahalli's piece also was liable
to censure : in the verse which prepares the way for the other he says that fertile and
steril grounds are not to be compared. Now, these qualities depend upon the presence or the absence of vegetation. Then, in the next verse, he assimilates the *izâr*
to ambergris; but what analogy is there between plants and ambergris? The manner of introducing the second verse is therefore faulty. This critical remark is similar to that already made on the piece which consists in three verses.—A number
of persons recited to me two (*other*) verses composed by al-Imâd al-Mahalli and which
I here give :

> They said to me : " The hair sports with the cheeks of the youth whom you admire;" and
> I answered : " That is not a defect. The glowing coal of his cheek has burned the ambergris
> " of his beauty-spot, and the smoke arising from it has formed the *izâr.* "

The idea then crossed my mind that the same critical remark which I made on the
other verses was applicable to these also. Observe that the poet, when told of the
hair's sporting with the youth's cheeks, does not disapprove of it, but says : That is
not a defect. He therefore admits that the hair was an excellent thing in its kind.
Why then does he say in the next verse that the glowing coal of the cheek has burned the ambergris, *etc.* and that the *izâr* was formed of the smoke? What analogy
is there between the smoke of ambergris and hair? To express the thought correctly, he should have said to those who spoke to him : That is not hair but the smoke
of ambergris.—I had at Aleppo a friend and fellow-student named Aûn ad-Din Abû
'r-Rabia Sulaimân Ibn Bahâ ad-Din Abd al-Majîd al-Ajami, who was a native of that
city. He composed two verses in which he came near to the idea above mentioned
and which I insert here :

> When the flame of his cheek appeared to my eyes, my heart flew into it like a moth (*into a
> candle*). Burnt by that flame, it formed a beauty-spot and there, on the borders (*of the cheek*),
> is the trace of the smoke.

Here the idea is well brought out and cannot incur a censure similar to the pre-

ceding, but the poet has fallen into another fault which deserves to be taken up : he
represents the *izár* as the smoke resulting from the burning of the heart, whereas,
al-Imâd al-Mahalli called it the smoke of the ambergris of the beauty-spot ; now,
there is certainly a wide difference between the two kinds of smoke; one smells
sweetly and the other badly.—Our article on Abd Allah Ibn Sâra ash-Shantarfai
(vol. *II. p. 59*) contains two verses in which that poet has expressed a very original
idea ; he says :

> (*I think of her*) whose waist was so slender and the borders (*lineaments*) of whose beauty
> so tender (*delicate*), that my heart was filled with a tender passion. It was not an *izár* which
> clothed her cheek but rather a tint cast upon it by the dark pupils of (*our*) eyes (4).

The original source of all the pieces of this cast is a poem in which the *kâtib* Abû
Ishak Ibrahîm as-Sâbi speaks of his page Yumn, who was of a swarthy complexion.
We have already given it (vol. *I. p. 32*), but we reproduce here what relates to our
subject :

> Thou hast a face which my right hand seems to have traced, and words which deceive my
> hopes. In it is the image of the full moon, but over it have been cast the shades of night.

The thought contained in Aûn ad-Dîn's two verses comes near to that which is
expressed in the following lines, composed by Abû 'l-Husain Ahmad Ibn Munîr at-
Tarâblusi (vol. *I. p. 140*) :

> Think not that the mole upon her cheek is a tear of blood fallen from my eyes. It was pro-
> duced by a burning coal from the fire in my heart; immersed in that (*cheek*), it was extin-
> guished and then rose to the surface.

I have here digressed from my subject and discoursed rather diffusely, but my observations are not devoid of utility.—Abû Saad as-Samâni says also (*in the work
above cited*) : " Yahya Ibn Nizâr al-Manbeji recited to me the following verses and
" gave them as his own :

> " Had she turned away from me through coquetry or through disapprobation, I should still
> " hope to gain her affection and should forgive her. But, if she rejects me through anxiety,
> " I cannot hope to make her relent; it is difficult to mend a glass, once it is broken. "

He (*Yahya Ibn Nizâr*) left other fine pieces of verse and expressed (*therein*) many

elegant ideas. The historical annals compiled by (Afíf ad-Dín) Abû 'l-Faraj Sadaka Ibn al-Husain Ibn al-Haddâd (5) contain a passage to this effect : " On the eve
" of Friday, the 6th of Zû 'l-Hijja, 554 (19th Dec. A. D. 1159], Yahya Ibn Nizâr
" al-Manbedji died at Baghdad and was buried in the Wardiya cemetery. It is said
" that he felt a weight (or obstruction) in one of his ears and called in an administra-
" tor of theriac (a quack-doctor) to treat him. This operator sucked his ear and
" drew out of it a portion of the brain; that was the cause of the patient's death."
As-Samâni says that he was the brother of Abû 'l-Ghanâim, the famous merchant.
Of the latter he gives an account in a separate article of the Zail, and praises him
highly.—Imâd ad-Din al-Mahalli was an elegant and refined literary scholar, if we
may judge from the anecdotes told of him. He left some good poetry, consisting of
short pieces only, and no kasídas. He knew by heart the Makâmas (of al-Harîri,
see vol. II. p. 490), and explained their difficulties. His death took place at Damascus, on the eve of Wednesday, the 14th of the first Rabî, 629 (9th January,
A. D. 1232). He was buried in the Sûfi cemetery. His birth is placed, by estimation, in the year 560 (A. D. 1164-5). His early youth was passed at al-Mahalla and,
from that place, he drew his surname. The denomination under which he was generally known was that of Ibn al-Jamâl. — I found among my rough notes, and in
my own handwriting, two verses attributed to Wajîh ad-Din Abû 'l-Hasan Ali Ibn
Yahya Ibn al-Hasan Ibn Ahmad, generally known by the surname of Ibn az-Zarawi
(vol. II. p. 555) the poet. Here they are :

> Her izâr is the smoke of the aloes-wood of her beauty-spot; her saliva, the water of the ro-
> ses of her cheek.

I then found the following verses attributed to Ibn Sana al-Mulk (vol. III. p. 589),
but they belong, in reality, to Asaad Ibn al-Mammâti (vol. I. p. 192):

> A brunette who surpasses all others in complexion, in shape and in the sweetness of her lips.
> Her breath is the vapour arising from the aloes-wood of her beauty-spot, and her saliva is the
> rose-water of her cheek. Were the moon to write her a letter of compliments, the signature
> would be " Your humble servant."

I found the following lines attributed to an inhabitant of Aleppo called Muhaddab
ad-Din Abû Nasr Muhammad Ibn Muhammad Ibn Ibrahîm Ibn al-Khidr, generally
known by the surname of Ibn al-Burhân at-Taberi; he was a native of Taberistân,
a calculator and an astronomer :

Her waist was slender, the radiance of her face dazzling and her aspect charming to the eye. With the fire of her cheek she heated the ambergris of her beauty-spot and, from the smoke of that ambergris, resulted the *izâr*.

I then perceived that al-Mahalli had borrowed his idea from one or the other of those persons just mentioned.

(1) For the meaning of this word, I refer to the first volume, Introduction, p. xxvi.

(2) The word ambergris is often employed as the synonym of *izâr*.

(3) See Introduction to vol. I. p. xxxvi.

(4) In the translation already given of this piece and the following, the meaning has been so much softened down and disguised, that the observations here made by our author do not apply to them. It was therefore necessary to render them more literally.

(5) See vol. I. p. 311.

YAHYA IBN AL-JARRAH

Abû 'l-Husain Yahya Ibn Abi Ali Mansûr Ibn al-Jarrâh Ibn al-Husain Ibn Muhammed Ibn Dâwûd Ibn al-Jarrâh, a native of Egypt, — this addition to the genealogy I found in the handwriting of a literary scholar, but am unable to certify its exactitude, and consider the first (*links of the chain*) as the surest, — was surnamed Tâj ad-Din (*crown of the religion*). During a long time he was employed as a writer (*kâtib*) in the correspondance office, under the government of Egypt. He wrote a great deal and in a beautiful hand. His talents, literary acquirements and varied information were of the highest order; his natural genius was fine, his poetry charming and his letters elegant. He heard Traditions in the frontier city of Alexandria, where he had for teachers the *hâfiz* Abû Tâhir as-Silafi (*vol. I.* p. 86) and Abû 'th-Thanâ Hammâd Ibn Hibat Allah al-Harrâni. Traditions were taught also by him to numerous auditors. An enigma was composed by him, of which the word was *damluj* (دملج), a term serving to designate the object worn by women (*the bracelet which encircles the ankle or the upper arm*). As this riddle is a remarkable thing of the kind, I am induced to insert it here; it is in prose and runs thus : " What is

" the thing (1), which, by inversion, becomes a stone; its face is a moon; if you
" reject it, it takes patience and goes apart from mankind (or from the skin); if you
" render it hungry, it will be satisfied with a date-stone; it folds itself around va-
" cuity; if you glut it, it kisses your foot and becomes the companion of your servants
" (your shoe-ties); if you perfume it, it is lost; if you take it to the bazar, it refuses
" to be sold; if you let it be seen, it renders (its) possession agreeable (to you) and
" embellishes the enjoyment (which it procures you); if you double its second
" (letter) and reject the finals, it troubles life and renders necessary an alleviation
" from praying; at the time of the asr, it causes anguish, at the fajr, it gives (you)
" alleviation and repose but, to its good termination is joined a bad trace; if you
" divide it, it prays for you and leaves a thing which, if you are borne upon it,
" affrights you, though it aids you to accomplish your wishes, increases your
" wealth and, by means of that which is a help for the poor, brings about for
" you a good result. Receive my salutations."— Any person, meeting with this
enigma and not knowing the way of solving it, would find great difficulty in
clearing it up; I shall therefore give here the elucidations which the subject
requires: The words: What is the thing which, by inversion, becomes a stone indicate the term dumluj (d. m, l, j, bracelet for the ankle or the upper arm), which,
being inverted, gives j, l, m, d (jalmad, stone). The words: whose face is a moon
mean that it is as round as the moon. In the expression: if you reject it, it takes
patience and goes apart from the skin (b, sh, r), the word bashar is the plural of
bashara (the skin of the body); now, when it is thrown off, it takes patience and
quits the skin, because it has not the faculty of resisting; it therefore has patience
and leaves the place where it was. If you render it hungry, it will be satisfied with
a date-stone (nawa); the word nawa has two significations, namely, remoteness and
a date-stone. In the provinces of Irák, it is the custom to grind down date-stones
with ripe or unripe dates and give them as forage to oxen; but here, the author,
intended to disguise the meaning which he gave to the word: when the dumluj
is taken off the arm or the leg, it may be said to be hungry because its belly (or
interior) is empty, and to be resigned to its nawa, or removal from the limb of its
owner. People say: " Such a one is satisfied with a nawa," when he is so poor
that he cannot procure a morsel to eat and makes up for that by sucking a date-
stone. This is often done by the inhabitants of Hijáz and of barren countries,
when provisions are scarce. The author of the enigma had these two significations

in view when he made use of the word *nuwa*, and, in that, consists the *tauriya* (or *disguising of the true meaning*). In the expression: *it folds itself around vacuity* (2), the word *khawa* means *emptiness*; and, effectively, when it (*the bracelet*) has its interior empty, it is really *khawi* (*vacuus*). The word *glutting*, in the expression: *if you glut it, it kisses your foot*, means putting it on, for the owner, when he does so, has filled its interior, and it is then over the foot, as if it was kissing it. In the words: *it becomes the companion of your servants*, we find also a *tauriya*; *khadam* (*servants*) is the plural of *khadim* and one of those plurals which occur very rarely. The active participle having the form *fáil* (*which is the type of the form khádim*) does not take a plural having the form *faal* (*which the type of* khadam) except in a few cases which are to be learned (*not from rules but*) by audition; such, for instance as *ghádib* (*absent*), *hárie* (*gardian*) and *jámid* (*solid*), of which the plurals are *ghaiyab*, *haras* and *jamad* respectively. It is by audition only that these plurals are to be learned. The same word *khadam* is also the plural of *khadama*, which means the strap bound round the pastern of the camel and to which is tied the thong which holds the leathern shoe (*on the animal's foot*). An ankle-bracelet is called a *khadama* because it is sometimes made of straps inlaid with gold and silver. Another plural of *khadama* is *khiddm*. The expression: *if you perfume it, it is lost* has another meaning which is here disguised (*though intended*): the word *dhda*, having for its noun of action *dhida*, means *to be lost*, and signifies, when applied to perfumes, that their odour escapes (*and spreads around*). The words: *if you take it to the bazar, it refuses to be sold*, have here another meaning: as the word *súk* signifies not only the place where things are bought and sold, but also the *legs*, (*the words which signify :*) taking it to the bazar, (*mean also*) entering the leg into it: It refuses to be sold, because it is customary not to offer for sale an object of that kind until it is taken off the leg; we may therefore say that, before it is taken off, it refuses to be sold. The words: *if you let it be seen, it renders its possession agreeable to you and embellishes the enjoyment (which it procures you)* are so clear that they require no explanation (3). *If you double its second* (letter), which is the *m*, and *reject the final*, you obtain the word *dummel* (boil, imposthume), which *troubles life* by the pain it gives and therefore *renders necessary an alleviation from* (the fatigues of) *praying*. *At the time of the asr, it causes anguish;* the word *asr* has a double signification : it designates one of the (daily) prayers, and is also the noun indicating the action expressed by the verb (asar, to press). Here again is a disguising of the meaning, and such is also the case with the word fajr which signifies the dawn of day and is, besides, the noun of action belonging to the verb fajar which signifies to let flow. When a man's tumour is pressed, he feels anguish and trouble, and when he lets the humour run out of it, he obtains alleviation and repose. To its good termination is joined a bad trace; here the author designedly opposes the idea of badness to that of goodness and, no doubt, the discharge of the humour is a good thing and the scar left on the place a bad (or ugly) one. If you divide it, it prays for you; that is, if you cut the word during in two, the first half is dum (endure!), which is prayer that a man may live long. And leaves a thing which, if you are borne upon it, affrights you; what is left is the syllable luj; now, the word lujj means the waves of the sea. In the first case, there is but one j and in the second, there are two; but licenses of this kind are pardoned when they occur in enigmas, conundrums (4) and riddles, and no attention is paid to them. As the sea is a fearful thing, the author said : it affrights you. It sometimes aids you to accomplish your wishes, because you arrive by it at the place to which you wished to go; it increases your wealth, because people embark for the purpose of trading. And, by means of that which is a help for the poor, it brings about for you a good result; by the words: that which is a help for the poor, is meant a ship, in as much as God said (Koran, sur. 18, verse 78) : but the vessel belonged to some poor people who worked upon the sea; this vessel was therefore a help for them in their need and kept them from poverty. The word result (ma' al) means the manner in which a thing terminates. God knows how far these explications are right. The word which signifies enigma has eight forms : loghz, loghus, laghz, laghaz, olghuza, loghghuzd and loghuzd.—What we have said here is rather long, but it was requisite that no doubts should be left in the reader's mind.—In a collection of pieces drawn up by a man of talent who was one of my acquaintances, I found two verses attribued to Yahya Ibn al-Jarrah and I give them there :

> I lift my hand towards my beard, with the intention of plucking out a white hair; but in-
> stead of the white one, it takes out a black. Since my own hand does not obey my wish, what
> must I think of my enemies ? (5)

He (Ibn al-Jarrah) was born on the eve of Saturday, the 15th of Shaabān, 541 (21st January, A. D. 1147), and died at Damietta (Dimyât) on the 5th of Shaabān

616 (16th October, A. D. 1219). The enemy (*the Crusaders under John of Brienne*), whose projects may God always confound! were then besieging that place.—*Jarráh* is to be pronounced with a double r preceded by an *a*.—The enemy took Damietta on Tuesday, the 27th of the month just mentioned (7th November), but God knows if this date be right. The Muslims retook it in the month of the latter Jumáda, 618 (A. D. July-August, 1221).—I give here a note which I found in the handwriting of the professor and philologer Muhaddab ad-Dín Abû Tálib Muhammad Ibn Ali, generally known by the surname of Ibn al-Khaimi. He was a native of al-Ililla (in *Mesopotamia*) and had settled in Misr (*Old Cairo*). He says: "The enemy landed be-"fore Damietta on Tuesday, the 12th of the first Rabî, 615 (8th June, A. D. 1218); "they landed on the eastern bank (*of the river*) on Tuesday, the 16th of Zû "'l-Kaada, in the same year (3rd February, A. D. 1219). This fortress was "taken on Tuesday, the 26th of Shaabân, 616 (6th November, A. D. 1219), and "was recovered from them on Wednesday, the 19th of Rajab, 618 (8th September, "A. D. 1221). From the time of their landing till that of their departure, three "years, three months and seventeen days elapsed. It is a remarkable coincidence "that they landed on a tuesday, blockaded the town on a tuesday and took it on a "tuesday. According to a tradition, God created on a tuesday all things disa-"greeable."—*Dimyát* is a Syrian word; its primitive form was *Dhimidt* (ذميد), with a point on the d (ذ), and is derived from دوذ, which means *the power of the Lord* (6). This seems an allusion to the junction of the two seas, that of fresh water (*the Nile*) and that of salt; but God knows best.

---

(1) Most of the words employed in this enigma have a double signification, one which is quite obvious but not appropriate, and the other, appropriate but less generally known. So the expressions of the author are, in themselves, a class of enigmas. The piece itself is a very poor one and not worth the long commentary in which Ibn Khallikan takes the trouble of explaining it.

(2) This idiomatical expression, when taken in its usual signification, denotes that a person supports patiently the sufferings caused by hunger.

(3) This phrase is so far from being clear that most of the copyists did not understand it; they write جمل in place of جمل and الاتباع or الامتداع in place of الامتناع.

(4) The word rendered by conundrum is تصحيف. It means in reality, changing the diacritical points of a word; the result of which is that the consonants of the word are changed and its meaning also.

(5) This passage, though given in the printed editions, is not to be found in our manuscripts.

(6) The ancient Egyptians called this town *Tamiati* and the Greeks *Tamiathis*. The meaning assigned to this name by our author has nothing to support it.

IBN MATRUH

Abú 'l-Husain Yahya Ibn Isa Ibn Ibrahim Ibn al-Husain Ibn Ali Ibn Hamza Ibn
Ibrahim Ibn al-Husain Ibn Matrúh, surnamed Jamâl ad-Dín (*beauty of religion*) was
a native of Upper Egypt (*Saîd*). He there passed his youth and, after residing for
some time in Kûs, he entered into the civil administration and filled successively
various offices till he got attached to the service of the sultan al-Malik as-Sâlih Abú
'l-Fath Aiyûb, surnamed Najm ad-Dín (*star of the religion*). This prince, who was
the son of the sultan al-Malik al-Kâmil (vol. III. p. 240) and the grandson of al-Aâdil
Ibn Aiyûb, was then acting in Egypt as his father's lieutenant. When al-Malik al-
Kâmil aggrandized his empire by the adjunction of the Eastern Countries (*Irak, Me-
sopotomia*, etc.) and obtained possession of Aâmid, Hisn Kaifa, Harrân, ar-Roha
(*Edessa*), ar-Rakka, Râs Ain, Sarûj and their dependencies, he sent there his son,
al-Malik as Sâlih, as his lieutenant. This took place in the year 629 (A. D. 1231-2)
Ibn Matrúh, who was attached to the service of that prince, accompanied him in all
his excursions throughout these provinces and continued to do so till his master returned to occupy the throne of Egypt. As-Sâlih made his entry into Cairo on Sunday, the 27th of Zû 'l-Kaada, 637 (19th June, A. D. 1240). In the beginning of the
year 639 (July-August, A. D. 1241), Ibn Matrúh came back to Egypt and received
from the sultan the intendance of the treasury. He continued to rise in favour and to
gain the good will of his sovereign till the latter obtained possession of Damascus for
the second time. This was in the month of the first Jumâda, 643 (Sept.-Oct. A. D.
1245). Some time afterwards, the sultan established commissaries (*nâibs*) in Damascus, and Ibn Matrúh, whom he sent there to act as vizir, rose thus to easy circumstances and an elevated position. Al-Malik as-Sâlih then set out for Damascus, where
he arrived in the month of Shaabân, 646 (Nov.-Dec. A. D. 1248), and then dispatched
an army against Hims (*Emessa*), for the purpose of taking that city from the commissaries who had been established there by al-Malik an-Nâsir Abû 'l-Musaffar Yusuf
(vol. II. p. 445), surnamed Salâh ad-Din. This prince was the son of al-Malik al-
Aziz, the son of al-Malik az-Zâhir, the son of the sultan Salâh ad-Din (*Saladin*), and
lord of Aleppo. He had taken by force (*the city of Hims*) from the hands of its former

possessor, al-Malik al-Ashraf Muzaffar ad-Din Abû 'l-Fath Mûsa (vol. *I.* p. 628), the son of al-Malik al-Mansûr Ibrâhîm and the grandson of al-Malik al-Mujâhid Asad ad-Dîn Shîrkûh. As this prince was devoted to al-Malik as-Sâlih, the latter set out from Egypt with the intention of reinstating him in the possession of Hims. He then took from Ibn Matrûh the office which he held at Damascus, and sent him off with the army which was marching against Hims. Whilst al-Malik as-Sâlih was remaining in Damascus, where he resolved to await the result of the expedition, he received intelligence that the Franks were assembling in the island of Cyprus, with the intention of invading Egypt. He in consequence sent off to the troops which were blockading Hims the order to raise the siege and return to Egypt for the purpose of guarding its territory. The army went back to that country, and Ibn Matrûh, who had continued in the service of al-Malik as-Sâlih, now incurred that sultan's displeasure, for some things which he had done. In the beginning of the year 647, the Franks landed in Egypt and, on Sunday, the 27th of Safar, in the same year (11th June, 1249), they obtained possession of Damietta (1). Al-Malik as-Sâlih encamped with his army at al-Mansûra, and Ibn Matrûh continued in his service notwithstanding the disfavour shewn to him. On the eve of the 15th of Shaabân, 647 (23 Nov. A. D. 1249) al-Malik as-Sâlih died at al-Mansûra and Ibn Matrûh went to Cairo (Misr) where he remained in his house till the day of his death. This is but a summary sketch of his history.—He possessed great talents, an amiable disposition and, to his merit and uprightness, he united the most estimable qualities of heart. An intimate friendship subsisted between him and me; when separated from each other, we kept up an epistolary correspondance and, when we met in a fixed abode (the city), we had sittings in which our time was passed in literary and amusing conversation. He composed a *diwân* of poetry, the greater part of which he recited to me. One of the pieces which I heard from him was a long and elegant *kasîda*, commencing thus :

Here is Râma (vol *I.* p. 200); take to the right of the valley, and let your swords repose in their scabbards; but beware of the glances shot from the large eyes of its residents! how many lions (*heroes*) have been struck down by those arms ! To him among you who feels sure of his heart (*I shall only say that*), in that place, I am not sure of my own. My two companions ! at the sand-hill, in the (*tribe's*) reserved grounds, a heart remains in captivity and has no one to redeem it. It was stolen from me on the day of the tribe's departure, by the glances of an eye whose lashes were darkened with collyrium. In the tribe of her for whose love I am dying, are eyes always watching the proceedings of lovers. There also is a sweet-voiced (maiden), with perfumed and honeyed lips, from whom, only for those jealous spies, I should have obtained my will. By what way can a meeting be effected with one who is so closely guarded by bright swords and yellow (shafted) spears? Her flowing hair dwells within a tent of hair, and her beauty always resides in the desert (2). They guard with the spear her whose waist, so slender and so gracefully bending, resembles the pliant (spear). A female (friend) said to me: The lock of hair pendant over her cheek and as strait as the letter alif (ﺍ), being joined to the mim (ﻡ) of her smiling mouth (3), will heal the thirst of the passionate lover.

The whole poem is very fine, but I limit my choice to this passage, through the necessity of being concise. Another piece of his is the following :

I am attached to a person of the family of Yarub, whose glances are sharper and more destructive than the swords of her noble Arab kinsmen. I have lodged her in the recess formed by my bosom, through love for her brilliant teeth and for the sweet water of her lips. Censors! you who blame the languor of her eyes; leave it for me; I am pleased with her very defects. She is pliant (in her movements), though the zephyr passes not by (to bend) her waist; she sheds perfume around, yet ambergris breathes not from her bosom.

Being taken ill, in one of his journeys, he stopped at a mosque on the road-side and said :

The doctor may be unable to cure me; so, thou, O Lord! who healest all woes, heal my illness though thy gracious bounty. I am detained here as thy guest, and beneficence towards guests is a quality of the generous.

After his death, these lines were found written on a piece of paper.—He related to me that he had, one day, a discussion with Abù 'l-Fadl Jaafar Ibn Shams al-Khilâfa (vol. I. p. 328), respecting a verse contained in a kasîda which had been composed by the latter and which began thus :

Who will bring to me that pliant branch (maiden) who is engirdled with eyes (4), whose qualities, whose lips and whose voice are all sweet? Rich (i. e. large) in haunches, poor (thin) in waist; did you ever hear speak, in the world, of a rich person being poor?

The verse which gave rise to the contestation was as follows :

I say : " O sister of the gazelle !" and she answers : " May the gazelle perish! may it not " survive !"

Ibn Shams al-Khilâfa pretended that it was his and that it belonged to one of the kasîdas which were contained in his diwân. Each of the disputants had then a certificate drawn up, attesting the verse to be his, and these documents they had signed by a number of witnesses. Ibn Matrûh declared solemnly, that he had composed it, and he was a man very cautious in his affirmations and never known to claim a thing which did not belong to him; but God knows the secrets of all things!—One of my acquaintances recited to me the following lines, declaring that Ibn Matrûh had taught them to him and had mentioned that they were by himself :

> O thou who hast forced me to put on the raiment of sickness, a sallow complexion marked with the red (blood) of tears! receive the last sighs of a heart which I should have expelled from my bosom, had it not melted away through grief for thy absence.

During the time of his remaining secluded in his house, whilst his mind was pre-occupied and his heart saddened at having no longer any place to fill, he caught a disorder in his eyes which finished by nearly depriving him of sight. I used then to visit him very often, but, as I was at that time acting as the deputy of the chief kadi and magistrate of all Egypt, whose names were Badr ad-Dîn Abû 'l-Mahâsin Yûsuf Ibn al-Hasan Ibn Ali, surnamed the Kâdi Sinjâr, I was under the necessity of suspending my visits for a short period. He therefore wrote to me these lines :

> O thou whom my eyes are longing to see; thou, the charms of whose society have never ceased to fill my heart! These eyes and this heart, in their present state, are always a dwelling for the moon and for the sun (5).

The following verses are taken from one of his long *kasîdas* :

> The (admiring) eyes which encircle that queen of beauty form her *yatak*; she takes our bosom for her tent and, in my heart, she has a *sabak*.

The idea expressed in the first verse is borrowed from al-Mutanabbi, who said :

> The glances of admirers are fixed upon her waist; so that she is encircled with a girdle of eyes.

Yatak يتاق is a Turkish word; it designates the company of soldiers who pass the night around the royal tent, and guard it when the prince is making an expedition (6). *Sabak* سبق means the king's tent; when he is on a march, a tent is sent forward to the place where he intends to halt, so that, on his arrival, he may find every thing prepared and not be obliged to wait till the tent in which he had already stopped is brought up. — In the following verses, he introduces, with great elegance, a verse of al-Mutanabbi's:

When she smiled and let me sip intoxication from her lips, I called to mind what had passed between al-Ozaib and Bârik (7); her slender stature and the flow of my tears made me think of our (slender) lances couched against the foe and of the rapid course of our steeds.

We give here al-Mutanabbi's verse, which forms the beginning of a long *kasida*:

> I called to mind what passed between al-Ozaib and Bârik : there our lances were couched ; there ran, with emulation, our rapid steeds.

Ibn Matrûh and Bahâ ad-Dîn Zuhair (vol. I. p. 542) were old friends. Their acquaintance commenced when they were boys and residing in Upper Egypt. They were as two brothers, neither of them having any wordly interest distinct from that of his companion. When they entered into the service of al-Malik as-Sâlih, they maintained their mutual friendship and carried on a written correspondance in verse, containing an account of whatever occurred to them. Bahâ ad-Dîn himself related to me that Jamâl ad-Dîn Ibn Matrûh wrote to him, one day, for the gift of a *darj* (a large sheet) of paper, being then in straitened circumstances. They were at that time in the East (Mesopotamia), as I believe. Here are the lines :

> Sir I I am in want of a leaf (in Arabic: *wrk*); bestow on me a sheet as fair as your reputation.— If it comes to me with some ink (I shall say :) " Welcome to the (fair) cheeks and the dark " eye."

Bahâ ad-Dîn informed me that the writer had placed two vowel points upon the r of the word w, r, k, so that it might be read either *warak* (leaf) or *warik* (money), and thus make known his distressed situation. Bahâ ad-Dîn answered in these terms :

> My master ! I send you what you wrote for : a little ink and some *warik*. Yet the small quantity (8) of that is precious in my sight, since you compared it to cheeks and eyes.

In the life of Bahâ ad-Dîn (vol. I. p. 544) I have given two verses which Ibn Matrûh wrote to him and I related, after Bahâ ad-Dîn's own statement, the motive which led the author to compose them. Since I wrote that, an accomplished literary scholar arrived in Egypt and I mentioned to him, in conversation, what Bahâ ad-Dîn had told me. I said also that he had recited to me the following verse, as having been composed by Ibn al-Halîwi (vol. I. p. 544):

> You compose verses well and you reward those who praise you in verse. Tell us then whether you are Zuhair or Harim?

Here, that person said to me : " The kasîda of which you speak was recited to me
" by the author, Ibn al-Halâwi, when we were in Mosul; but I read the verse in a
" different manner, for I heard it thus pronounced by him who composed it :

> " You make verses well and you remunerate those who bring verses to you. Tell us then
> " whether you are Zuhair or Harim?"

Ibn Al-Halâwi may, perhaps have composed this verse in the form given to it
by Bahâ ad-Dîn and, afterwards, modified it in the manner indicated by the literary scholar; or, perhaps, one or other of these relaters may have made a mistake;
but the verse is very good, both ways.   The history of Zuhair Ibn Abi Sulma al-Muzani (9) is so well known that we need not leave our subject for the purpose of
giving a long account of this anteislamic poet.   He used to compose poems in praise
of Harim Ibn Sinân al-Muzani, a famous Arab chieftain in the times of paganism.
Harim frequently bestowed rich presents on Zuhair and even swore that, every time
the poet saluted him , he would give him, out of his property, something very fine,
such as a horse, or a camel, or a male slave, or a female slave.   Zuhair, not wishing
to be onerous to Harim, never afterwards passed by a company where that chief was,
without saying : " Salutation to you all, this morning! with the exception of Harim:
" the best among you, I leave him out. "—Let us resume our account of Ibn Matrûb : I have been informed that, before his elevation to power, he wrote a petition to
a râis (or chief of a government office), requesting him to take charge a certain
affair for one of his friends.   The râis sent out to him the paper with the following
answer written on it: "To arrange such an affair would be a toil for me."   To this
Ibn Matrûb wrote as a reply : "Were it not for toiling etc."   The râis understood
the allusion and did the business.   These words belong to a verse of al-Mutanabbi's
which runs as follows :

> Were rank to be gained without toil, every man would be a râis; (but they know that) libe-
> rality impoverishes, and hardly daring is often fatal.

The hint was really very delicate.—Jamâl ad-Dîn Abù 'l-Husain Yahya Ibn Abd
al-Azîm Ibn Yahya Ibn Muhammad Ibn Ali, a learned and highly accomplished philologer, who was generally known by the surname of al-Jazzâr al-Misri, recited to me
an elegant kasîda which he had composed in honour of Ibn Matrûb.   It is rather
long, so I shall merely give the amatory part of it :

Here is her vernal abode which my soul was longing to see again; stop the caravan so that I may fulfil my duty towards that spot (*in offering it my salutations*). According to the laws of love, it would be disgraceful for me if I treated with ingratitude a place which procured me so much happiness. I shall never forget the nights passed therein with her whom I loved, and those happy hours. If, since their departure, I am become the mere shadow of myself, yet the love which I feel for her has never ceased to be a reality. My friend, sincere and noble! at such a moment as this, the generous man never forgets his friends. Place your hand upon my heart; you may perhaps alleviate its palpitations within my bosom. My eyes have shed torrents of tears, since they last saw this abode of love, and how often have they wept when they saw *(from afar)* the lightnings (*of the beneficent rain-cloud*) glimmer over it. They have exhausted the pearls of their tears, and now, they scatter on the ground their rubies (*drops of blood*). Stay with me, and tell the caravan to wait; if it will not, let it go forward on its way; this a country which we can seldom hope to attain, and we have never missed attaining (*overtaking*) a caravan. How often, in these tracts, have I endeavoured to see her who, when she called her sister, astonished the moon (*who thought that the call was addressed to her*). The rose is disgraced by the redness of her cheeks, and the juice of the grape wishes to resemble (*in flavour*) the moisture of her lips. For her, beauty is well adapted and has always been so; and real worth has always been adapted to (*the character of*) Ibn Matrúh.

Ibn Matrúh was born at Usyút on Monday, the 8th of Rajab, 592 (8th June, A. D. 1196); he died in Old Cairo on the eve of Wednesday, the 1st of Shaabán, 649 (19th October, A. D. 1251) and was buried at the foot of Mount Mukattam. I was present at the funeral service and the interment. One of his last injunctions was that the following quatrain (*dú-bait*), composed by himself during his last illness, should be inscribed on the headstone of his grave :

I am deposited, like a pledge, in the bottom of an excavation, possessing no other worldly goods than a shroud. O thou who includest all thy servants in thy mercy, I am one of thy servants who were sinners.

It is stated that, when he had breathed his last, a paper, on which were written the following lines, was found under his head :

Why standest thou in such terror of death, since the mercy of the Lord may always be hoped for? Hadst thou been guilty of every crime which mortals ever committed, the mercy of God can extend over them all.

The chief kádi Dadr ad-Dín Yúsuf, he of whom we have spoken above, died in Cairo on Saturday, the 14th of Rajab, 663 (14th June, A. D. 1265), and was interred in the mausoleum which bears his name and lies near the mosque founded by him in the lesser Karáfa cemetery. He told me more than once, that he was born in the mountains near the town of Arbela and that he drew his descent from a *zerzár* (or Greek patrician). — *Usyût* is a town in Upper Egypt; some persons suppress the first letter of the name and pronounce it *Suyût*.

(1) According to other accounts, saint Louis took Damietta on the 23nd of Safar (8th June).

(2) The translator may have perhaps mistaken the meaning of this verse.

(3) These two letters form the word *má*, which signifies *water*.

(4) The meaning of these words is : on whom all eyes are fixed. The same idea is similarly expressed by al-Mutanabbi in a verse which is given in the next page.

(5) There is here an allusion to Ibn Khallikán's title of Shams ad-Dín (*the sun of religion*). By the moon is perhaps meant the kádi Sinán who, as we have seen, bore the title of Badr ad-Dín (*the moon of religion*).

(6) The primitive signification of the Turkish word *yalak* is *bed*.

(7) These are the names of two places in Arabia, but they signify also *sweet water* and *fastling*, by which terms poets sometimes designate the moisture of the lips and the whiteness of the teeth.

(8) To obtain the measure and the meaning of this verse, we must read *yaḍru* ـــ .

(9) For the history of Zuhair, the author of one of the *Moallakas*, see Caussin de Perceval's *Essai sur l'Histoire des Arabes*, tome II, page 327 et seq.

IBN JAZLA

Abû Ali Yahya Ibn Isa Ibn Jazla, the physician, was the author of the *Kitáb el-Minháj*, a work drawn up in alphabetical order and containing the names of plants, drugs, medicaments, etc., in great quantity. He was a Christian, but became a Moslim and then composed an epistle in which he confuted the Christians, exposed the foulness of their doctrines and extolled Islamism. In it he set forth arguments to prove that the latter was the true religion and adduced passages which he had read in the Pentateuch and the Gospel and which spoke of the apparition of Muhammad as a prophet to be sent by God. (*According to him, these passages*) were concealed by the Jews and the Christians, who never made them public and whose turpitudes he then enumerates. It is an elegant epistle and displays great talent. In the month of Zû 'l-Hijja, 485 (January, A. D. 1093), it was read (*by students*) under his direction (1). The manner of his conversion was, that he went to study (logic?) under Abù Ali Ibn al-Walid the Motazelite, whose lessons he attended assiduously and who never ceased exhorting him to embrace Islamism, adducing evident proofs which attested the truth of that religion. This continued till God directed him, and he then became a good musulman. He studied medicine under Abù 'l-Hasan Said Ibn Hibat Allah Ibn al-Husain (2) and profited by that doctor's tuition. He possessed a superficial knowledge of polite literature and wrote a good hand. A great number of works were composed by him for the imàm (khalif) al-Muktadi bi-amr Illah, such as the Takwìm al-Abdàn (regimen of the body), the Minhàj al-Baiyàn etc. (highway of exposition, treating of the (plants and simples) made use of by man), the Ishàra fì talkhìs il-Ibàra (indication concerning the abridgment of the Ibàra (3), an epistle in praise of the medical art, demonstrating its accordance with the divine law and refuting the attacks directed against it, an epistle addressed to Alya (Elias(?)) the priest, when he (the author) became a Moslim. There are other works of his besides the above. He was one of those doctors who were famous for their theoretical knowledge of medicine and for the practise of that art. Abù 'l-Muzaffer Yùsuf Sibt Ibn al-Jauzi (vol. I. p. 439) mentions him in the historical work entitled Miràt az-Zamàn, and says: " When he became a Moslim, Abù " 'l-Hasan, who was then kàdi of Baghdad, deputed to him the task of engrossing " the judgements pronounced in court. He (Ibn Jazla) acted as doctor to the " inhabitants of his quarter and the persons of his acquaintance; he took from " them no retribution and carried to them gratuitously the potions and medicines " which they required. He sought out poor people and made them the objects of " his charity. Some time before his death, he made a wakf (4) of his books and " deposited them in the mash-hed (or funeral chapel) of Abù Hanifa (vol. III. p. 555)." — All this is mentioned under the year 493 (A. D. 1099-1100), and it was customary with that historian to place each of his biographical notices under the year in which the individual died; his book being drawn up in the form of annals. The author of the work entitled Aïtàb al-Bustàn al-Jàmé li-tawàrìkh az-Zamàn (the Garden, being a collection of historical dates) (5) states that Ibn Jazla died in the year 493, and Abù 'l-Hasan Ibn al-Hamadàni (vol. I. p. 280) informs us, besides, that his death occurred towards the end of Shaabàn (beginning of July, 1100). This indication is borrowed from him by Ibn an-Najjàr in the History of Baghdad (vol. I. p. 11). Another author states that his conversion to Islamism took place in the year 466, to which Ibn an-Najjàr adds: " On Tuesday, the 11th of the latter Jumàda

(11th February, A. D. 1074).—*Jazla* is to be pronounced with an *a* after the *j*; it takes no vowel after the *z*, but the *l* is followed by an *a*.

(1) The Arabic may also signify : " it was read (*before witnesses, so that it might serve as a proof*) against " him (*in case he relapsed*)." This may, perhaps, be what Ibn Khallikân, or his authority, meant.

(2) Said Ibn Hibat Allah, a celebrated doctor of Baghdad, was employed between the years 470-500 (A. D. 1077-1106), as physician to the khalifs al-Muktadi and al-Mustazhir Billah. Some of his pupils, such as Ibn Jazla, Abhad az-Zaman and Ibn at-Talmid, became highly distinguished.—(Wüstenfeld's *Arabische Aerzte*, n° 140).

(3) The *Irshad* and the *Tabra* treated probably of medicine; Hâjji Khalîfa does not indicate them in his Bibliographical dictionary.

(4) See vol. I, p. 69.

(5) This work is not noticed by Hâjji Khalîfa.

_____

SHIHAB AD-DIN AS-SUHRAWARDI

Abû 'l-Futûh Yahya Ibn Habash Ibn Amirek, surnamed Shihâb ad-Dîn (*flambeau of religion*), was a native of Suhraward and a philosopher; the same who was put to death at Aleppo. Some say that his name was Ahmad (*not Yahya*), and others assert that the surname Abû 'l-Futûh was his real name. Abû 'l-Abbas Ahmad Ibn Abi Osaibia al-Khazraji (1), the philosopher who composed the work called *Tabakât al-Atibba* (*classified dictionary of medical men*), gives to this Suhrawardi the name of Omar and does not mention that of his father. The true name is, however, the one which I have indicated, and I have therefore placed his article here (*among the Yahyas*). I found in the handwriting of some persons versed in this branch of science (*biography*) that such was his name, and I received the same information from a number of others, the exactness of whose knowledge could not be doubted. That fortified my opinion and led me to place as-Suhrawardi's article here.—He was one of the most learned men of that age. He studied philosophy and the fondamentals of jurisprudence under the *shaikh* Majd ad-Dîn al-Jîli, who was then teaching in the city of Marâgha, one of the governments in Adarbaijân, and he continued with him

till he attained pre-eminence in these two sciences. This Majd ad-Dín al-Jílí was
the professor under whom Fakhr ad-Dín ar-Rázi (vol. II. p. 652) studied with such
profit and completed his education; he was considered as a great master (imám) in
all those branches of science. The author of the *Tabakát al-Atibbá* says, in that
work : " As-Suhrawardi was the first man of his time in the philosophical sciences,
" all of which he knew perfectly well. In the science of the fundamentals of
" jurisprudence he stood pre-eminent; he was gifted with great acuteness of mind
" and the talent of expressing his thoughts with precision. His learning was
" greater than his judgment." He then states that he was put to death towards the
close of the year 586; at the age of thirty-six years. At the end of this article we
shall give the true date of his death. After this, he says : " It is reported that he
" was acquainted with the art of *símía* (*natural magic*), and the following anecdote
" was related by a Persian philosopher who happened to travel with him from
" Damascus : ' When we reached al-Kábún, a village which lies near the gate
" ' of Damascus, on the road leading to Aleppo, we came up to some Turkomans
" ' who had with them a flock of sheep. We said to the *shaikh* (*as-Suhrawardi*) :
" ' Master! we would like to have one of those sheep to eat (2).' He replied : ' I
" ' have with me ten dirhems (6 *shillings*); take them and buy a sheep.' We
" ' bought one from a Turkoman and proceeded on our journey, but we had not
" ' gone far whom a companion of this herdsman came up to us and said : ' Give
" ' back the sheep and take a smaller one ; for that fellow (*whom you got it from*)
" ' did no know how to sell it to you; this sheep is worth more than the sum
" ' given for it.' We talked with him on the subject, and the *shaikh* said to us, on
" ' perceiving what was going on : ' Take the sheep and walk off with it; I shall
" ' , stay with the man and give him satisfaction.' We proceeded on our way whilst
" ' the *shaikh* entered into conversation with the fellow, endeavouring to tranquil-
" ' lize him. When we had got to a short distance, he left him and followed
" ' us. The Turkoman ran after him, calling out to him to stop, but the *shaikh*
" ' did not mind him. Finding that could get no answer, he ran up to the *shaikh*
" ' in a passion and pulled him by the left arm, exclaiming : ' Do you mean to go
" ' ' away and leave me thus?' The arm separated from the shoulder and remained
" ' in his hand, with the blood running out. Astounded at the sight, and for-
" ' getful of what he was about, the Turkoman threw down the arm in terror.
" ' The *shaikh* turned back to the arm, took it up with his right hand and then

" ' followed us. The other continued to retreat, and the *shaikh* kept looking at
" ' him till he disappeared. When he came up to us, we saw in his right hand
" ' a towel and nothing else.' " —A great number of similar anecdotes are related
of him, but God knows if they be true. He composed some works, such as the
Tankíhát (*enucleations*), treating of the fundamentals of jurisprudence, the *Talwíhát*
(*elucidations*), the *Kitáb al-Haiákil* (*book of temples*) (3), the *Kitáb Hikma til-Ishrák*
(*the philosophy of illuminism*) (4), an epistle entitled : *al-Ghurba tal-Gharíba* (*extraordinary peregrination* (?)) and drawn up on the plan of Avicena's *Epistle of the bird*
(see vol. I. p. 443) and on that of the *Hai Ibn Yakzán* composed by the same author (5). This epistle, which is elegantly written, treats of (*what is called*) the
discourse of the mind (i. e. *its ambitious suggestions*) and whatever, in the system of
the philosophers, is connected with that subject. Here are some of his sayings :
" Let your reflection be turned towards such an image of sanctity as may be a gra-
" tification to the seeker of enjoyment." —" The tracts of sanctity are an abode on
" whose (*floor*) the ignorant cannot tread." —" For the bodies darkened (*by sin*),
" the realm of the heavens is forbidden. Declare therefore the unity of God and
" be filled with veneration for him; remember him, for you are naked, though
" clothed in the raiment of existence." — " Were there two suns in the world, its
" columns would be destroyed." — " The order (*of nature*) refuses to be otherwise
" than it is."

" I hid myself and said : ' I am not visible;' and by my effort, I let myself be seen by all
" things that have being." —" If I was sure that we (*and God*) were never to meet, I should
" satisfy my passion in the enjoyment of Salma (6)."

" I implore thee, O Lord! to deliver my subtle part (*the soul*) from this dense (or
" *material world*)." —Some poems are attributed to him, one of which is on the soul
and in the same style as the verses rhyming in *aín* which were composed by al-Husain Ibn Sina and which we inserted in his article (vol. I. p. 443). This philosopher (as-*Suhrawardi*) said (*on the subject*) :

*   She divested herself of the temple (*the body*) at the sand-hill of the park (*the world*), and aspired with ardour to regain her former abode. Impelled by passionate desire, she turned towards that dwelling-place, that vernal residence of which even the crumbling ruins had disappeared. She stopped to question it, and the echo (or screech-owl) replied : " There is no way
(to effect) your meeting." She is like a flash of lightning glimmering over the park, and then
disappearing, as if it had not gleamed.

A well known piece of his is the following :

Our souls are always turned towards you with tender affection; to meet with you would be
their company and their wine (7). The hearts of your lovers yearn for you and aspire after the
pleasure of that meeting. O how lovers are to be pitied! they must conceal their feelings, and
yet their passion betrays them. If they let their secret be known, they risk the shedding of
their life's blood; for this only is shed the blood of lovers. Whilst they hide (their feelings),
flowing tears tell their secret to the jealous spies. The symptoms of (love's) malady appear in
their looks, and that suffices to dispel every doubt concerning them. (Your devoted lover humbly) abstains the wing before you; it would be no crime in you to abase the wing (with indulgence) before him. To meet with you, his heart is always yearning; to please you, his eyes
are ever watchful. Replace the darkness of your cruelty by the light of your kindness; your
aversion is night, and your benevolence is day. She (the beloved) acted sincerely towards her
lovers, and their hearts were sincere towards her; the light (shining) from those (hearts) was
like a lamp burning in a niche. Their desires are ardent; the hour favours your approach;
clear is the wine and clear are the goblets (for the feast). My friend ! the lover is not to be
blamed if the morning ablow (if his joy appears) in the horizon of (happy) meeting; lovers
are not in fault if their ardour overcomes their secrecy, so that their passion is increased and
they reveal it. In risking their lives, they were prodigal, not sparing; for they knew that
such prodigality was (followed by) success. The herald of (mysterious) truths called unto them
and, from morning till evening, they continued obedient to that call. Whilst they rode along
the way of fidelity, their tears formed an ocean on which the seamen were their passionate desires. By Allah ! they sought not permission to approach the door of the beloved, till they were
invited thither and had received the key. Never do they find pleasure in discourse of which the
beloved is not the subject; all their time is therefore (continual) happiness. They appeared in
the (beloved one's) presence, though every sign which could attest the existence of their persons
had disappeared and, when they saw the beloved, they stood revealed and uttered a loud cry.
He (the beloved) annihilated them from before him; the veils of existence which shaded them
were removed and their souls were dissolved (H). Try to resemble them, if you are not like
them; to resemble the generous (brings) good success. Arise, my boon companion ! and bring
the wine in its cup; for the goblets have already passed round; (let it be the produce) of the vine
of nobleness (drawn) from the tun of piety; let it not be such wine as has been trod out by the
husbandman.

He left some other elegant pieces, in prose and in verse; but we need not length-
en this article by inserting them. He was a follower of the rite introduced by as-
Sháfi (vol. II. p. 569) and had received the title of al-Murid bal-Malakút (the aspirant
who desires the sight of the divine glory). He was suspected of holding heretical
opinions, of disbelieving in God and of following the system professed by the philosophers of ancient times. These suspicions became so general that, when he arrived
in Aleppo, the ulemá of the city issued a fetwa in which they declared that he might
be slain with impunity; so pernicious did his opinions appear to them. The most
ardent of the assembly for his condemnation were the two shaikhs Zain ad-Dîn and

Majd ad-Dîn, the sons of Jahyel. The shaikh Saif ad-Dîn al-Aamidi (vol. II. p. 235) relates as follows : " I met with as-Suhrawardi in Aleppo, and he said to me that " he should certainly become master of the earth. I asked him how he learned that, " and he replied : ' In] a dream ; methought I drank up the waters of the ocean.' " I observed to him that the dream might signify being celebrated for learning, or " something of that kind ; but I saw that he would not give up the idea which he " had in his mind. It seemed to me that he possessed great learning and little " judgment. "—It is related that when he was convinced that he should be put to death, he often recited these lines :

I see that my foot has shed my blood ; my blood is now worthless ; alas ! of what avail was my repentance?

The idea in the first hemistich is borrowed from Abû 'l-Fath Ali Ibn Muhammad al-Busti (vol. II. p. 314), who said :

My foot bore me towards my death ; I see that my foot has shed my blood ; I did not cease to repent, but repentance has been useless to me.

This occurred in the reign of the sultan al-Malik az-Zàhir (vol. II, p. 443), son of the sultan Salàh ad-Din (Saladin) and sovereign of Aleppo. As-Suhrawardi was imprisoned by his order and then strangled, in pursuance to the sultan Salàh ad-Din's advice. It was in the castle of Aleppo, on the 5th of Rajab, 587 (29th July, A. D. 1191) that the execution took place. As-Suhrawardi was then eight and thirty years of age. Bahà ad-Dîn Ibn Shaddàd, the kàdi of Aleppo, speaks of him, towards the commencement of his Life of Salàh ad-Din (9). After mentioning how orthodox that sultan was in his belief, he enters into a long discourse in which he praises him for the scrupulous observance of his religious duties and then adds : " He ordered " his son, the sovereign of Aleppo, to put to death a youth just grown up, whom they " called as-Suhrawardi and who was said to be an adversary of the divine law. " (Az-Zàhir) had him arrested as soon as he was told of it, and acquainted his father " with the circumstance. The latter ordered the prisoner to be put to death, which " was done." The body was exposed on a cross during some days. Sibt Ibn al-Jauzi (vol. I. p. 439) has inserted in his historical work the following statement, which had been made by the same Addi, Ibn Shaddàd : " On Friday, the 29th of " Zù 'l-Hijja, 587 (17th January, A. D. 1192), after the hour of prayer, the corpse " of Shihàb ad-Din as-Suhrawardi was carried out of the prison of Aleppo, and all "the partisans of that man dispersed and left him." I must here add that, when I was residing in Aleppo, where I passed some years, studying the noble science (the divine law), a great difference of opinion existed among the inhabitants respecting the character of as-Suhrawardi. Each of them spoke according to the dictates of his fancy : some declared him to have been a Zendik (10) and an infidel; others took him for a saint and one of those favoured persons who were gifted with miraculous powers; they said also that, after his death, they had witnessed things (prodigies) which justified their opinion. But the public, in general, considered him to have been an infidel who believed in nothing (11). May God pardon us our sins, grant us health (of mind) and preserve us from evil in this world and the next! may he permit us to die in the belief of those who know the truth and are rightly directed! — The date of his death given here is the true one, though it disagrees with that which I inserted, on another authority, in the beginning of this article. According to a third statement, his execution took place in the year 588, but that indication is of no value. — Both syllables of Habash are pronounced with an a. — Amirek is a Persian word signifying petty emir; that people add the letter k to the end of nouns in order to form the diminutives. — We have already spoken of Suhrawardi in our article on the shaikh Abû Najîb Abd al-Kâhir as-Suhrawardi (vol. II. p. 150), and to that we refer the reader.

(1) Abû 'l-Abbâs Ahmad Ibn al-Kâsim Ibn Khalîfa Ibn Abi Osaibia (اسم), surnamed Muwaffak ad-Din and a member of the Arabic tribe of Khazraj, was born in Damascus, where his father was an oculist and his uncle, Rashîd ed-Dîn Abû 'l-Hasan Ali, director of the hospital for the treatment of the maladies of the eyes. He studied philosophy under Rîfa ad-Dîn al-Jîli, and profited greatly by the lessons of Abû Muhammad Abd Allah Ibn Ahmad Ibn al-Baitâr, with whom he made a number of botanical excursions. Ibn al-Baitâr is the author of the Dictionary of Simples, a deservedly celebrated compilation of which Dr. Sontheimer published a German translation, at Stuttgard, in the year 1840. Ibn Abi Osaibia kept up for some time an epistolary correspondence with the celebrated physician and philosopher, Abd al-Latîf. In the year 634 (A. D. 1236-7), he got an appointment in the hospital founded at Cairo by the sultan Salâh ad-Dîn (Saladin). Some years after, he accompanied the emir Izz ad-Dîn Aidmor to Sarkhad, in Syria, and he died there, aged upwards of seventy years. His history of the physicians, entitled Oyûn al-Anbâ fi Tabakât al-Atibbâ (sources of information concerning the physicians of divers classes), contains a number of curious and highly interesting articles. The list of its chapters has been given by Mr. Wüstenfeld in his Geschichte der Arabischen Aerzte, No. 237, and from that work are taken the indications given here. In the catalogue of the Bodleian library, tome II. p. 131 et seq. will be also found this list of chapters.

(2) The Arabic text has here, and farther on, " a head of sheep "; the word " head " is employed also in English to designate one individual of a species; we say : three head of oxen. In Arabic historians we some-

times meet with the expression : " he brought back many bands of prisoners," which means simply : many prisoners. In Turkish and in Persian, expressions of this kind are very common; " three chains of elephant " means three elephants.

(3) This work was probably a treatise on mysticism.

(4) For the signification of the word *wârid* see my French translation of Ibn Khaldûn's *Prolegomena*, tome III. p. 167.

(5) Another work bearing the title of Hai Ibn Yakzân (or Yakdhân) was composed by Ibn Tufail and published by Pocock.

(6) That is : were I sure that there was no future life, I should indulge in sensual pleasures during this life. —The preceding sentences are evidently borrowed from the Sûfis.

(7) All this piece has a mystic import : the beloved is God.

(8) The ultra-sûfi doctrine of the soul's being absorbed into God and of its then losing the consciousness of its individuality is openly declared in this verse.

(9) See Schultens's *Vita et res gestæ Saladini*, pag. 7.

(10) The followers of Zoroaster's doctrine were called *Zendiks* by the Musulmans; for them, this term is the equivalent of infidel.

(11) As-Sohrawardi was evidently a Sûfi, and very far advanced in pantheistical speculations.

ABU JAAFAR *THE KORAN-READER*

Abû Jaafar Yazîd Ibn al-Kakâa, the *reader* (1), was a *mawla*, by enfranchisement (2) of Abd Allah Ibn Aiyâsh Ibn Abi Rabîa al-Makhzûmi (3), and bore the surname of al-Madani (*the inhabitant of Medina*). He learned the manner of reading the Korân from Abd Allah Ibn Abbâs (*vol. I. p.* 89), by reciting it under his direction (عرض), and received instructions on the same subject from his patron, Ibn Aiyâsh, and from Abû Huraira (*vol. I. p.* 570). He heard it read by Abd Allah, the son of Omar Ibn al-Khattâb (*vol. I. p.* 567), and by Marwân Ibn al-Hakam (*afterwards, the fourth Omaiyide khalif*). It is said that he read the Korân under Zaid Ibn Thâbit (*vol. I. p.* 372). Korân-reading was taught on his authority by Nâfê Ibn Abd ar-Rahmân Ibn Abi Noaim (*vol. III. p.* 522), Sulaimân Ibn Muslim Ibn Jammâz (4), Isa Ibn Wardân (5) and Abd ar-Rahmân Ibn Ziâd Ibn Aslam. He is the author of a system of readings. Abû Abd ar-Rahmân an-Nasâi (*vol. I p.* 58) said : " Yazîd Ibn al-Kakâa is a sure authority. He taught korân-reading

" to the people in Medina before the catastrophy of al-Harra (6)."—Muhammad
Ibn al-Kâsim al-Mâliki said : "Abû Jaafar Yazîd Ibn al-Kakâa was a mawla of Omm
" Salama, one of the Prophet's wives." He said also : "Some say that he was the
" same person as Jundub Ibn Fîrûz, a mawla of Abd Allah Ibn Aiyâsh al-Makhzûmi,
" and that he was a most holy man."—Sulaimân Ibn Muslim said : "Abû Jaafar
" Yazîd Ibn al-Kakâa informed me that he taught korân-reading in the mosque of
" the Prophet at Medina, before the affair of al-Harra; and that battle (said he)
" took place towards the end (7) of the year 63, in counting from the time of the
" Prophet's arrival in Medina (8). He told me that he used to hold the (sacred)
" volume before his patron, Ibn Abbas (for him to read it). He was an excellent
" reader. Every day, I used to look over what he read (to us) and (thus) learned
" from him his system of reading. He related to me that, when he was a child,
" they brought him to Omm Salama, who stroked his head and invoked God's
" blessing on him."—"I asked him," said the same Sulaimân, "at what time
" he commenced korân-reading?" and he said to me : "Do you mean teaching it
" ' or learning it?' I answered : 'Teaching it;' and he replied : 'O! it was long
" ' before al-Harra; in the days of Yazîd Ibn Moawia (the second Omaiyide khalif).'
" The battle of al-Harra was fought fifty-three years after the death of the Prophet."
—Nâfê Ibn Abi Noaim said : "When the body of Abû Jaafar Yazîd Ibn al-Kakâa,
" the reader, was washed after his death, they perceived that all the space from the
" neck to the heart was (smooth and white) like a leaf of the Korân, and every one
" present was convinced that it was the light of the Korân (which had produced that
" appearance)." Sulaimân Ibn Muslim related as follows : "Yazîd Ibn al-Kakâa
" told me that, when Nâfê passed near him, he would say : 'Do you see that fellow?
" ' when a boy still wearing long hair, he used to come and read (the Korân) under
" ' my direction, but he afterwards treated me with ingratitude.' In relating this, he
" laughed." Sulaimân said also : "The concubine of Abû Jaafar declared that the
" whiteness which reached from his neck to his heart became (afterwards) a white
" spot between his eyes." He related again as follows : "I saw Abû Jaafar in a
" dream, after his death. He appeared to be on the top of the Kaaba, and I said :
" ' Is that Abû Jaafar?' He replied : 'It is I; offer to my brethren a salutation
" ' from me and tell them that God has placed me among the living witnesses who
" ' obtain regularly a portion (of the divine favour). Offer my salutation to Abû
" ' Hâzim (9) and tell him that Abû Jaafar says to him : 'Prudence! prudence!

" ' for Almighty God and his angels are present, every evening, at your sittings.' "
— Mâlik Ibn Anas (*vol. II. p. 515*) said : " Abû Jaafar the reader was a holy man
" and acted as *mufti* (*casuist*) for the people of Medina."— Khalifa Ibn Khaiyât
(*vol. I. p. 492*) said : " Abû Jaafar Yazîd Ibn al-Kakâa died at Medina in the year
" 132 (A. D. 719-750)." According to another tradition, he died in the year 128.
Abû Ali 'l-Ahwâzi (10) says, towards the commencement of his treatise on the
readings entitled *al-Iknâa* (*the satisfactory*) : " Ibn al-Jammâz said that Abû Jaafar
" never ceased to be for the people their *imâm* (*great master*) in Korân-reading, till
" the year 133, when he died at Medina. Some say that his death took place in the
" year 130, but God knows best."— As al-Harra has been mentioned in this article
more than once and as some readers, not knowing anything about it, may wish to
obtain information on the subject, I shall here say that the word *harra* (حرّة), in its
primitive signification, designates every spot of ground which is covered with black
stones. A tract of this kind is called a *harra* (*the plural of which is* hirâr); there are
a great number of hirârs. That which is here mentioned is the *Harra* of *Wâkim*,
which lies near Medina, to the east of the town. When Yazîd the son of Moawîa
Ibn Abi Sofyân held the supreme authority, he dispatched against Medina an army
commanded by Muslim Ibn Ocba al-Murri. That chief sacked the place, and the
inhabitants, who had gone out to this harra, engaged in a battle the details of which
would take us too long to relate; besides, they are to be found in the books of
annals (11). It is said that, after the catastrophy of al-Harra, upwards of one thousand unmarried girls of Medina gave birth to children, in consequence of the infamous treatment which they had undergone. When Muslim Ibn Ocba had massacred the inhabitants of Medina, he set out for Mekka and was seized by death
at a place called the Thaniya (*or defile of*) Harsha (حرشة). On this, he called in
Hosain (حسين) Ibn Numair as-Sakûni and said to him : " Come here, you ass (12)!
" you are to know that the Commander of the faithful ordered me, in case I was on
" the point of death, to give you the command; and now, that I am dying, I am
" unwilling to disobey him (*though I ought to do so*) (13)." He then prescribed to
him a number of things which he should execute, after which he said : " If I go to
" the fire (*of hell*) after (*my good action of*) having slain the people of al-Harra, I
" shall be very unfortunate indeed!"— Wâkim (وَاكِم) is the name of one of the
otoms of Medina. Al-Otom (الأطم) is a building like a castle and situated near al-
Harra; that place was (*usually*) called the *Harra* of *Wâkim* (14).

(1) In the first century of Islamism, the true manner of reading the Koran could only be learned by oral instruction. The reason of this has been already given, vol. I, p. 162.

(2) See the introduction to the second volume, page ix.

(3) Abû 'l-Hârith Abd Allah Ibn Aiyâsh Ibn Abi Rabîa al-Makhzûmi, the Koran-reader, is said to have seen the prophet. He learned the readings from some of the prophet's companions and taught them to a great number of other persons. It is stated that he was killed, in the service of God, A. H. 78 (A. D. 697-8), in Sijistân; but, by another account, he lost his life subsequently to the year 70. — (Tabakât al-Kurrâ, MS. of the Bib. imp., ancien fonds, n° 748, fol. 8). — The author of the Nujûm says that he was killed in India, A. H. 48 (A. D. 668-9).

(4) The reader, Abû 'r-Rabî (الربيع) Sulaimân Ibn Muslim Ibn Jammâz was a mawla of the tribe of Zuhra and a native of Medina. He generally followed the system of reading adopted by Nâfi. — (Tab. al-Kurrâ, fol. 84 verso. The date of his death is not given.)

(5) Abû 'l-Hârith Isa Ibn Wardân al-Haddâ (الحذّاء, the camel-driver) was a native of Medina and a reader. He died probably before Nâfi. — (Tab. al-Kurrâ, fol. 85 verso.)

(6) Farther on, our author speaks again of the battle of al-Harra.

(7) The Arabic expression râs as-sina (the head of the year) means the end of the year. Ibn Khaldûn designates the end of a century by the words râs al-miya.

(8) The battle of al-Harra was fought towards the end of the last month of the Moslem year. According to Abû 'l-Fedâ, in his Annals, it took place on the 27th of Zû 'l-Hijja, A. H. 63 (27th of August, A. D. 683).

(9) By the surname of Abû Hâzim may perhaps be meant a disciple of Muhammad's companions and a Traditionist of good repute whose name was Abû Hâzim Salama Ibn Dinâr. He was a native of Medina and a mawla of the tribe of Khazrâj. He died A. H. 135 (A. D. 752-3), according to an-Nawawi, in his Tahdîb (Wüstenfeld's edition), or, in 140, according to the author of the Tabakât al-Huffâz.

(10) According to Hajji Khalîfa, in his bibliographical Dictionary, the author of this treatise on the Koran-readings which bears the title of al-Hudâ, was Abû Ali Hasan Ibn Ali al-Ahwâzi, who died A. H. 446 (A. D. 1054-5).

(11) See Abû 'l-Fedâ's Annals, tome I, p. 395, and Dozy's Histoire des Musulmans d'Espagne, tome I, p. 199 et seq. where a full and satisfactory account of this battle is given.

(12) Literally : You ass' packsaddle!

(13) See Dozy's Hist. des Musulmans d'Espagne, tome I, page 197.

(14) The text of this passage is probably incorrect; if translated literally, it would signify : which place was therefore called the Harra of Wâkim. It is here rendered in a manner which excludes the absurdity.

YAZID IBN RUMAN, THE KORAN-READER

Abû Rûh Yazid Ibn Rûmân, the Korân-reader (1), was a *maula* of the family of az-Zubair Ibn al-Awwâm (vol. *II. p.* 199) and a native of Medina. He learned how to recite the Korân correctly by reading it aloud under the direction of Abd Allah Ibn Aiyâsh Ibn Abi Rabîa al-Makhzûmi (*see page 162 of this volume*), and he heard it read by Ibn Abbâs (vol. *I. p.* 89) and Orwa Ibn az-Zubair (vol. *II. p.* 199). Korân-reading was learned from him by Nâfê Ibn Abi Noaim (vol. *III. p.* 522), who read aloud the text under his direction. Yahya Ibn Main (*see page 24 of this col.*) declared that Yazid Ibn Rûmân was a sure authority. Wahb Ibn Jarîr (2) stated that his father related to him as follows: "I saw Muhammad Ibn Sirîn (vol. *II.* "p. 586) and Yazid Ibn Rûmân counting on their fingers the number of verses "from the Korân which they recited during the prayer (3)." Yazid Ibn Rûmân related as follows: "I was praying by the side of Nâfê, the son of Jubair Ibn "Mutim (4), and he made me a sign to prompt him; and we were then praying (5)". He stated also that, in the time of (*the khalif*) Omar Ibn al-Khattâb, the people made twenty-three prostrations during the prayer, when they were in the month of Ramadân (6). Yazid Ibn Rûmân died in the year 130 (A. D. 747-8).

(1) See vol. I, p. 111, note 1.

(2) Abû 'l-Abbâs Wahb Ibn Jarîr, a traditionist of Basra, died A. H. 206 (A. D. 821-2). (*Tabakât al-Huffâz Nujûm.*)

(3) When the Musulman performs the ceremonies of the canonical prayer, he must recite, in a low voice, at least three verses of the Korân. Devotees repeat even a whole chapter or a considerable number of verses, ten, twenty, one hundred, etc., each time. It appears from the anecdote here related, that counting on the fingers the number of the verses, as they are recited, was authorized by the example of two very eminent doctors, although it was probably considered as an irregular proceeding.

(4) The Kuraishide, Jubair Ibn Mutim an-Naufali, one of the Companions, embraced Islamism subsequently to the battle of Badr, and then accompanied Muhammad in some of his expeditions. His authority as a Traditionist is acknowledged by al-Bukhâri and Muslim. He was one of the most learned of the Kuraishide chiefs. His death took place at Medina, A. H. 54 (A. D. 673-4), according to the author of the Nujûm, and of the Tahdîb al-Asmâ. — Nâfê, the son of Jubair, was considered as an *imám* of great merit and a learned and sure Traditionist. He died A. H. 99 (A. D. 717-8). — (*Tahdîb.*)

(5) This anecdote seems adduced to prove that the Musulman, in reciting a portion of the Korân during the prayer, may have himself prompted by his neighbours, in case his memory fail him.

(6) These prostrations are made in addition to those which are required in the ordinary form of prayer. The Hanifites make twenty; the Shafites, thirty-six. We learn here that, in the time of Omar, twenty-three was the usual number.

YAZID IBN AL-MUHALLAB

Abû Khâlid Yazîd al-Azdi was the son of al-Muhallab Ibn Abi Sofra. We have already mentioned his father, under the letter *M* (vol. *III*, p. 508), and, as we have there traced up and spoken of his genealogy, we need not repeat our observations here. Ibn Kutaiba (vol. *II*. p. 22) states, in his *Kitâb al-Madrif*, and a number of other historians also relate as follows : "Al-Muhallab, on dying, designated "Yazîd as his successor. The latter was then thirty years of age. Abd al-"Malik Ibn Marwân (*the Omaiyide khalif*) dismissed Yazîd from office by the advice "of al-Hajjâj Ibn Yûsuf ath-Thakefi (vol. *I*. p. 356), and appointed in his place, as "governor of Khorâsân, Kutaiba Ibn Muslim al-Bâhili (vol. *II*. p. 514). Yazîd then "fell into the hands of al-Hajjâj." I must here make some observations: Al-Hajjâj, who was married to Hind, the sister of Yazîd and the daughter of al-Muhallab, had conceived a great dislike for his brother-in-law, as he apprehended, from what he saw of his noble character, that the place which he then filled might, one day, be occupied by Yazîd. So, to protect himself against his attacks, he never ceased to evil-entreat him. He was always consulting astrologers and other persons who cultivated the art (*of divination*), in order to learn by whom he should be succeeded, and they used to answer: "By a man named Yazîd." He was then governor of the two Irâks and saw no one capable of replacing him in that office except this Yazîd. And thus it fell out; on his death, Yazîd obtained the command. So say the historians. Let us now resume our extract from the *Madrif* and finish it. "Al-Hajjâj inflicted tortures on Yazîd, who at length escaped from prison and went "to see Sulaimân Ibn Abd al-Malik, who was then in Syria. That prince inter-

" ceded with his brother (the khalif) al-Walid Ibn Abd al-Malik, and obtained a free
" pardon for Yazid. This put a stop to al-Hajjāj's conduct towards the latter.
" When Sulaimān obtained the khalifate, Yazid received from him the govern-
" ment of Khorāsān and then took (the cities of) Jurjān and Dihistān. Having
" set out for Irāk, he learned the death of Sulaimān Ibn Abd al-Malik and pro-
" ceeded to Basra, where he was arrested by Adi Ibn Artā (اِرْطَاة), who bound
" him in chains and sent him to Omar Ibn Abd al-Aziz. Yazid was imprisoned by
" that khalif, but, having effected his escape, he went to Basra. On the death of
" Omar, he revolted against the new khalif Yazid Ibn Abd al-Malik, who then sent
" against him his brother Maslama (Ibn Abd al-Malik). This general slew Yazid
" (on the field of battle)". — The hāfiz Abû 'l-Kāsim, generally known by the surname of Ibn Asākir (vol. II. p. 252), says, in his greater historical work : " Yazid,
" the son of al-Muhallab, had been appointed to govern Basra in the name of Su-
" laimān Ibn Abd al-Malik. Some time after, Omar Ibn Abd al-Aziz conceived a
" dislike for him and was still incensed against him when Adi Ibn Artā, to whom
" he had given the government of Basra, brought Yazid to him." — Yazid Ibn al-
Muhallab taught some traditions which he had learned from Anas Ibn Malik (vol. II.
p. 587), Omar Ibn Abd al-Aziz and his own father al-Muhallab. Traditions were
handed down on his authority by his son Abd ar-Rahmān, by Abû Oyaina, the son
of al-Muhallab, by Abû Isbak as-Sabil (vol. II. p. 392) and by others. — Al-Aamāi
(vol. II. p. 123) related that al-Hajjâj, having arrested Yazid Ibn al-Muhallab, inflicted on him grievous tortures and would not consent to suspend them unless he
received, every day, from the prisoner, the sum of one hundred thousand dirhems
(£ 2,500). When the money was not paid in, al-Hajjâj put Yazid again to the
torture, that very day, and continued to torment him till the night set in. One day,
Yazid had collected one hundred thousand dirhems, for the purpose of buying off
that day's tortures, when the poet al-Akhtal (1) came in to him and said :

> Abû Khâlid ! Khorāsân has perished since your departure, and the needy all exclaim :
> " Where is Yazid ?" Since you are gone, the two Marws have not received a drop of rain :
> not a tree is verdant in the two Marws. The throne of government has no splendour since your
> absence; beneficence has ceased, and there is no generous man to shower down his gifts.

By the two Marws, the poet meant Marw as-Shāhjān, which is the greater, and
Marw ar-Rûd, which is the less. They are both well-known cities of Khorāsān.

We have already spoken of them in this work (vol. *I. p.* 50).—"On this," says al-Asmái, "Yazid gave the poet the one hundred thousand dirhems, and al-Hajjáj, "being informed of the circumstance, sent for him and said: 'Native of Marw! "'art thou still so generous though in such a state? Well! I shall hold thee quit "'of the tortures of this day and of those which follow it.'" So the anecdote is related by Ibn Asákir, but the more received opinion is that the author of the verses, he to whom this happened, was al-Farazdak (vol. *III. p.* 612); and I since found the verses in the collected poetical works of Ziád al-Aajami *(vol. I. p.* 631). God knows best!—The same *háfis (Ibn Asákir)* related as follows: "When Yazid fled from al-"Hajjáj and went to find Sulaimán Ibn Abd al-Malik, who was then at ar-Ramla, "he passed, on his way through Syria, by the tents of some Arabs and said to his "servant boy: 'Go to those people and ask them to give us a drink of milk.' "When the milk was brought, he drank it and said: 'Give them one thousand "'dirhems (£·25).' The boy observed to him that these people did not know who "he was *(and that he need not give them so much)*; and he replied: 'But I know "'who I am; give them the thousand dirhems.' And that was done." The same author says: 'Yazid Ibn al-Muhallab made the pilgrimage and *(to conclude the* "*rites and ceremonies)* he sent for a barber to shave his head. When the ope-"ration was finished, he ordered him a recompense of one thousand dirhems. "The man was amazed and astounded, but at length said: 'With this sum I shall "'go and ransom from slavery my mother, such a one.' Yazid said: 'Give him "'another thousand.' The barber exclaimed: 'May my wife be divorced from "'me if I ever shave any one's head after this!'—'Give him two thousand more,' "said Yazid." Al-Madáini said: Said Ibn Amr Ibn al-Aási (2) bore a fraternal affection to Yazid Ibn al-Muhallab. When Omar Ibn Abd al-Azíz caused the latter to be imprisoned and gave orders that no person should be allowed to see him, Said went to him and said: "Commander of the faithful! Yazid owes me the sum of fifty thousand dirhems, but you hinder me from seeing him; will you per-"mit me to go and exact from him the payment?" The khalif consented, and Said entered into the chamber of Yazid, who was rejoiced to see him. "How did you "get in?" said he. Said informed him of the stratagem. "By Allah!" exclaimed Yazid, "you shall not go away without that sum." Said refused, but Yazid de-clared in the most solemn manner that he should accept the money and sent to

his house for fifty thousand dirhems which he gave to him. — Another author,
in relating this anecdote, adds: A poet said on that subject:

> I never saw a noble prisoner give presents to a visitor, except Yazid. He bestowed fifty
> thousand on Said (the Amr, who went to see him; and the money was paid down without de-
> lay to Said.

Abû 'l-Faraj al-Moâfi Ibn Zakariya an-Nahrawâni (vol. III. p. 374) relates, in his
Kitâb al-Anis wa 'l-Jalis, an anecdote which he learned from Abd Allah Ibn al-Kûfi
and which we insert here: Sulaimân Ibn Abd al-Malik (the Omaiyide khalif) required from Omar Ibn Hubaira (3) the payment of one million of dirhems (£. 25.000),
out of (what the latter had gained in) his expeditions on sea. Omar (not being able
to pay that sum) went to see Yazid Ibn al-Muhallab (4), who had been appointed
governor of Irâk, and took with him Othmân Ibn Haiyân al-Murri, al-Kakâa (القعقاع)
Ibn Khâlid al-Absi, al-Hudail Ibn Zufar al-Kilâbi and some other persons belonging
to (the tribe of) Kais. When they arrived at the door of Yazid's pavilion, the chamberlain obtained permission to introduce them (adana ishom al-hâjib) and informed
them that his master was washing his head. Yazid at length came in, threw
himself upon his bed and then said: "What has brought you all together?"
Othmân replied: "Here is our shaikh and master, Ibn Hubaira; al-Walid (the late
"khalif) furnished him with money and troops when he was about undertaking an
"expedition on sea, and a debt of one million of dirhems is now made out against
"him. We therefore said: Yazid is the chief of the Yemenites, the vizir of Su-
"laimân and the lord of al-Irâk; he has delivered from similar difficulties persons
"who were far from being similar to us. By Allah! if the wealth of the tribe of
"Kais had been sufficient, we should have taken the payment upon ourselves."
Al-Kakâa then spoke and said: "Son of al-Muhallab! this is an excellent affair
"sent to you by God, and no one deserves such a favour more than you. Act
"therein according to your former doings; let not stint or parcimony hinder you
"from fulfilling this duty; we have come to you with Ibn Hubaira, on account of
"a debt with which he is loaded. Give therefore to us our money and hide our
"shame from the Arabs." Al-Hudail Ibn Zufar then spoke as follows: "Son of
"al-Muhallab! had I found a pretext for not coming to you, now, that you have
"riches in Irâk, I should have staid away. You once came to us when you feared
"danger and you remained with us as a guest; did we then allow you to retire in

" sorrow? By the right hand of God I though we left (*neglected to visit*) you when you
" were in Syria, we have now come to you (*landtlannak*) in Irak; that (*distance*) is
" only a short step and renders indispensable the fulfilling of our duty (*towards*
" *you*)." Ibn Khaithama then spoke and said : "I shall not repeat to you, son
" of al-Muhallah! what the others have just said ; (*for their words would give me to*
" *understand*) that you (*anna anta*) are not strong enough to deliver Ibn Hubaira
" from his burden ; and on whom then could we count? By Allah ! the case is not
" so (*and I shall merely say that*) the tribe of Kais is not in a situation to help
" him ; their wealth is insufficient, and the khalif will grant him no respite." Ibn
Hubaira then spoke and said : " As for me, my affair is done if my request succeed,
" and (*I am done for*) if it be rejected ; since I find no one (*to whom I could think of*
" *applying*), either before or after you. This business did indeed preoccupy my
" mind, but (*I am convinced that*) you have already arranged it." On hearing
these words, Yazid laughed and said : " Hesitation is the brother of avarice ; there
" shall be no difficulties raised (*by me*) ; juge (*for yourselves and say how much you*
" *require*)." Al-Kakâa said : " The half of the sum," and Yazid replied : " I
" take charge of it. Boy ! let us see what there is for breakfast." The repast was
brought in and we (*said the narrator*) let our disappointment appear to him more
than we were aware of (*fankarna mdho akthar mamma arafna*). When we had finished (*falamma faraghna*), he ordered us to be perfumed and arrayed in handsome
robes. The narrator continues his recital thus : We then withdrew and, as we
passed (*the door*), Ibn Hubaira said : " Tell me who, after Ibn al-Muhallab, will take
" charge of paying the remainder? God has (*surely*) reduced your credit and your
" influence ! By Allah ! Yazid knows not the difference between half and whole ;
" for him, one is the same as the other. Go back and speak to him of what re-
" mains (*to be paid*)." The narrator continues in these terms : Yazid suspected
that they would come back to him for the entire sum, and he therefore told the
chamberlain to admit them, if they returned. When they came and were introduced, Yazid said to them : " If you regret your agreement, I shall cancel it, and if
" you think the sum which I offered too little, I shall increase it." Ibn Hubaira
then said : " Son of al-Muhallab ! when a camel is heavily loaded, his very ears are
" a weight for him, and I am heavily loaded with what remains for me to pay."
Yazid replied : " I take the whole burden on myself." He then rode to Sulaimân
and said : " Commander of the faithful ! you established me in authority for the

" purpose of attaining your ends through my means; I hesitate at nothing, as long
" as the money (which you furnish me) is sufficiently ample; but I have not now in
" my hands even the least trifle belonging to you, wherewithal I may render ser-
" vices (to the needy) and (thus) erect monuments of (your) generosity; were you not
" there to help me, the undertaking of the smallest thing would cripple me." He
then said : " Ibn Hubaira has come to see me, with his principal companions."
Sulaimán (here interrupted him and) said : " Take care and touch not the money
" which belongs to God (the money of the state); that man is all duplicity and
" cunning, a collector (of wealth) and a refuser (of it to others), a deceiver and a
" miser, a man to be avoided. And what did you do?" Yazíd answered : " I
" undertook to pay his debt (kál : hamalto ánho." — "(You were in the wrong),"
said Sulaimán; " you should have carried the money (kál : aḥmilo) to the public
" treasury." — " By Allah!" replied Yazíd, " I did not take charge of it with the
" intention of defrauding (the state); I shall carry the money to the treasury to-
" morrow." This he did, and Sulaimán, being informed of it, sent for him.
When he saw him (come in), he laughed and said : " It is for you that my fire has
" burned and that my tinder-box gave out sparks (ذكت بك نارى وورِيت بك زنادى);
" the charge is for me and the honour for you. My oath (that the cash should be
" paid in) is fulfilled (قد وفت لى يمينى). Go now and take back your money."
This he did. — Yazíd said, one day : " By Allah! I prefer life to death and an ho-
" nourable reputation to life; could I obtain a gift never yet granted to mortal, I
" should wish to have an ear by means of which I might hear what people say of
" me after my death." We have mentioned this saying in the life of his father
al-Muhallab (vol. III. p. 508), to whom we attributed it, and not to Yazíd; God
knows best! — Abú 'l-Hasan Ali al-Madáini (vol. I. p. 436) said : " One of Yazíd
" Ibn al-Muhallab's intendants sold, for the sum of forty thousand dirhems (£ 1,000),
" the melons produced in one of that emir's farms. When Yazíd was informed of
" the circumstance, he said to the intendant : ' You have converted us into green-
" ' grocers! were there not old women enough in the tribe of Azd among whom
" ' you might have shared them?'" — Omar Ibn Lajá (5) the poet praised Yazíd
in the following terms :

Trace up the genealogy of the Muhallabs; you will find them all, from father to son, noble
and generous. How many the caitiffs who detested them unjustly for their merit, and who
could not reach, nor even approach, the height to which that family has risen by its virtues.

But you always see illustrious chiefs exposed to envy whilst no one envies the vile. Were it said to Glory : " Turn from them and leave them; since thou art all-powerful in the world;" she would not obey. Noble sentiments are souls of which no men but the Muhallabs are the bodies.

Al-Asmái relates that some members of the tribe of Kudáa went to visit Yazid Ibn al-Muhallab, and one of them recited to him these verses :

By Allah ! if the request which we address to you fails, we know not to whom we can direct our prayer. We have travelled over many lands and found none but you who had the reputation of being generous. Persevere in the conduct to which you have accustomed us; or, if not, tell us towards whom we shall go.

He ordered one thousand dinars to be given to the poet, who, the following year, came back and said :

Why are the doors of other men abandoned whilst yours is crowded like a market? Is it through affection that they come to you or through respect? or did they leave distant countries in search of a pasturage, announced by the lightnings of beneficence which they saw flashing from your hands? I know that you take pleasure in noble deeds and that those who do so are very few.

Yazid ordered ten thousand dirhems to be given to the poet. — Persons versed in history all agree that, under the Omaiyides, the most beneficent family was that of the Muhallabs, and, under the Abbasides, that of the Barmekides. God knows best ! They displayed great bravery in many famous conflicts. Ibn al-Jauzi (vol. II. p. 96) relates, in his Kitáb al-Azkiá (book for the intelligent), that a serpent fell (from the roof of a house) upon Yazid Ibn al-Muhallab and that he did not push it away; on which, his father said to him : " You have lost your judgment in retaining your courage." — When Abd ar-Rahman Ibn al-Ashath Ibn Kais al-Kindi took up arms against al-Hajjáj, — the history of this event is well known (6), — he went to Toster where many persons joined him and, mention being made of the Muhallab family, much abuse was directed against its members. On this, Abd ar-Rahman said to Harish Ibn Hilál al-Kuraiéi (7), who was one of the company : " What is the matter with you, Abu Kudáma? why do you not speak out your " mind?" and received from him this answer : " By Allah ! I know of none who " are so careful of themselves as they when they are in easy circumstances, and " so indifferent for their personal safety when they are in distress." — Abd ar-

Rahmán Ibn Sulaim al-Kalbi went to visit al-Muhallab and, seeing that all his sons, from the oldest to the youngest, were on horseback, he said to them: " May " God accustom the Moslims to see a continual series of you; by Allah! though you are " not grandchildren of the Prophet, your are grandchildren of a malhama (8). — Habib, one of al-Muhallab's sons, lost a male child and charged Yazid to recite the funeral service over the corpse. On this, some person said to him : " Why do you " confide that duty to your brother? are you not his elder and is not he that is " dead your son?" Habib replied : " My brother is honoured by the people ; he " bears a high reputation among them, and all the Arabs have their eyes fixed on " him. I should regret to abase that (reputation) which God has exalted." — Mutarraf Ibn Abd Allah Ibn as-Shikhkhir (9), seeing, one day, Yazid Ibn al-Muhallab walking about in a silk robe, of which the train swept the ground, said to him : " What meaneth this manner of walking? it is odious to God and to his Prophet!" — " Dost thou know me?" said Yazid. — " I do," replied the other, " thy com- " mencement was a filthy drop (of sperm), thy end shall be a nasty carcass, and, " during the interval, thou wearest the excrement (of a worm)." — This thought has been versified in the following manner by Abû Muhammad Abd Allah Ibn Muhammad as-Sâmi, a native of Khorasán :

> I gazed with wonder on him who was proud of his shape and who, before that, was but a turdy drop. To-morrow, when that handsome shape is gone, he will be a filthy carrion in the earth. Nay, with all his self-love and pride, he carries excrements between his flanks.

The háfiz generally known by the surname of Ibn Asákir (col. II. p. 252) says, in that article of his greater historical work which treats of Abù Hirásh Makhlad, the son of Yazid Ibn al-Muhallab: "This Makhlad was one of those whose liberality " procured them universal praise. He went to see Omar Ibn Abd al-Azis for the " purpose of speaking to him in favour of his father; who had been imprisoned by " that khalif. He had been appointed by his father to the government of Jurján. " On his way, he passed near Kûfa and there received the visit of Hamza Ibn Baid " al-Hanafi (10), who came to him with a number of the inhabitants. This famous " poet then stood before him and recited these verses :

> " We are come to you for an affair which we request you to arrange; say to us : ' Wel- " come !' so that another welcomer may answer you. Refer us not to people who, when they " make a promise, tell a lie. You are the head of a family before whom the East and the

" West have been in submission and under whose care you were educated; excellent, I de-
" clare, were the lessons which they gave! In your eleventh year, you possessed that
" wisdom which is rarely acquired but by hoary chieftains; your thoughts were always turned
" towards serious affairs, whilst the thoughts of those as old as you were fixed on sport and
" play. You were so beneficent that I exclaimed : ' Does there yet remain a petitioner to ask
" ' a favour? an applicant who has something to demand?' From you, gifts flowed upon soli-
" citors, and also from those in your antechamber, when their generosity was invoked.

" ' Let me hear your affair;' said Makhlad. He immediately arranged it and
" then ordered one hundred thousand dirhems (£. 2,500) to be given to the poet."
—A man who had already visited Makhlad and received from him a present
adequate to his deserts, went to see him again, and Makhlad said to him : " Did
" you not already come to us, and did we not make you a gift?" "It is true;"
replied the visitor.—"What then," said Mukhallad, "has brought you back?"
—"Those words," replied the man, "which al-Kumait (vol. III. p. 373) pro-
" nounced, in speaking of you :

" He gave, then gave again; we returned to him and he gave; then I returned, and he re-
" newed his gift. (This happened) many times. I never return to him but he receives me
" with smiles and treats me with honour (11).

" This reply obtained for him that made it a gift double of the former."—
Kablsa Ibn Omar al-Muhallabi related as follows : " Yazid Ibn al-Muhallab effected
" the conquest of Jurjàn and Tabaristàn, and took prisoner one their great chiefs
" named Sûl."—I may here observe that this Sûl was the prince of Jurjàn and the
grandfather of two celebrated and good poets, Ibrahim Ibn al-Abbàs as-Sûli (vol. I.
p. 22) and Abû Bakr Muhammad Ibn Yahya as-Sûli (vol. III. p. 68).—Yazid found there
a great quantity of treasure and other valuable objects. He therefore wrote to (the khalif)
Sulaimàn Ibn Abd al-Malik a letter in which he said : "I have taken Tabaristàn and
" Jurjàn, places which none of the Chosroes dynasty and none of their successors
" had ever been able to conquer. I am sending you so many files of camels (12) load-
" ed with money and presents that, when the first of them reaches you, the last will
" be still here with me." Omar Ibn Abd al-Aziz, who succeeded to the khalifat on
the death of Sulaimàn, required of Yazid the fulfilment of this promise and cast him
into prison. Makhlad, the son of Yazid, went to intercede with Omar in favour of the
prisoner.—Kablsa continues thus : "From the time of Makhlad's leaving the city of
" Marw Shâhjàn till he reached Damascus, he gave away in presents one million of

"dirhems (£. 2,5000). When he was about to appear before Omar, he put on a
"suit of shabby clothes (which he tucked up), and a dirty old cap (13). Omar, on
"seeing him, said: 'I perceive that you have tucked up your clothes;' to which
"Makhlad replied: 'If you tuck up yours or let them hang down, we shall do the
"'same.' He then addressed him thus: 'You have extended your clemency to
"'all men; why then keep you this man in prison? If there be a legal proof
"'of his culpability, adduce it and then pronounce sentence; if not, make
"'him take oath (that he is not guilty), or else be reconciled with him on condition
"'of his giving up to you all his landed estates.' Yazid, on hearing this,
"exclaimed: 'As for the oath, it shall never be said by the Arabs that Yazid, the
"'son of al-Muhallab, was obliged to take one by necessity; as for my landed
"'estates, they are of sufficient value to pay what is claimed of me.' Makhlad
"died at the age of twenty-seven years and (on this occasion) Omar said: 'Had
"'God meant well towards the father, he would have left this youth with
"'him.' — It is stated that Makhlad died of the plague. The funeral service
"was recited over him by Omar Ibn Abd al-Aziz, who said, on finishing: 'To-day
"'is dead the most gallant youth of all the Arabs.' He then pronounced the
"following lines of a poet, applying them to the circumstance:

"Our souls are going off in sighs for the loss of Amr, and the faces of all the people are
"darkened and soiled with dust."

—An elegy, composed on his death by Hamza Ibn Baid al-Hanafi, the poet above
mentioned, contains the following lines:

The thrones (of state) will no longer be occupied by you; and, to-day that your (grace-) clothes only, (not your chamberlains,) prevent you from being seen, the only throne on which
you repose is the bier (14). The last time we saw you was at Dâbik, on the day in which they
poured upon you the crumbling mould (of the grave).

Al-Farazdak (vol. III. p. 612), said, in an elegy on his death:

Never did the bier which they carried off hold the like of Makhlad! Never did grave-clothes
cover a man like him. Thy father is one whose name sufficed to put a hostile squadron to
flight, though he it (every lance-head) (15) was fully a span in length. The foe knew that,
when he girded his loins, he was the lion of the forest that never fled from danger (بالمرد).

The passage given above proves that Makhlad, the son of Yazid, died on or about
the year 100 (A. D. 718-9), for Omar Ibn Abd al-Aziz was raised to the khalifate

in the month of Safar, A. H. 99 (Sept.-Oct. A. D. 717) and died in the month of Rajab, 101 (Jan.-Feb. A. D. 720) (16). It was in Omar's residence that he expired. Hamza's elegy proves also that Makhlad died at Dâbik, which is a village situated in the government of Aleppo, and to the north of the city. It gives its name to a large meadow (marj) in the neighbourhood. • Sulaimân Ibn Abd al-Malik died at that place and there also is his tomb, a well-known monument. — Let us resume our account of Yazid. Abû Jaafar at-Tabari (vol. II. p. 597) says, in his great historical work: " Al-Mughîra, the son of al-Muhallab, acted as his fa- " ther's lieutenant at Marw, and held the government of that city and of the " province." — He died in the month of Rajab, 82 (August-Sept. A. D. 701), as we have said in the life of al-Muhallab. — " When this news reached Yazid, he told " it to the military (chiefs), but kept it from al-Muhallab's knowledge; preferring " that he should learn it from the women. Al-Muhallab, hearing their lamenta- " tions, asked what was wrong and, being informed that al-Mughîra was dead, he " exclaimed : ' From God we came, and to God we must return !' His grief was " so excessive that he let it appear, and was reprimanded, for that reason, by one " of his domestic officers. He then called in Yazid and sent him off to Marw, " after giving him instructions for his conduct. During all this time, his tears " were trickling down over his beard. Al-Hajjâj wrote to him a letter of condo- " lence for the loss of al-Mughîra, who was truly an able chief." — I may here mention that al-Mughîra had a son named Bishr of whom Abû Tammâm (vol. I. p. 318) speaks in the first part of his Hamdsa (p. 119), and some of whose poetry he inserts in that work. One of these pieces, composed by him on (his uncle) Yazid, we here give :

The emir (al-Muhallab) has treated me ill and so did al-Mughîra; Yazid also has turned his back upon me. All of them have got (governments) wherewith to sate their appetite; yet it is disgraceful for a man to be sated when his companion suffers from hunger. Use me gently, dear uncle ! and employ me when an untoward event arrives; time (as you know) is an assemblage of vicissitudes. I am your sword and, though swords may sometimes rebound (without cutting), yet the sword of a man like me will never rebound, to the detriment of your cause. At what door shall I ask permission to enter, if I be repelled from the door of which I was the guardian ?

Let us return to at-Tabari's narration : " On the day of al-Mughîra's death, al- " Muhallab was stopping at Kish (or Kiss), in Transoxiana, being engaged in war

" with the people of that place. Yazíd set out with sixty horsemen and met, in
" the desert, with a body of five hundred Turks. A desperate conflict ensued, and
" Yazíd was wounded in the thigh by an arrow. After that, al-Muhallab made
" peace with the inhabitants of Kish, on receiving from them a (sum of money, as)
" redemption. He then left them and set out for Marw. On arriving at Zághúl,
" which is a village in the government of Marw or-Rúd, he was attacked by pains
" in the bowels. He then called in Habíb and such of his other sons as were
" with him. Some arrows, tied up so as to form a bundle, were brought in, by
" his order. ' What think you?' said he, ' could you break them all, now that they
" ' are tied together?' They answered that they could not. ' And if they were
" ' separated?' — ' Certainly,' said they, ' we could break them.' — ' Such,' conti-
" nued he, ' is the effect of union!' He then made them a long exhortation," —
which it is needless for us to repeat here, — "and finished by saying : ' I nominate
" ' Yazíd as my lieutenant and appoint Habíb to the command of the jund (the
" Arab troops), until he led them to Yazíd, whose authority they will all ac-
" knowledge. His son al-Mufaddal then said: ' Had you not placed him at
" ' our head, we ourselves would have done so.' Habíb received his dying in-
" junctions and, after saying the funeral prayer over the corpse, he proceeded
" to Marw. Yazíd wrote to Abd al-Malik, informing him that al-Muhallab
" was dead and had chosen him as his successor."—This nomination was confirmed by al-Hajjáj, who afterwards, in the year 85 (A. D. 704), revoked it and
gave the government to al-Mufaddal, Yazíd's brother. His motive for so doing was
this : Having gone (some years before) to visit (the khalif) Abd al-Malik, he passed
on his way back by a monastery at which he halted. Being then informed that a
very old and learned Christian was residing there, he had him brought in and said
to him : " Tell me, shaikh! do you find in your books any thing concerning you
and us?"—"I have," replied the other; "we find therein all that has already
" happened to you and the mention of your present state and of what it will be."
—"Are we designated by our names or are we merely described?" — "All is
" described without being named, but there is a name without a description."—
" What description do you find of the Commander of the faithful?" — " We find
" that, for the time in which we are, he is a bald sovereign before whom every one
" who stands in his way must fall prostrate."—" What do you find next?"—A man
" named al-Walíd (17)."—" And what then?"—" A man whose name is that of

" a prophet and by whom God will display his power to men."—That was Sulaimân,
the son of Abd al-Malik. — "Do you know what will happen to me?" — "I do."
— "Who will succeed to me in the authority?" — "A man called Yazîd." — "Will
" that be in my life-time or after my death?" — "I do not know."—Do you know
his description?" — "He will act with perfidy; that is all I know." — The person
(who related this anecdote) said: Al-Hajjâj was struck with the idea that the person
thus indicated was no other than Yazîd, the son of al-Muhallab and, during the
remainder of his journey, which required seven days, he never ceased thinking of
the old man's words. On his arrival, he wrote to Abd al-Malik, requesting permission to resign the government of Irâk and received from him a letter containing these words: "I see very well what your intention is; you wish to discover
" how you stand in my opinion." He then vainly employed every means for
the purpose of bringing about Yazîd's deposition, till one of al-Muhallab's
cavalry officers, named al-Khiâr Ibn Sabra and who was then in the service of
Yazîd, came to see him and was asked by him how that emir was getting on. Al-
Khiâr replied: "His obedience (towards the khalif) and the mildness of his
" administration are most exemplary." — "That is a fib!" exclaimed al-Hajjâj,
" tell the truth." His visitor then said: "God alone is greater and more mighty
" than he; he has saddled (the steed of independence) and has put no bridle on (to
" restrain it)." — "You now speak the truth!" replied al-Hajjâj, and, at a later
period, he gave to al-Khiâr the government of Omân (in Arabia, or of Ammân, in
Palestine?) (18). He then wrote to Abd al-Malik, blaming the conduct of Yazîd and
of all the Muhallab family; in short, he addressed him so often on that subject
that he received from him a letter containing these words: "You are always
" speaking against Yazîd and the family of al-Muhallab; point me out another
" man capable of governing Khorâsân. Al-Hajjâj named Majâa (or Mujjâa) Ibn
Saad as Saadi. To this, Abd al-Malik returned the following answer: "The same
" motive which impels you to effect the ruin of the Muhallab family has induced
" you to propose Mojâa Ibn Saad. Look out for a man of decision, and capable
" of executing your orders." Al-Hajjâj sent him the name of Kutaiba Ibn Muslim
al-Bâhili (vol. II. p. 514) and received for answer: "Appoint him." When Yazîd
learned that al-Hajjâj had effected his deposition, he said to the members of his
family: "Who, do you think, will receive from al Hajjâj the government of Kho-
" râsân?" They answered: "Some man of (his own tribe) the Thakif." — "Not

"at all!" replied Yazíd, "one of you will receive from him a letter appointing "him to that place and, when I am gone to meet him (and am in his power), he "will replace that person by another, and Kutaiba Ibn Muslim is the fittest man." The narrator of this anecdote said: When al-Hajjáj obtained from Abd al-Malik the authorisation to depose Yazíd, he felt that he would do wrong if he announced to him by a letter that the command was taken from him, and therefore wrote to him a dispatch in which he said: "Leave (your *brother*) al-Mufaddal as your lieutenant "and come here." Al-Hosain (الحسين) Ibn al-Mundir, whom Yazíd consulted on receiving this letter, advised him to give a pretext for remaining where he was, "Because," said he, "you stand very high in the good opinion of the Commander "of the faithful. This is a stroke aimed against you by al-Hajjáj. If you delay "your departure, I am in hopes that the khalif will write to him the order to con-"firm you in your post." To this Yazíd replied: "We are of a family whose "fidelity (*towards the khalifs*) has always been for it a benediction; I detest "disobedience and opposition to orders." He then commenced making prepara-tives for his departure. Al-Hajjáj, thinking that he delayed too long, wrote these words to al-Mufaddal, Yazíd's brother: "I have appointed you to the government "of Khorásán." Yazíd, whom al-Mufaddal then pressed most earnestly to depart, said to him: "Al-Hajjáj will not leave you in place, once I am gone; his only "motive in acting as he does is the fear of my resisting his orders." — "You are "mistaken," replied al-Mufaddal, "and are jealous of my good fortune." — "I am "not jealous of you," replied Yazíd, "and that you shall soon have reason to "know." In the month of the latter Rabí, 85 (April-May, A. D. 704), Yazíd left Khorásán, and al-Hajjáj replaced al-Mufaddal by Kutaiba Ibn Muslim. — Hosain Ibn al-Mundir, or according to another statement, Fírúz Ibn Hosain, said, in speaking of Yazíd:

I advised you to take a decided step, but you would not wear me; and now, that you are strip-ped of your commandment, you regret (your *folly*). But I shall not weep for you through fondness, neither shall I pray that you return home safely.

When Kutaiba Ibn Muslim arrived in Khorásán, Hosain was asked by him what he had said of Yazíd and made the following answer:

I advised you to take a decided step, but you would not hear me; blame then yourself, if you mean to blame. If al-Hajjáj learns that you resist his orders, you will find that his power is overwhelming.

Kutaiba then asked him what was the advice he gave, and Hosain replied:
" I told him not to keep a single yellow or white (piece of money), but to send them
" all to the emir (al-Hajjáj)." — The following verses by Abd Allah Ibn Hammám
as-Salûli were composed on the replacement of Yazid by Kutaiba:

> We said, Kutaiba! the morning you came here: " Assuredly, we have got in you a one-
> " eyed substitute for Yazid. Your father is no way resembled al-Muhallab; your (family),
> " compared to his, is mean and despicable. Wide is the difference between one who rose to
> " fortune by castanets and one who brandished the sword amidst the fires of war. Here came
> " the squinting Azdilites under whose domination liberality has perished and infamy flourishes.

The expression *a one-eyed substitute* (badal aawar) is figuratively applied to a
man generally despised who succeeds, in office, to one who always deserved praise.
They say also, in the same sense: *a one-eyed successor* (khalaf aawar). The word
castanets alludes to the fact that Kutaiba, in his youth, was a (public dancer and)
player on those instruments. Kutaiba is here called a *squinter* (ahwal), and so
he was; the plural form of this adjective is analogous to those of aswad, ahmar, etc.
which are sûddn, humrân.—Some say that these verses were composed, not by
Abd Allah Ibn Hammám, but by Nahár Ibn Tausla al-Yashkuri (19).—At-Tabari
says, under the year 90 (A. D. 708-9): " Al-Hajjáj went forth against the Kurds,
" who had occupied the entire province of Fars. He took with him Yazid and
" his brothers al-Mufaddal and Abd al-Malik. When he encamped, he had them
" placed in a tent, near his own lodgings, and under a guard of Syrian troops; this
" tent was surrounded with a sort of ditch. He exacted from them a sum of six
" millions (£ 150,000) and put them to the torture (in order to enforce payment).
" Yazid suffered those pains with such firmness as provoked the anger of al-Hajjáj.
" It is said that he (Yazid) had been wounded by an arrow, the head of which
" remained in his thigh, and that, if any thing touched him there, he would cry
" out; even if it was moved in the slightest manner, he would utter a cry. Al-
" Hajjáj ordered him to be tormented and receive strokes on the thigh. This
" was done; Yazid cried out, and his sister Hind, who was then with her husband
" al-Hajjáj, heard the cry and began to scream and to lament. On this, al-Hajjáj
" divorced her. He afterwards let them alone and began to ask money from
" them. They commenced furnishing it and, during that time, they made
" arrangements for effecting their escape. Having sent to (their brother) Marwán
" Ibn al-Muhallab, who was then in Basra, they told him to put horses at their

" disposal and to give the public to understand that he meant to offer them for
" sale; they bade him also ask so high a price for them that no one would buy
" them. 'They will be for us,' said they, 'a means of escape, if we succeed
" 'in getting out of this place.' Marwân did so, whilst his brother, Habíb,
" also was undergoing tortures at Basra. Yazîd then ordered a copious repast to
" be served to the guards and had them provided with wine. Whilst they were
" drinking and unmindful of their charge, he put on the clothes of his cook,
" placed a false white beard over his own and went out. One of the guards saw
" him and said : 'That is Yazîd's manner of walking (20).' He then went up,
" looked at him in the face,—it was in the night,—and seeing the white beard, he
" turned away, saying : 'This is an elderly man.' Al-Mufaddal followed his
" brother without being remarked and they went to a boat which was kept ready
" for them in the swamps (al-Batath) by their directions. They were then at the
" distance of eighteen parasangs from Basra. When they reached the boat, they
" waited for Abd al-Malik who had met with something to detain him, and at
" length Yazîd said to al-Mufaddal : 'Get into the boat with us and let him fol-
" low.' To this, al-Mufaddal, who was born of the same mother as Abd al-Malik,
" replied : 'By Allah! I shall not stir from this spot till my brother come, even
" 'should I be taken back to prison.' Yazîd stopped till Abd al-Malik came up;
" they then embarked and voyaged the remainder of the night, until daybreak.
" The next morning, the guards discovered that their prisoners had escaped and
" sent to inform al-Hajjâj of what had happened : He was dismayed at the news
" and, imagining that they had fled in the direction of Khorâsân, he sent off, by
" the post horses, to Kutaiba Ibn Muslim, a dispatch in which he gave him warning
" of their approaching arrival, ordered him to make preparations for resisting
" them and to send messengers to the commanders of all the districts (kûrân) and
" frontier stations, enjoining them to hold themselves in readiness and to keep
" a look-out for the fugitives. He sent also another dispatch to (the khalif) al-
" Walîd Ibn Abd al-Malik, informing him of their evasion and expressing his
" opinion that they intended to go to Khorâsân, and not elsewhere. He continued
" thinking of what they intended to do and would sometimes say : 'I am sure
" 'that Yazîd's mind prompts him to act like Ibn al-Asbâth.'"—I may here
observe that Ibn al-Asbâth, whose names were Abd ar-Rahmân Ibn Muhammad Ibn
al-Ashâth Ibn Kais, of the tribe of Kinda, revolted against Abd al-Malik Ibn

Marwàn. His history is well known and is to be found in the books of annals. —
" When Yazid " (and his companions), says at-Tabari, " drew near to al-Balkih (21),
" the horses which had been kept in readiness were brought to them, and they
" rode off with a guide who took the way which crosses (the desert) of as-Samàwa.
" Two days later, al-Hajjàj learned that they were on the road to Syria, that their
" horses were fatigued with the journey and that a person had seen them travelling
" towards the desert. He immediately sent off this news to al-Walid. Yazid
" continued his route till he reached Palestine and there he stopped at the
" dwelling of Wohaib Ibn Abd ar-Rahmàn al-Azdi, a person whom Sulaimàn Ibn
" Abd al-Malik (the khalif's brother) held in high esteem. Wohaib took his guest
" to Sulaimàn and said : ' Here is Yazid; his brothers are at my house; they have
" ' fled hither from al-Hajjàj and they seek refuge under your protection.'—' Bring
" ' them to me,' said Sulaimàn, ' I answer for their safety. He (al-Hajjàj) shall
" ' never lay hands on them, as long as I live.' — Wohaib brought them and thus
" placed them out of danger. Al-Hajjàj then wrote to al-Walid Ibn Abd al-Malik,
" saying : ' The family of al-Muhallab have defrauded the treasury; they esca-
" ' ped from me and are now with Sulaimàn.' When al-Walid knew that Yazid
" was with Sulaimàn, his uneasiness of mind was diminished to a certain degree,
" but he was greatly incensed at the loss of the money and therefore wrote to his
" brother Sulaimàn, asking where Yazid was. ' He is with me,' replied Sulaimàn,
" ' and I have engaged myself for his safety. He owes no more than three mil-
" ' lions of the six which al-Hajjàj required of them. They have paid three and owe
" ' three, which I shall take upon myself.' Al-Walid returned this reply : ' By
" ' Allah! I shall not pardon him till you send him to me chained.' To this,
" Sulaimàn answered : ' If I send him to you, I will go with him; but, for God's
" ' sake! do not dishonour me or bring me into disgrace.'—Al-Walid wrote back
" as follows : ' By Allah! if you bring him to me, I shall not forgive him.'—
" Yazid then said (to Sulaimàn) : ' Send me to him; by Allah! I do not wish to
" ' raise enmity and hostile feelings between you and him, or to let you and your
" ' brother gain a bad reputation on my account. Send me to him; let your
" ' son come with me and write to him (the khalif) as mild a letter as you can.'
" Sulaimàn dispatched his son Aiyùb with him and, as al-Walid had ordered
" the prisoner to be brought in chains, he said to his son : ' When you enter
" ' into the khalif's presence, appear before him bound in the same chain as

" 'Yazid.' When they reached the place where al-Walid was, they appeared
" before him in that state, and the khalif, on seeing his brother's son attached
" to the same chain as Yazid, exclaimed : 'By Allah! we have offended Sulai-
" 'mân!' The youth (Aiyûb) then handed him his father's letter and said : 'Com-
" 'mander of the faithful! may my life be laid down to save yours! do not cast
" 'dishonour on my father, you who are our natural protector; do not deprive
" 'us of the hope that people shall always continue to expect safety under the
" 'protection of us who are so closely allied to you; do not disappoint those who
" 'hope to gain honour in becoming attached to us who derive our honour from
" 'you.' He then read his father's letter, which ran as follows : 'To the servant
" 'of God, al-Walid, Commander of the faithful; from Sulaimân, the son of Abd al-
" 'Malik. Here is the point : Commander of the faithful! I certainly think that,
" 'if an enemy who revolted against you and resisted were to solicit my protection
" 'and place himself under my safeguard, you would not dishonour my guest
" 'and bring my right of protection into discredit; how then should it be if the
" 'person whom I received as my guest had always been devotedly obedient
" 'to your will and rendered. not only he but his father and all the mem-
" 'bers of his family, the most signal services to Islamism? I have now sent
" 'him to you and, if you wish (taghzâ) to come to a rupture with me, to annul
" 'my credit as a protector and to injure me in the gravest manner, you have
" 'the power of doing so and may do it. But I implore you, in God's name! to
" 'avoid a rupture, to refrain from casting a blemish on my honourable reputation
" 'and to continue the kindness and friendship which you have hitherto shown me.
" 'By Allah! Commander of the faithful! you know not how long my life
" 'and yours may endure, neither do you know when death shall part us.
" 'If the Commander of the faithful, whose happiness may God prolong! be in-
" 'clined to retard the moment of my death, to act kindly towards me, to
" 'respect my rights and to abstain from hurting me, I pray him to do so.
" 'By Allah! Commander of the faithful! there is nothing in the world, after my
" 'duty towards God, in which I find more delight than in your good will and
" 'your happiness; it is by deserving your benevolence that we all hope to
" 'obtain the favour of God. Commander of the faithful! if you deign, even
" 'for a single day, to give me joy, to be friendly towards me, to maintain my
" 'honour and to respect my rights, you will pardon Yazid for my sake, and all

" ' you reclaim of him shall be paid by me.' When this letter was read, the khalif
" said : ' We have been too severe on Sulaimân.' He then called his nephew over
" to him, and Yazîd began a speech in which, after extolling the Almighty and
" praising the Prophet, he said : ' Commander of the faithful! we appreciate to the
" ' utmost degree the kindness you have always shown us; others may forget favours,
" ' but we, never; others may be ungrateful, but we cannot. The toils which we
" ' have undergone in the service of your noble family, the strokes we have inflicted
" ' on your enemies in many great battles, both in the Eastern countries and in
" ' the West, are surely good titles to your benevolence.' The khalif then
" made him sit down, granted him a full pardon and left him free. Yazîd
" returned to Sulaimân, and his brothers tried to raise the money which was
" claimed of him. Al-Walîd wrote to al-Hajjâj, saying : ' I did not attempt
" ' to touch Yazîd and the members of his family, because they were with
" ' Sulaimân (and under his protection). So do you let them alone and cease
" ' writing to me about them.' When al-Hajjâj received this letter, he discon-
" tinued his attacks against them and even renounced to one million of dirhems
" which were owing to him by Abû Oyaina (another of al-Muhallab's sons). He
" also set at liberty Habib, the son of al-Muhallab. Yazîd passed nine months
" with Sulaimân, enjoying an agreeable life and great tranquillity of mind   His
" protector never received a present (of money), but sent him the half of it.
" Being asked by one of his usual companions why he did not build a house for
" himself, he replied : ' What should I do with it? I have always a dwelling
" ' ready prepared for me.' — ' Where is that dwelling?' said his friend. He
" answered : ' If I hold a commandment, it will be the government palace; and
" ' if I be out of place, it will be the state prison.' He said also : ' I should feel
" ' no pleasure in being free from worldly cares and having fortune submissive to
" ' my will;' and, being asked his reason, he answered : ' Because I should
" ' detest adopting lazy habits.' In the month of Shauwâl, A. H. 95 (June—
" July A. D. 714) and subsequently to these events, al-Hajjâj died. Some say
" that his death took place on the 25th of Ramadân, and that he had then
" reached his fifty-third or fifty-fourth year. When he was on the point of
" death, he charged Yazîd Ibn Abi Kabsha to replace him in the administra-
" tion of the two cities (al-Misrâni), that is, of Kûfa and Basra, and to take
" the direction of military affairs and the presidency of the public prayer.

"To Yazid Ibn Abi Muslim (*see next article*) he confided the administration
"of the land-tax (*kharāj*). Those two nominations were confirmed by al-Walid,
"who approved also of all the other appointments made by al-Hajjāj. According
"to another account, it was from al-Walid himself that they received their
"appointment. Al-Hajjāj held the government of the two Iráks during twenty
"years. Al-Walid Ibn Abd al-Malik died on Saturday, the 15th of the lat-
"ter Jumáda, A. H. 96 (25th February, A. D. 715) at Dair Narán."—I may
observe that this monastery is situated on the slope of Kásiún, the mountain
which lies near Damascus. He was buried in the cemetery outside the gate
called Báb as-Saghir. Sulaiman Ibn Abd al-Malik was proclaimed khalif on
the day of his brother al-Walid's death and, in that year,—I mean the year 96,
—he took the government of Irák from Yazid Ibn Abi Muslim and gave it to
Yazid, the son of al-Muhallab. Khalifa Ibn Khaiyát (*vol. I. p.* 492) says: "In the
"year 97 (A. D. 715-6), Yazid united in his own hands the commandment of
"the two cities,"—meaning Kúfa and Basra. God knows best. "Sálih Ibn
"Abd ar-Rahmán received from him the administration of the land-tax with
"the order that he should put to death the members of the Akil (22) fa-
"mily, that to which al-Hajjāj belonged. He, in consequence, arrested them
"and had then put to the torture, under the direction of Abd al-Malik, the
"son of al-Muhallab."—Al-Walid intended to have taken from Sulaimán the
right of succeeding to the khalifate and of transferring it to his own son Abd
al-Aziz. Al-Hajjāj had taken a solemn engagement to second the khalif and
so also did Kutaiba Ibn Muslim al-Báhili, the same who replaced Yazid Ibn
al-Muhallab in the government of Khorásán. When Sulaimán obtained the
khalifate, Kutaiba was apprehensive that his government would be taken from
him and given to Yazid Ibn al-Muhallab. He therefore wrote to Sulaimán
congratulating him on his accession, condoling with him on the death of al-Walid,
mentioning the services which he himself had rendered to the state and vaunting
his fidelity to Abd al-Malik and al-Walid. He then added that he would be equally
serviceable and obedient to the new khalif, provided that the government of
Khorásán were not taken from him. He addressed to him also another letter in
which he spoke of the conquests he had effected, of his elevated position and of his
influence over the foreign kings, "whose bosoms, said he, are filled with terror
"at my name." He then attacked the sons of al-Muhallab and declared solemnly

that if Yazid was named governor of Khorâsân, he himself would repudiate the
authority of the khalif. In a third letter he declared that he had repudiated
his authority. These three dispatches he sent off by a man of his tribe to whom he
gave the following instructions: " When the khalif has read the first letter, he
" may probably hand it to Yazid, if the latter be present. In that case, give him
" the second letter and, if he hand it also to Yazid, after reading it, give him the
" third. If, on the contrary, he reads the first letter and put it up without passing
" it to Yazid, do not give him the two others (but keep them up)." The narrator
says: Kutaiba's messenger arrived, found Yazid Ibn al-Muhallab with Sulaimân and
delivered the first letter to the khalif, who read it and passed it to Yazid. He then
gave the second letter which was read and passed also to Yazid. On this, he gave
the third. Sulaimân read it, changed colour and, having called for (sigillary) clay,
he sealed it up and kept it in his hand. According to Abû Obaida Mâmar Ibn al-
Muthanna (vol. III. p. 388), the first letter contained an attack on Yazid, accusing
him of perfidy, ingratitude and thanklessness; in the second was an eulogium
on the same person and, in the third, were written these words: " If you do not
" confirm me in the place which I now occupy and give me the positive assurance
" that I have nothing to fear from you, I shall cast off your authority as I cast off
" my slippers, and shall certainly fill it (the land) with horse and foot to attack
" you." — Sulaimân then ordered Kutaiba's messenger to go down to the guest-
house, and, when the evening set in, he sent for him and gave him a purse of
dinars (gold pieces), saying : " This is to requite your trouble and here is a diploma
" containing your master's nomination to the government of Khorâsân; set out,
" and a messenger of mine shall accompany you." The Bâhilide (Kutaiba's
emissary) departed with the khalif's messenger and, on reaching Hulwân, they
were told by the people that Kutaiba had revolted. On this, Sulaimân's agent
turned back after delivering the diploma to Kutaiba's man, who pursued his
journey. When Kutaiba saw the messenger, he consulted his brothers on the
line of conduct which he should follow, and they replied : " After what has
" occurred here, Sulaimân can no longer have any reliance on you." Some
time after, Kutaiba was slain, as we have related in our account of him (vol. II.
p. 516); this occurrence we mentioned in a summary manner, because the
details would have led us too far. — Yazid Ibn al-Muhallab, having then obtained
the government of Irâk, reflected (on the state of that province) and said to himself :

"Irâk has been ruined by al-Hajjâj; the people of that country place all their
"hopes in me, yet, if I go there and begin to exact the payment of the khardj
"(land-tax), I shall be obliged to act with great severity, become (for them) as bad
"as my predecessor and plunge them into a civil war. God forbid that I should
"bring down upon them again the afflictions from which He has just delivered
"them! and yet, if I did not furnish to Sulaimân the same amount (of revenue) as
"he received from al-Hajjâj, he would reject what I send, though it came from
"me." He therefore went to the khalif and said: "I can point out to you a
"man who well understands the administration of the khardj and to him you
"might confide that duty. His name is Sâlih Ibn Abd ar-Rahmân, and he is
"a mawla of the tribe of Tamîm." Sulaimân replied: "I accept your recom-
"mendation." Yazîd then set out for Irâk, whither Sâlih had preceded him and
was then stopping at Wâsit. On drawing near the town, he met all the inhabitants,
who had gone forth to receive him, but Sâlih did not appear till he had nearly
reached the place. It was only then that Sâlih set out, preceded by (a guard of)
four hundred Syrians. He returned to the town with Yazîd and, on entering, said
to him: "There is a house which I have cleared out for you." Yazîd stopped
there, and Sâlih proceeded to his own residence. (From that moment) he stinted
Yazîd (in money matters) and would not allow him to meddle, even in the slightest
degree (with the finance department). Yazîd caused one thousand tables to be got
ready, so that he might give a repast to the inhabitants; Sâlih took them from him
(and did not restore them) till Yazîd said: "Write down the expense to my own
"account." Yazîd purchased a great quantity of objects and, having drawn bills
on Sâlih for the amount, he sent to have them cashed. They were not accepted,
and the bearers returned to Yazîd, who got into a passion and said to himself:
"This is of my own doing." Soon after, he received the visit of Sâlih and made
room for him on his own seat. "What are those bills?" said Sâlih, "the khardj
"administration cannot take charge of them; a few days ago, I accepted a bill of
"yours for one hundred thousand dirhems (£. 25,000) and I have already advanced
"you the amount of your salary. Other sums you asked of me, and I gave them.
"Matters cannot go on so; the Commander of the faithful will never approve of
"these proceedings and you will be certainly called to an account." Yazîd replied,
in laughing: "Come now, Abù 'l-Walîd! accept these last bills," and wrought him
into a so good humour that he said: "Well! I shall accept them, but do not draw

" two many on me."   " I shall not," replied Yazid."—Sulaimán, having given to
Yazid the government, not of Khorásán but of Irák, said to Abd al-Malik, the son of
al-Muhallab : " How would you act were I to appoint you to the government of Kho-
" rásán?"   Abd al-Malik replied : " Commander of the faithful! you would always
" find me acting according to your wishes."   The khalif then turned the conversation to another subject, and Abd al-Malik sent to some of the military chiefs in
Khorásán, who were attached to him, a letter in which he said that the Commander
of the faithful had offered to him the government of that province.   Intelligence of
this reached Yazid, who was disgusted with the government of Irák on account
of the restraint in which he was held by Sálih, with whom he found that he
could do nothing.   He therefore called in Abd Allah Ibn al-Ahtam and said to
him : " I want your advice concerning an affair which preoccupies my mind,
" and wish you to free me from the uneasiness it gives me."   Ibn al-Ahtam
answered : " I shall obey whatever order you are pleased to give."   Yazid
then spoke to him in these terms : "You see in what restraint I am kept here
" and may imagine the annoyance which it gives me.   Now, the government of
" Khorásán is vacant and I have been informed that the Commander of the faithful
" spoke of it to Abd al-Malik Ibn al-Muhallab   Is there any means (by which I
" might obtain it)?"—"There is, most certainly;" replied the other,—"send me
" to the Commander of the faithful and I am sure that I shall return here with your
" appointment to that post."—"It is well," said Yazid, "but be careful not
" to speak of what I have told you."   He then wrote a letter to Sulaimán in which
he described the state of Irák and praised highly Ibn al-Ahtam, as being a man
perfectly well acquainted with the affairs of Khorásán.   He authorised Ibn al-
Ahtam to travel by post and gave him thirty thousand dirhems (£. 750).   Ibn
al-Ahtam was seven days on the road.   On arriving, he went to Sulaimán's
residence with the intention of delivered to him Yazid's letter.   Being introduced,
he found him at breakfast and therefore sat down in a corner of the room.   Two
(roasted) pullets were then brought to him and, when he had finished eating,
Sulaimán said to him : " You shall have an audience later, do not miss it."   One
third (of the day) had passed when the khalif sent for him and said : " Yazid Ibn
" al-Muhallab informs me by his letter that you are well acquainted with the state
" of Irák and of Khorásán, and he speaks of you with commendation.   How
" did you acquire your information respecting these countries?"   Ibn al-Ahtam

replied : ' No man knows them as well as I do; I was born and brought up
" in Khorásán."—" Ah!" said Sulaimán, "the Commander of the faithful is in
" great want of a man like you, whom he may consult respecting these two pro-
" vinces. Whom would you recommend as a fit person to govern Khorásán?"
Ibn al-Ahtam replied : "The Commander of the faithful knows whom he would
" like to appoint; if he deign to name the person, I shall tell him whether he is
", fit for the place or not." Sulaimán mentioned a man of the tribe of Kuraish,
and the other said : "That it not the man for Khorásán." The khalif then named
Abd al-Malik, the son of al-Muhallab. Ibn al-Ahtam replied : "He will not
" answer till he knows how to levy a body of troops (23)." Among the last whom
the khalif named was Wakî (وكى) Ibn Abi Sûd. "Commander of the faithful!"
said the other, " Wakî is a man of great bravery, decision and gallantry, but he is
" not of that (country) and, besides, he has never commanded a body of three
" hundred men and has always been under the orders of a superior." —
" You say true," replied Sulaimán, "but come now! tell me who is the fittest
" man." Ibn al-Ahtam answered : "One whom I know, but whose name you
" did not pronounce."—" Who is that?" said the khalif.—" I shall not mention
" his name unless the Commander of the faithful promise to keep the secret to
" himself and to protect me against the ill-will of that person."—" I promise it to
" you," said the khalif, " name him."—" Yazîd, the son of al-Muhallab ;" replied
Ibn al-Ahtam. The khalif said : "But that man is in Irâk and prefers residing
" there to being in Khorásán."—" You know him well, Commander of the
" faithful!" replied the other, " but you may oblige him to accept and authorise
" him to leave a lieutenant in Irak when he is about to set out." — " You have hit
" on it! exclaimed Sulaimán. He then had a diploma drawn up, by which Yazîd
was constituted governor of Khorásán, and, to it he joined a letter in which he
said : "Ibn al-Ahtam is, as you mentioned, a man of intelligence, piety, talent
" and judgment." Ibn al-Ahtam received the letter with the diploma and, after
a journey of seven days, he rejoined Yazîd : " What news do you bring with you?"
said the latter. Ibn al-Ahtam handed him the letter. "Nonsense, man!"
exclaimed Yazîd, "have you any news?" The other handed him the diploma.
Yazîd immediately gave orders to make preparations for his departure and, having
called in his son Makhlad, he sent him on before, to Khorásán, that very day.
Yazîd then set out and stopped in Khorásán three or four months, after which

he invaded and took Jurján, Tabaristán and Dihistán. This was in the year 98 (A. D. 716-7). Having lost five thousand men in besieging one of the fortresses of Jurján, he swore, by a most solemn oath, to slay so many of the enemy that the blood would suffice to turn a mill. He therefore massacred numbers, but it was necessary to pour water on the blood in order to make it flow and turn the mill. He then eat bread made of the flour which had been ground by means of their blood. Sulaimán Ibn Abd al-Malik died soon after. His death took place, at Dábik, on the eve of Friday, 19th of Safar, A. H. 99 (1st October, A. D. 717), or, according to another statement, on the 10th of that month. *Dábik is a village lying to the north of Aleppo.* Omar Ibn Abd al-Azîz, whom he appointed as his successor, took the government of Khorásán from Yazîd and gave it to Adî Ibn Artá 'l-Fazári, who immediately arrested his predecessor, bound him in chains and send him to the new khalif. Omar Ibn Abd al-Azîz detested Yazîd and all the members of that family: "They are a domineering set," said he, "and I do not like such " people." Yazîd, on his part, declared that he thought Omar to be a hypocrite. When Yazîd was brought before Omar, the latter said to him : " What has become " of the money about which you wrote to Sulaimán Ibn Abd al-Malik?" Yazîd answered : " You know on what footing I was with Sulaimán ; I wrote him that " (story) merely that he might tell it to the people, for I knew very well that he " would be incapable of calling me to an account, if he heard any thing against " me, or of treating me in a manner which I should not like." Omar replied : " I see that this affair of yours will bring you to prison. Have therefore the fear " of God before your eyes and pay the money which is claimed of you; it belongs " by right to the Moslim people and I cannot possibly avoid exacting it." He then sent him back to prison (24).— Al-Baládori (vol. I. p. 338) states, in that chapter of his *Book of Conquests* which treats of Jurján and Tabaristán, that Yazîd, having finished with Jurján, went to Khorásán and received on the way the usual presents. He then confided to his son Makhlad the government of Khorásán and went to see Sulaimán, after writing to him that he had with him twenty-five millions of dirhems. This letter fell into the hands of Omar Ibn Abd al-Azîz who, in consequence, arrested Yazîd and cast him into prison. God knows the exact truth !—Omar then sent for al-Jarráh Ibn Abd al-Malik al-Hakami and dispatched him to Khorásán. Makhlad, the son of Yazîd, then came to Omar and had with him the conversation which we have already related. When Makhlad left the

room, Omar said : " In my opinion, that youth is better than his father."   Makhlad
died very soon after.   As Yazid refused to pay the money which was claimed of
him , Omar had him clothed in a woollen cloak and placed on the back of a
camel.   He then said : " Take him off to Dahlak."—Dahlak is an island in the
Sea of Aidâb (the Red Sea), and not far from Sawâkin.   The khalifa used to confine
there the persons with whom they were displeased.—The narrator continues:
When Yazid was taken forth and saw the people passing near, he exclaimed :
" Good God! have I not relations and friends enough to prevent me from being
" taken to Dahlak, where none are sent but scandalous criminals?"   Salâma Ibn
Noaim al-Khaulâni (who heard these words) went in to Omar and said : " Com-
" mander of the faithful! let Yazid be taken back to prison; for I fear that, if you
" send him off to Dahlak, his people will take him by force out of our hands.   I
" saw some of them, and they were indignant at the manner in which he was
" treated."   Yazid was taken back to prison and there he remained till he was
informed of Omar's sickness.   It is said that Adi Ibn Artâ had caused Yazid's
hands to be chained to his neck and his legs to be fettered; after which, he
delivered him up to Wakl Ibn Hassân Ibn Abi Sûd at-Tamîmi, who had orders to
transport the prisoner to Ain at-Tamar, whence he was to be taken before Omar.
A troop of Azdites stopped Wakl, with the intention of taking Yazid from him by
force; but he drew his sword, cut the cable of the boat, took away the prisoner's sword and said : " I declare my wife divorced if I do not strike off his
" head! therefore disperse and leave him."   Yazid then called out to them and
informed them of Wakl's oath, on which they dispersed.   Wakl pursued his route
and delivered the prisoner to the jund (or detachment of Arab troops) at Ain at-
Tamar.   The jund took him to Omar, who put him into prison.   When Yazid was
detained in Omar's prison, he received the visit of al-Farazdak the poet who,
seeing him in chains, recited these lines:

> Your chains hold in bondage (liberality and beneficence, the man who payed for others the
> price of blood and who wrought every virtuous deed; one who never gave way to insolent joy
> when worldly goods were heaped upon him; one who is patient under affliction and refers his
> cause to God.

On this, Yazid exclaimed : " Alas! what have you done? you have done me
" harm."—" How so!" said the poet.   Yazid replied : " You praised me and I
" in such a state!"   Al-Farazdak answered : " I saw that you were now held cheap

" and I meant to obtain you (your favour) in exchange for my (poetical) merchan-
" dise." Yazid then threw him his ring and told him to sell it: "That," said
" he, " is worth one thousand dinars, which will serve as the interest of a
" capital to be paid to you later." He remained in prison till the year 101 (A. D.
719-20, when Omar was taken ill, and he was filled with dread at the prospect
of Yazid Ibn Abd al-Malik's succeeding to the khalifate. When he, the son of
al-Muhallab, had obtained the government of Irák, he had cruelly persecuted, as we
have already said, the family of Abû Akîl, the same of which al-Hajjâj was a member.
The mother (niece) (25) of al-Hajjâj was the daughter of Muhammad Ibn Yûsuf Ibn
al-Hakam Ibn Abî Akîl and had married Yazid Ibn Abd al-Malik. She bore him
a son named al-Walîd, the same who was (afterwards) called the Fâsik (debauched
reprobate) of the Omaiyide family. She was the daughter of al-Hajjâj's brother.
He, Yazid Ibn Abd al-Malik, had promised her that, if ever God placed Yazid Ibn
al-Muhallab in his power, he would cut off one of his limbs. The son of al-Muhallab, fearing that this threat would be executed, took measures for escaping from
prison and sent to his clients the order to keep camels in readiness, so as to
facilitate his flight. Omar Ibn Abd al-Azîz fell sick at Dair Samân. When the
illness grew serious, Yazid descended from the prison, went to the place were the
camels were stationed, according to agreement, and rode off. When he had
got out of danger, he wrote these words to Omar: " By Allah! if I was sure that
" you would survive, I should not have left my prison; but I cannot be otherwise
" than afraid of Yazid Ibn Abd al-Malik." On this, Omar said : " Almighty God!
" if Yazid mean to be wicked towards the people, protect them from his wickedness
" and turn his artifices against himself." It was thus that Yazid Ibn al-Muhallab
effected his escape.—Al-Wâkidi (vol. III. p. 61) says that Yazid did not fly from
prison till after the death of Omar. I found in the rough copy of the kâdi Kamâl
ad-Dîn Ibn al-Adîm's History (vol. I. p. 247) that Omar imprisoned Yazid Ibn al-
Muhallab and his son Moawla at Aleppo and that their evasion took place there.
God knows best! Omar Ibn Abd al-Azîz died at Dair Samân on Friday,—some say
on Thursday,—the 25th of Rajab, 101 (10th February, A. D. 720). Others say
that he died on the 20th of that month. He was then aged thirty-nine years and
some months. Other accounts say that he died at Khunâsira, an ancient village
in the neighbourhood of Aleppo and of which al-Mutanabbi has spoken in the
following line :

I love the country between Emesa and Khunásira; every man loves the spot where he passed his early life.

Omm Aâsim, the mother of Omar Ibn Abd al-Aziz, was the daughter of Aâsim, the son of (the khalif) Omar Ibn al-Khattâb. He (Omar Ibn Abd al-Aziz) was called the Omaiyide with the scar on the forehead; having been wounded in that part by one of his father's horses. Nâfé (vol. III. p. 521) the mawla of (Abd Allah), the son of Omar Ibn al-Khattâb, relates as follows: "The son of Omar was often "heard to say: 'I should be glad to know that descendant of Omar who is to have "'a mark on his face and who will fill the earth with (his) justice.'"—Sâlim al-Aftas related as follows: "Omar Ibn Abd al-Aziz received a kick from a horse, "at Damascus, when he was a little boy. He was taken to his mother Omm "Aâsim, who clasped him in her arms and began to wipe the blood off his face. "She had not finished, when seeing his father come in, she turned towards him "in a passion, and began to reproach and upbraid him: 'You have killed my "'child,' said she, 'because you would not give him a servant or a nurse to "'protect him from accidents such as this.' He replied: 'Be silent, Omm "'Aâsim! what a benediction will it be for you if this boy turn out to be the "'Omaiyide with the scarred forehead.'"—Hárúmid Ibn Zaid made the following relation: "Omar Ibn al-Khattâb passed by an old woman, in the milk-market, "who had milk to sell, and he said to her: 'Old woman! deceive not the true "'believers and the visitors of God's holy house, by mixing water with your "'milk.' She replied: 'I shall obey.' Some time after, he passed near her "again and said: 'Old woman! did I not forbid you to water your milk?' "She answered: 'By Allah! I never do so.' 'Her daughter, who was within the "booth, then spoke to her and said: 'Is it thus that you draw down upon "'yourself the double reproach of fraud and falsehood?' Omar overheard her "and intended punishing the old woman, but spared her on account of her "daughter's words. He then turned to his two sons and said: 'Which of you will "'marry that girl? Almighty God may produce from her an offspring as virtuous "'as herself." His son Aâsim replied: 'I will marry her;' and did so; and she "bore him a daughter whom they named Omm Aâsim. This daughter became the "wife of Abd al-Aziz Ibn Marwân and bore him Omar Ibn Abd al-Aziz. After "her (death), her husband took another wife whose name was Hafsa, and of whom "it was (proverbially) said: Hafsa is not one of the women who are like Omm

" *Adsim.*"—The *shaikh* Shams al Din Abù 'l-Muzaffar Yûsuf Ibn Kizoghli (*vol. I.*
p. 439), a daughter's son to Jamàl ad-Dìn Abù 'l-Faraj Ibn al-Jausi (*vol. II. p. 96*),
states in his *Kitâb Jauhara toz-Zamân fi taskira tis-Sulûn* (26), that Ibn Omar
related as follows: " Whilst my father was patrolling at night the streets of Medina,
" he heard a woman say to her daughter : ' Rise, my girl! and water the milk.'
" The other answered : ' O Mamma! did you not hear the Commander of the
" ' faithful's public cryer forbid the mixing of milk with water?' To this the
" mother replied : ' His cryer is far from you now!' and the daughter answered :
" ' If he see me not, the Lord of that cryer will see me.' Omar wept and, when
" the morning set in, he sent for the two women and asked the daughter if she was
" married. The mother answered that she was not, and Omar then said to me :
" ' O Abd Allah! marry that girl; if I stood in need of a wife, I myself would take
" ' her.' To this I replied that I (*was already provided for and*) could do without
" her. He then said : ' Abù Aàsim! do you marry her." Abù Aàsim (*whose other*
" *name was*) Abd al-Asiz the Omaiyide, married her and she became the mother of
Omar Ibn Abd al-Asiz."—On the death of Omar Ibn Abd al-Asiz, Yazîd Ibn Abd al-
Malik was raised to the khalifate. Yazîd Ibn al-Muhallab then proceeded to Basra,
seized on that city, imprisoned Adî Ibn Artâ, the officer who governed it in the
name of the new khalif and, having openly rejected the authority of Yazîd Ibn
Abd al-Malik, he aspired to obtain the khalifate for himself. One of his concubines
then went to him, kissed the ground before him and said : " Hail to the Commander
" of the faithful!" On which he recited this verse :

> Return to your place ! wait till you see what will happen when this dark thunder-cloud clears
> off.

—I must observe that this verse is taken from a piece composed by Bishr Ibn
Katin (?) al-Asadi. It is not necessary for us to give the particulars of this event
(*the revolt of Yazîd*), which we here indicate in a summary manner.—Yazîd Ibn
Abd al-Malik then placed his brother Maslama and his nephew al-Abbâs Ibn al-
Walîd at the head of the troops and sent them against Yazîd Ibn al-Muhallab.
This chief marched forth to encounter them and established his son Moawia in
Basra, as his lieutenant, leaving with him troops, money and the prisoners. He
sent on before him his brother Abd al-Malik, who proceeded to al-Akr, where he
halted (27). This place is called also the *Akr of Babel*; it lies near Kûfa and not far

from Kerbela, the spot where al-Husain, the son of Ali, was slain. *Al-Air* was originally the name of this castle. There are four places which bear this name, but we need not mention the others, as Yákút al-Hamawi (*see page 9 of this vol.*) has noticed them in his *Mushterik.*—At-Tabari says: Maslama Ibn Abd al-Malik advanced and took position opposite to Yazíd Ibn al-Muhallab. The troops drew up in line and engaged the combat. The people of Basra charged those of Syria, threw them into disorder and forced them to retreat, but their adversaries rallied, attacked them and put them to flight. Abd al-Malik, who commanded the van-guard, retreated after this check and went to join his brother Yazíd. The people (*of Basra*) had taken the oath of fealty to Yazíd and sworn, on the Book of God and the *Sunna* of his prophet, that they would support him, provided that he hindered (*his*) troops from entering into their territory or their city (مصرهم) and that he should not recommence towards them the conduct followed by that reprobate al-Hajjáj. Marwán Ibn al-Muhallab, who was in Basra, excited the people to march against the Syrians and join his brother Yazíd. Al-Hasan al-Basri (*vol. I.* p. 370) tried to dissuade them and said, in one of his public sittings: "I marvel "at a reprobate from among the reprobates, an impious man from among the "impious, who has passed some time in submitting this people to every dishonour, "and that too, in the name of God, and who, in God's name also, commits every "sin. What they (*his partisans*) devour is devoured by him, what they take is "taken by him and, when a mouthful is refused him, he swallows it (*by force*). "He said to you: 'I am filled with (*a virtuous*) anger (*for the cause of God*), and "'be you also filled with anger.' He has set up a long cane with a rag tied to it "(*for a standard*) and drawn after him a fickle (رعاع), wild and silly band of youths, "who have not the least intelligence. He says: 'I summon you to follow the "'path traced by Omar Ibn Abd al-Azíz!' but were that path followed, he would "be fettered in chains and cast into the place where Omar had already put him." Here a man said to him: "How now, Abú Saíd! are you making an apology for "the Syrians?"—meaning the Omaiyides.— To this he replied: "I make their "apology? may God never forgive them! Saíd, the son of al-Abbás, related as "follows: 'The Prophet of God said: 'Almighty God! I declare sacred in Medina "'all those things which You declared sacred in your town of Mekka.' And yet "the people of Syria entered into it for three days, and not a door was locked but "they burned it (*the house*) and all that was in it; things went so far that (*vile*) Copts

" and Nabateans intruded upon Kuraishide women, tore their veils off their heads
" and their bracelets off their ancles. Their swords were suspended from their
" shoulders whilst the Book of God was trodden by them under foot! Shall I let
" myself be killed for the sake of (one or other of) two reprobates who dispute the
" possession of (worldly) authority? By Allah! I should be delighted if the earth
" were to swallow them both up." Yazid Ibn al-Muhallab, being informed of what
al-Hasan had said, disguised himself, with some of his cousins, and went to the
mosque where he held his sittings. After saluting, they took him aside, and the
assembly looked on with apprehension. Yazid then commenced with him a discussion in which he was joined by one of his cousins. Al-Hasan said to the
latter : "Who are you? what do you mean, you son of a sluttish mother!" The
other drew his sword and, being asked by Yazid what he intended to do, he replied :
" To kill that fellow."—" Sheath your sword," said Yazid, " for, by Allah! if
" you kill him, the people who are now for us will turn against us."—I may here
observe that Yazid Ibn al-Muhallab is the person meant in that verse of the
Duraidiya, or Makstra, of Ibn Duraid (vol. III. p. 37), which runs thus :

And, before my time, Yazid aspired to reach the height of power, and he was neither feeble
nor irresolute.

The commentators of the Duraidiya have all discoursed on this verse and related
the history (of Yazid).—Yazid Ibn al-Muhallab remained (with his army) in position
during eight days, from the time of his meeting (the army of) Maslama. On Friday,
the 14th of Safar, 102 (24th August, A. D. 720), the boats were burned by the
order of Maslama; the two armies met and the fire of war was lighted up. When
(Yazid's) people saw the smoke and were told that the bridge of boats was burning,
they fled in disorder. Yazid, being informed that they had taken to flight, asked
why they did so and, having learned that the bridge was on fire and that not one of
them had kept his ground, he exclaimed : " May God curse them for mosquitoes,
" that fly away before smoke!" He himself had not the slightest thought of
retiring. Being then informed that his brother Habib was slain, he said : " Life
" will have no value for me after the loss of Habib; I abhorred the idea of
" retreating when my troops took to flight, and now, by Allah! I abhor it more than
" ever! March forward!" One of his companions said (afterwards) : " We knew
" that the man intended to get killed, so those who disliked fighting hung back

" and went off, one after the other. But a good troop still followed him whilst he
" dashed forward. Every band of horsemen which he met was put to rout; not a
" troop of Syrians but turned aside to avoid him and the lances of his companions.
" Abû Rûba 'l-Murji then went up to him and said : ' The rest of our people are
" ' gone off; what think you of returning to Wâsit, where you may hold out till you
" ' receive reinforcements from the people of Basra and till the people of Omân
" ' and Bahrain come to you in their ships. You might entrench yourself (and
" ' wait for them)!' Yazîd replied : ' Confound your advice! do you pretend to say
" ' that my death will be easier there than here?' The other answered : ' I fear
" ' for your life; see you not the mountains of iron (the masses of armed men) which
" ' surround you!'—' I care not for them,' exclaimed Yazîd, ' no matter whether
" ' they be mountains of iron or of fire. Leave us, if you are not inclined to fight
" ' on our side.' He then advanced against Maslama, without caring to attack any
" other, and the latter, on seeing him approach, called for his horse and mounted
" him. The Syrian cavalry gathered round (Yazîd) and his companions; Yazîd
" was slain with his brother Muhammad and a number of his partisans. Al-Kahl
" (الكهل) Ibn Aiyâsh al-Kalbi exclaimed, on seeing Yazîd : ' I shall kill him or he
" ' shall kill me but, as it will be difficult to get at him, some of you must charge
" ' with me and occupy his companions till I reach him.'—' We will charge with
" ' you'; exclaimed some of his comrades. They dashed on in a body and, after an
" hour's fighting, when the dust cleared off, the two parties separated, leaving
" Yazîd dead and al-Kahl Ibn Aiyâsh at his last gasp. Al-Kahl made a sign to his
" companions, pointing out where Yazîd was lying. The head of Yazîd was brought
" in by a mawlu of the Murra family who, being asked if it was he who slew him,
" answered : ' No.' — Whilst the combat was going on, al-Hawâri Ibn Ziâd saw a
" horse without a rider and exclaimed : ' Hurrah! there is the horse of that repro-
" ' bate, the son of al-Muhallab; God grant that he may be dead!' They looked for
" him, and his head was brought to Maslama, who did not recognise it. On this,
" Haiyân an-Nabati said : ' Think what you please, but think not that the man has
" ' fled; he has most certainly been killed."— " What sign is there of that?" said
" ' Maslama. The other replied : " In the time of Ibn al-Ashath, I heard him
" ' say : ' Shame on Ibn al-Ashath! raising dust (in flying before his enemies) was
" ' his main occupation. How could he prove himself superior to death unless he
" ' died honorably?" — I may here observe that the emir Abû Nasr Ibn Mâkûla

says, in that section (*of the work entitled* al-Ikmâl) which is headed by the words *el-Kahl, al-Fahl*: "*Kahl* is similar (*in its written form*) to *fahl*, except that the first let-"ter has two points (*instead of one*). He (*al-Kahl*) was the son of Aiyâsh Ibn Hassân "Ibn Samîr Ibn Sharâhîl Ibn Ozair. He slew Yazîd Ibn al-Muhallab. Each of "them struck his adversary and slew him". — When Yazîd's head was carried to Maslama, no person could say whether it was his or not; some one then advised him to have it washed and a turban put on it. That was done, and he recognised him. Maslama sent it to his brother Yazîd Ibn Abd al-Malik; the bearer was Khâlid Ibn al-Walîd Ibn Ochm Ibn Abi Moait.— Khalîfa Ibn Khaiyât says : "Yazîd, the son of "al-Muhallab, was born in the year 53 (A. D. 673); he was killed on Friday, the "12th of Safer, 102 (22nd August, A. D. 720)." God knows best!—When those who fled reached Wâsit, Moawia, the son of Yazîd, had thirty-two prisoners in his power. These he caused to be brought out of prison and beheaded. One of them was Adi Ibn Artâ. He then marched out of the town, and the people (*his soldiers*) said to him : "Out upon you ! we see clearly that you intend to have us all killed ; has "not your father been killed ?" He advanced as far as Basra, carrying with him the money and the treasures. Al-Mufaddal, the son of al-Muhallab, and the other members of the family were all assembled at Basra, as they feared the disaster which really took place. They then prepared sea-going ships and embarked all sorts of military stores. Moawia wished to obtain the commandment over the rest of the family, but they assembled and chose al-Mufaddal for their chief. "Al-Mufaddal", said they, "is our senior and you are still a boy like some others of the family." Al Mufaddal held the commandment over them till they reached Kermân where there were many scattered bands of soldiers who had escaped from the battle, and he united all those troops under his orders. An army, sent in pursuit of them by Maslama Ibn Abd al-Malik, overtook them at a defile in (*the province of*) Fars and attacked them with great vigour. Al-Mufaddal and a number of his officers lost their lives in that combat. All the other members of the Muhallab family were afterwards killed, with the exception of Abû Oyaina and Othmân Ibn al-Mufaddal who took refuge at the court of the Khâkân (*chief of the Khazars*) and of Reibîl (*prince of Kabul*). Maslama sent their heads to his brother Yazîd who was then encamped near Aleppo. When the heads were stuck up on poles, Yazîd went out to look at them and said to his companions : "That is the head of Abd al-Malik; that is the head of al-Mufad-"dal; by Allah ! he looks (*as tranquil*) as if he were sitting with me and conversing."

— Another author, not at-Tabari, says: " When the head of Yazid Ibn al-Muhal-
" lab was brought to Yazid Ibn Abd al-Malik, one of the courtiers began to depre-
" ciate the character of Yazid, the son of al-Muhallab; but the khalif said to him :
" ' Hold your tongue! Yazid aspired to greatness, encountered dangers and died ho-
" ' norably." — When Maslama had finished the war against the Muhallabites, he
obtained from his brother Yazid, that very year, the united governments of Kûfa,
Basra and Khorâsân. —The death of Yazid Ibn al-Muhallab was lamented in a number of fine elegies composed by his favorite poet, Thâbit Kutna. In one of these
pieces he said :

> All the (Arab) tribes swore to second you in what you undertook; they followed you and
> marched (to battle). But when the lances shocked together and you exposed your troops to the
> point of the spear, they abandoned you and fled. You were slain, but not disgracefully ; and
> how many the violent deaths which are disgraceful!

This Thâbit was one of the best poets and warriors of Khorâsân. He lost one of
his eyes and, as he kept its socket always filled with cotton (kutn), he became known
by the name of Thâbit Kutna. Having received, at one time, from Yazid Ibn al-
Muhallab the government of a canton in Khorâsân, he mounted into the pulpit, but
felt so confused and troubled that he was unable to utter a word and got down. The
people having then gone to visit him at his house, he said to them :

> I cannot stand up among you as your orator, but, when battle rages, I am an able orator with
> my sword.

When they heard this, they exclaimed : " By Allah! had you said so when in the
" pulpit, you would have been the very best of orators." — Ibn Kutaiba speaks of
him in the Tabakât as-Shuaard. It was against Thâbit that Sâhib al-Fîl al-Hanafi,
with whom he was often engaged in satirical conflicts, directed these lines :

> Abù 'l-Alâ (you met on Friday last with a misfortune : you were troubled and like to choke.
> Your tongue turned (in your mouth) when you were going to speak, and made a slip like that
> of a man who tumbles down from a mountain's top. When the eyes of the congregation were
> fixed on you in broad day-light, you were nearly arranged in clearing your voice.

Ibn al-Kalbi (vol. III. p. 608) says, in his Jamhara : " This Thâbit (came of a
" very noble family being) the son of Kaab Ibn Jâbir Ibn Kaab Ibn Kermân Ibn Tarafa
" Ibn Wahb Ibn Mâsin Ibn Tamîm Ibn al-Asad Ibn al-Bârith Ibn al-Atîk Ibn al-Asad

" Ibn Imrân Ibn Amr Muzaikiya Ibn Aâmir Mâ as-Samâ.—An author, but not al-
Tabari, says that Yazid was killed by al-Hudail Ibn Zufar Ibn al-Hârith al-Kilâbi.—
Al-Kalbi says also : " When I was a boy, the people used to say : ' The Omaiyides
" ' exposed religion (to ignoming) on the day of Kerbela (when al-Hussain, the son
" ' of Ali, was killed), and they injured generosity on the day of al-Akr!"—Muhammad Ibn Wâsl (واسل) related as follows : " When we received the news of al-Yazid's
" death, a woman of Omân, who was a professional weeper at funerals, came to
" me and made in my presence a lament for those of the Muhallab family who
" had been killed."—Ibn Abbâd said : " During more than twenty years after
" the death of the Muhallabs, not a girl was born in our family and not a boy
" died (28)."—Khalifa Ibn Khaiyât says : " In the year 102, on Friday, the 12th of
" Safar (22nd August, A. D. 720). Yazid, the son of al-Muhallab, was slain, at the
" age of forty-nine years. He was illustrious by his noble character, his genero-
" sity, his rank and his bravery." — It is related that the khalif Yazid received a
visit from his brother Maslama, at the time of Yazid Ibn al-Muhallah's revolt, and,
seeing him dressed in coloured robes (as if to enjoy a party of pleasure), he said to
him : " Why do you wear such clothes, you who are one of those whom the poet de-
" signated in this verse :

    " People who, when engaged in war, tighten their garments around them (and abstain) from
    " women; leaving them to pass the night in a state of purity.

    " Maslama answered : " We fight against our equals, those who belong to the
" Kuraish family; but, when a raven croaks, we do not mind it."—I may add that
the author of this verse was al-Akhtal at-Taghlibi, a Christian and a celebrated
poet.

(1) See vol. III, p. 138, note.

(2) This Said must have been the son of the conqueror of Egypt, but I can find no information respecting
him.

(3) Omar Ibn Hubaira 'l-Fazâri was one of the most active generals and provincial governors whom the
Omaiyides had in their service. He died in the year 106 (A. D. 724-5).

(4) The recital which follows is omitted in the edition of Bûlâk. I give it after three manuscripts and indicate the corrections which should be made in the lithographied text of Wüstenfeld. The piece is curious, as
it offers specimens of the sententious and elliptical style of speaking for which the ancient Arabs were remarkable.

(5) Omar Ibn Lajâ was a contemporary of the poet Jarîr, whom he sometimes satirised. — (Ibn Duraid's *Ishtikâk*.)

(6) The fullest account which we have of Abd ar-Rahmân Ibn al-Ashath's revolt is given by Price, in his *Retrospect of Mahommedan History*, vol. 1, p. 455 et seq.

(7) This Harîsh belonged to the tribe of Tamîm and was one of their bravest warriors. He distinguished himself highly in Khorâsân. — (Ibn Duraid's *Ishtikâk*.)

(8) These last words appear to mean : you are a hand which will bring about a catastrophe.

(9) Motarrif Ibn Abd Allah Ibn as-Shikhkhîr was the son of one of the Prophet's companions. He died subsequently to the year 97 (A. D. 708). — (Ibn Kotaiba's *Maârif*.) From what is related of him here, he seems to have been a rigid and puritanical Moslim.

(10) The poet Hazm Ibn Said al-Hasafî was a native of Kûfa. He celebrated the praises of al-Muhallab, of that emîr's sons and of the Adîd Bilâl Ibn Abî Burda. The gifts which he received for his eulogiums were immense. — (Kitâb al-Aghânî.)

(11) The expression here rendered by *treating with honour* signifies literally : *doubling the cushion*; which was done probably for the purpose of seating the visitor more commodiously. It occurs again in the article on Yazîd Ibn Omar Ibn Hubaira.

(12) The manuscripts all read أظار. This plural form of the word أظار is not mentioned in the dictionaries.

(13) The austerity of Omar Ibn Abd al-Azîz, his detestation of worldly pomp, and his rigid piety are well known.

(14) The word *amîr* signifies throne and bier. The poet employs it here in the two meanings.

(15) This parenthesis is supplied by conjecture.

(16) This passage is important in a philological point of view : it proves that the expression حدود فى al-guides on an orient.

(17) The son and successor of Abd al-Malik.

(18) Khâlid was put to death at Omân by Zîâd, the son of al-Muhallab. — (*Ishtikâk*.)

(19) Habîb Ibn Tamîm was one of al-Muhallab's favorite poets. He died A. H. 103 (A. D. 721-2).

(20) Yazîd had been killed by an arrow.

(21) The causeway marches which extend from Basra to the Persian gulf were called the *Batîh*.

(22) According to Ibn Duraid, in his *Ishtikâk*, the name خُلَيْل should be pronounced *Khalîl*. In the life of al-Hajjâj (vol. I, p. 356), it has been transcribed *Okail*. In the genealogy given there Ibn Okail must be replaced by Ibn Abî Akîl.

(23) The arabic text says : till he can count ten.

(24) This relation is taken from the *Annals of Tabari*.

(25) This passage is not found in most manuscripts. The indication given in it, and confirmed by the translator, is evidently erroneous.

(26) This work is not mentioned in Hajji Khalîfa's bibliographical dictionary. The title signifies : *Gem of the age, being a commemoration of the sultan*. I do not know of what subject it treats.

(27) The recital is evidently taken from at-Tabari's *Annals*.

(28) This seems to mean that the death of the Muhallabites brought good luck to the people.

YAZID IBN ABI MUSLIM

Abû 'l-Alâ Yazîd Ibn Abi Muslim Dînâr, a member, by enfranchisement, of the tribe of Thakîf, was a mawla of al-Hajjâj Ibn Yûsuf (vol. I. p. 356) and his secretary. It was for the talent and abilities which he displayed in the management of affairs, that al-Hajjâj raised him to eminence. We mentioned, in the life of Yazîd Ibn al-Muhallab (page 183 of this vol.), that al-Hajjâj, in his last illness, appointed Ibn Abi Muslim to act as his deputy in the administration of the kharâj (land-tax) of Irâk. On the death of al-Hajjâj, he was confirmed in that post by (the khalif) al-Wa-lîd Ibn Abd al-Malik, and no modifications were made in his attributions. Some say that he held his appointment from al-Walîd, subsequently to the death of al-Hajjâj, and that al-Walîd said : " I am, with regard to al-Hajjâj and Ibn Abi Mus-" lim, like a man who lost a piece of silver and found a piece of gold." Sulaimân, the brother and successor of al-Walîd, dismissed Ibn Abi-Muslim from office and sent Yazîd Ibn al-Muhallab to replace him. Ibn Abi Muslim was brought before the kha-lif with his hands and neck enclosed in a wooden collar (جامعة). Being low-set, and ungainly (قصد), with an ugly face and a large belly, he presented to the eye a very despicable appearance. Sulaimân, on seeing him, said : Are you Yazîd " Ibn Abi Muslim?" The other replied : " I am; may God direct the Commander " of the faithful !"—" The curse of God be on him," exclaimed Sulaimân, " who " shared his trust with you and confided to you authority on his own responsi-" bility." — " Commander of the faithful!" replied Ibn Abi Muslim, " make " not (such a wish); you see me now that things have turned badly for me, but, if " you saw me in prosperity, you would admire, not despise, think highly of me and " not scorn me." On hearing these words, Sulaimân exclaimed : " Curse on the " fellow! what a quick intelligence he has and what a sharp tongue!" He then said to him : " Tell me, Yazîd! your master al-Hajjâj is he still falling down to hell, " or has he already reached the bottom of it?" He replied : " Commander of the " faithful ! say not such things; al-Hajjâj was a foe to your foes and a friend to your " friends; he lavished his blood for you, and his place, on the day of the resurrec-" tion, will be on the right hand of Abd al-Malik and on the left of al-Walîd; so,

" put him where you think fit."—According to another relation, he replied : " To-
" morrow, on the day of the resurrection, he will be between your father and your
" brother; so, place them where you will."—" Curse on the fellow!" said Sulaimán, " how devoted he is to his master! it is such men as he that should be admitted
" into favour." One of the khalif's social companions here said : " Commander
" of the faithful! take that man's life; do not spare it." Ibn Abi Muslim asked
who that person was and said, on bearing his name : " By Allah! I have been told
" that his mother had not always her ears hidden by her hair (1)." Sulaimán, on
hearing these words, could not refrain from laughing and ordered the prisoner
to be set at liberty. He then caused an enquiry to be made into his conduct and
thus learned that he had not defrauded the state even of a dinar or of a dirhem. He
even thought of taking him for his secretary, but Omar Ibn Abd al-Azîz (who was
afterwards khalif) said to him : " Commander of the faithful! I implore you, in
" God's name, not to revive the recollections left by al-Hajjáj by taking his secretary
" for yours." Sulaimán replied : " Abù Hafs! I had his conduct examined into
" and have not found in it the least trace of peculation." Omar replied : " I could
" find for you an individual who cares as little as he for dinars and dirhems." —
" Who is that?" said the khalif.—"Satan;" replied Omar; " he handles neither di-
" nars nor dirhems, and yet he brought ruin upon mankind." Sulaimán abandoned his project.—Juwairiya Ibn Asmá (2) related as follows : " Omar Ibn Abd al-
" Azîs, being informed that Yazîd Ibn Abi Muslim had set out on an expedition with
" some Moslim troops, wrote to the admil (or superintendant) of the army, an order
" for his recal. 'I detest,' said he, 'the thought of gaining victories by means of an
" ' army in which that man is.'"—The háfiz Abù 'l-Kásim Ibn Asákir (vol. II. p. 252)
gives, in his (biographical) history of Damascus, an article on Yazîd Ibn Abi Muslim,
in which he relates as follows, on the authority of Yákùb (3) : " In the year 101
" (A. D. 719-20), Yazîd was appointed to the government of Ifrîkiya (Mauritania),
" in which post he replaced Ismall Ibn Obaid Allah Ibn Abi 'l-Muhájir, a mawla of
" the tribe of Makhzùm. Yazîd acted in the most commendable manner and was
" killed in the year 102." Here is, however, what at-Tabari (vol. II. p. 597) relates,
in his great historical work : " He resolved, it is said, on acting towards them (the
" Musulmans of Mauritania) in the same manner as al-Hajjáj Ibn Yùsuf had treated
" those members of the population of Sawâd (Babylonia) who had embraced Isla-
" mism and settled in the cities of Irâk : al-Hajjáj sent them back to the districts of

" which they were natives and exacted from them the poll-tax, such as they had
" to pay before their conversion. Yazid resolved on doing like him, but the people
" consulted together and decided on killing him, which they did. They then pla-
" ced at the head of affairs Yazid's predecessor in the government and wrote to (the
" khalif) Yazid Ibn Abd al-Malik a letter in which they said : ' We have not cast off
" ' our allegiance', but Yazid Ibn Abi Muslim treated us in a manner which neither
" ' God nor the Musulmans could brook. We therefore slew him and reinstated
" ' in office your former governor.' To this, Yazid Ibn Abd al-Malik replied by a
" letter in which he said : ' I disapprove of Yazid Ibn Abi Muslim's conduct and
" ' confirm the appointment of Muhammad Ibn Yazid to the government of Ifrikiya.
" ' This was in the year 102." Al-Waddah Ibn Khaithama related as follows :
" Omar Ibn Abd al-Aziz ordered me to set at liberty some people who were in prison,
" and Yazid Ibn Abi Muslim was among them. Him I left where he was, but let
" out all the others. This he could never forgive me. When we were in Ifrikiya,
" we heard that Yazid was coming to act as governor, and I therefore took to
" flight. He, being informed of the place where I was, sent persons to arrest me
" and bring me to him. When I was taken before him, he said : ' For a long time
" ' I have been asking Almighty God to place you in my power.' To this I replied :
" ' For a long time I have been asking Almighty God to protect me from you!' —
" ' God has not protected you," said Yazid, " and, by Allah! I shall kill you. Were
" ' the angel of death to come for you, I should hasten to take your life before he
" ' did.'" He then called for the sword and the naṭâ (4). They were brought
in, and al-Waddah was placed on the naṭâ by his order, with his hands tied behind his back. A man holding a sword stood behind him and (at that very moment) was heard the call to prayer. Yazid went out to join the congregation and,
as he was making the prostration, the swords (of the conspirators) took away his life.
A man then came in to al-Waddah, cut his bonds and set him at liberty. Muhammad Ibn Yazid, a mawla of the Ansars, was re-established in the government. — So
says at-Tabari; he names Muhammad Ibn Yazid, but Ibn Asakir gives that of Ismail
Ibn Obaid Allah. God knows best! — I may here observe that al-Waddah was
chamberlain to Omar Ibn Abd al-Aziz. Being ordered by that khalif, who had been
taken ill, to set at liberty all the prisoners, he let every one of them out, with the
exception of Yazid. On the death of Omar, al-Waddah fled to Ifrikiya, through fear
of Yazid, and then took place what has been related.—Omar fell sick at Khonakira.

—The word جامعة (*jámeá*) employed above, where mention is made of Yazid Ibn Abi Muslim's being brought before the khalif, means a collar by which the hands are fastened to the neck.—The د in the word دميم *damîm* which occurs in the expression (rendered by) *low-set* and ungainly, is written without a point and signifies *ugly*. Omar (*the khalif*) said : " Give not your daughters in marriage to ugly (دميم) men, for that " which, in men, pleases women is the same which, in women, pleases men (i. e. " *beauty*)." ذميم (*zamîm*) with a point on the ذ signifies *blamable*. Ibn ar-Rûmi (*vol. II. p. 297*) employed the word rightly when he said :

> Like the fellow-wives of a handsome woman; they say of her face, unjustly and through envy, that it is ugly (*damîm*).

I have indicated the right orthography of the word because it is often incorrectly written.—*Khundeira* is the name of an ancient village in al-Abass, which is a district in the province of Aleppo. It lies to the south-east of that city, near Kinnisrîn. Omar Ibn Abd al-Aziz acted there as governor, in the name of (*the khalif*) Abd al-Malik Ibn Marwân and in that of Sulaimân, the son of Abd al-Malik. It is this place which is meant in the following verse of el-Motanabbi :

> I love the country between Emesa and Khunfeira; every man loves the spot where he passed his early life.

The celebrated poet Adi Ibn ar-Rikâ al-Aâmili (5) mentions also this place in his well-known *kasîda* which rhymes in *d*; he says:

> When the vernal flowers follow in succession, may the rains water abundantly the Khundeira of al-Abass.

(1) This seems to mean that her hair had been cut off at one time to punish her for being a prostitute.

(2) The Traditionist Juwairiya Ibn Asmâ, a member of the Dabaah (الضبعة) tribe, died A. H. 173 (A. D. 789-90).

(3) A number of Traditionists bore the name of Yakûb, but we have not means of determining which of them it was whose authority is cited by Ibn Aalkir.

(4) The neck was a circular carpet of leather, having round the border a running string by means of which it might be drawn up into the shape of a bag. The executioner made use of it to receive the blood of those whom he beheaded.

(5) Adi Ibn Rikâ al-Aâmili, one of the numerous poets who flourished in the reign of al-Walîd Ibn Abd al-Malik, had frequently satirical encounters with the celebrated Jarîr (*vol. I. p. 294*). He usually resided in Damascus.

YAZID IBN OMAR IBN HUBAIRA

Abû Khâlid Yazîd Ibn Abi 'l-Muthanna Omar Ibn Hubaira Ibn Moaiya Ibn Sukain Ibn Khadlj Ibn Baghîd Ibn Mâlik Ibn Saad drew his descent from Adî, the son of Faadra, whose genealogy is so well known (1) that we need not lengthen this article by its insertion. According to Ibn Duraid (vol. *III.* p. 37) *Moaiya* (اميه) is the diminutif of *mian* (امي) which itself is the singular of the word *amda*, which signifies the *intestines*. This opinion is, however, rejected by others who consider the word as the diminutive of *(the proper name) Moaela*.—The vowels of *Sukain* are an u and ai ; in *Khadlj* and *Baghîd* the first vowel is an a. The other names are so generally known that it is not necessary for us to mark their pronounciation.— According to the *hâfiz* Abû 'l-Kâsim Ibn Asâkir (vol. *II.* p. 252), he *(Yazîd)* was a native of Syria and governed Kinnisrîn in the name of *(the khalif)* al-Walîd Ibn Yazîd Ibn Abd al-Malik. He accompanied Marwân Ibn Muhammad, the last of the Omaiyides, when that prince took the city of Damascus (A. H. 127, A. D. 744-5), and then obtained from him the government of all Irâk. He was born in the year 87 (A. D. 705-6). Ibn Aiyâsh (vol. *I.* p. 553) mentions him in the list of those governors who ruled in Irâk and held under their orders al-Misrain *(the two cities)* that is to say, al-Basra and al-Kûfa. —Ibn Kutaiba (vol. *II.* p. 22) says the same thing in his *Kitâb al-Maârif,* where he names those emirs who governed simultaneously the two Irâks. The first name on the list is that of Ziâd Ibn Abîh (vol. *I.* p. 364) who acted there as the lieutenant of Moawia Ibn Abi Sofyân, and the last is that of Yazîd Ibn Omar Ibn Hubaira, the subject of this article. The same writer adds : " No other, after these, " ever held the united governments of the two Irâks." In the same work, he had already spoken of him, in the article on Omar Ibn Hubaira. There he says: " Abû " Jaafar al-Mansûr besieged Yazîd in Wâsit during some months and obtained the " surrender of the city by granting him amnesty and protection. When Yazîd rode " forth, at the head of his household, to meet him, he said : ' No empire could " ' prosper with such a man in it;' and had him put to death."— Khalîfa Ibn Khaiyât (vol. *I.* p. 492) says : " In the year 128 (A. D. 745-6), Marwân Ibn Mu- " hammad dispatched Yazîd to Irâk, as governor. This was subsequently to the

" death of ad-Dabbák. " — He means ad-Dahhák as-Shaibáni Ibn Kais the khárijite (2).— " Yazid went as far as Hit, and there stopped. He was tall and corpu-
" lent, brave, liberal, a good orator and a great eater, but inclined to envy."—
Abù Jaafar at-Tabari mentions him in his History, under the year 128 : " In this
" year," says he, " Marwán Ibn Muhammad sent Yazid Ibn Omar Ibn Hubaira
" to Irák, for the purpose of warring against the Khárijites who were in that
" country." He then, under the year 132 (A. D. 749-50), speaks of the revolt got
up by Kahtaba Ibn Shabib, one of the Abbaside missionaries (or political agents),
subsequently to the triumph of that party in Khorásán and the adjoining countries.
Abù Muslim al-Khorásáni, the same of whom we have already spoken (vol. II. p. 100),
was the principal abettor of that movement and continued to be its main-spring till
the Abbasides had fully established their authority. The history of these events is
well known, and, as we have given some account of them in our article on Abù Muslim, we need not enter into further particulars. Kahtaba revolted in Irák and marched
against Yazid Ibn Omar Ibn Hubaira. Some encounters, too numerous to be related, took place between them, and we may state, in a summary manner, that
Kahtaba forded the Euphrates (with his army), in the neighbourhood of al-Falùja, a
well-known village in Irák, and advanced to attack Ibn Hubaira, who was on the
opposite bank of the river. Kahtaba was drowned. This occurred on Wednesday
evening, the 8th of Muharram (27th Aug. A. D. 749), towards sunset, and his son,
al-Hasan, replaced him as chief of the army. This is not a fit place for relating
this celebrated battle, as a full account of it would be too long. Maan Ibn Záida as-
Shaibáni (vol. III. p. 396) was one of Yazid Ibn Hubaira's partisans and his ablest
assistant in all affairs, either of war or otherwise. It is said that in the night (of
the battle), he struck Kahtaba Ibn Shabib with his sabre on the head or, according
to another statement, on the shoulder, so that he fell into the water. He was taken
out alive and said (to his people) : " If I die, let the water be my grave, so that no
" one may know what has become of me." Other relations are given respecting
the manner in which he was drowned, and God best knows the truth ! — Let us return to our account of Ibn Hubaira : Seeing his troops vanquished and put to flight by
the army of which Kahtaba, and then al-Hasan, the son of Kahtaba, was the commander, he took refuge in Wásit and fortified himself in that city. Abù 'l-Abbás Abd
Allah, the son of Muhammad Ibn Ali Ibn Abd Allah Ibn al-Abbás Ibn Abd al-Muttalib, and surnamed as-Saffáh, then arrived from al-Humaima with his brother Abù

Jaafar Abd Allah Ibn Muhammad (*the same who was*) surnamed al-Mansûr. The
village of *al-Humaima*, situated on that part of the Syrian frontier which extends
from the territory of al-Balkâ to Kûfa, was then the residence of the Abbasides, and
there were assembled a number of their partisans, their agents and the persons who
were assisting them in establishing the Abbaside dynasty and overthrowing that of
the Omaiyides. The chief of the latter dynasty and the last of its sovereigns was, at
that time, Marwân Ibn Muhammad Ibn Marwân Ibn al-Hakam. He bore the surname of al-Jaadi and was designated familiarly by the nickname of al-Ilimâr (3).
When they arrived at Kûfa, Abû 'l-Abbâs as-Saffâh was solemnly acknowledged as
sovereign. The inauguration took place on Friday, the 13th of the latter Rabî, 132
(29th November, A. D. 749). Another account places that event in the month of the
first Rabî, but the preceding date is the true one. The cause of the Abbasides then
began to triumph and their power augmented whilst that of the Omaiyides declined.
(*Abû Jaafar*) al-Mansûr, being then dispatched by his brother, as-Saffâh, with the
order to besiege Yazîd Ibn Omar Ibn Hubaira in Wâsit, joined the army which was
then posted near the city, under the orders of al-Hasan Ibn Kahtaba. At-Tabari
says, in his great historical work : " Frequent messages passed between Abû Jaa-
" far al-Mansûr and Ibn Hubaira. The latter then demanded by letter that an
" *amân* (or *full pardon*) should be given to him. A paper to that effect was drawn
" up and sent to him. He passed forty days in consulting doctors of the law (*on
" its validity*), before he consented to accept it. Abû Jaafar, to whom it was then
" brought back, sent it to as-Saffâh, who ordered him to ratify it in Yazîd's favour.
" Abû Jaafar's intention was to fulfil all the conditions granted, but as-Saffâh never
" took a decision without the approbation of Abû Muslim al-Khorâsâni, who was the
" chief director of the Abbaside party and had a spy who informed him by letter of
" all as-Saffâh's proceedings. Abû Muslim then wrote these words to as-Saffâh :
" ' The best of roads is a bad one if there be stones on it, and, by Allah! no
" ' road is good in which one meets with Ibn Hubaira.' When the letter of am-
" nesty was signed, Ibn Hubaira left the city at the head of thirteen hundred Naj-
" jârites (4) and was proceeding to enter on horseback into the enclosure (*sur-
" rounding Abû Jaafar's tent*), when the door-keeper stood up and said : ' Welcome,
" ' Abû Khâlid! dismount quietly!' Ten thousand of the Khorasanide troops were
" then drawn up about the enclosure. Yazîd dismounted, asked for a cushion so
" that he might sit down and then, at his request, the chiefs of the troop who came

" with him were admitted. The door-keeper now said to him : Abû Khâlid! you
" ' may go in.' The other replied: ' Do you mean me and those who are with
" ' me?' The door-keeper answered : ' I asked permission for you alone to enter.'
" Yazîd stood up and went in. A cushion was placed for him and he conversed
" for some time with him (Abû Jaafar). As he was withdrawing, Abû Jaafar kept
" his eyes fixed upon him till he disappeared. (Yazîd) then went to visit him every
" second day, accompanied by a troop of five hundred horse and three hundred foot.
" Yazîd Ibn Hâtim (see the next article) then said to Abû Jaafar : ' Emir! this
" ' Ibn Hubaira is capable of coming and intimidating (our) troops, for he has lost
" ' none of his influence.' Abû Jaafar, in consequence, ordered the door-keeper
" to inform Ibn Hubaira that, in coming again, he ought not to bring with him all
" his troop, but merely his usual attendants. Ibn Hubaira changed colour on re-
" ceiving this message and came (the next time,) with a suite of about thirty persons.
" On this, the door-keeper said to him : ' You seem to have come prepared (for
" ' whatever may happen).' The other replied : ' If you tell me to come on foot,
" ' I shall do so.' — ' Nay,' said the door-keeper, ' I mean nothing disrespectful,
" ' and the emir has given no orders but for your advantage.' After that, Yazîd
" made his visits every third day. Muhammad Ibn Kathîr related as follows:
" One day, in a conversation between Ibn Hubaira and Abû Jaafar, the latter
" made use of the expression : ' I say, you sir !' or : ' I say, my man !' and
" then added, as if to correct himself : ' Emir! I merely employed the terms in
" ' which I not long ago heard people address you, and my tongue has outrun
" ' my thought.'—Abû 'l-Abbâs as-Saffâh insisted on Abû Jaafar's putting Ibn Hu-
" baira to death and, on his persisting to refuse, he wrote to him these words: ' By
" ' Allah! you must kill him, or else I shall send a person who will take him out
" ' of your enclosure and put him to death.' This letter decided Abû Jaafar on ta-
" king Yazîd Ibn Hubaira's life. He therefore caused all the rooms of the public
" treasury (in Wâsit) to be sealed up and sent for the principal officers in Ibn Hu-
" baira's service. When they came, his door-keeper stepped forward and called out
" the names of two eminent chiefs, Ibn al-Hauthara and Muhammad Ibn Nubâta.
" They stood up, went in, and were immediately deprived of their swords and hand-
" cuffed by three officers whom Abû Jaafar had posted within the precincts of his tent,
" with one hundred men. Then two other chiefs were introduced and treated in
" the same manner. Two others were then let in and underwent a similar treatment.

" This was done also with the rest. Músa Ibn Akíl (*who was one of them*) said : ' You
" ' took an engagement with us in God's name and have betrayed us; but I hope that
" ' God will punish you.' Ibn Nubáta (*intending to express his contempt*) made a
" noise with his lips, as if breaking wind (5), on which Ibn al-Hauthara said to him :
" ' That will avail you nothing.' The other replied : ' This I had almost foreseen.'
" They were all put to death and their signet-rings taken off. Házim, al-Haitham
" Ibn Shaba and al-Aghlab Ibn Sálim then took with them about one hundred men
" and, having gone to Ibn Hubaira's residence, they sent in to him this message :
" ' We must have your treasures.' He told his door-keeper to go with them and
" point out where they were deposited. They placed guards at each of the doors
" and began to search every corner of the house. Ibn Hubaira had then with
" him his son Dáwúd, his secretary Omar Ibn Aiyúb, his door-keeper, some of his
" mawlas and, in his arms, he was holding a young child, one of his sons.
" Alarmed at the sight of these people, he exclaimed : ' I declare, by Allah! that
" ' the looks of those men portend nothing good.' They went up to him, the
" door-keeper placed himself before them and said : 'Stand off!' on which al-
" Haitham Ibn Shaba gave him a blow on the shoulder (*with his sabre*) and brought
" him to the ground. Dáwúd then attacked them but was killed; the mawlas also
" lost their lives. On this, he (*Ibn Hubaira*) laid down the child, exclaiming : Take
" care of the boy! and prostrated himself (*in prayer*). He was slain whilst in that
" position. Abú Jaafar, to whom their heads were carried, ordered a general am-
" nesty to be proclaimed. Abú 'l-Alâ as-Sindi, whose real name was Marzúk or Aflah,
" and who was a mawla of the tribe of Asad, lamented Ibn Hubaira's death in the
" following lines :

" The eyes which shed not over thee abundant tears, on the (*fatal*) day of Wásit, were sorely
" congealed. On that evening the female mourners stood forward, whilst bosoms and cheeks
" were torn in the presence of the assembly. The court before thy dwelling is now deserted,
" but often did visitors station there, hand after hand. From those who came to visit thee,
" thou didst never keep away; but alas! how far away are those who repose under the earth."

I may observe here that Abú Tammám at-Taî (vol. I. p. 348) has given this piece
in his *Hamása*, section of elegies. Here finish the indications borrowed from at-Tabari; they are roughly put together, having been extracted from different parts of his
work. Another author says : " When Abú Jaafar joined al-Hasan Ibn Kahtaba
" (*under the walls of Wásit*) the latter gave up his tent to him and went some where

" else. Hostilities continued for some days; Ibn Hubaira, seconded by Maan Ibn
" Zaida, held out firmly and sustained a long siege. Abû Jaafar happened to say
" that Ibn Hubaira, in sheltering himself behind ramparts, acted like a woman, and
" the latter, who was told of this, sent him a message to the following effect : ' If
" ' you said so and so, come out and meet me (in single combat). You will then see
" ' (what I am).' Abû Jaafar answered in these terms : ' I know of nothing to
" ' which I and you can be compared except a lion who met a wild-boar. The boar
" ' said to him : ' Come and fight me ; ' the other answered : ' You are not my equal
" ' in rank; if I encounter you and get a hurt, I should be disgraced, and, if I kill-
" ' ed you, it would only be the killing of a boar, and I should obtain for that
" ' neither praise nor honour.' The boar said : ' If you come not out to fight me, I
" ' shall tell the other animals that you were afraid to meet me.' The lion answer-
" ed : ' It will be easier for me to bear with your false imputations than with the
" ' disgrace of defiling my claws with your blood.' Al-Mansûr, having opened a cor-
" respondence with Ibn Hubaira and the other chiefs, they asked to capitulate and
" drew up a model of a treaty of peace and safeguard. Al-Mansûr sent this docu-
" ment to his brother, as-Saffâh, who ratified it, after inserting the following
" clause : ' If Ibn Hubaira break his word or infringe this agreement, the engage-
" ' ments taken with him and the amnesty granted to him shall be null and void.'
" Al-Mansûr's intention was to act with good faith towards Ibn Hubaira."—Abû 'l-
Hasan al-Madâini (vol. I. p. 438) says : " When the treaty of peace was written out,
" Ibn Hubaira went to visit al-Mansûr, who had a curtain drawn before him, and
" spoke in these terms : ' Emir ! your dynasty has only commenced; so, let the
" ' people taste of its sweetness and spare them its bitterness ; love for your fa-
" ' mily will thus penetrate into their hearts and the mentioning of your names will
" ' be agreeable to their tongues. We always thought your cause would succeed.'
" When he had finished, al-Mansûr caused the curtain to be drawn from between them
" and said to himself : ' How strange that he (my brother) should order me to kill such
" ' a man as this !' Ibn Hubaira, in his last days, went to dine and sup with al-
" Mansûr, taking with him only three of his companions, and was treated with the
" utmost regard (8). It is said that he engaged in a correspondence with Abd Allah,
" the son of al-Hasan, the son of al-Hasan, the son of Ali Ibn Abi Tâlib, that he
" tried to gain partisans for the cause of the Alides and intended to overthrow the
" power of the Abbasides. He (as-Saffâh) then received a letter from Abû Muslim,

"urging him to put Ibn Hubaira to death, and as-Saffáh, in consequence, wrote to
"al-Mansûr the order to take his life. Al-Mansûr replied : ' I shall not do so: I
"' am engaged towards that man by a treaty and a promise of protection; these I
"' shall not break at the word of Abû Muslim.' As-Saffáh answered : ' I do not
"' order his death in consequence of a word from Abû Muslim, but because he has
"' infringed the treaty and is carrying on a secret intrigue with the family of Ali
"' Ibn Abi Tálib; his blood is lawfully forfeited.' To this al-Mansûr returned no
"answer, declaring that such a deed would be the ruin of the empire. As-Saffáh
"then wrote to him, saying : ' If you do not put him to death, I shall break off all
"' connection with you.' Al-Mansûr then said to al-Hasan Ibn Kahtaba : ' Do you
"' kill him?'—' I will not,' replied al-Hasan. On this, Hâzim Ibn Khuzaima
"declared that he was willing to do the deed. He therefore took with him some of
"the Khorassanide chiefs, entered into the castle where Ibn Hubaira was and found
"him in company with his son Dâwûd, his secretary and his mawlas. He had on
"an Egyptian shirt and a rose-coloured mantle; a barber was with him and about
"to cup him. When he saw them come in, he prostrated himself (in prayer) and
"was slain by them, as also his son Dâwûd, his secretary and those who were with
"him. His head was borne to al-Mansûr. Maan Ibn Záida escaped the same fate,
"being then with as-Saffáh. Al-Mansûr sent the head to his brother. This took
"place in the year 132 (A. D. 749-50)."—Al-Haitham Ibn Adi (vol. III. p. 633)
related as follows : " When Ibn Hubaira was killed, a Khorassanide said to one of
"that chief's followers : ' What an enormous head your master had !' and received
"this reply : ' Your granting him a safeguard was even more enormous.' "—The
khatîb Abû Zakariya at-Tabrîsi says, in his commentary on the Hamdsa, section of
elegies, after giving the verses rhyming in d which were composed by Abû Atâ
as-Sindi on the death of Ibn Hubaira : " Al-Mansûr had sworn to act with good faith
"towards him and confirmed that engagement by a most solemn oath (7). When he
"killed him, the head was brought to him and he said to the guard (who come with
"it) : ' Look at the enormous size of his head;' and to this, the guard replied :
"' The safeguard granted to him was a greater enormity than his head.' Al-Man-
"sûr destroyed the castle of Wâsit."—The hâfiz Ibn Asâkir says, in his greater history : " Every morning, when Ibn Hubaira awoke, they brought him an dus (جرّ),
—this word means a large bowl,—" containing some honey, or else some sugar, on
"which milk had been drawn (from the camel). He would drink it off and towards

" the hour of morning prayer, would remain seated in the oratory till the proper
" time for saying it came. After that he would retire and, when the milk ope-
" rated, call for breakfast. At this repast he eat two fowls, two *adhids*,"—or young
pigeons,—" half a kid and flesh-meat dress in a variety of ways. He then went out,
" examined into the applications made to him, and, at noon, when he retired, he
" would send for some of his officers and of the chief men of the place, and then call
" for dinner. Placing a napkin over his breast, he would swallow large morsels
" without stopping. When he finished, the company retired and he went in to
" the women, with whom he remained till the hour of the after-noon prayer. He
" would then come out to pray, after which, he would give audience to applicants,
" examine into their affairs and say the *asr* prayer. A throne being then set up
" him and chairs placed for the others, all sat down, and bowls (*irds*) of honied milk
" and other drinks were brought in. The cloth being spread for the people and co-
" vered with dishes of meat, a table was set on an estrade for himself and his compa-
" nions. They eat with him and, after sunset, they went to attend the evening
" prayer. When the prayer was over, the persons who were to pass the evening with
" him would assemble in a room and sit there till called in. Conversation would
" then be carried on till the night was far advanced. Every evening, he allowed ten
" services to be asked of him, and these were all granted the next morning. His
" (yearly) salary was six hundred thousand dirhems (£.15,000). Every month he
" would distribute large sums to his companions, to the legists and to the members of
" respectable families. Abd Allah Ibn Shuburma ad-Dabbi, the *kadi* and juris-
" consult of Kûfa, who was one of those who were admitted to his evening conver-
" sations, said:

" When the night was advanced and sleep was overcoming us, Aiyâd would bring to us one
" of the two reliefs.

" Aiyâd was his door-keeper and the two reliefs were the permission of going in
" (to the emir) or of retiring. (At these social meetings) he had no napkin and,
" when he called for one (it was a signal for) the company to rise up (and retire)."
A *sheikh* of the Kuraish tribe related as follows : " On a very hot summer's day, Yazîd
" Ibn Omar Ibn Hubaira admitted some people (who were waiting to be introduced).
" He had on an old tunic the breast of which was patched. They looked at him

" with wonder and he, remarking their astonishment, recited this verse of Ibrâhîm
" Ibn Harma's (8), applying it to himself :

A gallant youth can attain to glory, though his robe be torn and his tunic patched.

His generous deeds, his noble qualities and the anecdotes related of him are numerous and well-known.— Khalîfa Ibn Khaiyât says : " Ibn Hubaira was put to death
" at Wâsit, on Monday, the 16th of Zû 'l-Kaada, 132 (26th June, A. D. 750)." —
In at-Tabari's historical work, the death of al-Hasan, the son of Kahtaba, is placed
under the year 181 (A. D. 797-8).

(1) This genealogy is given by Mr Caussin de Perceval in his *Essai sur l'Histoire des Arabes*. According
to the tables, Fazâra drew his descent from Maad Ibn Adnân, by Ghatafân.

(2) There were two generals bearing the names of ad-Dahhâk Ibn Kais. One of them was a Kuraishite, of
the family of Fihr; he governed the district of Damascus in the name of Moawia Ibn Abi Sofyân, joined the
party of Abd Allah Ibn az-Zubair, then had himself acknowledged as khalif by his own troops, the Kaisites.
He was slain at Marj Râhit, A. H. 64 (A. D. 683-4) in fighting against the khalif Marwân the first (see vol. I,
p. 180). The other belonged to the tribe of Shaibân. He put himself at the head of the Kharijites, a branch
of the Khârijite party in Mesopotamia, took the city of Kûfa from Abd Allah, the son of Omar Ibn Abd al-Azîz,
and then marched against Marwân the second. He was slain in battle at Kafraîbîs in the month of Safar,
128 (November, A. D. 745). — Notwithstanding Reiske's recommendation, one of these chiefs has been
sometimes confounded with the other, a fault of which there is an example in this work, vol. II, p. 103; the
note (11) should be struck out.

(3) *Al-Rimda* means *the ass*. Marwân received this nickname for the tenacity of his character.

(4) The Najjârites formed a branch of that religious and political party, the Khârijites, who may be considered as the Puritans of Islamism.

(5) The Arabic signifies literally : *pepedit in barba sua*. This noise, made with the lips, was probably
meant to express contempt.

(6) Literally : and the cushion was doubled for him. See page 190, note (11) of this volume.

(7) This passage is omitted in Freytag's *Hamdsa*. It must have existed in the larger Hamdsa, but not a
copy remains of that work.

(8) Abd Lahâk Ibrahim Ibn Ali Ibn Harma, a member of the tribe of Kuraish, inhabited Medina and bore
a high reputation as a poet. He was born A. H. 90 (A. D. 708-9); in A. H. 140 (A. D. 757) he recited to
the khalif al-Mansûr a kasida of his composition. He was notorious for his fondness of wine and his avarice.
His death took place in the year 150 A. D. 602. — (*Kitâb al-Aghânî; Nujûm*.)

YAZID IBN HATIM AL-MUHALLABI

Abû Khâlid Yazîd was the son of Hâtim Ibn Kabîsa Ibn al-Muhallab Ibn Abi Sufra al-Azdi. The rest of the genealogy has been already given in our article on his (great-) grandfather al-Muhallab (vol. III. p. 508). We have spoken of his brother Rôh Ibn Hâtim (vol. I. p. 529), of his father's uncle, Yazîd Ibn al-Muhallab (p. 164 of this vol.) and of his descendant, the vizir Abû Muhammad al-Hasan Ibn Muhammad al-Muhallabi (vol. I. p. 410). They belonged to an eminent family which produced a great number of illustrious and distinguished men. Ibn Jarîr at-Tabari vol. II. p. 597) says, in his Annals, that the khalif Abû Jaafar al-Mansûr took the government of Egypt from Humaid Ibn Kahtaba and gave it to Naufal Ibn al-Farât, whom he replaced, A. H. 143 (A. D. 760-1) by Yazîd Ibn Hâtim. In the year 152 (A. D. 769), al-Mansûr appointed Muhammad Ibn Saîd as the successor of Yazîd. Abû Saîd Ibn Yûnus (vol. II. p. 93) says, in his Annals, that Yazîd Ibn Hâtim obtained the government of Egypt in the year 144, and another author adds : " in " the middle of the month of Zû 'l-Kaada." " Then," says he (at-Tabari), " in " the year 154 (A. D. 771), al-Mansûr went to Syria and visited Bait al-Makdis (the " house of the holy place, Jerusalem) and, from that place, he dispatched Yazîd Ibn " Hâtim to Ifrîkiya, with an army of fifty thousand men, for the purpose of carrying " on the war against the Kharijites, who had killed Omar Ibn Hafs, his governor in " that country (1). Yazîd held the government of Ifrîkiya from that moment (till his " death). He vanquished the Kharijites and then made his entry into Kairawân, " A. H. 155 (A. D. 771-2), the year of his arrival in Ifrîkiya. By his liberality and " his princely disposition he drew numerous visitors to his court; all spoke loudly " in his praise and a number of poets who extolled his merits received from him " magnificent rewards." Abû Osâma Rabîa Ibn Thâbit ar-Rakki (vol. I. p. 530), a member of the tribe of Asad, or, by another account, a mawla of the tribe of Sulaim, went to visit Yazîd Ibn Osaid, who was then governor of Armenia and who held that place for a long time under the khalifate of Abû Jaafar al-Mansûr and of that prince's son and successor, al-Mahdi. The genealogy of this Yazîd is as follows : Yazîd Ibn Osaid Ibn Zâfir Ibn Asmâ Ibn Osaid Ibn Kunfud Ibn Jâbir Ibn Kunfud

Ibn Mâlik Ibn Aûf Ibn Amr il-Kais Ibn Buhtha Ibn Sulaim Ibn Mansûr Ibn Ikrima Ibn Khasafa Ibn Kais Ghailân Ibn Modar Ibn Nizâr Ibn Maadd Ibn Adnân. He held a very high rank in the tribe of Kais, of which he was one the bravest warriors and the ablest politicians. The Rabia above mentioned praised him in a poem of considerable merit but, not having received from him an adequate retribution, he composed another on Yazid Ibn Hâtim, the subject of this article, and was treated by him with the utmost munificence. He, in consequence, recited a kasîda in which he extolled Yazid Ibn Hâtim and depreciated Yazid Ibn Osaid. As the latter had an imperfection in his speech, he alluded to this defect in the poem and said :

> I declare by an oath which will admit of no subterfuge, by the oath of a man who swears without intending to prevaricate, that wide is the difference in generosity between the two Ta-zids, him of the tribe of Sulaim and the illustrious son of Hâtim ! Yazid of Sulaim is a saver of money, but that hero, the brother of the Azdites, is not a saver of his. Profusion is the Azdite hero's only aim, but the Kaiside's passion is to hoard up dirhems. Let no the stammerers suppose that I satirize him; I merely assign pre-eminence to men of merit. O thou who strivest to reach the bright station by him whose generosity is (not less copious than) oceans full to overflowing! Thou hast vainly endeavoured to imitate, in munificence, the son of Hâtim; thou wert often remiss, but the Azdite was no saver. Be satisfied with (admiring) the edifice of noble deeds raised by the son of Hâtim whilst he toiled in delivering captives and faced the greatest dangers. Son of Osaid! strive not to rivalize with the son of Hâtim; if you do, you will gnash your teeth with regret. He is the ocean; if you attempt to enter it, you will perish in the shock of its waters. I foolishly hoped to find honour in the tribe of Solaim; what an idle, what a visionary thought! But the family of Muhallab is a brilliant constellation and, in war, it leads yours (like a camel) by the bridle. The family of Muhallab are as the nose on the face; all others are as the soles of the feet, and the nose is far exalted above the soles. I have declared them worthy of all glory and justly pronounced them superior to all other men. They alone possess the noblest of qualities, liberality and bravery in battle. Even in adversity, they set no value on their money; even when borne on the bier, they gave protection to every outlaw.

Dibil Ibn Ali 'l-Khuzâi, the poet of whom we have already spoken (vol. I. p. 507), related the following anecdote : "I said to the poet Marwân Ibn Abi Hafsa : 'Tell "'me, Abû 's-Simt! who is the best of all your modern poets?' He replied : 'The "'man who, of them all, composed the simplest of verses!'—'Who is that?' said I. "' — He answered : 'The man who said :

> "'How different in generosity are the two Yazids, he of the tribe of Solaim and the illus-
> "'trious son of Hâtim.'"

I already gave some of these verses in the life of Rûh Ibn Hâtim (vol. I. p. 530),

Yazid's brother, but since met with a more complete copy of the poem and then decided on giving a separate notice of Yazid himself; for, in the case of a person so important, the slight account of him which we inserted in the life of his brother was really insufficent.—Rabia Ibn Thâbit ar-Rakki had gone to visit Yazid some time before this, but did not obtain from him the favorable reception which he expected. He therefore composed a piece of verse in which was the following line :

> I render God due thanks; but here I am returning with the boots of Husain (?), as a gift from the son of Hâtim.

When Abû Jaafar al-Mansûr gave the government of Ifrikiya to Yazid (Ibn Hâtim) Ibn al-Muhallab and that of Egypt to Yazid (Ibn Osaid) of the tribe of Sulaim, they both set out together, and the former defrayed the expenses of the troops (which escorted them). To this, Rabia ar-Rakki alluded in these verses :

> Yazid the bountiful! your namesake, the Yazid of our tribe, is not so lavish of his gifts as you.
> He leads a troop of horse; you, another; yet both of them are payed by you.

This proves that Sulaim was the tribe to which Rabia belonged, for he says that Yazid (Ibn Osaid) was of his tribe.   Ashab (3), he who was so notorious for his cupidity, visited Yazid (Ibn Hâtim), who was then in Egypt, and sat down with the company assembled in the saloon.   Seeing him whisper to a servant-boy, he went over to him and kissed his hand.   " Why do you so?" said Yazid.   Ashab replied : " Because I saw you whisper to your boy and thought that you were telling him to " give me something."   Yazid laughed and said : " I told him no such thing, but " I shall do it."   He therefore made him a present and treated him with kindness. — At-Tortûshi (vol. II. p. 685) says, in his Siráj al-Mulûk : " Sabnûn Ibn Said " (vol. II. p. 131) declared that Yazid Ibn Hâtim was truly a sage because he used " to say : ' By Allah! I fear nothing so much as a man whom I may have wronged " ' and who, to my knowledge, has no one to protect him except God.   What I " ' dread is, that he may say : ' May God call you to an account I may be judge be- " ' tween me and you!' "—Abû Saad as-Samâni (vol. II. p. 156) says, in his Kitáb al-Ansáb : " The poet al-Mushahhar at-Tamimi went to visit Yazid, who was then in " Ifrikiya, and recited to him these lines :

> " That I might reach you sooner, I shortened my prayers by half, during a month's jour-

" ary and another mouth added to that. I fear not that the hopes which I placed on you
" shall be frustrated; but the sweetest gift is that which comes soonest.

" On this, Yazid gave orders to bring money for the troops which he had in his
" pay and which formed an army of fifty thousand men. He then said : ' Those
" ' who wish to please me will lay aside two dirhems out of his pay for this man who
" ' has come to visit me.' He thus made up for him the sum of one hundred thou-
" sand dirhems, to which he himself added as much more."—I must here observe
that I found these two verses attributed to Marwán Ibn Abi Hafsa.—Abú 'l-Kásim
Ibn Asákir (vol. II. p. 250) says, in his History of Damascus, after giving an account of Yazid's life and mentioning the government which he held : " Yazid Ibn
" Hátim said to the persons who were sitting in his company : ' Let me hear from
" ' you three choice verses.' Safwán Ibn Safwán, a member of the Banú Harith
" family, which is a branch of the tribe of Khazraj, said to him : ' Must they be on
" ' you?' — ' Let them be on whom you please'; replied Yazid.   One would have
" thought that the poet had them ready in his sleeve, for he recited immediately
" these lines :

" I never knew what beneficence was except by hearsay, till I met with Yazid, the asylum
" of mankind (an-Nás).   I then met the most beneficent of those who walk upon feet; he was
" arrayed in an ample robe of liberality and bravery (as 'l-Bás).   If glory could be procured
" by beneficence (á), you would be its (sole) possessor and be more worthy of it than...

" There I stop, (said the poet) —' Finish the verse', said (Yazid) by the words the
" Abbasides (aali Abbási)'.   The poet answered : ' That would not be proper'. —
" He (Yazid) then said : ' Let no one ever hear you recite this piece.'"—Yamút
Ibn Muzarra (5) related as follows : " I went, one day, to salute al-Asmái (6) and hear
" him recite pieces composed by the good eulogistic poets of Moslim times, and I
" said to him : ' Tell me, Abú Othmán! Ibn al-Mawla, was he a good eulogistic
" ' poet?'   To this he replied : ' He was; and I have been kept awake all last night
" ' by that fine passage in which he praises Yahya Ibn Hátim and says :

" ' If honour could be bought or sold, others might sell it but Yazid would be the purcha-
" ' ser.   When the lightning prepares to flash from the cloud of his (beneficence), the hands
" ' of those who invoke such showers are held forth before the flash appears.   When you
" ' (Yahya) do a noble act, you accomplish it with hands whose generous gifts are always
" ' unalloyed.   When people count those who are the bravest among the horsemen, every
" ' finger points you out as one of the number.' "

Ibn al-Mawla went to see Yazid, when the latter was governor of Egypt, and recited to him the following verses :

> Thou who, of all the Arabs, standest alone, without an equal! did another like thee exist, there would not be a poor man in the world.

Yazid, on hearing these verses, called for his treasurers and asked them how much money he had remaining in his chests. They replied : "There are gold and "silver pieces to the amount of twenty thousand dirhems (£. 500)"; he told them to give the whole sum to the poet, whom he then addressed in these terms : "Brother! I ask pardon of God and next of you; did I possess more, I should not "with hold it from you." *Ibn al-Mawla* was the surname of the poet Abû Abd Allah Muhammad Ibn Muslim. Al-Asmâi (vol. *II. p.* 123) related also (7) that, when Yazid was in Ifrikiya, a courier came with the news that a son was born to him in Basra. On hearing this, he said : "I give him the name of al-Mughira." (The *poet*) al-Mushahhar at-Tamimi, who was present, exclaimed : "God grant that this "child be a blessing to you and that his sons be as great a blessing to him "as his father has been to his grandfather." — Yazid held the government of Ifrikiya till his death. He died at Kairawân, on Tuesday, the 18th of Ramadân, 170 (13th March, A. D. 787), and was buried near the city gate called Bâb Salm. His son, Dâwûd, was appointed by him as governor of Ifrikiya, but was removed from office, in the year 172 (A. D. 788-9), by Hârûn ar-Rashid. His successor was Rûh (Rauh) Ibn Hâtim.

---

(1) See Ibn Khaldûn's *History of the Berbers*, vol. I, p. 114 of the French translation.

(2) See vol. III, p. 273.

(3) Ashab Ibn Jobair, a native of Medina, was always expecting to receive presents, even from persons whom he did not know. Numerous anecdotes are related of his infatuation. See Abû 'l-Fedâ's *Annals*, t. II, p. 113, and Freytag's *Meidani*, t. II, p. 64. He died A. H. 164 (A. D. 774).

(4) The text says : If beneficence could be obtained by glory. All the manuscripts agree in the reading, but it is not satisfactory.

(5) The life of Yazid will be found in this volume.

(6) This is certainly a mistake; al-Asmâi died eighty-eight years before Yazid, and we find, lower down, that the latter gives him the surname of Abû Othmân, not of Abû Saîd. Our author probably meant to name Abû Othmân al-Jâbis (vol. II, p. 111), who was Yazid's uncle.

(7) The insertion of the word *also* (أيضا) is probably a mistake of the author's. See the preceding note.

YAZID IBN MAZYAD AS-SHAIBANI

Yazid, surnamed Abû Khâlid and Abû Zubair, was the son of Mazyad Ibn Zâida as-Shaibâni and the nephew of Maan Ibn Zâida, bim whose life we have already given (vol. III. p. 398). The remainder of the genealogy is there set forth in full, so, we need not repeat it here. This Yazld was a famous chieftain, renowned for bravery. He was governor of Armenia, but, in the year 172 (A. D. 788-9), he was deposed by Hârûn ar-Rashid. Eleven years later, that khalif appointed him to the united governments of Armenia and Adarbaijân. We have already related something of his history in our account of al-Walîd Ibn Tarîf (vol. III. p. 668); it was Yazld who conducted the war against that Khârijite and slew him. Al-Walîd took up arms against Hârûn ar-Rashid in the year 178 (A. D. 704-5). He revolted in al-Jazîra (Mesopotamia), the province situated between the Euphrates and the shatt (or river) of Mosul (the Tigris). His partisans, the Shurât, became so numerous that they overran all that country and killed the governor of Diâr Rabîa, who had marched against them. They then invaded Diâr Modar and besieged Abd al-Malik Ibn Sâlib Ibn Ali the Abbaside (vol. I. p. 316) in ar-Rakka. Ar-Rashid asked the advice of Yahya Ibn Khâlid the Barmekide, as to whom he should send to carry on the war against the insurgents. Yahya replied : " Send Mûsa Ibn Hâsim of the tribe of " Tamim, for Pharaoh's real name was al-Walîd and he was drowned by Mûsa (Moses)." Ar-Rashid placed this chief at the head of a numerous army and sent him off. Al-Walîd and his partisans advanced against him, put his troops to flight and slew him. When this news reached ar-Rashid, he dispatched against him Mamar Ibn Îsa al-Abdi. A number of encounters took place between the two armies, in the territory of Dârâ (a city) in Diâr Rabîa ; hostilities continued for a considerable time, and the bands of al-Walîd increased to such a degree that he became extremely powerful. Ar-Rashid then said : " No person is capable of conducting this war " except that bedwin Arab, Yazîd Ibn Mazyad as-Shaibâni. The poet Bakr Ibn an-" Nattâh (1) said :

"Send not against (the tribe of) Rabîa any other than a Rabîanite; iron cannot be cut except
by iron."

Ar-Rachîd placed Yazîd at the head of a numerous army and ordered him to go and give battle to the rebel. Yazîd went in pursuit of al-Walîd who, being full of craft and cunning, endeavoured to circumvent him. A number of conflicts ensued; ar-Rashîd, being informed that Yazîd was dilatory in his movements, sent him one troop of cavalry after another, and then dispatched an officer to reprimand him. Yazîd went therefore in pursuit of the enemy and, having stopped in order to say the morning prayer, he was surprised, before finishing, to see al-Walîd come up with his troops. The cavalry, on both sides, fell into rank, the soldiers marched forward and the battle was engaged. At that moment, Yazîd called out and said : " Al-Wa-" lîd! why do you take shelter behind your men? come out and fight with me."— " That I will!" replied al-Walîd. On this the armies halted, and not a man stirred from his place; the two champions tilted against each other, and the conflict lasted for some hours, without any advantage to either. At last, Yazîd found an opportunity, and gave his adversary such a stroke on the leg that he felled him to the ground. He (Yazîd) then cried out to his cavalry, which dashed forward, and they cut off his (al-Walîd's) head.—Abû Yâkûb Ishak Ibn Ibrahîm, surnamed Ibn al-Kirâb (2) al-Harawi, says, in the historical work of which he is the author, that al-Walîd Ibn Tarîf was killed by Yazîd Ibn Mazyad at al-Hadîtha, a place situated near Aâna (آنة), in the territory of the Euphratian al-Jazîra (Mesopotamia). It is called Hadîtha tan-Nûra, lies at the distance of some parasangs from al-Anbâr and must not be confounded with the Hadîtha of Mosul. Yazîd sent his son Asad (اسد) to ar-Rashîd with al-Walîd's head and a letter announcing the victory. On this occasion, the celebrated poet, Muslim Ibn al-Walîd al-Ansâri (vol. I. p. 25), who was wholly devoted to Yazîd, pronounced these verses :

> The khalif found among the descendants of Medar a sword so sharp that it separated bodies
> from heads. Were it not for Yazîd, — and causes has always a motive,—al-Walîd would have
> flourished many more years than two. Noble is Yazîd, and so were his fathers before him!
> To perpetuate their glory, they left (the recollection of) battle-days followed by battle-days.

When Yazîd returned to court, ar-Rashîd called him forward, assigned to him a place of honour and said : " Yazîd! most of the Moslim emirs belonged to your " tribe." To this, Yazîd replied : " They did; but, instead of mounting into pul-" pits (to say the khotba, as they hoped to do), they were mounted upon trunks of " palm-trees." By these words he meant the posts to which their bodies were atta-

ched when they lost their lives.—Al-Walid Ibn Tarif was slain in the year 179 (A. D.
795), as we have said in his article. Al-Fárɛa, his sister, lamented his death
in those admirable verses which we have there given and alluded again to it in the
following piece :

> Children of Walil the sword of Yazid has cast you into affliction by striking al-Walid. Had
> another sword than that of Yazid attacked him, it would not have been so fortunate. The chil-
> dren of Walil cannot be slain but by each other; iron cannot be notched except by iron.

It is related that Hárûn ar-Rashid, on sending Yazid Ibn Mazyad against al-Walid,
gave him Zû 'l-Fakâr, the sword which had belonged to the Prophet. "Take it,
" Yazid! by it you will be victorious." He took it, departed, and then occurred what
we have related of al-Walid's defeat and death. To this, Muslim Ibn al-Walid alludes, in the following verse of a kasida composed by him in praise of Yazid :

> You caused the Prophet's sword to recollect his way of acting and the bravery displayed by
> the first (Musulman) who ever prayed and fasted.

By these last words he meant Ali, the son of Abû Tálib, for he was the person who
dealt blows with it.—Hishâm Ibn al-Kalbi (vol. III. p. 608) mentions, in his Jamhara tan-Nisab, something which refers to Zû 'l-Fakâr and, as it is a piece of useful information, I insert it here. In treating of the genealogy of the Kuraish family,
he says : "Munabbih and Nabih, the sons of al-Hajjâj Ibn Aâmir Ibn Hudhaifa Ibn
" Saad Ibn Sahm the Kuraishide, were the chiefs of the Sahm family previously to
" the introduction of Islamism. They were slain at the battle of Badr and died in
" their infidelity. As chiefs, they were greatly respected. Al-Aâsi, the son of Na-
" bih, was killed with his father. To him belonged Zû 'l-Fakâr. Ali slew him on
" the day of Badr and took that sword from him." Another author says that Zû 'l-
Fakâr was given to Ali by the Prophet. I must observe that fakâr, with an o after
the f, is the plural of fakdra, which means a vertebra of the back. The plural forms
are fakdr and fakârât. The name of this sword is also pronounced Zû 'l-Fikâr; the
word fikâr is the plural of fikra (vertebra). We find in the language no other word
of a similar form in the singular having such a plural form except ibra (needle),
the plural of which is ibâr.—Let us return to our account of Zû 'l-Fakâr. The manner in which it came into the hands of Hárûn ar-Rashid is thus related by at-Tabari
(vol. II. p. 597), in a traditional account which he traces up to Omar, the son of

(*the khalif*) al-Mutawakkil. The mother of that prince had been in the service of Fâtima, the daughter of al-Husain, the son of Ali, the son of Abû Tâlib. She said : " Zû 'l Fakâr was borne by Muhammad Ibn Abd Allah Ibn al-Hasan Ibn al-Hasan Ibn " Ali Ibn Abi Tâlib on the day in which battle was given to the army of Abû Jaafar al- " Mansûr the Abbaside."—The history of this event is well known (3). —" When " he felt death to be near, he gave Zû 'l-Fakâr to a merchant who had followed him " and to whom he owed four hundred dinars (£ 200). ' Take this sword,' said " he, ' any member of the Abû Tâlib family whom you may meet with will buy it " ' from you and give you the sum to which you are entitled.' The sword remained " with the merchant till (*the Abbaside prince*) Jaafar the son of Sulaimân Ibn Ali Ibn " Abd Allah Ibn al-Abbâs Ibn Abd al-Muttalib obtained the governments of Ye- " men and Medina. He, being informed of what had happened, sent for the mer- " chant, took the sword and gave him four hundred dinars. It remained with " Jaafar till al-Mahdi, the son of al-Mansûr, was raised to the khalifate. This " sovereign, having learned where the sword was, got possession of it. From him " it passed to Mûsa al-Hâdi and, from Mûsa, to his brother Hârûn ar-Rashîd."—Al-Asmâi (*vol. II. p.* 123) related as follows : " I saw ar-Rashîd at Tûs with a sword " suspended from his neck, and he said to me : ' Asmâi ! would you like see Zû " ' 'l-Fakâr!'—I replied : ' Most willingly; may God accept my life as a ransom for " ' yours!' He then bade me draw the sword which he was wearing. I did so " and found on it eighteen *fakdras* (4)." — We have digressed from our subject, and must now return to the history of Yazîd Ibn Mazyad. The *khatîb* Abû Bakr Ahmad Ibn Ali Ibn Thâbit al-Baghdâdi (*vol. I. p.* 75) relates, in his History of Baghdad, that Yazîd, having gone to visit ar-Rashîd, was addressed by him in these terms : " Tell me, Yazîd ! who was the person that composed on you these lines :

" No perfumes are on his hands or on his hair, neither does he wipe antimony powder from " his eyes. He has taught the birds (*of prey*) a custom to which they have full confidence; so " they follow him in all his expeditions.'

Yazîd replied that he did not know, and ar-Rashîd exclaimed : " How can it be " that verses such as these should be composed in your honour without your " knowing the author?" Yazîd felt quite abashed and, having returned to his dwelling, he said to the chamberlain : " Is there any poet at the door?' The other answered : " Muslim Ibn al-Walîd al-Ansâri is there." — " How long have you

" kept him waiting?" said Yazid.—" For a long time," replied the chamberlain,
" I prevented him from coming in because I knew that you were not now in easy
" circumstances."—" Let him in," said Yazid. The poet was introduced and recited to him the entire kasida. When he had finished, Yazid said to his intendant :
" Sell such and such a farm of mine; give the poet one half the price obtained for
" it and put up the remainder for my own expenses." The property was sold for
one hundred thousand dirhems, of which Yazid gave fifty thousand to Muslim.
Ar-Rashid, being informed of the circumstance, sent for Yazid and questioned him
on the subject. Having learned the particulars, he said : "I shall order you a sum
" of two hundred thousand dirhems; with one hundred thousand you may repurchase
" your farm; add fifty thousand to those which you gave to your poet and keep fifty
" thousand for yourself."—Abû Bakr Ibn al-Anbâri (vol. III. p. 53) said : " My fa-
" ther declared that Muslim Ibn al-Walîd stole the idea from an-Nâbigha ad Dub-
" yâni (5) who said (in one of his poems) :

" When those chiefs go on an expedition with their troops, flocks of birds, led on by other
" flocks, hover in circles over them. They accompany them till the inroad be effected; for
" they are well trained and accustomed to blood. They are ready to swoop down, being cer-
" tain that the tribe of those (chiefs) will be victorious, when two hostile troops meet in battle.
" They have learned from those (chiefs) a custom and know well to practise it when the lance
" is conched (and projects) over the horse's shoulder (kawdthib)."

Kawdthib is the plural of kâthiba and signifies that part of the horse's back which
is before the pommel of the saddle.—Muslim's poem began thus :

I roamed, free as a libertine, and courted the fair (6), whilst my amorous thoughts to upbraid
me but abstained.

The eulogistic part of it contains this passage :

The khalif possessed, in one of the sons of Matar, a sword of which the blade corrected
those who swerved (from their duty). Dew many were the (princes) who, but for the Yazid
of the tribe of Shaibân, had never domineered from the exalted pinnacles of an empire. When
war shews its carved teeth, the imâm (khalif) shews his by (erring forward) Yazid, a chief
who smiles in the heat of battle (7), when the faces of the bravest warriors change colour. He
obtains by mildness what defies the efforts of all other men; like death, he attains quickly to his
aim, though he proceeds with slowness. People would not travel (to obtain gifts), were there
not to his tent (an object which), like the temple (of Mekka), forms the meeting-point of every
road. He clothes his swords in the souls (the blood) of those who break their engagements,

and, with their hands, he makes crowns for his pliant spears. In the morning, he marches forth, bearing death on the points of his lances which, when couched, announce to the foe that his last hour is come. When a band (of rebels) is too proud to advance and do homage to the (khalif), he holds their death (ready prepared and) hidden behind his swords and spears. Even in peace, you will always find him armed in a double coat of mail; for he trusts not Fortune and is ready to act at the first call.

Abú 'l-Faraj al-Ispahâni (vol. II. p. 249) relates as follows in the article on Muslim Ibn al-Walîd which he gives in his Kitâb al-Aghâni : " Ar-Rashîd, " said Yazîd Ibn Mazyad, " sent for me one day, at an hour in which it was not usual " (for him) to require the presence of (chiefs) such as me. So, I went to him with all " my armour on and ready to execute whatever he might order. When he saw " me, he laughed and asked me who was the person that composed the following " verses in my praise :

" Even in peace, you will always find him armed in a double coat of mail; for he trusts not " Fortune and is ready to act at the first call. God established on earth (the family of) Hâ- shim as a mountain (of glory); and the supports of that mountain are you and your son.

" I replied that I did not know; on which he exclaimed : ' It is a shame for you, " ' the chief of a great people, not to know the person from whom you received such " ' an eulogy. It has come to the knowledge of the Commander of the faithful; " ' he has heard it recited and recompensed the author. That man is Muslim Ibn " ' al-Walîd.' On my return home, I sent for the poet, made him a present and " treated him kindly. " — The two verses here mentioned are taken from the ka- sîda of which we have just given a fragment. It is related that Maan, the son of Zâida, preferred his nephew Yazîd to his own children, and was reproached by his wife for doing so. " How long, " said she, " will you continue to put forward " your nephew Yazîd and keep back your sons? if you advanced them, they would " get on well; if you raised them to some authority, they would continue to rise in " rank. " He replied : " Yazîd is nearly related to me and has a right to my treat- " ing him as a son, for he is my nephew. Nevertheless, my own children are " dearer to my heart and nearer to my affection, but I do not find in them that " talent of being useful which is possessed by Yazîd. If the services which he did " me (ﻣﺎ ﺻﻨﻊ ﺑﻪ) were rendered to a stranger, he would gain his affection and, if " rendered to an enemy, he would convert him into a friend. This very night, I " shall let you see something which will induce you to excuse me : Page! go and

" send here Jemád, Záida, Abd Allah, " — he here named all his sons. In a short
time, they came, dressed in perfumed waistcoats and Sindian shoes, though more
than one third of the night had gone by (8). They saluted and sat down. He then
said : " Page ! go and call Yazíd." Very soon after, Yazíd arrived, sheathed in
armour and, leaving his lance at the door, he entered into the saloon. " Abú Zu-
" hair ! " said Maan, " why are you thus appareled ? " The other answered :
" Emir ! a messenger came to me from you, and my first impression was that you
" required my presence for some important affair; I therefore put on my armour
" and said to myself : ' If my conjecture be right, I shall not be obliged to return
" ' back, and, if I be mistaken, it will be very easy for me to strip off this appa-
" ' rel.'" Maan then said : " You may all retire and God protect you ! " — When
they had withdrawn, his wife declared that he well deserved to be excused. On
this, he recited the following lines, applying them (to his nephew) :

Islam's noble mind raised Islam to power, taught him to advance and charge the foe, and made
of him a princely hero (9).

It was to this circumstance that Muslim Ibn al-Walíd alluded when he said :
" Even in peace, you will always find him arrayed in a double coat of mail." It
is related that, when Muslim came to this verse in reciting his poem, Yazíd, in
whose honour it had been composed, said to him : " Why did you not express your-
" self {in the same manner as the Asha of (the tribe of) Bakr Ibn Wáil did (10)
" when he celebrated the noble deeds of Kais, the son of Madi Karib ? He said :

" When a troop of horse approaches, so dark and serried that warriors clothed in mail show
" its encounter, you dash forward, without even taking a shield, and, proclaiming your name,
" you strike down the bravest with your sword."

Muslim replied : " What I said is better; for that poet extolled his patron's im-
" prudence (khurk), " — this word signifies ignorance of the right manner of acting, — " and I extolled your resolution. " — The Kais whom al-Asha eulogised
was the father of al-Ashath Ibn Kais al-Kindi, one of the Prophet's Companions. —
We have already mentioned the verse :

He has taught the birds a custom in which they have full confidence etc.

And stated that the idea was borrowed from an-Nábigha; the same was done

by a number of other poets, Abû Nuwâs, for instance. Omar al-Warrâk related
as follows : " I heard Abû Nuwâs recite his *kasîda* which rhymes in *r* and begins
" thus :

> " O them who art visited by a demon! thou shalt not be of my evening parties nor with those
> " who converse therein. I drive not birds away from a tree of which I found, by experience,
> " that the fruits were bitter.

" These verses excited my jealousy (*but I suppressed my feelings*) till he came to
" the following passage :

> " When the lances were dripping with gore and death appeared in her proper form, then at
> " evening, came home, proudly stalking in (*yushcani fi*) his coat of mail, a lion, the points of
> " whose claws were stained with blood. The birds of prey journey forth on the morning of
> " his departure, being certain of being gorged with the (*flesh of*) his victims.

" I then said : ' You have left to an-Nâbigha nothing out of that verse of his :

> " When those chiefs go on an expedition with the troops, *etc.!*

" To this he answered : ' Hold your tongue! if I am not good at invention, I am
" ' not bad at imitation.' " — The same idea was taken up by Abû Tammâm Habîb
Ibn Aûs at-Tai (*vol. I. p. 348*), who said :

> In the morning, the eagles of his standards were overshadowed by eagle-birds, accustomed to
> quench their thirst in blood; they kept close to the standards and seemed like a part of the army,
> only they did not fight.

Abû 't-Taiyib al-Mutanabbi also said (*something similar*) in the following verse :

> The birds (*of prey*), encouraged by their frequent feeding on the slain, were ready to swoop
> down upon the living.

In the description of a troop given by the last-named author, we find an idea
which comes near to the preceding; he says :

> (*On came,*) with a stunning noise (*a troop of hunters*), before which the possessors of wings
> fled but could not escape, and from which the wild beasts, starting from their coverts, were not
> safe. The sun passed over that (*troop*), but with a feeble light, and he could scarcely be seen,
> for the wings of the vultures. When his rays found an opening through the (*crowded flock of*)
> birds, his round disk appeared like a dirhem over the helmets.

When Yazíd held the government of Yemen, he received the visit of Marwán Ibn Muhammad, a well-known poet who was a mawla to Marwán Ibn Muhammad al-Jaadi, the last of the Omaiyide khalifs. This poet's surname was Abú Muhammad, but he was usually known by the appellation of Abú 's-Shamakmak (*the son of the man tall and active*). He arrived on foot, in ragged attire, and recited to Yazíd an eulogium, in which he described his own state of misery, saying :

> Those who are in search of beneficence saddle their camels to visit you, but the camel which bore me to you were my sandals (11). I took them for my steed, having no other, in order to get through my journey. That steed outruns even the most active and, in its rapid course across the desert wilderness, it leaves behind the meḥari camels, thin-flanked and full-chested. It goes to visit him who has the noblest reputation of all the family of Wáil, (*him who is*) a dome erected to the glory of that tribe. It is Yazíd whom I mean, the sword of the family of Mohammad, Yazíd who dispels every misfortune which a man can dread. He has two days (*for acting*); one luxuriant with gifts and favours, the other, copious with bloodshed and the taking of lives. I have come to him with confidence, being assured that he will hear an eulogium and not defer its recompense.

To this he replied : " You say the truth ; I never, on receiving an eulogium, " defer its recompense ; give this man one thousand dinars (£ 500)." — A long and excellent poem, rhyming in b, was composed in his praise by Abú 'l-Fadl Mansúr Ibn Salama an-Namari (12), a well-known poet. It contains this passage :

> Had the tribe of Shaibán no other title to honour than Yazíd, it would yet surpass all the others. Men know full well that liberality repels competency, but he (*not content with being munificent*), dilapidates his wealth.

Abú 'l-Abbás al-Mubarrad (vol. III. p. 31) relates, in his Kámil, that Yazíd Ibn Mazyad, meeting, one day, with a man who had a great flowing beard which covered his breast and was dyed (*with hinna*), said to him : " That beard of yours " must put you to some expense." The man replied : " It certainly does and, for " that reason, I say :

> " Every night, it costs me a dirhem for poonstum and another for hinna; thus one piece (*of " money*) outruns the other. Were it not for the gifts of Yazíd Ibn Mazyad, the scissors (*ja- " lamáni*) would have to twang around its borders."

Hárún ar-Rashíd said to him one day : " I count upon you, Yazíd ! for an impor- " tant business," and received this reply : " Commander of the faithful ! God has " prepared for you, in me, a heart sincerely devoted to your service, a hand ready

" to obey you and a sword whetted to slay your foes. If you have any order to give,
" speak." Al-Masûdi states, in his *Murûj ad-Dahab wa Maddin al-Jauhar* (meadows of gold and mines of jewels), that this conversation passed between Hârûn ar-
Rashîd and Maan Ibn Zâida, the uncle of Yazîd; then, farther on, he adds that, according to some, it took place between ar-Rashîd and Yazîd Ibn Mazyad. I must
observe that it could not possibly have passed between ar-Rashîd and Maan, because the
latter lost his life when Abû Jaafar al-Mansûr was khalif, as we have already mentioned
in his (Maan's) biographical notice, and, though there be some difference of opinion
respecting the precise date, it is certain that the event occurred not long after the year
150 (A. D. 767). How then could he have held this conversation with ar-Rashîd who
did not obtain the khalifate till the year 170 (A. D. 786-7)? Ibn Aûn relates the following anecdote in his work entitled *al-Ajwiba al-Muskita* (*silencing answers*) (13) :
" Ar-Rashîd was one day playing at mall and told Yazîd to take the side of Isa Ibn
" Jaafar (14). On Yazîd's refusing, he got angry and said : ' Are you too proud to
" ' be his partner?' Yazîd replied : ' I swore to the Commander of the faithful that
" ' I would never be against him, either in sport or in earnest." — I read in a compilation of anecdotes that some person related as follows : " I was one night with
" Yazîd Ibn Mazyad and we heard a voice exclaim : ' O! Yazîd Ibn Mazyad!' He
" ordered the man who uttered that cry to be brought into his presence and then
" said to him : ' What induced you to call out that name?' The other replied :
" ' I used up my mule and spent my stock of money; then hearing a poet recite a
" ' verse, I drew a good omen from it.' Yazîd bade him repeat the verse, and he
" recited as follows :

" If honour, generosity and beneficence require a supporter, call with a loud voice upon
" Yazîd Ibn Mazyad.

" When Yazîd heard these words, he treated the man with affability and asked
" him if he knew that Yazîd. The other replied : ' By Allah! I do not.' — ' Well,'
" said Yazîd, ' I am he.' He then gave him one hundred dinars and a pied horse
" which was a great favorite of his." — We have been rather prolix in this article but discourse will branch into digressions, each of them connected with the
other. The anecdotes told of Yazîd's noble conduct are very numerous. He
died in the year 185 (A. D. 801). An elegy was composed on his death by Abû
Muhammad Abd Allah Ibn Aiyûb (15), a well-known poet of the tribe of Taim; some

persons attribute it to the well-known poet Muslim Ibn al-Walîd al-Ansari, but
they are mistaken. We give it here :

> Is it true that Yazîd is no more? Tell us, you who announce so kindly tidings of death!
> Do you know him whose death you proclaim? how have your lips been able to utter his name?
> may your mouth be (for ever) filled with clay (16). Is the champion of (our) glory and of Isla-
> mism dead? Woe be to thee, o Earth! why hast thou not shuddered? See if the pillars of
> Islamism be not shaken and if the children's hair has not turned grey (with affright). See if
> the swords of the tribe of Nizâr be reposing in their scabbards and if the saddle-cloths have
> been taken off the horses. See if the heavy clouds continue still to water the land with their
> showers and if the trees are still covered with verdure. When he died, did Nizâr not feel the
> shock? It did, and its edifice of glory has fallen to the ground. When he was laid in the
> grave, the glory he had acquired and his hereditary honours were there entombed. By Allah !
> my eyes shall never cease pouring forth floods of tears for his loss. The vile may abstain from
> weeping, but the eyes of worthy men shall never remain dry. Can the female mourners be
> parcimonious with their tears after the death of Yazîd? can they spare their cheeks (and not
> tear them)? Let the pavilion of Islamism lament him, for the cords of that tent are now wea-
> kened, as also its support. A part from whom he never withheld his wealth now weeps over
> him, and laudatory poems have lost their value. Yazîd is dead; but every living being is
> near to death or is hurried towards it. Let it be a consolation for (the tribe of) Rabia that it
> never again can meet with (so sad) a day as this.

The idea enounced in the last verse has been employed by a number of poets.
Mutî Ibn Iyâs (vol. I. p. 438) said, in an elegy on the death of Yahya Ibn Ziâd al-
Hârithi (vol. II. p. 403) :

> (Say to Death:) You may now carry off whom you please ; misfortunes can no longer give
> us pain, now that Yahya is no more !

Abû Nuwâs (vol. I. p. 391) said, in a lament composed on the death of (the khalif) al-Amîn :

> His death was the only thing I feared, and nothing now remains for me to dread.

Ibrahîm Ibn al-Abbâs as-Sûli (vol. I. p. 22) said, on the death of his father :

> Thou wast dear to me as the apple of my eye; for thee (alone) my eyes shed their tears. Die
> now who may, since thou art gone; thou wast my only care.

The article on Muslim Ibn al-Walîd, which Abû 'l-Faraj al-Ispahâni (vol. II.

p. 249) has given in the *Kitâb al-Aghâni*, contains the following piece of information, which is traced up by the author of that work to Ahmad Ibn Abi Said. "Yazid
"Ibn Mazyad was eating his dinner when he received the present of a slave-girl.
"Immediately on finishing, he had intercourse with her and died in her arms. He
"was then in Bardâa and there he was buried. He had with him Muslim Ibn al-
"Walîd and a number of his ordinary companions. Muslim lamented his death
"in these lines :

"There is a tomb in Bardâa and, in the grave which it covers, is hidden worth unequalled.
"On his death, Fortune left (*the tribe of*) Rabîa in such sorrow that, by Allah! it will never
"be exchanged (*for joy*). He always led on the Arabs in the path of glory; how much then
"were they astounded when death overtook him! On his death, the saddles (*the travellers*)
"lost every hope of gaining wealth (17), and the cities recalled those who had left them
"in order to visit him. Depart (*in peace, o emir!*) depart like the rain-cloud, which leaves
"the plains and the hills extolling its beneficence."

This last verse is said to be most the most expressive of any that are to found in
an elegy. The piece itself is given in the *Hamdsa*, section of elegies. بردعة (*Bardâa*)
is the name of town situated at the furthest extremity of Adarbaijân; so I find it
mentioned in books of history, but natives of that place say that it is in the province
of Arrân. *Bardâa* is written with a pointed or an unpointed *d* (د or ذ), and such
also is the case when the same word is employed to designate the pad which is placed under the saddle. — Some say that this elegy was composed by Muslim Ibn al-
Walîd on the death of Yazîd Ibn Ahmad as-Sulami (18). According to another
statement, he composed it on the death of Malik Ibn Ali al-Khuzâi, and the first
verse ran thus : *There is a tomb in Hulwân, etc.;* the person whose death he lamented having died in that place. *Hulwân* is a city in Sawâd (*Babylonia*), or in one of
the governments into which Irâk is divided. God knows best which of these statements is true! Abù Abd Allah al-Marzubâni (*vol. III. p. 67*) says, in his *Mojam
as-Shuwará (alphabetical dictionary of poets)*, that Abù 'l-Balhâ Omair Ibn Aâmir,
who was one of Yazîd's *mawlas*, composed the following lines :

How excellent the hero by whose death the vicissitudes of time brought down affliction upon
his brethren, on the day he was interred (19). The access to his court was easy when you alighted at his door; his hands were prodigal and his servants polite. When you see his friends and
his brothers, you cannot tell which of them are his blood-relations (*they are all so deeply afflicted*).

Abû Tammâm at-Tai has given this piece in his *Hamdsa*, section of elegies (20),
and attributes it to Muhammad Ibn Bashîr al-Khâriji (21).   According to some, we
must read *Yasîr* (يسير) in place of *Bashîr* (بشير).   *Yasîr* is an adjective derived
from *yosr* (opulence); *Bashîr* comes from *bishâra* (good news).   He bore the surname of al-Khâriji, not because he was a Kharijite, but because he belonged to the
tribe of Khârija, a branch of that of Adwân.   God knows best! — Here is another
elegy on the death of Yazîd; it was composed by Mansûr an-Namari and is given in
the *Hamdsa* (page 440) :

> Abû Khâlid! what an awful stroke fell upon (*the descendants of*) Maadd, on the day in which
> you were consigned to your last home! By my life! if the enemies (*of the empire*) now look
> cheerful and and display an insulting joy, they must have passed by the court of your dwelling
> and found it empty. Time hastened to terminate your existence, but your renown will exhaust
> (*the efforts of*) time.

Yazîd Ibn Mazyad had two sons, both of them illustrious by their noble character
and exalted rank.   One of them was the Khâlid Ibn Yazîd whose praises were celebrated by Abû Tammâm at-Tâi.   This poet composed in his honour some beautiful
pieces which we should insert here, were they not to be found in his collected poetical works.   The other son was Muhammad Ibn Yazîd, who was noted for his liberality : he never sent away an applicant (*empty-handed*); if he had not money to give,
he would never say " No," but " Later," and would then hasten to fulfil his promise.   Ahmad Ibn Abi Funan Sâlih Ibn Said composed verses in his praise.   I since
found the following lines in the *Kitâb al-Bâri*, where they are attributed to Abû's-
Shîs (الشيص) al-Khuzâi (23):

> Noble actions were his passion and the occupation of his time; but few are those who love to
> do noble deeds. He opened a market for (*the purchase of*) eulogy, but markets for eulogy are not
> considered as markets. He scattered good offices throughout the land, and thus drew, from all
> quarters, a rich harvest of praise.

Khâlid Ibn Yazîd was appointed governor of Mosul by (*the khalif*) al-Mâmûn.   He
arrived there in company with Abû 's-Shamakmak, the poet already mentioned in
this article.   When he entered Mosul, the staff of his standard, which had been
planted on the top of the city gate, was broken in two.   He was about to draw a bad
omen from this accident, when Abu 's-Shamakmak extemporized to him these
lines :

The breaking of the standard denotes neither danger to be feared nor evil to come suddenly. Being deprived it of its force at the aspect of this petty government, it declared that Mosul was much too small.

The khalif, being informed of what had passed, wrote these words to Khâlid : " We have added to your government that of all Diâr Rabîa, because your standard " found Mosul too small." Yazîd was delighted with the news and bestowed an ample reward on the poet. In the reign of al-Wâthik, the affairs of Armenia fell into great disorder, and Khâlid Ibn Yazîd was dispatched to that province with a numerous army. Being taken ill on the way, he died at Daibil, a town in Armenia. This was in the year 230 (A. D. 844-5).

(1) Abû Wâlî Bakr Ibn an-Nattâh, a member of the Temenite tribe of Ranîe, led for some time the life of a vagabond and then entered into the service of Abû Dulaf (vol. II, p. 103), one of al-Mâmûn's generals, who admitted him into the jand, or armed militia and assigned to him a regular pay out of the coffers of the state (riâsa soltaniah). Ibn an-Nattâh was an excellent horseman, esteemed for courage and intrepidity, and possessing a good talent for poetry. In his verses, he frequently vaunted his own prowess. He always remained attached to Abû Dulaf. — (Kitâb al-Aghânî.)

(2) In the manuscripts this seems to written in various manners; one reads الترَاب (el-Kirâb or al-Kerrâb), another الفُرَاب (al-Furâb), a third الفُرَات (el-Ghawât), etc. Hajî Khalîfa does not mention this author in his Bibliographical Dictionary.

(3) This is the celebrated Alide surnamed an-Nafs az-Zakiya, who revolted against the khalif al-Mansûr in the year 145 (A. D. 762-3).

(4) The words fobdes must here designate either a sort of waving ornament engraved on the blade or else a notch on its edge. It is doubtful which is meant, probably the latter.

(5) De Sacy has given an account of the antiislamite poet, an-Nâbigha ad-Dubyânî, in the second volume of his Chrestomathie arabe.

(6) The true reading of this hemistich appears to be اجررت حبل خليع في الصبا غزل.

(7) Literally : when war shows its teeth.

(8) They had been at a party of pleasure.

(9) Iâlm, was visir to en-Nomân, the king of Hîra. See de Sacy's Chrestomathie arabe, t. II, p. 424.

(10) For the history of this poet, who was a contemporary of Muhammad, see de Sacy's Chrestomathie arabe, t. II, p. 471.

(11) Literally : and I travelled towards you on a sandaled camel.

(12) Abû 'l-Fadl Mansûr, qualifié d'en-Nomri parce qu'il était issu de Nemr Ibn Kâsit, poète du temps des Abbassides, sa patrie était la Mésopotamie. El-Fadl, fils de Yahya, le fit venir à Bagdad, à Haroun-er-Rashid dont Mansûr avait blamé les bonnes grâces. Mansûr avait compris le goût de Haroun en fait de poésie par la faveur que ce prince accordait à Merwân, fils d'Abû Hafsa. Il avait senti que le calife désirait qu'on joignit à son éloge quelques traits contre la famille d'Ali, comme le faisait Merwân, de manière à montrer qu'on se ralliait à cette famille aurait droit à l'imâmat. Mansûr imita Merwân en suivant cette voie ; mais il se laissa aux

Aliden que des traits indirects et ménagés, parce qu'il était au fond leur partisan, tandis que Marwân attaquait franchement et avec énergie les descendants d'Ali, contre lesquels il était animé de sentiments hostiles par conviction autant que par ambition.

Mamûr an-Nemri mourut à Râs-el-Ain sous le règne de Haroun. (Mr. Caussin de Perceval, gives this note on the authority of the *Kitâb al-Aghâni*. The author of that work says that the name of Mamûr's father was Zibrikân.)

(13) A work bearing this title is attributed to Abû Hâmid al-Ghazzâli (*ent. II, p. 411*) by Hajji Khalifa in his *Bibliographical Dictionary*, but that author takes no notice of Ibn Abâ.

(14) Isa Ibn Isalar was the grandson of the khalif al-Mamûr.

(15) Abû Muhammad Abd Allah Ibn Aiyûb, a member of the tribe of Taim Allât, was one the poets who flourished under the Abbasides. He was patronised by al-Amin. Died A. H. 200 (A. D. 814-5). — (*Nujûm.*)

(16) The expression : earth in your mouth! is equivalent to : I wish you were dead!

(17) This verse is cited by our author so incorrectly that it scarcely admits of a reasonable explication. See it correctly given in Freytag's *Hamâsa*, p. 192.

(18) We should perhaps read : Yazîd Ibn Ouaid as-Salami (*member of the tribe of Sulaim*). See p. 212 of this volume.

(19) Literally : on the day of al-Baki. Al-Baki was the name of the principal cemetery of Medina, but the poet employs it here to designate the cemetery of Bardâa, the town where his patron died.

(20) See *Hamâsa*, p. 274.

(21) Mohammed, fils de Bechir, qualifié d'el-Khârediji parce qu'il descendait de Khâredja, fils d'Adwân, poète de Ridjla. Son prénom était Abû Souleymân. Il vécut sous les Omeyiades (et peut-être aussi sous les Abbâsides, ambè je l'ignore). Il fut particulièrement attaché à Abû Obeyda, fils d'Abd Allah, fils de Rabia, Coraychite de la famille d'Abd el-Ozza. Les panégyriques et élégies funèbres qu'il a composées pour ce personnage sont les meilleures de ses poésies. Il habitait le plus ordinairement les déserts voisins de Médine et l'endroit nommé er-Rauhha (الروحّا). — (Note by Mr. Caussin de Perceval.)

(22) According to the author of the *Nujûm*, the poet Abû 'n-Shis Muhammad Ibn Ruzin died A. H. 196 (A. D. 811-2).

IBN MUFARRIGH

" Abû Othmân Yazîd was the son of Ziâd Ibn Rabia Ibn Mufarrigh Ibn Zi 'l-
" Ashîra Ibn al-Hârith IbnDallâl Ibn Aûf Ibn Amr Ibn Yazîd Ibn Murra Ibn Marthad
" Ibn Masrûk Ibn Zaid Ibn Yahsub al-Himyari (*the Himyarite*). The remainder of

" the genealogy, from Yahsub upwards, is well-known, so, there is no need of our
" giving it." It is thus that Ibn al-Kalbi (vol. III. p. 608) traces up Yazid Ibn
Mufarrigh's genealogy in the Kitáb al-Jamhara, but he does not mention his surname which, however, is given by the author of the Aghâni (vol. II. p. 219). Most
of the literati say that this Yazid was the son of Rabia and the grandson of Mufarrigh; thus suppressing the name of Ziad. The author of the Aghâni says : " His
" grandfather Mufarrigh received this name because he made a wager that he
" would drink the whole contents of a skin filled with milk, and he did not lay it
" down till he emptied it. He was therefore called Mufarrigh (the emptier)." The
same author relates, in the article of the Aghâni which contains the history of
as-Saiyid al-Himyari (col. II. p. 241), who was Mufarrigh's grandson, that Ibn
Aticha (1) said : " Mufarrigh was the same person as Rabia; Mufarrigh being
" merely a surname. Those who say that Rabia was the son of Mufarrigh are mis-
" taken." — God knows best! — Al-Fadl Ibn Abd ar-Rahmân an-Naufâli says that
Mufarrigh was a blacksmith in Yemen; he made a lock for his wife on the condition
that, when he had finished it, she would bring him a skin of milk. She did so
and, when he had drank some of its contents, he laid it down. She told him to give
her back the skin, and he replied : " I have nothing to empty it in." She insisted on having it and he emptied it into his belly. "O!" said she, " you are an emptier (mufarrigh)!" and, by this nickname he became generally known. According
to the members of his (Yazid's) family, he belonged to the tribe of Himyar. Ibn al-
Kalbi and Abû Obaida (vol. III. p. 388) state that Mufarrigh followed the trade of a
patcher and mender at Tabâla. I must here make some observations : Tabâla is a
village on the road which leads from Mekka to Yemen. It is situated in a very fertile
spot and is often mentioned in historical relations, proverbs and poems. This was
the first government which al-Hajjâj Ibn Yûsuf ath-Thakafi (vol. I. p. 356) ever
obtained. Till that time, he had never seen it. He set out for it and, on getting
near it, he asked whereabout it was. They answered : " It is behind that hill."
On this, he exclaimed : " A government that can be hidden by a hill is worth no-
" thing!" and he turned back and left it. From that time the Arabs said proverbially of any thing despicable : It is more contemptible than Tabâla was for al-Hajjâj.
The narrator (of Ibn Mufarrigh's adventures) (2) says : He pretended that he drew his
descent from Himyar. He was affiliated by oath to the family of Khâlid Ibn Osaid
Ibn Abi 'l-Iis (العاص) the Omaiyide. According to another statement, he was a

slave to ad-Dahhák Ibn Aûf al-Hilâli by whom he was treated with kindness. Ya-
síd was a poet and composed good amatory (and satirical) pieces. One of his descendants was as-Saiyid al-Himyari, whose name was Ismaîl and whose father, Muhammad, was the son of Bakkâr and the grandson of this Yazid. So it is stated by
Ibn Mâkûla (vol. II, p. 248) in his Ikmál. His title was as-Saiyid (the chief) and his
surname Abû Hâshim. He was one of the heads of the Shîite party. The history of
his proceedings in that cause and the poems composed by him in support of it are
well known. — One of the finest passages in Yazid's poems is to be found in a
kasída containing the praises of the Omaiyide prince Marwân Ibn al-Hakam, by
whom he had been generously treated. Here it is :

> You opened a market for (the purchase of) eulogy, at a time that eulogy was not considered
> as a marketable ware.   God seems to have granted to you the privilege of taking lives and of
> distributing gifts.

The first of these verses has been given in our article on Yazíd Ibn Mazyad Ibn
Zaida (page 230 of this vol.); it is there attributed to Ahmad Ibn Abi Fanan and said
to be taken from a kasída in which that famous poet (3) extolled the merits of Khâlid, the son of Yazíd Ibn Mazyed. God knows best! — When Said, the son of (the
khalif) Othmân Ibn Affân, was appointed governor of Khorâsân, he invited Yazíd
Ibn Mufarrigh to accompany him thither. Yazid refused, as he preferred becoming
the retainer of Abbâd (4), the son of Ziâd Ibn Abîh (5). On this, he said to him :
"Since you refuse bearing me company and prefer following Abbâd, hearken to
"the advice which I here give you : Abbâd is a man of a low mind; avoid there-
"fore being too familiar with him, although he encourage you to make free; for
"he then only means to delude you. Visit him seldom, for he is greatly in-
"clined to find irksome (the presence of visitors). Do not bandy arguments with
"him, even though he attack you, for he will not bear with such observations
"coming from you as you would bear with if they came from him."
He then sent for some money and gave it to him, saying : "Let this help to defray
"your travelling expenses. If you perceive that you are not on a good footing with
"Abbâd, recollect that, with me, you shall always find a favorable reception and come
"to me." Said then departed for Khorâsân, and Ibn Mufarrigh set out with Abbâd.
When Obaid Allah, the son of Ziâd and the governor of the two Iráks, was informed that his brother Abbâd was taking Yazid with him, he felt very uneasy and went

out with the people to see him off. Whilst they were saying farewell to the travellers, he went to take leave of his brother and, having called Ibn Mufarrigh over to him, he said: " You asked Abbád to take you with him and he granted your request; " now, that is a thing which annoys me greatly. " — " God protect the emir! " said Ibn Mufarrigh, " why should that annoy you? " — Obaid Allah replied : " A poet is not to be satisfied with such attentions as ordinary men shew one to ano- " ther; he is led away by his imagination, what he imagines he takes for certain " and he never overlooks an affront, even when he ought to do so. Now, Abbád is " going to a country which is the seat of war, and he will be so greatly taken up " with the direction of his troops and the collecting of the landtax that he will not " think of you. Such neglect you will not forgive and (in your satires) you will co- " ver us all with obloquy and shame. " Yazid answered : " Emir! I am not what " you think; I am profoundly grateful for the kindness which he has already shewn " me, and, besides, if I forget myself (in my conduct towards him), I shall always " find a ready pardon. " — " That you will not; " replied Obaid Allah, " so you " must promise me that if he delays giving what you expect from him, you will not " hasten to attack him but write to me. " — " That I promise you; " said the poet. — " It is well; " said Obaid Allah. " so, now depart under favorable auspices." The narrator (in the Kitáb al-Aghání) continues thus : Abbád arrived in Khorásán, or as some say, in Sijistán, — and was there so deeply engaged in warfare and in the collecting of the imposts that Ibn Mufarrigh thought the attention to which he was entitled very long in coming. So, without writing a letter of complaint to Obaid Allah, as he had engaged to do, he gave free career to (the virulence of) his tongue and attacked Abbád with sarcasms and satire. That emir had so great a beard that it resembled a fodder-bag. The poet was travelling with him, one day, and, seeing the beard shaken and tossed about by the wind, he laughed and said to a man of the tribe of Lakhm who was (riding) at his side :

O, that his beard was hay! we might then fodder all the Moslim cavalry.

Abbád, to whom the Lakhmite perfidiously related what the poet had said, flew into a passion : " It does not become me now, " said he, " to chastise him whilst " he is in my company; but, though I defer his punishment, I intend later to " gratify my revenge ; many are the times in which he cast abuse on my father. " Ibn Mufarrigh, being informed of this, said : " I perceive the odour of death

"(for me proceeding), from Abbâd!" He then went in to him and said : " Emir !
" I was with Saîd Ibn Othmân, whose good opinion of me you have learned; you
" know also the favorable impression which he has left on my mind. I preferred
" you to him, but, as yet, I have derived from you no advantage. I therefore
" request permission to depart; I have no need of being your retainer. " Abbâd
replied : " As you chose me, so also did I choose you; I took you into my service
" because you asked me to do so. You now hasten to prevent me from taking pro-
" ceedings against you, and therefore you ask permission to depart. But you mean
" to return to your people and give them the most unfavorable opinion of my cha-
" racter. Well, you have that permission and may make use of it when I have
" treated you according to your deserts." Being then informed that his honour
and reputation were attacked by Ibn Mufarrigh, he encouraged some of the poet's
creditors to cite him before (the tribunal presided by) himself, and the result was
that he put him into prison and had him severely beaten. After that, he sent to him
this message : " Sell me al-Arîka and Durd. " Al-Arîka was a female musician belonging to Ibn Mufarrigh and Durd was his slave-boy. He had brought them up from
their childhood and was greatly attached to them. The poet sent back by the same
messenger an answer to this effect: " Ask the emir, if a man can possibly sell him-
" self or his child. " Abbâd them took them from him (by force) or, according
to another account, he sold them, against their owner's will, to a native of Khorâsân. When the two slaves entered into this man's house, Burd, who was very intelligent and had received a good education, said to him : " Do you know what
" you have bought? " The other answered : " I do; I have bought you and that
" girl. " — " No, by Allah ! " replied Durd, " you have bought for yourself no-
" thing but shame, ruin and contumely, which will endure as long as you live, "
The man was alarmed at these words and exclaimed : " Woe betide you! how can
" that be? " Burd answered : "We belong to Yazîd Ibn Mufarrigh, and, by Allah !
" nothing has reduced him to the state in which he now is but his evil tongue. You
" are aware that he dared to satirize Abbâd, who is the emir of Khorâsân (6), whose
" brother, Obaid Allah, is the emir of the two Irâks, and whose uncle is the khalif
" Moawia Ibn Abi Sofyân. (He attacked him) because he thought him too slow
" (in granting favours); will he then withhold his tongue from you that have
" bought me and a girl who is as dear to him as his heart within his bosom.
" By Allah ! I know of no man into whose dwelling has entered a more fatal ·

" acquisition than that which has now entered into yours. " The man answered :
" I take you to witness that I declare you and her to be still his property; if you
" wish to go away, you may depart; I fear greatly for myself if Ibn Mufarrigh
" learns what has happened; if you wish to stay with me, both of you, you may. "
Burd said to him : " Write those words to my master. " The man wrote to Ibn Mufarrigh, who was still in prison, informing him of what he had done, and the
other replied by a letter in which he thanked him for his conduct and requested
him to keep the two slaves at his house till such time as God should set their master
at liberty. Abbád then said to his chamberlain : " I do find that the fellow, " —
meaning Ibn Mufarrigh. — " is much annoyed at being in prison; sell his horse,
" his arms, all his effects, and distribute the price between his creditors. " This order was executed, but there still remained unpaid a part of the debt for which Ibn Mufarrigh was imprisoned. He composed the following lines on the selling of his slaves :

I sold (*sharítá*) Burd, and, had his sale depended upon me, I should not have sought an advantage for myself in selling him. Were it not for that bastard (*Abbád*) and for the misfortunes
which have befallen me, I should never have been separated from him. O Burd! never before
did time bring on me so painful a stroke as this; never before did it oblige me to sell (*one whom
I considered as*) my child.

Sharítá here means : *I sold;* it is one of those verbs which have two opposite significations, as it means *to sell* and *to buy*. — The piece to which these verses belong
contains many more, but I omit the remainder. — Ibn Mufarrigh, having (at *length*)
perceived that, if he continued, whilst in prison, to insult and satirize Abbád, he
would only do more harm to himself, used then to answer in these terms to the persons who asked him what was the cause of his imprisonment : " (*I am*) a man to
" whom his emir is giving a lesson, for the purpose of correcting his extravagance
" and allaying his violence. That, I declare, is better than if he drew the skirt of
" his robe over the traces of his retainer's faults. " Abbád, being informed
of this, took pity on him and let him out of prison. Yazíd then fled till he reached
Basra, whence he proceeded to Syria, where he continued to err as a fugitive from
one city to another, and to recite satires against Ziád and his son (*Abbád*). In one
of those pieces, which we give here, the poet alludes to his abandoning Saíd Ibn
Othmán Ibn Affán for the purpose of following Abbád Ibn Ziád, and he mentions in
it the forced sale of Burd :

After some days passed at Rima, you (O poet !) broke the bonds which attached you to Imáma. The winds drop tears for her affliction whilst the lightning smiles from the cloud. O! how I regret committing an act which has terminated in repentance. I left the generous Saïd and his palace which is supported by lofty columns; (I left him who is) a lion in battle and who gives up the pleasures of love for the purpose of marching against the foe. Samarkand was conquered by his prowess and, in its precincts, he erected his pavilions, whilst I followed a slave belonging to the family of Iláj (7). Such things are signs foreboding the end of the world. With him (with the poet) went an Abyssinian maid so small of ears (sakkâ) that she might be taken for an ostrich; one of those dark-complexioned females whose faces bear the mark of an inferior race. I sold Bard! O that, after (losing) Bard, I had become an owl (R) or its female, which invokes the echos between al-Mushakkar and al-Yamáma. But a man must encounter what he most fears, if he wish to escape from ignominy and oppression. Slaves only should be beaten with the stick; a reprimand had sufficed to correct a freeman.

The family of Iláj belonged to the tribe of Táif. We shall speak of it again, in this article, when we give an account of al-Hárith Ibn Kalada. Abù Bakr Ibn Duraid (vol. III. p. 37), makes a similar statement in his Kitâb al-Ishtikâk (9), and cites the following lines to prove the fact:

Come to your senses, family of Abù Bakr! is the son to be compared with a candle? It is better to be a mawla to the Prophet than to claim relationship with the family of Iláj.

We shall speak of Abù Bakra Nafia Ibn Hárith in this article and mention the circumstance which gave rise to these verses. (Ibn Mufarrigh) says, in the last (10), verse of his piece that this Abyssinian maid resembled an ostrich in the smallness of her ears. They (the Arabs of the desert) say of a small ear, that it is sakkâ; this word designates also such female animals as have no (apparent) ears. The same Arabs say: "Every sakkâ lays eggs, and every sharkâ brings forth its young alive." By the word sharkâ is meant animals having long ears. These Arabs consider it as a general law that every animal having visible ears is viviparous and that every animal without visible ears is oviparous. — The narrator continues in these terms: Ibn Mufarrigh then persisted in satirizing (Abbâd) Ibn Ziâd, so that his poems were publicly sung by the people of Basra. Obaid Allah (Ibn Ziâd) caused an active search to be made for the poet, who narrowly escaped being taken and succeeded in reaching Syria. — Narrators do not agree as to the person who delivered the fugitive to (Obaid Allah) Ibn Ziâd; one says it was Moawia Ibn Abi Sofyân; another contradicts him and declares that it was Yazîd, the son of Moawia. It must have been the latter, for he was already reigning when Abbâd was appointed to the government of Sijistân.

— The author of the *Aghâni* relates, farther on, that Saîd, the son of Othmân Ibn Affân, went to visit (*the khalif*) Moawia Ibn Abi Sofyân and said to him: " Why have " you nominated (*your son*) Yazid as your successor, to my exclusion? By Allah! my " father was a better man than his; my mother was better than his, and I am better " than he. We raised you to power and have not deposed you; through us you " obtained what you have." To this Moawia replied : " You are right in saying that " your father was a better man than his; I freely acknowledge that Othmân was better " than I am; you say that your mother was a better woman than his; (*to that I re-* " *ply*) : a woman's worth must be appreciated by her remaining with her family, by " her deserving the good will of her husband and by giving birth to noble-minded " boys. You say that you are better than Yazid. To this, my son! I answer that, " if I was offered in exchange for Yazid as many persons like you as would fill the " Ghûta (11), I should feel no pleasure in accepting the proposal. You say that " your people raised me to power and did not depose me; (*to that I answer that*) I " received my (*first*) command from one who was better than you, from Omar Ibn " al-Khattâb, and your people confirmed my nomination. Moreover, I have not " been a bad governor for you: I revenged your wrongs, killed the murderers of " your father, elevated you to power and authority, enriched those among you who " were poor and raised the lowest of you to high stations. " Yazid then spoke in his favour and obtained for him the government of Khorâsân. — Let us return to the history of Ibn Mofarrigh. The narrator says: He continued passing from one town of Syria to another and satirizing the sons of Ziâd. His poems having reached Basra, Obaid Allah Ibn Ziâd, the emir of the two Irâks, wrote on that subject to (*the khalif*) Moawia, or, by another and more correct account, to Yazid (*the son and successor of Moawia*). In this letter he said : " Ibn Mofarrigh has " satirized Ziâd and the sons of Ziâd; calumniating the former in his grave and co- " vering the latter with eternal dishonour. From them he has passed to Abû Sofyân, " whom he stigmatizes as a fornicator, and whose sons he attacks in the foulest lan- " guage. He escaped from Sijistân, and I caused such strict search to be made for " him that he fled the country (12). He has now reached Syria where he mangles " our reputation (13) and tears our honour to pieces. I send you the satires which " he has directed against us, so that you may be induced to do us justice." He then sent (*to the khalif Yazid*) all the poems that Ibn Mofarrigh had composed on them. Yazid gave orders that search should be made for the offender who, being thus obliged to fly from one place to another, was driven out of Syria. He then went to Basra and stopped at the house of al-Ahnaf Ibn Kais. — Of this person, whose real name was ad-Dahhák, we have already spoken (vol. *I.* p. 635); his prudence became proverbial. — Al-Ahnaf, of whom he asked protection, replied in these terms : " Were I to promise you my protection against the son of Sumaiya (14), I " should only be deceiving you (*faughirraka*); I can protect any man against his " own family but not against the person under whose authority he is (15)." The poet then went to others, none of whom would engage to protect him, but he at last obtained from al-Mundir Ibn al Járúd al-Abdi (16) a promise to that effect. As Obaid Allah Ibn Ziád was the husband of al-Mundir's daughter and respected no man so much as her father, the latter, presuming on his influence over him, gave, inconsiderately, an asylum to the poet. Obaid Allah was already informed of the fugitive's arrival in Basra, when he learned that he had taken refuge at al-Mundir's. He sent for the latter and, when he appeared before him, he dispatched to his house some of the police guards. The dwelling was searched, Ibn Mufarrigh arrested, and his protector knew nothing of the matter till he saw the prisoner standing beside him. On this, he rose up, went over to Obaid Allah and spoke to him in favour of his guest. " Emir! " said he, " I implore you, in God's name, not to discredit my right of protection : I promised that man to be answerable for his " safety." Obaid Allah answered : " Mundir Allah ! (17) I have no objection to that " man's composing verses in praise of your father and you, but he has satirized " both me and my father, and yet you try to screen him from my vengeance. God " forbid that he escape me! that shall never be, and I shall not pardon him. " Al-Mundir replied in an angry tone and received this answer: " You presume too much " on your daughter that *is* with me; by Allah! if I please, I shall separate " from her and signify to her a full and absolute divorce. " Al-Mundir retired and Obaid Allah then turned towards the poet and said : " Evil for Abbád has been your " fellowship with him." The prisoner replied : " Evil for me has been his fel-" lowship! I preferred him to Saïd Ibn Othmán and spent, in accompanying him, " all that I possessed. I imagined that he was not devoid of intelligence such as " Ziád's, of mildness such as Moawia's and of liberality such as that of the Kuraish; " but he disappointed all my expectations, treated me with indignity and made " me suffer every thing disagreeable, imprisonment, *(prosecution for)* debt, upbraid-" ings and beatings. I was like the man who watched delusive lightnings proceed-

" ing from a cloud without rain; he hoped that it would pour showers upon him
" and he died of thirst. I fled from your brother because I feared that he would
" act in a manner of which he would have to repent. Now, I am in your power;
" do with me what you please." Obaid Allah sent him to prison and then addressed
to Yazid Ibn Moawia a letter in which he asked permission to put the poet to death.
Yazid wrote back to him in these terms : " You must avoid putting him to death,
" but you may inflict on him a chastisement that may serve him for a lesson and
" make your authority to be respected, without endangering his life. He has rela-
" tions in my army (jund) and among the persons of my court : were he put to death,
" they would be displeased with me and nothing would calm them except retaliating
" on you. Avoid that; know that all things are taken seriously by them and by me
" and that they would make you responsable for his death. Without going so far as
" to take his life, you have sufficient latitude for satisfying your anger." Obaid
Allah, on receiving this letter, gave orders that the prisoner should be obliged to
drink some sweet nabid (grape-juice) containing an infusion of shubrum (euphor-
bia), — or, as some say , of turbid (turbith). This produced a diarrhea and, whilst
he was in that state, they paraded him through the city, with a she-cat and a sow
tied on his (shoulders). The drug began to operate and the little boys ran after him,
hooting and shouting. The evacuation persisted with such violence that he lost his
strength and fell to the ground. Obaid Allah being then told that they could not
answer for his life, ordered him to be washed and taken back to prison. When
they were washing him, he recited this verse :

Water can wash away what I have done, but my words (satires) shall remain, even when your
bones are mouldered into dust.

Obaid Allah, being asked why he chose such a punishment for the poet, answered :
" He cast his filth on us and I intended that the sow should discharge her filth on
" him " (18). Out of the numerous verses directed by Ibn Mufarrigh against
" Abbâd Ibn Ziâd, we may cite the following :

Now, that Moawia, the (grand-) son of Harb, is dead, announced to your vase (your informer ?)
already cracked, that it will soon be (completely) broken. I now declare, (O Zaid!) that
your mother (did not lay) aside her veil (her dress) in order to have intercourse with Abû
Sofyân; but a thing occurred of a doubtful nature, and in (a moment of) great fear and trepi-
dation.

The following verses are by the same poet :

Come! announce to Moäwia, the son of Sakhr (Abú Sofyän), a message from the man of Yemen (19). Are you angry when people say that your father was chaste, and pleased, when they call him an adulterer? (Is that so?,) I declare that your relationship (rihm) to Zild is like that of the elephant to the foal of the ass. I declare that the female gave birth to Zaid and that Sakhr never approached Somaïa.

The expression : *I declare that your relationship to Zidd,* etc., is borrowed from the following verse, belonging to a poem which was composed by Hassân Ibn Thâbit al-Ansâri (20), surnamed Abù 'l-Walid, or, according to some, Abû Abd ar-Rahmân :

I declare that your relationship (ill) to the family of Koraish is like the relationship of the young camel (sakb) to the young ostrich (rál).

The word *ill* has the same meaning as *rihm; sakb* means a camel's foal ; *rál* means a young ostrich. — The following verses were composed by Hassân Ibn Thâbit on Abû Sofyân (Ibn al-Hârith) (21) :

Come! announce to Abû Sofyân a message from me to him; for that which was hidden has been brought to light. I'm Mahommed and I answer in his defence; my recompense for that I shall find with God. How dare you attack him, you that are not his equal? May the worst (sharr) of you two be sacrificed to save the best (khair)! Assuredly, my father, my father's father and my honour are sufficient to protect the honour of Mohammed against your insults.

The phrase : *may the worst of you two,* etc., gave rise to a discussion among the learned, because the words khair and sharr are terms which express superiority and require to be associated (with a complement) (22). Hassân Ibn Thâbit composed this answer by order of the Prophet. — I may here observe that, in the Prophet's family were five individuals who resembled him in their looks; namely, this Abû Sofyân (Ibn al-Hârith Ibn Abd al-Muttalib), al-Hasan Ibn Ali Ibn Abi Tâlib, Jaafar Ibn Abi Tâlib, Kotham Ibn al-Abbas Ibn Abd al-Muttalib, and as-Sâib Ibn Obaid Ibn Abd Yazid Ibn Hâshim Ibn Abd al-Muttalib Ibn Abd Manâf, the ancestor of the imâm as-Shâfi (23). This Abû Sofyân became a Moslim on the day in which Mekka was taken; that happened in the eighth year of the Hijra. His subsequent conduct attested the sincerity of his conversion. He accompanied the Prophet during the campaign of Talf and Hunain. When the Moslims were routed at the battle of Hunaîn, Abû Sofyân was one of the seven who stood firm and remained with the Prophet, till those who had fled rallied and came back. They then obtained the victory and a booty of five thousand captives. These the Prophet set at liberty. An account of this (battle) would form a long narrative, for which this is not a fit place. On that day, Abû Sofyân held the Prophet's mule by the bridle, without ever letting go his hold; and the Prophet used to say : '' I hope to find in him one capable of '' replacing Hamza Ibn Abd al-Muttalib. '' He declared also that Abû Sofiân would be one of those who were to enter into Paradise. He said also : '' Abû '' Sofyân Ibn Al-Hârith is one of the youths of Paradise, '' or (according to another statement) , '' the chief of the youth of the people of Paradise.'' Most of the learned consider the surname (Abû Sofyân) to be his real name and say that he had no other; but some of them declare that his name was al-Mughîra. Others again say that al-Mughîra was the name of his brother, that he was called Abû Sofyân and nothing more. It is stated that, from the time of his conversion to Islamism, he never dared to look the Prophet in the face, so much was he ashamed of having satirized him at a former period. — Let us resume our account of Ibn Mufarrigh. He is one of the poets who are mentioned in the Hamdsa. We find there (24) this piece of his :

> Behold! Zainab visited me towards the close of the night (and I said to her) : '' Blessings be
> '' upon you! are they come back, the (happy) days I passed (with you)? '' She replied : '' Avoid
> '' us and approach us not. '' (I answered) : '' How can I avoid you who are the sole object of
> '' my wishes? People ask if the sports of love continue when thirty years are passed, and I
> '' answer : Can they exist before the thirtieth year. The arrival of hoariness would be a great
> '' misfortune if, when it appears, the palanquin (-riders?) were precluded from every
> '' sport. ''

The Spanish author al-Muzaffar(25) says, in his great historical work, that, joined to those verses (min jumla hadi 'l-abydt) were the following :

> Were my body (26), when it grows weak, to become the sport of noble princes (?) or (the
> prey) of lions or of wolves, that (though) would alleviate my sufferings and console me in my mis-
> fortune; but (I cannot be consoled forever) she who was the most cruel to me (27) exists no
> more.

When al-Husain, the son of Ali Ibn Tâlib, was informed of Moawia Ibn Abi

Sofyán's death and the accession of Yazid, the son of Moawia (to the khalifate), he resolved on proceeding to Kûfa, whither he had been invited by a letter addressed to
him by a number of the inhabitants of that city. This is one of the well-known
circumstances of the affair which cost al-Hosain his life. During that time, he often
recited and applied to his own case the following verses of a poem composed by
Yazid Ibn Mufarrigh :

May I never spread terror through the flocks and herds by an incursion made at morning's
dawn, if I call not Yazid (to simple combat) on the day in which, not without fear, he does (me)
an injustice! May the fates watch (to seize) me, if I avoid (the combat) (28).

The persons who heard him discovered from this that he intended to have a struggle with Yazid Ibn Moawia for the supreme power. He set out for Kûfa and, when
he drew near it, the governor, Obaid Allah Ibn Ziad, sent against him a body of
troops commanded by Omar Ibn Saad Ibn Abi Wakkâs. Al-Husain was slain at
Tall and then happened what happened. It is related that (before this) Moawia had
written to him in these terms : " I am certain that you have taken into your
" head the idea of assailing (our government) and that you will be unable to conceal
" it. If I be then living, I shall most willingly forgive you." It is stated that
(the Omaiyide khalif) Omar Ibn Abd al-Aziz said : " Were I one of al-Husain's
" murderers and were God pleased to pardon me and to admit me into Paradise, I
" should not enter there, so much I would feel ashamed in the presence of God's
" apostle." Obaid Allah Ibn Ziad said to al-Hâritha Ibn Badr al-Ghudâni (29) :
" What think you will happen to me and to al-Husain on the day of the resurrection? "
Received from him this answer : " His father and his grandfather will intercede for
" him; your father and your grandfather will intercede for you. Learn from that
" what you want to know ! " — The Mirât az-Zamân (mirror of time), a historical
work drawn up in the form of annals and composed by Shams ad-Din Abû 'l-Muzaffar Yûsof Ibn Kizoghli, surnamed Sibt Ibn al-Jauzi (30), because he was the son of Abû
'l-Faraj Ibn al-Jauzi's (vol. II. p. 96) daughter, and the autograph of which, in forty
volumes, I saw at Damascus, contains, under the year 59 of the Hijra, an account of
what passed between Yazid Ibn Mufarrigh and the sons of Ziad. He then adds :
" Yazid Ibn Mufarrigh died in the year 69, "that is to say, of the Hijra (A. D. 688-9).
God knows best (31)! Abû 'l-Yakzân (vol. II. p. 578) says, in his Kitâb an-Nisab
(book of patronymics) : " Abbâd Ibn Ziad died A. H. 100 (A. D. 718-9) at Jârûd."

— *Járûd* is a village situated in the dependencies of Damascus and lying in the government of Hims (*Emessa*). Onagers are extremely abundant in that country. When the division of Egyptian troops entered into Syria, A. H. 660 (A. D. 1261-2) and marched against Antioch with the troops of Syria, it halted for a short time at Damascus, where I then was, and from that it returned back. The army entered into Damascus towards the end of the month of Shaabân of that year (July, 1262). A person belonging to that army related to me a circumstance so curious that it may very well be mentioned here. They had halted at Járûd, the place of which we are speaking, and hunted down a great number of onagers. So, at least, they said. A soldier, having killed one of them, proceeded to cook its flesh in the usual manner. Being unable to bring it to a proper state of coction, he added wood to the fire and augmented the flame; but that produced no effect, although the fire was kept up for a whole day. Another soldier then rose, took up the animal's head and found on the ear an inscription which, when he read it, proved to be the name of Bahrâm Gûr. When they arrived at Damascus, they brought me the ear. I found the mark to be quite visible, the hair on the ear being as fine as the smallest shreds. The writing was Kûfic. This Bahrâm Gûr was one of the (ancient) kings of the Persians and lived a long time before our prophet. When that prince took more animals at the chase than he required, he would mark some of them and let them go. God knows how old this onager was when Bahrâm captured it and to what age it would have reached, had they set it at liberty and not killed it. The fact is that the onager is one of the long-lived animals. This individual must have lived upwards of eight hundred years (32). — In the territory of Járûd is situated the famous mountain called al-Mudakhkhan. It is mentioned by Abû Nuwâs (vol. I. p. 391) in the poem wherein he names the places at which he halted on his way to Egypt, where he intended to visit al-Khasîb (33). He says :

Towards the East I saw the temples of Tadmor (*Palmyra*) and found them empty; they are walls facing the summit of al-Mudakhkhan.

This name must be pronounced *Muddakhan* (34). The mountain was so called because it is always capped with clouds which appear like a mass of smoke (*dukhán*). —I since read the following passage in the *Mafátíh al-Olûm* (*the keys of the sciences*), a work composed by Muhammad Ibn Ahmad Ibn Muhammad Ibn Muhammad Ibn Yûsuf al-Khowâresmi : " Bahrâm Gûr was the son of Bahrâm, the son of Sâpûr

" al-Junûd, the son of Sâpûr Zû 'l-Aktâf.   He was called *Bahrâm Gûr* because he
" was fond of hunting the *ofr*.   This last word serves to designate both the wild
" and the domestic ass (35)."   Having calculated the duration of their dynasty
from that period to the Hijra, I found it to be two hundred and sixteen years.   This
onager must therefore have lived for more than eight hundred years, if we count
from the time it was marked by Bahrâm Gûr till the year 660, when it was killed.
But God knows best! — In this article, frequent mention has been made of Ziâd, of
his sons, of Sumaiya, of Abû Sofyân and of Moawia, as also of the poems composed
upon them by Ibn Mufaerigh; now, as readers not acquainted with the facts may
desire some information respecting them, I shall give here a summary account of
the affair.   There was a king of Yemen called Abû 'l-Jabr, of whom Ibn Duraid
(vol. *III. p.* 37) has spoken in the following verse of his celebrated *kasîda* which is
entitled the *Makûra* :

> And sadness mingled with the soul of Abû Jabr, till death joined him to the number of those
> whom it had already seized.

The surname Abû-'l-Jabr was his real name; some say that his name was Yazîd
and that he was the son of Shurahbîl the Kindite; others state that Abû-'l-Jabr was
really his name and that he was the son of Amr.   Having been dethroned by his
subjects, he went to Persia for the purpose of obtaining from Kisra (*Chosroes*) the
assistance of a body of troops.   The Persian king sent with him a band of his
Asâwira (*cavalry*).   When they reached Kâzima and saw the sterility and unpro-
ductiveness of Arabia, they said : " Where is this man taking us to? " and then
delivered some poison to his cook, promising him, at the same time, an ample recompense, if he put it into the meat which was to be served before the king.   This
was done, and the food had no sooner settled in his stomach, than he felt intense
pain.   When the Asâwira were informed of this, they went in to where he was and
said to him : " Since you are reduced to such a state, give us a letter for king
" Chosroes, in which you declare that you have authorised us to return. " He wrote
a letter for them to that effect and, feeling some alleviation, he proceeded to Tâif,
the town situated in the vicinity of Mekka, and put himself under the care of al-
Hârith Ibn Kalada the Thakifite, who was the great physician of the Arabs and who
resided there.   Ibn Kalada treated and cured him, for which service he received from
his patient a rich present   which in were included (a slave-girl named) Sumaiya and

(a slave named) Obaid. Kisra had given them to Abû 'l-Jabr. The latter then set out for Yemen but, having had a relapse, he died on the way. Ibn Kalada gave Sumaiya in marriage to Obaid, and she had a son whilst Obaid was still living (36). Her son was called by various names, such as Ziâd Ibn Obaid, Ziâd Ibn Sumaiya, Ziâd Ibn Abîb *(Ziâd, the son of his father)* and Ziâd Ibn Ommih *(Ziâd the son of his mother)* (37). These were the appellations by which he was known before his adoption *(into the Omaiyide family)* by Moawia, an occurrence of we shall speak farther on. Sumaiya had also by al-Harith Ibn Kalada a son named Abû Bakra Nafî (نفيع) Ibn al-Harith, whom some persons call Nafî Ibn Masrûh and who became known, under the name of Abu Bakra, as one of the Prophet's companions. She had also two other sons, one named Shibl Ibn Mabad, and the other Nâfî (نافع) Ibn al-Harith. These were the four brothers who bore witness against al-Mughîra Ibn Shoba as being an adulterer. When we finish our account of Ziâd, we shall speak of that affair. In the time of heathenism, Abû Sofyân Sakhr Ibn Harb the Omaiyide and the father of Moawia Ibn Abi Sofyân, had incurred *(disreputable)* suspicions in consequence of his frequent visits to Sumaiya. It was in the time of their acquaintance that she gave birth to Ziâd, but she had still her husband Obaid (38). When Ziâd grew up, he displayed great talents and command of language, and became an orator whose eloquence, sagacity and intelligence filled the Arabs with admiration. It was for that reason that Abû Mûsa al-Ashari, on being appointed to the government of Basra by Omar Ibn al-Khattâb, took Ziâd Ibn Abîb for his secretary. Some time after, Ziâd brought a message from Abû Mûsa to Omar, who was so highly pleased with him that he ordered him a present of one thousand dirhems (£. 25). When Ziâd was gone, Omar thought of the money *(he had given)* and said : " There is one thousand lost, since Ziâd has " gotten it. " The next time that Ziâd came to see him, he said to him : " What " has become of your thousand? " Ziâd answered : " I purchased a little slave (obaid) " with them and gave him his liberty." By the word obaid he meant his own father *(who was so called)*. Omar replied : " Your thousand has not been spent uselessly. " Will you bear to Abû-Mûsa al-Ashari a letter in which I order him to take another " secretary in place of you? " Ziâd answered : " Most willingly; provided that the " order does not proceed from a feeling of anger *(against me)*." — " It does not " proceed from any feeling of anger; " replied Omar. " Why then, said Ziâd, do " you send him such an order? " [When dispatches were brought to Omar from

Basra, he preferred that Ziåd should be the bearer of them, because he was sure of obtaining from him satisfactory information.] He then gave him a government in the dependancies of Basra and, soon after, took it from him, saying: " It is not " as a disgrace that I depose you, but I am unwilling that your superior intelli- " genco should contribute to the oppression of the people *(an ahmit alá'n-nåsi fadl* " *aklik)*." Abû Mûsa, having dismissed Ziåd, took for secretary al-Husain Ibn Abi 'l-Hurr al-Anbari. A dispatch, written by the latter, was received by Omar who, finding in it a fault of orthography, wrote back these words to Abû Mûsa : " Give a flogging to your secretary." Ziåd, being sent by Omar to quell some troubles which had broken out in Yemen *(accomplished his mission so promptly that he)* had scarcely arrived when he set out again. On his return, he addressed the people in a speech the like of which they had never heard before. Amr Ibn al-Aási then said : " By Allah! did that youth belong to the family of Kuraish, he would *(force the* " *Arabs to obey and)* drive them before them with his stick." Abû Sofyân, hear- " ing this, said : " By Allah! I know the man who deposited him in his mo- " ther's womb." — "Tell me," said Ali Ibn Abî Tâlib, " who he was. " — " It was I." replied Abû Sofyân. — " Take care of what you say, Abû Sofyân! " said Ali. To this the other answered by the following lines :

> By Allah! were I not afraid, O Ali! that a certain person might look on me as his enemy, I, Sakhr Ibn Harb, should reveal the secret, even had there been no question of Ziåd. Long ago I was on good terms with *(the tribe of)* Thakîf and I then left among them a proof of my affec- tion (59).

When Ali obtained the supreme authority, Ziåd was sent by him to Persia, where he reduced all the country to obedience, protected it against attacks, collected the imposts and remedied abuses. Moawia then wrote to him with the intention of turning him against Ali, but this letter had no effect and was sent to Ali by him whom had received it. In it were some verses which I abstain from inserting here. Ali wrote back to Ziåd in these terms: " I appointed you to " the commandment which you hold, because I thought you worthy of it. In " your present career, you cannot obtain the object you have in view unless you " act with patience and a sincere conviction. Under the rule of Omar, Abû " Sofyân committed a fault by which no relationship or right of inheritance " can be established. As for Moawia, he can circumvent any man; so, be on your

" guard against him; be on your guard! Receive my salutation." When Ziâd read this letter, he exclaimed: " I swear by the Lord of the Kaaba, that the father of al-" Husain (i. e. Ali) bears witness in favour of me." It was this (communication) which emboldened Ziâd and Moawia to act as they (afterwards) did. Al-Hasan, the son of Ali, having obtained the khalifate after the murder of his father, gave up the supreme authority to Moawia, a fact which is well known. Moawia then endeavoured to gain over Ziâd and acquire his good will, so that he might be induced to serve him with the same fidelity that he had shewn to Ali. This, joined to the words which escaped from his father in the presence of Ali and Amr Ibn al-Aâsi (produced the desired effect and), in the forty-fourth year of the Hijra (A. D. 664-5), Ziâd was acknowledged by Moawia (as his brother) and became known by the name of Ziâd Ibn Abi Sofyân. When Abù Bakra was informed that his brother had been adopted, with his own consent, into the family of Moawia, he declared most solemnly that he would never speak to him again. "That fellow," said he, " declares his mother to be an adulteress and " disavows his father. By Allah! I do not think that Sumaiya ever saw Abù " Sofyân. Evil befall him! how will he manage with Omm Habîba, the daughter " of Abù Sofyân and the widow of the Prophet? If he goes to visit her, she will re-" fuse him admittance, and thus disgrace him, and, if she receive him, she will be " guilty of an act injurious to the profound respect which all have for the Prophet." Under the reign of Moawia, Ziâd went to Mekka for the purpose of making the pilgrimage and meant to visit Omm Habîba under the pretext that he and Moawia considered her as his sister; but he then thought of what Abù Bakra had said and abandoned his intention. According to another account, Omm Habîba refused to receive him, and, if we are to believe another statement, he made the pilgrimage but paid no visit in consequence of the words uttered by Abù Bakra. " May God reward Abù Bakra! " said he, " he never, in any case, gives bad advice. " — Having gone to see Moawia, for whom he was acting as lieutenant, he took with him a magnificent present containing, amongst other objects, a coffer of pearls so valuable that it excited Moawia's admiration. He then addressed him in these terms: " Commander of the " faithful! I have subdued for you that country," — meaning Irâk, — " I have col-" lected for you its tribute, both by land and by sea, and have brought you " the almond with its shell." On this, Yazîd Ibn Moawia, who was sitting in the room, said to him: " If you have really done that, we shall transfer you from (the " tribe of) Thakif to (that of) Kuraish, from Obaid to Abù Sofyân and from the rank

" of a secretary to that of a governor (40)." Moawia, on hearing these words,
said to Yazid : " That is quite enough! you are the flint I wanted for striking fire
" from my steel (41)." — Abû 'l-Hasan al-Madâini (vol. I. p. 438) states that
the kâtib Abû 'z-Zubair told him that Abû Ishâk related to him what follows :
" Ziâd, after purchasing his father Obaid, went to see Omar, who said to him :
" What did you do with your pay, the first time you received it? " Ziâd replied :
" I purchased my father with it." This answer gave great pleasure to Omar. The
anecdote (told above concerning Yazid and Ziâd) is in contradiction with the statement that it was Moawia who declared Ziâd a member (of the tribe of Kuraish). —
When Moawia acknowledged Ziâd (as his brother), the Omaiyides went to see him
(and remonstrate). One of them, named Abd ar-Rahmân Ibn al-Hakam, and brother
to Marwân Ibn al-Hakam, then addressed him in these terms : " Moawia! had you
" found none but negroes (Zenj) to adopt, you would have (taken them for members
" of your family and) outnumbered us by (an act of) meanness and degradation."
Moawia (on hearing this reproach), went up to Marwân, Abd ar-Rahmân's brother,
and said : " Turn out that blackguard." Marwân replied : " By Allah! (for you to
" say) that he is a blackguard is not to borne." Moawia answered : " By Allah!
" were it not for my mildness and clemency, I should teach you that it must be
" borne. Did he not send me verses composed by himself against Ziâd and me?
" Hear them from my lips :

" Come! say to Moawia, the son of Sakhr : ' We cannot suffer what you have done. Are
" ' you angry when people say that your father was chaste and pleased when they say he was an
" ' adulterer? ' "

We have already given the rest of this piece (page 242 of this vol.) and attributed it
to Ibn Mufarrigh; but there is a difference of opinion respecting its author : some say
that it was composed by Ibn Mufarrigh, and others, by Abd ar-Rahmân Ibn al-Hakam.
In the former case, the first verse is that which has been previously given; in the
latter, it must be read as it is here. — Ziâd, on his adoption by Moawia, was treated
by him with great favour, obtained a commandment and became one of his most
effective supporters in the contestations with the sons of Ali Ibn Abi Tâlib. It is
related that, when he was governor of the two Irâks, he caused active search to be
made for a man named Ibn Sarh who was a partisan of al-Hasan, the son of Abû Tâlib. The name of this person had been included in the act of amnesty granted to the

companions of al-Hasan, when the latter abdicated the khalifate in favour of Moawia.
Al-Hasan, in consequence, wrote the following letter to Ziad : " From al-Hasan to
" Ziad : You know that we obtained an amnesty for our partisans, and yet Ibn Sarh
" informs me that he has been exposed to your attacks.   I therefore request that you
" act towards him only for his good.   Receive my salutation."   This letter commenced by the writer's name and did not give to Ziad the surname of *the son of
Abû Sofyân.*   Ziad was offended at it and replied in these terms: " From Ziad,
" the son of Abû Sofyân, to al-Hasan : I received your letter concerning a re-
" probate who is now harboured by others, by partisans of yours and of your fa-
" ther.   By Allah! I shall pursue and arrest him, even were he (*hidden*) between
" your skin and your flesh.   The flesh that I most wish to devour is that of which
" you are a part."   When al-Hasan received this epistle, he sent it to Moawia who,
on reading it, was so indignant that he wrote to Ziad a letter containing these words :
" From Moawia, the son of Abû Sofyân, to Ziad: Al-Hasan, the son of Ali, has sent
" to me a letter written by you in answer to one in which he spoke to you concern-
" ing Abû Sarh.   Its contents surprised me greatly and I perceived by it that you
" have two ways of judging matters, one which you inherited from Abû Sofyân, and
" the other from Sumaiya.   That which you owe to Abû Sofyân is all prudence and
" precaution; the other, for which you are indebted to Sumaiya, is just such as
" should be expected from one like her.   It was the last which produced the letter
" in which you revile al-Hasan and treat him as a reprobate.   Now, by my life!
" you are more deserving of that epithet than he.   If, through a sentiment of su-
" periority, he commenced his letter by his own name, that could not derogate
" from your merit; but, by rejecting the application made by him in favour of a
" person whom he thought deserving of his intercession, you have thrown off your
" own shoulders a task which shall be executed by one who has a better right to ac-
" complish it than you.   On the receipt of this, my letter, restore to Ibn Sarh the
" property of his which is in your hands and do not attempt to injure it.   I have
" written to al-Hasan, informing him that, if he pleases, the fugitive may either
" stay with him or return to his own country, and that you have been prohibited
" from harming him either by word or deed.   In your letter to al-Hasan, you call
" him by his name without mentioning of whom he is the son; I therefore let you
" know, inconsiderate fellow! that al-Hasan is above the reach of contempt (48).
" Did you then think that his father was so contemptible a person? but that person

" was Ali the son of Abû Tâlib; or did you think it (not) worth while to join his name
" to that of his mother? but his mother was Fâtima, the daughter of the Apostle
" of God, and, if you have any intelligence remaining, you must acknowledge
" that therein he excels us all.   Receive my salutation." — The word *rajewdni* is
a dual which (*has a plural signification and*) means *places of danger.* — I must here
observe that the same anecdote is related in another form, and shall therefore give
it here : Said Ibn Sarh was a *mawla* to Kuraiz Ibn Habib Ibn Abd Shams, one
of Ali Ibn Abi Tâlib's partisans.   When Ziâd, the son of his father (*Ibn Abih*)
arrived at Kûfa in the capacity of governor, he persecuted Ibn Saad and caused
strict search to be made after him.   Ibn Saad then went to Medina and alighted at
the door of al-Hasan Ibn Ali, who said to him : " What has forced you to quit your
" residence and come here?"   The fugitive told his story and described the conduct of Ziâd towards him.   Al-Hasan therefore wrote to Ziâd in these terms :
" You engaged towards a certain Musulman that he should partake of all the advan-
" tages enjoyed by those of his belief, and incur the same obligations which are im-
" posed on them.   Yet you have pulled down his house, seized on his property and
" arrested the members of his family.   Therefore, when this, my letter, reaches
" you, rebuild his house, and restore to him his property and the members of his
" family; I have given him hospitality and have been requested by him to interfere
" in this matter."   To this Ziâd replied : " From Ziâd, the son of Abû Sofyân, to
" al-Hasan the son of Fâtima : I received your letter, in which you commence by
" placing your own name before mine, and yet you request of me a service; you,
" a man of the people, from me, a sovereign (*sultân*)!   You write to me in favour
" of a reprobate whom none would harbour except a reprobate like himself : and,
" what is still worse, he has found in you a patron (*tawallihi tydka*)!   You have al-
" lowed him to reside with you, him disaffected (*to government*) and taking pleasure
" in being so!   But, by Allah! you shall not save him from me, even were he hid-
" den between your skin and your flesh; and certainly the flesh that I should most
" like to devour is that of which you are a part.   Deliver him up by the halter (43)
" to one who has a better right to him than you.   If I then pardon him, it shall
" not be in consequence of your intercession and, if I put him to death, it shall be
" on account of the love you bear him. "   When al-Hasan read this epistle, he wrote
to Moawia an account of Ibn Sarh's affair and enclosed in the letter (*a copy of*) his
own to Ziâd and the answer which he had received.   He wrote also a letter to Ziâd

(and addressed it) thus : " From al-Hasan, the son of Fàtima, who was the daughter
" of the Apostle of God, to Ziàd, the son of Sumaiya, who was a slave of the tribe of
" Thakîf, (to Zîdd) legitimate by birth and yet the son of an abandoned adulterer. "
When Moawia read al-Hasan's letter (he was so much ashamed that) Syria seemed too
narrow to hold him, and he wrote to Ziàd in the terms which we have already mentioned (51). — Obaid Allah Ibn Ziàd declared that, of all the verses directed against
him, none wounded his feelings so much as the following, which were composed by
Ibn Mufarrigh :

> Reflect ! for reflection may give you a moral lesson. Are you not indebted for all your ho-
> nours to your nomination as governor? As long as Sumaiya lived, she never suspected that her
> son belonged to the tribe of Koraibb.

Kalàda (vol. II. p. 513) relates that Ziàd, when on the point of death, said to his
sons : " O, that your father had been a shepherd leading his flocks to countries far
" and near, and that what he came by had never befallen him ! "— The verses directed by Ibn Mufarrigh against Ziàd and his sons are all of the same cast : he treats
them as pretenders and goes so far as to say of the sons of Sumaiya :

> Ziàd, Nàfi and Abû Bakra are for me a cause of wonder. These three were formed in the
> same womb and had all the same father, yet one says that he is a Koraishide, the other is
> an enfranchised slave, and the third has an Arab for his uncle.

As these lines require explanation, I shall give here what is related by persons
versed in history : Al-Hàrith was the son of Kalada Ibn Amr Ibn Ilàj Ibn Abî Salama Ibn Abd al-Ozza Ibn Ghiara Ibn Aûf Ibn Kasi. This last was the same person
as Thakîf. It is thus that Ibn al-Kalbi exposes this genealogy in his *Jamhara*.
Al-Hàrith was a celebrated physician among the Arabs. He died soon after the
promulgation of Islamism, but the fact of his conversion has not been ascertained.
It is related that the Prophet of God ordered Saad Ibn Abi Wakkàs to go and take
the advice of al-Hàrith Ibn Kalada on a malady by which he had been attacked.
This proves the lawfulness of consulting, on medical questions, persons who are
not Moslims, provided they be of the same nation as the sick man (45). His son,
al-Hàrith Ibn al-Hàrith, was one of those *whose hearts had been reconciled* (46),
and he counts as one of the Prophet's companions. It is said that al-Hàrith Ibn
Kalada was incapable of begetting children and that he died in the khalifate of Omar.

The Prophet, when he laid siege to Tâif, made this declaration : " Whatever slave " lets himself down (from the wall) and comes to me shall be free." Abû Bakra then lowered himself down from the fortress by means of a bakra (pulley), — which is a thing traversed by a rope and placed over a well for the purpose of drawing water. It is called a bakara by common people, but this pronounciation is not correct, although the author of the Mukhtasir al-Aîn (abridgment of the Aîn) (47) gives it as good. It has, however, so little to recommend it that no other philologer ever authorised it. — The narrator continues : He received therefore from the Prophet the surname of Abû Bakra (the pulley-man), and used to say that he was a mawla of the Prophet of God. His brother, Nâfi, was also going to lower himself down when al-Hârith Ibn Kalada said to him : " Remain, and I adopt you as my " son." He therefore remained and was surnamed Ibn al-Hârith. Abû Bakra, before his conversion to Islamism, bore also that surname, but, when he became a good Musulman, he gave it up. On the death of al-Hârith Ibn Kalada, Abû Bakra abstained, through self-mortification, from receiving any part of the inheritance. — This, I must observe, might have been the case, were we to admit the statement of those who say that al-Hârith died a Musulman, for, if he did not, Abû Bakra would have been excluded from inheriting, on account of the difference of religion (48). — (The narrator continues :) Ibn Mufarrigh was induced to compose the three verses above-mentioned because Ziâd pretended to be a Kuraishide on the plea of his adoption by Moawia; because Abû Bakra declared himself a mawla of the Prophet, and because Nâfi used to say that he was the son of al-Hârith Ibn Kalada, of the tribe of Thakîf. They were, besides, born of the same mother, the Sumaiya already mentioned. It was also for that reason that the poet composed on the family of Abû Bakra the two verses which commence by the words : Come to your senses, family of Abû Bakra! (page 238 of this vol.). Hâj was the grandfather of al-Hârith Ibn Kalada, as we have already stated. This is an abridged account of the affair of Ziâd and his sons. — I must again make an observation : these words of Ibn Mufarrij in the second verse : they had the same father, are not true, for no one ever said that Ziâd was the son of al-Hârith Ibn Kalada; on the contrary, he was the son of Obaid, having been born on his bed (in his lifetime). As for Abû Bakra and Nâfi, they were considered as the sons of al-Hârith. How then could the poet say with truth that they had all the same father? Weigh these observations. — Ibn an-Nadîm (49) says, in the work entitled the Fihrest, that Ziâd was the first person who compiled a work containing things disreputable to the Arabs. Ziád Ibn Abíh having been calumniated and seeing his genealogy impugned, composed that book for the use of his sons and said to them : "Defend yourselves with this against the Arabs, " and they will cease to attack you." — The anecdote concerning al-Mughíra Ibn Shoba the Thakifide and the evidence given against him must now be related : Al-Mughíra, having been named governor of Basra by Omar Ibn al-Khattáb, used to go out of the government palace every day, at the hour of noon. Abú Bakra, having met him said : " Where is the emir going?" and received this answer. " I am going on business." To this Abu Bakra replied : " An emir receives visits " but never makes any." He (al-Mughíra) was going, it said, to see a woman named Omm Jamíl, who was the daughter of Amr and the wife of al-Hajjáj Ibn Atík Ibn al-Hárith Ibn Wahb al-Jushami. — Ibn al-Kalbi states, in his Jamhara, that Omm Jamíl was the daughter of al-Afkam Ibn Mihjan Ibn Amr Ibn Shatba Ibn al-Huzam, and he counts this family among those of the Ansárs. Another author furnishes this additional information : " Al-Huzam was the son of Ruwaiba Ibn Abd Allah Ibn Hilál " Ibn Admir Ibn Saada Ibn Moawla Ibn Bakr Ibn Hawázin." God knows best! — The narrator continues : Abú Bakra was in an upper room with his brothers, Náfi, Ziád and Shibl Ibn Mabad, who were all sons of the same mother, her who was named Sumaiya. Omm Jamíl was in a chamber opposite to theirs, and, the wind happening to blow open her door, they saw al-Mughíra in the act of carnal intercourse with her. On this, Abú Bakra said : " There is a calamity for you! look at that." They looked till they were convinced, and Abú Bakra then went down stairs and sat there, waiting till al-Mughaira came out. When he saw him, he said: " You know " full well what you have done, so you had better quit us (and leave the city)." — The narrator says (farther on) : Al-Mughíra went to say the afternoon (ashr) prayer at the head of the congregation, and Abú Bakra rose to go out, saying : " By Allah! " you shall not preside at our prayer after what you did!"—" Let him go on with " the prayer," said (some of the) people, "for he is our emir. Write down your com- " plaint and send it to (the khalif) Omar." He and his brothers did so, and Omar summoned al-Mughíra to appear before him, and them also as witnesses. When they arrived, Omar took his seat and cited them all forward. Abú Bakra advanced, and (the khalif) said to him (50): " Vidistine illum inter femora mulieris?" Respondit : " Per Deum! latera duo femorum divaricata adhuc mihi videre videor." Tunc eumdem (testem) compellavit al-Mughíra dixitque : " Callide aspexisti!" Res-

pondit Abû Hakra : " Moriar si non declarem id propter quod te Deus ignominia
affecturus est." Dixit Omar : " Quinimo oportet te eum vidisse penem intromit-
" tentem in vulvam, sicut stylum in pyxidem." Respondit Abû Bakra : " Illud vidi
" et attestor." Tune dixit Omar : " Væ tibi, Mughira! effugit quarta pars (vitæ
" tuæ." Tunc Nafiam advocavit et ei dixit : " Quid est testimonium tuum ? " Respondit : " Sicut testimonium Abû Bakra." Dixit Omar : " Necesse est declarare illud scil.
" mentulam)in mulierem intromissum fuisse, sicut stylum in pyxidem." Respondit :
" Certe intromissum fuit usque ad radicem (hudad)." — Vox hudad sagittæ pennam
" significat. — Tunc dixit Omar : " Væ tibi, Mughira! effugit dimidium tuum."
" Postea (testem) tertium appellavit et ei dixit : " Quid est testimonium tuum ? " Res-
" pondit : " Idem est quod socii mei duo præstiterunt." Dixit Omar : " Væ tibi,
Mughira! effugit (vitæ) tuæ dodrans." Tunc scripsit (Omar) ad Ziadum qui nondum
compareurat, et postquam eum vidit, consedit in moscheo, ducibus Muhajirorum
et Ansariorum congregatis. (Mughira), Ziadum intrantem aspiciens, dixit : " Video
"hominem cujus lingua, Deo volente, Muhajirum ignominia afficere nolet." Sus-
tulit Omar caput dixitque : " Quid novisti, otidis pulle! " Fertur quoque al-Moghi-
ram surrexisse ad Ziadum et dixisse : " Post Arusam aromati loculus non est (51)."
— Dico hanc locutionem proverbium esse, Arabibus notum, sed illud exponere haud
convenit, præsertim cum in hoc capite oratio nostra latius diffusa sit. — Tradidit
narrator : Dixit ei al-Mughira : " Ziade! Dei excelsi memor esto coram quo staturus
" es in die resurrectionis. Certe Deus, et liber ejus, et Propheta ejus et im-
" perator fidelium effusionem sanguinis mei prohibebunt, dummodo de iis quæ
" vidisti ad ea quæ non vidisti transire noles ; cave ne propter rem turpem quam vi-
" disti transeas ad rem quam non vidisti. Per Deum! si inter ventrem meum et ven-
" trem illius (mulieris) fuisses, me mentulam in illam intromittentem haud vidisses."
Tradidit narrator : " Tunc Ziadus, cujus oculi lacrymabant et facies rubore suffun-
" debatur, dixit : " Imperator fidelium! verum esse quod alii pro vero dederunt, di-
" cere non possum ; sed vidi consessum, audivi suspiria crebra et occasionem arrep-
" tam ; vidi illum super illam recubantem." Dixit Omar : " Vidistine rem inser-
" tam in vulva sicut stylum in pyxide?" Respondit: " Haud vidi." Fertur etiam
Ziadum dixisse : " Vidi illum pedes mulieris sustollentem ; vidi testiculos ejus oscil-
" lantes super femora mulieris, cum impetu vehementi." Omar then exclaimed :
" Praise be to God! " Al-Mughira, being told by him to go over and beat them
(for having borne false witness against him), inflicted on Abû Bakra eighty strokes

and flogged also the (two) others. Ziâd gave, by his deposition, great satisfaction to Omar, as it averted from al-Mughîra the penalty (of lapidation) fixed by the law. Abû Bakra exclaimed after undergoing his punishment : " I bear witness that al-" Mughîra did so and so " (repeating his former evidence). Omar was about to have him chastised a second time; when Ali Ibn Abi Tâlib said to him : " If you beat " him, you must lapidate your friend (52)." He therefore let him alone and told him to repent of his sin. " Do you bid me repent," replied Abû Bakra, " so that " you may receive whatever evidence may be given by me later?" Omar answered : " Such is my motive," and Abû Bakra replied : " I shall (therefore) never serve as " a witness between two parties, as long as I live." When he was undergoing the legal penalty, al-Mughîra addressed him thus : " Glory and praise be to God who has " thus brought shame upon you ! " Not so," said Omar, " but may God bring shame " upon the place in which these (people) saw you ! " — Omar Ibn Shabba (vol. II. p. 375), states, in his history of Basra, that, when Abû Bakra was beaten, his mother caused a sheep to be flayed and the skin applied to his back. This made people say that, assuredly, the strokes must have been very heavy. Abd ar-Rahmân, the son of Abû Bakra, related that his father swore never to speak to Ziâd as long as he lived. One of Abû Bakra's dying injunctions was that Ziâd should not be allowed to say the funeral service over him, and that Abû Barza al-Aslami, a person to whom he had been united in brothership by the Prophet of God, should discharge that duty. When Ziâd was informed of this, he (left the place and) went to Kûfa. Al-Mughîra was greatly pleased with Ziâd's conduct (at the trial) and testified to him all his gratitude. At a later period, when the pilgrims had assembled in Mekka, Omar received the visit of Omm Jamîl and said to al-Mughîra, who was present : " Tell " me, Mughîra! do you know this woman ! — " I do," replied the other, " she " is Omm Kulthûm, the daughter of Ali." On hearing these words, Omar exclaimed : " Do you intend to make me believe that you do not know her? by Allah ! " I now think that Abû-Bakra did not accuse you wrongfully and, when I see you, I fear lest stones should be thrown down on me from heaven (for saving you from lapidation)."—The Shaikh Abû Ishak as-Shirâzi (vol. I. p. 9) says, in his Muhaddab, towards the commencement of the chapter on the number of witnesses (required by law): " Testimony was given against al-Mughîra by three persons : Abû " Bakra, Nâfi and Shibl Ibn Mabad. As for Ziâd (the fourth witness), he (merely) said : " ' Vidi oulum resilientem, (audivi) anhelitum fortem et (vidi) pedes duos (erectos) ad

" ' instar aurium asini; quid fuerit ultra, nescio! Omar caused therefore the three
" witnesses to be chastised and did not punish al-Mughira."—Legists have discussed
what Ali meant when he said: " If you beat him, you must lapidate your friend; "
and Abû Nasr Ibn as-Sabbâgh (vol. II. p. 164) writes, in his Shâmil, a treatise on
the (Shafite) system of jurisprudence: " He (Ali) meant to say: ' That sentence (of
" ' yours) can only be (applicable) in case of your counting what he said for another
" ' (a fourth) deposition; but then, the number (of depositions requisite for the con-
" ' demnation of al-Mughira) would be complete; if it (your sentence) applies to the
" ' first deposition (made by Abû Bakra, it cannot be executed, because) you have al-
" ' ready punished him for it. "—Omar Ibn Shabba relates as follows, in his history
of Basra : " Al-Abbâs, the son of Abd al-Muttalib, said to Omar Ibn al-Khattâb: "The
" Prophet of God made me a grant of (the province of) al-Bahrain! — ' Who was
" ' witness to that?' replied Omar.   Al-Abbâs named al-Mughira Ibn Shoba, but
" Omar refused to admit such an evidence."—This article has run to a great length,
but it contained a number of facts that required elucidation, and our statements
took therefore a wide spread.   They are not, however, devoid of utility.

(1) Abû Abd ar-Rahmân Abd Allah Ibn Mohammad was generally known by the surname of Ibn Aisha,
because he was the son of Aisha, the daughter of Talha Ibn Obaid Allah at-Tamimi, one of Mohammad's
principal Companions and the same who was slain at the battle of the Camel, A. H. 86 (A. D. 656).   As a
traditionist and a transmitter of historical and literary information, he enjoyed a high reputation.   It was at
Baghdad that he gave his lessons.   To his natural talents, philological knowledge, piety and a perfect acquaintance with the history of the days (or encounters) of the desert Arabs, he joined great bodily strength.   It
would appear that he was an orthodox Mussulman, believing that the Koran was God's uncreated word, for it
is stated that the khalif al-Mâmûn, a great adversary of that doctrine and a cruel persecutor of those who
professed it, had him severely flogged.   An accident which happened to him whilst undergoing this punishment gave to that reprobate poet, Abû Nawâs (vol. I. p. 391), the idea of composing on his misadventure
a piece of verse which became generally known.   He died A. H. 228 (A. D. 842-3).—(Nujûm.)

(2) The Kitâb al-Aghâni has a long article on Ibn Molarrigh.   That is the source from which our author
has extracted, verbatim, the greater part of the information which is contained in this article.

(3) Of Ibn Abi Fanan little or no information has yet been found, except a few indications given by Ibn
Khallikan and the author of the Kitâb al-Aghâni.   He seems to have been one the poets who flourished in the
time of Hârûn ar-Rashid.

(4) Abbâd Ibn Ziâd was named governor of Sijistan by Moawia in A. H. 88 (A. D. 673), and he was still
holding that place in the year 66 (A. D. 680-1).—(Nujûm.)

(5) In this article will be found an account of Ziâd's origin.

(6) The narrator probably meant to say : of Sijistan.

(7) Abbád's grandfather was a slave. The history of his origin is given further on.

(8) One of the superstitious ideas of the pagan Arabs was that the souls of the dead passed into the bodies of screech-owls.

(9) See page 106 of Wüstenfeld's edition of that work.

(10) The verse to which our author refers is now followed by others which have been added at a later period.

(11) The country surrounding Damascus and covered with gardens is called the Ghūta.

(12) Literally: that the country spat him out, i.e. rejected him, was too hot to hold him.

(13) Literally: where he devours our flesh.

(14) Ziād, the father of Abbád, was the son of Samaiya. See her history farther on.

(15) Lit.: but not against his sakoe.

(16) Abū 'l-Ashath al-Mundir Ibn al-Jārūd al-Abdī was appointed governor of Istakhar by Ali Ibn Abī Tālib; and, in the year 66 (A.D. 664-5), he was nominated to the government of Sind by Obaid Allāh Ibn Ziād, who was then emir of Irāk. Al-Mundir died in Sind.—(Maārif, Nujūm, Balādori.)

(17) Mundir Allāh means: monitor of God. Was that Ibn al-Jārūd's real name?

(18) From this we should infer that it was not the poet but the son, which had taken the purgative draught. Moslim writers are sometimes very inattentive.

(19) The poet was proud of belonging by birth to the powerful party of the Yamanites.

(20) Hassān Ibn Thābit, one of the poets employed by Muhammad to satirize his adversaries, lived to the age of one hundred and twenty years, as his father, grandfather and great-grandfather had done before him. He died A.H. 54 (A.D. 673-4).—(Nujūm.)

(21) See lower down, in the same page.

(22) The author seems to say that they are really adjectives in the comparative degree, although they have not the form proper to such adjectives. Formed according to rule, they would have been akhyar and asharr.

(23) This genealogy agrees with that given by Ibn Duraid in his Ishtikāk. The same genealogy, as it occurs in the Sila of as-Shāfi (vol. II, p. 359), is faultive,—some of the names being incorrectly spelled.

(24) See Freytag's Hamāsa, page 372.

(25) Abū Bakr Muhammad Ibn Abd Allāh Ibn Muhammad Ibn Maslama, the second Abbāside sovereign of Badajoz, bore the title of al-Muzaffar (the victorious). He composed a work in fifty volumes, forming an encyclopaedia of all the sciences, historical annals, biography, literature, etc. This immense compilation was named after him the Mozafferian. The author died A.H. 460 (A.D. 1068).—(Makkari, vol. II, p. 353 and 749 of the Leyden edition, and vol. I, p. 147 of the English translation by Gayangos.)

(26) Literally: my flesh.

(27) Lit.: the most ardent in worrying my flesh.

(28) In this place the words us la desunis Yazida mean equivalent to illa (or in la) desunis Yazida. The translator adopts this opinion the more readily as the expression la unis hada wa la min hada does not mean: neither of this nor of that; but: not only this but that. For example, see the Arabic text of Ibn Khaldūn's Prolegomena, Paris edition, tome I, p. 447 and 367, and tome III, p. 276.

(29) Al-Ghuddūn (الغُدَّانيّ) is the right reading: see Ibn Duraid's Ishtikāk, page 148. That author informs us that al-Hārith Ibn Badr, surnamed Abū 'l-Anbas, was distinguished for his courage, his love of good wine and the rectitude of his judgment. Ziād (Ibn Abīh), with whom he was a great favorite, had his name inscribed on the roll of the Koraishide troops (in order that he might receive a higher pay). He had been designated by Omar Ibn ar-Rabī as commander of the troops which were to be sent against the Azāriks (vol. II.

p. 514) of al-Ahwâz, but al-Mahallah (vol. *III. p.* 506) frustrated him, (he was drowned at that place). For more information respecting the character, conduct and death of this Arabic chieftain, see the first volume of Dozy's *Histoire des Musulmans d'Espagne*, tomes I, pages 189, 140, 141 et seq.

(30) See vol. I, p. 431.

(31) Here the author finishes his account of Ibn Mufarrigh, without informing us what became of him when he was delivered up to Abbâd. Had he continued his extracts from that poet's biography as given in the *Kitâb al-Aghâni*, he would not have left his readers in the dark. In order to repair his omission I insert here an abridged account of Ibn Mufarrigh's subsequent adventures, as related in the *Aghâni*. During his detention in the prison to which Obaid Allah had sent him, he never ceased composing satires on the family of Ziâd. Obaid Allah, being informed of this, had him taken, under escort, to his brother Abbâd. (Here, in the *Aghâni*, the names of the two brothers are displaced, one being put for the other.) The guards had orders to pass with him to every caravanserai (*khân*) at which he had stopped on flying from Abbâd, and to force him to efface all the satirical verses which he had written on the walls of the chambers in which he had lodged. As they would allow him no instrument with which he might scratch out the writings, he had to employ his nails and, where these were worn out and the tips of his fingers came to the bone, he was obliged to efface the obnoxious lines with his blood. Abbâd, to whom he was thus delivered, put him into close confinement. The poet succeeded, however, in discovering a man who, for a recompense, went to Damascus and there recited aloud, in one of the most public places, (the vol. has دربُ صفلق) two verses by which the Yemenite troops were informed that their countryman and relative was kept in prison by the son of Ziâd. These Arabs, yielding to the spirit of party which animated the Yemenites against the Kaisites, could not suppress their indignation and carried their complaints before the khalif Moawia. He at first refused to grant what they demanded and sent them away, but then, listening to the dictates of his usual prudence, he had them called back and granted their request. A letter sent by him to Abbâd procured the poet his liberty. Ibn Mufarrigh then waited on Moawia and obtained from him a full pardon with a gift of two thousand dirhems (£. 940), on the condition of his not attacking the family of Ziâd. Having received from him also the permission of inhabiting whatever province he pleased, he proceeded to Mosul and from that to Basra. He then went to see Obaid Allah Ibn Ziâd and offered him his excuses. These were well received and procured for him the authorization of going to the province of Kermân. Some time after, he reverted to Irâk and continued passing from one place to another till he at length obtained the favour of Masûr Ibn al-Hakam (?). He returned to Basra when Obaid Allah fled from that place to avoid being murdered by the inhabitants who, seeing the troops of Abd Allah Ibn az-Zubair every where victorious, had resolved on taking their governor's life. Obaid Allah was killed at the battle of the Zâb, A. H. 67 (A. D. 687), in fighting against al-Mukhtâr. For the history of the latter, the first volume of Dozy's brilliant and conscientiously written work on the Spanish Musulmans may be usefully consulted. When Ibn Mufarrigh returned to Basra, he renewed his attacks against the Ziâd family. Some time afterwards, he received abundant presents from Obaid Allah, the son of Abû Bakra, and settled at al-Ahwâz where he continued to spread his wealth with the greatest liberality. — The article of the *Kitâb al-Aghâni* is very long and contains a great quantity of verses, anecdotes and digressions which are here omitted.

(32) The inscription was perhaps traced on the ear after the death of the animal.

(33) Abû Nasr Khasîb Ibn Abd al-Hamid was appointed intendant of the finances in Egypt, by the khalif Hârûn ar-Rashid. According to Elmacin (*al-Makin*), page 110, and the author of the *Raud al-Akhyâr*, cited by Reiske in the Annals of Abulfeda, t. III, p. 751, Khasîb's nomination took place in the year 190 (A. D.

(33-3). This fact I do not find mentioned in the *Nujûm*, a work of which the main subject is the history of Egypt. Al-Khadib was noted for his generosity and highly praised by the poets of the day.

(34) This appears to be an error: the measure of the preceding verse requires the redoubling of the third consonant, not of the second.

(35) *Gûr* is the Persian name of the onager or wild ass. Our author has written *Jâr*.

(36) Literally: she brought forth a son on the bed of Obaid. The Moslim law term: a child born on the bed of such a one, indicates that it was born in wedlock.

(37) The three last denominations indicate that he was considered as a bastard, begot by an unknown father. Ziâd was so named by his enemies.

(38) Lit.: she brought him forth on Obaid's bed.

(39) Lit.: the fruit of my heart.

(40) Literally: from the pen to the pulpit. In the manuscripts we read *menâbir* (*pulpits*).

(41) That is: you hit precisely on my idea.

(42) The Arabic words have this meaning, but their literal signification is: the two sides (*rejected*) cannot handy him about; that is, he is not to be cast from side to side. Lower down, the author explains *rejected* by its figurative signification.

(43) This is a common proverbial expression; it refers to the practice of leaving the halter on the animal which is sold, in order that the purchaser may lead it away without difficulty.

(44) The edition of Bûlâk and some of the manuscripts insert here another copy of Moawia's letter, with a few slight changes in the wording of the text. As these alterations are of no importance, the letter is suppressed in the translation.

(45) The text may also signify: provided they be regular physicians.

(46) After effecting the conquest of Mekka, Muhammad made large presents to some of the vanquished who had embraced his religion. He thus hoped to *gain their hearts*. (*Korân*, sur. IX, verse 60.)

(47) The author of this work was Abû Bakr az-Zubaidi, see vol. III, p. 33.

(48) According to the Moslim law, persons of different religions cannot inherit one of the other.

(49) Abû 'l-Faraj Muhammad Ibn Ishak, surnamed Ibn an-Nadîm (*the son of the boon companion*) and Ibn Abî Yakûb al-Warrâk (*the stationer*), was a native of Baghdad. He composed in the year 377 (A. D. 987-8) a sort of encyclopedia, full of literary, bibliographical, biographical, and historical information, to which he gave the title of *Fihrest* (*list or index*). The fullest and most satisfactory account of this highly important and rare work has been given by professor Flügel in the thirteenth volume of the German Oriental Society's journal (*Zeitschrift der Deutschen Morgenländischen Gesellschaft*).

(50) The rest of the story, containing an account of the trial and the evidence of the witnesses, cannot be rendered into English; so it is given here in a latin translation. That the observations addressed by Omar to al-Mughîra may be well understood, it is necessary to recal to mind that the Moslim law punishes adultery by lapidation and that a most formal declaration by four eye-witnesses is requisite for the proof of the crime. Omar, with all his austerity and uprightness, tried every means to save his friend and had the witnesses severely punished although he well knew that their depositions were true. His conduct in that business was very unfair and not such as his great reputation for integrity would have led us to expect.

(51) This proverb is explained by al-Maidâni; see Freytag's edition, vol. II, p. 422. The speaker meant to say that he would be a lost man if Ziâd, the fourth witness, deposed against him.

(52) These words of Ali's are explained farther on.

IBN AT-TATHRIYA

" Abù 'l-Maksbùb Yazid Ibn Salama Ibn Samura Ibn Salama tal-Khair Ibn Ku-
" shair Ibn Kaab Ibn Rabîa Ibn Aâmir Ibn Sasâa, generally known by the surname
" of Ibn at-Tathriya and a celebrated poet." It is thus that Abû Amr as-Shaibâni
(vol. I. p. 182) traces up his genealogy. The appellation of al-Khair (the good) was
given to his (great-) grand-father because Kushair had another son who was called
Salama tas-Sharr (Salama the bad). The same author states that the name of this
Yazid's father was al-Muntashir Ibn Salama. According to Ibn al-Kalbi (vol. III.
p. 608), Yazid was the son of Simma, who was one of the sons of Salama tal-Khair.
The learned men of Baṣra held him to be the son of al-Aawar Ibn Kushair, which
person is spoken of by Abù 'l-Hasan Ali Ibn Abd Allah at-Tûsi (1) towards the commencement of Ibn at-Tathriya's Diwân (collected poetical works) of which compilation he was the author.   Here are his words : " Ibn at-Tathriya was a poet by na-
" ture, intelligent, elegant in language, well-educated and of a noble, manly dispo-
" sition; never did he incur either reproach or blame.   He was liberal, brave, and
" held, by the nobleness of his family and character, a high rank in his tribe, which
" was that of Kushair.   The Omaiyides had him for one of their poets and treated
" him with great favour." Another author says : " Yazid Ibn at-Tathriya was sur-
" named al-Muwaddik (the exciter) on account of his handsome face, the beauty of
" his poetry and the sweetness of his discours.   People used to say that, when he sat
" in the company of women, he excited them to love.   In speaking of a female, the
" verbs istaudakat (in the tenth form) and wadakat (in the first form) are employed to
" signify that a female desires the approach of the male.   This verb, taken in its
" primitive signification, was only applied to animals having hoofs, but it was subse-
" quently employed in speaking of human beings.   A muwaddik is a person who
" inspires woman with an inclination for him.   He frequented the company of fe-
" males and liked conversing with them. It is said that he was impotent, incapable of
" having intercourse with a woman or of begetting children." Abù Tammâm at-Tai
(vol. I. p. 348) mentions this highly distinguished poet in different places of his Hamâsa; thus, in the section of amatory poetry (p. 588), he has inserted as his the following lines :

(*I think of*) that Okailide female whose (*ample forms*) enveloped in her gown are (*in shape, smoothness and colour*) like a sand-hill, and whose waist is like a wand. She passes the summer within the tribe's reserved grounds and, in the afternoon, she makes her siesta at Naamán, in the valley of Arák. The glance which I cast at her, is it for me a very slight (*satisfaction*)? By no means! a (*pleasure coming*) from her is never slight. Friend of my soul! thou except whom I have no other sincere friend! O thou for whose sake I have concealed my love, disobeyed (*the advice of thy*) enemies and placed no faith in the words of those (*intriguers*) who interfered against thee! Is there no way of reaching a place near thee, where I may complain of the great distance (*which lay between us*) and of the dread (*in which I stood*) of (*jealous*) foes? May my life be the ransom of thine! numerous are my enemies, wide is the distance (*between us*), few are the partisans whom I have near thee. (*If I die of grief,*) take not the fruit thereof upon thyself, for thou art too weak (*to bear it*); to answer for my blood on the day of judgment would be a heavy responsibility! When I went (*to see thee,*) I had always a pretext, but now, that I have exhausted all my pretexts, what can I say? I have not every day a business which may take me to your country; every day, I cannot send there a messenger.

Abû 'l-Faraj al-Ispahâni, the author of the *Kitâb al-Aghâni*, formed also a *diwan* of Ibn at-Tathriya's poetry and attributes to him the following piece:

I should sacrifice my father for the safety of one who inspired me such love that my body is quite exterminated; for one on whom all eyes are fixed and who is the object of my passion! for one whose charms never cease augmenting desire and who is never to be seen unless under the protection of a watchful guard. If I am forbidden to hold converse with her, if I should have to encounter enemies and combats in case I tried to meet her, yet I shall continue to extol the beauty of Laila in eulogiums brilliant with the ornaments of rhyme and sweet to hear from the lips of the public. Dearest Laila! take care not to diminish my strength (*by thy disdain*) and permit me, though far away and an outcast, to hope that I retain a share in your affection. Let me still give lasting trouble to jealous spies, as they have given constant annoyance to me. If you fear that you cannot support the bitterness of love, restore to me my heart; our visiting place is near.

The same author attributes to Ibn at-Tathriya the piece which here follows:

I should sacrifice my life for the safety of one whose cool hand, if passed over my breast, would heal my pains. (*I devote myself*) for her who always fears me and whom I always fear; for her who never grants me a favour and from whom I never ask one.

Abû 'l-Hasan at-Tûsi gives the following verses as Ibn at-Tathriya's:

I should blush before God were I to be seen succeeding to another in the affections of a female or replaced therein by a rival. (*I should be ashamed*) to quench my thirst at a lake of which the borders are become like a beaten path, or to be a suitor for such love as you could grant, love too weak to endure.

I met these verses elsewhere and found that, after the first, was inserted another which I give here :

> Water filled with dregs and troubled by the frequent visits of those who come to drink inspires me with disgust.

At-Tûsi gives also the following verses as his :

> Many hope for a thing and cannot obtain it, whilst it is granted to others who sit (quietly and make no effort). One man toils for a favour and another receives it; he to whom it is granted had given up all hopes when it came.

The same author extracts this passage from a piece of verse composed by our poet :

> I persist in turning away from her, though much against my will; and, when she is absent, I avoid listening to those who saw her or heard of her. Love for her came to me before I knew what love was, and it found a lasting abode in a heart till then unoccupied.

He gives also the following verses by the same poet :

> And (I pronounced) a word which, when she (whom I loved) accused me of numerous crimes, dissipated every foul imputation. (I said) : " If I am innocent, you do me wrong; if guilty, I " have repented and merit pardon." When she persisted in rejecting my excuses and let herself be pushed to the utmost extreme by the lies of vile defamers, I discovered that indifference could console me when suffering from her disdain, and I no longer wished to approach one who refused me her love. I acted like the man who, afflicted with a malady, looks for a physician and, not finding one, becomes his own doctor.

The piece which we now insert is given as Ibn at-Tathriya's by Abû Abd Allah al-Marzubâni in his *Mojam as-Shuaará* (vol. *III.* p. 67), and is also to be found in the *Hamása* (page 584); but some persons attribute it to Abd Allah Ibn ad-Dumaina al-Khathami (2) :

> I should sacrifice my life and my family for the safety of her who, when unjustly wronged, knew not what to answer. She tried not to justify herself as one would do who is innocent, but remained astounded, so that people said : " How very suspicious ! "

In the same work, al-Marzubâni gives also as his the piece (which begins) as follows (3) :

Though you long to see Raiya, you postpone the day of your meeting with Raiya? and yet you both belong to a branch of the same tribe!

I must here observe that, in this piece, the poet has attained the height of tenderness and elegance. It is given by Abû Tammâm in his *Hamâsa*, towards the commencement of the section which contains the amatory poetry. That author attributes it, however, to as-Simma Ibn Abd Allah al-Kushairi; God knows if he be right! Abû Amr Yûsuf Ibn Abd al-Barr, the author of the *Istîâb*, which work contains the history of the Prophet's Companions, — we shall give his life (*wa saydtî dhikruhu*), — says in (*another work of his*), the *Bahja tal-Majdlis* (*the beauties of sittings, or conferences*) : " As-Simma Ibn Abd Allah Al-Kushairi composed the " following lines :

" Had you remembered me as faithfully as I remember you, I declare that you would not " have refrained from tears. She replied : " By Allah! 'tis quite the contrary; (*I ever remem-* " *ber you and the sadness of*) that recollection would burst even a solid rock (b)!' "

Farther on, the same writer says : " Most of the literati consider him to be the " author of : *Though you long to see Raiya*." He then gives all the verses, just as they are to be found in the *Hamâsa*, and adds : " Some persons however attribute them " to Kais Ibn Darih (5); others consider them as the production of al-Majnûn (6), " but the majority say that as-Simma is the author. God knows best! " From this we see the difference of opinion respecting the person who composed these verses ; was it Ibn at-Tathriya, or as-Simma Ibn Abd Allah al-Kushairi, or Kais Ibn Darih, or al-Majnûn? God knows best! — Al-Marzubâni mentions our poet in his *Muwath-thak* (7) and says : " Abû 'l-Jaish recited to me the following lines as the composi- " tion of Yazid Ibn at-Tathriya :

" After nightfall, my camel moaned through (*grief and*) longing for its companion; O what " dismay I felt, whilst her moans cast despondency into my heart! I said to her : Suffer with " patience; the female of every couple must, sooner or later, be separated from the male. "

He gives also the following verses and attributes them to the same author :

How can I receive consolation (*when separated from you*) who are the most amiable of beings that walk (*on earth*)? My soul is afflicted and your dwelling-place far away. My life is in your hands, if you wish to take it; my soul you can heal, if you choose to heal it. When

Falja is the name of two places, one lying between Mekka and Basra, and the other in (*the valley of*) al-Akik. — The combat (*which cost Ibn at-Tathriya his life*) took place in the year of al-Walid Ibn Yazid the Omaiyide's death. Now, al-Walid was killed on Thursday, the 27th of the latter Jumâda, 126 (16th April, A. D. 744), at *el-Bakhra*. Abû 'l-Hasan at-Tûsi says, in speaking of this combat, that the standard was borne by Yazid Ibn at-Tathriya. When al-Mundalith was killed and his partisans were routed, Ibn at-Tathriya stood his ground with the standard. He was dressed in a silk gown which got entangled in an oshara-tree (*asclepias gigantea*). — The *oshara* is a thorny plant and produces gum. — This accident caused him to fall, and the Banû Hanîfa then kept striking him till he died. This combat is mentioned subsequently to the account of al-Walid's death and in the same year; so, the death of Ibn at-Tathriya must be placed between that of al-Walid and the end of the year 126. Abû 'l-Faraj al-Ispahâni says, towards the commencement of the volume (*diwân*) in which he has given the collection of Ibn at-Tathriya's poetical works, that he was killed by the Banû Hanîfa under the khalifat of the Abbasides; but the former indication is nearer to the truth. The following elegy was composed on the poet's death by al-Kuhaif Ibn Omair (10 Ibn Sulaim an-Nida Ibn Abd Allah al-Okaili :

> Let the noble sons of Koshair weep for the loss of their chief and their hero. O Abû 'l-Makhûb; now that you are gone, who is there to protect (*us*)? who is there to harry on the (*war-*) camels whose feet are already tired and worn by travel?

Al-Kuhaif composed also a lament on the death of al-Walid Ibn Yazid. The following verse on the death of Ibn at-Tathriya was composed by his brother Thaur Ibn Salama :

> I see that the tamarisk, my neighbour in the valley of al-Akik, still holds itself erect (*and yields not to grief*), though fate has taken Yazid by surprise and overwhelmed him.

This verse belongs to a choice piece of poetry which Abû Tammâm has inserted in the *Hamâsa* (page 468). He attributes it to Zainab Bint at-Tathriya, but others say that it was composed by the poet's mother. At-Tûsi states that the combat above-mentioned was fought at al-Akik. We find in Yâkût al-Hamawi's *Mushtarik* that there were ten places of this name. According to al-Asmai (*col. II. p. 123*) the *Aikka* (which word is the plural of akik) are valleys in which there is running

water. In enumerating the places bearing this name, Yákút says : " The third is
" the Akik of Aárid, in al-Yamáma. It is a large valley near al-Arama, and into it
" flow all the streams of al-Aárid. It abounds in sources and villages. " He then
says : " Al-Akik, a town in al-Yamáma, belongs to the Banú Okail. It is called
" the Akik of Namira and lies on the road leading from al-YamAma to Yemen. "
The valley of al-Akik mentioned in the foregoing verse, is perhaps the first of the
places thus indicated, or perhaps the second. God knows best! — Ibn al-Tathriya
was called Abú 'l-Makzhúh because he had on his kashh a scar caused by a burn.
The word kashh signifies the side. — Yazid's mother was called at-Tathriya(11) and
he was surnamed after her. She was one of the children of Taibr Ibn Ans Ibn
Wáil.   " The word taihr signifies fertility and abundance of milk. It is said that
" she was born in a year of which that was the distinguishing character, but others
" contradict this statement and say that she gave birth to her son in a year of that
" kind.   Others again relate that she toiled in extracting butter from milk and was
" named at-Tathriya because the taihr of milk is its butter. "   This account is, in
itself, quite objectionable : all say that the poet's mother was of the family of Taihr
Ibn Ans, whence we must conclude that she was named after that tribe, and declare
that the words " she was born in a year of such a character" or " she gave birth
" to him in a year of such a kind" or " she extracted butter from milk " are here
quite inapplicable.   We submit these remarks to the reader; but it is evident that
there were two opinions on the subject; according to one, she was named after her
tribe and, according to the other, for the reasons stated in the second place. — A
great number of poems are attributed to Zainab Bint at-Tathriya, the sister of Yazid.
Such is the eulogistic piece which we here give :

> He is proud when you go to ask of him a favour, and he bestows on you whatever he holds
> in his hand.   Had he nothing to give him his life, he would bestow it; so let those who apply to
> him take care lest (by taking away his life), they offend God.

These verses have been attributed to Ziád al-Aajam (vol. I. p. 631).   The second
is also to be found in the diwân of Abú Tammám's poems, where we meet with it
in the kasîda which begins by these words :

> Vernal abode! those of which the inhabitants have departed! it is, alas! too true that the rains (?)
> have effected upon thee that (destruction) which they intended.

But, in all that, God best knows the truth!

(1) Abú 'l-Hasan Alí Ibn Abd Allah Ibn Sinán at-Táīī (of the tribe of Taim Allāh) at-Táī (a native of Taī), was a man of learning and a narrator of anecdotes concerning the (Arabian) tribes, of poems and of (the adventures of) heroes (fuhúl). He met (and was taught by) the great masters (mashaīkh) who professed at Basra. The preceptor whose sittings he most frequented and from whom he received the greater part of his information was Ibn al-Aārābī. (Fihrist.) — Ibn al-Aārābī died A. H. 231 (A. D. 845). (See vol. III, p. 24.) We have learn from Ibn Khallikān that at-Táī collected the poems of Ibn at-Tathrīya into a dīwān.

(2) Abú Allah Ibn ad-Dumaina al-Khathamī was one of the early Moslem poets and lived probably in the first century of the Hijra. Having learned that Moahhim Ibn Kais of the tribe of Saláil was paying court to his wife, he assassinated the lover, repudiated the woman some time afterwards, and then killed his young daughter because she wept for her mother. He was detained for a long time in the prison of Tabāla (page 823 of this vol.), but was finally liberated because the charge could not be made out against him. At a later period he was killed by the son of him whom he had murdered. — (Aghānī, Sharḥ Shawāhid al-Moghnī).

(3) This piece consists of nine verses and is to be found in the Ḥamāsa, page 818.

(4) Literally: Nay, by Allah! a recollection which, if poured upon the solid rock, it (the rock) would split asunder.

(5) Abú Zaid Kais Ibn Darīḥ ولابن al-Lakhī, belonged to a bedwin family which lived in the desert outside of Medina, and was the foster-brother of al-Ḥusain, the son of Alī. He married Lubna, the daughter of al-Ḥubāb, but as their union was not fruitful, he was forced by his father to divorce her after two years' cohabitation. He then took another wife of the same name, but more against his will and, soon after, he died of grief for being separated from his first love. He composed on Lubna a number of poems, passages of which are given in the article of the Kitāb al-Aghānī wherein his history is related. An abridged and tolerably fair translation of the prose accounts offered by the Aghānī will be found in the second volume, page 419, of von Hammer-Purgstall's Literaturgeschichte der Araber. The author of the Nujūm states that Ibn Darīḥ died on or about the year 68 (A. D. 684-5).

(6) Al-Majnūn (the insane, the possessed) is the surname by which was designated a poet whose love for Laila became proverbial. His name, it is said, was Kais Ibn al-Maʿūh, but his existence has been generally doubted. De Sacy, in his Anthologie grammaticale arabe, page 159, has a note on this subject. Be that as it may, a number of amatory poems pass under the name of al-Majnūn.

(7) The orthography of this name is not certain.

(8) It appears, from the Kitāb al-Aghānī, that the tribe of Bakila and that of Ghazī had, for some time, being carrying on a galam each other a war of surprises and predatory incursions. In one of these encounters Ibn at-Tathrīya lost his life.

(9) A town cannot have a pulpit or cathedral mosque, unless it be the capital of a province or of a considerable district. The governor, who is also the khalif's representative, has alone the privilege of pronouncing the khotba from the pulpit.

(10) The Paris ms. of the Aghānī reads Ḥuwayr instead of Omair. In this translation the reading of Ibn Khallikān and of the author of the Kāmūs is adopted. De history of al-Kuhail, who was a contemporary of Ibn at-Tathrīya and belonged to the same tribe as he, offers nothing deserving of being noticed here.

(11) According to the author of the Kāmūs, this name should be pronounced at-Tathrīya, with an a after the th.

YAKUB AL-MAJISHUN

Abû Yûsuf Yakûb, the son of Abû Salama Dinâr, or Maimûn, according to some, bore the surname of al-Mâjishûn and stood allied (by clientship) to the Banû Taim, a branch of tribe of Kuraish (al-Kurashi at-Taimi). He was a mawla of the Munkadirs, a family of Medina. Traditions were taught to him by Ibn Omar (vol. I. p 567), Omar Ibn Abd al-Aziz (afterwards khalif), Muhammad Ibn al-Munkadir (vol. II. p. 110) and Abd ar-Rahmân Ibn Hormuz al-Aaraj (1); traditions were taught on his authority by his sons Yûsuf and Abd al-Aziz, and by his nephew Abd al-Aziz Ibn Abd Allah Ibn Abi Salama .   "Al-Mâjishûn," says Yakûb Ibn Shaiba (2), "was a mawla of the Hudair family (3)."   When Omar Ibn Abd al-Aziz was governor of Medina, Yakûb al-Mâjishûn knew him and used to converse with him familiarly.   Omar, on his elevation to the khalifate, said to al-Mâjishûn, who had come to visit him : " I have given up your acquaintance, because I have given up wearing " silk clothes," and then turned away from him (4).   Mohammad Ibn Saad (vol. III p. 64) says, in his Tabakât, that Yakûb Ibn Shaiba related as follows : " Musab " (vol. I. p. 186) said : Al-Mâjishûn used to side with Rabia tar-Râi (vol. I. p. 517) " against Abû 'z-Zinâd (vol. I. p. 580), because the latter was hostile to Rabia, and " that Abû 'z-Zinâd was heard to say : ' What passes between me and Ibn al-Mâjishûn " ' is similar to that which is related of the wolf.   That animal used to enter into " ' a village and devour children   The inhabitants, at last, assembled and went " ' after him, but he fled away and they gave up the pursuit. · One of them, a " ' dealer in earthen ware, continued, however, to follow him, on which the wolf " ' stopped and said to him : ' I can excuse the others [for pursuing me], but what " ' ' have I done to you?   I never broke a single pot of yours!'   Now, as for that " ' al-Mâjishûn, I never broke any of his kabars (tambourines) or of his bar- " ' hats (guitars)!'"   Al-Mâjishûn's son related as follows : " The soul of al-Mâ- " jishûn was taken up aloft (i. e. his animation was suspended) and we placed the " body on a bench, so that it might be washed (according to the prescription of the " law).   We then informed the people that we were going to carry forth the corpse " (to the grave), when the washer (of the dead) came in and perceived, whilst he was

" operating, that an artery was still beating in the lower part of the font. He came
" out to us and said : ' I find an artery still beating; so, I advise you not to hasten
" ' the interment.' On this, we induced the people to retire by informing them of
" what we had seen and, the next morning, when they returned, the washer went
" in and found the artery beating as before. We again made excuses to the people,
" and, during three days, my father remained in the same state. He then sat up
" and said : ' Bring me some porridge.' We brought it and, when had supped it
" up, we asked him if he could tell us what he had seen? He replied, ' I can;
" ' when my soul was taken away, the angel mounted with me to the heaven of this
" ' earth and ordered the door to be opened. It was opened to him and he pro-
" ' ceeded (successively) through the other heavens till he reached the seventh.
" ' There he was asked whom he had brought with him, and he answered : ' Al-
" ' ' Mâjishûn.' On this, a voice said to him : ' He has not yet received permission
" ' ' to come here, he has still to live such and such a number of years and of
" ' ' months and of days and of hours.' Whilst I was a carrying down, I saw the
" ' Prophet, with Abû Bakr on his right hand, Omar on his left, and Omar Ibn Abd
" ' al-Azîz (sitting) at his feet. I said to the angel who was with me : ' Tell me
" ' ' who is that?' and he answered : ' Omar Ibn Abd al-Azîz.' On this, I said :
" ' ' He is allowed to sit very near the Apostle of God '" and I received this answer :
" ' ' He acted uprightly in an age of perversity, as the two others did in an age
" ' ' of righteousness.' ' " This relation is given by Yakûb Ibn Shaiba in his article on al-Mâjishûn. Abû 'l-Hasan Muhammad Ibn Ahmad al-Kauwâs al-Warrâk
states that Yakûb al-Mâjishûn died in the year 164 (A. D. 780-1). — I have
taken all this information from the work designed, by the *hâfiz* Abû 'l-Kâsim
Ibn Asâkir (*vol. II.* p. 252), to serve as a (biographical) history of Damascus. — Ibn
Kutaiba says, in the article on Muhammad Ibn al-Munkadir which he has given in
the *Kitâb al-Maârif* (5), that one of Ibn al-Munkadir's *mawlas* was Yakûb Ibn
Mâjishûn. He states also that he (Yakûb) was a legist, and then adds : " Al-Mâ-
" jishûn had a brother named Abd Allah Ibn Abi Salama, whose son, Abd al-Azîz
" Ibn Abd Allah, was surnamed Abû Abd Allah. He (al-Mâjishûn) died at Bagh-
" dad; (the khalif) al-Mahdi said over him the funeral service and had him buried
" in the Kuraish cemetery. This was in the year 164." — We have already given
in this work an article on his (nephew's) son and mentioned there what has been said
by the learned respecting the signification of al-Mâjishûn; it is therefore needless to

repeat their words here. — In the expression : "*I never broke any of his kabars or*
"*of his barbats,*" occur two words which require explanation. The *kaber* is a drum
having only one *face* (or *head*), and the *barbat* is a sort of lute (*aūd*), the musical
instrument so called. Its name is derived from *bar*, which signifies *breast* in
Persian, joined to the (*Arabic*) word *batt* (*duck*), the well-known fowl so called. As
this instrument bears a resemblance to the breast of a duck, it was so denominated.
In Arabic, it is called *al-aūd* and *al-mizhar*; in Persian, it bears the name of *burbat*,
as we have just said.

(1) Abū Dawūd Abd ar-Rahmān Ibn Bormus, surnamed al-Aaraj (*the lame*), was a native of Medina and
a *mawla* of a Kuraish family, that of al-Hārith Ibn Abd al-Mottalib, or that of Omar Ibn Abi Rabia. He handed down a quantity of traditions, most of which he had received from Abū Huraira (vol. *I*, p. 610). Traditions were given on his authority, which was considered as perfectly sure. He died at Alexandria, A. H.
117 (A. D. 735-6). — (Dahabi's *Tabaḳāt*.)

(2) Abū Yūsuf Yakūb Ibn Shaiba Ibn Aafur, of the tribe of Sadūs and a native of Basra, fixed his residence
at Baghdad and composed a *musnad*, or collection of authenticated Traditions, which work was very extensive,
but remained unfinished. As a Traditionist, he was considered to be a good authority. His *Musnad* formed
five volumes, and a collection of traditions, which he traced up to Abū Huraira, filled two hundred quires of
paper. He was nominated kādi of Irak but did not fill that office. His death took place in the first Rabī,
246 (May-June, A. D. 860). — (Dahabi's *Huffāz*.)

(3) Al-Mankadir Ibn Abd Allah, the father of Muhammad Ibn al-Monkadir, was the son of al-Hudair. —
(Kāmil.)

(4) It appears from this and from an anecdote related lower down, that al-Majishūn was a man of pleasure
who drowned finely and was fond of music.

(5) See the *Kitāb al-Hadris*, page 321.

THE KADI ABU YUSUF

The *kādi* Abū Yūsuf Yakūb al-Ansāri (a *descendant of one of the proselytes of Medina*)
was the son of Ibrahim, the son of Habib, the son of Khunais, the son of Saad, the
son of Habta, who was one of the Prophet's Ansārs. "Saad was known amongst
"the Ansars by the surname of Ibn Habta (*the son of Habta*); being thus denomi-

'' nated after his mother. Malik, the father of Habta, belonged to the family of Amr " Ibn Aûf the Ansarian. Aûf, the father of Saad Ibn Habta, was the son of Bahir, " who was the son of Moawia, the son of Salma, the son of Dajlla, who was allied, " by an oath of fraternity, to the family of Amr Ibn Aûf the Ansarian. " It is thus that the genealogy of Saad Ibn Habta is traced up in the *Istiâb* (1). The Khatîb Abû Bakr al Baghdâdi (rol. *I*. p. 75) says, in the historical work composed by him, that Saad was the son of Bahir, the son of Moawia, the son of Kuhâfa, the son of Balll, the son of Sadûs, the son of Ahd Manâf, the son of Abu Osâma, the son of Shahma, the son of Saad, the son of Abd Allah, the son of Faddâd, the son of Thalaba, the son of Moawia, the son of Zaid, the son of al-Ghauth, the son of Bajila. Abû Yûsuf, a *kâdi* and a native of Kûfa, was one of Abû Hanîfa's (vol. *III*. p. 555) disciples, a legist, a learned scholar and a *hâfiz (possessing great traditional information)*. He heard Traditions from the lips of Abû Ishak as-Shaibâni (2), Sulaimân at-Taimi (3), Yahya Ibn Saîd al-Ansâri (vol. *II*. p. 549), al-Aâmash (rol. *I*. p. 587), Hishâm Ibn Orwa (rol. *III*. p. 606), Atâ Ibn as-Saîb (4), Muhammed Ibn Ishak Ibn Yasâr (vol. *II*. p. 677) and other Traditionists of the same class; he attended also the sittings (*or lectures*) of Muhammed Ibn Abd ar-Rahmân Ibn Abi Laila (vol. *II*. p. 584) and afterwards, those of Abû Hanîfa an-Nomân Ibn Thâbit (vol. *III*. p. 555). The system of jurisprudence taught by Abû Hanîfa was that which he preferred, though he differed, in many points, from that master. Traditions were delivered on his authority by Muhammad Ibn al-Hasan as-Shaibani al-Hanafi (vol. *II*. p. 590), Bishr Ibn al-Walîd al-Kindi (5), Ali Ibn al-Jaad (vol. *I*. p. 476), Ahmad Ibn Hanbal (vol. *I*. p. 44), Yahya Ibn Maîn (*page* 24 *of this vol.*) and others. Whilst he resided at Baghdad, he acted there as a *kâdi* during the reigns of three khalifa, al-Mahdi, al-Hâdi, the son of al-Mahdi, and Hârûn ar-Rashîd. By the latter he was treated with great honour and respect, and he continued to enjoy under him the highest favour. He was the first who bore the title of *Kâdi'l-Kudât* (*the kâdi of the kâdis, Chief Justice*), and it is said that he was also the first who changed the dress of the learned (*the ulemâ*) and gave it that form which it retains to this day. Before his time, persons of all classes dressed in the same manner, so that they had nothing in their attire to distinguish them one from the other. Yahya Ibn Maîn, Ahmad Ibn Hanbal and Ali Ibn al-Madîni (vol. *II*. p. 242) agreed in considering him a sure and trustworthy Traditionist. Abû Omar Ibn Abd al-Barr, the author of the *Istiâb*, says, in his work entitled *Kitâb al-Intikâ fi faddâil ath-thalátha tal-Fukahá (the choice selection, treating of the merits of the three le-gists)* (6., that Abú Yûsuf was eminent as a *háfiz*, his memory being so retentive that he would attend the lessons of a Traditionist, learn from him fifty or sixty Traditions, then stand up and go to dictate them to other scholars. The quantity of Traditions which he knew by heart was very great. " Some Traditionists, " says Ibn Jarîr at-Tabari *(col. II. p.* 597), " mistrusted the Traditions delivered by him, because he " was much inclined to resolve points of law by rational deduction (*rái*), drawing " consequences from the maxims of the divine law; besides which they disappro- " ved of his having frequented men in power (*sultán*) and undertaken to fill the du- " ties of a *kádi* (7). " — The Khatîb Abû Bakr states, in his history of Baghdad, that Abû Yûsuf related as follows : " When I first applied to the study of Traditions " and law, I was very poor and ill dressed. One day, whilst I was at Abû Hanîfa's " (*lectures*), my father came, took me out and said to me : ' My son ! I do not try to " march in step with Abû Hanîfa; he has always his bread ready baked, whilst you " are in need, without the means of subsistence.' In consequence of this, I abstain- " ed from the pursuit of knowledge, thinking it preferable to shew obedience to " my father. Abû Hanîfa, having remarked my absence, asked what had become " of me; so, I recommenced attending his sittings. The first day of my appearing " there after a considerable absence, he said to me : ' What kept you away from us " ' so long ? ' and I answered : ' Seeking a livelihood and shewing obedience to a " ' father. ' I then took my place and, when the class broke up, he handed to me a " purse saying : ' Make use of this.' I looked into it and found there one hundred dir- " hems (£2. 10 s). He then said : ' Follow my class regularly and, when you have emp- " ' tied that, let me know.' I attended the class assiduously, and soon after, he gave " me another hundred. From that time, he continued to repeat his gifts without my " ever informing him of my penury or of my having spent what I had received. When- " ever my money was gone, it was as if he had been informed of the circumstance, " (*and these acts of beneficence continued*) till I was able to do without assistance and " had become rich." The Khatîb then says : " According to another statement, " Abû Yûsuf was a child when his father died, and it was his mother who disappro- " ved of his attending Abû Hanîfa's lectures. " Farther on, the same author gives a relation which he traces up, through an unbroken series of narrators, to Ali Ibn al-Jaad (8), who said that the *kádi* Abû Yûsuf made to him the following state- ment : " My father died, leaving me an infant in my mother's arms. Some time

" after, she put me to service with a fuller, and I used to leave (the shop of) my
" master and go to Abû Hanîfa's class, where I would sit down and listen. My mo-
" ther sometimes came, took me by the hand and led me back to the fuller. My
" assiduity in attending Abû Hanîfa's lessons and my zeal for acquiring knowledge
" interested him in my favour. My mother finding, at length, that those escapades
" of mine were too frequent and too long, said to him : ' You alone are the ruin of
" ' this boy; he is an orphan possessing nothing; I procure him food with the
" ' produce of my spindle, and my sole hope is that he may soon be able to
" ' gain a penny for his own use. ' Abû Hanîfa answered her in these
" terms : ' Go away, you silly talkative woman! your son is here learning how to eat
" ' falûdaj (9) with pistachio oil. ' On this she turned away from him and went
" off, saying : ' You are an old dotard and have lost your wits. ' From that time
" I attended Abû Hanîfa's lessons regularly and, with the help of God, I acquired
" learning, rose in the world, obtained the kadiship, was admitted into the society
" of ar-Rashîd and ate at his table. One day, some falûdaj was set before ar-Rashîd
" and he said to me : ' Abû Yakûb! eat of this; it is not always that the like of it is
" ' prepared for us. ' I said to him : ' What is it? Commander of the faithful! '
" He replied : ' Falûdaj with pistachio oil. ' On hearing this, I laughed.
" ' What makes you laugh ? ' said he. I answered : ' Commander of the faith-
" ' full it is all right (it is nothing). ' He said : ' You must tell me, ' and he insist-
" ed to such a degree that I related to him the whole story, from beginning to end.
" It pleased him so much that he exclaimed: ' By Allah! science is profitable in this
" ' world and in the next. May the mercy of God light upon Abû Hanîfa! he could see
" ' with the eye of his intelligence that which was invisible to the eye of his
" ' head.' " — Ali Ibn al-Muhassin al-Tanûkhi (vol. II. p. 567) states that his father said to him : My father related to me as follows : " Abû Yûsuf's intimacy with
" ar-Rashîd was brought about in the following manner. The former came to
" Baghdad subsequently to the death of Abû Hanîfa, and a certain kâid (military
" chief), who was afraid of having committed a perjury, was then looking out for a
" mufti (casuist) whom he might consult on the matter. Abû Yûsuf being brought
" to him, declared that the oath was not infringed, and the kâid bestowed on him
" some gold pieces and procured for him a house near his own. Some days after,
" the kâid went to visit ar-Rashîd and, finding him in low spirits, asked him the cause
" of his sadness. (The khalif) replied : ' What afflicts me is a matter which concerns

" ' religion ; look out for a legist whom I may consult. ' The káíd brought him
" ' Abû Yûsuf. Here is the latter's account of what passed : ' When I entered the
" ' alley which lies between the (two lines of) houses (forming the khalif's resi-
" ' dence), I saw a handsome youth of a princely appearance, confined in a chamber.
" ' He made signs to me with his finger as if asking me to assist him, but I did
" ' not understand what he wanted. When I was brought into the presence of ar-
" ' Rashîd and stood before him (waiting for what he had to say), he asked me my
" ' name and I answered: ' Yakûb; may God favour the Commander of the
" ' faithful ! ' — ' What say you, said he, ' of an imâm (khalif) who saw a man
" ' commit adultery ? must he inflict on him the punishment fixed by law (10)?' I
" ' replied : ' No. ' When I pronounced that word, ar-Rashîd prostrated himself on
" ' the floor, so, it struck me that he had seen a member of his family committing
" ' that act, and that the young man who made signs to me as if imploring my as-
" ' sistance was the guilty person. Ar-Rashîd then asked me on what authority I had
" ' pronounced my decision and I answered : ' From those words of the Prophet :
" ' Reject (the application of) penalties in cases of doubt. Now, in this case there is a
" ' doubt which suppresses the penalty.' On this, Ar-Rashîd said : ' How can there be
" ' doubt, since the act was seen. " I answered : " Seeing is not more effective than
" ' knowing for authorising (the application of) a penalty, and the simple knowing (of
" ' a crime) is not sufficient to authorise its punishment. Besides, no one is allow-
" ' ed to do justice to himself even though he knew (that the right was on his side).'
" ' The khalif made a second prostration and then ordered me a large sum of mo-
" ' ney. He told me also to remain in the house (the palace?), and I did not leave
" ' it till a present was brought to me from the young man, another from his mo-
" ' ther, and others from the persons attached to his service. That was the foun-
" ' dation of my fortune. I continued to remain at the house and one servant
" ' would come to consult me on a case of conscience ; another, to ask my ad-
" ' vice, and I at length rose so high in ar-Rashîd's favour that he invested
" ' me with the kadiship (of Baghdad). ' " — I must here observe that this statement is in contradiction with that which I have already given and in which it
is said that he held the kadiship under three of the khalifs. God knows the
truth ! — Talha Ibn Muhammad Ibn Jaafar (11) said : " The history of Abû Yûsuf
" is well known and his great merit is evident to all. He was Abû Hanîfa's pupil ;
" the ablest legist of that time, and none of his contemporaries surpassed him

" (in talent). He attained the highest point in learning, in wisdom, in authority
" and in influence. It was he who, the first, composed works on the fundamentals
" of jurisprudence, according to the Hanifite system. He dictated and developed
" the problems of which that science treats, and he spread the doctrines of Abù
" Hanifa over all parts of the world. " — " Of all Abù Hanifa's disciples, there
" was none, " said Ammár Ibn Abi Málik, " who could be compared with Abù
" Yùsuf. Had it not been for him, no one would ever have heard of Abù Hanifa
" or of Muhammad Ibn Abi Laila (vol. II. p. 584). It was he who put their opi-
" nions into circulation and spread abroad their learning. " — Muhammad Ibn
" al-Hasan (vol. II. p. 590), one of Abù Hanifa's disciples, said : " Abù Yùsuf was
" taken so dangerous ill, whilst Abù Hanifa was still living, that fears were enter-
" tained for his life. Abù Hanifa then went to visit him and we went with him.
" On retiring he put down his hand on the threshold of the door and said : " If that
" youth die, the most learned of those who are on that " — pointing to the ground,
" — will disappear. " — Abù Yùsuf related the following anecdote : " Al-Aàmash
" (vol. I. p. 587) questioned me on a point of law and I resolved it for him. ' Where
" ' did you find that solution? ' said he. I replied : ' I took it from one of the
" ' Traditions which you taught us; " and then repeated it to him. ' Yakùb. '
said he, ' I learned that tradition by heart before your father ever consorted with
" ' your mother, but I did not understand its application till now ! " — Hilâl Ibn
Yahya [12] related as follows : " Abù Yùsuf knew by heart the explanations of the
" Korân, the history of the (Moslim) wars and of the encounters which took place
" between the Arabs of the desert; the science of which he knew the least was that
" of law. Amongst the disciples of Abù Hanifa, there was not one to be compared
" to Abù Yùsuf. " — In the work entitled al-Jelís wa'l-Anís, the author, Abù 'l-
Faraj al-Moâfa an-Nahrawâni (vol. III. p. 374) states that as-Sháfi (vol. II. p. 569)
made the following narration : The kádi Abù Yùsuf absented himself from Abù Hanifa's lessons for some days, in order to hear Muhammad Ibn Ishak (vol. II. p. 677)
and others relate (traditional accounts of) the expeditions (undertaken by the early
Moslims). When he returned to Abù Hanifa's lessons, the latter said to him : " Abù
" Yùsuf! tell me the name of Goliath's standard-bearer. " Abù Yùsuf replied :
" You are an imdm (a master of the first rank); yet, if you do not abstain from
" making such questions, I declare by Allah ! that I shall ask you in the presence of
" all the class, which of the combats occurred first, that of Badr or that of Ohod?

" I am sure that you do not know which of them preceded the other. " Abû Hanîfa then let him alone. — It is stated in the same work that Ali Ibn al-Jaad related the following anecdote : " The *kâdi* Abû Yûsuf was one day writing a letter,
" and a man who was (sitting) at his right hand kept looking over what he was
" writing. Abû Yûsuf perceived this and, when he had finished, he turned round
" to the man and asked him if he had remarked any faults in the letter. The other
" answered : ' By Allah! not a single word misspelt. " Abû Yûsuf then said
" ' to him : ' I am much obliged to you for sparing me trouble of revising my let-
" ' ter, ' and recited this verse :

" One would think, from his bad education, that he had been converted to Islamism by (*the*
" *lecture of that chapter in the book of Traditions which is entitled : On*) bad manners [13]. "

Hammád, the son of Abû Hanîfa (*vol. I. p.* 469) said : " I saw Abû Hanîfa one day,
" with Abû Yûsuf on his right hand and Zufar (14) on his left. These two were dis-
" cussing a question and one could not advance an assertion without being refuted by
" the other. This continued till after the hour of noon, when the *mueddin* called
" to prayers. Abû Hanîfa then rose his hand, clapped Zufar on the thigh and
" said : ' Hope not to obtain the first place as a legist in any town where Abû Yûsuf
" ' may be; " declaring thus that Abû Yûsuf had the advantage over Zufar.
" After the death of Abû Yûsuf, Zufar had not his equal among the disciples of
" ' Abû Hanîfa. " — The following anecdote was related by Tâhir Ibn Ahmad
az-Zubairi : " There was a man who attended Abû Hanîfa's lessons without
" ever uttering a word. Abû Yûsuf at length said to him : " Do you ne-
" ' ver intend to speak (*and ask a question*)? ' The man answered : ' By no
" ' means; and I shall now ask you at what time he who keeps a fast should
" ' break it? ' Abû Yûsuf replied : ' When the sun has set. ' — ' Well ' said the
" man, ' and if he do not set till midnight?' Abû Yûsuf laughed and said : ' You
" ' were right in remaining silent, and I was wrong in asking you to speak.'
" ' He then pronounced the following verses as applicable to the circumstance :

" I admired the indifference of that man who was so careless about himself, and wondered at
" the silence of a person who knew well how to speak. For the indifferent man, silence serves
" as a veil (*to hide his ignorance*), and for him who can speak well it is a dorket indicating his
" talent. "

One of Abû Yûsuf's sayings was : " Associating with one who fears neither dis-
" grace nor shame, will be the cause of disgrace and shame on the day of the resur-
" rection. " — He said also : " There are three chief blessings : that of being a
" Moslim, without which, no other blessing is complete; that of health, without
" which there is no pleasure in life, and that of wealth, without which life cannot
" be completely enjoyed. " Ali Ibn al-Jaad related that he heard Abû Yûsuf say :
" Science will not give to you a portion of itself unless you give yourself totally up
" to it; and if you do so for the purpose of obtaining (15) a mere portion, you com-
" mit a grave error. " — Abû Yûsuf was one day riding, and his servant-boy was
running on foot after him. A man then said to him : " Does the law permit you
" to make your boy run after you and not give him whereon to ride? " Abû Yûsuf
replied: " Do you admit that I may consider my boy in the light of a mu-
" kâri (16)? " The other replied : " I admit that you may. " — " Well, " said
Abû Yûsuf, " in that case, he must run at my side, as a mukâri should do. " —
Yahya Ibn Abd as-Samad relates that al-Hâdi, the Commander of the faithful, brought before the kâdi Abû Yûsuf a suit relative to a garden of which
he was in possession. His claim, at first sight, appeared just, but it was, in reality, ill founded. (Some time after,) he said to the kâdi : " What have you done in the
" affair which we submitted to your judgment? " The kâdi answered : " The
" Commander of the faithful's adversary requires of me that I make you declare,
" upon oath, that your witnesses have truly deposed. " — " Do you think that he
" has a right to do so ? " said al-Hâdi. — " Ibn Abi Laila is of that opinion, " said
the kâdi. " Then, " replied al-Hâdi, " let the garden be restored to the man. "
This was a device imagined by the kâdi (in order to get out of the difficulty),
for he knew that al-Hâdi would not swear. — Bishr Ibn al-Walîd al-Kindi
states that the kâdi Abû Yûsuf made to him the following relation : " Yesterday
" evening, when I had got into bed, I heard a violent knocking at the door. I
" wrapped the sheet about me and went to see who was there, and lo! it was Har-
" thama Ibn Aâyan (17). I saluted him and he merely said to me : ' Answer the
" ' call of the Commander of the faithful.' I replied : ' Abû Hâtim! I know that you
" ' have some regard for me; the time is now late, as you see, and I am afraid
" ' that the Commander of the faithful wants me for some serious matter. Could
" ' you not try and have the affair put off till tomorrow morning? perhaps he may
" ' then have changed his mind.' Harthama answered : ' That I have not in my power

" ' to do.' I asked him then what was the cause of his being sent, and he replied :
" ' The eunuch Masrûr came out and ordered me to bring you before the Comman-
" ' der of the faithful.' I said to him : ' Will you allow me to make the (funeral) lo-
" 'tion and perfume myself; if the affair be grave, I shall be prepared for the
" ' worst, and that (precaution) will do me no harm if God, in his bounty, deliver
" ' me from danger.' Having obtained his consent, I went into my chamber, put
" on new clothes, perfumed myself with such odours as were at hand. We then
" went out together and proceeded to the residence of the Commander of the faith-
" ful, Hârûn ar-Rashîd. We found Masrûr standing there, and Harthama said to
" him : ' I have brought you the man.' I then addressed Masrûr in these
" terms : ' Abû Hâshim! (I owe you) my humble respects, my service and my
" ' friendship. This is a painful moment; can you tell me what the Commander
" ' of the faithful wants me for?' He answered that he could not. I then asked him
" ' who was with the khalif, and he replied : ' Isa Ibn Jaafar (18).' — ' And who
" else? ' said I. — ' There is no third person,' was the answer. He then said to
" me : ' Go forward and, when you are in the vestibule, you will find him sitting
" ' in the porch. Scrape your foot on the ground; he will ask who is there and
" ' you will answer : ' It is I.' I went in and did as I had been told. He (Ar-
" Rashîd) said : Who is that? ' and I answered : ' Yakûb.' He told me to enter
" and, when I went in, I found him seated, with Isa Ibn Jaafar on his right hand.
" I made him the salutation ; he returned it and said : ' I think that we must
" ' have alarmed you.' I replied : ' You did, by Allah! and have alarmed
" ' those also whom I left behind me.' — ' Sit down,' said he. I sat down
" and, when my apprehensions were allayed, he turned towards me and said :
" ' Abû Yakûb! do you know why I sent for you? ' I replied : ' I do not.' — ' I
" ' sent for you,' said he, ' so that you might receive the declaration which I am
" ' going to make against this man who is here. He possesses a slave-girl; I asked
" ' her from him as a present, and he refused; I asked him to sell her to me, and
" ' he refused. Now, by Allah! if he do not (consent to my demand), I shall take
" ' his life. ' On this, I turned towards Isa and said : ' See what God has effected
" ' by means of a girl (19)! you refuse giving her to the Commander of the faithful
" ' and are therefore reduced to this extremity.' He replied : ' You have spoken
" ' before knowing what I have to say. ' I asked him what he could say for himself,
" and he answered : ' I am bound by oath to divorce my wife, to liberate my slaves

" ' and to distribute to the poor all I possess, in case I sell that girl or give her away. '
" Ar-Rashid then turned towards me and said : ' Has he any means of getting
" ' out of that ? ' I replied that he had. ' And how so ? ' said he. I answered :
" ' Let him give you the half of her and sell you the other half; he will then have
" ' neither given her nor sold her. ' Is that the law ? ' said he. I replied that
" ' it was. ' Then, ' said he, I take you to witness that I give him the half of her
" ' and sell him the other half for one hundred thousand dinârs (£. 50,000). '
" Ar-Rashid answered : ' I accept the gift and purchase the half of her for that sum.
" ' Bring in the girl. ' She was brought in and the money also. Isa then said :
" ' Commander of the faithful! receive her, and may you find in her a blessing
" ' from God. ' When he had taken the money, ar-Rashid said : ' Abû Yakûb!
" ' one thing still remains to be done. ' — ' What is it ? ' said I. — ' She is a
" ' slave, ' said he, ' and I cannot approach her till she has had her next monthly
" ' infirmity; now if I do not pass this night with her, I think my soul will quit
" ' my body. ' I replied : ' Commander of the faithful! declare her free and
" ' marry her; for a freewoman is not bound by that obligation. ' He said : ' I
" ' declare her free; who will marry me to her ? ' I answered : ' I.' On this, he
" ' called in Masrûr and Husain (to serve as witnesses). I recited the khotba
" ' (invocation), praised God and then married them, on the condition of his giving
" ' her a dowry of twenty thousand dinârs (£. 10,000). He sent for the money and
" gave it to her, after which, he said to me : ' Yakûb! you may retire. ' He
" then looked up to Masrûr, who replied : ' I am at your orders. ' To him he
" said : ' Carry to Yakûb's house two hundred thousand dirhems (£. 10,000) and
" ' twenty chests of clothing.' That was done. Here Bishr Ibn al-Walîd said : ' Abû
" Yûsuf then addressed me, saying : ' Do you see anything wrong in what I did ? '
" I answered : ' No. ' ' Then, ' said he, take your fee (for this consulta-
" ' tion). ' I asked him how much was my fee, and he replied : ' The tenth (of
" ' the whole). ' I thanked him, prayed for his happiness and was about to stand
" up (and withdraw) when an old woman came in and said : ' Abû Yûsuf (one
" ' who considers herself as) your daughter sends me to salute you and to say, in her
" ' name : ' By Allah! all I received last night from the Commander of the faithful
" ' was the dowry which you know of; I here sent you the half of it and reserve
" ' the rest for my own use. ' The kâdi said to the woman : ' Take the sum
" ' back to her; by Allah! I shall not accept it. I delivered her from servitude,

" ' married her to the Commander of the faithful, and she thus shows me her sa-
" ' tisfaction' (20).— I and my uncles remonstrated with him till he accepted, and he
" then ordered one thousand dinárs to be taken out of the sum and given to me. "
— Abù Abd Allah al-Yùsufi related as follows : " Omm Djaafar Zubaida, the
" daughter of Jaafar (21) and the wife of ar-Rashid, wrote a letter to Abù Yùsuf in
" which she asked his opinion relatively to something ' the legality of which, ' said
" she, ' is, for me, highly desirable. ' He returned her a favorable decision,
" and she sent him a silver case containing a number of silver boxes pla-
" ced one over the other and containing, each of them, a different species of per-
" fume. With that came a vase filled with silver money, in the midst of which
" was another vase filled with gold. One of the company then reminded him
" that the Prophet had said : When a man receives a present, his companions (22)
" must be sharers in it. To this (hint), Abù Yùsuf replied : ' Those words were
" ' said at a time when the usual presents consisted of milk or dates. ' " —
Yahya Ibn Main (gives us another version of the same story); he says : " I was
at the kádi Abù Yùsuf's, and with him were a number of Traditionists and
" other (learned) men. A present was then brought to him from Omm Jaafar :
" it consisted of boxes containing flowered and plain stuffs, liqueurs, perfumes,
" little figures composed of odorous paste for fumigations, and other objects. One
" of the persons who were in the room then repeated to me the saying of the Pro-
" phet : When a man receives a present, the by-sitters must be sharers therein. Abù
" Yùsuf overheard these words and said : ' How can that apply? The Prophet said
" ' so a time when presents consisted of curds, or dates, or raisins, and not of objects
" ' such as these. Up with them, boy! and take them to the store-room."— I shall
now give a passage which I found in a work bearing the title of al-Latíf (the Miscellany), but in which the name of the author is not mentioned : " Abd ar-Rahmàn
" Ibn Mus-hir, the brother of Ali Ibn Mus-hir (23), was the kádi of al-Mubàrak." —
Al-Mubàrak is a village situated on the bank of the Tigris, between Baghdad and
Wàsit. — " This kádi, having learned that ar-Rashid was going to Basra, in his
" barge, with Abù Yùsuf, requested the inhabitants of his village to speak in praise
" of him when the khalif and Abù Yùsuf would be passing by. As they refused to
" do so, he put on his (outside) clothes, with a high-peaked cap and a black scarf
" (thrown over it). He then went to the landing-place and, when the barge ap-
" proached, he bawled out : ' Commander of the faithful! we have an excellent

" 'kádi, a kádi of sterling worth.' From that he proceeded to another landing-
" place and repeated the same words. On this, ar-Rashid turned round to Abù
" Yûsuf and said : ' The worst kádi on earth must be here I a kádi who, in the place
" ' where he resides, can find only one man to speak well of him.' Abù Yûsuf
" replied : ' The Commander of the faithful would be still more surprised if he
" ' were told that it was the kádi who praised himself.' Ar-Rashid laughed hear-
" tily and said : ' He is a clever fellow and must never be dismissed from office.'
" From that time, whenever he thought of this kádi, he would say : ' That
" fellow shall never be deposed.' Abù Yûsuf was asked how he could have
" nominated such a man, and he replied : ' He was for a long time (a suitor)
" ' at my door, complaining of poverty, and I therefore gave him an appoint-
" ' ment.' " — Abù 'l-Abbás Ahmad Ibn Yahya, surnamed Thalab (vol. I. p. 83)
says, in his Faïth : " One of my companions informed me that ar-Rashid said to
" Abù Yûsuf : ' I am told that all those whose depositions you receive when they
" ' appear before you to give evidence, are considered by you as hypocrites and that
" ' you say so.' The kádi answered : ' That is the truth.' — ' How so?' said ar-
" Rashid. The kádi replied : ' People who are really respectable and truly honest
" ' have no occasion to know us, nor we them; those whose (profligacy) is evident
" ' and whose (bad) character is well known never appear before us as witnesses,
" ' neither would their evidence be received. One class only remains, and those
" ' are the hypocrites who put on the appearance of virtue in order to hide their
" ' vices.' Ar-Rashid smiled and said : ' That is the truth.' " — Muhammad
Ibn Samáa (24) relates that he heard Abù Yûsuf utter these words on the day of his
death : " I declare, my God! that I never pronounced intentionally an unjust sen-
" tence, when judging between two of Thy servants; in my decisions I always en-
" deavoured to follow the prescriptions of Thy book and those of Thy Prophet's
" Sunna; in every case which was doubtful, I placed Abù Hanîfa between me and
" Thee, for I solemnly declare that I considered him to have been a man well ac-
" quainted with Thy commandements and never deviating from the truth, when he
" knew it. " There is here an idea borrowed from a saying of Abù Muhammad
Abd Allah, the son of al-Hasan and the grandson of al-Hasan Ibn Ali Ibn Abi
Tálib : He passed his hand over his boots (when making the ablution for prayer,
and did not take them off in order to wash his feet), and a person said to him : ' Do
" you pass your hand over your boots?' His reply was : ' I do; Omar Ibn al-Khattáb

" did so; and he who places Omar between himself and God has secured himself
" from danger. " It is Ibn Kutaiba who mentions this in his *Kitáb al-Maârif*,
where he speaks of Ali. — The anecdotes related of Abû Yûsuf are very numerous,
and the doctors of the law enlarge upon his merit, his preeminence and the respect
to which he is entitled. In the Khatîb's greater history of Baghdad, we find things
said of Abû Yûsuf which are shocking to hear and which we therefore abstain from
mentioning. They are given on the authority of Abd Allah Ibn al-Mubârak (*col. II.*
p. 12), Waki Ibn al-Jarráh (*col. I. p. 374*), Yazîd Ibn Hârûn (*col. I. p. 374*), Muhammad Ibn Ismail al-Bukhâri (*vol. II. p. 594*), Abû 'l-Hasan ad-Dârakutni (*col. II.*
p. 239) and others. God knows best! — The *kâdi* Abû Yûsuf was born in the year
113 (A. D. 731-2); his death took place at Baghdad on Thursday, the 5th of the first
Rabî A. II. 182 (26th April, A. D. 798), at the first hour of the afternoon; some
say, but erroneously, that he died in the year 192. He was appointed *kâdi* in the
year 166 (A. D. 782-3), and died in office. — His son Yûsuf studied and practised
the application of rational deduction (*râi*) to questions of law. He learned Traditions
from Yûnus Ibn Abi Ishak as-Sabîî (25), as-Sari Ibn Yahya and others. He was appointed *kâdi* of the western suburb of Baghdad in his father's lifetime and, by the
order of ar-Rashîd, he presided at the Friday prayer in the city of al-Mansûr (*the*
suburb of al-Karkh). He held the kadiship till his death. That event occurred at
Baghdad, in the month of Rajab, 192 (May, A. D. 808). — The Khatîb of Baghdad
states that, when the *kâdi* Abû Yûsuf died, ar-Rashîd nominated in his place Abû
'l-Bakhtari Wahb Ibn Wahb al-Kurashi, the same of whom we have given an account
(*col. III. p. 673*). Abû Yakûb al-Khuraimi a poet of some celebrity and an intimate friend of Abû Yûsuf and his son, having heard a man say, on the death of the
former : " To-day jurisprudence is dead, " recited the following lines :

> O thou who announcest the death of jurisprudence to the members of its family, because
> Yakûb has ceased to live, thou art not aware that jurisprudence is not dead but has merely
> passed from one bosom to another; from Yakûb to Yûsuf; from goodness to purity. Whilst
> he (*Yusuf*) remains and wherever he stops, it will stop (*with him; when he dies*), it will
> descend to the tomb.

— *Khunais* is the diminutive form of *akhnas*, which (*adjective*) signifies : having
the nose sunk into the face and the point of it slightly prominent. The masculine is
akhnas and the feminine *khonas*. This form of the diminutive is called the apoco-

pated (tarkhím); to obtain it, the rule is that the servile letters are to be suppressed and that the regular diminutive form is to be given to what remains of the word. It is thus that Ashar, Aswad and Ahmad have for apocopated diminutives Zuhair, Suwaid and Humaid (26). — Instead of the name Bahír, some persons read Bujair, but they are in the wrong. — I turned over law-books and other treatises in hopes of discovering the meaning of the word Habta, but did not succeed in my search. — The other names (in the genealogy) are so well known that we need not indicate their orthography. — Saad Ibn Khabta was one of those volunteers who, on account of their extreme youth, were dispensed by the Prophet from fighting at the battle of Ohod. The others were al-Dará Ibn Aázib (27) and Abù Saíd al-Khudri (vol. II. p. 208). — At the battle of the Intrenchment, the Prophet remarked Saad Ibn Khabta who, though very young, was fighting with great bravery. He called him over to him and asked him his name. The other replied : " Saad (happiness), the " son of Habta; " on which the Prophet stroked his head and said : " May God " grant you happy fortune. " — Hunais was the person after whom was named the open place in Kúfa which is called the Tchihár Súh ul Khunais. Tchihár Súh are persian words and mean four streets. This place was effectively an open square from which streets branched off in four directions.

(1) See the life of Ibn Abd al-Barr, in this volume.

(2) Abù Ishak Sulaimân Ibn Firûs, a member of the tribe of Shaibân, a traditionist and a native of Kûfa, died A. H. 141 (A. D. 756-9), or 142. — (Nujûm.)

(3) Abù 'l-Kasim Sulaimân Ibn Tarkhân at-Taimi, one of the Tábís, or disciples of Muhammad's Companions, was most assiduous in the practice of piety. The author of the Nujûm places his death in the year 143 (A. D. 760-1).

(4) Abù 'l-Gáih Atá Ibn as-Sáib Ibn Málik, a member of the tribe of Thakîf and a native of Kûfa, was a traditionist of good authority. He died in the year 136 (A. D. 153-4), or thereabouts. — (Nujûm.)

(5) Abù Bakr Bishr Ibn al-Walid Ibn Khálid al-Kindi, one of the most eminent of Abù Ha..ifa's disciples, was highly distinguished for his learning, his piety and the austerity of his life. In the year 209 (A. D. 853), he was appointed by al-Mamûn to act as a kádi in the quarter of Baghdad which was then called Askar al-Mahdi, and which became afterwards known by the name of ar-Rusáfa. When he held that place, he incurred the displeasure of Yahya Ibn Aktham (page 33 of this vol.), because he refused to exercise a judgment pronounced by that powerful magistrate. Being cited for that reason before al-Mamûn, he declared that the unfavorable character which he had received of Yahya from that kádi's own townsmen prevented him from obeying his mandates. Yahya asked the khalif to depose the kádi, but his request was not granted. Bishr Ibn al-Walid became kádi of Baghdad and of the suburb of al-Karkh under the khalifate of al-Motasim, but was afterwards persecuted and confined to his house by that prince because he refused to declare that the Koran, which is the word of God, was created and not eternal. The khalif al-Motawakkil set him at liberty

and authorised him to give opinions on points of law and teach Traditions. He lived to an advanced age and died A. H. 238 (A. D. 852-3). — (*Lives of the Hanifite doctors*; ms. of the Bib. imp. of Paris, supp'ément, n° 699, fol. 99. — *Nujûm*.)

(6) The three imâms of which this work treats were Mâlik, Abû Hanîfa and as-Shâfi.

(7) See vol. I, p. 215.

(8) Abû 'l-Hasan Ali Ibn al-Jaad Ibn Obaid al-Jauhari, one of Abû Yûsuf's disciples, died A. H. 188 (A. D. 749-50), at the age of ninety-six years. — (*Lives of the Hanafites*, fol. 104.)

(9) *Faludej*, in French *nougat*, is a cake or hard paste made of almonds and honey.

(10) An adulterer cannot be punished unless four witnesses declare that they saw him in the act. Here the question is, if the khalif, as chief of the religion, had the right of inflicting the punishment, because he witnessed the commission of the crime.

(11) Talha Ibn Muhammad Ibn Jaafar was one of the witnesses to the act by which the Khalif al-Muti abdicated in favour of his son at-Tâi. This document was signed the 13th of Zû 'l-Kaada, 363 (5th August, A. D. 974). — (*Nujûm*.)

(12) Hilâl Ibn Yahya Ibn Muslim, a native of Basra and surnamed Hilâl ar-Râi (*river-sighted Hilâl*) on account of his great learning and intelligence, studied jurisprudence under Abû Hanîfa and Zufar (*see note 14*). He died A. H. 245 (A. D. 859-60). — *Lives of the Hanafites*, fol. 97.)

(13) The translation of the last verse is conjectural.

(14) The imâm Zufar Ibn Hudhail Ibn Kais, a native of Basra and an eminent doctor of the Hanifite sect, was one of Abû Hanîfa's ablest disciples. He was appointed to the kadiship of Basra, the inhabitants of which place esteemed him highly, and he died there in the year 158 (A. D. 774-5), at the age of forty-eight years. — (*Lives of the Hanifites*, fol. 99.)

(15) The word *min* seems to stand here for *fi*.

(16) The *mukâri* keeps an ass, a horse or a mule for hire, and accompanies on foot the person who hires the animal.

(17) Harthama Ibn Aäyan was one of ar-Rashîd's principal generals.

(18) Isa Ibn Jaafar was the grandson of the khalif al-Mansûr and the cousin of ar-Rashîd.

(19) The arabic expression is here translated by conjecture.

(20) It is not clear whether the *kadi* thought the sum too little or meant to show his disinterestedness.

(21) This Jaafar was the son of the khalif al-Mansûr.

(22) Literally : his by-sisters.

(23) Ibn Duraid informs us, in his *Ishtikâk*, that Ali Ibn Mas-hir was kâdi of Mosul. We see from the passage quoted by our author, that he lived under the khalifate of Hârûn ar-Rashîd.

(24) The imâm Abû Abd Allah Muhammad Ibn Samâa Ibn Obaid Allah at-Tamîmi, a learned Traditionist and doctor of the Hanifite sect, studied jurisprudence under Abû Yûsuf. He composed a number of works such as the *Guide for Kadis* (*Adab al-Kâdi*), the *Conventions* (*Muhâdarât*), models of acts (*Sijillât*) and *Amâidates* (*Nawâdir*). In the year 192 (A. D. 807-8), on the death of Yûsuf, the son of Abû Hanîfa, he was appointed kâdi of Baghdad by al-Mâmûn. He died in the year 233 (A. D. 847-8), at the age of one hundred and three years. — (*Lives of the Hanifites*, fol. 99.)

(25) According to ad-Dahabi, the Traditionist Yûnus Ibn Abi Ishak as-Sabîî died in the year 159 (A. D. 775-6).

(26) The regular declinations of these words would be Ushaiya, Uraiyid and Uhmayid.

(27) Abû Omâra al-Barâ Ibn Aâzib, one of the Ansars, died A. H. 71 (A. D. 690-1). — (*Nujûm*.)

YAKUB AL-HADRAMI

Abû Muhammad Yakûb Ibn Ishâk Ibn Zaid Ibn Abd Allah Ibn Abi Ishâk al-Hadrami (a hadramite) by clientship and a native of Basra, was a celebrated teacher of the Koran-readings (vol. I. p. 152) and the eighth of the ten Readers (1). The system of readings taught by him (2) is well known and has been regularly handed down by oral transmission. He came of a family which produced men learned in the Readings (3), in grammar and in the (pure) language of the Arabs, men distinguished for having transmitted down a great quantity of various readings and for their knowledge of the law. Yakûb was one of the most eminent Readers, and those of the two holy cities (Mekka and Medina), of the two Iraks, of Syria and of other countries, learned his system by heart, either with or without the isnâds (vol. I. introd. p. xxii). He obtained a full acquaintance with the readings (or editions) by reciting them aloud to able masters, such as Sallâm Ibn Sulamân at-Tawîl (4), Mahdi Ibn Maimûn (5) and Abû 'l-Ashhab al-Otâridi (6). He taught some lections (hurûf) (7) which he had learned from Hamza (vol. I. p. 478); he heard lections taught by Abû 'l-Hasan al-Kisâi (vol. II. p. 237) and he heard also (traditions taught by) his grandfather Zaid Ibn Abd Allah and by Shoba (vol. I. p. 493). The isnâd of the reading adopted by him reaches up to the Prophet in the following manner : he read under Sallâm's tuition, Sallâm under that of Aâsim Ibn Abi 'n-Nujûd (vol. II. p. 1), Aâsim under that of Abû Abd ar-Rahmân as-Sulami (vol. II. p. 1), Abû Abd ar-Rahmân under that of Ali Ibn Abi Tâlib, and Ali under that of the Prophet. A number of Readers handed down that reading after learning it from Yakûb and reciting it under his direction; such were Rauh Ibn Abd al-Mumin (8), Muhammad Ibn al-Mutawakkil (9), Abû Hâtim as-Sijistâni (vol. I. p. 603) and others. Az-Zafarâni (10) heard it from his (Yakûb's) lips and, after the death of Abû Amr Ibn al-Alâ (vol. II. p. 399) the most eminent of the Basra literati approved the choice which he had made, and all or most of them adopted his system. Tâhir Ibn Abd al-Mûmin Ibn Ghalbûn, the imâm of the great mosque of Basra, never recited (to the congregation) any other reading of the Koran than that of Yakûb. According to Abû 'l-Husain Ibn al-Munâdi (p. 77 of this vol.),

Yakûb read the Koran under the tuition of Abû Amr, but there he is mistaken. Abd ar-Rahmân Ibn Abi'l-Hâtim stated that Ahmad Ibn Hanbal (*vol. I.
p. 44*), being asked his opinion of Yakûb al-Hadrami, answered : " Veracious " (!!), and Abû Hâtim as-Sijistâni said : " Of all the persons whom we have
" seen or met with, Yakûb al-Hadrami is the best acquainted with the *lections*, the
" differences (*observable in the text*) of the noble Koran, the manners of conciliating
" these differences and the systems followed by the grammarians in analyzing the
" text of the Koran. " He (*Yakûb*) composed a work which he entitled the *Jámi*
(*collector*) in which he noted all the differences which exist between the various
manners of reading the Koran, and indicated the persons to whom each of those
readings could be traced up. In a word, we may say that, in his time, he was for
the people of Basra, the chief doctor in the Readings. He would sometimes question his disciples respecting the number of verses contained in the Koran and, if
any of them made a mistake in the enumeration, he would order him to stand up
(*and leave the class*). He died in the month of the first Jumâda, 205 (oct.-nov.
A. D. 820); those who place his death in the month of Zû 'l-Hijja are mistaken.
He, his father Ishak, and his grandfather Zaid, lived each of them to the age of
eighty-eight years. His father's grandfather, Abd Allah Ibn Abi Ishak al-Hadrami,
was one of those great and distinguished doctors (*in law and grammar*) whom all
point at, for their learning. Abû Obaida Mamar Ibn al-Muthanna (*vol. III. p. 388*)
says, that the first person who laid (*the foundations of*) Arabic grammar was Abû 'l-
Aswad ad-Duwali (*vol. I. p. 662*); after him came Maimûn al-Akran (12), who was
succeeded by Anbasa tal-Fil (13), who was followed by Abd Allah Ibn Abi Ishak al-
Hadrami. In another version of this statement, Anbasa's name is placed before that
Maimûn. God knows best which reading is preferable. Abd Allah Ibn Abi Ishak
was a contemporary of Isa Ibn Omar ath-Thakafi (*vol. II. p. 419*) and Abû Amr Ibn
al-Alâ, but died before them. Abû Allah Ibn al-Marzubâni (*vol. III. p. 67*)
says in his *Muktabis* (*information picked up*), which work contains an account of the
celebrated grammarians, that al-Mubarrad (*vol. III. p. 31*) said : " All agree in
" considering Abû 'l-Aswad ad-Duwali as the first who laid down the principles of
" Arabic grammar and that he learned them from Ali Ibn Abi Tâlib. Abû 'l-As-
" wad taught them to Anbasa Ibn Maadân al-Mabri, who transmitted them to Mai-
" mûn al-Akran by whom they were communicated to Abul Allah (*Ibn Abi Ishak*)
" al-Hadrami, from whom they passed to Isa Ibn Omar (14), then to al-Khalil

" Ibn Ahmad (*vol. I. p.* 493), then to Sîbawaih (*vol. II. p.* 390) and then to al-
" Akhfash. " Bilâl Ibn Abi Burda (*vol. II. p.* 2), the son of Abù Mùsa 'l-Ashari
(*vol. III. p.* 633), was governor of Basra when he brought about a conference between
Abd Allah (*Ibn Abi Ishâk*) and Abù Amr Ibn al-Alà. The latter said (*in his account of
what then passed*) : " Ibn Abi Ishak got the better of me in a discussion concerning
" the (*letter*) hamza, but I afterwards studied the question and attained supe-
" riority. " This Abd Allah frequently objected to al-Farazdak (*vol. III. p.* 612) the
faults which he committed in his poems, and the latter at length said ; " By Allah!
" I will compose against him a satirical verse which will obtain currency among
" literary men and be quoted by them as a proverb. " He then made this verse :

If Abd Allah was a (*simple*) mawla, I should satirize him ; but Abd Allah is a mawla of a family which are mawlas.

He said so because Abd Allah was a *mawla* of the Hadramis, which family was con-
federated by oath (*halîf*) with that of Abd Shams Ibn Abd Manâf. The Arabs of the
desert say that the word *halîf* is the equivalent of *mawla*, and they cite verses in proof
of their assertion. Some of these passages I should give here were I not apprehensive
of lengthening this article too much ; besides which, this is not a fit place for them.

---

(1) We find frequent mention of seven principal Readers and also of ten. Were we to class the ten by
the dates of their deaths, Yakûb would hold, not the eighth place, but the ninth, and we should obtain a list
arranged in this order : Ibn Aâmir, Ibn Kathir, Aâsim, Yazid, Abù Amr, Hamza, Khlf, al-Kisâi, Yakûb and
al-Bazzâr. The biographers place Yakûb as the eighth on the list and create thus a difficulty of which the
solution has not yet been found by the translator. The list called that of *the seven Readers*, should be arranged thus, if the chronological order were to be followed : Ibn Aâmir, Ibn Kathir, Aâsim, Abù Amr, Hamza,
al-Kisâi and Nâfi. To make up the list of ten, the names of Yazid, Yakûb and al-Bazzâr were added.

(2) The Reading, or rather, the system of readings or lections adopted by each of the seven or ten Readers, may be considered as an edition of the Koranic text.

(3) See vol. 1, page 152.

(4) Abû 'l-Mundir Sallâm Ibn Sulaimân, a native of Basra and a *mawla* of the tribe of Mazins, was known
as a Reader and a grammarian. He spoke with elegance and was considered as veracious (*wathî*) in what
he taught. His death took place in the year 171 (A. D. 787-8). Persons not well informed have confounded
him with Abû Sulaimân Sallâm al-Tawîl al Maddini as-Saadi, surnamed al-Khorâsâni. — (*Kitâb Nam ife tal-
Kurrâ*, ms. of the Bib. imp., n° 742, fol. 30.) — Has the Khatibân fallen into the mistake pointed out by
Shams ad-Din Muhammad Ibn Ahmad ad-Dahabi, the author of the *Kurrâ*?

(5) Abû Yahya Mahdi Ibn Maimûn al-Azdi, a *mawla* and a native of Basra, is placed by ad-Dahabi among
the Traditionists. He died A. H. 171 (A. D. 787-8) or 172. — (*Nufân.*)

(6) Abû 'l-Ashhab Jaafar Ibn Haiyân al-Otâridi died in Basra, towards the year 155 (A. D. 771-8), at a very advanced age. — (Kitâb al-Maârif, Hoffds.)

(7) The word *harf* is employed as a technical term in the science of the Readings and has then two different significations. It designates the system of Koran-reading, that is, the editions of the Koranic text taught by the great masters, and also the various readings or lections which are found in the different texts of the Koran. The plural is *horûf*.

(8) Abû 'l-Hasan Banh Ibn Abd al-Mumin, a native of Basra and one of Yakûb's disciples in Koran-reading, died towards the year 224 (A. D. 818-9). — (Aïrri, fol. 59, verso.)

(9) Muhammad, the son of the khalif al-Mutawakkil, was distinguished as a poet and died A. H. 282 (A. D. 895-6). He may perhaps be the person indicated here.

(10) Abû Muhammad Abd Allah Ibn Muslim az-Zafarâni (a native of the village of Zafarân near Baghdad), was a teacher of the readings. The date of his death is not given by the author of the Aïrri.

(11) *Muftis*, or casuists, when consulted on a doubtful point, always draw up their answer in the most concise manner possible.

(12) Little or nothing is known of Maîmûn al-Ahras.

(13) Little is known of Abû 'l-Aswad Anbasa Ibn Maâdân al-Fîl. He possessed some grammatical knowledge and transmitted down orally a great number of poems, amongst which were many composed by Jarir and al-Farazdak. He must therefore have lived in the second century of the Hijra. His father was called Maâdân al-Fîl, because he had received one of those animals as a present from the governor of Irâk, Zaîd Ibn Ablh, of whose children he was the preceptor. The title of al-Fîl passed to his son. — (Fluegel's Grammatische Schulen der Araber.)

(14) The grammarian Isa Ibn Omar of the tribe of Thakîf died at Basra A. H. 111 (A. D. 791-39). For details see Fluegel's Gramm. Schule der Ar., p. 22.

ABU AWANA *THE HAFIZ*

Abû Awâna Yakûb Ibn Ishak Ibn Ibrahîm Ibn Yazîd, an inhabitant of Naisâpûr (Naisâpûri) and afterwards of Isfarâin (Isfarâini), is the author of the book entitled al-Musnad as-Sahîh (collection of authentic Traditions), the materials of which he extracted from the work of Muslim Ibn al-Hajjâj (vol. III. p. 348). He was one of those *hafizes* who travelled about and gathered up a great quantity of Traditions. He rambled over Syria and Egypt and visited Basra, Kûfa, Wâsit, Hijâz, Mesopotamia, Yemen, Ispahan, Rai and Fars. The hâfiz Abû 'l-Kâsim, generally known by the surname of Ibn Asâkir (vol. II. p. 252) says of him, in the History of Damascus:

"Abù Awàna heard, at Damascus, the lessons of Yazîd Ibn Muhammad Ibn Abd
"as-Samad, Ismail Ibn Muhammad Ibn Kîr it (1), Shoaib Ibn Shoaib Ibn Ishak
"and others. In Egypt, he heard Yùnus Ibn Abd al-Aala (2), Ibn Akhi Ibn
"Wahb (3), al-Muzani (vol. I. p. 200), ar-Rabî (vol. I. p. 519), Muhammad Ibn
"al-Hakam and Saad Ibn al-Hakam. In Irâk he heard Saadàn Ibn Nasr, al-Hasan
"az-Zafarâni (vol. I. p. 373), Omar Ibn Sbabba (col. II. p. 375) and others. In
"Khorâsan, his teachers were Muhammad Ibn Yahya ad-Dhuhli, Muslim Ibn al-
"Hajjàj, Muhammad Ibn Rajâ as-Sindi and others. In Mesopotamia he heard Ali
"Ibn Harb and others. Traditions were taught on his authority by Abû Bakr al-
"Ismalli (vol. I. p. 8), Ahmad Ibn Ali ar-Râzi (4), Abû Ali al-Husain Ibn Ali, Abû
"Ahmad Ibn Ali, Sulaimân at-Tabarâni (vol. I. p. 592), Muhammad Ibn Yakûb
"Ibn Ismail the hâfiz, Abû 'l-Walid the legist and his own son Abû Musab Muham-
"mad Ibn Abi Awàna. He made the pilgrimage five times." — "When I was at
"al-Missîsa, "says Ibn Abi Awàna, "my brother, Muhammad Ibn Ishak, wrote to
"me a letter in which were these lines :

        " If we meet before (our) death, we shall care our souls of the pains caused by one mutual
        " reproaches; and if the hand of death anticipates us, (we can only say :) how many of our
        " absent friends are now under ground. "

Abû Abd Allah al-Hakim (vol. II. p. 681) declared Abû Awàna to be a learned
and most exact Traditionist, one of those who travelled over the regions of the earth
in search of Traditions. He died in the year 316 (A. D. 928-9). Hamza Ibn Yûsuf
as-Sahmi (col. I. p. 25) mentioned that, in the year 292 (A. D. 904-5), Abû Awàna
was seen in Jurjàn. The hâfiz Abû 'l-Kàsim Ibn Asàkir states that the following
narration was made to him by the holy and fundamentally learned shaikh (as-
Shaikh as-Sâlih al-Asîl) Abû Abd Allah Muhammad Ibn Muhammad Ibn Omar as-
Saffàr, a native of Isfarâin : "The tomb of Abû Awàna, at Isfaràin, is visited by all
" pious people, and considered as bringing a blessing on those who go to it. At the
" side of it is the tomb of the scholar by whom his Traditions were handed down,
" I mean Abû Noaim Abd al-Mâlik Ibn al-Hasan al-Azhari of Isfaràin. These
" tombs are in the same mausoleum; it lies within the city, on the left
" hand of the person who enters by the gate of Naisâpûr. Near that mausoleum
" is another containing the tomb of the ustàd (or master) Abû Ishak al-Isfaràini
" (vol. I. p. 8); it is on the right hand of the person who enters the city by the gate

" just mentioned. Beside it is the tomb of Abû Awâna's disciple and inseparable
" companion in life and death; I mean the *ustâd* *(master)* Abû Mansûr al-Baghdâdi,
" who was eminent as an *imâm*, a legist and a dogmatic theologian. They both
" assisted each other in defending religion by means of arguments and logical
" proofs. I heard my grandfather, the *imâm* Omar Ibn as-Saffâr, to whom God be
" merciful! say, after looking at the tombs which surrounded that of the *ustâd* Abû
" Ishak, and pointing at the mausoleum : ' It is said that forty *imâms* and legists
" ' of the Shafite sect are there reposing, every one of whom was worthy of govern-
" ' ing the sect and of giving opinions conformable to his, as-Shâfi's, views and
" ' decisions. ' The people visit the mausoleum of the *imâm* Abû Ishak more fre-
" quently that of Abû Awâna, that great *imam* and Traditionist whose worth they do
" not appreciate because he died a long time ago; they know Abû Ishak's merit
" because he died but lately. Abû Awâna was, however, the first to make known at
" Isfarâin the doctrine of the *imâm* as-Shâfi. This he did on his return from
" Egypt, where he had studied under Abû Ibrahîm al-Muzani *(vol. I. p.* 200).
" When my grandfather passed near the mausoleum of the *ustâd (Abû Ishak),* I re-
" marked that he never entered into it, through a feeling of reverence, and that he
" was satisfied with kissing the threshold, to which there were a number of steps
" leading up. He would remain there standing for some time, like a man pene-
" trated with respect and veneration, and then pass on with the look of a man who
" has just said farewell to a person of high dignity. When he reached the mau-
" soleum of Abû Awâna, he would display more respect, reverence and veneration
" than he had done at the other, and would remain there a longer time. " — As
we have already spoken of the adjectives *Naisâpûri (col. I. p.* 61) and *Isfarâini*
(col. I. p. 55), we need not repeat our observations here.

(1) Ismail Ibn Muhammad Ibn Îlrâl the Traditionist died A. H. 987 (A. D. 1006–7). — *(Najûm.)*

(2) The life of Yûnus Ibn Abd al-Aalâ will be found in his volume.

(3) The manuscripts offer the reading which we give here; the edition of Boulac has : Ibn Abhî Wahb.

(4) Abû Bakr Ahmad Ibn Ali ar-Râsi *(a native of Rai),* was an eminent hâfiz. He died in the year 489
(A. D. 1012–1). — *(Neffâs.)*

IBN AS-SIKKIT

Abû Yûsuf Yakûb Ibn Ishak, generally known by the surname of Ibn as-Sikkit (*the son of the taciturn*), is the author of the (*philological work entitled*) *Islâh al-Mantik* (*the correcting of the language*) and other treatises. The hâfiz Ibn Asâkir (*vol. II. p.* 232) says of him, in the History of Damascus : " He delivered (*this philo-* " *logical*) information on the authority of Abû Amr Ishak Ibn Mirâr as-Shaibâni " (*vol. I. p.* 182), Muhammad Ibn. Mubanna , and Mubauimad Ibn Subh Ibn " as-Sammâk the preacher. The same information was received from him " and taught to others by Ahmad Ibn Farah al-Mukri (1), Muhammad Ibn Ajlân " al-Akhbâri, Abû Ikrima ad-Dabbi, Abû Saîd as-Sukkari (2), Maimûn Ibn Hârûn " the kâtib, and others. He gave lessons to (*the khalif*) al-Mutawakkil's sons, " and he said : ' Muhammad Ibn as-Sammâk uttered this saying : ' He who " ' knows mankind humours them ; he who has not that knowledge thwarts " ' them, and the main point, in humouring mankind, is to abstain from thwart- " ' ing them (3).' " Ibn as-Sikkit taught also philology on the authority of al-Aamâi (*vol. II. p.* 123), of Abû Obaida (*vol. III. p.* 388), of al-Farrâ (*p.* 63 *of this vol.*) and of many others. His works are good and full of sound informa tion. Such are the *Islâh al-Mantik,* the *Kitâb al-Alfâz* (*vocabulary*), the *Madni's-Shiar* (*ideas currently used in poetry*) and the treatise on grammatical permutations and substitutions (*al-Kalb wa 'l-Ibdâl*). As a grammarian, he wanted penetration. In his religious belief he inclined towards the opinions and doctrines of those (*the Shîites*) who assigned preeminence to Ali Ibn Abi Tâlib. The following rela tion was made by Ahmad Ibn Obaid (4) : " Ibn as-Sikkit consulted me on the " propriety of his becoming one of al-Mutawakkil's social companions, and I ad- " vised him to refuse. He attributed my counsel to envy and accepted the proposal " made to him. One day, whilst he was with al-Mutawakkil, (*that prince's two sons*) " al-Motazz and al-Muwaiyad came in, and al-Mutawakkil said to him : ' Tell me, " ' Yakûb ! which you like best, these two sons of mine or al-Hasan and al-Husain " ' (*the sons of Ali*)? ' Ibn as-Sikkit answered by depreciating the merit of the two " princes and giving to al-Hasan and al-Husain the praise to which they were well

" entitled. On this, al-Mutawakkil ordered his Turkish guards to chastise him,
" and they (threw him down and) trod on his belly. He was then carried to his
" house, where he died two days afterwards. This happened in the year
" 244 (A. D. 858-9). " Abd Allah Ibn Abd al-Aziz, a person who also had advised Yakûb (Ibn as-Sikkit) not to enter into the service of al-Mutawakkil, said on
this occasion :

> I advised you, Yakûbl to avoid the proximity of a gazelle which, if it attacked a lion, would
> overcome him. Taste therefore and swallow that which you preferred to drink (mo stahsai-
> tahu'l I shall not say, if you miss your footing : " God set you up again! " but shall say :
> " May you fall dead and flat) on your hands and your mouth! "

It is related that al-Farrà asked Ibn as-Sikkit what was his native place and received
this answer : " I am a Khûzian, God bless you! and come from Daurak. " Daurak
is a village in Khûzistân and forms a district in the province of al-Ahwâz. — I
may here observe that Ahwâz forms also a part of Khûzistân. — Al-Farrà then remained in his house during forty days, without letting himself be seen by any of his
acquaintances, and, being asked why he did so, he replied : " May God be glorified !
" I should be ashamed to meet with Ibn as-Sikkit, for I asked him what was his
" country and, though he answered me truly, there was in his reply a shade of re-
" prehension (5). " — Abû'l-Hasan at-Tûsi (6) related as follows : " We were at a
" sitting held by Abû'l-Hasan Ali al-Lihyâni (7), who proposed dictating to the com-
" pany such rare and curious philological anecdotes as he was acquainted with, though
" very feeble he was in the art of dictating. One day, he said : The Arabs (of the
" desert) make use of this expression : ' A heavily loaded (لقَب camel) helps itself
" ' up with its chin (بذنَة bi-dekenihi).' On this, Ibn as-Sikkit, who was then a mere
" youth, rose up (went over) to him and said : ' Abû'l-Hasan ! the correct expression
" ' is : A heavily loaded (camel) helps itself up with its two flanks (بذى bi-deffaihi);
" ' and it means that, when a camel rises with its load, it gets up with the help
" ' of its two sides.' Abû 'l-Hasan ceased dictating that day. Having resumed his
" lessons at another sitting, he said : ' The Arabs (of the desert) say : Such a one is my
" ' next-door neighbour (mukdshir); on which Ibn as-Sikkit again stood up to him
" ' and said : God bless you, sir! what does mukdshir mean? the right expression
" ' is : Such a one is my mukdsir; in as much as the kasr, or side of his tent tou-
" ' ches the kasr of mine. ' Al-Lihyâni ceased to dictate and never commenced

" again." — " Never," said Abù 'l-Abbâs al-Mubarrad, did I meet with a work
composed by a Baghdadian which surpassed Ibn as-Sikkit's treatise on the lan-
" guage."— Ahmad Ibn Muhammad Ibn Abi Shaddâd related as follows : ' I com-
" plained to Ibn as-Sikkit of being in narrow circumstances, and he asked me if
" I had ever spoken (in verse)? I answered that I had not, on which he said :
" But I can do so; and he then recited to me these lines :

> " I desire things which I cannot possibly obtain as long I remain in apprehension of what
> " destiny may bring about. Travelling (as a merchand) in search of riches is not travelling
> " (and fatigue); it is your remaining in a state of misery that is really travelling (i. e. fa-
> " tiguing). "

Ibn as-Sikkit related that a man wrote to a friend of his in these terms : " A case
" of necessity has occurred which obliges me (to have recourse) to you (kibalak). If
" I succeed, I shall find therein my share (of good fortune) and the rest shall be your
" share. If you ask to be excused (I shall only say that every thing) good may
" always be expected of you and that I now offer beforehand my excuses. (Receive
" my) salutation (8). " — The following anecdote was copied from a note in his
(Ibn as-Sikkit's) handwriting : Sulaimân Ibn Rabîd al-Bâhili (9) was reviewing
his cavalry (man by man) and, when Amr Ibn Madi Karib az-Zubaidi (10) passed
before him on horseback, he said to him : " Your horse is of a base breed. " —
" Nay, " replied Amr, " he is a blood-horse." On this, Sulaimân ordered that
the animal should be kept from water till it got thirsty, and had then a large basin
brought out, filled with water. The blood-horses to which it was offered drank out
of it, and so did the horse of Amr, but in bending the leg. " Do you see that?" said
Sulaimân. " I do;" replied Amr, "one base-born animal has recognised another. "
Omar Ibn al-Khattâb, to whom this was told, wrote to Amr in the following terms :
" I have been informed of what you said to your superior officer, and am told
" that you have a sword which you call Simsâma. Now, I also have a sword the
" name of which is Simsim and, by Allah! if I lay it across your head, I shall not
" withdraw it till it has reached your rakâba. If you wish to know whether I say
" truth or not, you have only to recommence. Receive my salutation. " The term
rakâba takes the same vowels as the word sahâba (cloud), and designates that bone of
the breast which is shaped like a tongue and is situated above the stomach. — Abû
Othmân al-Mâzini said : " I met Ibn as-Sikkit at the house of the vizir Muhammad

" Ibn Abd al-Malik as-Zaiyât (vol. III. p. 210), and the latter said to me : Pro-
" pose a question to Abû Yûsuf (Ibn as-Sikkît). Being unwilling to do so, I hesi-
" tated and delayed, fearing to displease Ibn as-Sikkît, who was my intimate friend.
" The vizir insisted and asked why I did not obey; so, I endeavoured to choose an
" easy question and thus do him a friendly act. I therefore said to him :
" What is the grammatical form of the verb nakial in that passage of God's
" book where it is said : Send our brother with us, so that we may have (corn) mea-
" sured to us. (Korân, sûr. 12, verse 63). He replied : ' Its form is nafâl.' On this,
" I observed to him that, if it were so, the preterite (or root) of the verb would be
" kalal. I do not mean that, said he, the form is naftail. On this, I asked him how
" many letters there were in naftail (when in Arabic characters), and he answered :
" ' five.'" And how many, " said I, are there in nakial? He answered : " Four. "
" How then, said I, can a word of four letters have the same form as one of five? "
" Being unable to answer, he coloured up and remained silent (11). " On this,
" Muhammad Ibn Abd al-Malik said to him : ' You receive, every month, a salary of
" ' two thousand dirhems (£. 50), and yet you cannot indicate the form of nakial.'
" When we withdrew, Yakûb (Ibn as-Sikkît) said to me : ' Abû Othmân! do you
" ' know what you have done?' I replied : ' By Allah! I endeavoured to find for you
" ' an easy question, and do you a service.' " — Abû 'l-Hasan Ibn Sîda (vol. II.
p. 272) states, in his Muhkam, towards the beginning of his preface, that this scene
passed in the presence of (the khalif) al Motawakkil. God knows best! — An author,
but not Ibn Asâkir, says that Ibn as-Sikkît and his father kept a school for children
of the lower order in that street of Madina tas-Salâm (Baghdad) which is called Darb
al-Kantara (Bridge-Street), and, wanting to gain something more, he applied to the
study of grammar. It is related that the father, having made the pilgrimage and the
circuits around the House (the Kaaba), and the running (between Safa and Marwa),
prayed God to render his son learned in grammar. (Ibn as-Sikkît), having studied
grammar and philology, used to visit regularly some persons who resided in (the street
of) al-Kantara, and he received from them, each time, the sum of ten dirhems (5 shillings) or somewhat more. He then went regularly (to teach) Bishr and Hârûn, who
were employed as scribes by Muhammad Ibn Abd Allah Ibn Tâhir al-Khuzâi (12), and
he continued to go to them and their children. Ibn Tâhir, being then in want of a
person capable of bringing up and educating his children confided them to the care of
Ibrahim Ibn Ishak al-Musâbi, and engaged Yakûb at a (monthly) salary of five hun-

dred dirhems, which sum be afterwards increased to one thousand. — Abû 'l-Abbâs Thalab (vol. I. p. 83) said : " Ibn as-Sikkît was skilled in various branches " of knowledge. His father, who was a virtuous man and had been one of Abû " 'l-Hasan al-Kisâi's (vol. II. p. 237) disciples, was well acquainted with pure " Arabic. The motive which induced people to attend Yakûb's sittings was this : " I found that he had collected the poems of Abû 'n-Najm al-Ijli (13) and amelio- " rated the text; so, I asked him to lend me the volume in order that I might copy " it. 'Abû 'l-Abbâs' said he,' I have sworn that my wife shall be divorced from me " ' if that volume ever gets out of my sight; but there it is before you; so, you may " ' (begin to) copy it (here) and return to me on Thursday next (to resume your task).' " My going to see him induced a number of persons to do the same, and the news, " having spread about, brought crowds to his lessons." Thalab said also : " Our " masters were unanimous in declaring that, since the time of Ibn al-Aârâbi (vol. III. " p. 23), there had not appeared a more learned philologer than Ibn as-Sikkît."— Being obliged by al-Mutawakkil to become the preceptor of his son al-Motazz Billah, he went to that prince's room and said, on taking his seat: " What does the emir wish " that we should begin by ?" To this al-Motazz replied: " By departing."— "Then, " said Yakûb, I shall rise (and retire)." — " I shall be more active in rising than " you, " said al-Motazz, and he stood up in such haste that his feet got entangled in his " trowsers, and he fell on the floor. Yakûb, to whom he then turned, quite ab- " ashed and blushing with shame, recited to him these lines :

" A man may be punished for a slip of the tongue, but is never chastised for the slipping " of his feet. A slip of the tongue may cost him his head, but a slip of the foot is cured by " repose.

" Al-Mutawakkil, to whom Yakûb went the next morning and related what had ' passed, ordered him a gift of fifty thousand dirhems but observed that he had al- ' ready heard these two verses." — Yakûb used to say : " I am a better gramma- ' rian than my father, but he surpasses me by his acquaintance with poetry and ' (pure) Arabic." — Al-Husain Ibn Abd al-Mujîb al-Mausili said : " I heard Ibn as- ' Sikkît recite the following verses at a sitting held by Abû Bakr Ibn Abi Shaiba (14) :

" There are persons who love you ostensibly with a love not to be diminished; and yet, if " you ask them for ten farthings, they would refer their dear friend to the bounty of the all- " knowing God. "

Ibn as-Sikkít composed some poetry capable of giving confidence to a dejected
mind. Such, for instance, was the following :

> When the heart is filled with despair and the widest bosom is too narrow to hold the grief
> which invades it, — when afflictions have lodged therein and taken up their dwelling, — when
> you find no means of escaping from misery and perceive that all the address of the most expe-
> rienced is useless, — assistance will come to you, whilst you are in despair, as a favour from the
> bountiful being who hears the prayers of the wretched. When misfortune has reached its
> height, deliverance is at hand.

It was said by the learned that the *Islâh al-Mantik* was a book without a preface
and the *Adab al-Kátib* of Ibn Kutaiba (vol. II. p. 22) a preface without a book; the
fact is that the preface of the latter work is very long, but it contains much useful
information. One of the learned said : " There never crossed the bridge (of boats)
" at Baghdad such a treatise on philology as the *Mantik*." It is certainly an instructive and useful work, containing a great quantity of philological information,
and there does not exist, as far as we know, a treatise of the same size and on
the same subject. A number of persons have made it the special object of
their studies : the visir Abû 'l-Kásim al-Husain Ibn Ali, surnamed Ibn al-
Magbribi (vol. I. p. 450), made an abridgment of it, the khatîb Abû Zakariya at-
Tibrisi (p. 78 of this vol.) remodelled it, and Ibn as-Sîrâfi (vol. I. p. 377), composed, on the verses cited in it, an instructive work. The other productions
of Ibn as-Sikkít are : The *Kitâb az-Zibrij* (book of precious ornaments), the
Kitâb al-Alfâz (a vocabulary), the *Kitâb al-Amthâl* (book of proverbs), the *Kitâb al-
Maksûr wa'l-Mamdûd* (on the short and the long final a), the *Kitâb al-Mudhakkar wa'l-
Muwannath* (on masculine and feminine nouns), the *Kitâb al-Ajnâs* (on the different
species of animals), which is a large work, the *Kitâb al-Fark* (on the difference between the names given to the members of the human body and to those of animals), the Kitâb as-Sarj wa'l-Lidjâm (on the saddle and bridle), the *Kitâb
faal w'Afaal* (on the difference of signification between verbs of the first and the
fourth form), the *Kitâb al-Hasharát* (on reptiles and insects), the *Kitâb al-Aswât* (on
the cries of men and animals), the *Kitâb al-Adhdâd* (on words which have two opposite significations), the *Kitâb as-Shajr wa'n-Nabât* (on trees and plants), the *Kitâb al-
Wuhûsh* (on wild beasts), the *Kitâb al-Ibl* (on camels), the *Kitâb an-Nawâdir* (on
expressions of rare occurrence), the *Kitâb Maâni 's-Shiar al-Kabîr* (the greater work

on the ideas occurring in poetry), the *Kitáb Sarakát as-Shuwará wa m'attafaka aleih* (*on the plagiarisms of poets and the thoughts in which they agreed unintentionally*), etc. The reputation of this author is so great that we need not expatiate on his merits. The manner of his death has been related otherwise than in the account which we have given : according to some, al-Mutawakkil often attacked the character of Ali Ibn Abi Tálib and of that khalif's sons, al-Hasan and al-Hussin. — His detestation of them has been already noticed in some verses which we inserted in the life of Abû 'l-Hussin Ali Ibn Muhammad surnamed Ibn Bassám (vol. *II.* p. 303). — Ibn as-Sikkit (*on the contrary*), shewed for them the utmost veneration and attachment. In the conversation of which we have spoken, he said (*it appears*), to al-Mutawakkil : " Kanbar, Ali's slave, was better than you and your sons." On this, al-Mutawakkil ordered his tongue to be plucked out from the back of his neck, and the order was obeyed. This occurred on the eve of Tuesday, the 5th of Rajab, 244 (17th october, A. D. 858); or according to others, in 243 or 246. God best knows the true date! Ibn as-Sikkit had then attained his fifty-eighth year. When he died, ten thousand dirhems were sent to his son by al-Mutawakkil, as the price of the father's blood. — The grammarian Abû Jaafar Ahmad Ibn Muhammad, generally known by the appellation of Ibn an-Nahhás (vol. *I. p.* 81), states that al-Mutawakkil's conversation with Ibn as-Sikkit began in a jesting tone, which then turned to earnest. According to another account, al-Mutawakkil ordered him to revile and disparage a certain Kuraishide and, perceiving his unwillingness to do so, he caused the Kuraishide to revile Ibn as-Sikkit. — The latter replied to this attack; on which al-Mutawakkil said to him : " I gave you an order and you refused to obey; and, on " being insulted by this man, you did what I wanted." He then had a beating inflicted on Ibn as-Sikkit, who was immediately afterwards carried out of the room and dragged (*home*) prostrate (*on the ground*). — God knows which of these accounts is the true one. — An anecdote similar to the one related above has been already given by us in the life of Abd Allah Ibn al-Mubárak (vol. *II. p.* 12), who had been questioned respecting the relative merits of Moawia Ibn Abi Sofyán and Omar Ibn Abd al-Azîz. — The surname of *as-Sikkit* was given to the subject of this notice because he was very taciturn and would remain a long time without speaking. All words of the forms *fáïl* and *fáïl* take an *i* after the first letter (15). — *Khúzi* means *belonging to Khúzistán*, which a region lying between Basra and Fars.

(1) Abû Jaafar Ahmad Ibn Farah Ibn Jîbrîl, a teacher of the Korân-readings, a Traditionist and an expositor of the Korân, was a blind man and a native of Baghdad. His vast learning and the exactitude of his information brought him into great repute. As a Traditionist, he is considered to be sure and trustworthy. He died A. H. 303 (A. D. 915-6) at the age of nearly ninety years. — (*Kurrå*, fol. 69.)

(2) Abû Saîd al-Hasan Ibn al-Husain as-Sukkari studied at the schools of Kûfa and Basra, acquired great philological, grammatical and historical information and published highly esteemed editions of the ancient poets. He composed some treatises on philological subjects and an extensive work on the poems of Abû Nuwâs. Born A. H. 818 (A. D. 827-8), died A. H. 975 (A. D. 888-9). — (*Fihrest*; Flugel's *Grammatische Schule der Araber*, p. 89.)

(3) This maxim is probably inserted here because the subject of it cost Ibn as-Sikkît his life.

(4) Abû Jaafar Ahmad Ibn Obaid, surnamed Abû Assîn, was one of the learned men of Kûfa and preceptor to al-Muntasir and al-Moazz, the sons of al-Motawakkil. He composed some philological works and died A. H. 275 (A. D. 888-9), or 278, by another account. — *Fihrest*; Flugel's *Gram. Schule der Ar.*, p. 191.)

(5) Al-Farrâ, on opening his course of lectures, asked each of his scholars what was his name and from what country he came. Ibn as-Sikkît answered frankly that he was from Khûzistân, a country the inhabitants of which, according to Yakût, were notorious for their avarice, their stupidity and the vileness of their inclinations. It was said that a year's residence in that country sufficed to change the cleverest man into an idiot. — (*Dictionnaire géog. de la Perse*, translated from the Arabic of Yâkut by Barbier de Meynard.)

(6) See p. 940 of this volume and Flugel's *Gram. Schule der Ar.*, p. 154.

(7) Abû 'l-Hasan Ali Ibn al-Mubârak al-Lihyâni, was al-Kisâi's servant-boy. Having had frequent opportunities of meeting with men of learning and Arabs of the desert who spoke their language with elegance, he picked up a great quantity of literary information, and composed some works. Abû Obaid al-Kâsim Ibn Sallâm (vol. II, p. 493) received lessons from him. He died probably towards the commencement of the third century of the Hijra (A. D. 815). — (*Fihrest*, fol. 64.)

(8) The epistolary style of the Arabs during the first and second centuries after Muhammad, was highly admired by philologers for the subtility of the thoughts and the elegant conciseness of the style. To Europeans this elliptical style appears obscure and affected.

(9) This was one of the khalif Omar's generals.

(10) This celebrated chieftain was a contemporary of Muhammad and the first khalifs. For his adventures, see Caussin de Perceval's *Essai sur l'histoire des Arabes*.

(11) Arabic scholars will easily understand the question; so, we shall merely state that Ibn as-Sikkît's second answer was right; unfortunately, he had forgotten that verbs having a vowel for one of their radicals, had it in the conditional mood.

(12) Abû 'l-Abbâs Muhammad, the son of the celebrated emir, Abd Allah Ibn Tâhir, left Khorasân in the year 237 (A. D. 851-2) and obtained from the khalif al-Motawakkil the government of Irak. He fixed his residence at Baghdad and, in the year 866 (A. D. 862-3) he was appointed commander of the *shorta* (the police guards), and received, in addition to the government of Irâk, that of the two holy Cities (Mekka and Medina). He died A. H. 295 (A. D. 867). His talents, literary acquirements, bravery and generosity rendered his name illustrious. — (*Nujûm*.)

(13) The poet Fadl Ibn Koddâma al-Ijli, surnamed Abû 'n-Najm (*the father of the star*), was contemporary with the Omaiyide khalif Hishâm Ibn Abd al-Malik. — (De Hammer's *Literaturgeschichte der Araber*, vol. II, p. 468.)

(14) The hâfiz Abû Bakr Abd Allah, surnamed Ibn Abi Shaiba, was a mawla of the tribe of Abs and a native of Kûfa. As a Traditionist, his authority is cited by al-Bukhâri, Muslim, Abû Dâwûd and others. He died in the month of Moharram, 235 (July-Aug. st, A. D. 849). — (Nojûr.)

(15) As examples of the first of these forms, we may give رِبْيق (ibrîk) اكليل (iklîl) and رِدِد (ridîd) and جبريل (jibrîl). For the second form we have سكّيت (sikkît) (nikhil), صدّيق (siddîk) (siddîk).

YAKUB IBN AL-LAITH AS-SAFFAR

Abû Yûsuf Yakûb Ibn al-Laith as-Saffâr al-Khâriji (*the insurgent*); of this chief and of his brother Amr, historians make frequent mention : they speak of the countries which they conquered, of the numbers which they slew and of the conflicts which took place between them and the khalifs. It is from these accounts that I have extracted the information given in the following pages. Abû Abd Allah Muhammad Ibn al-Azhar al-Akhbâri (1) says : " Ali Ibn Muhammad, a person well-
" acquainted with the proceedings of (*Yakûb*) Ibn al-Laith as-Saffâr and with the
" history of his wars, related to me as follows : Yakûb and his brother Amr were
" *saffârs* (*coppersmiths*) in their youth and, at that time, they made a great show of
" piety. A native of Sijistân then attracted attention by undertaking, of his own
" accord, to wage war against the Khârijites (2). This volunteer in God's service
" (*mutawwê*) came from the town of Bust and bore the name of Sâlih Ibn an-Nadr
" al-Kinâni (*of the Arabic tribe of Kindra*). The two brothers became his partisans
" and rose to fortune by his means. Yakûb, having lost his brother, who was slain
" by that sect of Khârijites which was called the *Shurât*, was appointed by the above-
" mentioned Sâlih to act as his lieutenant. On the death of Sâlih, another of the
" volunteers (*Mutawwê*) named Dirhem Ibn al-Husain occupied his place, and
" Yakûb remained with him, as he had done with Sâlih. Dirhem, having then fal-
" len into a snare which had been laid for him by the governor of Khorâsân, was
" sent by him to Baghdad and there imprisoned. When set at liberty, he entered
" into the sultan's service, but afterwards confined himself to his house and mani-

" fested great piety, devotion and the intention of making the pilgrimage.
" This continued till Yakûb became powerful. " — Our professor Izz ad-Dîn
Abû 'l-Hasan Ali Ibn Muhammad, surnamed Ibn al-Athîr (vol. II. p. 288), says,
in that section of his Annals which contains an account of Yakûb's first proceedings and which is placed under the year 237 (A. D. 851-2) : " In this year,
" a native of Bust whose name was Sâlih Ibn an-Nadr made himself master of Sijistân.
" With him was Yakûb Ibn al-Laith.   Tâhir Ibn Abd Allah Ibn Tâhir Ibn al-Hussain,
" the governor of Khorasân, marched against him and delivered the province from the
" invaders.   Some time after, a man named Dirhem Ibn al-Hussain, who was also
" one of the volunteers, made his appearance in the same country and subdued it,
" he was, however, unable to provide for his troops, and so glaring was his incapa-
" city that his partisans rallied around Yakûb Ibn al-Laith, who held the command
" of the army, and placed him at their head, having already remarked the talent
" with which he administered, governed and maintained order. — Dirhem, being
" informed of this, offered no resistance and abdicated in favour of Yakûb.   The
" new chief subdued all the country and became very formidable; reinforcements
" came to him from every quarter, and his authority increased in the manner which
" we shall relate. " — Let us resume and terminate the recital made by Ali Ibn Muhammad : " When Dirhem Ibn al-Hussain arrived in Baghdad, Yakûb took the com-
" mand of the volunteers, and continued the war against the Shurât Khârijites.
" These sectaries he succeeded in vanquishing and destroying, and in laying waste
" their villages.   By his skill and address he obtained from his partisans such obe-
" dience as they had never shown to his predecessors.   His power and might then
" became so great that he was able to effect the conquest of Sijistân, Herât, Bu-
" shandj and their dependencies.   There was in the frontier territory of Sijistân a
" Turkish tribe called the Parâri and governed by a king named Retbîl (see page 196
" of this vol.).   Yakûb, incited by the inhabitants of Sijistân, who stated that this
" people did even more harm than the Shurât Khârijites and better deserved to
" be punished, marched against them, slew their king and three princes, all of them
" bearing the title of Retbîl.   He then returned to Sijistân with the heads of these
" princes and some thousands more.   Having become formidable to all the kings
" of the countries around him, he obtained the humble submission of the sovereigns
" who reigned over Multân, ar-Rukhkhaj, at-Tabassin, Zâbulistân, as-Sind, Mekrân
" and other places.   His expedition against Herât and Bûshanj took place in the

" year 253 (A. D. 867). At that time, the emir of Khorásán was Muhammad Ibn
" Táhir Ibn Abd Allah Ibn Táhir Ibn al-Husain al-Khuzái. The officer who com-
" manded for him in these cities, and whose name was Muhammad Ibn Aûs al-
" Anbári, marched against the invader at the head of a numerous force, magnifi-
" cently equipped and armed. In the battle which ensued, he fought bravely and
" kept his ground, till Yakûb, by a skilful manœuvre, intercepted his communica-
" tions with Bûshanj and thus obliged him to make a precipitate retreat. It is said
" that (Yakûb), in all his battles, never met with a more obstinate resistance than
" that offered by Ibn Aûs. He then occupied Bushanj and Herât. Having got into
" his power a number of Taherians, persons so called because they were attached
" to the family of Táhir Ibn al-Husain al-Khuzái, he took them with him to Sijistán
" and kept them prisoners. The khalif al-Motaz Billah obtained their liberty by
" sending to him a letter, the bearer of which was a Shîîte named Ibn Balam. I was
" informed, said Ibn al-Azhar al-Akhbári, by Muhammad Ibn Abd Allah Ibn Marwán,
" that Ibn Balam related to him as follows: I set out with a letter for him from al-
" Motaz Billah and, on arriving at Zaranj, — the capital of Sijistán, — I asked
" permission to see him. The authorisation being granted, I went in without sa-
" luting and sat down in his presence without his inviting me to do so. I then
" delivered the letter to him and, when he received it, I said to him: Kiss the
" letter of the Commander of the faithful.' That he did not do, but broke the
" seal and opened it. I then retired walking backwards, towards the door of the
" saloon in which he was, and said: ' Salutation to the emir and the mercy of
" ' God (3). He was so much pleased with this that he lodged me well, made me a
" ' present and set the Taherians at liberty.' The same Ibn Balam related as fol-
" lows: I went, one day, to visit Yûsuf as-Saffâr, and he said to me: ' There is a
" ' man coming to me from Fars, or that quarter, for the purpose of obtaining my
" ' protection, and he has with him three or four others; nay, there are
" ' five in all.' This declaration of his I did not believe and remained silent; yet,
" before I was aware, the chamberlain entered and said: — 'Emir! there is a man
" ' at the door who comes to ask protection, and with him are four others.' The
" visitor being introduced by Yakûb's order, informed him, after saluting, that he
" had with him four companions. These also were admitted. I turned to the
" chamberlain and asked him if this was a juggling trick of his? He replied with
" a solemn oath that the men had arrived quite suddenly and that no one had been

" aware of their coming. Some time after, I asked Yakúb about it: ' Emir I said I,
" ' I remarked something said by you which was really surprising; how did you know
" ' of this suppliant's coming with his companions?' He replied : ' I was thinking of
" ' Fars when I saw a raven alight on a spot fronting the road which leads to that
" ' country, and I felt in one of my toes a twitching which passed successively to
" ' each of the others. Now, as toes are not noble members of the body, I
" ' knew that some people from that quarter would come to see me, either sup-
" ' pliants or envoys of little consequence.' Ali Ibn al-Hakam related as follows :
" I asked Yakúb Ibn al-Laith as-Saffár how he came by the scar which disfigured
" him so much and which extended from the bridge of his nose across his cheek.
" He replied that he got the wound in one of his encounters with the Khárijites; a
" man whom he had wounded with his lance turned upon him and struck off (with
" a sabre) one half of his face. The piece was then replaced and sewed on. ' Du-
" ' ring twenty days' said he, ' I remained with a tube in my mouth, which had to be
" ' maintained open lest the inflammation should extend to the head, and my food
" ' consisted of liquids which were poured down my throat.' His chamberlain
" added : ' Notwithstanding this wound, the emir went out as usual to direct the
" ' movements of his troops and fought (like the others).' — Yakúb sent to al-
" Motazz Billah a magnificent present and, amongst other objects, a portative
" mosque made of silver and large enough to hold fifteen persons at prayers. He
" asked that the province of Fars should be given to him, and engaged (to
" pay a yearly tribute of) fifteen millions of dirhems in case he succeeded in expell-
" ing from that province Ali Ibn al-Husain Ibn Kuraish, him who governed
" it (b). Yakúb, having sent this letter to al-Motazz, left Sijistán with the intention
" of proceeding to Kermán, and halted at Bam." — This place marks the point
which separates Sijistán from Kermán. — " Al-Abbás Ibn al-Husain Ibn Kuraish,
" the brother of the above-mentioned Ali Ibn al-Husain, then departed from Ker-
" mán with Ahmad Ibn al-Laith al-Kurdi and took the road of Shíráz. Yakúb
" placed a body of troops under the orders of his brother Ali Ibn al-Laith and sent
" him forward to as-Sirján whilst he himself remained at Bam," — As-Sirján is a
town in Kermán. — " Ahmad Ibn al-Laith al-Kurdi then turned from his way, with
" a numerous body of Kurds and other troops, and proceeded to Darabjird." — This
name is common to three localities, of which the first is the capital of a vast district
in Fars, and the second a village of Fars, in the district of Istakhar, at which there

is a mine of quicksilver. It must have been to one of these two places that
they went, for the third is at Naisápúr in Khorásán, to which province it is probable that they did not go, since it has no connection with Fars. — The narrator
continues thus : " Ahmad Ibn al-Laith then met with a band of Yakúb's troops
" who were on a foraging party, killed some of them and put the rest to flight.
" The heads of the slain he sent to Fars, where they were stuck up by Ali Ibn al-
" Husain. Yakúb, on learning what had happened, entered into Kermán. Ali Ibn
" al-Husain sent against him Tauk Ibn al-Mughallis at the head of five thousand
" Kurds and the troops which Ahmad Ibn al-Laith al-Kurdi had brought with him.
" He marched to Onás (5), a city in the province of Kermán and there halted. Tauk
" then received a letter from Yakúb in which he was told that he had made a
" mistake in coming into a province which did not belong to him, and to this he
" replied : ' You are more skilled in the working of copper than in the work
" ' of war. ' This gave great offence to Yakúb. There was in Tauk's army three
" hundred of the Abná (6). When Yakúb reached the city of Onás, he gave battle
" to Tauk, killed part of his troops and put the rest to flight; but the Abná stood
" their ground so bravely that Yakúb had pity on them and offered to spare their
" lives. This proposal they rejected and continued fighting till they died. In
" this battle, Yakúb slew two thousand men, took one thousand prisoners and,
" with them, Tauk Ibn al-Mughallis. The latter he put into light chains and
" provided abundantly with food and other necessaries, but obliged him to
" deliver up his treasures. Having then left Onás, he entered into the go-
" vernment of Fars, and Ali Ibn al-Husain retrenched himself in Shiráz. This
" took place on Tuesday, the 17th of the latter Rabi, 255 (14 April, A. D. 869).
" Ibn al-Husain then wrote to Yakúb a letter in which he declared that he had
" not ordered Ibn al-Mughallis to act as he had done and that hostilities had been
" commenced by that chief without authorization. 'If you intend to take Kermán,'
" said he, ' you have turned your back to it; if you wish to obtain possession of
" ' Fars, produce a letter from the Commander of the faithful ordering (me) to
" ' give it up; then I shall retire. ' Yakúb answered that he had a letter from the
" sultan (7), but would not deliver it till he had entered the town and that, if he (Ali
" Ibn al-Husain) would evacuate the place and give it up, he would do an act of
" piety and remove all cause of evil. If not, said he, ' the sword must
" decide between us, and our place of meeting shall be the marj of Senkán. '

— This is a large and moist tract of land at the distance of three; parasangs from Shiráz. — "The post-master and the chief men of the place then wrote to "'Yakûb, saying: For you to whom God has given a spirit so devoted to his service "'and so zealous for the interests of religion, for you who have slain the Khárijites "'and expelled them from the provinces of Khorâsân and Sijistân, it is not befit-"' ting to be hasty in the shedding of (Moslim) blood. Ali Ibn al-Husain will not "'give up the town unless he receives a written authorisation from the khalif.' The "people of Shiráz then prepared to sustain a siege. When the troops of Tauk had "been put to flight, three of Yakûb's partisans fell into the hands of the fugitives "and were imprisoned by Ali Ibn al-Husain. As for Tauk, he had purchased, "previously to marching against Yakûb, a house in Shiráz for which he payed "seventy thousand dirhems (£. 1.750) and had allotted another sum of money to be "spent upon it. He now wrote these words to his son (who was in the town): 'Do "'not suspend the work of the masons; for the emir Yakûb treats me with honour "'and kindness. Obtain the liberation of his three partisans; that is what he "'asks for. And he has promised, if it be done, to set me at liberty.' Ali Ibn "al-Husain (being informed of this), said : 'Write to Yakûb and tell him that he "'may crucify Tauk Ibn al-Mughallis, for I prize the meanest of my slaves more "'than him.' Tauk, whom Yakûb questioned respecting the means of which "Ali Ibn al-Husain could dispose, represented them as very inconsiderable and, to "gain Yakûb's favour, he offered him the money which he had in Shiráz and "said that he would write to his family the order to send it. 'This,' said he, 'will "'help you to war against him.' Being told to do so by Yakûb, he wrote to his "son, but the letter fell into the hands of Ali Ibn al-Husain, who immediately "seised on the money and other things which were in Tauk's house, and had "them carried to his own. Yakûb then began his march and Ali Ibn al-Husain "levied troops." Ahmad Ibn al-Hakam relates as follows : "Yakûb said to me: "'Ali Ibn al-Husain is he a Moslim or not?' I answered that he was. On this he "said : 'How can you consider him to be a Moslim who brings into the land of "'Musulmans troops of infidel Kurds, for the purpose of killing the true belie-"'vers, carrying off their women and seizing on their wealth ? Know you not that "'Ahmad Ibn al-Laith al-Kurdi put seven hundred men to death in Kermân, to "'avenge the murder of a single individual, that the Kurds violated two hundred "'virgins of the best families and carried out of the country upwards of two thou-

" ' and women? Do you consider him to be a Moslim who permits such doings?'
" I replied that Ahmad had acted so without Ali's orders. In another conference,
" Yakûb bid him take this message to Ali Ibn al-Husain : ' I have brought with me a
" ' people of freemen, and cannot send them away unless I give them what they
" ' want. Let me have therefore wherewithal to satisfy them and send me also
" ' such a gift as is fitting for a person of my rank. If you do so, I shall be for
" ' you as a brother and lend you my assistance against those who may attack you ;
" ' I shall deliver Kermân over to you, so that you may gorge upon it, and shall
" ' return to my own government.' Yakûb, having departed, halted at a village
" called Rbûaistân (sic) and, on Tuesday, the 8th of the first Jumâda of that year
" (24th April, A. D. 869), Ahmad Ibn al-Hakam rejoined Ali Ibn al-Husain, and
" delivered to him Yakûb's letter. Ali Ibn al-Husain, said Ibn al-Hakam, was so
" greatly astounded at the news which I brought him that he could understand
" nothing of it. The contents of the letter were, in a summary manner, what we
" here relate : The writer began by good wishes for the person to whom it was ad-
" dressed and then said : ' I have well understood the purport of your letter and
" ' your allusion to my arrival at this most important town without having received
" ' the Commander of the faithful's authorisation. Know that I am not one of those
" ' persons whose minds aspire to act unjustly ; I am not capable of such conduct ;
" ' so I thus deliver you from the trouble of ruminating over that point. The
" ' town belongs to the Commander of the faithful, and we are his servants who
" ' act by his orders throughout his land and his dominions, and who are obedient
" ' towards God and towards him. I have heard the observations of your envoy,
" ' and leave to him the task of delivering to you my answer to the message which
" ' you charged him with, and of communicating to you a reply which, I hope, will
" ' tend to your advantage and to mine. If you act as I advise, you will assure
" ' your own welfare, please God! and, if you refuse, (recollect) that the will of God
" ' is not to be resisted or avoided. As for us, we place ourselves under the pro-
" ' tection of the Almighty, so that we may be saved from perdition ; we have
" ' recourse to Him against the dictates of injustice and the strokes of disappoint-
" ' ment. We hope that, in His bounty, he will assure our happiness in this world
" ' and in the next. May God grant you long life! Written on Monday, the 1st of
" ' the first Jumâda, 255 (17th April, A. D. 869).' The two armies then marched
" against each other; that of Ali Ibn al-Husain consisting of fifteen thousand

" men. On Wednesday morning, the 4th of the same month, he sent forward
" Ahmad Ibn al-Laith with the vanguard. On Thursday, Yakûb's vanguard came
" up and the two armies met. The first charge had no result, but, in the second,
" Ali Ibn al-Husain's partisans were driven from their positions and, after an obsti-
" nate conflict, they were thrown into disorder and every man of them fled without
" once looking back. Ali Ibn al-Husain followed his troops, crying after them :
" ' Stop, in the name of God! come back!' but they did not mind him, and he
" remained with only a few of his companions. The fugitives reached the gates of
" Shîrâz on the evening of the same day. It was shortly after the hour of noon
" that the battle took place. The gates being too narrow to admit the crowd,
" numbers of them ran through the outskirts of the town, nor did they stop till
" they reached al-Ahwâz. In that battle they lost about five thousand men. Ali
" received three wounds from some of Yakûb's cavalry, who hacked at him with
" their sabres, brought him out of the saddle to the ground, and were just going
" to kill him outright when he exclaimed : ' I am Ali Ibn al-Husain.' On this,
" they took off his turban-cloth, tied it about his waist and led him to Yakûb.
" The soldier who took him prisoner asked for a reward and was offered ten thou-
" sand dirhems (g. 250), but rejected that sum, and Yakûb said to him : ' You
" ' brought me a dog which you took, and I have nothing more for you than what
" ' I offer.' The man went away. Yakûb then gave the prisoner, with his own
" hand, ten strokes of a whip over the head, seized his chamberlain by the beard
" and plucked nearly all of it off; having then ordered that Ali should be fettered
" with irons of twenty pounds' weight, he had Tauk Ibn al-Mughallis fettered also
" and confined them both in the same tent. Immediately after, he marched towards
" Shîrâz, and the partisans of Ali Ibn al-Husain fled in all directions. He made his
" entry into that city with drums beating before him, and the inhabitants, think-
" ing that he would do them harm, by shedding their blood and plundering
" their wealth, because they had warred against him, did not dare to utter a word.
" He had, in fact, promised to his troops that they should have permission to sack
" the city, in case he was victorious. The people, being aware of that, shut them-
" selves up in their houses. He returned to his camp, the same night, after
" having perambulated the city and, the next morning, he caused an amnesty to be
" proclaimed, and the inhabitants, being informed that they might go out into the
" market-places, took advantage of the permission. He then announced by procla-

" mation that whoever sheltered any of Ali Ibn al-Husain's secretaries would be out-
" lawed by the fact. When Friday came (*he went to the mosque and*) offered up the
" prayer for the *imâm* (*khalif*) al-Motass Billah, but without naming himself, and,
" as this was remarked to him, he replied : ' The emir [*or governor*] has not yet ar-
" rived (R). He said to them also : ' I shall stay with you only ten days and then re-
" turn to Sijistân." His brother, whom he sent to the house of Ali Ibn al-Husain,
" took out of it the carpets and other furniture, but was unable to discover where
" the money was hid. On this, he (Yakûb) had Ali brought before him and indu-
" ced him, by threats and promises, to declare that he would point out the place
" where he had concealed his treasures. Ali, being then taken to his house, drew
" forth four hundred *badras* (0), or one thousand, according to another account.
" This sum Yakûb distributed to his troops, instead of the pillage which he had
" promised them, and each man obtained for his share three hundred dirhems (£. 7,
" 10 s). He them inflicted on Ali tortures of various kinds, caused his testicules to be
" compressed and bound the two glands (7) to his cheeks. The prisoner said to
" him : ' You have already taken from me furniture and other objects, to the value
" ' of forty thousand dinars (£. 20,000); ' but Yakûb persisted in torturing him
" and had him bound in fetters of forty pounds' weight. Ali then pointed out
" to them a place in his house where they found four millions of dirhems
" (£. 100,000) and a great quantity of jewels. He was again tortured and in-
" formed that he (Yakûb) would not be satisfied unless he obtained (*an additional*
" *sum of*) thirty thousand dinars £. 15,000). Ali, though now deranged in
" mind by the violence of his sufferings, was delivered over to al-Hasan Ibn Dirhem,
" who beat, tortured and reviled him; Tauk Ibn al-Mughallis, was tortured also
" by Ibn Dirhem, and shut up with Ali in the same chamber. On Sa-
" turday, the 28th of the first Jumâda of the same year (14th May, A. D. 869),
" Yakûb departed from Shirâs for his own country, and took with him Ali Ibn al-
" Husain and Tauk Ibn al-Mughallis. On reaching Kermân, he had them dressed
" in party-coloured clothes, with women's bonnets on their heads, and paraded them
" about whilst a public cryer walked before, announcing who they were. After
" that, he cast them into prison and went on to Sijistân. On the third of Rajab,
" the same year (17th June, A. D. 869), the khalif al-Motass Billah was deposed,
" and, on the same day, the *imâm* al-Muhtadi Billah was raised to the khalifate. This
" prince also was deposed, on the afternoon of Tuesday the 16th of Rajab, 256

" (19th June, A. D. 870), and al-Motamid ala Allah was solemnly acknowledged
" as khalif. During the khalifate of al-Muhtadi, Yakûb as-Saffâr did nothing
" of importance; he merely continued making predatory incursions, warring
" against the neighbouring princes who reigned in Sijistân and its dependancies,
" and making irruptions into the districts of Khorâsân, those of Kûbistân which
" were in that vicinity and those dependancies of Herât and Bûshanj which
" were contiguous to Sijistân. He then returned to Fars and, having gathered
" in its crops, he returned to Sijistân with about thirty millions of dirhems
" (£ 750,000). Muhammad Ibn Wâsil was left by him in Fars to direct the mili-
" tary operations in that country, collect the taxes, correspond with the khalif
" and transmit to him part of the money which he gathered in. The kharâj
" (or land-tax) of Fars, which he was to send to his master every year was fixed at
" five millions of dirhems (£ 125,000). That country he [Yakûb] held by right
" of conquest, and the khalif would not have confirmed him in its possession had
" he found amongst his dependants any one capable of taking his place. In the
" month of the latter Jumâda, 259 (April-May, A. D. 873), news was received (at
" Baghdad) of Yakûb's entry into Balkh. From that city he proceeded to Naisâpûr,
" where he arrived in the month of Zû 'l-Kaada, 259 (Aug.-Sept. A. D. 873), and
" made prisoners Muhammad Ibn Tâhir al-Khuzâi, the emir of Khorâsân and a
" number of Taherides. In the month of Muharram, 260 (Oct.-Nov. A. D. 873),
" he left that country, taking with him as prisoners Muhammad Ibn Tâhir and
" upwards of sixty persons attached to that family. He then marched towards
" Jurjân, with the intention of encountering the Alide prince, al-Hasan Ibn Zaid,
" who was the emir of that country and of Tabaristân. Al-Hasan, being informed
" that Yakûb was coming to attack him, raised thirteen millions of dirhems
" (£ 325,000) out of the land-tax (kharâj), by calling in the arrears and exacting
" advances on the imposts of the following year, after which, he retired from
" Jurjân to Tabaristân. Yakûb entered into Jurjân and dispatched some of his
" partisans against Sâriya, (the capital) of Tabaristân, which place they took. In
" Jurjân the daily rations of his cavalry amounted to one thousand bushels (kafîz)
" of barley. He then set out for Tabaristân, and al-Hasan Ibn Zaid marched
" against him with a large body of troops. Yakûb, having declared to his parti-
" sans that he would put to death whoever fled from the enemy, set out to fight,
" accompanied with five hundred of his slaves, and, having encountered the troops

" of al-Hasan, he charged them with such vigour that he put them to rout. Al-
" Hasan Ibn Zaid, who was a heavy, corpulent man, had already provided for his
" safety by causing horses and mules to be kept in readiness at each village on the
" road by which he intended to retreat. Yakùb, having rallied his partisans, set
" out at the head of five hundred horse (djarida) in pursuit of al-Hasan who,
" however, effected his escape. The treasures which the latter had with him and
" which consisted of three hundred (horse-) loads of wealth, most of it coined
" money, fell into the hands of Yakùb and, besides that, a number of persons des-
" cended from Ali Ibn Abi Tàlib. These he treated with great cruelty and cast
" into prison. This encounter took place on Monday, the 26 thof Rajab, 200 (17th
" May, A. D. 874). After this victory, Yakùb pushed forward and entered Aamul,"
— the capital of Tabaristàn. — " Al-Hasan Ibn Zaid fled to a city called Sàlùs,
" but, not obtaining from the inhabitants as favorable a reception as he had been
" led to expect, he departed and left them. Yakùb set out from Aamul in pursuit
" of al-Hasan and had already made one day's march when he received intelli-
" gence of the occupation of Marw ar-Rùd by al-Hussin Ibn Tàhir Ibn Abd Allah
" Ibn Tàhir, aided by the lord of Khuwàrezm at the head of two thousand Turks.
" This obliged him to give up his project and cease advancing into the heart of the
" country. He, in consequence, abandoned the pursuit of al-Hasan Ibn Zaid
" and retraced his steps. In the month of Zù 'l-Hijja, 260 (Sept.-Oct. A. D.
" 874), he wrote to the emir of Rai the order to leave that place, stating that
" he himself had been appointed governor of it by the khalif. When the khalif
" was informed of this, he declared Yakùb's assertion to be false and chastised
" such of the dependants of that chief as were in Baghdad, by casting them into
" prison and seizing on their money. In the month of Muharram, 261 (Oct.-
" Nov. A. D. 874), Yakùb, who was in Tabaristàn, set out for Jurjàn and had an
" encounter with al-Hasan Ibn Zaid, whom he met near the (Caspian) sea and
" who had with him a body of troops from Dailam, al-Jibàl and Tabaristàn.
" Al-Hasan dispersed Yakùb's partisans, killed all those whom he was able to over-
" take and obliged their chief to take refuge in Jurjàn. A terrible earthquake then
" occurred by which two thousand of Yakùb's men lost their lives. Al-Hasan Ibn
" Zaid retook Tabaristàn, that is, Aamul, Sàriya and their dependancies. Yakùb
" remained in Jurjàn where he oppressed the people by levying heavy taxes (khardj)
" and seizing on their wealth. The earthquake lasted three (days), and a number

" of the inhabitants of Jurjân retired to Baghdad. These refugees being asked
" what Yakûb as-Saffâr was doing, spoke so loudly of his tyranny and oppression that
" the khalif resolved on marching against him, and made preparations accordingly.
" As-Saffâr (Yakûb) had returned to the neighbourhood of Rai, and the pilgrims
" were come back from the fair (of Mekka) when the khalif al-Motamid ala
" Allah wrote to Obaid Allah, the son of Abd Allah Ibn Tâhir Ibn al-Hosain, who
" was then governor of Irâk, ordering him to assemble the pilgrims of Khorâsân,
" Tabaristân, Jurjân and Rai, and to read to them a letter which he sent to
" him. Obaid Allah assembled those pilgrims who had come from the farthest
" parts of the empire, and read to them a letter by which the Commander
" of the faithful ordered the people to war against as-Saffâr. Thirty copies of
" this document were drawn up, one of which was given to the people of
" each province, so that the news might be spread throughout all the country.
" When Yakûb as-Saffâr was informed of the imprisonment of his servants and
" learned that Obaid Allah had assembled the pilgrims at his palace and delivered
" to them copies of this letter, he perceived evidently that the khalif intended to
" march against him and, judging that his troops were not sufficiently numerous
" to resist those of his adversary, he returned to Naisâpûr. On his arrival in that
" city, he extorted money from the inhabitants and, in the month of the first
" Jumâda, 261 (Feb. — March, A. D. 875), he set out for Sijistân. When he arri-
" ved there, letters came from the khalif by which all the princes of Khorâsân and
" all the men possessed of means and influence were declared, each of them, go-
" vernor of the place in which he resided. When these letters arrived, as-Saffâr's
" partisans were scattered (in detachments) throughout the province of Khorâsân.
" As-Saffâr then went to Askar Mukram, in Khûzistân, and (having collected his
" troops, he) wrote to the khalif a letter in which he demanded the governments of
" Khorâsân, Fars and all the provinces which had been possessed by the family of
" Tâhir Ibn al-Hosain el-Khozâi. He asked also for the commandment of the
" shurta of Baghdad and that of Sarra-man-râa, and required his nomination to
" the governments of Tabaristân, Jurjân, Rai, Kermân, Adarbaijân, Kazwîn, Sijistân
" and Sind. He demanded also that those to whom had been read the letter copies
" of which had been made at the palace of Obaid Allah Ibn Abd Allah Ibn Tâhir should
" be assembled and another letter read them, annulling the former. All this was
" done by al-Muwaffak Billah Abû Ahmad Talha, the son of al-Mutawakkil ala

" Allah and the brother of the khalif al-Motamid ala Allah.   This al-Muwaffak was
" also the father of al-Motadid Billah, the khalif who succeeded to al-Motamid. The
" entire direction of public affairs was in the hands of al-Muwaffak, who left nothing
" of the khalifian authority to his brother except the mere title.   He (al-Muwaffak)
" granted to him (Yakûb) what he demanded, and, having assembled the people,
" he read to them a dispatch by which he complied with as-Saffâr's request and
" nominated him to the offices for which he asked.   This answer, rendered in the
" khalif's name, to what was exacted by as-Saffâr, caused great perturbation among
" the Mawlas (10) (in garrison) at Sarra-man-râa and threw them into a ferment. As-
" Saffâr cared so little for what was granted to him that he entered into Sûs, a city
" forming one of the districts of Khusistân and situated near Askar Mukram.   On
" arriving there, he took the resolution of attacking the khalif al-Motamid
" who, on his side, made preparations for embarking (with his troops) on
" the Tigris and going down to give him battle.   When the two armies
" advanced against each other, the Mawlas, struck by the conduct of al-Muwaf-
" fak, thought that as-Saffâr's approach was the result of the letters which
" he had sent him : ' If it be not so,' said they, ' it is most extraordinary that
" ' a rebel should set out from Zaranj,' — the capital of Sijistân, which country
" separates Sind from that of the Turks and Khorâsân, — ' should come into
" ' Irâk with an army well-equipped, for the purpose of waging war against
" ' the khalif whose empire, of old, extended from the eastern to the west-
" ' ern extremities of the earth.   As-Saffâr alone advances with his army, ha-
" ' ving no other chief to support him or to share with him in this enterprise. '
" The khalif, being informed of what passed, called for the mantle and the rod
" (or sceptre) which had belonged to the Prophet, took his bow with the intention
" of being the first who shot an arrow (against the enemy), and pronounced a male-
" diction on as-Saffâr.   By this, he quieted the minds of the Mawlas.   On Sunday
" morning, the 9th of Rajab A. H. 262 (8th April, A. D. 876), as-Saffâr's troops arrived,
" in order of battle, at a village called Istarband and situated between as-Sib and Dair
" al-Askûl, in the province of central Nahrawân.   He then assembled his compa-
" nions, with the intention of leading them to the charge as he used to do, and
" proceeded forward, wearing a tunic of black brocade.   When the two armies
" were in presence, the kâid Khishûj, who was one of the Mawlas, advanced be-
" tween the two armies, and harangued as-Saffâr's troops in these terms : ' Men

" for bravery and intrepidity, stood beside the khalif. The archers advanced before
" him, shooting off their arrows, and his brother al-Muwaffak, having uncovered
" his head, cried out : ' I am the boy of the Hashemides!' and charged upon the
" partizans of as-Saffâr. Numbers were slain on both sides. As-Saffâr, seeing
" how matters were turning, retreated from the field, leaving there his treasures,
" wealth and riches, and fled strait before him, without being accompanied by any
" of his followers. Not a man of his army but received an arrow-wound,
" and such was the disorder and press that, when the night overtook them, they
" fell into the canals and were covered with wounds. Abû 's-Sâj Dîvdâd (11) Ibn
" Dost, the same whose name was borne by the Sâjite jund at Baghdad, said to as-
" Saffâr subsequently to his flight : ' You did not show the least skill in war; how
" ' could you expect to vanquish an adversary after placing in your front the bag-
" ' gage, the treasure and the prisoners and invading a country with which you
" ' were ill-acquainted ? You had not even a guide to show you the way through
" ' the marshes and canals. You fought on a Sunday, and had the wind in your
" ' face; you took forty days to march from as-Sûs to Wâsit with an army badly
" ' provided for, and, when they received provisions and money and were brought
" ' into good order, you marched them from Wâsit to Dair al-Aâkûl in two days,
" ' and then retreated at the moment you had an opportunity of obtaining the
" ' victory. You fled when you should have kept your ground.' To this as-Saffâr
" replied : ' I did not think that I should have been obliged to fight; I had no
" ' doubt of obtaining what I wanted, and imagined that envoys would come to me
" ' in order to avert the danger (which threatened the khalif) and that I then might
" ' have obtained whatever I pleased!'" — End of the extract from Ibn al-Azhar's
recital. What follows I have taken from the work composed by Abû 'l-Hussain
Obaid Allah as a continuation of his father Ahmad Ibn Tâhir's (vol. I. p. 291) history of Baghdad. As the accounts given by that writer are very prolix, we
abridge them and suppress the repetitions : " Yakûb Ibn al-Laith," says he,
" having attacked Dirhem Ibn an Nadr,"—so the last name is written (instead of al-
" Hussain). — took Sijistân from him on Saturday, the 5th of Muharram, 247 (21st
" March, A. D. 861). Dirham had governed three years, after having expelled
" from that country, in the month of Zû 'l-Hijja, 237 (May-June, A. D. 852) (12),
" Sâlih Ibn an-Nadr, an Arab of the tribe of Kinâna. Yakûb remained in Sijistân,
" where he continued to wage war against the Shurât and the Turks, in the osten-

" sible character of a volunteer in God's holy cause.   He set out for Herât in the
." year 253 (A. D. 867) and then proceeded to Bushanj, which place he besieged and
" took by assault.   This happened in the khalifate of al-Motazz.   When al-Motazz
" died, no change had taken place in Yakûb's conduct, and things continued so
" till the reign of al-Motamid ala Allah.   He then entered into Balkh, whence he
" marched to Râmhormuz, making, all the time, an outward show of obedience to
" the khalif al-Motamid.   This was in the month of Muharram, 262 (Oct-Nov. A.
" D. 875).   He then dispatched envoys to Baghdad, where they made their entry
" on the 14th of the latter Jumâda of the same year (15th March, A. D. 876).   After
" that, he went to Wâsit where he installed a lieutenant.   On Saturday, the 8th of
" Rajab (7th April, A. D. 876), he proceeded to Dair al-Aakûl and from that to
" Istarband where he made a halt.   Al-Motamid, being informed of what was going
" on and learning that Yakûb was directing his march towards Baghdad, assembled
" troops from all quarters for the purpose of combating the invader, and, having
" left Sarra-man-râa, he entered Baghdad on Sunday, the 24th of Zû 'l-Hijja, of
" that year (18th September, A. D. 876).   Abû 'l-Faraj, who was secretary to the
" kâdi Abû Omar, related as follows: When the khalif set out to attack as-Saffâr, he
" continued, during his march, to dispatch letters by which that chief was ordered
" to retire, warned of the danger to which his conduct exposed him and informed
" that the Commander of the faithful was in march with troops, arms and ammu-
" nition, for the purpose of encountering him.   The answers returned by him
" were all of this cast : ' I know that the Commander of the faithful has set out,
" ' but it is with the intention of doing me honour and indicating the high esteem
" ' in which he holds me.'   The khalif then drew up his troops in order of battle at
" the village above-mentioned, and caused the road by which as-Saffâr has passed
" to be laid under water.   This was the main cause of his (as Saffâr's) defeat, for he
" was not aware that his retreat had been cut off.   The two armies then drew up
" for action and attacked each other in repeated charges till (that of) as-Saffâr was
" put to flight.   An immense quantity of baggage fell into the hands of the victors
" who, thinking that it had been left there as a snare to entrap them, did not pur-
" sue as-Saffâr, as they should have done.   A person who had been present at this
" battle informed me that the number of arrows shot off in it by the regiment of
" Mawlas amounted to twenty thousand.   The khalif returned full of joy at the
" victory which God had granted him.   Amongst the persons who, on that day,

" were delivered from the captivity in which as-Saffâr held them was Abû Abd Allah
" Muhammad Ibn Tâhir, the emir of Khorâsân. The khalif before whom he appeared
" with his chains still on, caused them to be struck off and clothed him in an im-
" perial robe. Al-Motamid related that, on the night before, he had a dream in
" which he saw a man come and inscribe on his bosom these words (of the Korân):
" *We have granted to you a signal victory.* He related this to his intimates
" and said : ' I reckon with confidence on the aid of the Almighty.' Previously to
" the battle, letters were received from as-Saffâr in which he gave the assurance of
" his profound submission and declared that he was merely coming to offer his
" humble respects to the Commander of the faithful, in whose presence he wished
" to have the honour of appearing and whose aspect he longed to contemplate. To
" this he added that he was ready to die at the side of the imperial stirrup. Al-
" Motamid said, on receiving this communication : ' We are still in the midst
" ' of his stratagems; let him know that I have nothing for him but the sword.'
" He gave orders also that a letter should be sent to Abû Ahmad Obaid Allah, the
" son of Abd Allah Ibn Tâhir and the uncle of Muhammad Ibn Tâhir Ibn Abd
" Allah Ibn Tâhir, informing him of the deliverance of his nephew. Abû Ahmad
" was then holding the commandment of the shurta of Baghdad in the capacity of
" lieutenant for his nephew; the latter being not only governor of Khorâsân but
" commander of the Baghdad shurta and that of Sarra-man-râa. " — As the paragraphs of this letter are very long, we shall give here a simple summary of its
contents : The writer enumerates the crimes of as-Saffâr, the favours and marks of
kindness which he had received from the khalif, who had invested him with the
government of Khorâsân and the countries of which mention has been already
made, who had raised him to a lofty station, who had ordered that, in the dispatches
addressed to him, he should be designated by a title of honour, who had conceded
to him a number of fine landed estates and who had done every thing possible in
order to gain his good-will. This, however, only served to increase his perversity
and disobedience : when things were refused to him which he demanded, he
would march against the seat of the empire, for the purpose of exciting troubles
and domineering (over the government). The Commander of the faithful, not thinking proper to comply with his demands, sent him letter after letter, enjoining him
to retire into the magnificent provinces of which he had been appointed governor,
and advising him not to attempt acts which would bring to an end all the blessings

conferred on him by almighty God. He was informed that if he persisted in the resolution of approaching the imperial residence, he would be guilty of an act of disobedience, of rebellion and of revolt. Another time, the Commander of the faithful sent a band of *kádis*, legists, and military chiefs to remonstrate with him on the same subject, thinking that this deputation would induce him to return to his duty. But he (as-*Saffár*) still persisted in following the same path, that of iniquity, contumacy and disobedience; he would not be turned from it by good advice, but allowed himself to be circumvented by Satan, who was leading him towards his ruin and making him swerve from the path of salvation towards the precipice of perdition. When the Commander of the faithful perceived that such was really the case, be thought fit to act towards him in the same (*hostile*) manner, and marched against him, putting his trust in God and convinced that, with the divine aid, he would turn from the execution of (*pernicious*) projects a reprobate who was advancing, by forced marches, towards the battle-field wherein he was destined to be vanquished. The rebel was already half-way between Baghdad and Wásit, bearing standards on some of which were crosses : he had called the poly-theists to his assistance against the true believers, and openly displayed the secret enmity which he bore in his heart towards God, so that the Lord might deliver him over by the bridle (*to the hands of perdition*). He abandoned the laws of Islamism and its maxims, broke every covenant, violated every engagement and let all men see that he was in open revolt. This obliged the Commander of the faithful to send forth his brother Abú Ahmad al-Muwaffak Billah, the acknowledged successor to the khalifate, and with him a body of those imperial *Mawlas* whose fidelity God had tested and whose views were fixed on the necessity of defending the empire. He accompanied them with his best wishes, praying God to assist them and render them victorious over the enemy. In all the times and all the conjunctures wherein God knew the sincerity of his heart, he pronounced maledictions against the rebel and abandoned him to the fatal consequences of his conduct. The Commander of the faithful continued to superintend the proceedings of his brother, of his *Mawlas* and of his partisans, and to send them reinforcements and supplies. Al-Muwaf-fak Billah took his station in the center of the army, whilst the accursed, the enemy of God, surrounded by those who partook his errors, had arrayed himself in the vest of disobedience and the trousers of iniquity, confiding in the number of his troops and the multitude of his followers. When the two armies were in presence, the enemy of the faith and his partisans brandished their arms and hastened to attack the *Mawlas* and the supporters of the Commander of the faithful; but, against that accursed and misguided man were directed the trenchant blades of the good cause, its piercing lances and its penetrating arrows. The wretch was covered with wounds, and his followers, seeing what had happened to him, hastened to cry out : "All is lost!" (*lit. woe and ruin!*) The Commander of the faithful's *Mawlas* and partisans followed in their pursuit, killing some and taking others prisoners, and God hurried to the fire (*of hell*) an immense number of the rebels. This continued till Abû Abd Allah Muhammad Ibn Tâhir, the servant of the Commander of the faithful, was delivered unharmed from the hands of the enemy, who had been driven from all his positions. The survivors took to flight in great disorder, without once looking behind them. God allowed them and the accursed to escape, but all their gains and plunder, gathered up in former days when God permitted them to hold the regions of the earth (*were taken from them*); treasures, goods, effects, camels, beasts of burden, mules and asses became the prey of the *Mawlas* and the other partisans of the khalif. Those objects the (*victors*) removed to the place where they had deposited their baggage. — As this letter is very diffuse, we have been obliged to abridge it. At the end of it were these words : " Written by "Obaid Allah Ibn Yahya, on Wednesday, the 12th of Rajab, 262 (11th April, A. " D. 876)." The historian then adds : " As Saffâr fled to Wâsit, and his troops " pillaged all the villages on the line of their retreat. The victorious army seized " on the arms and baggage of the vanquished, but the *Mawlas* did not con- " tinue the pursuit, fearing that as-Saffâr might turn and attack them; they were, "besides, too much occupied in collecting the booty and the spoil. The khalif " returned to his camp, and as-Saffâr went back to as-Sûs, where he levied contri- " butions. From that he proceeded to Tustur, which place he besieged and took. " Having installed there one of his lieutenants, he assembled again a multitude of " troops and set out for Fars, in the month of Shauwâl (July). The khalif returned " to al-Madâin, where he stopped two days, and then departed for Baghdad, whence " he proceeded to Sarra-man-râa. He arrived there on Friday, the 13th of Shabân " (12th May, 876)." The historian then mentions that, on Tuesday, the 14th " of Shauwâl (11th of July), the khalif received the news of Yakûb Ibn al-Laith's death. The quantity of money found in his treasuries amounted to four millions of dinars (£. 2,000,000), in gold pieces, and fifty millions of dirhems (£. 1,250,000)

in silver. On Thursday, the 22nd of Shauwâl, Ahmad Ibn al-Asbagh arrived there. He had been sent by the khalif for the purpose of arranging matters with Yakûb and was just reaching Wâsit, on his return, when he learned the news of that chief's death. Yakûb had been acknowledged by the khalif as governor of Khorâsân, Fars, Kermân, Rai, Kumm and Ispahân; he was commander of the two shurtas, that of Baghdad and that of Sarra-man-râa, and was authorised to place these troops under the orders of whom he pleased. In return, he engaged to pay in two thirds of the taxes furnished by all the provinces which he governed. His brother Amr Ibn al-Laith succeeded to his authority by the unanimous consent of the army, and then wrote to the khalif's brother, al-Muwaffak, a letter in which he declared himself the humble and obedient servant of the khalifate, provided that he was confirmed in the possession of the offices held by his brother. To this a favorable answer was returned and his nomination took place in the month of Zû 'l-Kaada of that year (July-August, A. D. 876). To judge from the context of this history, Yakûb Ibn al-Laith as-Saffâr died in the latter part of the year 262, for the author says, in relating the events of that year : " Shortly af-
" ter Yakûb's defeat in the month of Shauwâl, news was received of his death. "
This appears to denote that he died in that year, but what I have learned from a number of historical works does not agree with that indication : Abû 'l-Husain as-Salâmi says, in his account of the governors of Khorâsân, towards the beginning of the chapter which he devoted to Amr Ibn al-Laith : " The cause of Yakûb Ibn
" al-Laith's death was this : he had an attack of colic and was advised to follow a
" treatment; but he refused and preferred dying. His death took place at Jundi
" Sâpûr, in Khuzistân, on Tuesday, the 14th of Shauwâl, 265 (9th June, A. D.
" 879). Abû 'l-Wafâ al-Fârisi relates that he read on the flag of marble which
" is placed over the tomb of Yakûb Ibn al-Laith :

" I ruled over Khorâsân and the regions of Fars; neither did I despair of ruling over Irâk.
" But now, farewell to the world and to the sweetness of its zephyrs! Yakûb no longer sits
" therein. " •

In some rough notes written by myself I found the following passage : " Yakûb
" Ibn al-Laith as-Saffâr died in the year 265 (A. D. 878-9) at al-Ahwâz. His bier
" was carried to Jundi Sâpûr and there he was interred. On his tomb were in-
" scribed these words :

" This is the tomb of poor Yakûb.

" You confided in Fortune because she favoured you, and you feared not the evils which
" destiny might bring on. Fortune befriended you and you were deceived by her; days of
" prosperity are followed by days of trouble. "

I then found in another note written by myself that he died at Jundi Sâpûr and
was interred in the hippodrome of that city. He was then on his way to Irâk. The
date of his death as before. " He died of a cholic; the doctor told him that there
" was no remedy for, it but an injection; this he refused to take and preferred
" dying. His malady, which was a cholic accompanied with hiccough, lasted six-
" teen days. He reigned over Sijistân and the provinces in that quarter during
" fourteen years and some months." Our shaikh Ibn al-Athîr (vol. II. p. 288)
says, in his Annals, under the year 265 : " Yakûb Ibn al-Laith died on the 19th
" of Shauwâl of this year (11th June, A. D. 879)." He mentions also the cholic
and Yakûb's refusing to take an injection, and then adds that he died at Jundi Sâpûr, which is a district in the province of al-Ahwâz. I may observe that Jundi
Sâpûr is a district of Khuzistân, lying between Irâk and the province of Fars. He
says also: " The khalif al-Motamid, being desirous of conciliating his good-will, sent
" him an agent with a letter by which he nominated him governor of Fars. When
" this envoy arrived, Yakûb, though unwell, held a sitting to receive him. At his
" side he had a sword, a small loaf made of unbolted flour and some onions. The
" ambassador being introduced, delivered his message and Yakûb answered him in
" these terms : ' Tell the khalif that I am sick and that, if I die, he and I will be
" ' delivered from the uneasiness which each of us gives to the other; but, if I recover
" ' my health, nothing shall settle matters between us except this sword. If he must try
" ' for vengeance, if he succeed in ruining my power and reducing me to poverty, I
" ' shall return, as before, to bread and onions such as these.' The messenger depart-
" ed and Yakûb died shortly after."—Ibn Haukal (13) says, in his work entitled al-
Masâlik wa'l-Mamâlik (routes and realms) : Jundi Sâpûr is a fortified city abounding
" in all the necessaries of life. Its date-tree plantations and tilled grounds are very
" extensive. Yakûb Ibn al-Laith chose it for his residence on account of its ample
" resources and the constant abundance of its supplies." — Yakûb was so steadfast in
purpose that the Alide prince, al-Hasan Ibn Zaid, designated him by the nickname of
as-Sindân (the anvil). He was seldom seen to smile and was noted for intelligence and
resolution. One of his sayings was : " If you keep company with a man during forty

" days without discovering his true character, you will not discover it in forty
" years." — Amr (Yakûb's brother), having obtained the supreme authority, governed his subjects with such ability that people said : " Since a very long time,
" no person attained to the height reached by Amr Ibn al-Laith in the art of admi-
" nistrating an army and practising the rules by which an empire should be go-
" verned." As-Salâmi, in his History of Khorâsân, speaks very often of his great
abilities and his skill in applying the maxims of good government, but I omit these
observations lest I should be led too far. He payed his troops every three months
and then never omitted to be present. When he passed them in review, he took
his seat and had the money placed before him in the presence of all the army. A
crier then called out the name of Amr Ibn al-Laith, who immediately sent forward
his horse fully equipped, and presented him for inspection. The agent examined
the animal and ordered the owner a donative of three hundred dirhems (£. 7,10s.),
measured by weight. This sum was carried to him in purse which he took and
kissed, saying : " Praise be to God who hath held me in obedience to the Commander
" of the faithful so that I deserved this gratification ! " He then placed it in one of
his boots and left it to the servant who pulled them off. All those who received a
fixed pay were then called forward, according to their rank, and they appeared before the inspector fully equipped and having with them their vigorous steeds. They
were then examined in order to obtain the certitude of their having about them every
object, large or small, which is requisite for a horseman or a foot-soldier; and, if
even one of those things was missing, the delinquent was deprived of his pay. One
day, at a review, Amr saw a horseman pass before him with a very lean steed, and
said to him : " Fellow! how dare you take our money and spend it all upon your
" wife? You fatten her up and allow the horse to grow lean on which you go to
" war and which gains for you your pay? Go off! I have nothing for you." The
trooper replied : " My life for yours! were you to pass my wife in review, you would
" find that my horse is fatter than she is." Amr laughed at this, and told the
man to take his pay and get another horse. — The Kâdi Kamâl ad-Din, better
known by the surname of Ibn al-Adîm of Aleppo (14), relates, in his history of that
city, an anecdote which deserves to be inserted here on account of its similarity
to the preceding : Kisra Anûshrewân, the son of Kobâd (and king of Persia) confided
the administration of the army to an eminent kâtib (or civil officer), highly distinguished for intelligence and talent, and whose name was Bâbek Ibn Nahrawân.

This officer then said to Kisra : " O king! you have charged me with a duty which,
" to be well executed, requires that you support patiently such severity as I may use
" towards you. I have to pass your men in review every four months; I must see
" that those of each class be provided with the arms required by their rank, and exa-
" mine the conduct of the instructors who teach the soldiers horsemanship and ar-
" chery, so that I may retribute them well if they do their duty and punish them if
" they neglect it. By that means, my administration will hold the course which it
" ought to follow." Kisra replied : " He whose request is now granted cannot be
" more happy than the granter; they both partake of the advantages (procured by
" that arrangement); the granter will still continue to enjoy repose, and therefore
" gives his assent to what you ask." A platform was then built by his order at the
place where the reviews were to take place, and over it were spread magnificent
carpets. The inspector took his seat upon it and a cryer summoned all the soldiers
to present themselves. When they were assembled, the inspector dismissed them
because he did not see Kisra among them. The next day, he acted in the same
manner, on account of Kisra's absence and, on the third day, he had a proclamation
made to this effect : " Let not a single soldier remain absent from the review, even
" were he one of those who are honoured with the diadem and the throne. It is a
" review in which no indulgence or respect of persons will be shown." Kisra,
being informed of this, put on his armour, got on horseback and passed before
Bâbek. Every horseman was obliged to exhibit a tijfâf (horse-armour), a coat of
mail, a breastplate, a helmet with its neck-piece in chain mail, two armlets, two
cuishes, a spear, a buckler, a mace stuck in the belt, a tabarzîn (battle-axe), a
mace, a case containing two bows with their strings, thirty arrows, and two bow-
strings rolled up and suspended behind the helmet. Kisra appeared completely
armed before the inspector who, missing the bow-strings which ought to have been
behind the helmet, did not inscribe his approval after the sovereign's name. Kisra
then recollected the bow-strings, attached them to his helmet and passed again before Bâbek, who then gave his approval and said : " For the chief of the men in
" armour, four thousand dirhems (£ 100) and one dirhem." The highest pay
was four thousand, but he gratified Kisra with one dirhem more. On rising from
his seat, he went in to the sovereign and said : " O king! blame me not for my se-
" verity; I only wished to introduce the custom of proceeding with justice and equity,
" and to eradicate the habit of showing respect to certain persons." Kisra replied :

" The man is not severe for us who acts with the intention of correcting our faults
" or of rendering a service to the government. Why should we not submit to
" his rigour as the sick man submits to take a nauseous medicine in the hope of its
" doing him good." — Let us resume our account of Amr Ibn al-Laith. As-Salámi says : " Ráfi Ibn Harthama was a follower of Abû Thaur, who was one of Mu-
" hammad Ibn Táhir's generals. When Yakûb as-Saffâr arrived at Naisâpûr, Abû
" Thaur was one of those chiefs who sided with him against Muhammad Ibn Táhir.
" Yakûb then returned to Sijistân, and Abû Thaur went with him, accompanied by
" Ráfi Ibn Harthama. The latter was an ugly man with a long beard and a stern,
" gloomy aspect. He went, one day, to see Yakûb who, when he had retired, said :
" ' I feel no inclination for that man ; let him leave us and go where he will ! ' Ráfi
" then sold all his effects and returned to his residence at Bâmîn, which is a village
" in the district of Kanj-Rustâk. There he remained till Ahmad Ibn Abd Allah al-
" Khojistâni sent for him." — Khojistân is a village in the mountains of Herât and
situated in the district of Bâdghis. — " Al-Khojistâni was one of Yakûb's followers,
" but, having repudiated his authority, he effected the conquest of Naisâpûr and
" Bistâm in the year 261 (A. D. 874-5). He affected to be inclined towards the
" Tâhirite party, in order to gain the good-will of the inhabitants of Naisâpûr, and
" went so far as to sign his letters with the words : Ahmad Ibn Abd Allah the Táhi-
" rite. He then wrote to Ráfi Ibn Harthama, who was still in his native place, in-
" viting him to come and join him. Ráfi complied and received from him the
" command of the troops." — The wars and battles in which al-Khojistâni was engaged are very famous, but it does not suit our purpose to speak of them here. —
" Some time after, two his (al-Khojistâi's) pages conspired against his life and
" murdered him whilst he was asleep and drunk. This happened on the eve of
" Wednesday, the 23rd of Shauwâl, 268 (16th May, A. D. 882). Ráfi, who was
" then absent, went to join al-Khojistâni's troops and was acknowledged by them
" as their chief. They took the oath of allegiance to him in the city of Herât, or
" of Naisâpûr, by another account. In the year 271 (A. D. 884-5), al-Muwaffak
" Billah deprived Amr Ibn al-Laith as-Saffâr of the government of Khorâsân and
" gave it to Abû Abd Allah Mohammed Ibn Táhir. The latter, who was then residing
" in Baghdad, appointed Ráfi Ibn Harthama to act as his lieutenant in that country,
" and Nasr Ibn Ahmad Ibn Asad as-Sâmâni was established by al-Muwaffak as Mo-
" hammed Ibn Táhir's lieutenant in the provinces of Transoxiana. Some time af-

" ter, Râfî received dispatches from al-Muwaffak by which he was ordered to make
" an expedition against Jurjân and Tabaristân, both of which had belonged to al-
" Hasan Ibn Zaid, the Alide, and had fallen, on the death of that prince, A. H. 270
" (A. D. 883-4), into the hands of his brother, Muhammad Ibn Zaid. In the
" year 274, Râfî marched against the latter and, finding that he had abandoned
" these places and taken refuge in Astarâbâd, he blockaded him in that city during
" two years. Muhammad then left it by night with a few partisans and fled to Dai-
" lem. In the year 277 (A. D. 890-1), Râfî was master of Tabaristân. In the
" month of Rajab, 279 (Sept. — Oct. A. D. 892), the khalif al-Motamid ala Allah
" died and the supreme authority passed into the hands of Abù 'l-Abbâs al-Motadid
" ala Allah, the son of al-Muwaffak (who had died two years before). On the death
" of Nasr Ibn Ahmad the Sâmânide, his brother, Abù Ibrahim Ismail was appoint-
" ed governor of Transoxiana by al-Motamid." — I may here observe that Nasr
died at Samarkand on the 23rd of the latter Jumâda, 279 (20th Sept. A. D.
892). — The historian continues : " He (al-Motadid) took from the above-men-
" tioned Nasr Ibn Ahmad the government of Khorâsân and gave it to Amr Ibn al-
" Laith. Râfî continued to reside at Rai and, having entered into friendly relations
" with the princes of the neighbouring countries, he gained their assistance
" against Amr Ibn al-Laith. He then marched towards Naisâpûr and, in the
" month of the latter Râbi, A. H. 283, (May-June, A. D. 896), he had an engage-
" ment with Amr and was defeated. Being closely pursued by the victor, who fol-
" lowed him to Ablward, he left that city with the intention of going either to Herât
" or to Marw. Amr having then learned that he was setting out for Sarakhs, resol-
" ved on taking the same direction and cutting off his adversary's retreat. Râfî,
" being informed of his design, departed from Ablward with a guide who led him
" across the mountains of Tûs and brought him to the gates of Naisâpûr. He entered
" into that city and Amr came back to besiege him. (A combat ensued in which) the
" partisans of Râfî were defeated, and that chief, accompanied by a small troop of
" adherents, all mounted on dromedaries, succeeded in reaching the province of Kho-
" wârezm with his baggage and his treasures. This took place on Saturday, the
" 25th of Ramadân, 283 (5th Nov. A. D. 896). The emir of Khowârezm dispatched
" an officer to render him every service and provide him with whatever he required
" till he reached (the capital of) the province; but that agent, finding Râfî accom-
" panied with a very feeble escort, took the opportunity and killed him. This oc-

" curred on Friday, the 7th of Shauwâl, 283 [17th Nov. A. D. 896]. He then cut
" off his head and sent it to Amr Ibn al-Laith, at Naisâpûr, by whom it was dispatch-
" ed to al-Motadid Billah. Râfi was not the son of Harthama (*as his surname
" seems to imply*); Harthama was his stepfather and, as his name was a usual one,
" Râfi adopted it as a surname. His real father bore the name of Tûmard."— Ibn
Jarîr at-Tabari says, in his Annals, under the year 283 : " On Friday, the 22nd of
" Zû 'l-Kaada [31st December, A. D. 896], letters were read from all the pulpits,
" announcing the death of Râfi Ibn Harthama, and, on Thursday, the 4th of Mu-
" harram, 284 [11th Feb. A. D. 897], a courier sent by Amr Ibn al-Laith as-Saffâr
" arrived at Baghdad with Râfi's head. Al-Motadid caused it to be set up in the
" eastern quarter of the city and, in the afternoon, it was removed to the western
" quarter, where it remained exposed till nightfall. It was then carried back by his
" order to the palace of the khalifs (*dâr as-saltân*)."— As-Salâmi says : " All Kho-
" râsân, up to the border of the Jaihûn, fell thus into the power of Amr Ibn al-
" Laith." — Al-Bohtori (vol. *III.* p. 657), the celebrated poet, composed an eulogium on Râfi Ibn Harthama, to whom he gives the surname of Abû Yûsuf. He sent
this poem to him from Irâk and received, in return, a gift of twenty thousand dirhems (£. 500). — As-Salâmi says : " When Amr Ibn al-Laith sent Râfi's head to
" al-Motadid, he demanded that the province of Transoxiana should be conceded to
" him on the same conditions by which Abd Allah Ibn Tâhir held his command-
" ments, and he received a promise to that effect. Some time after, whilst he was
" in Naisâpûr, a magnificent present was sent to him by al-Motadid, but this he re-
" fused to accept unless the promise already made was executed. The messenger
" who brought those gifts wrote back to al-Muktafi Billah, the son of al-Motadid,
" informing him of Amr's declaration. That prince was then at Rai with a num-
" ber of his father's officers, and it was decided by them that the diploma of Amr's
" nomination should be made out. This document was brought to him with the
" presents which he had refused to accept and among which were seven robes of
" honour. When all was placed before him, the envoy clothed him in the seven
" robes, one after the other, and, as each was put on, (*Amr*)prostrated himself and
" made a prayer of two *rukas*. The diploma being then presented to him, he asked
" what it meant, and the envoy informed him that it was the thing he asked for.
" To this Amr replied : 'Of what use will it be to me? Ismail Ibn Ahmad will not
" ' deliver up that province unless (*I enforce my demand*) by one hundred thousand

" ' swords.' To this the envoy answered : ' It was yourself who asked for it ; so,
" ' get ready to take possession of the province and govern in his place.' Amr
" then received the diploma, kissed it and laid it down before him ; after which,
" he sent to the envoy and his suite a gift of seven hundred thousand dirhems
" (£. 17,500) and dismissed them. He then equipped an army for the purpose of
" attacking Ismail Ibn Ahmad ; who, on learning this, crossed the Jaihûn, to meet
" them, cut to pieces a part of them and put the rest to flight. Amr Ibn al-Laith was
" then in Naisâpûr. This engagement took place on Monday, the 17th of Shauwâl,
" 286 (26th Oct. A. D. 899). Ismail returned to Bokhara, a city forming one of
" the districts of Transoxiana." — " Amr Ibn al-Laith, " says as-Salâmi, " had
" charged Muhammed Ibn Bishr (15) to lead this army against Ismail.   When the
" latter crossed the Jaihûn, Mûsa as-Sijazi (16) went into the place where Ibn Bishr
" was and, finding that he was getting his head shaved, he said to him : ' Did you
" ' obtain leave from Ismail to have your head shaved ?' giving him thus to un-
" derstand that by attempting to contend with Ismail, he had already rendered that
" chief the master of his head.   To this Mohammed Ibn Bishr replied : ' Begone
" ' out of my sight, and may the curse of God light upon you !' The next morning,
" Mohammad's troops were put to rout and he himself was taken prisoner and had
" his head cut off.   Ismail, to whom this and the other heads were brought, char-
" ged some of Muhammad's partisans to examine them and point out the head of
" their chief. One of these persons then related to Ismail what Mûsa as-Sijazi had
" said, and this ill-omened prognostic caused him great surprise." — In at-Taba-
" ri's Annals, under the year 287, is a passage to this effect : " On Wednesday,
" the 25th of the first Jumâda (28th May, A. D. 900), the sultan (17) received, it is
" said, a letter announcing that a battle had taken place between Ismail Ibn Ahmad
" and Amr Ibn al-Laith, that the army of the latter had been completely routed and
" that he himself had been taken prisoner. Here is an account of what passed be-
" tween them: The sultan, being asked by Amr for the government of Transoxiana,
" granted his request and sent to Naisâpûr, where he (Amr) was residing, the robe
" of investiture and the standard under which he was to hold that province and
" carry on the war against Ismail Ibn Ahmad. On this, Ismail wrote to him (Amr)
" in these terms : ' You have obtained the government of a vast country and I pos-
" ' sess Transoxiana; be satisfied with what you have and let me remain in this
" ' frontier province.' Amr refused to accept his proposal and, being spoken to, rea-

" pecting the river of Balkh (*the Oxus*) and the difficulty of crossing it, he answer-
" ed : ' Were I inclined to make a dike across it with bags of money and pass
" over on that, I could do so.' Ismail, having given up the hope of turning Amr
" from his project, assembled all the dihkáns (*landed proprietors*) who were under
" his authority and crossed over to the western side of the river, whilst Amr Ibn al-
" Laith posted himself in Balkh. He then occupied the neighbouring country, and
" Amr, perceiving that he was in some measure blockaded, regretted what he had
" done and, it is said, requested a suspension of arms. This, Ismail refused to
" grant, and, although no considerable combat took place between them, Amr
" found himself obliged to make a hasty retreat. On his way, he came up to a
" jungle and, being informed that a shorter road passed through it, he told the
" main body of his troops to follow the highway, and then engaged in the wood
" with a small escort. The animal which he rode got into some marshy ground and
" fell, leaving him without the means of escape, whilst his companions pushed for-
" ward without minding him. Some of Ismail's troops then came up and took him
" prisoner. When al-Motadid was informed of what had passed, he praised Ismail's
" conduct, blamed that of Amr and said : ' Let Abù Ibrahîm Ismail be invested by
" ' patent with all the authority which appertained to Amr!' The robes of investi-
" ture were then sent off to him." — At-Tabari says, under the year 288 : " On
" Thursday, the 1st of the first Jumáda (23rd April, A. D. 901), Amr Ibn al-Laith
" arrived in Baghdad. I have been told that Ismail Ibn Ahmad gave him the
" choice of remaining with him as a prisoner or of being sent to the Commander
" of the faithful, and that he was taken to the Commander of the faithful because he
" preferred it." —As-Salámi says, in his History of Khorásán : " Amr, having pro-
" ceeded to Balkh, had there an encounter with Ismail and was taken prisoner. This
" happened on Tuesday, the 15th of the first Rabi 287 (20th March, A. D. 900).
" Ismail had him put into irons and taken to Samarkand." — This city lies (in
" Transoxiana), on the other side of the river which is called the Jaihùn. —
" His (*Ismail's*) brother, Abù Yùsuf, being placed by him at the service of the priso-
" ner, remained with him till Abd Allah Ibn al-Fath arrived with Ismail's nomi-
" nation to the government of Khorásán, bringing with him the diploma, the stan-
" dard, the diadem and the robe of investiture. This was in the year 288. He
" was accompanied by Ashnás (18) who was charged to transport Amr Ibn al-Laith
" to Baghdad. The prisoner was given to him by Ismail and taken to that city."

— Ibn Abi Tâhir (vol. *I. p.* 291), the historian already cited, says : " Amr Ibn
" al-Laith as-Saffâr was defeated and a great number of his partisans were slain.
" The battle was fought at the gates of Balkh, on Wednesday, the 17th of the latter
" Rabî, 287 (21st April, A. D. 900). Previously to the encounter, his secretary,
" Ibn Abi Habla, passed over to Ismail, and was accompanied by one of the generals
" with a large body of troops. On the morning of the day on which the
" battle took place, Amr was informed of this desertion and, finding that most of
" his partisans had gone over to Ismail, he lost courage and took to flight. Ismail,
" whose attention was engaged by the state of his army, sent a detachment after
" Amr. They found him on horseback, but at a full stop (19), and took him priso-
" ner. Ismail, to whom they brought him, sent a dispatch to al-Motadid, inform-
" ing him of what had occurred and stating that Amr should be sent to Samarkand
" (*and be detained there*) till the Commander of the faithful's answer arrived. The
" khalif was highly pleased at this news and granted to Ismail, in addition to the
" government which he already held, all the provinces over which Amr had extend-
" ed his authority. Abd Allah Ibn al-Fath then set out for the purpose of
" receiving the prisoner. When he arrived, Ismail had Amr brought in and
" sent him off bound in chains. One of his soldiers was placed at the side of Amr,
" with a drawn sword in his hand, and to Amr was said : ' If the people attempt to
" deliver you, we shall throw to them your head.' Not a man stirred. They ar-
" rived at Nahrawân on Tuesday, the 26th of the second Rabî, 288 (19th April, A.
" D. 901) and there took off Amr's chains. On Thursday, the 1st of the first Ju-
" mâda (23rd April), the troops (*of the city*) rode forth to meet him. He arrived
" in a palanquin the curtains of which were let down (*so as to prevent him from
" being seen*). On arriving at (*the gate called*) Bâb as-Salâma, he was taken out of
" that conveyance, clothed in a brocade gown and placed, with the *bonnet of
" displeasure* (20) upon his head, on the back of a camel with two humps (a *drome-
" dary*), an animal which, when large and strong, is called a *fâlij*. This camel
" was one of the presents which had been formerly sent by him to the khalif; it was
" (*then*) covered with silk housings and adorned with tresses and harness, all
" inlaid with silver. They led him through Baghdad, down the high street, till they
" reached the *Kasr al-Hurna* (*the abode of bliss*), which was then the khalif's resi-
" dence. During that time, he held his hands up in prayer and uttered words of
" resignation and humility; but that was through craftiness, for the purpose of

" exciting commiseration. Effectively, the people abstained from reviling him.
" He was then taken before the khalif, who held a special sitting for the purpose
" of receiving him and had convoked to it a great number of persons. He stopped
" at the distance of about fifty cubits from the khalif, who merely said to him : 'This
" is what you have been working for, O Amr!' After that, he was led to a cell
" which had been prepared for him." — Yakûb as-Saffâr married an Arab woman
of Sijistân who, after his death, became the wife of his brother Amr. She died without children and had then in her possession one thousand seven hundred female
slaves. — A person of that time related as follows : " I was with the Traditionist Abû
" Ali al-Husain Ibn Muhammad Ibn Fahm (21), when a student in Traditions came
" in and said : Abû Alil I saw yesterday Amr as-Saffâr mounted on one of the
" dromedaries which he sent, three years ago, to the khalif as a present! On this,
" Abû Ali pronounced the following lines :

> " As a man of talent and of rank it is sufficient to indicate as-Saffâr. Morning and evening
> " he marches at the head of an army. He gave camels as presents, but knew not that he
> " should be mounted upon one and led as a prisoner. "

Ali Ibn Muhammad Ibn Nasr Ibn Bassâm, a poet of whom we have already
spoken (vol. II. p. 301), composed the following lines on the same subject :

> O thou who art deluded by thy worldly prosperity! didst thou see Amr? After possessing a
> kingdom and great power, he was forced to ride on a dromedary and to wear the bonnet of
> displeasure as a humiliation. With hands raised up, he prayed God aloud and in his heart,
> begging to be saved from death and allowed to work again in copper.

Al-Tabari says : " Al-Motadid Billah died on the eve of Monday, the 21st of
" the latter Rabî, 289 (5th April, A. D. 902). The khalifate devolved to his
" son, al-Muktafi Billah Abû Muhammad Ali, who was then absent, at ar-Rakka.
" After his return to Baghdad, he gave orders, on Tuesday, the 8th of the latter
" Jumâda (20th May), that the subterraneous cells which his father had caused to be
" made for the reception of criminals should be filled up. The next morning, Amr
" Ibn al-Laith as-Saffâr died and was buried in the neighbourhood of the Kasr al-
" Husna. When Motadid was lying speechless on his death-bed, he ordered by signs
" and indications that Amr should be executed. Those signs he made by placing his
" hand on his neck and then on his eye; they meant : 'Kill the one-eyed man ! 'Amr

" had lost an eye. Sâfi al-Harami to whom this order was given, did not fulfil it,
" being unwilling to take Amr's life because he knew that the khalif would soon
" breathe his last. It is related that al-Muktafi had no sooner arrived in Baghdad
" than he asked of (the vizir) al-Kâsim Ibn Obaid Allah (vol. II. p. 300) if Amr was
" still alive, and was highly pleased to learn that he was. 'I wish,' said he,
" 'to do him good.' During his residence at Rai, in the life-time of his father,
" he had received from Amr a great quantity of presents and numerous marks
" of good-will. It is said that al-Kâsim, disliking to be questioned about the
" prisoner, caused him to be murdered. Amr governed nearly twenty-two
" years." — Yakûb was called as-Saffâr because he had been a worker in sufr
(copper), that is to say, in nahâs (brass). At that time, his brother Amr kept
asses for hire. The syndic of the copper-smiths related as follows : " When
" Yakûb was a boy, in the shop, learning to work in copper, I often perceived
" between his eyes the sign of his future greatness." Being asked what he had
remarked, he said : "I used to look at him from a place in which he could
" not perceive me, and I always saw him with his eyes cast down, like a person full
" of thought and absorbed in his reflections. After that, he became what we have
" seen." The kâtib Ali Ibn al-Marzubân al-Ispahâni made the following relation : " I once asked a partisan of the Saffaride family what had been the trade
" of Amr Ibn al-Laith, the brother of Yakûb. Amr was then imprisoned in
" Madîna tas-Salâm (Baghdad). The man returned me no answer, but, on the
" death of Amr, he said to me : " It would not have been prudent in me, had I
" ' given you any information on that subject whilst Amr was still to be feared or
" ' to be hoped in. But now, I may tell you that he continued to hire out asses till
" ' his brother rose to power and got possession of Khorâsân. He then went to
" ' join him and gave up that trade!" — A number of historians relate, in their
works, that Abû Ahmad Obaid Allah Ibn Tâhir Ibn al-Husain al Khuzâi, the same
person of whom we have spoken (vol. II. p. 79), would sometimes say : " Three are
" the wonders of the world; first, that which happened to al-Abbâs Ibn Amr al-
" Ghanawi (vol. III. p. 417) and his army of ten thousand men : they were all put
" to death and he alone had his life spared; secondly, Amr Ibn al-Laith's army of fifty
" thousand men; all of them escaped and he alone was taken prisoner; thirdly, my
" being out of office and my son Abû 'l-Abbâs being employed to administer (the
" tolls received at) the two bridges of boats which are at Baghdad." The history of

al-Abbás Ibn Amr al-Ghanawí was this : When the Karmats became powerful, they invaded the neighbouring countries and indulged to the utmost in the shedding of blood.   In the year 287 (A. D. 900), al-Motadid Billah sent against them an army under the orders of al-Abbás al-Ghanawí.   A battle ensued in which Abú Saíd al-Kirmiti (vol. I. p. 427), the chief of the Karmats, took al-Abbás and all his army prisoners.   The next day, he had them all brought before him, put them to death and had their bodies burned.   Al-Abbás, whom he set at liberty, was the only one of the army who returned to al-Motadid.   This was towards the end of Shaabán (end of August), in that year.   The encounter took place between Basra and al-Bah-rain, and furnished matter to a long and well-known relation.   We present here a mere summary of it, because this is not a fit place for entering into particulars. If it please God, we shall give a full relation of it in our great historical work (22). — The first of the two verses which were said to have been inscribed on Yakúb's tomb and which we have already given, terminates with a hemistich borrowed from the piece of verse which was sung by Moawia Ibn Abi Sofyán the Omaiyide, when he had established his domination in Syria and received the visit of Jarír Ibn Abd Allah al-Bajali, who had been sent to him from Kúfa by Ali Ibn Abi Tálib. Moawia heard the message from Jarír and, when the sitting was over, had him lodged in a chamber near his own.   That night, he sung the following verses, so that Jarír might hear them and repeat them to Ali :

> Long and uneasy is my night, vague the suppositions which assail me, since the arrival of a visitor who came to me with vain and futile talk (*turrahát baidbís*).   Jarír has come, though events are crowding on, with proposals equivalent to the acquitting of our noses.   I bear with him, but the sword is still between me and him; for I am not a man to put on the raiment of ignominy.   Syria has offered me the same obedience which I already received from Yemen, and the chiefs of that country declare it loudly in their assemblies.   If they act (*as they promise*), I shall attack Ali with a band (*jabha*) which shall break down, to his harm, all the branches, green or withered (*which afford him shelter*).   I hope for the greatest advantage which any man ever obtained, neither do I despair of ruling over Irák.

— The word *turrahát* signifies *futilities*; in its primitive acceptation, it designates the paths which branch off a highway.   *Turraha*, its singular form, is a Persian word arabicised (*turréhé*).   Being subsequently employed to signify *futilities*, it gave rise to the expression *turrahát baidbís*. — The word *jabha* means a troop of men. The poet, in using it, gave to understand that he would attack Ali with a body

of horse and foot. The other words of the poem are so well known that they do not
require explanation. — I found the following indications in the handwriting of a
person who cultivated this branch of science (history) : When Amr Ibn al-Laith
was taken prisoner, his grandson, Tâhir Ibn Muhammad Ibn Amr obtained the
government of Fars. This took place on the 17th of Safar, 288 (10th February,
A. D. 901). In the year 290 (A. D. 902-3), he and his brother Yakûb Ibn Muhammad were arrested by Sebuk as-Sebukri, a chief who had been one of their grandfather's pages, and were sent by him to Madîna tas-Salâm (Baghdad). The authority then passed to al-Laith Ibn Ali Ibn al-Laith, a nephew of Yakûb and
Amr, who made the conquest of Sijistân, A. H. 296. A number of conflicts had
passed between Tâhir and Sebuk as-Sebukri, who finally obtained possession of
the country. Al-Muaddel (Ibn Ali) Ibn al-Laith, who governed Sijistân in the name
of his brother al-Laith (Ibn Ali), then invaded Fars, and Sebuk fled to the khalif for
assistance. In the month of Ramadân, 296 (May-June, A. D. 909), al-Muktadir Billah sent off troops, under the orders of Mûnis al-Muzaffar, Badr al-Kabîr and al-
Husain Ibn Hamdân. These generals encountered al-Laith Ibn Ali, routed his army
and took him prisoner with his brother Muhammad and his son Ismaîl. Mûnis returned to Baghdad with the prisoners and arrived there in the month of Muharram,
297 (Sept.-Oct. A. D. 909). Al-Laith Ibn Ali was paraded through the city on an elephant, and al-Muaddel Ibn Ali obtained the government of Sijistân. Ahmad Ibn
Ismaîl the Sâmânide then marched against him with a numerous army of horse and
foot, and deprived him of that province. After that, Sebuk as-Sebukri possessed it
for some time and was subsequently carried prisoner to Baghdad with Muhammad
Ibn Ali Ibn al-Laith. Thus ended the power of the Saffârides.

(1) [footnote text illegible]

(2) Nearly all the provinces of the Moslim empire were, at that time, in the power of chiefs who, though acknowledging the supremacy of the khalifs, were, in fact, independent sovereigns. Such were the Taherides in Khorasan and the Tulunides in Egypt, whilst the Alides of Taberistan, the Kharijites of Mosul and of the countries to the north of Persia rejected completely the authority of the khalifs. The south of Irâk was ravaged by the Zenj.

(3) The singular proceeding was perhaps conformable to the etiquette observed by all the khalif's ambassadors.

(4) Ali Ibn al-Hosein Ibn Koraish had been appointed governor of Fars by the khalif, but, though he acknowledged the authority of the court of Baghdad, he acted as an independent prince.

(5) The editions and the manuscripts read *Aycls* ايلس (instead of *Onâs* انّاس), but the orthography given by the geographical dictionary entitled the *Merâsid*, seems preferable.

(6) The word *abnâ* signifies *sons*. It was generally employed to designate persons one of whose parents was an Arab and the other of a foreign race. At the time of Muhammad and afterwards, there was in Yemen a great number of *abnâ* whose progenitors were Persians and whose mothers were Arabs.

(7) It is remarkable that in this ancient relation and in the account given by the historian at-Tabari, the khalif is designated, not by the title of *imâm*, but by that of *sultan*. This latter term generally serves to indicate sovereigns who possess, not the spiritual, but the civil authority.

(8) Tahir wished to propitiate the khalif by refusing to take the title of emir, till authorized to do so by the court of Baghdad.

(9) The *bedra* or *purse* contained one thousand dirhems (L. 2b), according to some, ten thousand, according to others.

(9 bis, p. 311) The word *ghilmân*, here rendered by *dependents*, means *boys*, *servants*, *pages*. Those whom Yakûb had in Baghdad were perhaps slaves or *mawlas* who traded there on his account.

(10) These *mawlas* were the Turkish slaves or mamlûks who formed the khalif's guard.

(11) The editions and manuscripts read *Abû 'r-Sâj Dêwdd*, but it is well ascertained that the name of this chief was *Dîwdâd* (God's gift). We have spoken of him in the first volume, p. 500. A history of the Sâjites has been published by M' Defrémery in the *Journal asiatique* for 1847. The Sâjite *junds* were probably regiments of cavalry which Abû 's-Sâj had formed and kept up at his own expense. Kamâl ad-Dîn Ibn al-Adîm takes notice occasionally of this chief in his history of Aleppo. See Freytag's *Selecta ex historia Halebi*.

(12) There is here some error in the dates.

(13) Abû 'l-Kâsim Mohammad Ibn Hawkal, a native of Baghdad and the author of a very remarkable geographical work, entitled *al-Mesâlik wa 'l-Memâlik*, put his last corrections to that treatise in the year 366, A. D. 976-7). He travelled over many countries and appears to have been a secret agent of the Fatimides. The date of his death is not known.

(14) Kamâl ad-Dîn Omar Ibn Ahmad, surnamed Ibn al-Adîm and chief kâdi of Aleppo, wrote a biographical dictionary in which he noticed all the remarkable men who had been in that city. Another great work of his, the History of Aleppo, has been analyzed by professor Freytag in the *Selecta ex historia Halebi*, which contains also a long extract from Kamâl ad-Dîn's treatise, with instructive notes. Kamâl ad-Dîn was born A. H. 388 (A. D. 1192), and died at Cairo, A. H. 660 (A. D. 1261-2). He had been driven from Aleppo by the invasion of the Tartars. For a full account of his life, see p. XXXVI of the introduction to Freytag's work. — The anecdote related by Ibn Khallikan is borrowed from Tabari.

(15) In the editions and the manuscripts this name is preceded by the word بن, which must be suppressed.

(16) The diacritical points of the word which I read Sijazi (native of Sijistân) vary greatly in the manuscripts.

(17) Here the word sultan is employed by Tabari to designate the khalif. See above, note (7).

(18) The orthography of this proper name is uncertain.

(19) The arabic words may also signify : they found him standing upon a horse. If this be the true meaning, the horse was his own, which had sunk into the mud.

(20) This was a sort of fool's cap which criminals were obliged to wear when exposed to public view.

(21) Abû Alî al-Husain Ibn Mohammad Ibn Fahm, a learned Traditionist and a native of Baghdad, died A. H. 289 (A. D. 902), aged seventy-eight years. — (Huffâz.)

(22) This work was probably never published.

YAKUB IBN YUSUF IBN ABD AL-MUMIN.

Abû Yûsuf Yakûb, the son of Abû Yakûb Yûsuf and the grandson of Abû Muhammad Abd al-Mûmin al-Kaisi al-Kûmi (1), was sovereign of Maghrib (2). We have spoken of his grandfather Abd-al-Mûmin (vol. II. pag. 182), and shall give an article on his father Yûsuf. [He was of a very light tawny complexion (3), rather tall (4) and well-looking; his mouth wide, his eyes large and very dark, his limbs bulky, his voice loud and his discourse fluent. He was the most veracious of men, the most elegant in language and the most fortunate in his suppositions. He managed affairs with skill whilst acting as visir to his father and watched over his provincial governors and other public officers so attentively that he acquired a perfect acquaintance with all the details of the administration.] On the death of his father, the shaikhs (or chiefs) of the Almohades and of the descendants of Abd al-Mûmin agreed on placing him at the head of affairs and, having tendered to him the oath of allegiance, they instituted him chief of the empire and saluted him by the appellation of Emir al-Mûminîn (Commander of the faithful) (5), the same which was borne by his father and his grandfather. They gave him also the surname of al-Mansûr (the victorious). He governed with great ability, displayed (*to the world*) the glory of the (*Almohade*) empire, set up the standard of the holy-war (*against the Christians*), settled the balance of justice on a firm basis and established throughout the land the application of the prescriptions enounced in the divine law. He watched over the interests of religion and of piety, corrected public morals by ordering the people to do what was commendable and avoid what was reprehensible; the penalties fixed by law were applied by him not only to his subjects in general but even to the members of his own family and to his nearest relations. His reign was therefore prosperous and his conquests extensive. When his father died (*A. H.* 580 — *A. D.* 1184, *at the siege of Santarem*), he was with him, and, from that moment, he took into his own hands the administration of the empire. In the space of two months, he re-established order in (*Muslim*) Spain, ameliorated greatly the state of that country, placed garrisons in the centers of administration and did all that might promote the welfare of the people. He gave directions that the *Fátiha*, when recited in the public prayer, should be preceded by the *Bismilla* (6), and orders to that effect were sent by him to all the Moslim countries under his rule. These orders some complied with, but others disobeyed. He then returned to Morocco, which city was the capital of the (*Al-mohade*) empire. After that, in the month of Shabán, 580 (Nov.-Dec. A. D. 1184), the Almoravide prince Ali Ibn Iskák Ibn Muhammad Ibn Ali Ibn Ghánla (7) departed from the island of Majorca and took possession of Bugia and the neighbouring country. The emir (8) Yakúb (*he who is the subject of this article*) sent against him a fleet and an army of twenty thousand horse; then, in the beginning of the year 583 (March, A. D. 1187), he set out himself and recovered the countries which had been taken from him. He then returned to (*the city of*) Morocco and, in the year 586, he learned that the Franks (*the Spanish Christians*) had obtained possession of Silves, a city in the west of Spain. He, in consequence, set out thither in person and, having retaken it, he immediately dispatched on an expedition a body of Almohade (*Berber*) troops and of Arabs. This army entered into the country of the Franks and took from them four cities of which they had effected the conquest forty years before. The sovereign of Toledo (*Alphonse IX, king of Castile*) then conceived such fear of Yakúb that he asked for peace and obtained a truce of five years. Yakúb then returned to (*the city of*) Morocco. The truce had nearly expired when some Franks, at the head of a numerous army, invaded the Moslim territory, plundering and slaying all before them and committing horrible depredations. When this news reached the emir Yakûb, who was then in Morocco, he levied a numerous body of troops among the Almohade (*Berber*) and Arab tribes, for the purpose of going to meet the enemy, and after a rapid march, he passed the Straits and landed in Spain. This was in the year 591 (A. D. 1195). The Franks, being informed of his approach, collected, from far and near, a great multitude (*of warriors*), and advanced to encounter him. — I must here relate that, towards the close of the year 668 (July, A. D. 1270), I saw, in Damascus, a note-book in the handwriting of Tâj ad-Dîn Abd Allah Ibn Hamawaih who had acted there in the capacity of *shaikh of the shaikhs* (*chief of the professors*) and who, having travelled to Spain, had written down, during his residence there, some notes concerning the proceedings of that (*the Almohade*) administration. The book of which I am speaking contained on that event, a chapter which must be inserted here :

" Towards the close the year of 590 (A. D. 1194), when the truce expired which the
" emir and sovereign of the West (*Morocco and Spain*), Abû Yûsuf Yakûb, the son of
" Yûsuf and the grandson of Abd al-Mûmin, had concluded with al-Adfonsh (*Al-*
" *phonso*) the Frank, who possessed the western part of the Spanish peninsula and
" who had Toledo for the seat of his government, the former, who was then in
" (*the city of*) Morocco, took the resolution of passing into Spain for the purpose of
" encountering the Franks. He, in consequence, wrote to the governors of his
" provinces and the chiefs of his troops, ordering them to join him. He then
" proceeded to Slâ (*Salles*), outside of which town the troops were directed to
" assemble. It happened, however, that he was taken seriously ill and the physicians
" lost all hopes of his recovery. This (*untoward occurrence*) interrupted the orga-
" nising of the army, and the emir Yakûb was carried back to Morocco. The
" (*nomadic*) Arabs and other tribes who stationed in that neighbourhood, being
" encouraged by this to ravage the country, spread, throughout all quarters, ruin
" and devastation, whilst Alphonso did the same in the territory of the Spanish Mos-
" lims. The result was that the army of the emir Yakûb had to be broken up and
" sent, in detachments, east and west, for the purpose of protecting these countries
" and quelling the insurrection. Alphonso then conceived such hopes of conquer-
" ing the provinces (*of Moslim Spain*) that he sent to the emir Yakûb an ambassa-
" dor charged to exact from him, by threats and menaces, the surrender of a cer-
" tain fortress (*or some fortresses*) situated in the vicinity of the Christian territory.
" He wrote to him also a letter which had been drawn up (*in Arabic*) by one of his

" vizirs named Ibn al-Fakkhâr and which ran thus : ' In thy name, O God!
" ' creator of the heavens and of the earth! His blessings be upon the Lord
" ' Messiah, the Spirit of God, his word and his eloquent messenger (9).
" ' Now, 'to the point (10) : It cannot escape the attention of whoever is gifted
" ' with a penetrating intellect and a good understanding that you are the emir of
" ' the hanifite (11) community as I am that of the Christian one. You well
" ' know how the chiefs of the Spanish Moslims have abandoned and deserted
" ' each other, how they neglect the care of their subjects and how greatly they
" ' are inclined to enjoy repose. (You know that) I make them undergo the law
" ' of the strongest, expelling them from their abodes, carrying their children into
" ' captivity and making an example of their men. You have at present no
" ' excuse to offer for not coming to their assistance, since the hand of Provi-
" ' dence has given you the means of doing so. You pretend that Almighty God
" ' has prescribed to you as a rule that, when we kill one of your people, you
" ' must kill ten of ours. But God has now alleviated you (from that necessity),
" ' because he knew that you have among you many men so weak and feeble
" ' that, if we were to slay ten of yours in order to avenge the death of one of ours,
" ' they would be incapable of resistance and unable to defend their lives. I was
" ' informed that you had prepared for war and ascended to the summit of the hill
" ' of battle (12) ; yet you procrastinate, year after year, making one step forward
" ' and the other backward. I know not whether you be detained by cowardice
" ' or by the intention of belying the promises made by thy Lord. But, being
" ' told that you could not find an opportunity of passing the sea on account
" ' of a circumstance which, as long as it subsists, will prevent your engaging
" ' in such an undertaking, I shall now make you a proposal which will set
" ' you at ease and deliver you from the blame of not fulfilling your promises
" ' and engagements and of not furnishing a great number of guarantees : send
" ' me some of your servants with ships, galleys, transports and mistics (13), so
" ' that I may pass over to you with my hands and fight with you in the place
" ' which you like best. If you gain the victory, an abundant spoil shall have
" ' thus been brought to you and a magnificent present set before you ; if I am
" ' victorious, I shall hold a high hand over you and deserve to be the emir of the
" ' two communities and the sovereign of the two continents. It is God who pre-
" ' pares success and who facilitates the accomplishment of wishes. There is no

" ' lord but he, no good but what comes from him; God's will be done! '
" The emir Yakûb, on receiving this letter, tore it to pieces and wrote these
" words on the back of one of the fragments : '*Return to them; for we shall
" ' certainly go unto them with troops which they shall not be able to withstand,
" ' and we will expel them from their (possessions), humbled and despicable (14). My
" ' answer you shall see, not hear!'* Under this, he wrote the following verse :

> " He has no letters to send but swords; no other ambassadors than the fivefold host (i. e.
> " *the army which is drawn up in five divisions*). "

— This is a verse of al-Mutanabbi's. — " He then dispatched letters, calling the
" people to arms and ordering up the troops established in the cities; on that very
" day, he caused his tents to be pitched outside the town. Having assembled his
" army, he proceeded to the sea which is called *Zokâk Sibta* (*the straits of Ceuta*),
" crossed from thence to Spain and penetrated into the country of the Franks.
" Having met the enemy, who were already assembled and prepared for battle, he
" made them suffer a most disgraceful defeat. This took place (at al-Arcos] in the
" year 592 (A. D. 1196). " — End of the extract made from the note-book above-
mentioned. — I then met with a work composed by Abû 'l-Hajjâj Yûsuf Ibn Muhammad Ibn Ibrâhîm al-Ansâri al-Baiyâsi (15) and entitled *Taskîr al-Adkil wa
Tanbîh al-Ghâfil* [i. e. *remembrancer for the intelligent and advertiser for the
negligent*), and, in it I found this letter ascribed to Adfonch Ibn Ferdiland (Alphonso
IX, the son of Ferdinand), who addressed it to the Commander of the Musulmans,
Yûsuf Ibn Tâshifîn, a sovereign whose life we shall give. Yûsuf's answer was
drawn up in the same terms as that which we have just given. God knows
where the truth lies! Al-Baiyâsi then adds an indication which seems to prove
that he borrowed them from a document in the handwriting of the Egyptian
kâtib Ibn as-Sairafi (16), and, if that be true, the message could not have been
sent to Yakûb Ibn Yûsuf, for as-Sairafi lived long before the time of that sovereign. I met with a number of learned Maghribins who considered the date
given above as incorrect (17) and related what we shall here expose : "The Franks,
" having assembled an immense army, marched against the emir Yûsuf who, being
" informed of their approach, hastened to encounter them, without being alarmed
" by what he had heard of their multitude and of their advancing against him. The

" two armies met in the Marj al-Hadíd (the iron meadow), which is a plain in the
" neighbourhood of Kalat Rabáh (Calatrava), and lying to the north of Cordova.
" This plain is traversed by a river which Yakûb passed in order to encounter the
" Franks and draw up his troops in order of battle. This was on Thursday, the 9th
" of Shabán, 591 (19th July, A. D. 1195). He thus followed the example of his father
" and grandfather who generally gave battle on a Thursday, and commenced their
" campaigns in the month of Safar. The engagement began by champions sallying forth
" to encounter their adversaries in single combat, whilst the armies kept their ground,
" till the emir Yakûb, at length, ordered the Almohade cavalry and the Arab chiefs
" to charge. They did so, routed the Franks and put them to the sword. All
" were exterminated, except their king, who escaped with a few followers, and, had
" the night not set in, not a man of the enemy had remained alive. The
" mass of booty taken by the Musulmans was immense; it is said that the num-
" ber of coats of mail which fell to the share of the Bait al-Mal (the public treasury)
" amounted to sixty thousand (18). Beasts of burden of all kinds were taken in
" such quantities that it was impossible to count them. Never was such a defeat
" heard of in Spain. It was the custom of the Almohades to make no prisoners when
" their adversaries were polytheists; even if they took a great king, they would
" strike off his head and those of the other captives, no matter how numerous they
" might be. The next morning, the Moslim army went in pursuit of the fugitives
" and found that they had evacuated Kalat Rabáh, so great was their terror. The
" emir Yakûb occupied the fortress, placing in it a wáli (governor) with a
" garrison. The quantity of booty which fell into the hands of the victors was
" so great that Yakûb was unable to advance farther into the territory of the Franks
" and therefore turned his arms against Toledo. This city he blockaded and
" attacked with great vigour; he caused the trees in the neighbourhood to be
" cut down, sent detachments to ravage the country all around and took a great
" number of castles situated in the environs of this place. The garrisons of these
" posts were put to the sword, the women carried into captivity, the walls and
" buildings demolished. After reducing the Franks to such an extremity that they
" did not once dare to make a sally against him, he returned to Seville, where he
" remained till the middle of the year 593 (April-May, A. D. 1197). He then
" entered, for the third time, into the country of the Franks and acted there as he
" had done before. That people, unable to resist him and finding the earth, wide

" as it was, too narrow for them (19), sent to ask for peace. He consented to
" their prayer on account of the news which had reached him respecting Ali Ibn
" Ishák (Ibn Ghánía) the Majorcan, " him of whom mention has been already made
in this article. " That chief had invaded the territory of Ifríkiya (20), ruined a
" number of its towns and was advancing towards al-Gharb (the west, i. e. the empire
" of Morocco), in the hope of taking the city of Bugia; for he knew that the emir
" Yakúb's attention was totally engaged by the state of Spain and by the holy war
" which he was carrying on in that country. He knew also that he had been
" absent from al-Gharb during three years. Yakúb granted therefore a truce of
" five years to all the Spanish kings, on the conditions which they themselves had
" proposed, and returned to (the city of) Morocco towards the end of the year 593
" (Oct.-Nov., A. D. 1197). On his arrival, he gave orders for the construction of
" cisterns and watering-places (on the line of his intended march), and to prepare all
" the materials and provisions necessary for an expedition into Ifríkiya. The
" shaikhs (chiefs) of the Almohades then waited on him and said : ' Sire! we have
" ' made a long absence in Spain; some of us have been there five years, others four,
" ' and others three. Favour us therefore with a respite and let the expedition be
" ' put off till the beginning of the year 595.' He granted their request and then
" went to Sla (Sallee) where he witnessed a magnificent pageantry got up for his
" reception. He had already founded near that place another large city to which
" he gave the name of Ribát al-Fath (the redoubt or station of victory, now called
" Rabát), and which he had constructed on the plan of Alexandria, the streets being
" wide, the quarters well distributed, the edifices solid, the whole city handsome
" and well fortified. It was built near the Surrounding sea (the Atlantic), on the
" southern bank of a river and opposite to Sla. After visiting all parts of that
" country and admiring its beauties, he returned to Morocco." — [I must here
observe (21) that accounts vary greatly respecting his proceedings after this epoch :
some say that he abdicated the throne and wandered through the land till he arrived
in the East, where the meanness of his appearance prevented him from being recognised, and where he died in obscurity. Other relate that, after his return to (the
city of) Morocco, he died there on the 1st of the first Jumáda, 595 (1st March, A. D.
1199), or on the 17th of the latter Rabí (15th February) or on the 1st of Safar
(3rd December, A. D. 1198). Some say that he died at Sla (Sallee). God knows best!
I may add that, in the year 680 (A. D. 1281-2), a number of persons spoke to me

at Damascus of a mausoleum situated close to al Hamâra, which is a village not far from al-Mijdal, a town in the dependancies of al-Bekâa al-Aulzi (*Cœlosyria*). This monument is called the tomb of the emir Yakûb, king of al-Gharb. The inhabitants of the place all agree on this point. The tomb is at the distance of two parasangs from al-Mijdal, in a south-western direction.] — Yakûb was a just and beneficent king and a strict observer of the holy law; he obliged all men, without respect of persons, to hold a laudable conduct; he presided regularly at the five public prayers and wore (*the simple*) woollen (*garment of the devotees*); he would stop to hear the complaints of women and of poor people, and render them justice. His dying injunction was that he should be buried at the road-side, so that the travellers who passed by might pray God to have mercy on him. I heard an anecdote respecting him which deserves to be inserted here: The emir and shaikh Abû Muhammad Abd al-Wâhid, who was the son of the shaikh Abu Hafs Omar and the father of the emir Abû Yahya Ibn Abd al-Wâhid (*the Hafside*), held the government of Ifrikiya. He had married the sister of the emir Yakûb, and she dwelt with him. A quarrel then arose between them, and she removed to the house of her brother, the emir Yakûb. The emir Abd al-Wâhid sent to bring her back and, on her refusal to return, he addressed a complaint to Abû Abd Allah Muhammad Ibn Ali Ibn Marwân (*kâdi of the community* (22) *at Morocco*). The kâdi had an interview with the emir Yakûb and said to him : " The shaikh Abd al-Wâhid demands that his wife (23) should be restored " to him." The emir Yakûb kept silent. Some days afterwards, Abd al-Wâhid met the kâdi in the emir Yakûb's palace at Morocco and said to him : " You are " the (*chief*) kâdi of the Moslims; I asked to have my wife restored to me, but she is not " yet come". On this the kâdi went to see the emir Yakûb and said to him : " Com- " mander of the faithful! here is twice that the shaikh Abd al-Wâhid has asked to " get back his wife." The emir Yakûb returned no answer. Some time after, the shaikh Abd al-Wâhid met the kâdi in the same palace, whither he had gone for the purpose of presenting his respects to the emir Yakûb, and said to him : " Kâdi " of the Moslims! I told you twice, and now tell you for the third time, that " I asked them to restore to me my wife and that they will not let me have her. " The kâdi had then an interview with the emir Yakûb and said : " Sire! the shaikh " asked that his wife should be restored to him and he has now renewed his request. " So you must either send her to him or accept my dismission from the kadiship." The emir Yusûf remained silent for a time, — or, according to another account, he said : "Abû Abd Allah ! this is really becoming too troublesome." — He then called forward an eunuch and said to him secretly : " Take Abd al-Wâhid's wife " back to him. " That was done the same evening. Yakûb was not offended with the kadi, neither did he say a word to displease him. In this, he acted according to the prescriptions of the divine law and executed its injunctions. It was a good action which (on the day of judgment), will surely be put to his account and to that of the kâdi. He certainly did his utmost to maintain erect the beacon of justice. The same emir was particularly strict in obliging his subjects to say the five daily prayers, and he sometimes put to death those who drank wine. He inflicted the same punishment on the governors who, by their misconduct, excited the complaints of those whom they administered. He gave orders that all the secondary maxims (deduced from the main principles of the law and received by the orthodox community) should be laid aside, and that the muftis (consulting-lawyers, casuists) should draw their decisions directly from the noble book (the Koran) and from the Sunna (or Traditions concerning the acts and opinions) of the Prophet. His injunctions were that they should pay no attention to the decisions of the mujtahid imâms who lived in former times, but judge according to the maxims which they themselves could deduce, by the exercise of private judgment, from the Koran, the traditions, the general agreement of the Moslim community and analogical deduction (24). A number of Maghribin doctors whom I met here (at Damascus) followed that system; such were Abû 'l-Khattâb Ibn Dihya (vol. II. p. 384), his brother Abû Amr (vol. II. p. 386, and Muhî ad-Dîn Ibn al-Arabi (25), a settler at Damascus. He (Yakûb) punished those who staid away from the (five public) prayers and had proclamations made in the streets ordering all to go to the mosque; those who absented themselves through inattention, or the necessity of working for their livelihood, received a sound flogging. His empire was vast and his realm so extensive that all the regions of Maghrib, from the Surrounding ocean to Barka, acknowledged his authority and formed provinces of his empire. He possessed besides a part of the Spanish peninsula. Yakûb was beneficent and friendly to the learned (in the law); he favoured literary men, listened willingly to poems composed in his praise and rewarded generously the authors. It was for him that Abû 'l-Abbâs Ahmad Ibn Abd as-Salâm al Jerâwi compiled the Safwa tal-Adab wa Dîwân al-Arab (Choice selection of literature and collection of poems composed by the Arabs). The pieces which form this miscellany are remarkably well chosen. The gold maghribin coins which are called Yakûbian were so named after this sovereign. In the year 587 (A. D. 1191-2), the sultan Salâh ad-Dîn (Saladin) Abû 'l-Muzaffar Yûsuf Ibn Aiyûb, a prince whose life we shall give, dispatched a member of the Munkid family as ambassador to the emir Yakûb, for the purpose of obtaining his assistance (26) against the Franks who had come from the countries of the West to invade Egypt and the maritime provinces of Syria. (In his dispatch) he did not give Yakûb the title of *Emîr al-Mûminîn* (*Commander of the faithful*), but that of *Emîr al-Muslimîn* (*Commander of the Muslims*). This gave Yakûb great offence and prevented him from granting the demand (27). The ambassador's names were Shams ad-Daula Abû 'l-Hârith Abd ar-Rahmân, the son of Najm ad-Daula Abû Abd Allah Muhammad Ibn Murshid. The rest of the genealogy has been already given in our article on his uncle, Osâma Ibn Munkid (28). The hâfiz Zaki ad-Dîn Abd-al Azim al-Mundiri (vol. I. p. 89) mentions him in his Takmila tal-Wafayât (*supplement to the Obituary*)(29) and says: " He died in Cairo, the year 600 (A. D. 1203-4); he was born at " Shaizar in the year 523 (A. D. 1128-9). He composed some pieces in prose and in " verse. "—Let us resume our account of Yakûb. One of the poets who frequented his court was Abû Bakr Yahya Ibn Abd al-Jalîl Ibn Abd ar-Rahmân Ibn Mujîr, a native of Murcia in Spain. I looked over his collected poetical works and found the greater part of them to be in praise of the emir Yakûb. In one of these poems he says :

Think you that the poet will cease to extol the fair whilst he is still in his youth and has reached the height of manhood? He was always captivated by the charms of graceful maids and, never, from the age of reason, did he allow indifference to occupy his heart. He cannot admire the character of him who, having once tasted (*the sweets of*) love, can become indifferent. You who censure me! little do I care! I am so occupied that I heed not your reproaches. My ear is deaf to your reprimands, though never deaf to the call of love. It can hear a fond discourse though held in whispers, but it cannot bear words of blame. My eyes, to their misfortune, directed (*towards her*) glances which (*for me*) were equivalent to death (31). On the morning in which I appeared before her, she left me as an example to show what love might be. Twas she who robbed me of (*the bloom of*) youth, (*so that the darkness of my hair disappeared*) and became the dark colouring of her eyelids (31). The magic of her glances annihilated the reality of all that belonged to me; that magic was not unreal. She turned from me through coquetry and, when she perceived my affliction, she turned away in confusion; as if she had been frightened by something which excited fear. She thought I meant to harm her, when she saw the grayness of my head shine like a flame. Noble chieftains of the tribe! you who are the fairest in the world to encounter the greatest dangers! we halted in your neighbourhood; we were grateful for your protection, and yet your gazelles (*maidens*) faced us boldly and filled us with fear and dread. You answered for the safety of your guests, but you did not provide for the safety of your roads.

You intended to ravish away our souls by scattering among them glances from (maidens') eyes. Better would it have been for us had we plunged into the midst of swords than to have encountered these large eyes! A band of your maidens attacked us and thus infringed the pact which we made (with you). They were Thoalites (skilful archers) with their glances, though they never heard of Thoal (32). These delicate nymphs levelled against us the graces of their movements when we levelled our pliant lances (for the fight). Their glances struck us successively, and we cast away helmet and spear. They shot at us with arrows, and yet we saw nothing about them but female ornaments and robes. Aided by beauty, they rifled all the hearts which had been ensnared in the toils of love. These graceful maids stripped me of my firmness, and yet I deck them with the jewels of amatory verse. I obliged my soul to face temptations and told her to be firm, but she could not resist them. She (who tempted me) then said : " You " most surrender your soul to love, either as a booty or as a gift; " and I replied : " She (my " soul) belongs to the Commander of the faithful, and (I shall) therefore not (give her up to " you). Never did a king like him appear before our eyes; he who sees him has attained his " utmost hopes. Benignity has established in his cheek a fountain of kindness whose waters " heal every indisposition; when he is moved by generosity, gifts burst forth from his right " hand and flow like a torrent. "

The kasída from which we have taken this extract is rather long, as it contains one hundred and seventy verses; so, we shall confine our choice to what we have here given. This poet died at Morocco in the year 587 (A. D. 1191-2), at the age of fifty-three years. [Abû Ishâk Ibrâhîm Ibn Yakûb al-Kânimi (33), a negro who was a good literary scholar and a poet, entered, one day, into the presence of the emir Yakûb and recited to him these verses :

He caused the curtain to be drawn which concealed him from my sight, yet he seemed to be still veiled by a curtain, such was the awe which he inspired. He allowed me, through condescendance, to draw near, and that awe (mahábatuhu) disappeared when I approached him.

The race of Negroes called the Kânim and that of the Takrûr are cousins. Neither of them derive their name from a maternal or a paternal ancestor : Kânim is the name of a town situated in the territory of Ghána, and is the metropolis of the Sûdán (or Blacks) who reside to the south of al-Gharb (the states of Morocco). The Kânim are so called after this town. Takrûr is the name of a territory and is borne also by those who inhabit it. They are all descended from Kûsh the son of Hâm, the son of Noah.] — When the emir Yakûb received the visit of death and expired, his son Abû Abd Allah Muhammad was proclaimed sovereign under the title of an-Násir (the defender). This prince marched into Ifrîkiya, routed the troops of Ibn Ghânia and recovered al-Mahdiya from the lieutenants of that adventurer. It had been taken by Ibn Ghânia when Yakûb was occupied in waging war against the enemies (of the faith). Muhammad (an-Nâsir), the son of Yakûb, then made an expedition into Spain and fought the battle of al-Okâb (Las Navas) in the year 609 (A. D., 1212). He died on the tenth of Shaabân, 610 (25th Dec., A. D. 1213). He was born in the year 576 (A. D. 1180-1). The Maghribins state that Muhammad Ibn Yakûb had told the slaves who were employed to guard his garden at Morocco, that they might lawfully kill whoever they found there at night. Wishing then to know what care they made of his orders, he put on a disguise, one night, and went to walk in the garden. When the slaves saw him, they attacked him with their spears, and, though he cried out to them : "I am the khalif! I am the khalif!" they would not believe him, but took his life. God knows if that be true (34). The supreme authority then passed to his son Abû Yakûb Yûsuf Ibn Muhammad, the grandson of the emir Yakûb, who took the title of al-Mustansir Billah. He was born on the first of Shauwâl, 594 (6th August, A. D. 1198). There was not, among all the descendants of Abd al-Mûmin, a handsomer man than he or a more eloquent pulpit orator; but he was so fond of his ease that he never stirred from his capital. Therefore, under his reign, the empire founded by Abd al-Mûmin began to decline. He died without issue in the month of Shauwâl (Oct.-Nov.), or of Zû 'l-Kaada, 620 (Nov.-Dec., A. D. 1223). The principal officers of the state then agreed to nominate as their sovereign Abû Muhammad Abd al-Wâhid, the son of Yûsuf and the grandson of Abd al-Mûmin. They fixed their choice on him because he was advanced in age and highly intelligent; but as he soon showed his inability to govern and knew not how to humour the inclinations of the chiefs who held a high rank in the administration, he was deposed by them and strangled, after a reign of nine months. When he was proclaimed sovereign at Morocco, his authority was rejected at Murcia by Abû Muhammad Abd Allah, the son of the emir Yakûb, who, thinking himself better intitled than he to the supreme power, invaded the Spanish provinces situated in the neighbourhood of his own, took possession of them without difficulty and assumed the (imperial) surname of al-Addil. When Abd al-Wâhid was strangled at Morocco, the army of this Abd Allah was attacked by the Franks and underwent a most disgraceful defeat. He himself took to flight and embarked with the intention of going to Morocco, after authorizing his brother Abû 'l-Alâ (or Olâ) Idrîs, the son of the emir Yakûb, to act at Seville, as his lieutenant. On his way to Morocco, he was greatly harassed by the nomadic Arabs and, on his arrival there, he found every thing turn against him and was imprisoned by the inhabitants of that city. A conference was then held by them respecting the choice of a person to whom they might confide the power, and they finished by electing Abû Zakariya Yahya, the son of Muhammad an-Nâsir and the grandson of Yakûb. This prince was incapable of governing, as might have been seen from his looks, and had not the least talent for business. A few days only elapsed from his accession to the throne when news arrived that Abû 'l-Alâ Idris had caused himself to be proclaimed khalif at Seville and received the oath of allegiance from the inhabitants of the Spanish provinces (*which belonged to the Almohades*). Yahya's affairs then took so bad a turn that he was besieged in Morocco by the Arabs; his troops underwent so many defeats that the people of the city got tired of him, lost patience and expelled him from the capital. He took refuge in the mountain of Deren (*the Atlas*) and then entered into a secret correspondence with some of the Moroccans for the purpose of obtaining his recal and the death of the chiefs who directed Ibn Abi 'l-Alâ's party in that city. He subsequently arrived there and had them all killed. Abû 'l-Alâ had now come from Spain, where the emir Muhammad, the son of Yûsuf Ibn Hûd al-Judâmi (35), had revolted and proclaimed the supremacy of the Abbasides. The popular feeling being in his favour, the cause of Abû 'l-Alâ Idris was abandoned (in *Spain*). The latter, on arriving at Morocco, found there the emir Yahya Ibn an-Nâsir and gave him battle. Yahya was defeated and fled to the mountain, whilst Abû 'l-Alâ took possession of Morocco. He then assembled a body of troops and marched against Abû 'l-Alâ, who was still in that city, but, being defeated in a number of encounters, he was forced to take refuge among some people who held a castle in the neighbourhood of Tilimsân (*Tlemcen*). A servant-boy (*ghulâm*) who was there, and who had to avenge the death of his father, lay in wait for Yahya, one day that he was riding out, and killed him (36). Abû 'l-Alâ, having then obtained the supreme authority, took the title of al-Mâmûn. He was brave, resolute, intrepid and audacious in his enterprises. He died a natural death, in one of his expeditions, but I have not been able to discover the date of that event. I have been since told by some people from that country that he died in the year 630 (A. D. 1232); God knows best (37)! His son Abû Muhammad Abd al-Wâhid concealed his death till he had made all requisite arrangements and provided for his own safety. He then assumed the title of ar-Rashid, subdued his older brother and took the supreme command. Abù 'l-Alà had caused the name of the Mahdi Abù Abd Allah Muhammad Ibn Tûmart (vol. III. p. 205) to be suppressed in the khotba, at Friday prayers, but this order was revoked by his son, who thus gained the hearts and the affection of the Almohades. Ar-Rashid continued to reign over Ulterior Maghrib and a part of Spain till the year 641 (A. D. 1243-4). What happened to him since, I am unable to say, having no knowledge of it. — Since this article was written out, I met a native of Morocco, a man of talent and information, who had lately quit that city, and I learned from him that, in the year 640 (A. D. 1242-3), ar-Rashid was drowned in a pond of his garden, at Morocco, the seat of the empire. His death was kept secret for some time by the chamberlain, so that the month in which it occurred is not known. Ar-Rashid was succeeded by his half-brother, Abù 'l-Hasan Ali Ibn Idris, who took the title of al-Motadid, but was generally known by the appellation of as-Said. Some time after, he made an expedition in the direction of Tilimsân (Tlemcen) and, having laid siege to a castle (Temzezdekt), at the distance of one day's march from that city, he was killed there, whilst riding about. This took place in the month of Safar, 646 (May-June, A. D. 1248). He was succeeded by el-Murtada Abù Hafs Omar, the son of Abù Ibrahim (Ishâk) and the grandson of Yûsuf. This was in the month of the latter Rabi (July-August) of that year (A. D. 1248). On the 21st of Muharram, 665 (22nd Oct. 1266) al-Wâthik Abù 'l-Ala Idris, the son of Abù Abd Allah Yûsuf Ibn Abd al-Mûmin (38), and generally designated by the name of Abù Dahbûs (the man with the club or mace) entered into Morocco, and al-Murtada fled from thence to Asemmor (39), a place in the dependencies of that city. The governor of Asemmor had him arrested, and sent a dispatch with this intelligence to al-Wâthik, who gave orders that the prisoner should be put to death. Al-Murtada was executed on one of the last ten days of the latter Rabi, 665 (between the 18th and the 28th of January, A. D. 1267), at a place called Ketâma and situated at the distance of a three days' journey from Morocco. Al-Wâthik maintained his power during three years and lost his life in the war which had broken out between him and the Merinides who reigned at Tilimsân (40). With him fell the dynasty which had been founded by Abd al-Mûmin. Al-Wâthik was killed at a place situated three days' journey north of Morocco, and in the month of Muharram, 668 (September, A. D. 1267). The Merinides then took possession of the empire. Their sovereign, at the present

time, is Abû Yûsuf Yakûb Ibn Abd al-Hakk Ibn Mammâma; but God knows best.
— Let us now speak of Ali Ibn Ishâk, (Ibn Ghânîa) the Majorcan of whom frequent
mention has been made in this article. His father, Abû Ibrahîm Ishâk Ibn Hammû
Ibn Ali the Sanhâjian, surnamed Ibn Ghânîa, was sovereign of Majorca, Ivica (Yâ-
bisa) and Minorca, three islands situated near each other and lying in the Western sea
(the Mediterranean). He died in the year 580 (A. D. 1184-5) and left four sons (41)
one of whom, named Abû Abd Allah Muhammad, proceeded to Spain, after the
death of his father, and joined the party of the Almohades. They received him with
the utmost cordiality and gave to him the city of Denia. Ali and Yahya, two other
of these brothers, left their country and invaded Ifrikiya, where they committed
such deeds of war and devastation as excited astonishment, and of which the recollection still subsists. Ali died, I know not in what year, but he was alive in the
year 591 (A. D. 1195) (42). His brother Yahya pursued the same career and continued it for a long time. The hâfiz Zakî ad-Dîn Abd al-Azim al-Mundiri mentions him (Yahya) in the Kitâb al-Wafayât and says: " He left Majorca in the month
" of Shabân, 580 (Nov.-Dec., A. D. 1184), conquered many countries and gained
" high renown by his courage and enterprising spirit. His death took place towards
" the end of the month of Shauwâl, 633 (June-July, A. D. 1236), in a desert
" region (situated at some distance from the city) of Tilimsân. His attacks were
" directed against the dynasty of Abd al-Mûmin (the Almohades). The youngest
" brother, Abû Muhammad Abd Allah, remained in Majorca till the year 599
" (A. D. 1202-3), when Muhammad an-Nâsir, the son of Yakûb, sent a fleet against
" him. The troops landed on the coast of Majorca, and Abd Allah, who was a noble-
" minded and brave warrior, advanced to give them battle. In the encounter, his
" horse fell under him, and he was beheaded by the invaders. His body was
" then suspended to the wall (of the city) and his head was sent to Morocco. Majorca
" was then conquered by the Almohades and remained in their possession till
" the year 627 (A. D. 1230), when it was taken by the Franks (the Catalonians).
" Horrible deeds were then perpetrated by them, such as massacring the inhabi-
" tants and reducing them to slavery." — Adfûnch (43) was the name borne by the
principal king of the Franks. He is now master of Toledo.

judge their real origin and readily found genealogists who could show that their family descended from one or other of the noble Arabian tribes. Ibn Khaldûn declares positively, in his *Histoire des Berbers*, t. I, p. 261, that the genealogy given as that of Abd al-Mûmin is a forgery.

(2) By *Maghrib* (*the West*) and *Maghrib al-Acsa* (*the ulterior West*) is meant the country which is now called the empire of Morocco.

(3) The text of this paragraph is not to be found in our manuscripts.

(4) For the signification of the expression ﺧﻄﺒﺔ see de Sacy's *Grammaire arabe*, t. I, p. 349.

(5) This title was given to khalifs only. The Almohades of Morocco and the Almohade Haïsides of Tunis considered their sovereigns as khalifs and designated them by that title.

(6) The *Fâtiha* is the first *sura* of the Khorân and contains only seven verses. The *bismilla* is the invocation placed at the beginning of all the *suras* except one, and which may rendered thus : *in the name of God, the merciful, the clement! &c* Is the orthodox Muslim prayer, the *Fâtiha* should not be preceded by the *bismilla*, but, in the Almohade sect, this, and a number of other irregularities were authorised.

(7) For a full account of the Ghâzia family and of their wars against the Almohades, see Ibn Khaldûn's *Histoire des Berbers*, tome II. The same volume contains a satisfactory account of the Almoravides and the Almohades.

(8) The orthodox Muslim historians give to the Almohade sovereigns the title of *amir* or *amir al-Muslimin*.

(9) This invocation has nothing in it to offend the orthodoxy of a Moslim. The letter was evidently drawn up by a Mussulman, but, from internal evidence, I am inclined to consider it as a forgery.

(10) This is the usual form by which, in Arabic letters, the writer enters into the subject, after commencing by a pious invocation or a series of compliments and good-wishes. It was approved of by Muhammad himself. In North Africa, the form ﺑﻌﺪ (*baâd, i. e. after which follows*), is very generally employed.

(11) Mohammad designated himself and his followers as *hanifites*, which term, according to the Moslim doctors, signifies the followers of the ancient orthodox religion.

(12) This metaphoric expression signifies : preparing for fight.

(13) Mistics are small vessels with lateen sails.

(14) Korân, sura 27, verse 37.

(15) An account of al-Belyâni will be found in this volume.

(16) The historian as-Saïraû was living A. H. 667 (A. D. 1112), as we have remarked in vol. II, page 376, note (2); and we learn here that he died a long time before the reign of Yakûb Ibn Yûsuf the Almohade, who mounted the throne A. H. 580 (A. D. 1184). We may therefore suppose that he died A. H. 525 (A. D. 1130-1).

(17) The date of the battle of Alarcos, given above, is certainly incorrect; the battle was fought on the 4th or the 9th Shabân, 591 (15th or 19th July, A. D. 1195).

(18) As the share of the Bak al-Mâl was a 80th, three hundred thousand Christian knights, if we are to believe the narrator, must have fallen in that battle. Moslim historians have no idea of numbers.

(19) This is a Coranic expression and signifies being reduced to despair.

(20) *Ifrikiya* or, as it is generally pronounced, *Frikiya*, is the name given to the province of Tunis. In former times, the kingdom of Ifrikiya included also the provinces of Tripoli, Constantina and Bugia.

(21) This passage is not to be found in our manuscripts.

(22) In Spain and in the states of North Africa, the chief or the *kâdis*, or lord chief-justice, was called the *kâdi* of the community.

(23) The *Ldds*, instead of saying *wife*, made use of the word *family* (*ahl*). A euphemism of this kind is absolutely required by Moslim delicacy: nothing can be more unpolite or more offensive than to speak to a man, in direct terms, of the female part of his family.

(24) This was putting aside all the questions which had been already resolved and established as precedents by the most learned doctors of the law, and permitting his own *kádís*, most of whom were ignorant men, to examine and settle them again as they thought fit.

(25) Mohí ad-Dín Muhammad Ibn Alí Ibn Muhammad al-Ḥátimí, surnamed Ibn al-Arabí, was one of the most voluminous writers on Ṣúfism that the Mohammedan world ever produced. He was born in the month of Ramadán, 560 (July-August, A. D. 1165) at Murcia, a city in Spain. After studying the law and the Koran in that country, he went to the East, made the pilgrimage, visited Cairo and other cities, and died at Damascus in the month of the second Rabí, 638 (Oct.-Nov. A. D. 1240). The number of works composed by him is enormous; see Ḥájji Khalífa's *Bibliographical Dictionary*, vol. VII, p. 1171. Of them the most remarkable is the *el-Fotúhát al-Makkíyát* (*revelations obtained at Mekka*), forming a very large and thick volume closely written, and filled with mystical reveries. His *Fuṣús al-Hikam* (*maxims of wisdom set as jewels*) is another work of the same kind. A long account of him is given by al-Makkarí, vol. I, p. 567 of the Arabic text, Leyden edition, and by M. de Hammer in the *Literaturgeschichte der Araber*, vol. VII, p. 499.

(26) That is, the assistance of his foot.

(27) For an account of this embassy, see Khaldún's *Histoire des Berbers*, vol. II, p. 513.

(28) This an oversight of the author: the genealogy is not given in that article.

(29) This was one of the numerous works composed as supplements to the *kádís* Abú Sulaimán Muhammad Ibn Abd Allah's *Wafayát an-Nahala* (*Necrology of persons who handed down traditional information*), which obituary extended from the time of the Hijra 80 A. H. 210 (A. D. 918).

(30) Such appears to be the poet's meaning, if the verse be correctly given. Even in that case, the absence of vowel points renders the reading and the sense very uncertain.

(31) The poet means to say that his hair was now gray, because the whom he loved best takes its darkness away and made use of it as *kohol*, or colouring matter, for her eyelashes.

(32) The tribe of Thoaï was celebrated for having produced the best archers in Arabia.

(33) The text of this passage is not to be found in our manuscripts.

(34) The accounts of an-Náṣir's death vary greatly. See the *Histoire des Berbers*, t. II, p. 226, note.

(35) See the translation of Makkari by Gayangos, vol. II, p. 320.

(36) In the *Histoire des Berbers*, vol. II, p. 241, Ibn Khaldún gives a different account of Yahya's death.

(37) According to Ibn Khaldún, the death of Abú 'l-Alá took place in that year.

(38) Abú Dabbús al-Wáthik, was the son of Muhammad, the son of Abú Hafs Omar, the son of Abd al-Múmin. — (*Hist. des Berb.*, vol. II, p. 332.)

(39) The fortress of Azammur is situated at the mouth of the Morbia, that is, the Omm-Rabia.

(40) The Merinides were then reigning at Fez, and at Tlemsen, which belonged to the Abd al-Wádites.

(41) According to Ibn Khaldún, *Hist. des Berbers*, t. II, p. 80, Lisán Ibn Ghánia left eight sons.

(42) He lost his life in a skirmish, A. H. 584 (A. D. 1188-9). — (*Hist. des Berbers*.)

(43) *Adfūnsh* or *Alfonso* is the Arabic transcription of *Adefons*, which in the old manner of writing *Alphonso*. See *Hist. des Berbers*, t. II, p. 76.

YAKUB IBN DAWUD, *THE VIZIR.*

Abû Abd Allah Yakûb Ibn Dâwûd Ibn Othmân Ibn Amr Ibn Tahmân was an adopted member of the tribe of Sulaim, being a mawla to Abû Sâlih Abd Allah Ibn Hâzim as-Sulaimi, the governor of Khorâsân (1). Yakûb was secretary to Ibrahîm Ibn Abd Allah Ibn al-Hasan Ibn al-Hasan Ibn Ali Ibn Abî Tâlib, the same who, stirred up a revolt, in the city and province of Basra, against Abû Jaafar al-Mansûr, and was put to death with his brother Muhammad, who had aided him in that attempt (2). This is not a fit place to speak of their enterprise which, being related in historical works, is well known. Dâwûd Ibn Tahmân, the father of Yakûb, and his (*Dâwûd's*) brothers were clerks employed in the office of Nasr Ibn Saiyâr, who was then governor of Khorâsân for the Omaiyides. After the death of Dâwûd, his sons Ali and Yakûb became eminent by their literary acquirements, their talents and their information in all the various branches of knowledge. When al-Mansûr defeated the above-mentioned Ibrahîm Ibn Abd Allah, he got Yakûb into his power and imprisoned him in the *Matbak* (3). This was in the year 144 (A. D. 761-2), or, by another account, in the year 146. The latter is probably the right date, because Ibrahîm was put to death in 145, as we have said elsewhere. We may suppose, however, that Yakûb was made prisoner anteriorly to the death of Ibrahîm, when the latter commenced his revolt; but God knows best! Yakûb was of a kind disposition, liberal, generous, charitable and always ready to oblige. Dibil Ibn Ali 'l-Khuzâi (*vol. I. p.* 507), the celebrated poet, mentions him in the book which contains the names of the poets. He was often visited by poets, some of them highly eminent, who came to eulogize him in their verses; such were Abû 's-Shais al-Kuzâi (4), Salm al-Khâsir (*vol. I. p.* 22), Abû Khumais and others. When al-Mahdi succeeded to the khalifate, on the death of his father al-Mansûr, Yakûb (*whom he had released from confinement*) endeavoured to ingratiate himself with the new sovereign and, having succeeded in gaining his favour, he attained so high a place in his confidence that he became a personage of great importance. An edict was even addressed to all the boards of administration, declaring that the Commander of the faithful had adopted as a brother Yakûb Ibn Dâwûd. This induced Salm al-

Khâsir to pronounce the following lines:

> Say to the imâm who obtained the khalifate by a title not to be contested: " Excellent is the
> " associate whom you have chosen to assist you in your devotions! your brother in God,
> " Yakûb Ibn Dâwûd. "

In the year 160 (A. D. 776-7) al-Mahdi made the pilgrimage and took Yakûb
with him. In 161, he permitted him to establish commissaries in all the provinces
of the empire, so that none of the governors should address dispatches to court
without his (Yakûb's) authorisation. Al-Mahdi had then for vizir Abû Obaid Allah
Moawia Ibn Abd Allah Ibn Yasâr al-Ashari at-Tabarâni, the same after whom the
square (murabbâ) of Abû Obaid Allah, in Baghdad, was so named. His grandfather
Yasâr was a mawla to Abd Allah Ibn Idâh (5) al-Ashari. Ar-Rabi Ibn Yûnus, the same
of whom we have already spoken (vol. I. p. 521) endeavoured to indispose al-
Mahdi against him (Abû Obaid Allah) and was the cause of that vizir's son's being
put to death, having furnished to the khalif proofs that the young man was a
zindik (an infidel). Some time after, he represented to al-Mahdi the danger of keeping about him such a man as Abû Obaid Allah: " Be on your guard against him, "
said he, " now that you have killed his son." He also spoke to him of Yakûb Ibn
Dâwûd's great talents and succeeded in having him appointed vizir. Abû Obaid Allah
was thus deprived of his place, and the only charge left to him was the direction of
the board of correspondence. This occurred in the year 163 (A. D. 779-780). Four
years after, al-Mahdi removed Abû Obaid Allah from that office and gave it to ar-
Rabi Ibn Yûnus. Abû Obaid Allah continued to visit al-Mahdi as usual, in order to
testify his sentiments as an humble and devoted servant. This induced a native of
Kûfa called Ali Ibn al-Khalîl to compose a poem in which was the following passage:

> Say to the vizir Abû Obaid Allah: " What resource have you left? Yakûb now disports him-
> " self in the direction of affairs and you turn away your eyes. You brought him into office
> " and he has prevailed over you; such misfortunes attend the great. By your remissness in
> " taking proper measures you have deliberately brought about your own ruin.

Yakûb then gained such influence over al-Mahdi that he took from him the direction of affairs. Al-Mansûr, in dying, had left in the treasure-chambers nine hundred millions and sixty thousand dirhems [£. 22,501,300], and Abû Obaid Allah

always advised al-Mahdi to be moderate in his expenses and spare the public money. When Abù Obaid Allah was deposed, his successor Yakùb flattered the inclinations of the khalif and encouraged him to spend money, enjoy all sorts of pleasures, drink wine and listen to music. By this means, he succeeded in obtaining the entire administration of the state. Dasbahàr Ibn Durd, the poet of whom we have already spoken (*vol. I. p. 254*), was induced by this to compose the following lines :

Awake, sons of Omaiya! your sleep has endured too long. It is Yakùb Ibn Dàwàd who is now khalif. Family (*of al-.Abbàs*)! your khalifate is ruined; if you seek for the vicar (*khalif*) of God, you will find him with a wine-flask on one side and a lute on the other.

Abù Hàritha an-Nahdi (6), the guardian of the treasure-chambers, seeing that they had got empty, waited on al-Mahdi with the keys and said : "Since you have spent "all your treasures, what is the use of my keeping these keys? give orders that "they be taken from me." Al-Mahdi replied : "Keep them still, for money "will be coming into you." He then dispatched messengers to all quarters in order to press the payment (*of the revenues*), and, in a very short time, these sums arrived. A slight diminution was then made in the expenses, and the sums paid in were so abundant that Abù Hàritha had enough to do in receiving them and verifying the amount. During three days, he did not appear before al-Mahdi, who at length said : "What is he about, that silly Bedwin Arab?" Being informed of the cause which kept him away, he sent for him and said : "What prevented your co-ming to see us?"—"The arrival of cash," replied the other.—"How foolish it was "in you, "said al-Mahdi, "to suppose that money would not come in to us!"— "Commander of the faithful!" replied an-Nahdi, "if some unforeseen event hap-"pened which could not be surmounted without the aid of money, we would not have "the time to wait till you sent to have cash brought in." — It is related that al-Mahdi made the pilgrimage one year and passed by a milestone on which he saw something written. He stopped to see what it was, and read the following line :

O Mahdi! you would be truly excellent had you not taken for a favorite Yakùb, the son of Dàwàd.

He then said to a person who was with him : "Write underneath that : (*It shall "still be so*) in spite of the fellow's nose who wrote that, bad luck attend him!" On "

his return from the pilgrimage, he stopped at the same milestone, because the
verse had probably left an impression on his mind; and such, in fact, appears to
have been the case, for very soon after he let his vengeance fall on Yakûb. Rumours unfavorable to this minister had greatly multiplied; his enemies had discovered a point by which he might be attacked and they reminded the khalif of his having seconded Ibrahim Ibn Abd Allah the Alide in the revolt against al-Mansûr.
One of his servants informed al-Mahdi that he had heard his master say : " That
" man (*the khalif*) has built a pleasure-house and spent on it fifty millions of dir-
" hems (£. 1,250,000) out of the public money." The fact was that al-Mahdi had
just founded the town of Isâbâd (7). Another time, al-Mahdi was about to execute
some project when Yakûb said to him : " Commander of the faithful! that is mere
" profusion." To this al-Mahdi answered : " Evil betide you! does not profusion
" befit persons of a noble race?" At last Yakûb got so tired of the post which he
filled that he requested of al-Mahdi the permission of giving it up, but that favour he
could not obtain. Al-Mahdi then wished to try if he was still inclined towards the
party of the Alides and sent for him, after taking his seat in a saloon of which all
the furniture was red; he himself had on red clothes and, behind him, stood a
young female slave dressed in red; before him was a garden filled with roses of all
sorts. " Tell me, Yakûb!" said he, " what you think of this saloon of ours. " —
The other replied : " It is the very perfection of beauty; may God permit the
" Commander of the faithful to enjoy it long!"—" Well," said al-Mahdi, " all that
" it contains is yours, with this girl to crown your happiness and, moreover, a
" sum of one hundred thousand dirhems (£. 2,500). " Yakûb invoked God's
blessing on the khalif, who then said to him : " I have something to ask of
" you." On this, Yakûb stood up from his seat and exclaimed : " Commander
" of the faithful! such words can only proceed from anger; may God protect me
" from your wrath!" Al-Mahdi replied : " I wish you to take the engagement of doing
" what I shall ask." — Yakûb replied : " I hear and shall obey. ,, — " Swear by
Allah, " said the khalif. — He swore. — " Swear again by Allah." — He swore.
— Swear again by Allah." — He swore for the third time, and the khalif then said
to him : " Lay your hand on my head and swear again." Yakûb did so. — Al-
Mahdi, having thus obtained from him the firmest promise that could be made,
spoke to him in these terms : " There is an Alide named " — such a one, the
son of such a one, — " and I wish you to deliver me from the uneasiness which he

" gives me and thus set my mind at rest. Here he is; I give him up to you." He
then delivered the Alide over to him and bestowed on him the girl with all the furniture which was in the saloon and the money (*which he had offered*). Yakûb was so
delighted to have got the girl that he lodged her in a room close to his own, so that he
might the more easily go and see her. The Alide, whom he had then brought in
and whom he found to be a man of intelligence and information, said to him :
" Yakûb! beware lest you have my blood to answer for before God; I am descended
" from Fâtima, the daughter of Muhammad, on whom God's blessings and favours
" always repose! " — To this, Yakûb replied : " Tell me, sir! if there be good in
" you." The Alide answered : " If you do good to me, I shall be grateful and
" pray for you happiness. — " Receive this money," said Yakûb, "and take what-
" ever road you like. " — " Such a road, " said the Alide, naming it, " is the
" safest." — " Depart with my good wishes," said Yakûb. — The girl heard
all this conversation and told a servant of hers to go and relate it to him (*al-Mahdi*)
and to say in her name : " Such is the conduct of one whom, in giving me to him,
" you preferred to yourself! such is the return which he makes you for your
" kindness!" Al-Mahdi had immediately the road occupied by guards, so that the
Alide was taken prisoner. He then sent for Yakûb and said to him, as soon as he
saw him : " What has become of that man? " — Yakûb replied : " I have deliver-
" ed you from the uneasiness he gave you." — " Is he dead? " — " He is." —
" Swear by Allah." — " I swear by Allah!" — " Lay your hand on my head." — Yakûb
did so and swore by his head. Al-Mahdi then said to an attendant : "Boy! bring
" out to us those who are in that room." The boy opened the door and there the
Alide was seen with the very money (*which Yakûb had received from the khalif*).
Yakûb was so much astounded that he was unable to utter a word and knew not
what to say. " Your life," said al-Mahdi, " is justly forfeited, and it depends on
" me to shed your blood, but I will not. Shut this man (*Yakûb*) up in the Matbak."
He had him confined in that dungeon and gave orders that no one should ever
speak to him or to any other about the prisoner. Yakûb remained there during the
rest of al-Mahdi's reign, which was two years and some months, and during the reign
of Mûsa al-Hâdi, the son of al-Mahdi, and during five years and seven months
of the reign of Hârûn ar-Rashîd. Yahya the Barmekide (*page 103 of this vol.*),
having then learned where he was, interceded in his favour and obtained his
deliverance. When Yakûb was taken out prison, he had lost his sight. Ar-Rashîd

treated him with great kindness, restored to him all his property and allowed him
the choice of a place of residence. Yakûb chose Mekka and, having received permission to go there, he remained in that city till his death. This event took place
in the year 187 (A. D. 803). — When he recovered his liberty, he asked for a
number of his dearest friends and, being informed that they were all dead, he pronounced these lines :

> All men have a cemetery near their residence, and, as their number diminishes, that of the
> tombs augments. But, though their dwelling be near at hand, the time of meeting them again
> (*the day of the resurrection*) is far distant.

These two verses are to be found in the *Hamâsa*, section of elegies. — I must
observe that the date of his death, as given above, is the same which is mentioned
by Abû Abd Allah Muhammad Ibn Abdûs al-Kûfî, generally known by the surname of al-Jibahlâri (vol. *II*. p. 137), in his *Târîkh al-Wuzarâ* (*history of vizirs*),
but another author states that Yakûb Ibn Dawûd died in the year 182 (A. D. 798-9);
God knows best! — Abd Allah, the son of Yakûb Ibn Dâwûd, related that, when
his father was imprisoned in a well by al-Mahdi, a cupola was built over it by that
khalif's order. He mentioned also that his father related to him as follows :
" Every day, during the fifteen years of my remaining there, a small loaf of bread
" and a pitcher of water were let down to me by a cord and the hours of prayer
" were announced so that I might hear the call. Towards the end of the thirteenth
" year, I saw in a dream a figure which came to me and said :

> " The lord took pity on Joseph and drew him forth from the bottom of a well, and of a
> " chamber where darkness was around him.

" I gave thanks to God and said : Deliverance is coming! I then remained
" another year without seeing anything, till the same figure visited me again and
" adressed me thus :

> " God may perhaps bring deliverance; every day, he does something for his creatures.

" I remained another year without seeing anything, but at the expiration of that
" time, the same figure came to me and said :

" The affliction in which you were yesterday may perhaps be followed by a prompt deli-
" verance from care. He that is in fear may cease to dread, the captive may be delivered and
" the stranger in a distant land may be taken back to his family.

" When morning came, I heard a voice calling on me, but thought it was the
" call to prayers. A black (camel-hair?) rope was lowered down and I was told to
" tie it about my waist. I did so and was drawn up. When I faced the daylight,
" my sight was extinguished. They led me to ar-Rashíd and bade me salute the
" khalif. I said : 'Salutation to the Commander of the faithful, the *well directed*
" (al-Mahdi), on whom be the mercy of God and his benediction!' The prince
" answered : ' I am not he.' I then said : 'Salutation to the Commander of the
" faithful, *the director (al-Hádi)*, on whom be the mercy of God and his benedic-
" tion!' He replied again : 'I am not he.' On this, I said : ' Salutation to the
" Commander of the faithful, *the rightly guided (ar-Rashíd)*, on whom be the mercy
" of God and his benediction!' To this ar-Rashíd replied : ' Yakúb Ibn Dáwúd! no
" one interceded with me in your favour, but, this night, as I was carrying one of
" my children on my shoulder, I remembered that you, formerly, used to carry
" me about in the same manner; so, I had compassion on you, thinking of the
" high position which you once held, and I ordered you to be taken out of confi-
" nement!" — When ar-Rashíd was a little boy, Yakúb used to carry him about
and play with him. — After Yakúb's imprisonment, Abú Jaafar al-Faid Ibn Abi
Sálih was appointed to the vizirate by al-Mahdi. He had been one of Abd Allah
Ibn al-Mukaffa's (vol. I. p. 431) servants and was noted for his excessive pride.
His father was a Christian. It was of al-Faid that a poet said :

O you who unjustly debar me from what I claim, may God oblige you to have recourse to
al-Faid's beneficence; to that man who, when he grants a favour, (shuffles about) as if walking
upon eggs!

— The name *Tahmán* is to be pronounced with an *a* after the *t;* the *h* is not followed by a vowel. — Abú Obaid Allah Moawia al-Ashari was born in the year 100
(A. D. 718-9), and died in the year 170 (A. D. 786-7), or 169. It is said that he
and (the khalif) Músa al-Hádi died on the same day. He breathed his last at
Baghdad and was interred in the Kuraish cemetery. — The vizir al-Faid died in
the year 173 (A. D. 789-790), and was replaced by ar-Rabí Ibn Yúnus vol. I.
p. 521). We have spoken of Yakúb Ibn Dáwúd in the life al-Bashshár Ibn Burd

(vol. I. p. 256) and stated that he contributed to the death of that poet. An elegy was composed on his (Yakúb's) death by Abu Hanash of the tribe of Hilál, or of that of Numair, according to another account. He was a native of Basra and his true name was Khudair Ibn Kais. He lived to the age of one hundred years. Some verses of his elegy are given in the *Hamása* (p. ٤٢٢). The first of them is this :

Yakúb! let us not lose you! O that you may escape from death ; otherwise, we shall have to weep for the days in which you ruled and which were so flourishing and so prosperous.

.

(1) Abû Sâlih Abd Allah Ibn Házim, a member of the tribe of Sulaim, governed Khorásán during ten years. He adhered to the party of Abd Allah Ibn az-Zubair and was killed, A. H. 71 (A. D. 690-1), by his own lieutenant Wahil رزوز. In a revolt which the latter got up against him at the instigation of the Omaiyide khalif Abd al-Malik Ibn Marwán. — (Tabari's *Annals*; Price's *Retrospect*).

(2) See De Sacy's *Chrestomathie Arabe*, vol. I, page 8 ; Abou 'l-Fedâ's *Annals*, tom. II ; page 18, and Price's *Retrospect*, vol. II, page 15. The revolt of An-Nafs az-Zakíya and his brother Ibrahim took place A. H. 145 (A. D. 762-3).

(3) The word *morbed* signifies anything which closes with a lid. It was the name given to the state-prison wherein political offenders were confined for life. (*Al-Fakhri*, page 210 of the Arabic text). It was a pit or under-ground chamber, communicating with the exterior by a deep and narrow passage like a well.

(4) Abû 'n-Shair (NÁLI?), or Abû Jaafar, Muhammad Ibn Abd Allah al-khuzâi was the cousin of the poet Dibil Ibn Ali al-Khuzâi. He died A. H. 194 (A. D. 815-2). See vol. I, page 310 of this translation, and Freytag's *Hamása*, page 692 of the Arabic text.

(5) According to Ibn Duraid, in his *Ishtikák*, Kilâb ركاب was a noble Arab chief who settled in Syria after the conquest (min ashráf ahli 'z-Sâdm). The vizir Abû Obaid Allah Moawîa Ibn Yasâr died A. H. 170 (A. D. 786-7). Some account of him is given in Ibn at-Tiktaka's *Fakhri*, page ٢٥٥.

(6) This surname is variously written in the manuscripts ; one of them gives *Biadi*, another *Mahdi*, etc. As the individual who bore it belonged to an Arabian tribe, the only plausible reading is that of *Nahdi*, (a member of the tribe of Nahd Ibn Kudâa). Farther on, it will be seen that al-Mahdi called him a Bedwin Arab.

(7) Isábád (*the dwelling of Isá*), was so named after Isá, the son of al-Mahdi. It lay to the east of Baghdad. — (*Mardsd.*)

YAKUB IBN KILLIS.

Abû 'l-Faraj Yakûb Ibn Yûsuf Ibn Ibrahim Ibn Harûn Ibn Dâwûd Ibn Killis, was vizir to al-Aziz Nizâr, son of al-Moizz al-Obaidi (vol. III. p. 377), and sovereign of

Egypt. In the first part of his life he professed the Jewish religion and pretended that he drew his descent from Hârûn (Aaron), the son of Imrân and the brother of Mûsa (Moses). According to another statement, he gave himself out for a descendant of the Jew Samauwel Ibn Âdyâ, the lord of the castle called al-Ablak, him who acquired such renown for his good faith. The history of his conduct towards Amro 'l-Kais al-Kindi and of the fidelity with which he preserved the objects confided to his care by that celebrated poet, is well known to men of learning (1). Yakûb was born at Baghdad and there he passed his youth. His residence was situated near the gate called Bâb al-Kass. When he had learned writing and arithmetic, his father took him to Syria and sent him from that to Egypt, in the year 331 (A. D. 942-3). Yakûb then paid assiduous court to an officer in the service of the ustâd Kâfûr al-Ikhshîdi (col. II. p. 524) and was chosen by the latter to direct the furnishing of his palace. He subsequently became Kâfûr's chamberlain and acted, in that capacity, with great honour, discernment, probity, intelligence and disinterestedness. His master did not fail to remark his conduct and, having admitted him into his intimacy, he appointed him to a seat in the privy council. Yakûb's duty being then to wait in Kâfûr's presence, receive his orders and control the public accounts (2), every affair passed through his hands. He rose to such a height in Kâfûr's favour that all the chamberlains and nobles stood up when he entered and showed him the deepest respect. He had no desire of gaining money; when his master sent him any, he always returned it and accepted nothing more than his regular appointments. Kâfûr then sent positive orders to all the boards of administration that not a dinar should be payed without a written authorisation from Yakûb, and thus placed all the public expenses under his control. A part of his modest emoluments Yakûb employed in acts of beneficence, and yet he continued to profess his religion. On Monday, the 18th of Shabân, 356 (29th July, A. D. 967), he became a convert to the Moslim faith and applied to the practise of prayer and the study of the Koran. Having engaged for a salary a learned shaikh, well acquainted with the august text of the Koran, skilled in grammar and knowing by heart the (grammatical) work of as-Sîrâfi (vol. I. p. 377), he passed the nights with him in the recitation of prayers and the reading of the Koran. His power and favour continued to augment till Kâfûr's death, when he was arrested with all the clerks and chiefs of the public offices by the visir Abû 'l-Fadl Jaafar Ibn al-Forât (vol. I. p. 319), whose jealousy he had excited and of whom he

had made an enemy. By the intervention of his friends and by bribes he obtained his liberty from the vizir, and, on leaving the prison, he borrowed money from his brother and other persons, packed it up and departed secretly for Maghrib. On his way, he met the *kdid* Jawhar Ibn Abd Allah ar-Rûmi (*vol. I. p. 340*), who was marching to Egypt with an army and large sums of money, for the purpose of reducing that country under the authority of his master al-Moizz al-Obaidi (*vol. III. p. 377*). Yakûb returned with him, or, according to another account, he continued his journey to Ifrikiya and entered into the service of al-Moizz, after which he returned to Egypt. He rose into such great favour (*with the Fatimides*) that he became the vizir of al-Aziz Nizâr, the son of al-Moizz Maadd, and obtained a high place in his esteem. Whilst he was thus favoured by fortune and whilst his door was besieged by crowds of people, he reorganised the administration of the empire, directed with ability the march of the affairs and (*gained such influence that*) no one dared to contradict him. Under the reign of al-Moizz, he had been employed in the civil administration and, on passing into the service of al-Aziz, he was nominated vizir. This took place on Friday, the 18th of Ramadân, 368 (19th April, A. D. 979). Ibn Zûlâk (*vol. I. p. 388*) says, in his History (*of Egypt*), after speaking of al-Moizz and giving the date of his death:
" Amongst the vizirs of al-Moizz, Yakûb Ibn Killis was the first who acted in Egypt
" for the Fatimide dynasty. After holding a place at the board of government,
" under (*the regence of*) Kâfûr, he joined the party of al-Moizz and served him with
" such zeal and obedience that he was raised to the vizirate." — Another author
says : " Yakûb was fond of learned men and liked to assemble them at his residence.
" Every Thursday night he held a sitting at which he read works of his own com-
" posing to an assembly of *kddis*, doctors of the law, professors of Koran-reading,
" grammarians, Traditionists, grandees and other persons of talent. When the
" sitting was over, the poets would advance and recite to him eulogiums. He kept
" in his palace a number of persons, some of whom were occupied in making copies
" of the Koran, and others in transcribing books of Traditions, jurisprudence, lite-
" rature and even medicine; these volumes they collated, adding also to the text
" vowel signs and diacritical points. One of the doctors who attended his sit-
" tings was al-Husain Ibn Abd ar-Rahîm, surnamed az-Zalâzili, the same who
" composed the *Kitâb al-Azjâa* (*the book of rhymes*). He kept also with him, at a
" fixed salary, a number of Koran-readers and *imâms* whose duty it was to pray in

" the mosque which he had constructed in his palace. Kitchens were established
" there for himself and his guests, and others for his pages, retainers and followers.
" Every day, a large table was laid out for the learned men, the clerks who were
" attached to his service, some of his chosen followers and the guests whom he had
" invited. A great number of other tables were set out for the chamberlains,
" the other clerks and the retainers. In the palace he had a closet arranged (with
" a fountain) for the purifications, and eight chambers were always kept ready for
" the reception of strangers. Every day, after the morning prayer, he gave audience
" to the public and received, with their salutations, the papers in which they
" exposed their wants or the acts of injustice which they had to complain of. He
" placed around his sovereign some officers to whom he assigned the rank of *káids*
" (*generals*) and whose duty it was to accompany him (*the khalif*) when he rode out
" in state; with them were a number of negro slaves to whom also it was obliga-
" tory to give the title of *káid*. One of these officers was the *káid* Abú 'l-Fatúh
" Fadl Ibn Sálih, the same whose name is borne by the *Munya* or *garden, of the*
" *káid Fadl*, which is a hamlet in the province of Jíza, in Egypt. This vizir
" then began to fortify his palace and the dwellings of his pages by means of
" *darbs* (3); there he set guards and laid in a large stock of arms and provisions.
" The neighbouring grounds got covered with shops for the sale of all sorts of
" goods, eatables, liquours and clothing. It is stated that his palace was situated
" in that part of Cairo which is now occupied by the *madrasa* (or *college*) that was
" founded by the vizir Safi ad-Dín Abú Muhammad Abd Allah Ibn Ali, surnamed
" Ibn Shukr (*vol. I. p.* 190) and which he appropriated to students of the Malikite
" sect. It is said also that the street of Cairo called *Hárat al-Waziríya* (*the street of*
" *the vizirians*) and situated (*at the entrance of the city*), within the Báb as-Saáda
" gate, was so named because his dependants resided there." The vizir Abú 'l-
" Fadl Ibn al-Furát was his constant visitor and inspired him with such confidence
that he was sometimes authorised to make the agents (*of government*) give in and
settle their accounts. At public audiences he was allowed to sit beside Yakúb,
who sometimes detained him for dinner, and yet he had acted towards him in the
manner which we have related (*vol. I. p.* 319) (4). The respect which Yakúb inspired was profound, his beneficence ample, and the eulogiums composed on him by
poets were very numerous. On looking over the collected poetical works of Abú
Hámid Ahmad Ibn Muhammad al-Antáki, surnamed Abú 'r-Rakamak (*vol. I. p.* 116),

I found that most of the eulogistic pieces were adressed to this vizir; such, for instance, is the *kasîda* of which we inserted a portion in our account of that poet. In the historical work composed by the emir al-Mukhtâr Izz al-Mulk Muhammed Ibn Abi 'l-Kâsim, generally known by the appellation of al-Musabbihi (*vol. III. p. 87*), I found a long article on Ibn Killis and, from it, I drew the greater part of the information given above. Yakûb composed a work on jurisprudence, containing the (*Shîite*) doctrines which he had learned from the lips of al-Moizz and of al-Azîz, that prince's son. In the month of Ramadân, 369 (March-April, A. D. 980), he held a sitting to which people of all ranks were convoked, and there he read to them the contents of this work. The vizir Ibn al-Furât was at the assembly. A number of persons then held sittings in the mosque called al-*Jâmê 'l-Atîk*, and decided points of law conformably to the principles enounced in that book. I heard some Egyptians relate that the vizir Yakûb had birds (*pigeons*) of so choice a kind and so excellent a breed that they outstripped all others. His sovereign al-Azîz had also some fine birds, remarkable for the rapidity of their flight. One day, the prince flew a bird of his against one of the vizir's and lost the prize. The displeasure which this gave him induced some of the vizir's enemies to think that they had found the means of ruining his credit, and they said to al-Azîz : " That man chooses for him- " self the best things of every kind and leaves nothing for you except those of inferior " quality. It is even so with regard to pigeons." By these words they meant to incense the prince against his minister, of whom they were all jealous, and turn his mind against him. Yakûb, being informed of what had passed, wrote to al-Azîz these lines :

> Say (*my letter!*) to the Commander of the faithful, to him whose glory is exalted and whose origin illustrious : " Your bird would have had the precedence but, before it, went its cham- " berlain (to do it honour). "

The prince was pleased with these verses, and the irritation which he felt against the vizir disappeared. So it is stated by Al-Kâdi ar-Rashîd Ibn az-Zubair (*vol. I. p. 143*), in his *Kitâb al-Jinân*, but, according to another author, the two verses were composed by Wali ad-Dawla Abû Muhammad Ahmad Ibn Ali, surnamed Ibn Khairân, a *kâtib* and Egyptian poet of whom we have spoken in our account of Abû 'l-Hasan Ali Ibn Nûbakht (*vol. II. p. 319*). I have not given a separate article to Ibn Khairân, because I never met with the date of his death, and because I made

it a rule not to insert, in this work, a notice on any person the year of whose decease
I could not discover (5). Abù 'l-Kàsim Ali Ibn Munjib Ibn Solaimàn, surnamed
Ihn as-Sairafi, a kátib and a native of Egypt, drew up a volume to which he gave
the title of Al-Ishàra fi man nàl al-Wizàra (the Indicator, treating of those persons
who obtained the vizirate), and in which he mentioned the visirs who administered
in Egypt, up to his time. In this work, he begins by speaking of Yakùb, the subject of the present article, and says: "He was a kátib and a jew, guarding himself
"(from vice), strict in the observance of his religious duties, and obliging towards
"the merchants with whom he had dealings. Kàfùr al-Ikhshìdi, to whose service
"he got attached, was so much pleased with his conduct, that he confided to him
"the direction of the diwan (or board of administration) for Egypt and Syria.
"That office he filled to his master's satisfaction. The cause of his high favour
"with Kàfùr was this: A jew told him that a sum of thirty thousand dinars was
"buried at Ramla, in the house of Ibn al-Bakri (6), who had just died. In conse-
"quence of this information, he addressed a memorial to Kàfùr, expressing his
"desire of setting out for Ramla, in order to bring back a sum of twenty thousand
"dinars, which was hidden in the house of Ibn al-Bakri. Kàfùr gave his consent
"to this request and sent with him a number of mules for the purpose of transport-
"ing the money. News having then arrived that the merchant Bukair Ibn Hàrùn
"was dead, Kàfùr charged Yakùb to make investigations into the property left by
"deceased. It then happened that a jew who had with him some bales of flax,
"had just died at al-Farama. Yakùb seized on the bales, opened them and found,
"in the interior, money to the amount of twenty thousand dinars. Kàfùr, to
"whom he announced in a letter this discovery, thought himself highly fortunate
"in having such an agent, and wrote back to him the order to carry off the money.
"Yakùb sold the flax, took with him all these sums, and, on reaching Ramla,
"had an excavation made in Ibn al-Bakri's house, and, from that, he took out
"money to the amount of thirty thousand dinars. On this, he wrote to his master
"saying: 'I informed your Lordship (usidd) that the sum was twenty thousand
"'dinars, but I have found it to be thirty thousand.' He thus acquired a still
"higher place in Kàfùr's esteem and a greater title to his confidence. Having
"closely examined into the inheritance left by Ibn Hàrùn, he took out of it a large
"sum which he carried off. Out of the ample donation which Kàfùr then sent
"to him, he accepted only one thousand dirhems (£. 25), and returned the rest with

" these words : ' What I have taken is a sufficiency.' His influence with Káfúr then
" rose to such a degree that he was consulted by him in almost every affair." —
Abd Allah Akbú Muslim the Alide related as follows : " I saw Yakúb standing to
" the right of Káfúr, and, when he retired, he (*Káfúr*) said to me : ' What a vizir
" is contained within that man's sides ! ' " He (*Yakúb*) travelled to Maghreb and
entered into the service of al-Moizz. On the first day of the month of Ramadán,
368 (2nd April, A. D. 979), he became prime minister of al-Aziz, and received from
him the title of vizir. Orders were then given by the sultan, that no person should
address Yakúb verbally or in writing except by that appellation. In the year 373
(A. D. 983-4), al-Aziz imprisoned him in the Kasr (*the citadel of Cairo*), but, some
months later, in the following year, he set him at liberty and restored him to his
former place. In the year 380 (A. D. 990-1), that of Yakúb's death, a paper containing the following lines was found in his house :

Be on your guard against the events of time! stand in dread of unforeseen misfortunes!
You think yourself secure against adversity; you sleep on, yet danger is often hidden by security.

When he read these verses, he exclaimed : " There is no power and no strength,
" except through the Almighty ! " and used in vain, every endeavour in order to
discover the author. Towards the end of the year just mentioned, when he was
in his last illness, he received a visit from al-Aziz, who came riding in state
to see him. " O ! " said that sultan, " I should give my kingdom to redeem
" you (*from death*); to ransom you (*from her grasp*), I should sacrifice my son !
" Have you any thing to ask of me, Yakúb ? " The vizir wept and replied :
" As to what concerns me personally, you can so well appreciate my deserts, that
" I need not refer you to them, and you have been so kind to those whom I am
" leaving behind me, that I need not recommend them to your benevolence. But
" I shall give you some advice touching the welfare of your empire : Remain in
" peace with the Greeks as long as they remain in peace with you ; he satisfied with
" the Hamdanides (*of Aleppo*), as long as they offer up the prayer for you from
" the pulpit and inscribe your name on the coinage; show no mercy to Mufrij
" (*Mufarrij?*) Ibn Dagbfal Ibn al-Jarráh (*vol. I. p. 406*), whenever the opportunity
" presents itself." When he died, al-Aziz gave orders that he should he buried
in the house where he (*Yakúb*) resided, and which was called the Palace of the

Vizirat. It was situated in Cairo, within the gate which bears the name of Bâb
an-Nasr (victory Gate), and it contained a mausoleum (kubba), which the vizir had
built for himself. Al-Azîz said the funeral service over him, and arranged the
body in the grave with his own hands. He then returned, sorrowing for his
loss, and ordered that all the public offices should remain shut for some days. The
appointments which he allowed to the vizir were one hundred thousand dinars
(£. 50,000) a year. In the property left by Yakûb were four thousand slaves, whites
and blacks, all of them young men, precious stones to the value of four hundred
thousand dinars, and drapery of all sorts to the value of five hundred thousand
dinars. Six hundred thousand dinars were owed by him to merchants, but this
debt was acquitted by al-Azîz, who drew the amount from the public treasury and
distributed it to the creditors over the vizir's grave. The háfiz Ibn Asákir (vol. II.
p. 252) mentions him in the History of Damascus and says: " He was a Jew of
" Baghdad, perverse and crafty, full of shrewdness and cunning. In the early
" part of his career, he went to Syria and settled in Ramla, where he became an
" agent of affairs. Having embezzled the property of the merchants, he fled to
" Egypt, and was chosen by Káfûr as his commercial agent. Káfûr soon re-
" marked his intelligence, his skill in the management of affairs, his perfect ac-
" quaintance with every thing concerning the [government] estates, and was heard
" to say: ' Were that man a Moslim he would be fit to be made a vizir.' The hope
" of obtaining the vizirship induced him to embrace Islamism, and he made his
" profession of faith, one Friday, in the great mosque of Misr. The vizir Abû
" 'l-Fadl Jaafar Ibn al-Furât perceived what he was aiming at and planned his
" ruin, on which he fled to Maghrib and joined some Jews who were with the per-
" son surnamed al-Moizz (7). When the latter set out for Egypt, he accompanied
" him, and, on that chief's death, he became vizir to the person surnamed al-Azîz,
" who was the son and successor of al-Moizz. This took place in the year 365
" (A. D. 975-6). He continued in the direction of affairs till the death of his
" master, which occurred in the month of Zû 'l-Hijja, 380 (Feb.-March, A.D. 991)."
—Another author says: " The last illness of the aforesaid vizir began on Sunday,
" the 21st of Zû 'l-Kaada, 380. He was seized by a palsy which continued to
" augment and become worse; then he recovered the use of his tongue; then,
" towards the morning of Monday, the 5th of Zû 'l-Hijja (23 February, A. D. 991),
" he breathed his last. His body was shrouded in fifty robes, and all the people

" assembled in the street leading from the citadel to his house. Al-Azis came forth,
" evidently much afflicted; he was mounted on a mule, and, contrary to his usual
" custom when riding out, no parasol was borne over him. He prayed over the
" corpse, wept and remained present till the grave was filled up. It is said that
" the shrouds and the perfumes used in embalming the body, cost ten thousand dinars.
" A person related that he heard al-Azis say: ' How long shall I grieve for thee,
" 'O Visir!' The kdid Jawhar (vol. I. p. 340) wept bitterly, but it was as if he
" were weeping for his own death, since he did not survive the visir more than a
" single year. The next morning, the tomb was visited by the poets, one hundred
" of whom, it is said, recited elegies over it. For these poems they received in
" exchange ample donations."—Some say that he died in his former religion and
was only a Moslim in appearance, but the truth is that he was a sincere and good
Musulman. At one of his assemblies, he spoke of the Jews in terms such as that
people could not have endured, and he proceeded to expose their infamy and the
corruptness of their religion. " Those people," said he, " hold opinions which
" have no foundation, and the name of the Prophet is mentioned in the Pentateuch,
" though they deny it." He was born at Baghdad, in the year 318 (A. D. 930-1),
near the gate called Bâb al-Kass.—The orthography of Killis, Samawwel and
Addyd is that which is given here. We have already spoken of the kdid Jawhar.
The kdid Fadl (8) was a man of talent and honour, praised by all. The garden
called Munyat al-Kdid, and situated in the district of Jiza, was so named after
him. It was in his praise that Abû 'l-Kâsim Abd al-Ghaffâr, the court poet of
al-Hâkim, the son of al-Azis, composed the following lines :

> Al-Fadl is a brilliant star on the foreheads of our eulogiums; ample in his gifts, the favours
> he bestows are odours which do not pass away. His hand is the crater of beneficence for
> travellers departing in the morning and arriving at eventide. All things prosper under the di-
> rection of the son of Sâlih.

Fadl enjoyed high favour under the reign of al-Hâkim; but, having incurred his sovereign's displeasure, he was cast into prison and there beheaded. This
event took place on Saturday, the 21st of Zû 'l-Kaada, 399 (17th July A. D. 1009).
He met his death with great fortitude. His body was rolled up in a mat and carried out of the cell where he had been confined.— The poet Abû 'l-Kâsim was
put to death by al-Hâkim, with a number of other distinguished men, on Sunday,

the 26th of Muharram, 395 (12 November, A. D. 1004). Their bodies were burned
by his order. All of them were executed together, in the same cell. God knows
how far these things may be true!

---

(1) See Rasmussen's *Additamenta ad historiam Arabum*, p. 11, and Caussin de Perceval's *Essai sur l'histoire des Arabes*, t. II, p. 319 et seq.

(2) الأمل, the plural of أمل, bears often the meaning of *vote*, *bet*, *account*.

(3) The darbs were lanes or passages closed at each end by a gate.

(4) It is a singular oversight of our author not to have mentioned the reconciliation of Ibn Killis and Jaafar Ibn al-Furât in the life of the latter.

(5) The author gave subsequently the date of Ibn Khairân's death in his article on Ibn Nûbakhti.

(6) According to another reading: al-Baladi. — This person was probably a commercial agent in the service of the Fatimide government.

(7) Ibn Asâkir, writing as he did, under the government of the Abbaside khalifs, gives here to understand that the Fatimides had no right to bear imperial titles.

(8) See page 342.

IBN SABIR AL-MANJANIKI.

Abù Yùsuf Yakùb Ibn Sâbir Ibn Barakât Ibn Ammâr Ibn Ali Ibn al-Husain Ibn
Ali Ibn Hauthara al-Manjaniki, surnamed Najm ad-Dîn (*the star of religion*), belonged to a family of Harrân, but was, by birth and by residence, a native of Baghdad. Abù Abd Allah Muhammad Ibn Saîd, surnamed Ibn ad-Dubaithi (*vol. III.
p. 102*), notices this distinguished poet in the historical work intended by him
to serve as a supplement to the work which the *hâfiz* Abù Saad Abd al-Karîm Ibn
as-Samâni (*vol. II. p. 156*) drew up as a continuation of the (*biographical*) history
of Baghdad, which was composed by the *hâfiz* Abù Bakr Ahmad Ibn Ali Ibn Thâbit
al-Baghdadi (*vol. I. p. 35*). Mention has been made of these three authors in the
present historical work. "This Yakùb," says Ibn ad-Dubaithi, "was at the head
"of those who practised his art,"—the writer means ballistics and the matters relating to that branch of science, — "he was a man of merit and could extemporise

" poetry. Some traditions were learned by him from the lips of Abû 'l-Muzaffar
" as-Samarkandi and of Abû Mansûr as-Shatranji. I wrote down some pieces of
" his poetry which were dictated to me by himself. (Thus for instance): The fol-
" lowing verses were recited to me by Abû Yûsuf Yakûb Ibn Sâbir, as being of his
" own composing :

> " I kissed her cheek and she, in her confusion, turned away her neck and inclined (from me)
> " her pliant waist. From her cheeks trickled down upon her breast drops of respiration like
> " the dew upon the myrtle (1). It was as if the breath of my sighs had obliged the rose of
> " her cheeks to shed its dew-drops.

" I asked him the date of his birth, and he replied that it was on Monday morn-
" ing, the 4th of Muharram, 554 (26th January, A. D. 1159)."— Another person
said : " Ibn Sâbir al-Manjaniki commenced his career by serving in the regular
" army (jundi), and became chief of the engineers stationed in the City of Welfare
" (Dâr es-Salâm), which is Baghdad. He laboured assiduously with the sword and
" the pen, and became noted for his studies and his military exercises. None of his
" contemporaries could cope with him in the knowledge of these last matters. He
" composed on that subject a book which he entitled Omdat al-Masâlik fi Sidset
" il-Mamâlik (the directing-post, marking the paths which lead to the government of
" kingdoms). This fine work, which remains unfinished, treats of every thing
" relating to war, orders of battle, taking fortresses, building castles, horse-
" manship, engineering, blockading strongholds, sieges, equestrian exercises, war-
" horses, the management of all sorts of arms, the construction of military engines,
" close fighting, the different sorts of cavalry and the qualities of horses. He drew
" up this treatise in sections, each of which is divided into a number of chapters.
" He was an elderly, good—humoured man, well-looking, pleasant and lively; agree-
" able in his conversation, noble-minded and modest; in his manners concilia-
" tory, kind and tranquil. He was, besides a prolific poet, gifted with original
" thoughts and composing not only detached pieces, but regular kasidas. His poe-
" tical works were united by him in a compendium to which he gave the title of
" Maghâni 'l-Madni (the abodes were striking thoughts abound). He composed
" poems in praise of the khalifs and held rather a high place in the favour of the
" imâm (khalif) An-Nasr li-Dîn Illah Abû 'l-Abbâs Ahmad, the (Abbaside) khalif who
" was then ruling. " — Whilst he was alive, we often received news of him;

the professional reciters of poems giving to the public the pieces of his which they had learned by heart and relating his doings, his adventures, and the passages composed by him on these matters, and in which he displayed great originality of thought. I never had an opportunity of seeing him, though the proximity of his residence to ours rendered us neighbours; he inhabited Baghdad and we dwelt in the town of Arbela, which places are near one to the other; but, as I heard accounts of him frequently during his life, as also the verses which he occasionally composed and which were recited on his authority, I may be considered as having been acquainted with him. I was always anxious to procure the occasional poems which he composed, so greatly was I pleased with his (style and) manner. Many were the friends of his with whom I met, and many also were the persons whom I heard repeating his verses. One of them was our master the shaikh Afíf ad-Dín (virtuous through religion) Abú 'l-Hasan Ali Ibn Adlán, of Mosul, surnamed al-Mutarjim (the interpreter). From him, I learned a great number of these pieces, such, for instance, as the following:

> I was engaged in studying ballistics and in employing machines fitted to destroy castles and to breach redoubts. Then I turned, through poverty, to the composing of verses; so, in both cases, I have been always aiming at a *k&tt* (a *wall, or something to fill the belly*).

Ibn Adlán recited to me also as Ibn Sábir's a piece, the idea of which, said he, never before occurred to any poet. Here it is:

> Trust not to him who restrains his anger through perfidy; fear the arrows of the deceitful. The sharp bows are never more killing than when their water (*their well-tempered blade*) sinks into the bosoms.

He communicated to me also the following piece, which the poet had composed on a dark-coloured Abyssinian girl with whom he was in love:

> That maiden, a daughter of the Abyssinians, shot from her eyelids glances at once powerful and languishing. I loved her through the impulse of youth, and passion turned my hair gray; a thing which I had no mind to. So, when I reproached her with her blackness, she reproached me with my grayness.

He recited to me also this piece, as being of Ibn Sábir's composition:

> A girl was weeping in (*the bustle caused by*) the running of the pilgrims round the Kaaba,

and her tears fell in abundance. I said to her: "Enter into the temple and be not afraid; it "always gives protection to those who are in fear. Its guardianship belongs to the family of " Shaiba (9)." She replied : " I am also afraid of shaibn (grey hair). "

Another of Ibn Sàbir's pieces which he (*Ibn Adlàn*) recited to me, was composed on a young girl (3), who was learning to swim in the Tigris, at Baghdad. She had put on blue drawers and tied to her back a bladder filled with air, as is customary with persons who are learning to swim. On this subject, the poet said :

O you men (*who hear me*) I my affliction (*shiklya*) proceeds from that bladder (*shikwo*) which holds closely to her whom I desire to possess and whom I love. It is filled with *hawa* (*air*) as I am filled with *hawa* (*love*), but it floats where my passion would weigh me down and drown me. Those drawers excite my jealousy whilst they embrace her charms; they are really a *blue enemy.*

This is an original thought. The (*desert*) Arabs, when they wished to describe a man whose hostility (*to another*) was very violent, used to say : " He is the *blue* " *enemy.*" This expression occurs frequently in their discourses and poems. Al-Hariri (*vol. H. p.* 490), made use of it, in the fourteenth (4) *Makáma*, where he says : " But since (*my*) green (*flourishing*) life has been soiled, and since the be-" loved yellow (*money*) has turned away, black have become my days (*once so*) white, " and white, my locks (*once so*) black ; so that pity is shewn to me (*even*) by the " *blue enemy!* Welcome (*were to me even*) red death." In an epistle, the au-thor of which I have not been able to discover, I found the following passage : " We quenched the thirst of our *dark* iron blades in the water of the little *red* rose " (*the heart*), belonging to that enemy of God, the *blue* (*-eyed christian*), one of " the sons of the *yellow* (Europeans)." — This is a subject offering so ample a stock of examples that we need not lengthen our article by adducing others. — He (*Ibn Adlàn*) recited to me the following piece as having been composed by Ibn Sàbir on a band of Sùfis (*dervishes*), to whom he had given hospitality and who eat up all that he set before them. In this piece, which he sent to their superior, he relates what had taken place between him and them :

My lord I you who are the *shaikh* of the convent and have manifested to the world your eminent merit and your noble feelings! To you I complain of the injustice committed by some Sùfis who passed the night with me as guests and friends. I offered them provisions in preference to myself, and I passed the night with my stomach complaining of hunger. When they walked, it was towards the bread; not like those saints whose custom was to walk upon the surface of the waters. They continue to be my guests up to the present moment. Send them, I beg you, bread and sweetmeats; or, if not, take them to you and deliver me from them; I have not a good opinion of people like them.

Here is another piece which the same poet composed on the Súfis and which was recited to me by Ibn Adlân..... (5). A person, but not Ibn Adlân, related to me as follows: "When Ibn Sâbir grew old and slow in his movements, he used to lean "on a staff in walking. Alluding to this, he said:

"In the time of my youth, I threw the staff out of my hand when I intended to make a "halt; and now, that hoary age calls on me to journey forth, I have taken that staff up "again.

"There was at Baghdad a man called Ibn Bishrân, who was always spreading "about reports and rumours. Being forbidden to do so, he took his seat at the "road side, and set up for an astrologer. On this, Ibn Sâbir said:

"Ibn Bishrân turned astrologer through fear of the sultan, and I blame him not. That "unlucky wight was formed by nature to be loquacious; and, not being allowed to speak of "what passes on earth, he talks to us of the heavens."

In the month of Ramadân, 638 (March–April, A. D. 1241), whilst I was in Cairo, Abû Abd Allah Mohammad Ibn Yûsuf Ibn Sâlim, surnamed Shihâb ad-Dîn (the flambeau of religion), and generally known by the appellation of Ibn al-Tallâfari, who was an eminent literary scholar and one of the good poets of the day, recited to me the following verses:

Hoariness! what do you mean? You hasten to invade my dark locks before the time of my youth has expired. Hasten not! for, by Him who changed into day the dark night of my locks, were my hair on the day of judgement to replace the book containing my actions (6) its whiteness, even then, would not rejoice my heart.

On hearing this, I said: "You have stolen from Ibn Sâbir the entire meaning of "the last verse and some of the expressions; you have even adopted his rhyme and "his measure. That poet said:

"If the beard of the gray-haired man were, on the day of the resurrection, the book of his "actions, its whiteness would displease him."

He swore that he had composed the above verses before he heard of this one.
God knows best! Ibn Sâbir's verse belongs to a piece which we give here :

> They say that hoariness is a brilliant light which clothes a man's face with brightness and
> dignity. But, when its grayness invaded the summit of my head, I wished I had not been deprived
> of darkness.   I began to cajole the marks of youth, so that they might remain, and I dyed them
> with a tint of black.   If the beard of the gray-haired man were, on the day of the resurrec-
> tion, the book of his actions, its whiteness would displease him.

A literary man informed me that Ibn Sâbir addressed the following verses to a
man of high rank in Baghdad :

> I come not to you with praises for the purpose of obtaining gifts; I am satisfied with what
> you have already bestowed on me and am thankful.   But I now come to you with a message
> from glory : She says that your efforts to obtain her favour shall not go unrewarded.

When I was in Cairo, I met with some quires of a book containing the poems of
Ibn Sâbir, who, in all his verses, displayed great talent.   I there found the famous
distich which has been attributed to different poets and of which the real author is
not known.   Here is that which I mean :

> Throw me into fire and, if it consume me, be then assured that I am not Yakût (a hyacinth).
> Every one who makes tissues is included in the term weaver; but, in that art, David was not
> equal to the spider (7).

In answer to those two verses, Ibn Sâbir composed the following :

> O thou who art so vain-glorious! leave glory to him who is the lord of greatness and of po-
> wer.   David's tissue would have rendered no service on the night of the Cavern; it was the
> spider who had all the honour.   The resistance of the samured (asbestus) (8) to the ardour
> of fire deprives the yakût of its merit.   The ostrich can swallow burning coals, though they
> are not its (natural) food.

The two verses given first of all have served as models to a number of our contemporaries.   Such, for instance, were the following, composed by Jamâl ad-Dîn
Abû Muhammad al-Kâsim Ibn al-Kâsim Ibn Omar Ibn Mansûr, a native of Wâsit
who had settled in Aleppo and who wrote a commentary on the Makâmas (of al-
Harîri) :

The silkworm, when it built over itself a house and died after spinning, was right in dying; for the spider has spun before (*and outdone it*).

It was thus also that a native of Mosul, named Muhaddab ad-Dîn Abû Abd Allah Muhammad Ibn Abi 'l-Hasan Ibn Yumn al-Ansâri, and generally known by the surname of Ibn Ardakhel, expressed a similar thought in these lines :

People said : « We see you frown when persons unworthy pretend to follow the religion of "love." I answered : " The silkworm was right in killing itself when its work was equalled by " the dwelling of the spider.

In these verses is an allusion to a thought which (two) other poets have expressed thus :

When you have, in any work, a vile fellow for a partner, you incur neither disgrace nor odium.   The class of animals necessarily includes Aristotle and the snappish cur.

The wasp and the falcon, like other animals that fly, have wings and can hover in the air. But great is the difference between what is captured by the falcon and what is caught by the wasp.

Having spoken of the silkworm, we cannot but mention what has been said of the *surfa* (*a sort of case-worm or caddis*).   In al-Jawhari's lexicon, the *Sahâh*, we read that the *surfa* is a little animal which constructs for itself a square house like a coffin, forming it with small bits of wood which it sticks together by means of its spittle.   It then enters into this case and dies.   The expression : *More industrious than the surfa*, is proverbial.   A person of merit told me that the *surfa* is the same as the *arda* (or *termite*); God knows ! — To the verses given above we cannot avoid adding these two :

When people have not at hand an able workman, they take one who is awkward and with- out skill.   When the chess-player is in want of a pawn, his custom is to replace it by a pebble.

The idea which pervades all these verses originates from one which al-Mutanabbi (*vol. I. p.* 102), has thus expressed :

The most worthless prey that my hand ever seized on was, when the yellow falcon and the vulture obtained equal shares.

Something similar is what Abû 'l-Alâ 'l-Maarri (vol. I. pag. 94) has enounced thus:

> How could the lion store up food for its daily wants, and then imitate the ant which gathers up subsistance for the year to come?

There is something in the verses given first of all which requires explanation; for it is not every person who reads them that can understand their meaning. What is said of the yakût, in the first verse, refers to the particular nature of that mineral; fire having no effect on it. Al-Hariri alludes to this in his forty-seventh Makáma; he has there three verses one of which is:

> The yakût may be long heated over burning coals; the coals will at last die out and the yakût remain as it was.

A poet said of a young page of his whose name was Yakût (Hyacinth):

> Yakût! Yakût! the heart of him that yearns after that (youth). — it is an act of generosity that food should not be withheld (from it) (9). Come and dwell in my heart (10); you need not fear the flame with which it burns; why should a yakût fear the flame of fire.

Ideas of this kind frequently occur in poetry; but it is now better that we should be brief. — In the second line of Ibn Sâbir's answer, the words David's tissue would have rendered no service, etc., allude to the flight of the Prophet from Mekka, with Abû Bakr as-Siddîk (the veracious). Apprehensive of being pursued by the infidels of that city, they entered into the cave of Thaur, a mountain situated between Mekka and Medina, but nearer to the former place. Immediately after, a spider wove its web across the entrance of the cave. When the infidels came and saw the work of the spider, they said: "There is nobody here; if any one had gone in, the spider "would not have woven its web so soon." The infidels had immediately hastened pursuit of them, and hoped to attain them, but God concealed the fugitives. This was one of the blessed prophet's miracles. In the third verse (of the same piece), the poet speaks of the samand, which resists the ardour of fire. The word samand, or samandel, as it is sometimes written (11), designates, it is said, a kind of bird which, if it falls into the fire, receives no injury. Napkins are made of its feathers and brought to our countries. When one of them is soiled, it is cast into the fire,

and that element eats away the impurities without harming the napkin or making
any impression on it. I saw a piece of thick cloth made of *samand*; it was in the
shape of a saddle-girth, having the same length as one and the same breadth. They
laid it on a fire, but no effect was produced on it; then they dipped one end of it into
oil and placed it over the (burning) wick of a candle. It took fire and burned for a
long time; when extinguished, nothing was found changed in its former state.
People say that it is imported from India, and that the bird of which we have spoken
is found in that country. There is something curious in that (experiment), which
we must notice here : the end of that piece of cloth was placed over the candle, and
left there for a long time, without its taking fire. One of the persons present, then
said : "Fire has no effect on it, but dip the end of it into oil and place it on the
"fire." They did so, and it blazed up. From this, it appears that, unless it be
dipped in oil, it resists the action of fire. I, afterwards, found in a copy of the auto-
biography composed by our shaikh Muwaffek ad-Din Abd al-Latif Ibn Yusuf al-Baghdadi (12), and in that doctor's hand-writing, that a piece of *samand*, one cubit in
breadth and two in length, was presented to al-Malik az-Zahir, son of Salah ad-Din,
sovereign of Aleppo. When it was dipped in oil and set on fire, it burned so that
the oil was consumed and it then became as white as before. God knows best !
Similar to the *samand*, is the *sarafat*, a little animal which lives in glass-furnaces,
when they are violently heated. There it lays its eggs and produces its young ;
never does it make its nest except in a place where fire is constantly burning.
Glory be to God, the creator of all things ! — In the fourth verse of the piece above
given, Ibn Sâbir speaks of ostriches swallowing burning coals; this is a fact which
we ourselves have often witnessed, and it is so well known that it no longer
appears curious. Here, after all, we have digressed from our subject, but one
observation brought on another, and they have spread to a great extent. — Ibn Sâbir
died at Baghdad, on the eve of the 28th of Safar, 626 (26th Jan. A. D. 1229), and
was buried on Friday, in the new cemetery of the western quarter of the city. His
tomb is near the entrance of the mausoleum which bears the name of Mûsa Ibn
Jaafar (vol. III. p. 463).—The word *howthara*, designated originally the *glans penis*,
and then became the name of a man. Ibn al-Kalbi (vol. III. p. 608), says, in his
Jamharat an-Nisab : "The name of *Howthara* was given to Rabiah Ibn Amr Ibn
"Aâf Ibn Bakr Ibn Wâil for the following reason : As he was making the pilgri-
"mage, he met a woman and bargained with her for a cup. She asked a high

" price for it, on which he said : ' By Allah ! I could stop it up with my *kaulharn*.'
" This word has here the same meaning as the word *kamera*." The relative adjective *manjaniki* is derived from *manjanik* (mangonel), the name of a well known
engine. As we have mentioned this word, we cannot avoid offering some remarks
concerning it, for, on this subject may be said a number of things little known.
First of all, the manjanik is a machine employed (*in war*) and transportable (*from one
place to another*). It is a general rule that, in words of this class (*names of instruments*), the letter m should be followed by the vowel i ; amongst the rare exceptions,
we may cite *munkhal* (*a sieve*), mudhun (*an oil-flask*), and *munt* (*an instrument for
introducing medicinal powders into the nostrils*). Ibn al-Jawaliki (*rol. III. p. 498*),
says, however, in his *Muarrab*, that this word has four forms : manjanik and min-
janik, both of them regular ; then *manjanik* and *manjalik*. It is stated on good
authority, that the m and the first n of this word, may take one or other of the three
vowels. It is also said that those two letters belong to the root of the word. According to another statement, the m is a radical, and the n a complementary letter ; God
knows best (13) ! The word *manjanik* is of foreign origin (14), for the letters j ($\mathrm{\check{g}}$)
and k (k), are never found together in any Arabic word. We thus recognize as
foreign, the words *jurmuk* (*slipper*), *jardak* (*gâteau*), *jausak* (*palace, kiosk*), *julahk*
(*ball of an arbalet*), *kabj* (*partridge*), and others. This is a general rule which
applies also to the letters j ($\mathrm{\check{g}}$), and s ($\mathrm{\bar{s}}$); they are never to be found together in an
Arabic word ; *sahrij* (*pond*), *jass* (*gypsum*), *justul* (?), and others are therefore of
foreign origin. When we put the word *manjanik* in the plural number, we begin
by suppressing one of the *nn*; if we take away the first, we obtain the plural *majânik*,
and, if we suppress the second, we obtain *mandjik*. Al-Jawhari says, in his
Sahâh, that the word *manjanik* is derived from (*the Persian*) man ji nik (15), which,
in Arabic, means : *how good am I*. I may add that *man* signifies *I*, *ji* is (*the
interrogative*) *what*, and *nik* is *good*. So the meaning is *I, what thing, good*,
" These words," says al-Jawhari, " being arabicised, become *manjanik*." Ibn
Kutaiba (*col. II. p. 22*), says, in his *Kitâb al-Madrif*, and Abû Hilâl al-Askari
(*vol. II. p. 440*), in his *Kitâb al-Awâil* (*book of origins*), that the first inventor of
this machine was Jadîma tal-Abrash (16), a king of the Arabs, who possessed (*the
town*) of Hira in former times. Al-Wâhidi (*vol. II. p. 246*), says, in his *Medium
Commentary*, on the Korân, *sûrat* of the Prophets : " When the infidels resolved
" on burning alive Abraham, the friend of God, they lighted a fire (*so great, that*

" *they could not approach it*), and did not know how to cast him into it. Iblîs
" (*Satan*), God's curse be upon him! then went to them and indicated the manner
" of constructing a manjanîk. This was the first ever made. They placed Abra-
" ham on it, and shot him off." God knows best! These paragraphs are a digres-
sion, and, as they are not devoid of useful information, my discourse, on the subject,
has been considerably extended.—Shihâb ad-Dîn at-Tallâfari, he of whom we have
spoken above, informed me that he was born at Mosul, on the 25th of the latter
Jumâda, 593 (15th May, A. D. 1197). He died at Hamâh, on the 10th of Shauwâl,
675 (17th March, A. D. 1277). I heard from his lips, the following verses, which
were the last he ever composed :

> When my bed at night shall be the grave and when I am near unto the Merciful, felicitate me,
> my dear friends! and say: "Rejoice! you have now gone into the presence of the bountiful Lord."

(1) In the translation of these verses, it was necessary to disguise their character by changing some of
the pronouns. The signification given by Arabic poets to the words *myrtle* and *tulu* has been indicated in
vol. I, *Introduction*, p. XLVI.

(2) The Shaiba family had the guardianship (*sadâna*) of the Kaaba even so far back as the reign of
Moawia Ibn Abi Sofyân.

(3) To render the following piece presentable, modifications of the nature indicated in note (1) have been
made in the translation.

(4) It is in the thirteenth *Makama* that the passage occurs.

(5) This piece and the following cannot be given by the translator : the grammatical construction of the
first and the wit contained in it he is unable to discover; the second piece, containing three lines, cannot be
translated.

(6) See Sale's Introduction to the Koran, sect. IV.

(7) The king and prophet David was celebrated for making coats of mail; the work of the spider is explained further on, page 375.

(8) This word is explained by our author further on.

(9) In the translation, the awkward grammatical construction of the Arabic text has been followed.

(10) The text has : you have dwelt in my heart.

(11) This word is evidently an alteration of the Greek *kalaptiptos*.

(12) This is the celebrated Abdallatif whose Description of Egypt has been published by Dr White and by
S. de Sacy. Ibn Khallikan was about nineteen years of age when Abd al-Latîf died.

(13) Here, in the Arabic text, is a passage out of its place and which will be found at the end of this biographical article. It is given in two of our manuscripts.

(14) *Manjanîk* comes from the Greek *μαγγανικ*.

(15) This lexicographer meant to write the Persian words نيك جه من (*men iche nik*).

(15) For the history of this antrislamite prince, who was king of Hira, see Pocoeke's *Specimen Hist. Arabum*, 2nd edition, page 67 et seq., and Caussin de Perceval's *Essai sur l'Hist. des Arabes*, tome II, p. 10 et seq. Pococke writes the name *Jodsima*, and Caussin *Djothema*, but this pronunciation is erroneous.

IBN AS-SAIGH *THE GRAMMARIAN.*

The grammarian Abû 'l-Baka Yaîsh Ibn Ali Ibn Yaîsh Ibn Abi 's-Saráiya Ibn Muhammad Ibn Ali Ibn al-Mufaddal Ibn Abd al-Karim Ibn Muhammad Ibn Yahya
Ibn Haiyân al-Kâdi Ibn Bishr Ibn Haiyân was a descendant of Asad (*the progenitor of
the Arabic tribe thus named*). He belonged to a family of Mosul, but was born and
brought up in Aleppo. This grammarian was surnamed Muwaffak ad-Din (*favoured
in religion*), and was generally known by the appellation of Ibn as-Sàigh (*the son of
the goldsmith*). He studied grammar under the direction of Abû 's-Sabnâ Fityân (1),
a native of Aleppo, Abû 'l-Abbâs al-Maghrebi and an-Nîrouzi. At Mosul he heard
traditions delivered by Abû 'l-Fadl Abd Allah Ibn Ahmad al-Khatîb at-Tûsi (*the
pulpit-orator of Tûs*) and Abû Muhammad Abd Allah Ibn Omar Ibn Suwaida of
Tikrît. At Aleppo, he learned traditions from Abû 'l-Faraj Yahya Ibn Mahmûd ath-
Thakefi, the kâdi Abû 'l-Husain Ahmad Ibn Muhammad at-Tarsûsi and Khalid Ibn
Muhammad Ibn Nasr Ibn Saghir al-Kaisarâni. At Damascus he received traditions from Tâj ad-Din al-Kindi (*vol. I. p 546*) and other masters, and, at Aleppo,
he taught them. In syntax and etymology he displayed great talent and skill.
On entering into active life he set out from Aleppo for Baghdad, with the intention of meeting there Abû 'l-Barakât Abd ar-Rahmân Ibn Muhammad, surnamed Ibn
al-Anbâri (*vol. II. p. 95*) and the other professors who flourished, at that epoch, in Irâk
and in Jazira (*Mesopotamia*). On reaching Mosul he learned that Ibn al-Anbâri
was dead.—In our article on that grammarian will be found the date of his death.
—He remained for a short time in that city and heard traditions taught there, after
which, he returned to Aleppo. Having then decided on becoming a professor of
literature, he travelled to Damascus and there met with Tâj ad-Din Abû 'l-Yumn
Zaid Ibn al-Hasan al-Kindi, a celebrated shaikh (*professor*) and imâm of whom we

have given a notice (vol. I. p. 546). He questioned him on some difficult points of Arabic grammar and asked him how he should construe the following passage, taken from the latter part of al-Hariri's tenth *Makáma* entitled the *Rahabiyan*: " Till, " when illuminated the sky (al-ufk) the tail of the wolf (the *twilight*,—in Arabic " *dhanab el-sirhán*), and arrived the time of the glimmering of the dawn." Al-Kindi was unable to resolve the difficulty, which was to determine whether the words *ufk* and *dhanab* were in the nominative case or in the accusative, or if *ufk* were in the nominative and *dhanab* in the accusative, or *vice versa*. " I know " what you at aiming at; " said he, " you wish to show how exalted a place you " hold in this science." He then wrote with his own hand a certificate in which he praised him in high terms, acknowledging his great proficiency in literature.— I may here state that the question admits the four solutions, but that which is preferred is the putting of *ufk* in the accusative and *dhanab* in the nominative. This opinion has been already expressed by Táj ad-Dín Abú Abd Allah Muhammad Ibn Abd ar-Rahmán al-Bundahi (vol. III. p. 99), in his commentary on the *Makámas*, and, were I not apprehensive of being led too far, I should explain all that here.— In the year 626, on Tuesday, the 1st of Zú 'l-Kaada (21st Sept. A. D. 1229), I arrived at Aleppo for the purpose of studying the noble science (*jurisprudence and divinity*). That city was then the capital of a principality and was filled with learned men and with students. The Muwaffak ad-Dín of whom we are here speaking was at that time the chief of the literary community and in it he stood without a rival. I began to study under him; he taught in the great mosque, and held his class in the northern *maksúra* (vol. II. p. 255), immediately after the *asr* prayer (vol. I. p. 594). In the interval between the two prayers (the *mughrib and the asha* (?)), he taught in the *Rawáḥya* college. A considerable number of students, who had already attained great distinction under his tuition, attended his sittings most assiduously and were never absent when he gave lessons. I commenced by Ibn Jinni's *Luma* (vol. II. p 192) and read over to him the greater part of that work, besides which, I listened to the lecture which he addressed to the assembly. This was towards the close of the year 627 (Oct.-Nov. A. D. 1230). I finished the *Luma* under another master,—circumstances having forced me to do so. He had a rare talent for explaining difficulties and rendering them intelligible; his tone was mild, his patience with beginners and proficients most exemplary, his character cheerful, his disposition pleasing and, with all his seriousness and gravity, he was inclined to pleasantry. I was one day at his class whilst a legist was reading the *Luma* under his direction and had come to the following verse of Zû 'r-Rumma's (*vol II. p.* 447), which is cited as an example in the chapter on the vocative:

Gazelle of the desert which lies between Jaldjil and an-Nakal is it you whom I see or Omm Sâlim?

Here the professor said to him: "The poet had so violent a passion for his mistress, " so ardent a desire to possess Omm Sâlim, her whom he loved and whom he had " often compared to a gazelle, conformably to the custom of poets in assimilating " handsome women to fawns and to gazelles, that his mind was quite confused, " and, knowing not whether the object which he saw was a woman or a gazelle, he " exclaimed: Is it you or Omm Sâlim?" He continued to discourse in this style, and in such clear terms that the dullest and most stupid of men might have understood his explanation. The legist listened to him with the utmost attention, so that any person who saw him would have thought, from his aspect, that he understood perfectly well what was said. When Muwaffak ad-Din had finished, the other said to him: "Tell me, master! what are the points of likeness between a hand- " some woman and a gazelle?" The professor replied: "Explanation in full: " The likeness lies in the tail and the horns (2)." These words threw all who were present into a fit of laughter, and the legist was so much abashed that I never again saw him at the lecture.—*Jaldjil* or *Juldjil* is the name of a place. There are two *jj* in the word.—We were one day reading in the Rawâhiya mosque, under Muwaffak ad-Din's direction, when a trooper (*jundi*) came in with a paper in which was written the acknowledgment of a debt; it should be known that the professor used to act as a witness to law papers. The man said to him: "Master! witness " this writing for me." Muwaffak ad-Din took the paper out of his hand and, find- ing that the first words of it were these: *Fâtima acknowledges*, he said to " the man: Are you Fâtima?" "The trooper replied: "She will be here in " a moment." He then went to the door of the college and, as he brought her in, he kept smiling at what the professor said.—An anecdote similar to this is related in our article on Aâmir as-Shâbi (*col. II. p.* 6): a person went into the room where he was and, finding a woman with him, said: "Which of you two is as-Shâbi?" to which the other replied: "She is the man."—We were one day reading under his direction, in his own house, when one of the persons present felt thirsty and asked

the servant boy for some water. When it was brought, he drank it off and said :
" That is merely cold water (3)." On this, the professor said to him : " Had it
" been warm bread, you would have liked it better."—Another day, we were with
him in the Nawáhiya college when the mueaddin came in and announced the asr
prayer, an hour before the time. The persons present said to him : " What does
" this mean ? you old fellow ! the hour of the asr is yet far off."—" Let him alone,"
said the shaikh Muwaffak ad-Din, " he may perhaps have business and is in haste."
—He was, one day, at the house of Bahá ad-Din Ibn Shaddád, the kádi of Aleppo,
—we shall give his life,—and the company happened to be talking of Zarka
'l-Yemáma (4), her who could distinguish objects at a great distance, that of
a three days' journey, it is said. Those who were present related the anecdotes
which they had learned respecting her, and the shaikh Muwaffak ad-Din said :
" I can distinguish an object at the distance of a two months' journey." The
company were surprised at this assertion but none of them dared to question him
on the subject, till the kádi asked him how that could be. He replied : " I
" can see the new moon." On hearing this, the kádi said : " You might
" as well have said : 'At the distance of such and such a number of years'
" ' journey. — " Nay," answered Muwaffak ad-Din, " had I said so, they would
" have known what I meant ; but my object was to puzzle them."—It would take
us too long to relate the numerous anecdotes told of this professor.—I was one day
with him at his house when a native of Maghrib, who was an eminent literary scholar
and who had just arrived from Musul, came in and took his place in the circle of
students which surrounded the professor. During the lesson, the stranger discussed
some questions with the ability which distinguishes a man of talent, and mention was
made of the controversies which he had at Mosul with some of the eminent scholars
who resided in that city. He then related as follows : " I was at the house of Diá
" ad-Din Nasr Allah Ibn al-Athir al-Jazari,"—we have give an article on this
person (vol. III. p. 541),—" and we engaged in a conversation during which we
" recited pieces of verse. On this occasion I repeated to him the following lines
" which had been composed by a native of Maghrib."—I may here observe that
Abû Ishak al-Husri (vol. I p. 34) has mentioned them also and attributes them to a
native of Kairawán whom he does not indicate :

" These youths, the vegetation of whose checks resemble pens of musk (blackness) dipped
" in khalúk (5), have united the violet (the dark hair of the cheeks) to the anemony (the

"*redness of the cheeks*) and ranged underneath the emerald (*the hair growing on the upper*
" *lip*) pearls (*white teeth*) and cornelians (*red lips*). They are such that when a maiden de-
" void of cares sees them, love towards them finds its way into her heart."

The (*latter*) half of the second verse contains an idea similar to that which Ibn
az-Zarawi (or ad-Darawi), the Egyptian, expressed in a piece of verse which is given
in our article on Mubárak Ibn Munkid (*vol. II. p. 555*), where he says :

Under the hyacinth (*the dark tress*) of his lips appears a row of pearls still humid, and he
displays a moustache of emerald.

In a piece attributed to Abú Muhammad al-Hasan Ibn Ali, generally known by
the surname of Ibn Waki' at-Tinnísi (*vol. I. p. 396*) we find this passage :

The qualities by which we may describe him are all taken from precious stones; so that the
greatest genius and the sharpest intellect are unable to conceive them. The moustache is
of emerald, the teeth are of pearl enclosed in a mouth of cornelian.

These verses remind me of two others which I knew by heart and which may
be appropriately mentioned here, after the preceding :

When (6) we stopped to say a mutual farewell and when the idea which we had formed of
(*the pains of*) love was realized, my friends shed pearls (*tears*) on the dark anemonies (*the
cheeks*) and I let drop cornelians (*tears of blood*) upon the marigold (*my pallid cheeks*).

The following verses, in the same style, were recited by al-Wáwá ad-Dimishki
(*vol. II. p. 340*) :

She rained down pearls from the narcissus (*the eyes*) and watered roses (*the cheeks*); she bit
the jujuba (*her brown lips*) with hailstones (*white teeth*).

In the same style are the following verses, composed by Muhammad Ibn Saíd
al-Ahmiri, a native of Damascus, but some persons attribute them to Ibn Waki' :

When we embraced to say farewell, dropping tears spoke our feelings in the clearest language; they separated veils from eyes (*caused the females to unveil*) (?) and united the violet to
the anemony. I should sacrifice my life to save that gazelle on the bowers (*ringlets*) of whose
face are fixed the pupils of our eyes.

Similar to this are the following verses attributed to Abù 'l-Fath al-Hasan Ibn Abi Hasina, a poet of some reputation and a native of Aleppo :

When we stopped to say a mutual farewell, and whilst her heart and mine were overflowing with passion and with love, she wept liquid pearls; my eyelids let fall cornelians, and both formed a necklace on her bosom.

My friend Husâm ad-Dîn Isa Ibn Sinjar Ibn Bahrâm al-Hâjiri (vol. II p. 434), who was a native of Arbela, recited to me the following piece as being of his own composing :

When we met again, after a long lapse of time, she saw that the tears in the corners of my eyes were drops of blood, and she said : " When I last saw those pearls, they flowed " like cornelians, but why (*should they do so now*) since this is (*the joyful hour of*) our " meeting. " I answered : Wonder not, my beloved! thou for whom I, living or dead, should " give my soul! The tears you first saw were those of our farewell; what you see now are the " last drops of those which were caused by our separation. "

[The *shaikh* (7) Muwaffak ad-Dîn often recited the following verses, which he attributed to Abù Ali al-Hasan Ibn Roshik (vol. I. p. 384), but I looked for them without success in the collected poetical works of that writer :

I did not approach you with the intention of deluding ; I did not praise you through arti- fice ; but, considering it my duty to extol you, even when that was not an obligation, I began a discourse of which you could not but see the merit, and I continued till my words were unequal to the grandeur of the subject. Let not unjust suspicions agitate your mind, for they are blamable ; leave to me the means of making my peace. If I were mistrustful of any other but you, I should give full career to the inclination which impels me to speak (my *mind*). By Allah, I did not discourse of you with prolixity, neither did I expose my ear to hear a word in your dispraise. I did myself honour (*in praising you*), exalting myself thus above contempt and humiliation. I have left (you), but enmity has not left (*my heart*) ; I have broken (*with you*), but my sincerity remains unbroken.]

There exist a great number of pieces similar, in their character, to those given above, and it is needless to expatiate farther on the subject.—Muwaffak ad-Dîn compo- sed a commentary on az-Zamakhshari's *Mufassal* (vol. III. p. 322) ; it is fuller and more complete than any other treatise of the kind. His commentary on Ibn Jinni's *Tasrîf al-Mulûki (the parsing of the Mulûki)* (8) is a fine work which has greatly con- tributed to the instruction of many natives of Aleppo, and other places. Amongst his pupils he had men who, at that time, filled high offices in the city. He was born at Aleppo on the 3rd of Ramadán, 553 (28th Sept. A. D. 1158), and he died there on the morning of the 25th of the first Jumáda, 643 (18th Oct. A. D. 1245). He was buried the same day within the monument which he had erected for himself in the Makàm (or *residence*) of Abraham (*situated within the citadel of Aleppo*).

(1) Abû 'a-Sahad Fityân, a man of a low family and a weaver at Aleppo, studied the science of grammar and, subsequently in the year 546 (A. D. 1151), when that city was besieged and nearly ruined by the Crusaders, he was the only learned man to be found in it. He died on or about the year 560 (A. D. 1164-5). Ibn as-Sáigh was one of his disciples.—(Suyûti, in his *History of the Grammarians*.)

(2) The professor might have spared the joke and given a direct answer to the logic's question. He had only to tell him that the large eyes and the graceful movements of a handsome girl are compared by poets to those of the gazelle.

(3) It would seem that water and nothing in one with it was called *cold water*.

(4) See Caussin de Perceval's : *Essai sur l'histoire des Arabes*, tome I, p. 161.

(5) The *khalûk* was a sort of perfume or unguent, coloured yellow with the crocus flower. The tint of the cheeks is compared to it.

(6) The manuscripts and the editions have لَوَلَا, but the rules of prosody require us to read لَوَلَا. The sense is the same in both cases.

(7) The passage placed between brackets is to be found in only one of our manuscripts.

(8) The *Maâdhi* was probably the same work as the *Kitâb al-Maûlâ* (*Book of Kings*), one of the numerous treatises composed by the grammarian al-Akhfash al-Awsat (see vol. I. p. 675).

YAMÛT IBN AL-MUZARRA.

[*Here is the genealogy of Yamût*] : Abû Bekr Yamût Ibn al-Muzarrá Ibn Yamût Ibn Isa Ibn Mûsa Ibn Sinán Ibn Hakim Ibn Jabala Ibn Hisn Ibn Aswad Ibn Kâb Ibn Aâmir Ibn Adi Ibn al-Hârith Ibn ad-Duîl Ibn Amr Ibn Ghanem Ibn Wadiah Ibn Lukaiz Ibn Afsa Ibn Abd al-Kais Ibn Afsa Ibn Domi Ibn Jadila Ibn Asad Ibn Rabiah Ibn Nizâr Ibn Maadd Ibn Adnán. He was a member of the tribe of Abd al-Kais (al-Abdi) and a native of Basra. In Ibn al-Kalbi's *Jamhara tan-Nasab* (col. III. p. 608) I find mention made of this Hakim Ibn Jabala, with a genealogy traced up in the same manner as we have just done, but, on the margin of the book I perceived the following note: " One of Hakim Ibn Jabala's descendants was " Yamút Ibn al-Muzarrá Ibn Yamút; he (*Ibn al-Kalbi*) has traced his genealogy up " to Hakim in a manner for which he alone must be answerable." In a collection of rough notes made by myself I found this passage in my own handwriting: " Yamút was the son of al-Muzarrá Ibn Yamút Ibn Odas Ibn Saiyár Ibn al-" Muzarrá Ibn al-Hárith Ibn Thalaba Ibn Amr Ibn Dhamra Ibn Dilháth Ibn Wadiah " Ibn Bakr Ibn Lukais Ibn Afsa." God knows best the truth in this matter! Yamút himself took the name of *Muhammad;* the Khatib of Baghdad (col. I. p. 75) mentions him among the Muhammads in his greater (*biographical*) history of that city, and he afterwards speaks of him under the letter Y. He there says: " His name " was Yamút; he was a sister's son to Abú Othmán al-Jáhiz (col. II. p. 405)." Yamút Ibn al-Muzarrá went to Baghdad in the year 301 (A. D. 913-4), and was then an old man (1). He there taught Traditions on the authority of Abú Othmán al-Mázini (col. I. p. 261), Abú Hátim as-Sijistáni (col. I. p. 605), Abú 'l-Fadl ar-Riáchi (col. II. p. 10), Nasr Ibn Ali al-Jahdami (col. I. p. 496), Abd ar-Rahmán, a brother's son to al-Asmái (col. II. p. 123), Muhammad Ibn Yahya al-Azdi (2), Abú Ishak Ibrahim Ibn Sofyán az-Ziádi and other masters. Traditions were delivered on his authority by Abú Bakr al-Kharáiti (col. I. p. 323), Abú 'l-Maimún Ibn Ráshid, Abú 'l-Fadl al-Abbás Ibn Muhammad ar-Rakki, Abú Bakr Ibn Mujáhid, the teacher of the Korán-readings (vol. I, p. 27), Abú Bakr Ibn al-Anbári (col. III. p. 53) and others. He was an accomplished literary scholar and well versed in history. A number of curious and interesting anecdotes have been handed down by him. He never fulfilled the duty of visiting the sick lest a bad omen might be drawn from his name (*Yamút* signifying, *he dies*) : " The name," said he, " which I received from my " father has been a great annoyance to me; so, when I go to visit the sick and am " asked my name, I answer: ' The son of al-Muzarrá,' and suppress my real " name." Mansúr, a blind jurisconsult (*ad-Darír*) who was also a poet, composed the following lines in his praise :

You keep (us) in life, and he whom you do not wish to live, dies. You are the twin-brother of my soul; nay, you are the nourishment of my soul's existence. You are a dwelling-place for wisdom; may our dwelling-places be never without your presence.

One of the historical anecdotes related by him was the following, which he
gave in the words of Abû 'l-Fadl ar-Rbâchi, from whose lips he had heard
it : " Al-Asmâi (*vol. II. p. 123*)," said Abû 'l-Fadl, " related to me as follows :
" Hârûn ar-Rashîd was incensed against (*his relative*) Abd al-Malik Ibn Sâlih, the
" son of Ali, the son of Abd Allah, the son of al-Abbâs, the son of Abd al-Muttalib
" (*col. I. p. 316*). This was in the year 188 (A. D. 803-4). I was with ar-Rashîd
" when Abd al-Malik was brought in, dragging after him the chain in which he
" was bound. Ar-Rashîd, on seeing him, said : ' Soho, Abd al-Malik ! methinks
" ' I see the cloud (*of destruction*) already dropping its rains! methinks I see its
" ' lightnings already flashing! methinks I see my threat (*executed and*) disclosing
" ' to view fingers separated from wrists and heads from shoulders. Gently!
" ' gently! O you children of Hâshim! for it was by me that, for you, the
" ' rugged was smoothed and the turbid clarified ; it was through my means, that
" ' power placed her own bridle in your hands. Beware of my wrath lest a cata-
" ' strophy befal you and come stumbling down upon you, tripped off its forefeet and
" ' its hind ones (3)! Abd al-Malik replied : ' Shall I speak to you in single or in
" ' double (4)?' — 'Let it be in double,' said ar-Rashîd. On this, the other spoke
" ' as follows : ' Commander of the faithful! respect God in what he has confided
" ' to your care; be mindful of him in tending the flock over which he has
" ' appointed you to be the shepherd. By Allah! it was by me that the rugged
" ' paths were smoothed for you and that all bosoms were rendered unanimous in
" ' the hopes and fears which you inspire them. I was like the person whom a
" ' poet of the Bani Jaafar Ibn Kilâb family described in these terms :

> Often did I widen a narrow place (*remove obstacles*) by eloquence and by reasoning.
> Were an elephant to stand forth with his rider and attempt to reach a station such as mine,
> he would retire humiliated. "

The narrator continued thus : " Yahya Ibn Khâlid the Barmekide, wishing to abate
" the high opinion in which Abd al-Malik was held by ar-Rashîd, then said to the
" former : ' Abd al-Malik! I have been told that you are of a malevolent disposition.'
" To this the other replied : ' May God direct the vizir! if malevolence consists in
" ' the lasting recollection of good and evil done to me, I avow that such recollec-
" ' tions remain always in my heart.' " Al-Asmâi here added : " Ar-Rashîd

"turned towards me and said: 'Asmáí! take note of that; by Allah! never before was
"an argument produced in favour of malevolence such as Abd al-Malik has just
"offered.' He then remanded the prisoner, after which"—said al-Asmáí,—
"he turned towards me and said: 'I assure you, Asmáí! that, more than once, I
"looked at that part of his neck which I meant to strike with the sword, but my
"merciful disposition towards every member of my family prevented me (from
"striking him).'" — I have already spoken of Abd al-Malik Ibn Sálih in the
life of the poet Abù Obàda al-Walîd al-Bohtori (vol. III. p. 657), and have there
given the date of his death.—Yamùt Ibn al-Muzarrà related as follows : "The
"kâtib Abù 'l-Hasan Ahmad Ibn Muhammad Ibn Abd Allah, surnamed Ibn al-
"Mudabbir, was a member of the tribe of Dabba and a native of Dastamîsàn (5).
"When a poet came to him with an eulogium, his custom was, if the verses
"did not please him, to say to his attendant : 'Take this man to the great
"mosque and do not let him go till he has accomplished a prayer of one hundred
"rakas (6).' All the poets, except a few, those of real talent, avoided his pre-
"sence for that reason." One day, a native of Egypt named Abù Abd Allah al-
Husain Ibn Abd as-Salàm and generally known by the surname of al-Jamal (7),
asked of him the authorisation to recite him a poem.   "You are aware of the con-
"dition?" said Ibn al-Mudabbir.   "I am," replied the other, and he began
thus :

> We wished to speak in praise of Abû Hasan, because eulogy is the means by which men is
> office are rendered the pasture (of the needy). We said : "He is the noblest of all creatures,
> "men or genii; nothing can equal him (in the copiousness of his gifts) except the (abun-
> dant flow of) the Tigris and the Euphrates."   On this, people said : "He receives praises but
> "repays them with prayers."   To which I answered : "To maintain my family, alms are neces-
> "sary, not prayers of mine.   Let him order for me, as a favour, that the first vowel of one
> "word be changed; then salât (prayers) will become silât (gifts) for me. "

Ibn al-Mudabbir laughed at this idea and asked the author where he borrowed
it? The reply was : "From a verse in which Abû Tammâm at-Tai (vol. I. p. 348)
says :

> "They are hamâm (pigeons), but if, in taking us angury, you pronounce the h with an i.
> "they will become himâm (death)."

This answer pleased Ibn al-Mudabbir and obtained an ample donation for the poet.
—Ahmad Ibn al-Mudabbir was administrator of the land-tax throughout Egypt.   In
the year 265 (A. D. 878-9), he was sent to prison by Ahmad Ibn Tûlûn (vol. I. p. 153)

and remained there till the month of Safar, 270 (Aug.-Sept. 883 (8), when he died.
According to another statement, he was put to death by Ibn Túlún; God knows best!
—*Mudabbir* is to be pronounced with an *i* after the second *b*.—(Yamút; Ibn al-Muzarrá stated that his maternal uncle, Abú Othmán al-Jáhiz, related to him the following anecdote : "Al-Motasim (*the khalif*) endeavoured to obtain a slave-girl belong-
"ing to the poet Mahmúd Ibn al-Hasan al-Warrák and bearing the name of
"Nashwa. He was greatly enamoured with her and had offered seven thousand
"dinars to purchase her. Mahmúd, who was also very fond of her, would not
"consent to the sale. After Mahmúd's death, the girl was bought for the khalif
"out of the inheritance, and the price given for her was seven hundred dinars.
"When she was brought to him he addressed her thus : 'Do you see that? I left
"'you there for a time and then purchased you for seven hundred dinars instead
"'of seven thousand.' To this she replied : 'Certainly, if the khalif waits for
"'(*the sale of*) inheritances before he gratifies his passions, (*such passions cannot
"'be very strong, and*) seventy dinars would then be a high price for me, let
"'alone seven hundred!'—The khalif, on hearing these words was greatly abashed."
—Yamút related also that a man spoke to him and said : "I saw in Syria a tomb-
"stone on which was written : 'Let no one be deluded by the (*vanities of the*)
"'world. I was the son of a person who sent forth the wind whither he pleased
"'and retained it when he pleased (9)!' Opposite to this stone was another,
"bearing this inscription : 'The miserable scoundrel has there told a lie (10).
"'Let no one suppose that the person spoken of is Solomon, the son of David;
"'the man was the son of a blacksmith who used to gather wind into a skin and
"'direct it upon lighted coals.' He then said : 'Never before did I see two tomb-
"'stones one of which insulted the other."—The historical recitals, stories and
curious anecdotes which have come down from Ibn al-Muzarrá are very numerous,
but our design is to be as concise as possible and avoid prolixity, unless our discourse happens to take a wide spread. Yamút had a son called Abú Nadla Muhalhil
Ibn Yamút, who was a good poet and of whom al-Masúdi said, in his *Murúj ad-
Dahab wa Maddin al-Jauhar (meadows of gold and mines of jewels)* : "He is
"a poet of the present time;" that was in the year 332 (A. D. 943-4). His
father addressed him in a piece of verse which we give here :

Muhalhil! you adorned for me the web of life (11) whilst stubborn fortune turned her face against me. I struggled with mankind in every way, till high and low submitted to me humbly. The most painful feeling which my heart encloses is (to see) a virtuous man ill-treated by malignant fortune. It is for me grief quite sufficient to see men of an old (and noble descent) reduced to ruin, whilst thrones are occupied by the sons of slaves. These eyes which were yielding to sleep, I kept open, fearing that you might be ruined when I was no more. But, through the grace of God, the Protector, I shall find consolation in you, whether I live or die. Travel over the earth; search it throughout for knowledge, and may no dire (12) calamity cut short your career! If a man of learning withholds from you (what he knows), humble yourself before him and let your rule be to keep silent. Say that your father freely bestowed his knowledge, and if people ask who was your father, say that he is dead (yamût). May your lore and adversaries acknowledge that you possess learning such as no calumniator can disprove.

Yamût Ibn Muzarrâ went to Egypt at different times; his last visit to that country took place in the year 303 (A. D. 915-6), and he left it the next year. Abû Saïd Ibn Yûnus as-Sadafi (vol. II. p. 93), the Egyptian, says in his shorter work on the foreigners who came to Egypt, that Yamût Ibn al-Muzarrâ died at Damascus in the year 304 (A. D. 916-7), but Abû Sulaimân Ibn Zain (13) states, in the historical work composed by him, that this event took place at Tiberias, in Syria. God knows best! —Muhalhil, the son of Yamût, is noticed by the Khatîb (vol. I. p. 75), in the History of Baghdad. We there read as follows: "Muhalhil was a poet; he composed pleasing "verses on amatory and other subjects and inhabited Baghdad. He transmitted "orally (his poetical productions) to others. His poetry was written down under his "dictation by Abû Badâ Ibrahim Ibn Muhammad, surnamed Tûzûn." After this, the same author adds: "At-Tanûkhi related to us what I here give: "Abû 'l-Husain "Ahmad Ibn Muhammad Ibn al-Abbas al-Akhbâri related to us as follows: "In the year 326 (A. D. 937-8) I was present at a sitting held by Tuhfa tal- "Kuwâla (14), who was a slave-girl belonging to Abd Allah Ibn Omar al-Bâzyâr. "I had on my left Abû Nadla Muhalhil, the son of Yamût, and, on my right, Abû "'l-Kâsim Ibn Abi 'l-Hasan, a native of Baghdad. Tuhfa then sung to us from "behind a curtain:

"I am too much preoccupied with him to neglect him, so greatly do I love him; yet he "affects to neglect me. Thinking that I wronged him, he turned away from me and let the "same (disdain) appear which he feared in me. He was pleased to see that I was mad on his "account, and I was pleased when my madness redoubled.

"Abû Nadla, on hearing these verses, said to me: 'It was I who composed "'them.' Abû 'l-Kâsim, who overheard him and had a dislike for him, told me

" to ask of him an additional verse for the same piece. I made the request to Abû
" Nadla in a polite manner, and he pronounced these words :

" By his beauty he creates such trouble (in our hearts) as gives me who love him every sort
of trouble."

The following piece is by Muhalhil :

His charms are so exalted that nothing can be compared to them, and are so great that no
one can describe them. Contemplate his beauty and dispense me from describing it; glory to
the Creator! glory to the Maker of all ! To that youth belongs the humid narcissus (the eyes)
and the rose just plucked; in his mouth is the (white) anthemis flower (like teeth), moist in
its brightness. By his glances he attracts my heart to my perdition, and it hastens towards him
submissively, obedient to his will. It goes there as the moth rushes towards a burning lamp
and throws itself into the flame.

Other pieces by the same author are given in the Khatîb's work, but I abstain
from inserting them here.—The name *Muzarrd* is to be pronounced with an *ain* after
the last *r;* so it is stated by the shaikh (*professor*) and *hâfiz* Zaki ad-Dîn Abd al-Azîm
Ibn Abd al-Kawi Ibn Abd Allah al-Mundiri (vol. I. p. 89).—*Hakîm* Ibn Jabala, the
person who is mentioned in the genealogy (*at the beginning of this article*), is named
by some *Hukaim* and his father *Jabal.* He was one of Ali Ibn Abi Tâlib's partisans.
Ali, on being proclaimed khalif, received the oath of allegiance from Talha Ibn
Obaid Allah at-Taimi and as-Zubair Ibn al-Auwâm al-Asadi. He then resolved to
nominate the latter as governor of Basra and the former as governor of Yemen; but
one of his female clients, happening to go out, overheard those two chiefs say : " We
" have sworn to him with our tongues, not with our hearts." Ali whom she
informed of this circumstance, exclaimed : " May God reject them! whoever
" breaks an oath does so to his own detriment." He then dispatched Othmân Ibn
Hunaif al-Ansâri to Basra in the capacity of governor and confided the government
of Yemen to Obaid Allah, the son of al-Abbâs Ibn Abd al-Muttalib. Ibn Hunaif
gave the command of the *shurta (police-guards)* to Hakim Ibn Jabala. Talha and
as-Zubair then went to Mekka and, having met there Aaisha (*the widow of Muhammad, and surnamed*) the Mother of the faithful (*Omm al-Muminîn*), they concerted
matters with her and proceeded to Basra, where Ibn Hunaif was. Hakim Ibn
Jabala went to the latter and advised him to hinder the two chiefs from entering into

the city. Ibn Hunaif refused to do so, saying that he did not know Ali's opinion on that subject. Talha and az-Zobair went into the city and, being well received by the people, they posted themselves in the Marbad (or public place) and began to discourse about the murder of Othmân Ibn Affân and the inauguration of Ali. A man of the Abd al-Kais tribe attempted to refute their insinuations, but was ill-treated by them and had his beard plucked out. The people then began to throw stones and raised a great commotion. Hakîm Ibn Jabala went to Ibn Hunaif and asked permission to charge the mutineers, but could not obtain it. Abd Allah, the son of az-Zubair, then went to the city (magazine), where the provisions were kept for the troops, and began to distribute them to his partisans. Hakîm Ibn Jabala went forth at the head of seven hundred soldiers belonging to the tribe of Abd al-Kais, but was attacked by the insurgents and killed with seventy of his companions. It is related that he had said to his wife, who belonged to the tribe of Azd : " I shall " to day treat your people in a manner such as will furnish a matter of talk of all men."—" Nay," replied the woman, " I think my people will to day strike you " such a blow as shall be a subject of talk for every one." Hakîm was then en- countered by a man called Suhaim, who struck him on the neck with his sword and so violently that the head was nearly separated from the body, to which it remained attached by a strip of skin. (Suhaim) then turned the head half-way round, so that the face was directed backwards. This occurred before the arrival of Ali and his army. When he came up, a conflict took place between the two parties, on a Thursday, towards the middle of the latter Jumâda, A. H. 36 (8th December, A. D. 656). The battle was fought on the spot where the castle (casr) of Obaid Allah Ibn Ziâd was (afterwards) built. Then came on the great engagement called the Battle of the Camel, which took place on Thursday, the 19th of the same month (13th December). The first arrival of the insurgents (at Basra) and the death of Hakîm Ibn Jabala had occurred some days previously. The total loss on both sides amounted to ten thousand men. Talha and az-Zubair were killed on that very day, but not in the battle. Were I not apprehensive of being led too far, I should relate how that hap- pened (15). Al-Mâmûni (vol. II. p. 334) says, in his History : " It is stated that " the people of Medina learned on that very Thursday, before sunset, that a battle " had been fought. This they became aware of by seeing a vulture hovering " around the city and bearing something suspended (from its beak). This " it let fall and, on examination, was found to be a hand on which was a

" ring inscribed with the name of Abd ar-Rahmán Ibn Attáb Ibn Asíd.
" Then, all who dwelt between Mekka and Medina, and all who lived about
" Basra, far or near, knew that a battle had taken place, from seeing the number of
" hands and feet which had been carried thither by vultures."— Kushájim (vol. I.
p. 304) says, in his work entitled *Al-Masdid wa'l-Matdrid*, that the vulture
dropped the hand of Abd ar-Rahmán into the city of Mekka, and the same statement is made in the law-book entitled *el-Muhaddab* (vol. I. p. 9), in the chapter
which treats of the prayer to be said over the dead. Ibn al-Kalbi and Abû Yakzán
(vol. II. p. 576) say, in their respective works, that the vulture dropped the hand
in (*the province of*) al-Yemáma.

(1) This passage and the following belong, perhaps, to the extract from the Khatîb's work.

(2) According to the author of the *Nujûm*, Muhammad Ibn Yahya Ibn Abd al-Karim al-Asdî died A. H. 299 (A. D. 864-7).

(3) This discourse is in rhyming prose, full of metaphors and uncommon expressions; an imitation, in fact, of the affected and sententious style for which the Arabs of the desert were at that time celebrated and admired.

(4) That is: in simple phrases or in double ones. We would say: in a plain style or in rhyming prose.

(5) This was the name of a large canton situated between Wàsit, Basra and al-Anbàr.

(6) See vol. I. p. 614.

(7) This poet had been a disciple of the imàm as-Sháfi. He died A. H. 214 (A. D. 815-9).—(*Nujûm*).

(8) Two manuscripts have ـــــ (ninety) in place of ـــــ (seventy). The more probable reading has been followed in this translation.

(9) This is an allusion to the words of the Koran: " And, unto Solomon (we subjected) a strong wind " which ran at his command." (Surât 21, verse 81.)

(10) Literally: mamalitas en (lle homo, clitoridem matris suae engere cravmine. This was a common form of insult with the ancient Arabs.

(11) Literally: You have ornamented the lines of my time.

(12) The reading of the Arabic word is very doubtful; here is its form ـــــ.

(13) One of the manuscripts reads *Zeid*, another *Zain*, and another *Zir*. I can find no information respecting this historian.

(14) This surname seems to signify: The choicest pearls from among the female speakers.

(15) Talha was mortally wounded in that battle by an arrow, shot purposely at him by Marwan Ibn al-Hakam, who was fighting on the same side as he. Az-Zubeir was flying to Medina when he was slain by Amr Ibn Jurmûz.

AL-BUWAITI.

Abû Yakûb Yûsuf Ibn Yahya al-Buwaiti, a native of Egypt and a disciple of as-Shâfi (vol. II. p. 569), was the most eminent of that imâm's pupils and the most distinguished for talent. As long as his master lived, he remained invariably attached to him and, on his death, he filled his place as professor and as jurisconsult. Traditions relating to the Prophet were taught to him by the legist Abd Allah Ibn Wahb (vol. II. p. 15) and by the imâm as-Shâfi. His own authority was cited for Traditions by Abû Ismâil at-Tirmidi (1), Ibrahîm Ibn Ishak al-Harbi (vol. I. p. 46), al-Kâsim Ibn al-Mughîra al-Jauhari, Ahmad Ibn Mansûr ar-Ramâdi (2) and others. During the persecution (of the orthodox musulmans) (3) under the reign of (the khalif) al-Wâthik Billah, he was carried (as a prisoner) from Old Cairo to Baghdad and summoned to declare that the Koran was created. On his refusal, he was imprisoned at Baghdad and there remained in chains till the hour of his death. He was a most virtuous man, living in the practice of piety, devotion and self-mortification. Ar-Rabî Ibn Sulaimân (vol. I. p. 519) related as follows : " I saw al-Buwaiti mounted " on a mule; round his neck was a wooden collar; on his legs were fetters; from " these to the collar extended an iron chain to which was attached a clog (4) " weighing forty pounds. Whilst (they led him on,) he continued repeating these " words : ' Almighty God created the world by means of the word kun (5); now, " ' if that word was created, one created thing would have created another. By " ' Allah! I shall willingly die in chains, for, after me, will be people who shall " ' learn that, on account of this affair, some men died in chains. Were I brought " ' before that man,'—meaning al-Wâthik,—'I should declare unto him the truth.'" —The hâfiz Abû Omar Ibn Abd al-Barr (see page 398 of this vol.) states, in his Intikâ (enucleation), a work treating of the preeminent merits possessed by the three legists (Mâlik, Abû Hanîfa and as-Shâfi), that Ibn Abi 'l-Laith, the hanifite kadi of Old Cairo, was jealous of al-Buwaiti and so hostile to him that, during the persecution to which the sacred Koran gave rise, he had him transported from Cairo to Baghdad with the other (doctors) who were sent thither. He was the only disciple of as-Shâfi who was expelled from Egypt. On arriving at Baghdad, he refused to make the declaration which was required of him, relatively to (*the creation of*) the Koran, and was therefore committed to prison ; " It is the word of God," said he, " his uncreated word! " and he was kept in confinement till he died. The shaikh Abû Ishak as-Shîrâzi (*vol. I. p. 9*) says, in his *Tabakât al-Fukahâ* (*classified list of doctors learned in the law*) : " Every time that Abû Yakûb al-Buwaiti heard, " during his imprisonment, the *muwaddin* call the people to the Friday prayer, he " would wash, dress, and go to the door of the prison. The jailor would then say " to him : 'Where are you going?' and he would reply: ' I answer to him who calls " ' in the name of the Lord.' To this the jailor would say : 'Back! God will pardon " ' you.' Then the prisoner would exclaim : ' Almighty God! you perceive that I " ' answered the call of your herald and that I was prevented from obeying.'"—Abû 'l-Walîd Ibn Abi 'l-Jârûd related as follows : " Al-Buwaiti was my neighbour " and, no matter at what hour I awoke during the night, I was always " sure of hearing him recite the Koran or say his prayers."—" Abû Yakûb," said ar-Rabl, " was constantly moving his lips in commemoration of the glory " of God. I never saw a man who drew from the book of God more " original arguments than Abû Yakûb al-Buwaiti."—" Abû Yakûb," said he again, " held a high place in as-Shâfi's esteem. When a man came to ask the solution of a " legal difficulty, as-Shâfi would tell him to consult Abû Yakûb; and, when the " answer was given, the man would bring it back to as-Shâfi, who would say : " ' The right answer is what he has given.'"—" A messenger from the chief of the " police guards (*shorta, who was also the magistrate in criminal cases*) would sometimes " come to ask as-Shâfi's opinion on a point of law, and the latter would send him " back with Abû Yakûb, saying : 'Here is my tongue.'"—The Khatîb of Baghdad (*vol. I. p. 75*) says, in his History : " When as-Shâfi was in his last illness, Muham- " mad Ibn Abd al-Hakam (*vol. II. p. 598*) went to the place where that imâm used " to give his lessons, and had the intention of contending for it with al-Duwaiti. " The latter said : ' I have a better right to it than you.'—' Nay,' replied the other, " ' I am better entitled to his place than you are.' Abû Bakr al-Humaidi (*vol. II.* " *p. 573*), who was then in Egypt, came forward and said : ' As-Shâfi has declared " ' that no one is better entitled to that place than Yûsuf al-Buwaiti, and that none " ' of his disciples are more learned than al-Buwaiti.' ' You tell a falsehood,' " said Ibn Abd al-Hakam. ' Nay,' replied al-Humaidi, ' you are the liar, and " ' your father was a liar and your mother also.' Ibn Abd al-Hakam flew into a

" passion and, leaving the place where as-Shâfi held his sittings, he went
" to take his seat in a niche higher up, which was separated from that of as-
" Shâfi by another niche. Al-Buwaiti then occupied that niche where his master
" used to hold his sittings."—Abû 'l-Abbâs Muhammad Ibn Yakûb al-Asamm (6)
related as follows : " I saw my father in a dream (7), and he said to
" me : ' My son! keep to al-Buwaiti's book; it is less faulty than any other.'—
" We were one day with as-Shâfi," said ar-Rabi Ibn Solaimân; " I was there, and
" al-Muzani (vol. I. p. 200) and Abû Yakûb al-Buwaiti. He (as-Shâfi) looked at
" me and said : ' You will die in (teaching) the Traditions; ' he then said of al-Muzani :
" ' That fellow is capable of confuting Satan himself and reducing him to silence,
" ' if he entered into a discussion with him.' To al-Buwaiti he said : ' You will
" ' die in chains.'" The same person related as follows : " I went to visit al-
" Buwaiti, during the persecution; I found him fettered up to the middle of his
" legs, and his two hands attached to the same (wooden) collar which confined his
" neck." He related also as follows : " Abû Yakûb wrote to me from his prison,
" saying : ' There are certain moments, in which I do not perceive that I have
" ' chains on my body till I happen to touch them with my hand. When you have
" ' read this, my letter, act with condescention towards (the students who form)
" ' your class, and be particularly careful in treating with kindness those who come
" ' from foreign parts. How often did I hear as-Shâfi apply to himself the following
" ' verse :

> I use condescention towards men; so that, through them I may be honoured. That man
> is never honoured which does not humble itself.

Numerous anecdotes are related of him (al-Buwaiti). He died in the prison, at
Baghdad, and in chains, on a Friday of the month of Rajab, 231 (March, A. D. 846),
before the hour of prayer. Another statement places his death in the year 232,
but the former is nearer to the truth. Ibn al-Furât (vol. I. p, 66) says, in his
History, that he died on a Thursday of that month; God knows best! — Buwaiti
means belonging to Buwait, which is a village in Lower Said, a province of Egypt.
—There are six manners of pronouncing the name of Yûsuf : the first syllable may
be a yû or else a yu' with a hamza (point of separation), and in each case the s may
be followed by an a or an i or an u. The name of Yûnus offers a similar variety of
pronunciations, as we shall indicate later.

(1) Abû Ismâîl Mohammed Ibn Ismâîl at-Tirmidi, a Traditionist remarkable for his learning and the correctness of the information which he handed down, studied under the most eminent teachers and transmitted what he had learned to an-Nasâî (vol. I. p. 58), Ibn Abî Dunya (vol. I. p. 481), al-Ajurri (?) and other eminent doctors in that branch of knowledge. He died in the month of Ramadân, 280 (Nov.-Dec. A. D. 893).—(Tabakât al-Huffâz.)

(2) Abû Bakr Ahmad Ibn Mansûr ar-Ramâdi, a native of Baghdad, travelled to different countries for the purpose of learning and collecting Traditions. One of his teachers was the celebrated imâm Ahmad Ibn Hanbal. As a traditionist, he was considered to be perfectly trustworthy. He died in the month of the latter Rabî, 265 (December, A. D. 878).—(Nujûm.)

(3) The Abbaside khalif al-Mâmûn and his two successors, al-Motasim and al-Wâthik, were inclined to the Shiite doctrines and rejected the eternity of the Koran, as God's word. To this opinion they summoned the orthodox doctors to subscribe, and, on their refusal, they tried to overcome their obstinacy by means of tortures and imprisonment.

(4) The Arabic word means a brick.

(5) In the Koran, sûrat 16, verse 42, God is stated to have said : "Verily our speech unto a thing, "when we will the same, is, that we only say unto it, Be (kun); and it is." This was one of the arguments adduced by the orthodox theologians to prove the eternity (a parte ante) of the Koran, considered as the word of God.

(6) Abû 'l-Abbas Mohammed Ibn Yahiâ al-Ammân (the deaf), a mawla to the Omaiyide family, a native of Naisâpûr and the chief Traditionist of that age in Khorâsân, taught during seventy-six years the knowledge which he had acquired. His death took place in the month of the latter Rabî, 346 (July, A. D. 957). He lost his hearing after having travelled and made his studies.—(Huffâz; Nujûm.)

(7) See vol. I. p. 46.

IBN KAJJ.

The kâdi Abû 'l-Kâsim Yûsuf Ibn Ahmad Ibn Yûsuf Ibn Kajj, surnamed al-Kajji ad-Dinaweri (the Kajjian, native of Dinawer) and one of the great Shafite imams, studied under Ibn al-Kattân (vol. I. p. 51), attended the sittings of Abû 'l-Kâsim Abd al-Azîz ad-Dâraki (vol. II. p. 137) and became the chief of the shafite sect and head-professor (1). People came from all parts to Dinawer for the purpose of studying under his tuition; so general was the desire of deriving profit from his erudition and the correctness of his speculations. In exposing the doctrines of

as-Shâfi, he followed a system peculiar to himself.   A number of works were composed by him and were studied with great profit by legists.   Abû Saad as-Samâni
(vol. *II.* p. 156) says: " When Abû Ali al-Husain Ibn Shoaib as-Sinji (vol. *I.* p. 419;
" returned from (*Baghdad where he had been studying under*) the *shaikh* Abû
" Hâmid al-Isfarâini (vol. *I.* p. 53), he passed through the town where Ibn Kajj
" dwelt and was so greatly struck with his learning (*in the law*) and his merit that
" he said to him : ' I declare, master! that, Abû Hâmid possesses the name of a
" ' man of science, but you possess the reality.'   To this Ibn Kajj replied : ' Baghdad
" ' exalted him and ad-Dinawer depressed me. ' "   He acted as a *kâdi* in his
native place and was living in opulence when he was murdered by the
banditti of that town.   This occurred on the eve of the 27th Ramadân, 405
(20th of March, A. D. 1015). — *Kajj* must be pronounced with an *a.* —
We have already spoken of *Dinaweri* (vol. *II.* p. 23) and need not therefore
repeat here what we have said.—The relative adjective *Kajji* was derived from the
name of his ancestor.

IBN ABD AL-BARR.

Abû Omar Yûsuf Ibn Abd Allah Ibn Muhammad Ibn Abd al-Barr Ibn Aâsim
an-Namari, a native of Cordova, was the *imâm* (*the greatest master*) of the time by
his knowledge of the Traditions, of ancient (*moslim*) history and of every thing

connected with these two branches of science. At Cordova, he taught Traditions on
the authority of the *háfiz* Khalaf Ibn al-Kásim (1). Abd al-Wárith Ibn Sofyán, Saīd
Ibn Nasr (2), Muhammad Ibn Abd el-Múmin, Abû Omar al-Báji, Abû Omar at-Ta-
lamanki, Abû 'l-Walîd Ibn al-Faradi (*vol. II. p.* 66) and others. Among the
doctors of the East who kept up an epistolary correspondence with him were Abû
'l-Kásim as-Sakati al-Makki, the *háfiz* Abd al-Ghani Ibn Saīd (3), Abû Durr al-
Harawi (4) and Abû Muhammad Ibn an-Nahhás al-Misri. The kádi Abû Ali Ibn
Sukkara (5) said : " I heard our professor, the kádi Abû 'l-Walîd al-Báji (*vol. I.*
" *p.* 593) declare that there was never in Spain the like of Abû Omar Ibn Abd al-
" Barr, as a Traditionist; and the same al-Báji said : ' Abû Omar was the best
" ' *háfiz* (*traditionist*) of all the people in the West.'" Abû Ali al-Husain Ibn
Ahmad Ibn Muhammad al-Ghassáni al-Jaiyáni, a doctor of whom we have spoken
(*vol. I. p.* 458), said : " We other students had for professor Ibn Abd al-Barr of
" Cordova; it was in that city that he made his studies and there also he learned ju-
" risprudence. One of his masters was the Sevillian legist Abû Omar Ahmad Ibn
" Abd al-Malik, whose lessons he wrote down in his presence ; another of his pro-
" fessors was Abû 'l-Walîd Ibn al-Faradi, from whom he obtained a great quantity
" of traditional and philological information. He was assiduous in the pursuit of
" knowledge and acquired such eminence in the different branches of science that
" he surpassed all the learned men who had preceded him in Spain." He (*Ibn
Abd al-Barr*) composed a number of useful treatises on the *Muwatta* (*vol. II.
p.* 549), such as the *, Tamhíd* (*arrangement*), in which he discussed the matters
and *isnáds* (*vol. I. p.* xxii) found in that work; it is arranged alphabetically,
according to the names of those Traditionists through whom Málik received his
information. Nothing of the kind had ever been composed before ; it consists
of seventy parts. Abû Muhammad Ibn Hazm (*vol. II. p.* 267) said : " As a critical
" appreciator of the credibility to which a Tradition may be entitled, I do not
" know any one like him, and much less any one who has surpassed him." The
Istidkár (*Remembrancer*), a work composed by him subsequently, treats of the
various opinions held by the legists in the great cities, relatively (*first of all,*) to
such articles of law as may be deduced, by private judgment, from the texts given
in the *Muwatta*, and (*secondly*) with respect to the historical facts which are indicated in that compilation. In the *Istidkár* he explains the *Muwatta* according to its
actual arrangement and in following the order of its chapters. He drew up also a

large and instructive treatise on the names of the Prophet's companions and entitled
it the *Istiâb* (*comprehensive*). In another of his works, he collected every thing
which had been said in explanation of what is meant by *science* and of its high value:
he there indicates the rules which are to be observed in transmitting knowledge
orally and in learning it by heart. His *Kitâb ad-Durar* (*book of pearls*) contains an
abridged account of the proceedings and military expeditions (*of the first Moslims*).
Another of his works treats of the intellect and intellectual men, and contains passages in which such persons are described. He left also a small work on the Arabian
tribes and their genealogies. Other treatises also were published by him. The
composition of works occupied all his thoughts; to that task he was entirely devoted,
and God rendered his labours useful to mankind. His profound knowledge of
history and his deep insight into the (*hidden*) meanings of the Traditions did
not prevent him from acquiring an extensive acquaintance with (*Arabian*)
genealogies. Having left Cordova, he travelled, for some time, in Western
Spain, and then passed into the Eastern part of that country. He resided for
a while in Denia, in Valencia and in Xativa. He filled the kadiship of Lisbon
and Santarem when al-Muzaffar (or el-Modaffar) Ibn al-Aftas (*king of Badajoz*) held those cities under his rule. His *Bahja tal-Majâlis wa Ins al-Jâlis* (*the
delight of assemblies and companion of the sedentary*) fills three volumes and contains
a mass of interesting anecdotes, such as are fit to be repeated at literary conferences
and social parties. Here are some extracts from it : "The Prophet dreamt that he
"entered into Paradise and saw there suspended a bunch of dates. His curiosity
"being excited, he asked for whom they were reserved, and was told that they were
"kept there for Abû Jahl. Deeply afflicted with this information, he exclaimed :
"'What has Abû Jahl to do with Paradise? By Allah! he shall never enter into
"'it! no soul can get in there unless that of a true believer.' Some time after,
"when Ikrima, the son of Abû Jahl, came to him and declared himself a Mu-
"sulman, he was greatly rejoiced, stood up to receive him and then understood
"that the fruit seen by him represented the son of Abû Jahl."—"Djaafar Ibn
"Muhammad, he who bore the surname of as-Sâdik (*vol. I. p. 300*), being asked
"what was the longest time which might elapse before the fulfilment of a dream,
"returned this answer : 'The blessed Prophet dreamt that he saw his blood
"'(*poured out*) and a speckled dog lapping it up. Now the dog represented Shamir
"'Ibn Zi-'l-Jaushan, him who slew al-Husain, the son of Ali Ibn Abi Tâlib, and who

" ' was a leper. So, the fulfilment of that dream was delayed fifty years.'" — The
" Prophet had a dream which he related to Abû Bakr as-Siddik : ' O Abû Bakr,'
" said he, ' methought that you and I were going up a flight of stairs and that I
" ' preceded you by two steps and a half.' Abû Bakr replied : ' Apostle of God!'
" ' when the Almighty shall have received you into his compassion and mercy, I
" ' shall survive two years and a half.' "—" A Syrian [Arab] said to Omar Ibn al-
" Khattâb : ' Methought I saw the moon and the sun fighting one against the other,
" ' and each of them was aided by a band of stars.' — ' On which side were you?'
" said Omar. The other replied that he had sided with the moon. ' Then,' said
" Omar, ' you sided with the sign which is subject to be effaced (6). By Allah!
" ' you shall never more hold a commandment under me.' That man was then
" deposed, and he subsequently lost his life at Siffin whilst fighting on the side of
" Moawia Ibn Abi Sofyân."—" Aâisha said to Abû Bakr : ' Methought that three
" ' moons fell into my lap.'—' If your dream be true,' said he, ' three of the best
" ' men upon earth will be buried in your house.' When the Prophet was inter-
" red there, Abû Bakr said to her : ' There is one of the moons which you saw, and
" ' the best of them.'"—" An Arab of the desert who, as some say, was the poet
" al-Hutaiya (vol. I. p. 209) formed the project of going to travel and said to his
" wife :

" Count my absence by years and wait with patience; leave out the months, for they are
" but short (kisârâ).

To this she replied :

" Remember my fondness of you and my passion; have pity on your daughters for they are
" little children (sighârâ).

" On hearing these words, he gave up his intention and remained at home."—
" Al-Haitham Ibn Adi (vol. III. p. 633) related that, being asked by Sâlih Ibn Haiyân
" who, of all the poets, was the best legist, he made this reply : ' On that subject
" ' opinions differ, but some say that it was Waddâh al-Yaman (7) who proved
" ' himself such when he pronounced these lines :

" I said to her : ' flirt with it (the wine)! Give it to me.' She smiled and answered : ' God "'preserve me from doing a thing forbidden!' Neither did she hand it to me till I humbled "myself before her and taught her how indulgent was God for venial sins."

"Aslam Ibn Zaràa was told that, if he fled before the partisans of Mirdâs (8), he "would incur the anger of the emir Obaid Allah Ibn Ziâd. To this he replied: 'I had "'rather that he should be angry with me, and I living, than that he should be "'pleased with me, and I dead.'"—"An Arab of the desert was insulted by "another and remained silent. Being asked why he held his peace, he answer- "ed: I know not that man's vices, and am unwilling to reproach him with "defects which he may not have." An idea similar to this has been enounced thus:

"If, when Amr insulted me, I insulted him, the insulted and the insulter would be "both reprehensible. But I spoke well of him and he spoke ill of me; each of us thus "told lies of his adversary."

"Ali (*Zain al-Aabidîn*, *vol. II*, *p.* 209), the son of al-Husain, on both of whom "be the blessing of God, said: 'A man who extols your good qualities without "'knowing them, will probably speak ill of you without knowing your defects.'" —"Al-Moghira Ibn Shôba (*vol. II*. *p.* 485) said of (*the khalif*) Omar: 'By Allah! "'he was too generous to deceive and too intelligent to be deceived.'"—"It is "related that, when Adam was sent out of Paradise and down to earth by Almighty "God, the angel Gabriel went to him and said: 'O Adam! God here sends you "'three qualities, so that you may select one of them for yourself and leave the two "'others.'—'What are they?' said Adam. Gabriel replied: 'Modesty, Piety and "'Intelligence.'—'I choose Intelligence,' said Adam. The angel then told Mo- "desty and Piety to return to heaven, because Adam had made choice of Intelli- "gence. They answered: 'We will not return.'—'How!' said he, 'do you mean "'to desobey me?' They replied: 'We do not, but our orders were, never to quit "'Intelligence wherever she might be.'" — "Abd al-Malik Ibn Abd al-Hamid (9) "said, in a piece of verse.

"Water has its price in the house of Othmân and bread is there the most precious of "things. Othmân is aware that praise costs money; yet he wishes to obtain it gratis. But "people are too knowing to praise a man unless they discover in him symptoms of liberality."

From the same work: "Ar-Riâshi (*vol. II*. *p.* 10) related as follows: "The

" people of Basra went out to watch for the appearance of the new moon (*which*
" *indicates the commencement of the month*) of (*fasting*,) Ramadân. One of them
" discovered it and continued pointing at it till some of his companions perceived it.
" When the moon which indicates the end of the fast was (*about to appear*), al-Jam-
" mâs, he who was so much noted for his witty sallies, went to the house of that
" man, knocked at the door and said : ' Come! Get up and take us out of the
" ' scrape into which you brought us.'"—I may here observe that al-Jammâs was
descended from one of Abû Bakr's *mawlas*; his surname was Abû Abd Allah, and
his name, Muhammad; his father, Amr, was the son of Hammâd, the son of Alî,
the son of Raiyân (?). This al-Jammâs was a sister's son to Salm (10) al-Khâsir: As-
Samâni (*vol. II, p.* 156) speaks of him in these terms : " His tongue was virulent;
" his sallies were clever. He was older than Abu Nuwâs (*vol. I. p.* 391)." Some
authors assign to him a genealogy different from that which we have given. Al-
Jammâs (*the dromedary, the mehdri camel*) was a nickname by which he was known.
Amongst the smart sayings attributed to him we may notice the following : " One
" rainy morning," said he, " I was asked by my wife what was best to be done on
" such a day as that, and I answered : ' Divorcing (*a troublesome wife*).' This
" stopped her mouth and made her leave me quiet."—An acquaintance of his went
to see him, one day, and found him eating out of a dish of meat which he had just
cooked. " Glory to God!" said the visiter, " what an extraordinary godsend ! "
Al-Jammâs answered : " Disappointments are sometimes more extraordinary; may
" my wife be divorced if you taste a mouthful of it! (11)" As-Sarawi (12) the poet
said to him one day : " Yesterday, my wife brought forth a child, (*as pretty*) as a
" gold-piece newly coined." Al-Jammâs replied : " (*That is not surprising;*) its
" mother was never considered to be barren."—Al-Jammâs composed some pieces
of poetry which he inserted in his *Kitâb al-Waraka* (*book of the leaf* (?)). One of
them, which he addressed to an acquaintance who, after being very assiduous in
frequenting the mosque, had ceased to go there, runs thus :

> You have ceased frequenting the principal mosque, and absence such as that always gives rise
> to unfavourable suspicions. Yo do an supplementary works of devotion; you serve not as a
> witness to law-writings (13). The news we have received of you is (*as publicly known as if
> it were*) inscribed on banners borne aloft. If you prolong your absence (*ghaiba*), we'shall
> prolong our talk of it (*ghîba*) more and more.

The following passages are taken from the *Bahia tal-Majâlis* : "Ardashîr said :

" ' Beware of being attacked by a noble-hearted man when he is hungry and by a " ' vile fellow who is sated with food. Be it known to you that the noble are firmer " ' in mind and the vile firmer in body.'" — All this is taken from the *Bahja* and, as it is quite sufficient, there is no need of dilating farther. — The *hâfiz* Abû Omar (*Ibn Abd al-Barr*) died at Shâtiba (*Xativa*), in Eastern Spain, on the last day of the second Rabî, 463 (3rd February, A. D. 1071). His disciple, Abû 'l-Hasan Tâhir Ibn Mufauwaz al-Maâfiri, the same who said the funeral service over him, related as follows : I heard Abû Omar Ibn Abd al-Barr say that he was born on Friday, the 25th of the second Rabî, 368 (29th Nov. A. D. 978), just as the imâm was reciting the *khotba*. In the life of the Khatîb Abû Bakr Ahmad Ibn Ali Ibn Thâbit al-Baghdâdi (*vol. I.* p. 75), we have mentioned that this person was the *hâfiz* of the East and Ibn Abd al-Barr the *hâfiz* of the west, and that they both died in the same year. They were masters in traditional knowledge. — *Namari* takes an *a* after the *n* and after the *m*. It means *sprung from Namir Ibn Kâsit*, the progenitor of a well-known (*Arabian*) tribe. This relative adjective offers a particular case of the *a* being employed after the second radical letter instead of the *i* (14). — We have spoken of *Kortuba* (*vol. I.* p. 94) and of Shâtiba (*vol. II. p. 501*); so, we need not repeat our observations. — Abû Omar mentioned that his father Abû Muhammad Abd Allah Ibn Muhammad Ibn Abd al-Barr died in the month of the latter Rabî, 380 (June-July, A. D. 990), and that he was born in the year 330 (A. D. 941-2). — Abû Muhammad Abd Allah Ibn Yûsuf, the son of Abû Omar Ibn Abd al-Barr, was highly distinguished for his knowledge of refined literature and the elegance of his style. He is the author of some pieces of verse, one of which is the following :

> Gaze not [too long] (*on handsome faces*), and hold in your glances with a tight rein. If you slacken the bridle to them, they will cast you into the arena of death.

It is stated that he died in the year 458 (A. D. 1065-6); but God knows best.

---

(1) Abû 'l-Kâsim Khelaf Ibn al-Kâsim, surnamed Ibn ad-Dallâgh, was one of those Spanish Moslems who travelled to the East for the purpose of acquiring traditional knowledge. He studied in Damascus and in Mekka. His authority as a Traditionist was highly appreciated. He died in the month of the latter Rabî, 393 (Feb.-March, A. D. 1003.)—(*Nujûm, Makkari*).

(2) Abû Othmân Saîd Ibn Nasr Ibn Omar Ibn Khalfûn, a native of Ecija in Spain, collected Traditions at

Cordova, al-Mekka and at Baghdad. He died in the last-mentioned city, probably towards the end of the sixth century.—(*Nakhaw.*)

(3) Abd al-Ghani Ibn Saad (?) al-Azdi, a native of Egypt, was held to be the chief of Traditionists of the age in which he lived. He died in the month of Safar, 409 (June-July, A. D. 1018).—(*Naffds.*)

(4) Abû Durr al-Harawi, surnamed Ibn as-Samanik, was professor in chief at Mekka (*sheikh al-Haram*). He died somewhat before the year 400 (A. D. 1018).—(*Hafds.*)

(5) Abû Ali al-Husain Ibn Muhammad as-Sairafi, surnamed Ibn Sukhara, was a native of Saragossa. In the year 431 (A. D. 1039) he travelled to the East for the purpose of studying, and visited Egypt, Basra, Wâsit and Baghdad, in which last city he passed five years. On his return to Spain he became a professor at Murcia and there acted also as a kadi, but much against his will. He was well-versed in the Koran-readings and had great skill in the critical appreciation of Traditions. Having resigned his places with the intention of taking a share in the war against the Christians, he lost his life, in the year 514 (A. D. 1120) at the battle of Cutanda.—(*Nakhawl.*)

(6) This is an allusion to a text of the Koran, *sur.* 17, verse 13, where it is said : " We blot out the sign of the night and we cause the sign of the day to shine forth."

(7) Waddâh al-Yaman (*Fair fair faced man of Yemen*); such was the surname given to Abd ar-Rihmân Ibn Ismaïl of Sanâa, on account of his beauty. He drew his descent from one the Persians who were sent into Arabia Felix for the purpose of expelling the Abyssinians and placing Saif Ibn Zi-Yazan on the throne. He was one of Muhammad's contemporaries and bore a high reputation as a poet. The *Kitâb al-Aghâni* contains a long article on Waddâh and numerous extracts from his poems. The author of the *Nujûm* places his death in the year 60 (A. D. 689-90). Waddâh was so handsome that he always wore a veil to preserve him against the evil eye.

(8) Abd al-Ali Mirdâs, a distinguished member of the tribe of Baddah and surnamed Ibn Udaiya (أديّة), lived under the reign of Moawia Ibn Abi Sofyân. Such was the fervour and rigidness of his devotion that he was always ready to join with any band of Sharijites which might take up arms against the Omaiyides for the purpose of re-establishing the Moslim government in its primitive simplicity. The year 61 (A. D. 680-1) witnessed the massacre of al-Husain, Muhammad's grandson, and most of his family, by Obaid Allah Ibn Ziâd who, at that time, governed Irak in the name of the Omaiyide prince, Yazid, the son of Moawia. In that same year, Mirdâs was at the head of a party and warring against the Omaiyides. Ibdâ Ibn al-Abdar was sent by Obaid Allah, with a body of troops, against the insurgents. The two armies met on a Friday. Mirdâs requested his adversary to defer the battle and give him time to accomplish the solemn prayer which al-Moslims are bound to make on that day. Ibdâ consented, but, when the Sharijites were prostrate in prayer, he charged upon them with his cavalry and cut them to pieces. Mirdâs fell with the rest. —(The Doraid's *Ishtikâk*; Ibn al-Athir's *Kâmil*.)

(9) I cannot discover who this Abd al-Malik was, nor who was the Othman whose avarice he attacks.

(10) See vol. I. p. 99.

(11) The text of the manuscripts is probably faulty : they read امرأته طالق ان ذكته .The right reading seems to be امرأتي. In the anecdotes told of Nasr ad-Din Khoja, an individual, half knave and half fool, who figures in the popular literature of the East, this saying is attributed to him on account of his simplicity. In the Arabic edition of these anecdotes, the reading is that which I have here proposed. The anecdotes of this buffoon exist also in Turkish.

(12) Abû 'l-Alâ as-Sarawi (السروي), a native of Tabaristan, stood pre-eminent as a prose-writer and as a

poet. He was one of those literary men who frequented the court of the vizir Ibn al-Amid (vol. III, p. 244).—(Tháliabi's Yetima).

(13) No man could be a witness to bonds or give evidence in court of justice unless his character as a pious and virtuous moslim was well established.

(14) This is not exceptional case; it falls under the general rule: Nemir forms Namari, as Maïth and Aabd form Maïabi and Aabadi.

YUSUF AS-SIRAFI.

Abû Muhammad Yûsuf Ibn Abi Saïd al-Hasan Ibn Abd Allah Ibn al-Marzubân as-Sîrâfi, was a grammarian, a philologer, a historian, a man of merit and the son of a man of merit. We have already spoken of his father (vol. I. p. 377). Abû Muhammad, being well acquainted with grammar, occupied, as a professor, the seat left vacant by the death of his father. We have already given the date of that event. He undertook all the occupations in which his father had been engaged, and, even in the latter's lifetime, he instructed students. The work which his father had left unfinished and which had received the title of al-Iknâa (the sufficiency) was terminated by him. It is one of the most important and instructive works of the kind; his father had begun by commenting Sibawaih's Kitâb (vol. II. p. 396), as we have already mentioned, and displayed in that task such erudition and research as never had been shown before by any of those persons who treated the subject; after that he drew up the Iknâa, which was thus the fruit of the information acquired by him during his researches and whilst he was writing out his work. He died before the termination of his task, and it was his son who completed it. Every impartial critic who may examine the book will not find any great difference between the style and manner of the father and those of the son. Yûsuf as-Sîrâfi composed afterwards a number of treatises in which he elucidated the verses adduced as examples in some (grammatical) works of great note; such, for instance, was his explanation of the verses cited by Sibawaih, and which is the best and the most extensive treatise on that subject. He wrote also a very good explanation of the verses quoted in the Islâh al-Mantik (page 293 of this vol.); another treating of the verses which occur in Abû Obaida's

Majâz (vol. III. p. 391); another on the verses of the *Madni (a work on the figurative expressions of the Koran)* by az-Zajjâj *(vol. I. p. 28)*, another on the verses quoted by Abû Obaid al-Kâsim Ibn Sallâm *(vol. II. p. 486)* in the *Gharîb al-Musannaf* (1). This list we might easily augment. The students to whom he gave lessons in philology went twice over the books of that science under his direction : the first time, they recited to him the text, and, the second time, they received from him its explanation. One of the works read to him was the *Kitâb al-Bâri (the surpassing, a philological work)*, composed by al-Mufaddal Ibn Salama *(vol. II. p. 611)*; it forms a number of volumes, the contents of which have been digested into the *Kitâb al-Aîn*, that philological work which is attributed to al-Khalîl Ibn Ahmad *(vol. I. p. 493)*. To this book he added a considerable quantity of philological observations. The copies which he made of the *Islâh al-Mantik* were written by him from memory (2). Abû 'l-Alâ al-Maarri *(vol. I. p. 94)* related as follows : " Abd as-Salâm " al-Basri, the keeper of the public library (3) at Baghdad, who was a man of " veracity and a good friend of mine, told me that he was present at one of Abû " Saîd as-Sîrâfi's sittings, whilst a student was reading aloud under his direction Ibn " as-Sikkît's *Islâh al-Mantik.* When he came to the verse in which Humaid Ibn " Thaur (4) says :

" And *(I was sometimes borne by)* a thin-flanked *(camel)* which, during *(the heat of)* the " day, took rest and, during the night, slung on at a trot.

" Abû Saîd here observed that the word *thin-flanked* should be put in the geni- " tive case, and then, turning towards us, he said : ' The conjunction *and*, being " ' here equivalent to *sometimes*, governs the genitive.' On hearing this I said : " ' God preserve you, kâdi! the verse which precedes shows that the word is in the " ' nominative.'—' What is that verse?' said he. I answered :

" God, who sent down from heaven the true direction, has brought me to you; my guides " were a *(heavenly)* light, kinsmen and a thin-flanked etc.

" On this, he went over the passage again and corrected the mistake. His son, " Abû Muhammad, who was present, changed colour on witnessing what had passed " and, standing up instantly, with every mark of displeasure in his looks, he retur- " ned to his shop,—he was a butter merchant,—sold that establishment and took

" to study. He continued to acquire information until he attained the highest rank
" in learning and then composed a treatise in which he explained the verses cited
" in the *Isláh al-Mantik*." Abû 'l-Alâ said also : ' A person who saw him whilst
" he was composing that treatise told me that he had then before him four hundred
" *diwans (or collections of poems)*."—Yûsuf as-Sirâfî continued to hold one uni-
form line of conduct, studying and teaching, till the day of his death. That event
took place on the eve of Wednesday, the 27th of the first Rabî, 385 (30th April,
A. D. 995). He was then aged fifty-five years and some months. The next
morning, he was buried, and the funeral service was said over him by Abû Bakr
Muhammad Ibn Mûsa al-Khuwâreami (vol. *I. p.* 60); so says Hilâl Ibn al-Mu-
hassan as-Sâbi (vol. *III. p.* 628) in his Annals. Another author states that he
(Yûsuf as-Sirâfî, was born in the year 330 (A. D. 941-2) and that he died on
Monday, the 27th of the above-mentioned month ; God knows best! Yûsuf
was a pious, virtuous man, very devout and living in the plainest manner. He had
frequent discussions and controversies with Abû Tâlib Ahmed Ibn Abi Bakr al-Abdi,
the grammarian of whom we have spoken (vol. *I. p.* 82). These conferences have
been (*preserved and*) handed down, but this is not a fit place for them. In the life
of his father we have spoken of the word *Sirâf* (vol. *I. p* 379) and need not therefore
repeat our observations. Ibn Haukal says, in his *Masâlik wa 'l-Mamâlik (roads and
realms)* (5) " Sirâf is a large sea-port town in Persia; its buildings are in teak
" wood. It is situated close to a hill which overlooks the sea, and possesses neither
" water, nor cultivated grounds nor flocks; yet it is one of the richest places in
" Persia (6). It lies in the neighbourhood of Jannâba and Najîrem. A traveller,
" on starting from Sirâf and following the shore-road, will arrive at the castle (him)
" of Ibn Omâra, a strong fortress on the border of the sea; there is not a stronger
" place in Persia. It is said that its (*former*) possessor was the person whom God de-
" signated by these words (*of the Koran; surát* 18, *verse* 78) : ' And there was
" ' behind them a king who took every ship by force.'"—Another author says that
the name of this king was al-Julunda, with a u in each of the first syllables and the
last syllable terminating in an a. It was he whom a certain poet meant in the
following lines, addressed to an oppressor of the people :

Julunda was a tyrant, but thou art a greater tyrant than he.

The statements on this subject differ and God alone knows the truth.

(1) This title, which is sometimes written *al-Gharîb al-Musannaf*, appears to signify : *the uncommon terms and expressions occurring in the Musannaf*. There were two works intitled *al-Musannaf*: one treating of the traditions and composed by Ibn Abi Shaiba, and the other by Ibn Sina (see *vol. II. p. 191* and Hajji Khalifa's *Bibliographical Dictionary*, tome II, p. 304) forming a commentary on the *Tasrîf*, or treatise on the conjugations and grammatical inflections, by Abû Othmân al-Mâzini (*vol. I. p. 364*). The hâfiz Abû Bakr Abd Allah Ibn Muhammad al-Absi, surnamed Ibn Abi Shaiba, was a Traditionist of the highest reputation. Al-Bokhâri, Abû Dawûd and Ibn Mâja have given Traditions on his authority. He taught at Damascus. His death took place in the month of Muharram, 235 (July-August, A. D. 849). —(*Haffâz, Nujûm, Hajji Khalifa.*)

(2) The text is more or less altered in the manuscripts and the printed editions. By combining the different readings, I obtain من طهر نسخه لكتاب اصلاح المنطق .ونقل من طهر. I consider من طهر as equivalent to من طهر القلب and, read muallâsha. If this word be pronounced muhhâtle the antecedent حَال, for هي , حلَّ, is to be understood. The meaning of the phrase is nearly the same in both cases.

(3) Literally : the treasurer of the house of knowledge.

(4) Hammâd Ibn Thaur al-Hilâli, a member of the tribe of Âmir Ibn Saâsâ and a contemporary of Muhammad, was a poet of some reputation.—(Ibn Duraid's *Ishtikâk*).

(5) This passage is given in the two editions and in only one of our manuscripts.

(6) The edition of Bûlâk has أقصى (the most distant); that of Mr Wüstenfeld أعبى, a word to which no appropriate signification can be assigned; the only manuscript of Paris which gives the passage reads أغبى (the most ignorant). The true reading seems to be أغنى (the richest), but the passage is not to be found in the copy of the Haukal's work which we possess at Paris.

ABU YAKUB AN-NAJIRAMI.

Abû Yakûb Yûsuf Ibn Yakûb Ibn Ismail Ibn Khurrâzd an-Najîrami, a philologer and a native of Basra, settled in Egypt. · He came of a family which produced a number of eminent literary scholars, all of them deeply versed in philology, gifted with every talent and possessing the most solid information on these subjects. Abû Yakûb taught traditions on the authority of Abû Yahya Zakariya Ibn Yahya Ibn Khallâd as-Sâji (*vol. III. p. 411*) and other masters of that time. The same information was transmitted down on his authority by Abû 'l-Fadl Muhammad Ibn Jaafar al-Khuzâi and others. He was the most remarkable man of all the family; his handwriting (*as a book-copyist*) was not good as to its form, but extremely correct, and nearly such also was that of his company (*his disciples*). The people of Misr (*Old*

Cairo) were so anxious and so eager to procure (books) written by him, that a copy
which he made of Jarir's poetical works was purchased at the price of ten dinars.(1).
In Egypt, the received texts of old works, treating of philology, Arabic poetry and the
battle-days of the (ancient) Arabs, are those which he had delivered orally and which
he himself had drawn up. Indeed, he was able to dictate from memory books of
that kind and was perfectly well acquainted with such matters. The members of
his family who were in Misr supported themselves by trading in fire-wood.
The grammarian Abû Abd Allah Muhammad Ibn Barakât Ibn Hilâl al-Misri (2) obtained his philological information from some of Abû Yakûb's disciples and was old
enough to have seen their master; but, being then a child, he was not capable of receiving lessons from him. Muwaffak ad-Dîn Abû 'l-Hajjâj Yûsuf Ibn al-Khallâl al-
Misri, the official correspondence writer to whom we shall assign an article
farther on, related that Ibn Barakât said to him : " I saw Abû Yakûb walking on the
" road which leads to the Karâfa (vol. I. p. 53). He was an elderly man of a tawny
" complexion, with a bushy beard and a large round turban. In his hand he held
" a book which he kept reading as he walked on. " This assertion is controvertible :
the hâfiz Abû Ishâk Ibrahîm Ibn Said Ibn Abd Allah, generally known by the appellation of al-Habbâl (the rope-maker) (3) says, in the Obituary (Wafaiydt) of which he
was the compiler, that the death of Abû Yakûb Kharrâzd an-Najtrami took place on
Tuesday, the 4th of Muharram, 423 (22nd Dec. A. D. 1031), and another author
places his birth on the 10th of Zù 'l-Hijja, 345 (15th march, A.D. 957). Now, Ibn
Barakât was born at Old Cairo in the year 420 (A. D. 1029) and died there in 520
(A. D. 1126); being at that time the chief grammarian of Egypt. This is even said
by Muwaffak ad-Dîn Ibn al-Khallâl. How then could Ibn Barakât have seen Abû
Yakûb as he describes? he was only three years old at the time of Abû Yakûb's death.
It was perhaps the latter's son whom he perceived; God knows! — The Kâdi al-
Fâdil (vol. II. p. 111) said that, in all Ibn Barakât's poems, there was nothing finer
than these two verses, composed by him on Muzâffir al-Auâr (4) :

> O thou whose neck is like that of a silver ibrîk (5) and whose waist is a pliant wand! Were you
> to disdain me and repel me, do you think you could ever get out of my heart?

Ibn Barakât obtained his grammatical information from Ibn Bâbshâd, a grammarian of whom we have already spoken (vol. I. p. 647). Al-Kâdi ar-Rashid Ibn az-
Zubair (vol. I. p. 143) mentions him with commendation in the Kitâb al-Jinân. —

Kharrádd; such is the orthography of this name according to the learned in Traditions. It is Persian; *ádd* means *son,* but *kharr,* with a double *r,* has no meaning;
so we must suppose that the people who spoke Arabic altered the orthography of the
name, according to their usual custom in such cases, and that it was primitively
Khdrsdd, which, in Persian, means *the son of a thorn.* *Khurshíd* signifies *the sun;*
if this was the word intended (*in the formation of the name*), the syllable *shíd* must
have been suppressed, and such a licence is indeed authorized (*in Persian*). We
must say that, in general, the Arabs tamper greatly with foreign names. — I have
since read, in that chapter of al-Balâdori's *Kitáb al-Buldán* (6) which contains the
account of Persia and its provinces, that *Ardashír Khurrah* means *bahá Ardashír*
(*the glory of Ardashír*) (7). — *Najtrami* is derived from *Najtram* on *Najdram.* Abû
Saad as-Samâni (*vol. II. p.* 156) says, in his *Ansáb,* that this is the name of a quarter
in the city of Basra. According to another authority, it is the name of a village in
the territory of Basra, lying on the road which leads to Fars and situated near
Siráf. God knows best! A similar statement is made in the *Masálik wa 'l-Ma-
málik* (8), which places this town on the coast of the Persian Gulf. The fact seems
to be that a number of persons belonging to Bajíram went to Basra and settled in a
quarter which then received the name of the place from which they came. God
knows best!

---

(1) The *Díwán* of Jarîr's poems which is in the university library at Leyden, fills about four hundred and
seventy pages. If the transcription of such a work cost six dinars and if the dinar be estimated at thirteen shillings and eight pence, each page would have brought in to the copyist somewhat more than two pence.

(2) Abû abd Allah Muhammad Ibn Barakát Ibn Hilál as-Saîdî, a native of Saîd, or upper Egypt, was known
as a grammarian and a philologer. He composed a (khitat or) work on the topography of Cairo, and died
A. H. 520 (A. D. 1126).—(*Yâfi's Annals.*)—See also the first volume of the present work, page 449, and, in
the third line, read *Saîdi* in place of *Saadi.*

(3) Abû Ishak Ibrahim Ibn Saîd an-Nomâni, a háfiz of good authority and noted for his piety, was a native
of Egypt and died in Old Cairo (*Misr*), A. H. 489 (A. D. 1069-96), aged ninety years.—(*Yâfi's Annals,
Nojûm*).

(4) This person is not known to the translator.

(5) The name of *íbrík* is given to a sort of ewer with a curved spout like that of a coffee-pot.

(6) See de Goeje's edition of the *Liber Expugnationis Regionum,* page 386 of the Arabic text.

(7) The author forgets to draw his conclusion; he evidently means to say that *Kharradd* may be derived
from *Khurreh-Zád* (*the son of glory*).

(8) See page 314 of this volume, note (19).

YUSUF AL-HAMADANI.

Abû Yakûb Yûsuf Ibn Aiyûb Ibn Yûsuf Ibn al-Husain Ibn Wahara al-Hamadâni, the jurisconsult, the man of learning, the ascetic, the divinely favoured, he who often enjoyed states (*of exaltation*) and possessed miraculous gifts (1), went to Baghdad in his youth, some time after the year 460 (A. D. 1067) and became the assiduous disciple of Abû Ishâk as-Shîrâzi (*vol. I. p. 9*). He studied law under that doctor till he mastered the fundamentals of jurisprudence (2), the system of doctrine (*peculiar to the Shafite sect*) and the examination of controverted questions. Traditions were received by him from the lips of the *kâdi* Abû 'l-Husain Muhammad Ibn Ali Ibn al-Muhtadi Billah, Abû 'l-Ghanâim Abd as-Samad Ibn Ali Ibn al-Mâmûn, Abû Jaafar Muhammad Ibn Ahmad Ibn al-Maslama and other teachers of that time. At Ispahân and Samarkand he heard traditions delivered and took down in writing the greater part of them. Having then abstained from that practice and given it up, he took to a life of self-mortification, devotional exercises, and efforts (in *pursuit of God's grace*); this he continued till he became as a religious hand-post, directing towards God. In the year 515 (A. D. 1121-2) he went (*again*) to Baghdad and opened in the Nizâmiya College a course of religious instruction which had the greatest success with the public. The venerable *shaikh* and preacher, Abû 'l-Fadl Sâfi Ibn Abd Allah, related as follows : " I was one day present at a sitting held by " our *shaikh* Yûsuf al-Hamadâni in the Nizâmiya College, and a multitude of people " were there assembled. A legist named Ibn as-Sakkâ then stood up, and vexed " the *shaikh* and proposed to him a question : ' Sit down,' said Yakûb, ' for those " words of yours smell strongly of infidelity, and you may probably die in ano- " ther religion than Islamism! Some time after the uttering of these words, a " Christian ambassador, sent to the khalif by the king of the Greeks, arrived (in " *Baghdad*). Ibn as-Sakkâ went to visit him, asked to become his follower and " said : ' It strikes me that I shall abandon the religion of islamism and adopt " yours.' The ambassador granted his request and took him to al-Constantiniya " (*Constantinople*), where he got attached to the service of the Greek king and died " a Christian. The *hâfiz* Abû Abd Allah Muhammad Ibn Mahmûd al-Baghdâdi,

" surnamed Ibn an-Najjár (vol. I. p. 11) says, in that article of his (biographical) his-
" tory of Baghdad which treats of Yûsuf al-Hamadáni : ' Abû 'l-Karam Abd as-Salâm
" ' Ibn Ahmad , a teacher of the Koran-readings, said in my presence : ' Ibn as-
" ' Sakkâ was a reader of the noble Koran and could psalmody it with great ele-
" ' gance. A person who saw him at Constantinople said to me : ' I found him
" ' lying on a sofa, sick and holding in his hand a sort of fan with which he drove
" ' away the flies from his face. I asked him if the Koran still remained in his me-
" ' mory, and he replied that he remembered nothing of it except this single verse :
" ' *The time may come when the infidels shall wish that they were Moslims* (surat 15,
" ' verse 2), and that he had forgotten the rest.' God preserve us from an evil des-
" ' tiny, from the loss of His grace and from the down-coming of His vengeance !
" ' We pray him to keep us firm in the religion of islamism; Amen ! Amen !' " —
Abû Saad Ibn as-Samâni (vol. II. p. 156) says : " Yûsuf Ibn Aiyûb al-Hamadâni
" was a native of Bûzanajird, a village situated in that part of the province of Hama-
" dân which is contiguous to Rai. He was an imâm noted for piety, living in the
" fear of God and the practice of devotion; according to what he knew he acted, ful-
" filling all his obligations. To him were granted frequent *states* and prolonged
" *stations* (in *religious extasy*); on him devolved the education of the novices who
" aspired sincerely (to a *devout life*). In his convent (ribat) at Marw was assembled
" such a number of persons who had renounced the world for the love of God, that
" the like of it could not be imagined, neither was it to be found in any other con-
" vent. From youth to old age he followed the approved path, the way of recti-
" tude and righteousness. Having left his village for Baghdad, he went to see the
" imâm Abû Ishak as-Shîrâzi (vol. I. p. 9) and, during his residence in that city, he
" studied jurisprudence under his direction and attended his lessons with the utmost
" assiduity. He thus acquired a superior knowledge of the law and, in the specu-
" lative part of it particularly, he surpassed all his contemporaries. Though still a
" youth, he was appointed to direct the studies of a large class of students by as-
" Shîrâzi, who had remarked his self-denial, his virtuous conduct and his exclusive
" application to the duties of religion (3). He subsequently abandoned the specula-
" tive studies which had absorbed his attention and betook himself to a more serious
" occupation, the practice of devotion, the calling of the people to the service of
" God and the conducting of his fellow-students in the path of righteousness. He
" then went to reside at Marw, whence he removed to Herât, where he remained

" for some time. Being invited to return to Marw, he proceded thither and, towards
" the close of his life, he paid a second visit to Herât. Having then resolved on
" going back to Marw, he set out on his journey but, when he reached Bâmayîn, a
" place situated between Herât and Baghshûr, he breathed his last. This happened
" in the month of the first Rabî, 535 (oct.-nov. A. D. 1140). He was buried there,
" but his body was afterwards removed to Marw. His birth is placed, not with cer-
" tainly but with probability, in the year 440 (A. D. 1048-9), or 441. He was born
" at Bûzanajird."—All that precedes was extracted by me from Ibn an-Najjâr's (biographical) history (of Baghdad). — Some words occur in this notice which require
elucidation : Wahura, the name of his ancestor, has no meaning in Arabic, as far as
I know. — Al-Kostantiniya, the great city of the Greeks (Rûm), was so called after its
founder, Kostantin (Constantine), who was the first of their sovereigns that embraced
Christianity.—Bûzanajird is a village in (the province of) Hamadân and at a day's
journey from that city. It lies near Sâwah; so says as-Samâni in his Ansâb. — Of
Marw we have already spoken (vol. I. p. 50). — Bâmayin is a small town in Khorâsân, according to the same author. — Herât we have already mentioned (vol. I.
p. 78); it is one of the four seats of government which exist in Khorâsân. The others
are Naisâpûr, Marw and Balkh. — Boghshûr is also a village in Khorâsân and lies
between Marw and Herât. We have mentioned in our article on the jurisconsult
al-Hasan Ibn Masûd al-Farrâ (vol. I. p. 420) that he drew his surname of al-
Daghawi from this place.

(1) For the explanation of these terms, which belong to the theory of that mystic devotion which was
practised by the Sûfis, see the preface of Jâmî in the twelfth volume of the Notices et Extraits.

(2) Ibn Khaldûn has a chapter on the fundamentals of jurisprudence in his Prolegomena. See my French
translation of that work, tome III, page 23.

(3) Literally : to what concerned him. Ibn Khaldûn says, in his Prolegomena, tome III, page 181 : " Le
législateur autorise tout ce qui dirige nos pensées vers la religion, parce qu'elle nous assure le bonheur d'une
l'autre vie; il permet les actes qui, en nous procurant la nourriture, assurent notre bien-être dans ce monde...
Quant aux actes qui ne nous intéressent pas et qui ne renferment rien de mal, l'homme qui s'en abstient se
éloigne pas de la faveur divine : le meilleur témoignage qu'on puisse donner de sa soumission à la volonté
de Dieu, c'est de s'abstenir des actes qu'on n'a aucun intérêt de faire."

AL-AALAM ASH-SHANTAMARI.

The grammarian Abû 'l-Hajjâj Yûsuf Ibn Sulaimân Ibn Isa, surnamed al-Aalam (the harelipped) was a native of Shantamariya in the West (1). He travelled to Cordova in the year 433 (A. D. 1041-2) and resided there for some time. Having studied under Abû 'l-Kâsim Ibrohîm Ibn Muhammad Ibn Zakariya al-Iflili, Abû Sahl al-Harrâni and Abû Bakr Muslim Ibn Ahmad an accomplished literary scholar, he became well acquainted with (pure) Arabic, philology and the ideas usually expressed in poetry. He possessed by heart all the passages illustrative of these subjects, to which he had applied with great assiduity. His extensive learning, the retentiveness of his memory and the correctness (of the texts which he dictated) procured him a wide reputation. To his pupils he furnished a great quantity of information, and he was the only teacher of that time whose renown attracted students from distant parts. One of his disciples was Abû Ali al-Husain Ibn Muhammad Ibn Ahmad al-Ghassâni al-Jaiyâni, the same of whom we have spoken (vol. I. p. 458). Al-Aalam, towards the close of his life, lost his sight. He composed a commentary the Jumal of Abû 'l-Kâsim az-Zajjâji (vol. II. p. 92) and a separate treatise on the verses (given as examples) in that work. A commentary on the poetical works of al-Mutanabbi (vol. I. p. 102) was drawn up by him with the assistance of his master, Ibn al-Iflili. He commented also the Hamâsa (vol. I. p. 348), as far as I can judge; for I once possessed an explanation of that work by one ash-Shantamari; I do not now recollect the (other) names of the author, but am inclined to think that it was the person of whom we are speaking. It is a very good work, whoever made it. Al-Aalam died at Seville, a city in the Spanish peninsula, A. H. 476 (A. D. 1083-4). He was born in the year 410 (A. D. 1019-20). The following relation was made by Abû 'l-Hasan Shuraih Ibn Muhammad Ibn Shuraih ar-Roaini, a native of Seville and the preacher in the great mosque of that city : "On Friday, the 15th of Shawwâl, 476 (25th February, A. D. 1084) took place the "death of my father, Abû Abd Allah Muhammad Ibn Shuraih. I went to inform "the professor and master Abû 'l-Hajjâj al-Aalam of that event, because they loved "each other as brothers. He wept bitterly on hearing the news, and exclaimed :

" ' We belong to God and unto him must we return!' He then said: ' I shall not
" ' survive him more than a month.' And so it happened.—In a document written
by the learned and virtuous teacher of Koran-reading, Muhammad Ibn Khair (2),
who was a native of Spain, I found the following note : " This Abú 'l-Hajjáj
" was surnamed al-Aalam because he was much disfigured by a slit in his upper lip."
I may here observe that a man who has that defect in his upper lip is called an
aalam, which word is derived from the verb alima, yalamu, alaman. A female
with this deformity is designated by the term almd. If the defect be in the lower
lip, the adjective is aftah, derived from the verb faliha, yaftahu, falahan. This is
conformable to the general rule for all verbs which designate bodily infirmities and
defects : the second radical letter is followed, in the preterite, by an i and, in the
aorist and the noun, by an a. Such are the verbs kharisa, yakhrasu, kharasan (to
be dumb), barisa, yabrasu, barasan (to be leprous), àmia, yàma, àman (to be blind).
In such verbs, the adjective indicating the person takes (in the masculine) the form
afál; so, they say : akhras, aalam, aftah. Abù Yazìd Suhail Ibn Amr al-Aàmiri, a
member of the tribe of Kuraish (and a contemporary of Muhammad) had a harelip.
When he was made a prisoner at the battle of Badr, Omar Ibn al-Khattáb said to the
Apostle of God : " Let me pluck out his fore-teeth so that he may never again stand
" forward to make speeches against you." The Prophet replied : " Let him alone;
" he may, one day, stand forward in a manner which you will approve of. " This
Suhail was a good orator, a correct and elegant speaker. It was he who came (from
Mekka) to al Hudaibia for the purpose of concluding a truce, and in that he succeeded.
Having subsequently embraced Islamism, he proved a sincere convert. The standing forward, which the Prophet foretold, really occurred : when he gave up his soul
to God, many of the Arabs apostatised and violent dissentions arose between them.
Suhail, who was then at Mekka, stood forward and addressed the people in a speech
which tranquillised them and put an end to their disputes. This was the praiseworthy standing-forth which the Prophet had foreseen. When Omar asked leave to
pluck out his fore-teeth in order to prevent him from making speeches, he was
aware that persons having a harelip and no front-teeth find great difficulty in pronouncing their words. — Antara Ibn Shaddàd al-Absi, the famous horseman (and
the author of one of the Moallakas), had a harelip and was surnamed al-falhd (which
is the feminine adjective), but, in his case, the word referred to the noun thafa (lip),
which is of the feminine gender. — Shantamariya is a city in western Spain. — Al-

Hudaibia is a place situated between Mekka and Medina; it was there that the Prophet received from his followers *the oath of satisfaction* (*bia tar-Ridwan*) (2). This name is sometimes pronounced *al-Hudaibiya*.

(1) There were in Spain two large towns called by the Arabs Shanta-Mariya (*Santa-Maria*): one of them, situated in the province of Algarve, was designated as the Shanta-Mariya of the West (*el-gharb*); the other, situated in the kingdom of Aragon was called the Shanta-Mariya of the Beni Razin (*Albarracin*).

(2) This took place in the sixth year of the Hejira.

THE KADI BAHA AD-DIN IBN SHADDAD.

Abú 'l-Mahásin Yúsuf Ibn Ráfi Ibn Temím Ibn Otba Ibn Muhammad Ibn Attáb al-Asadi, surnamed Bahá ad-Dín (*lustre of religion*), was a legist of the Sháfite sect and *kádi* of Aleppo. When a child, he lost his father and was brought up in the family of his maternal uncles, the Beni Shaddád. This Shaddád was his mother's grand-father. He (*Bahá ad-Dín*) bore at first the prenomen of Abú 'l-Izz, which he afterwards replaced by that of Abú 'l-Mahásin, as we have indicated above. He was born on the eve of the 10th of Ramadán, 539 (5th March, A. D. 1145) at Mosul, and there, in his youth, he learned by heart the noble Koran. When Abú Bakr Yahya Ibn Saadún of Cordova, the *shaikh* of whom we have given a notice (*p. 57 of this vol.*), went to Mosul, Abú 'l-Mahásin attended his lectures with great assiduity, read under his direction the seven *ways* (or *editions*) of the Koranic text (1) and obtained a solid acquaintance with its various readings. He, himself, says in one of his works : " The first (*professor*) from whom I took lessons was the *háfis* (*traditio-*
" *nist*) Sáin ad-Dín Abú Bakr Yahya Ibn Saadún Ibn Tammám Ibn Muhammad al-
" Azdi al-Kortubi; may God have mercy on his soul! I studied Koran-reading
" under him, without discontinuing, during the space of eleven years. I read over,
" also, under his direction, the greater part of the works which he used to teach and
" which treated of the different readings, the manner of reciting the noble Koran,
" and the text of the Traditions, with explanations and commentaries of his own.

" He then drew up for me, with his own hand, a certificate attesting that none of his
" scholars had read under his tuition more than I did. I possess also, in his hand-
" writing, nearly two quires (forty pages) in which were indicated all that I had read
" under him and the matters which he himself had taught orally and which I might
" teach on his authority. Amongst the works mentioned in this list are those of al-
" Bukhári (vol. II. p. 594) and Muslim (vol. III. p. 348), with the indication of the
" different channels through which the texts of these works had come down to him.
" Besides that were mentioned most of the (standard) works on Traditions and philo-
" logy. The last treatise which he authorised me to teach was his commentary on
" the Gharib, composed by Abû Obaid al-Kâsim Ibn Sallâm (vol. II. p. 486). I read
" it under his direction during a number of sittings, the last of which took place in the
" last third of the month of Shabán, 567 (April, A. D. 1172)." — I may here observe
that this was the year in which the shaikh of Cordova (Ibn Saadán) died. — " Another
" of my professors, " continues he, " was Abû 'l-Barakat Abd Allah Ibn al-Khidr Ibn
" al-Hussin, generally known by the surname of as-Shaji (2). I heard him explain a
" part of ath-Thalabl's (vol. I. p. 60) commentary (on the Koran), and I received from
" him a licence to teach on his authority all that he had taught orally, touching
" the various readings. A certificate, drawn up by him to that effect and inscrib-
" ed by him in the album (or catalogue) containing the list (fihrest) of texts which I
" had heard taught, is dated the 5th of the first Jumáda, 566 (14 January, A. D.
" 1171). This doctor was noted for his learning in the science of Traditions and in
" that of jurisprudence. He acted as a kádi in Basra and taught in the Old Atábe-
" kiya (college)." — The writer means the Atábekiya of Mosul. — " Another of my
" masters was the shaikh Majd ad-Dîn Abû 'l-Fadl Abd Allah Ibn Ahmad Ibn Abd
" al-Kábir at-Tûsi, the preacher of the great mosque in Mosul. He was so highly
" renowned as a Traditionist that people came from all countries for the pur-
" pose of hearing him. He lived upwards of ninety years." — I may add that Abû
'l-Fadl Ibn at-Tûsi was born on the 15th of Safar, 487 (5th March, A. D. 1094), in
the quarter of Baghdad called Báb al-Marátib and that he died at Mosul on the eve
of Tuesday, the 14th of the month of Ramadán, 578 (11th January, A. D. 1183).
He was interred in the cemetery contiguous to the gate called Báb al-Maidán
(hippodrome-gate). Let us resume Abû 'l-Mahásin's relation and finish it : — " I
" heard from him," — meaning the preacher just mentioned, " most of the texts
" which he had learned from the lips of his masters and, on the 26th of Rajab, 558

" (10th june, A. D. 1163), I received from him a licence to teach all that he used
" to deliver from memory. Another of my professors was the *hâfiz* Fakhr ad-Dín
" Abû'r-Rida Said Ibn Abd Allah as-Shahrozûri. I heard from his lips the
" *Musnad (or collection of authenticated traditions made)* by as-Sbâfî (*vol. II. p. 589*),
" that of Abû Awâna (*p. 28 of this vol.*), that of Abû Yala 'l-Mausili (*vol. I. p. 212*)
" and the *Sunan* of Abû Dâwûd (*col. I. p. 589*). He gave me a certificate to that
" effect and inscribed it in my album. I heard him also recite the text of Abû Isa
" al-Tirmidi's *Jâmi* (*vol. II. p. 679*), and received from him a licence to teach all
" that he himself taught. This document is in his hand-writing and bears the date
" of the month of Shawwâl, 567 (may-june, A. D. 1172). Another of my profes-
" sors was the *hâfiz* Majd ad-Dín Abû Muhammad Abd Allah Ibn Mohammad Ibn
" Ali al-Ashtri as-Sanhâji (3). He gave me licence to teach all the texts which he
" had dictated from memory, notwithstanding the great variety of their subjects. I
" have in my album a certificate to that effect, dated in the month of Ramadân,
" 559 (July-Aug. A. D. 1104). His own album contains the same document and
" is also in my possession."— I must here add that Abû Muhammad Abd Allah al-
Ashtri died in Syria, in the month of Shawwâl 561 (August, A. D. 1166), and was
interred at Baalbek, outside the Gate of Emessa (*Bâb Hims*), on the northern side of
he town. — " Amongst them also was the *hâfiz* Siraj ad-Dín Abû Bakr Muhammad
" Ibn Ali al-Jaiyâni (4). At Mosul I read under his tuition the *Sahih* of Muslim,
" from the beginning to the end, as also the *Wasit* of al-Wâhidi (*vol. II. p. 246*).
" He authorized me to teach the same texts as he did, and his certificate bears the
" date of 559 (A. D. 1163-4). These were the teachers whose names come to my
" recollection; there were a number of others whom I heard, but now, that I am
" compiling this treatise, I cannot call to mind on whose authority they gave their
" lessons. Their names were Shuhda tal-Kâtiba (*col. I. p. 625*) at Baghdad,
" Abû 'l-Mughith in al-Harbiya (5), Rida ad-Dín al-Kazwini, who professed in the
" Nizâmiya college, and some others who obtained their information through chan-
" nels the recollection of which has escaped me. I need not give their names, as
" those whom I have mentioned are quite sufficient." End of Abû 'l-Mahâsin's
personal statement. — According to another account, he studied under Abû 'l-Barakât Abd Allah Ibn as-Sizaji, the chief logist of Mosul, and the same of whom mention has been made; he was noted for learning, self-denial and austerity of life.
His death occurred at Mosul, in the month of the first Jumâda, 574 (Oct.-Nov. A D.

1178). He was interred outside the city. He (Abú 'l-Mahásin) then studied the controverted points of jurisprudence under Dia ad-Dîn Ibn Ali Házim, the disciple of that Muhammad Ibn Yahya an-Naisápúri who died a martyr (vol. II. p. 628). He then practised the art of controversy under the ablest (mutkini) masters, such as Fakhr ad-Dîn an-Naukâni, al-Darruwi, Imâd ad-Dîn an-Naukâni, Saif ad-Dîn al-Khuwâri and Imâd ad-Dîn al-Mayânji. He had attained the highest proficiency when he went down to Baghdad and put up at the Nizâmiya college, where he shortly afterwards was appointed to act as an under-tutor (6). That office he held about four years, during the professorship of Abú Nasr Ahmad Ibn Abd Allah Ibn Muhammad ash-Shâshi. In the month of the latter Rabî, 566 (Dec.-Jan. A.D. 1170-1), ash-Shâshi had been appointed chief professor in the Nizâmiya college, and towards the end of Rajab, 569 (Feb.-March, A. D. 1174), he was dismissed from office. To him, and on the date just given, succeeded Rida ad-Dîn Abú 'l-Khair Ahmad al-Kazwîni. Abú 'l-Mahásin continued to act as under-tutor and, in that office, he had for a colleague as-Sadîd as-Salamási (vol. II. p. 843). He went up to Mosul in the same year, and was appointed to the professorship in the college which had been founded by the kâdi Kamâl ad-Dîn Abú 'l-Fadl Muhammad Ibn ash-Shahrozûri (vol. II. p. 640). He there continued his learned occupations and a number of students derived profit from his lessons. In the beginning of a work which he composed on law-cases and entitled Maljá 'l-Hukkâm and Iltibâs al-Ahkâm (the resource for judges in doubtful cases), he says that he made the pilgrimage in the year 583 (A. D. 1186) and, after fulfilling that duty and visiting the (tomb of the) Prophet (at Medina), he went, in pious devotion, to al-Bait al-Mukaddas (the consecrated dwelling, that is Jerusalem) and to (Hebron, where he saw the tomb of Abraham) al-Khalîl (the friend of God). He then entered into Damascus, whilst the sultan Salâh ad-Dîn was besieging Kalat Kaukab (7). Being sent for by that prince, who had been informed of his arrival, he thought that he would have been questioned about the manner in which the emir Shams ad-Dîn Ibn al-Mukaddam met with his death. This officer commanded the pilgrim-caravan of that year in the name of Salâh ad-Dîn and was killed at Mount Arafât in an affray of which there is a long account, but this is not the place to give it (8). When he (Abú 'l-Mahásin) appeared before the sultan, he was received by him in the most honourable manner, and no other questions were asked of him except about his journey and the learned men, practisers (of virtue), whom he had met with. The

sultan having then expressed the wish of reading over some traditions under his direction, he produced a (small) volume in which he had collected the azkâr (or pious
invocations) handed down by al-Bukhâri, and this book was read aloud to
him by the prince. When Abû 'l-Mahâsin retired, the kâtib Imâd ad-Dîn
al-Ispahâni (vol. III. p. 300) overtook him and said : " The sultan sends you word
" that, if you resolve on coming back here after your return from the pilgrimage (9),
" you must inform him (of your arrival), because he wishes to communicate to you
" something important. " On his return, he let the sultan know of his arrival and
received the order to go and see him. During the interval, he had composed a
work in which he enumerated the merits to be acquired by warring against infidels,
and indicated the promises which God had made in favour of those who engage in
holy war. This treatise filled about thirty quires (600 pages). He undertook the
journey, found the sultan encamped in the plain (at the foot of the fortress called)
Hisn al-Akrâd (the Castle of the Kurds), and presented to him this book. " I inten-
" ded," said he, " to renounce the world and take up my residence in the Mash-
" hid (10) which is outside of Mosul, as soon as I could get there." In the beginning of the first Jumâda, 584 (end of June, A. D. 1188), he went to present his
respects to the sultan Salâh ad-Dîn who, some time after, appointed him kâdi of the
army (kâdi 'l-Askar) and nominated him hâkim (11) of Jerusalem.—In one of
the months of the year 666 (A. D. 1267-8), whilst I was hâkim in the city of Damascus, a deed came into my hands which had been authenticated (and witnessed) in
the presence of the kâdi Abû 'l-Mahâsin, whilst he was acting as Salâh ad-Dîn's
kâdi 'l-Askar. Its validity had been impaired by the demise of the witnesses and, in
my opinion, could hardly be reestablished. This document I read through to the
very end because it interested me greatly as being a memorial of our professor Abû
'l-Mahâsin, him who had taught us so much and whose assiduous disciples we had
been.— Let us now return to the account which he gives of himself : " On going to
" offer my respects to Salâh ad-Dîn, I had for travelling-companions the shaikh of
" the shaikhs (chief of the professors), Sadr ad-Dîn Abd ar-Rahîm Ibn Ismaîl
" and the kâdi Muhi ad-Dîn Ibn as-Shahrozûri, who had been sent to him
" on a mission. The death of al-Bahâ ad-Dimishki, which happened at that time,
" left vacant the chief professorship in the Nandzil al-Izz college at Old Cairo and
" the office of preacher in that city. Salâh ad-Dîn offered me the professorship, but
" I did not accept it. The second time that I appeared before the sultan, I had been

" sent to him on a mission from Mosul and found him at Harrán. He was then
" sick."... " After the death of Saláh ad-Din, at which I was present, I proceeded
" to Aleppo for the purpose of reestablishing harmony between his sons and
" inducing them to swear that they would support each other. Al-Malik az-Záhir
" Ghíath ad-Din, one of these brothers and the sovereign of Aleppo, then wrote
" to his brother al-Malik al-Afdal Núr ad-Din Ali, the lord of Damascus, demand-
" ing I should be sent to him. On my arrival az-Záhir dispatched me to Cairo
" for the purpose of obtaining the adhesion of his brother, al-Malik al-Aziz
" Imád ad-Din Othmán. He then offered me the chief magistracy of Aleppo,
" but I would not accept it. After my return from this mission, I consen-
" ted to accept the kadiship of Aleppo, that place having become vacant by the
" death of him that filled it." Such is the relation made by Abú 'l-Mahásin
in his *Maljá 'l-Hukkám*. — The *kádi* Kamál ad-Din Abú 'l-Kásim Omar Ibn
Ahmad, surnamed Ibn al-Adím (*p.* 334 *of this vol.*), says in his smaller work on
the history of Aleppo to which he gave the title of *Zubda tal-Halab fi Tárikh Halab*
(*the cream of new milk*, *being a treatise on the history of Aleppo,* : " In the
" year 91, " — that is, in 591 (A. D. 1195), — " the *kádi* Bahá ad-Din Abú
" 'l-Mahásin Yúsuf Ibn Ráfi Ibn Tamím, entered into the service of al-Malik
" az-Záhir, having come to see him at Aleppo. That prince confided to him
" the kadiship of the city with the administration of the *wakfs* (12), after deposing
" the *kádi* Zain ad-Din Abú 'l-Bayán Baná Ibn al-Bányási, who had been acting as
" the deputy of Muhl ad-Din Ibn az-Zaki. Bahá ad-Din then obtained the places
" of vizir and privy-counsellor to that prince. " End of the extract. — I may here
observe that [the *kádi* Baná was the son of al-Fadl Ibn Sulaimán al-Humri (or *al-
Himyari*), that their family was known at Damascus by the name of al-Bányási, and
that] (13) Muhl ad-Din Muhammad Ibn az-Zaki, the person above mentioned, had
been appointed *kádi* by the sultan Saláh ad-Din and had afterwards taken for his deputy Zain ad-Din Baná Ibn al-Bányási, who remained in place till the above-mentioned date. At that time, there were but few colleges (or *high schools*) in Aleppo and
learned men were very rare. Abú 'l-Mahásin was therefore induced to reorganise
these institutions and provide them with teachers, learned in the law. During
his lifetime, a great number of colleges were thus established. Al-Malik az-Záhir
granted to him a rich *iktá* (14) which produced a very ample revenue. The *kádi*,
having neither children nor relatives, did not spend much, and the rest of his in-

come was so abundant that he was able to found a college near the Gate of Irâk and opposite to the college opened for Shâfite students by Nûr ad-Dîn Mahmûd Ibn Zinki (vol. III. p. 338). I saw the date of its erection inscribed on the ceiling of the mosque attached to it, in the place allotted to the giving of lessons. That date was 601 (A. D. 1204-5). He then founded in the neighbourhood of this college a school for the teaching of the Traditions concerning the Prophet and, between the two establishments, he erected a mausoleum in which he intended to be buried. This edifice has two entrances, one on the side towards the college and the other on the side towards the Tradition school; they are opposite one to the other and each of them is closed by a (metal) grating, so that a person standing at one end of the monument can see through it to the other. When Aleppo was brought into this (prosperous) state, legists arrived there from all quarters, studies became active and the number of persons who came to the city was very great. A close intimacy, a sincere and friendly attachment subsisted between my deceased father and the kâdi Abû 'l-Mahâsin, from the time in which they were fellow-students at Mosul. When I went to (study under) this kâdi, a very short time after my brother had gone to him, a letter of recommendation, drawn up in the strongest terms, was sent to him by the sovereign of our city (Arbela). This prince (whose names and titles were) al-Malik al-Muazzam Muzaffar ad-Dîn Abû Saîd Kôkubûri, the son of Ali and the grandson of Bektikin (the valourous bey), has been already spoken of (vol. II. p. 535). In this letter he said : " You know what is necessary to be done with these boys : " they are the sons of one who was for me as a brother and who was also a brother " for you. To this I need not add any stronger recommendation." The writer continued in this style to some length. The kâdi Abû 'l-Mahâsin, being very obliging, received us most honourably and treated us as well as he possibly could and in a manner worthy of himself. He lodged us in his college, inscribed us on the list of those who received commons and placed us in the class of the elder boys, though we were still very young and merely beginning to study. In the life of the shaikh Muwaffak ad-Dîn Yaîsh the grammarian (page 380 of this vol.) I mentioned the date of my arrival at Aleppo and need not therefore repeat it here. I and my brother remained with him (Abû 'l-Mahâsin) till the day of his death, an event of which the date shall be given farther on. During all that time there was not a general course of lectures in the college, because the professor, Abû 'l-Mahâsin himself, was much advanced in years and so very weak that he could hardly move, much less commit his lessons to memory and deliver them. He therefore confided to four legists of merit the duty of going over the lessons with the students, and it was under the tuition of these doctors that all the school pursued their studies. I and my brother read our lessons under the *shaikh* Jamâl ad-Dîn Abû Bakr al-Mâhâni, because he was our townsman and had been a fellow-student of my father's under the shaikh Imâd ad-Dîn Abû Hâmid Muhammad Ibn Yûnus (vol. II. p. 656). He (al-Mâhâni) died on the 3rd of Shawwâl, 627 (15 August, A. D. 1230), aged upwards of eighty years. I then attended the lectures of the *shaikh* Najm ad-Dîn Abû Abd Allah Muhammad Ibn Abi Bakr Ibn Ali, generally known by the appellation of Ibn al-Khabbâz (15), who was a native of Mosul. This legist and *imâm* was then professor in the Saifiya college. I read under his direction al-Ghazzâli's (*law-treatise, the*) *Wajîz* (vol. II. p. 622), from the beginning of the work to the chapter on affirmations (*ikrâr*) (16). But, after all, these observations, each of them bringing on another, have led us away from our subject.—The *kâdi* Abû 'l-Mahâsin (*being nominated vizir*), obtained the entire and absolute direction of affairs, and no person in the state dared to remonstrate with him. The sovereign, at that time, was al-Malik al-Azîz Abû 'l-Muzaffar Muhammad, the son of al-Malik az-Zâhir and the grandson of Salâh ad-Dîn (*Saladin*). As he was still a child, he remained under the care of the eunuch Shihâb ad-Dîn Abû Saîd Togbrul, who acted as his *atâbek* (*guardian*) and administered the principality under the direction of Abû 'l-Mahâsin. Every thing was regulated by the authority of these two persons. During the administration of Abû 'l-Mahâsin, legists were treated with the highest respect and consideration, particularly those who were attached to his college : they were authorized to assist at the sultan's private parties and, during the month of Ramadân, they broke their fast every day at his table. As he taught Traditions, we went regularly to his house for the purpose of hearing him. He had there a winter-alcove, arranged purposely for himself, and in it he sat, winter and summer. The fact was that old age had produced its effect on him and rendered him as weak as a little bird just hatched. It was with the greatest pain and difficulty that he was able to stir for the purpose of saying his prayers or for any other motive. As he was often afflicted with a catarrh, he never left his alcove; in winter, he had always beside him a large brasier filled with a great quantity of lighted coals, and yet he was never free from defluxions. He constantly wore a pelisse lined with Bortasian furs (17) and a number of tunics; under him was a very soft cushion placed upon a pile of carpets thickly wadded. When we were with him, the heat inconvenienced us greatly, but he did not feel it, so completely was he overcome by the cold which accompanies decrepitude. He never went out to perform his devotions at the mosque unless during the great heats of summer, and when, with extreme difficulty, he stood up to pray, he was always ready to fall. One day, whilst he was standing at prayer, I looked at his legs, and they had on them so little flesh that they were like thin sticks. After Friday prayers, those who had been present went to his house in order to hear him repeat Traditions, and this gave him great pleasure. His conversation was agreeable and, in his discourse, which was highly elegant, literature was the prevailing subject. He frequently quoted at his sittings the following verse :

To escape from (*the charms of*) Laila and her fair neighbour, you must never, in any case, pass near their place of meeting.

He often quoted proverbially a line from one of Surr Durr's (vol. *II.* p. 321) long *kasîdas*, in which that poet says :

The promises made by them in the sands (*of the desert*) have been broken; so fails whatever is built upon sand.

He repeated it, one day, in the presence of his pupils and one of them said : "Master! Ibn al-Muallim al-Iráki has expressed that idea with great elegance."—"Is that Ibn al-Muallim," said he, "the same who was surnamed Abû 'l-Ghanâim? (*vol. III.* p. 168)." Being informed that it was, he replied : "He was my comrade; what did he say?" The other recited as follows :

They failed to fulfil their engagements, but every thing built by the hands of love in the sands of the desert cannot but fail.

"Not bad!" said he, "and the expression *by the hands of love* comes in gracefully." The same student then said : "Master! be employed again the same thought in another *kasîda*."—"Let us have it," said he, and the other recited this line :

The promise was not built on sand; how then could it fail?

This verse also obtained his approbation. He frequently repeated to us a piece of

verse composed by Abû 'l-Fawâris Saad Ibn Muhammad, surnamed Hais Bais (vol. I.
p. 559) and declared that he gave it on the authority of that poet, because he had
heard it from his lips.   In our article on Surr Durr we have given this piece, so we
need only mention here the first verse :

> Strive not to abuse exalted worth when you yourself are pointed at with respectful admi-
> ration.

He stated also that, whilst he and al-Kadi'l Fâdil (vol. II. p. 111) were at (the siege
of) the castle of Safad (18), the latter recited to him a verse composed by a poet and
which ran as follows :

> I said to the defluxion (which afflicted me and) which was beginning to affect my tonsils :
> " Leave my throat, I implore you! for it is the vestibule of my life. "

These two verses are attributed to Ibn al-Habbâriya (vol. III. p. 150).—As often as
Abû 'l-Mahâsin looked at himself and considered the state of weakness he was in,
being unable to stand up, or to sit down, or to pray, or to make any movement whatever, he would say :

> Let him who wishes for a long life arm himself with fortitude, so that he may support the
> death of friends.   He that lives long finds in himself all the pains which he could wish for his
> enemies.

These two verses are attributed to Zâhir ad-Dîn Abû Ishak Ibrahim Ibn Nasr Ibn
Askar, the kâdi of as-Sallâmiya whose life we have given towards the commencement
of this work (vol. I. p. 15).   So it is mentioned by my friend Ibn as-Shâir al-Mausili, in the article on az-Zâhir which he has inserted in the Ohûd al-Jumân (collars of
pearls) (19).   The thought is borrowed from Abû 'l-Alâ al-Maarri (vol. I. p. 94),
who said :

> Our lips wish long life to him for whom our hearts feel the utmost love.   We would rejoice,
> were his existence prolonged, and yet, in that prolongation, he would meet every thing that he
> dislikes.

All these verses derive from a passage in which a poet said :

My spear (stature) never yielded to whatever tried to bend it; it yielded only to the succession of nights and days. I ardently implored the Lord to preserve my life, and now I find that life itself is an evil.

A Maghribin named Abû 'l-Hajjâj Yûsuf, who had just come from his native country to Aleppo and who was a man of talent, well versed in literature and philosophy, went to visit him one day, and, on seeing him greatly emaciated and worn away, recited to him these lines :

If people knew what would happen (you), were you allowed to live for their advantage, they would weep because you would be stripped of the garment of youth. Were they able to give up part of their existence (in order to lengthen yours), they would consent to redeem you (from death) with nothing less precious than their lives.

These words gave the *kâdi* great pleasure, and tears came to his eyes as he thanked the speaker. — One of my acquaintances told me that, one day, he heard the *kâdi* relate the following anecdote to his assembled auditors : " Whilst we were in the " Nizâmiya college, at Baghdad, four or five of the law-students agreed on swallow-" ing kernels of the *belâdor* nut (20) for the purpose of sharpening their wits and " their memory. So, they went to a physician, asked him what was a sufficient " dose for a man and the way in which the drug should be taken. After that, they " went and purchased the quantity which he had indicated and drank off the decoc-" tion in a place situated outside of the college. They then became delirious, sepa-" rated one from the other and each of them went his way. Nobody knew what had " become of them till a few days after, when one of them, a very tall fellow, return-" ed to the college. He was in a state of nudity, having not even a rag to conceal " his privy parts, but, on his head, he wore a high-peaked cap (21) the tail of which " was extravagantly long and hang down his back as far as his ancles. He remained " tranquil and silent, looking calm and grave, but neither jested nor spoke. One " of the legists who were present asked him what had happened and received this " answer : ' We met together and drank an infusion of *belâdor* kernels; my com-" ' panions became insane and I was the only one who kept his senses. ' He con-" tinued to evince great intelligence joined to a profound gravity. All the assem-" bly laughed at his appearance, but that he did not perceive and, thinking that he " escaped from what had befallen his companions, he paid not the least attention to

" those who were around him."— Some of the students who had been with Abù 'l-
Mahàsin before we went to him made me the following relation : " An eminent poet
" and literary scholar of Cordova whose names were Nizàm ad-Din Abù 'l-Hasan Ali
" Ibn Muhammad Ibn Yùsuf Ibn Masùd al-Kaisi and who was known by the appel-
" lation of Ibn Kharùf (the son of the lamb) came to see Abù 'l-Mahàsin and addres-
" ed to him a letter commencing with some verses in which he asked him for the
" gift of a furred cloak (22); the epistle ran thus :

"   " Lustre of religion (Bahà ad-Din) and of the world, refulgent in glory and public esteem!
"   " I fear the inclemency of the weather and ask of your bounty the skin of my father.
"   " Your worship knows that I am the lamb (harùf) so eminent in literature. May you always
"   " milk the teats of prosperity and may the milk (halab) which I obtain in Aleppo (Halab) be
"   " pure!

"   " He to whom belongs eminent respect and an illustrious origin, he who
"   " causes happiness (as-sarrà) to sweep proudly on in its progress and who likes
"   " grammarians for the sake of al-Farrà (page 63 of this vol.), — may he bestow
"   " upon an eminent lamb the skin of its father; a skin dyed red and lately tanned.
"   " The person who undertook to curry it was not mistaken, neither did he lose
"   " (his pains). Nay! the praise of him who prepared it has been published and
"   " spread abroad. The fibres of its wool are compact, and it derides the efforts of
"   " every violent and impetuous storm. When that fur appears, cold dreads
"   " and fears it; no other garment is like it when frost and snow descend;
"   " man has nothing to equal it when the tender branches are stripped of
"   " their foliage. It is not like the hood (tailasàn) of Ibn Harb nor like the skin of
"   " Amr which had been lacerated by beating. It is like the skin of the sheep (the
"   " constellation of Aries) in the starry heaven (al-jarbà), which sees beside it the
"   " moon and the stars (najm); not like the skin of the mangy (al-jarbà) sheep
"   " which feeds on (the leaves of) trees and grass (najm). In species, it is a cloak;
"   " in odour, a perfume. (Let me have it) so that it may sometimes serve me for a
"   " coat, and sometimes for an overall; in both cases, it will give life to heat and
"   " death to cold. May the donor never cease to be happy and to accomplish his
"   " promises towards friends, his threats against enemies. Such be the will of God!
"   " Salutation.' " In our article on Abù 'l-Fath Muhammad Sibt Ibn at-Taàwizi
(vol. III, p. 165) we have inserted an epistle which he addressed to the kàtib Imàd

ad-Din in the hope of obtaining a furred pelisse also.   Both letters are very original
in their kind.   That which we have just given contains some expressions which
require to be explained : the words *not like the tailasân of Ibn Harb* refer to a saying
which was current among the literary men of that period ; when an object was much
used, they said it was like Ibn Harb's tailasân.   As we are therefore obliged to
notice it, we shall here speak of it.   Ahmad Ibn Harb, the nephew of Yazid, the son
of al-Muhallab (*p. 164 of this vol.*), gave to Abû Ali Ismail Ibn Ibrahim Ibn Ham-
duyah al-Hamdûi, a poet and literary scholar of Basra, a worn-out tailasân.   Numerous epigrams were composed on the subject by the poet and passed from mouth
to mouth.   Amongst them we may notice the following lines belonging to a piece
which contains a number of verses :

> Ibn Harb! you have clothed me in a tailasân which had got tired of being time's companion
> from days of old and given up his company.   It has been so often taken to the darner that, if
> we sent it there alone, it would not miss its way.

In another piece he said :

> It became such an annoyance (*khilaf*) to the darner, that he almost wished it could learn
> from him to darn itself.

He said also :

> Ibn Harb! you clothed me in a time-worn tailasân, quite decrepid.   As often as I darned it,
> it said to me : "Glory to them *who restores life to bones that have mouldered into dust* (Coran,
> " *sur.* 36, *verse* 78)."

He said again :

> Ibn Harb! you have incurred my lasting hatred by obliging me to darn a tailasân which I
> could well have done without.   Whilst I mend it, I compare it to the family of Pharaoh which
> deserved *to be cast into the fire, morning and evening* (Coran, *sur.* 40, *verse* 49).

Again he said :

> Ibn Harb! we have seen your tailasân; it is a new humiliation to a man already humbled.
> When the darner mends it in one part, the rest hastens to split open.   When a friend embraces
> me, he pulls away a hand's breadth of it and, when I return his embrace, I tear off from it

so ill. I turn my eyes from one end of it to the other, examining it in length and breadth, and can see nothing but darns. I have no doubt but that in former times, it served as a sail to Noah's ark. For me, it is quite enough to see the rest of it falling to tatters on my shoulders. Stop a little longer, o hyæna! before your departure; let not your station here be for the purpose of saying a long farewell (23).

In a piece addressed to a man in high station he resumed the subject and said :

Let me weep for my garment, now, that it has bidden me farewell; I must persist in weeping since it persists (in leaving me). Son of al-Husain! see you not how my vest has become a rag which, through long use, has fallen (into ruin) and become (a network) like a coat of mail. It has so many rents that the zephyr, in breathing upon it, would disperse it like a cloud. My tailasān declares, by its tattered state, that, from it my vest learned to get used and be worn away. May it not obtain the favour of God! it was always a foe to my other garments and made them fall to pieces. The mountains should praise God, for, had they been as old as it, they would now be split open and fallen down.

He said also on the same subject :

Ibn Harb! you clothed me in a tailasān which is for the darner as if he sowed corn in a salt marsh. He that first mended it is dead; his sons are dead also, and his grandsons are now turning gray and becoming old men.

By the same on the same subject :

O that my tailasān had a voice where people think that (what we say of it) is a lie! It is like the Tūr (Mount Sinai) which was shattered in its strength and in its foundations when God manifested his presence. We so often mended it when it was torn, that nothing now remains but the patches; all the (original) tailasān is gone.

By the same :

Ibn Harb! I see in a corner of my chamber one of those things with which you clothed so many. It is a tailasān which I darned and darned, and of which I repatched the patches. Obedient to decay, it was headstrong and obstinate for him who tried to mend it. When any curious enquirer sees me wear it, he takes me for an apprentice in the art (of darning).

By the same :

Tell Ibn Harb that the people of Noah used to talk of his tailasān. It has never ceased passing down as a heritage through by-gone generations. When eyes are fixed upon it, their glances seem to read it still more. It will perish if I mend it not, and, if I mend it, it will not last. It is like a dog; whether you attack him or let him alone, he will be always gaping.

It is stated that the poet composed on this tailasân two hundred pieces, each of them containing an original thought. — As for the words of the letter : *nor like the skin of Amr which had been lacerated by beating*, we may observe that they allude to the example cited by grammarians : *Zaid beat Amr*, and which is employed by them, to the exclusion of all others (in order *to illustrate the double action of the verb*). So it might be said of them that they tore to pieces the skin of Amr by frequent beatings. — Al-Hamdûi conceived the idea of composing these epigrams on reading some verses which *Abû Humrân as-Sulami* had made on a tailasân which was worn out to a shred. Here is the piece :

> Tailasân of Abû Homrân! existence is for you an affliction, and in it you can find no pleasure. Every second day, patching must be recommenced; how foolish to think that what is old can be rendered new! When I put you on with the intention of being present at a festival or an assembly, people turn aside lest their glances might do it harm.

The idea expressed in the third (and last) of these verses is taken from a piece composed by the Motazelite doctor, Abû Ishâk Ibrahim Ibn Saiyâr an-Nazzâm al-Balkhi (vol. *I*, p. 186), and in which he described a youth of a very slender shape :

> He is so slender that, if his trousers were taken off, he would become light enough to remain suspended in the air. When people look at him, their glances hurt him, and he complains when pointed at with the finger.

In the month of Ramadân, 626 (July-August, A. D. 1229), a literary man at Mosul recited to me the following verses in which a poet had expressed a similar thought :

> My eyes saw her in imagination and, the next morning, her cheek bore the impress which my imaginary glances had left upon it. My heart took her by the hand and caused her fingers to bleed; in touching her fingers, my heart left on them a wound.

The sûfi shaikh Aidmor Ibrahim as-Sulami (24) recited to me a quatrain composed by himself on this subject, and which I give here :

> When the zephyr blew from Irâk, she (whom I love) charged it to bear her salutations to

me, if it could. And it said to me, fearing for her cheek (25): " If you pass near it, it will be
" wounded and complain. "

A literary man in decayed circumstances made a piece of verse in which he
complained of his poverty and his thread-bare clothes. One of these verses contains
an idea similar to the preceding and runs as follows :

My clothes are so completely worn out that I dare not wash them, lest that, whilst I wring
them, the last shreds may go off with the water.

The same idea has been often expressed in poetry, but here, brevity is preferable.
Let us return to our subject. — The kádi Abû 'l-Mahásin followed the habits of the
Baghdad (court) in his mode of living, in his usages and even in his dress. The
men in office who went to visit him dismounted at his door and took, each of them,
the place regularly assigned to him, without daring to pass on (and take a higher
one). He subsequently travelled to Egypt for the purpose of bringing to Aleppo the
daughter of al-Malik al-Kâmil Ibn al-Malik al-Aádil, whose marriage with al-Malik
al-Aziz, the sovereign of Aleppo, he had negotiated. He set out towards the beginning of the year 629 (november, A. D. 1231), or the end of 628, and returned with
her in the month of Ramadán (june-july, A. D. 1232). On his arrival, he found
that al-Malik al-Aziz was no longer under guardianship and had taken all the authority
into his own hands. The atâbek Toghrul had left the castle and retired to his house
at the foot of the fortress. Al-Aziz then let himself be governed by some of the
young men who had been his companions and associates; it was them only whom he
minded. The kádi Abû 'l-Mahásin, not receiving such countenance as he had a
right to expect, retired to his house and never stirred out till the day of his death;
but he continued to fill the place of hákim and receive the revenue of his iktâ.
The utmost to be said on the subject is that his word had no longer any influence
with the government and that his advice was never asked for. He then opened his
door every day to students who wished to hear him deliver Traditions. His intelligence at length became so feeble that he could no longer recognise those who
came to see him; when a visitor stood up and retired, he would ask who he was.
He remained in this state for a short time, was then sick for a few days and died at
Aleppo on Wednesday, the 14th of Safar, 632 (8th november, A. D. 1234). He
was buried in the mausoleum of wich we have spoken. I was present at his inter-

ment and at what passed afterwards. The works composed by him were the *Maljá 'l-Hukkám* and *Iltibás il-Akkám* (*the resource for magistrates when the texts of the law are doubtful*), treating of (*unforeseen*) law-cases, in two volumes; the *Daláil al-Ahkám* (*indication of the sources from which are drawn the articles of Moslim law*), in which he treats of the Traditions from which such articles were deduced, in two volumes; the *al-Mujaz al-Báhir* (*eminent compendium*) on jurisprudence. Amongst the other works of his we may indicate the *Kitáb Sírat Saláh ad-Dín* (*the history of Saladin* (26). He left his house to the Súfis as a convent (*khanqah*), not having any heir. The legists and Koran-readers frequented his mausoleum for a long time and recited the Korân beside his tomb. Before each of the trellises which we have mentioned, he established seven readers, so that every night, the whole of that book might be read over his grave. Each of the fourteen readers went over one fourteenth part of the volume after the last evening prayer. On the 23rd of the latter Jumáda (14th march, A. D. 1235) I set out for Egypt, leaving things in this state, but, since then, great changes have taken place, as I am told, and all these establishments are broken up. — The shaikh Najîn ad-Dîn Ibn al-Khabbáz died at Aleppo on the 7th of Zú 'l-Hijja, 631 (3rd september, A. D. 1234), and was buried outside the city, near the Arbaîn gate. I was present at the funeral service and the interment. He was born on the 29th of the first Rabî, 557 (18th march, A. D. 1162), at Mosul. — The atábek Shihâb ad-Dîn Toghrul died at Aleppo on the eve of monday, the 11th of Muharram, 631 (17th october, A. D. 1233), and was buried in the Hanefite college, outside the Arbaîn gate. He was a slave and, by birth, an Armenian; fair in complexion, virtuous in conduct, praiseworthy in all his actions. I was present at the funeral service and enterment. — Abú 'l-Hasan Ibn Kharûf, the literary man of whom we have spoken, lost his life at Aleppo, in the year 604 (A. D. 1207-8), having fallen into a cistern.

(1) See vol. I, page 139.

(2) *Ar-Sítají* means *native of Sítaj*, a village in Sijistán. Some manuscripts read *as-Sábjí*, which word signifies a *dealer in sesame oil*. It is worthy of remark that not one of Bahâ ad-Dîn's professors is noticed in the manuscript, n° 641, *entière fonds* of the imperial library, which gives a chronological account of the principal Shafite doctors. The date of as-Sírají's death is given farther on.

(3) These last titles indicate that the bearer was a member of a Sanhajian family, that of the Zírides which reigned at Ashîr, a town of Algeria, from the middle of the fourth till the middle of the sixth century of the Hejira.— See my translation of Ibn Khaldûn's history of the Berbers, in french, vol. II. p. 9 *et seq.*

(4) According to Makkari, the Traditionist Abû Bakr Muhammad Ibn Alî Ibn Yâsir al-Jaiyâni, a native of Jann, in Spain, was born in the year 489 (A. D. 1089-1090). He travelled to the East, visited Irak, rambled over the province of Khorâsân and settled in Balkh. In the year 649 (A. D. 1151-2) he arrived at Samarkand and there taught Traditions. The date of his death is not given.—(Makkari.)

(5) The quarter of Baghdad called al-Harbiya took its name from the Bâb Harb, one of the city gates.

(6) The Arabic term is mold; see vol. II. p. 582.

(7) Saladin laid siege to Kalat Kaukab, A. H. 583 (A. D. 1187-8) and took it in 584.—Ibn al-Athîr.)

(8) A dispute for precedence took place between Ibn al-Mokaddem and Mujîr ad-Dîn Tashtikîn, chief of the pilgrim-caravan from Irak. A scuffle ensued in which the Syrian caravan was attacked and plundered by that of Irak. Ibn al-Mokaddem lost his life in the skirmish.—(Ibn al-Athîr.)

(9) As Abû Mahâsin had just made the pilgrimage to Mekka, we must suppose that the pilgrimage which he now intended to accomplish was the visiting of the holy places in Syria.

(10) The mashî-hid, or funeral chapel, outside of Mosul, was probably the pretended tomb of Jonas at Nineveh.

(11) The hâkim was a magistrate with full executive authority.

(12) See vol. III, p. 387.

(13) This passage is given in only one of the manuscripts.

(14) The revenue of any property belonging to the state, such as houses and lands, and the product of certain taxes might be conceded by the sultan as an iktâ (detached portion) to any individual whom he chose a favour. The iktâs were often granted for life and, in some cases, became hereditary. Iktâs were granted as fiefs, or benefices, to military chiefs, under the condition that these officers should maintain a certain number of troops and furnish them to the sultan, when required.

(15) The date of this professor's death is given by our author, at the end of the article.

(16) The chapter on verbal declarations, by which an obligation is acknowledged or an intention expressed, is placed, in most Moslem codes, towards the middle of the volume. It is preceded by the chapter on law-suits and followed by that which treats of compromises.

(17) Berda was a town situated to the north of the Caspian sea.

(18) Safad was besieged and taken by Saladin A. H. 584 (A. D. 1188-9).—(Ibn al-Athîr.)

(19) According to Hajji Khalîfa, the Okûd el-Jumân (collars of pearls) contained an account of the poets who were the author's contemporaries. It was drawn up by Ibn as-Shâîr, a native of Mosul, who died in the year 654 (A. D. 1256). In the second volume of this translation, page 359, his name is incorrectly spelled.

(20) According to Dr Sontheimer, in his german translation of Ibn al-Baitâr's dictionary of simples, the balddor is the semecarpus anacardium. The remarkable qualities of the nut which it bears are noticed by authors whose observations are given by Ibn al-Baitâr.

(21) In Arabic balpdr. The description which follows indicates clearly what such a piece of dram was and removes every thing doubtful in the note (6) of vol. III. page 899.

(22) The word قرط or قرص signifies a marten or scroll, but the words فروة القرص seem to indicate merely a cloak lined with fur, no matter of what nature.

(23) Why a tattered band should be thrown to a hyæna cannot readily be answered. Yet all the manuscripts agree in giving the reading خباءنا. In general, these epigrams are insipid and full of far-fetched ideas; but such is usually the case with moslem anecdotes.

(91) The name of this sbb or derrich, who was an acquaintance of our author's, has been already mentioned in vol. II. p. 884.

(92) It is difficult to say why the poet said ـــــــ. The true reading seems to be ـــــــ.

(98) The text of this work, with a latin translation, was published at Leyden by A. Schultens in 1789.

YUSUF IBN OMAR ATH-THAKAFI.

Abù Abd Allah Yùsuf Ibn Omar Ibn Muhammad Ibn al-Hakam Ibn Abi Akil Ibn Masùd was a member of the tribe of Thakif (*Thakaf*). The rest of his genealogy will be found in our article on al-Hajjâj Ibn Yûsuf, who was his cousin, descended from the same ancestor, al-Hakam Ibn Abi Akil (1). Khalifa Ibn Khaijât (vol. I. p. 492) relates as follows: "Yùsuf Ibn Omar being appointed governor of Yemen by "(the khalif) Hishâm Ibn b d al-Malik, arrived in that province on the 27th of Re- "madân, 106 (15th Feb. A. D. 725). This post he held till the year 120 (A. D. "738), when Hishâm sent to him a diploma by which he appointed him to the go- "vernment of Irâk. Yùsuf then left his son as-Salt Ibn Yûsuf in Yemen, to act "there as deputy-governor." Al-Bukhâri (vol. II. p. 594) says that Yùsuf Ibn Omar was appointed to the government of Irâk in the year 121 (A. D. 739) and that he held it till the year 124. Another author relates as follows: "When Hishâm "Ibn Abd al-Malik wished to dismiss Khâlid Ibn Abd Allah al-Kasri (vol I. p. 484) "from the government of Irâk, a courier came to him from Yùsuf Ibn Omar ath- "Thakafi, the governor of Yemen. He had the messenger brought in and spoke to "him in these terms: 'Your master has passed the bounds in asking for a thing "'much above his merit.' He then ordered the man's clothes to be torn off and "had him flogged with a whip. 'Now,' said he, 'go back to your master, and may "'God treat you as you deserve (2).' He then called in Sâlim al-Yamâni who was "a mawla to Sâlim Ibn Anbasa, a grandson of (the khalif) Abd al-Malik and who, "at that time, was chief of the board of correspondence. 'Here,' said he, 'is an "'order of mine which must be sent to Yùsuf Ibn Omar; write it out and bring me

" ' the letter.' Sálim retired and drew up the dispatch whilst Hishám, who remai-
" ned alone, wrote with his own hand to Yúsuf Ibn Omar a short note, containing
" these words : ' Go to Irâk, for I have appointed you its governor. Take care not
" ' to let any one know what you are about, and rid me of that Christian woman's
" ' son,' — meaning Khálid, — ' and of his intendants.' This note he held in
" his hand and, when Sálim returned and presented to him the dispatch which he
" had written, he (Hishám) slipped his own note into the cover of the other letter,
" without being perceived and, having sealed all up, he gave orders that the packet
" should be delivered to Yúsuf's messenger. Sálim obeyed and the messenger de-
" parted. When Yúsuf saw him arrive, he said to him : ' What news? (3)' The
" other replied : ' Bad! the Commander of the faithful is incensed against you and
" ' caused my clothes to be torn off and myself to be whipped. He wrote no ans-
" ' wer to the letter which you sent him, but here is a dispatch from the chief of
" ' the board (of correspondence).' Yúsuf broke the seal, read the dispatch and, on
" finishing, perceived the little note. He, in consequence proceeded to Irâk and
" left his son as-Salt to act as his lieutenant in Yemen. Sálim was, by this time,
" replaced in the board of correspondence by Bashír Ibn Abi Talha, a member of
" one of the (Arab) families established in (the military colony of) Urdonn (the
" Jordan). This officer, being very intelligent, understood what Hishám's in-
" tentions were and said to himself : ' This (ill-treatment of the messenger) is a mere
" ' stratagem; he has certainly appointed Yúsuf Ibn Omar to the government of
" ' Irâk.' He in consequence wrote the following lines to Iyâd, the intendant of
" (the territory called) Ajma Sálim, for whom he had a sincere affection : ' Your
" ' people have just sent you the Yemanite cloak (4); when it reaches you, put it on
" and let thanks be given to God.' He (Iyâd) told this news to Tárik, the inten-
" dant who had been charged by Khálid Ibn Abd Allah al-Kasri with the adminis-
" tration of Kúfa and its dependancies. Bashír then regretted what he had done
" and wrote again to Iyâd, saying : ' They were thinking of sending you the Yemanite
" ' cloak.' Iyâd communicated this news also to Tárik, who said : ' The truth is
" ' in the first letter, but your friend repented of what he had written, fearing that
" ' his conduct might be discovered.' He immediately rode off and informed
" Khálid of what was passing. Khálid said to him : ' What think you best to be
" ' done?' Tárik replied : ' My advice is that you ride off this very instant to the
" ' Commander of the faithful; your presence will make him ashamed of what he is

" ' about and dissipate that prejudice against you which weighs on his mind.' As
" Khálid did not accept this advice, Tárik said : ' Allow me, in that case, to go and
" ' appear before him; I shall then take the engagement that all the revenue (of the
" ' province) for the present year shall be paid to him immediately.' Khálid asked
" to how much it would amount, and the other replied : ' To one hundred millions
" ' of dirhems (5). I shall then bring you a diploma confirming you in your
" ' place.' — ' Where will you get the money?' said Khálid, ' by Allah! I do not
" ' possess ten thousand dirhems.' Tárik replied : ' I and Said Ibn Ráshid will
" ' undertake to pay forty millions of dirhems' — this Said was then holding the
" perceptorship of Saki 'l-Furát (the lands irrigated by the Euphrates), — ' az-Zai-
" ' nabi and Abbán Ibn al-Walid will engage to furnish twenty millions and we shall
" ' make the repartition of the rest amongst the other intendants.' Khálid re-
" plied : ' I should be considered as a low-minded man were I to recal favours al-
" ' ready granted.' — ' Nay,' said Tárik, ' we save not only you but ourselves by
" ' giving up a part of our property; the advantages which you and we enjoy will
" ' then continue, and it is better for us to renew our efforts in the pursuit of wealth
" ' than to let you be prosecuted for the non-payment of the money. The mer-
" ' chants of Kûfa have cash of ours in their hands (let us force them to give it up),
" ' for they will be tempted to delay the payment and wait to see what may become
" ' of us; in that case, we shall be the authors of our own ruin and, when we lose
" ' our lives, they will keep the money and spend it.' Khálid refused to follow
" this advice and Tárik then bade him farewell, saying : " This is the last time we
" ' shall see you.' Yûsuf Ibn Omar then arrived among them; Tárik was tortured
" to death, and Khálid with all his intendants suffered every sort of ill treatment.
" A number of them were tortured to death, and the money extorted from him and
" from his agents by Yûsuf amounted to ninety millions of dirhems. " — In our notice on Khálid Ibn Abd Allah al-Kasri we have given some account of what happened
to him, and to that article we refer the reader. In our notice on Isa Ibn Omar ath-
Thakafi (vol. II. p. 521) we have related what passed between him and Yûsuf Ibn
Omar, when he was questioned about the deposit confided to him. Abû Bakr Ahmad
Ibn Yahya al-Balédori (6) says, in his Ansáb al-Ashráf (the genealogies of the descendants of Muhammad) and their history : " Hishám Ibn Abd al-Malik's mind was turn-
" ed against Khálid Ibn Abd Allah al-Kasri in consequence of some reports which
" came to his ears concerning him. He was much displeased on learning how

" wealthy he had got and how numerous were his houses and lands; he was also
" highly offended at some things which Khálid had openly said of him. He there-
" fore resolved on dismissing him from office, but concealed his intention. The
" province of Yemen being then governed in his name by Yúsuf Ibn Omar ath-
" Thakafi, he wrote to that functionary, ordering him to set out for Kúfa with
" thirty men. Yúsuf having received this letter, to which was joined the act of his
" nomination to the government of Irák, set out on his journey, reached Kúfa after
" a march of seventeen days and halted, for the night, in the neighbourhood of the
" city. Tárik, to whom Khálid al-Kasri had confided the collectorship of the land-
" tax (kharáj), had just circumcised his son and, on this occasion, he (Khálid?)
" sent him a present of one thousand blood-horses, one thousand male slaves and
" one thousand female slaves, besides a quantity of money, clothes and other objects.
" It was then that a man came to Tárik and said : ' I have just seen some people
" ' whose looks I do not like, and who pretend to be travellers. '' In the mean
" time Yúsuf Ibn Omar went to the quarter where the Arabs of the Thakif tribe were
" residing and told one of them to assemble and bring him as many Modarite
" Arabs (7) as he could. This was done and, at the dawn of day, Yúsuf entered into
" the mosque and ordered the muwazzin to recite the ikáma (and thus indicate that
" the imám was already at the head of the congregation). The muwazzin replied :
" ' Wait till the imám comes; ' but, being intimidated by Yúsuf's threats, he at
" length obeyed. Yúsuf then placed himself at the head of the assembly, directed
" the prayer and recited (these verses of the Koran) : When the inevitable (day of
" Judgement) shall suddenly come, etc. (sur. 56, verse 1), and : A person asked (to see
" God's vengeance arrive) (sur. 70, verse 1). He then caused Khálid and Tárik to
" be arrested with all their people and at length, the pot boiled over. ''—Abú Obaida
" (vol. III. p. 388) related as follows : '' Yúsuf imprisoned Khálid but was indu-
" ced to release him and his companions by Alibán Ibn al-Walid, who offered him
" nine millions of dirhems (£ 225,000). He then regretted having done so; yet, on
" being told that, if he had refused the offer, one hundred millions would have been
" given, he replied : ' I am not a man to retract an engagement, once it is taken by
" ' my tongue. ' Khálid, being informed by his friends of what they had done, said
" to them : ' You did wrong in offering so great a sum at the outset; I am sure that
" ' he will accept it and then come down upon you for more. Go back (and speak)
" ' to him. ' They went to Yúsuf and said : ' We have mentioned to Khálid the

" ' amount of the sum for which we assessed ourselves in order to pay you, and be
" ' has declared that he does not possess so much.' Khâlid replied:' Do you know
" ' better than your master the state of his fortune? by Allah! I do not ask you for
" ' more, but if you wish to go back from your engagement, I will not hinder you.'
" They replied, that they would retract. 'Well!' said he, ' I declare by Allah! that
" ' I shall not be satisfied with nine millions of dirhems nor with twice as much.'
" He then mentioned thirty millions, or, by another account, one hundred millions."
—Al-Aabras, who was a mawla of the Banû Asad family and who traded for Yûsuf
Ibn Omar, made the following relation : " A letter came to us from Hishâm; Yûsuf
" read it, concealed from us its contents and said : ' I shall go and make the Omra
" ' (see vol. III, page 248). ' We set out with him whilst his son as-Salt remained
" behind, as governor of Yemen during his absence. Not a word passed between
" us till we reached al-Ozaib (vol. III, page 445), when he made his camel
" kneel down, (dismounted) and said : ' Ashras! where is your guide?'—' Here he
" ' is,' said I. He asked him concerning the road, and the guide answered :
" ' This takes to Medina and that to Irâk. ' I then said : ' By Allah! for this time
" ' we are not making the Omra; ' but he (Yûsuf) made no reply, neither did he
" open his lips till we halted, one night, at a place situated between al-Hira and
" Kûfa. Having then lain down on his back, he crossed one leg over the other
" and said :

Our camels were not long in bearing us unto a distant land which we had visited not
long ago.

" ' Ashras ! ' said he, ' find me a man from whom I can obtain information. '
" I brought him one. ' Ask that fellow, 'said he,' what the son of the Christian
" ' woman ' — meaning Khâlid al-Kasri, — ' is about. '—I said to the man :
" ' What is Khâlid doing?' He answered : ' He is at al-Hamma (8); as he was
" ' complaining (of some illness), he went there. ' ' Ask him, ' said Yûsuf, ' what
" ' Târik is about. ' The man replied:' He has been circumcising his sons and is
" ' now giving a great dinner to the people of Hira, whilst his lieutenant, Aliya Ibn
" ' Miklâs (مكلاس) is doing the same at Kûfa. — ' Let the fellow go, ' said
" Yûsuf. He then mounted (his camel), proceeded to the public place (rahaba),
" entered into the mosque and said his prayers. After that, he laid down on his

" back and we passed there a long night. The muëzzins at length came, made
" the call to prayer and pronounced the salutation. Ziäd Ibn Abd Allah al-Härithi,
" who was then acting in Kûfa as Khâlid's deputy, for the presidence of the
" prayer, came into the mosque and, as the commencement of the prayer had been
" just announced, he went to take his place at the head of the congregation. Yûsuf
" then said : ' Ashras! remove that man. ' I told Ziäd to give up his place to the
" emir, and he did so. Yûsuf, who could recite the Koran with great elegance,
" then took the presidency, repeated the verses : When the inevitable shall come,
" and : A person asked to see God's vengeance arrive, and accomplished the prayer
" of day-break. The kâdi then stepped forward, offered to God praise and thanks-
" giving, said a prayer for the khalif and asked of us what was our emir's name.
" Being told it, he prayed for his welfare. All the people (of the city) had joined
" the congregation before it separated. Yûsuf lost not a moment in sending
" for Khâlid, and for Ahbân Ibn al-Walid who was in Fars, and for Bilâl Ibn Abi
" Burda (vol. II, p. 2) who was in Basra, and for Abd Allah Ibn Abi Burda,
" who was in Sijistân. Hishâm had given orders that all Khâlid's lieutenants
" should be deposed, with the exception of al-Hakam Ibn Awâna who was
" governing the province of Sind. This officer was confirmed in his place
" and there he remained till he was killed by Nakeber (9). He lost his life
" on the same day as Zaid Ibn Ali (10). Khâlid, on arriving, was informed
" that Yûsuf was now the emir, on which he exclaimed : ' Let me alone with
" ' your emir! is the Commander of the faithful still alive? ' Being answered
" in the affirmative, he said : ' In that case, I have nothing to fear. ' Yûsuf,
" before whom they brought him, sent him to prison and ordered thirty strokes of
" a whip to be inflicted on Yazid, the son of Khâlid. Hishâm then wrote to Yûsuf,
" saying : ' I declare solemnly before God that if Khâlid receives (from you) even
" ' the scratch of a thorn, I shall have your head struck off.' Khâlid, being allowed
" to depart with his family and bagage, went to Syria, took up his residence
" there and continued, till the death of Hishâm, to accompany, every summer,
" the usual expeditions made against the infidels. " — Some persons state that
Yûsuf applied to Hishâm for the authorisation of putting Khâlid to the rack,
but did not obtain it. He insisted however in his demand, pretenting that the
public revenue had been embezzled by Khâlid and his agents, and received at
length permission to torture him, but once only. The khalif sent a soldier

of the guard to witness what would he done, and swore that, if Khâlid died during
the operation, he would take Yûsuf's life. The latter then sent for Khâlid and,
having taken his seat in a trader's stall at Hîra, he convoked the people and
caused him to be tortured. Khâlid did not utter a word till Yûsuf spoke to him
tauntingly and called him a son of a diviner, meaning the celebrated diviner Shikk,
who was one of Khâlid's ancestors. — We have spoken of Shikk in our article on
Khâlid. — Let us resume the narration : On this, Khâlid said : '' You are a silly
'' fellow to reproach me with what does me honour; but you are the son of a *sabbá;*
'' your father was a mere *sabbá,* ' or dealer in wine. Khâlid was then taken back
to prison, and he remained there for eighteen months. In the month of Shawwâl,
121 (september-oct. A. D. 739), Hishâm wrote to him (*Yûsuf*), ordering the prisoner
to be set at liberty. Khâlid then set out with part of his family and some other
persons. On reaching al-Karya, a place in the territory of ar-Rusâfa, he stopped
there during the remainder of the month and the months of Zû 'l-Kaada, Zû
'l-Hijja, Muharram and Safar, but was unable to obtain from Hishâm the authorisation of going to see him. — Al-Haitham Ibn Adi (vol *III*, p. 633) related as
follows : '' Zaid, the son of Ali Zain al-Aâbidîn (*vol. II*, p. 209), who was the son
'' of al-Husain and the grandson of Ali Ibn Tâlib, revolted against Yûsuf Ibn Omar
'' who, in consequence wrote the following lines to Hishâm : ' Your cousins
'' ' of that family were dying of hunger and not a man of them had any other
'' ' thought than to procure his daily food, till Khâlid, on receiving the government
'' ' of Irâk, strengthened them with money to such a degree that their minds
'' ' aspired to the khalifat. Zaid would not have revolted without Khâlid's per-
'' ' mission, and Khâlid's sole motive for remaining at al-Karya is his wish to be
'' ' on the high-road, so that he may readily obtain news of his proceedings. '
'' Hishâm replied to the bearer of this message : ' You lie and so does your master;
'' ' whatever our suspicions may be with respect to Khâlid's conduct, we have never
'' ' had any doubts of his fidelity. ' He then caused the messenger's throat to be
'' compressed (*till he was half-strangled*). Khâlid, on learning what was going on,
'' set out for Damascus. ''—Abû 'l-Hasan al-Madâini (*vol. I*, p. 438) says : '' Dilâl,
'' the son of Abû Burda (*vol. II*, p. 2) and the grandson of Abû Mûsa 'l-Ashâri,
'' was the person whom Khâlid al-Kasri entrusted with the government of Dasra.
'' He was tortured by order of Yûsuf Ibn Omar till he engaged to pay three hundred
'' thousand dirhems. He offered bail for the amount and, when it was given

" in, he fled to Syria. There he was discovered by the circumstance of his
" servant-boy's going to buy a francolin. According to another account, his servant
" was roasting a francolin and let it burn ; for this, he was beaten by his master and
" therefore betrayed him. Bilál, being taken before Yúsuf Ibn Omar, was kept
" exposed to the sun by that emir's order. He requested to be taken before the
" Commander of the faithful, saying : ' Let him treat me as he pleases; ' but he
" (the khalif) refused to receive him and sent him back to Yúsuf, who caused
" him to be tortured to death. Abd Allah, the brother of Bilál, said to the jailor :
" ' When you give in the names of the prisoners who die, inscribe that of my bro-
" ' ther (ﺍﺧﻮ) on the list.' He did so, but, being ordered by Yúsuf to produce the
" corpse, he smothered the prisoner. According to another statement, it was Bilál
" who asked the jailor to inscribe the name on the dead-list, promising him a sum
" of money if he did so. The jailor then gave in his name as dead. Some say that
" it was Abd-Allah who was tortured to death. God knows best ! " — Yúnus the
grammarian (11) related as follows : " Bilál's cunning cost him his life : by the offer
" of money he induced the jailor to inscribe his name on the dead-list, but, as
" Yúsuf ordered the corpses to be produced, the jailor smothered Bilál and then
" showed his body."—The following anecdote is related by al-Madáini : " Sálih Ibn
" Kuraiz had been appointed to a commandment by Yúsuf Ibn Omar. The exami-
" nation of his accounts proved that a sum of thirty thousand (gold pieces?) was due
" by him to government and, for that reason, he was sent to prison. Bilál Ibn Abi
" Burda, who was then in the same place of confinement, said to him : ' The man
" ' who directs the application of the torture is called Sálim, but people give him the
" ' nickname of Zenbíl (haunched like a female). Take care not to call him Zenbíl,
" ' for he will be displeased.' Bilál repeated to him this recommendation very often.
" Sálih, being put to the torture, forgot Sálim's name and surname, and began to cry
" out : 'O Zenbíl! spare me for the love of God.'(12). During the tortures inflicted
" on him he continued to repeat these words whilst he (Sálim) kept exclaiming :
" ' Kill the fellow!' so great was his anger. When Sálih was let go, Bilál said to
" him : ' Did I not tell you to avoid uttering the name of Zenbíl?' To this Sálih replied : " Who taught me that name except yourself? I had known nothing of it were
" ' it not for you. You will never give over your wicked tricks, either in prospe-
" ' rity or in adversity."—The same al-Madáini said : " The chief of Yúsuf Ibn
" Omar's police-guards was al-Abbás Ibn Saíd al-Murri; his secretaries were Kabram

" (13) Ibn Sulaimân Ibn Zikwân and Ziâd Ibn Abd ar-Rahmân, who was a mawla
" to the Thakîf tribe; his chamberlain and the chief of his body-guard was Jundub.
" It was to him (Yûsuf) that the poet alluded in this verse :

" An emir of extreme severity has come to us : the very chamberlain of his chamberlain
" has for himself a chamberlain (لحاجب حاجب حاجب).

The hâfiz Abû 'l-Kâsim Ibn Asâkir (vol. II. p. 252) says, in his History of Damascus : " I have been informed that Yûsuf Ibn Omar, when arrested with the other
" members of al-Hajjâj Ibn Yûsuf's family and tortured in order to make him give
" up his money, obtained permission to be taken out of prison so that he might ask
" (of his friends pecuniary assistance). He made his rounds under the guard of al-
" Hârith Ibn Malik al-Juhdami, who was noted for his negligence. On coming to
" a certain house which had two entrances, he said to al-Hârith : " Let me go into
" ' this house; I have there an aunt to whom I wish to apply." Having obtained
" permission, he went in, passed out through the other door and made his escape.
" This took place when Sulaimân Ibn Abd al-Malik was khalif. Yûsuf Ibn Omar
" followed the example of al-Hajjâj Ibn Yûsuf, his father's cousin, in the firmness
" and severity with which he directed public affairs and treated the people; this line
" of conduct he followed till his dismissal from office. "— Omar Ibn Shabba (vol. II.
p. 375) relates, in his History of Basra, that Yûsuf Ibn Omar, having weighed a
dirhem and found it too light by one grain, wrote to all the coining establishments
in Irâk, ordering the persons employed there to be chastised; and it was reckoned
that one hundred thousand lashes were applied on account of the deficiency of a
single grain. Yûsuf's conduct as a governor was highly reprobated; he was fan-
tastic and cruel, but his hospitality was great. He used to have five hundred tables
set out, and to these were admitted people from all quarters, far and near; the native of Irâk would partake of the repast with the native of Syria. On every table was
placed a cake of bread (furniya) sprinkled over with sugar. The guests at one of
these tables happening, one day, to complain that their cake was not sugared, Yûsuf
ordered the baker to be chastised, and three hundred lashes were inflicted on him
whilst the company were at their meal. Ever after, the baker would go about with
the sugar-boxes and add sugar wherever it was wanted. —Al-Hakam Ibn Awâna related that his father said to him: " There is none like (the tribe of) Kalb for strength-
" ening an empire; none like Kuraish for mounting into the pulpit; none like

" Tamím for taking vengeance; none like Thakíf for leading flocks (*governing the*
" *people*); none like Kais for defending frontiers; none like Rabía for exciting revolts,
" and none like Yemen for collecting imposts."—Al-Asmái (*vol. II. p.* 123) relates
as follows : " Yúsuf Ibn Omar said to a man whom he had nominated to the govern-
" ment of a district: ' Enemy of God! you have eaten up the wealth which belonged
" ' to God.' The man replied : ' Tell me whose wealth I have been eating from the
" ' day in which I was created till now? By Allah! if I asked from Satan a single
" ' dirhem, he would not give it to me.' "—Nasr Ibn Saiyár al-Laithi was appointed
to the government of Khorásán by Yúsuf Ibn Omar, and he held that post till the last
days of the Omaiyide dynasty. His battles and engagements with Abú Muslim al-
Khorásáni (*vol. II. p.* 100) are set forth in their proper places (*the books of annals*).
It was on Yúsuf that Sawwár Ibn al-Ashar (14) composed these lines :

> Khorásán, after its alarms, was delivered from the tyranny of its numerous oppressors; Yúsuf,
> being informed of what it suffered, chose Nasr Ibn Saiyár for its protector (*nasr*).

The following anecdote was related by Simák Ibn Harb (15) : " Yúsuf Ibn Omar,
" when governor of Irák, sent to me this message : ' One of my intendants has
" ' written to me, saying that he has cultivated for me every *khukk* and *lukk*.
" ' What do these words mean ?' I replied : *Khukk* signifies a low ground, and
" *lukk* a high one."—Here ends the anecdote, but I must observe that al-Jauhari
(*vol. I. p.* 22) says, in his *Sahâh* : " *Khukk* means a soil rendered dry by draining
" off its waters; *lukk* means a long stripe, or, according to some, a deep excava-
" tion in the earth." *Khukk* is written with a pointed *kha.* — Yúsuf Ibn Omar
was remarked for the extraordinary length of his beard and the shortness of his stature; his beard reached lower down than his navel. He held the government of
Irák during the rest of Hishám Ibn Abd al-Malik's reign. That khalif died on Wednesday, the 6th of the latter Rabí, 125 (6th February, A. D. 743), at ar-Rusáfa, in
the district of Kinnisrin, and there he was buried. He lived to the age of fifty-five
years, or fifty-four, by another account, or fifty-two; God knows best! His surname was Abú 'l-Walíd. He was succeeded by his nephew al-Walíd Ibn Yazíd Ibn
Abd al-Malik, who confirmed Yúsuf Ibn Omar in the government of Irák. Al-Walíd
was killed on Thursday, the 27th of the latter Jumáda, 126 (16 April, A. D. 744).
He intended to have replaced Yúsuf Ibn Omar by Abd al-Malik Ibn Muhammad, the

grandson of al-Hajjáj Ibn Yúsuf ath-Thakafi. Al-Walíd Ibn Yazíd's mother, surnamed Omm al-Hajjáj (16), was the daughter of Muhammad Ibn Yúsuf and therefore
niece to al-Hajjáj. The following letter was then sent to Yúsuf Ibn Omar by
" al-Walíd : You have written to me, stating that Khálid Ibn Abd Allah al-Kasri had
" ruined the province of Irák, and yet you used to send loads (of wealth) to Hishám.
" It must be then that, by reviving agriculture, you have restored that country to
" its former state. Come therefore to us and bring with you such a convoy (of
" money) as may confirm our favorable opinion respecting your efforts in forwarding
" the prosperity of the province. We shall then acknowledge your preeminent
" merit, and that the more readily, on account of the relationship which exists bet-
" ween us; you are our uncle by the mother's side and have more right than any
" other man to our consideration. You are aware that we have augmented the do-
" natives to which the people of Syria (the Arabic troops established in that country)
" are entitled and that we made gifts to our family in consequence of His-
" hám's harshness towards them. The result has been the impoverishment of our
" treasury." In consequence of this invitation Yúsuf set out to visit al-Walíd Ibn
Yazíd, and took with him such a quantity of treasure, merchandise and vases
as was never before brought from Irák. At the time of his arrival, Khálid Ibn Abd
Allah al-Kasri was still in prison. Hassán an-Nabáti (vol. I. p. 674) had an interview with him (Yúsuf) by night and informed him that al-Walíd had the intention of
appointing Abd Allah Ibn Muhammad Ibn al-Hajjáj (to the government of Irák) and
that he should by all means arrange the affair of his (Hassán's) nomination to the
vizirship. Yúsuf answered that he had no money, on which Hassán said : " I have
" five hundred thousand dirhems (about £ 13,500) which, if you wish, I shall give
" you as a present, or, if not, (as a loan which) you will repay to me when you got
" rich." Yúsuf replied : " You know the people (at court) better than I, and can
" well appreciate the extent of their influence over al-Walíd. Do you therefore
" distribute that money amongst them, in proportion to what you know of their
" credit." Hassán did so, and Yúsuf, on his arrival, was highly extolled by all the
party. It was then agreed upon between him and Abbán Ibn Abd ar-Rahmán an-
Numairi that the latter should offer (to the khalif) forty millions of dirhems
(more than one million sterling) to obtain that Khálid Ibn Abd Allah al-Kasri
should be delivered up to him. Al-Walíd (having received Yúsuf's visit,) told him to
return to his government. Abbán then said to him : " Deliver Khálid up to me and

" I shall pay you forty millions of dirhems."—" Who goes security for you?" said the khalif. Abbás replied: " Yúsuf."—" Do you become security for him?" said al-Walíd to Yúsuf. The answer was : " Deliver him (Khálid) up to me and I " shall force out of him fifty millions of dirhems." He (al-Walíd) gave up the prisoner to Yúsuf, who enclosed him in a litter without cushions, bore him to Irák and put him to death in the manner already related (vol. I. p. 486).—When al-Walíd Ibn Yazíd was killed, his cousin, Yazíd Ibn al-Walíd Ibn Abd al-Malik, obtained the supreme authority, brought under his command the people of Syria (the Arab troops settled there), and succeeded in consolidating his power. The government of Irák was then offered by him to Abd al-Azíz Ibn Hárún Ibn Abd al-Malik Ibn Dibya Ibn Khalífa al-Kalbi, who replied that, unless troops were given to him, he would not accept. On this, Yazíd turned away from him and nominated Mansúr Ibn Jumhúr.—According to Abú Mihnaf (17), al-Walíd was slain at al-Bakhrá (18), on the date above mentioned. Yazíd was proclaimed khalíf at Damascus, and Mansúr Ibn Jumhúr set out for Irák with six companions, on the day of al-Walíd's death. Yúsuf Ibn Omar, being informed of his approach, took to flight. Mansúr Ibn Jumhúr arrived at Ultra some days after the commencement of Rajab, took possession of the treasure houses (the state treasury), distributed money to those who were entitled to donatives or to pensions, and appointed governors to all the provinces of Irak. He remained there during the rest of the month of Rajab, the whole of Shabán, and was dismissed from office towards the end of Ramadán. Yúsuf Ibn Omar took the road of as-Samáwa and continued his flight till he reached al-Balká, where he found a place of concealment. As his family were residing there, he dressed himself in women's clothes and took his seat among the females. Yazíd Ibn al-Walíd, having learned where he had gone, sent a person to arrest the fugitive and bring him to the capital. The messenger made every search, and Yúsuf was at length found by him, dressed in female attire and seated amongst his women and children. He was put into bonds and carried to Yazíd who sent him to the place in which al-Hakam and Othmán, the sons of al-Walíd Ibn Yazíd, were imprisoned by his orders. On the death of their father, Yazíd had shut them up in the Green House (al-Khadrá), a well-known palace in Damascus which was situated on the south side of the principal mosque and which is now destroyed; its place is, however, well-known to the people of the city. Yazíd Ibn al-Walíd then took the government of Irák from Mansúr Ibn Jumhúr and gave it to Abd Allah Ibn Omar Ibn Abd al-Azíz.

Yûsuf Ibn Omar remained in confinement during the rest of Yazîd's reign. That khalif died in Zû 'l-Hidjja, 126 (Sept.-Oct. A. D. 744), but statements differ greatly as to the day of the month : some say it was the first, others the tenth, and others the last day of Zû 'l-Kaada. He had designated as successor to the throne his brother Ibrâhîm Ibn al-Walid, and ordered that the supreme authority should pass from the latter to Abd al-Azîz Ibn al-Hajjâj Ibn Abd al-Malik. During the reign of Ibrâhim Ibn al-Walid, Yûsuf Ibn Omar remained in prison. Marwan Ibn Muhammad, the last sovereign of the Omaiyide dynasty, having made his apparition with the troops of Mesopotamia and Kinnisrîn, got possession of the empire, dethroned Ibrahim, took his place and put to death Abd al-Azîz Ibn al-Hajjâj Ibn Abd al-Malik. Ibrâhim reigned four months and was deposed in the month of the latter Rabî, 127 (Jan.-Feb. A. D. 745). According to another statement he reigned seventy days only. Yazîd, the son of Khâlid Ibn Abd Allah al-Kasri, had sided with Ibrâhim Ibn al-Walid. When the revolt of Marwan broke out, a conflict took place between his troops and those of Ibrahim. The latter were defeated and returned to Damascus. Ibrâhim's partisans were pursued by Marwan and, being apprehensive that, if he entered into the city, he would deliver from prison al-Hakam and Othmân, the sons of al-Walid, for the purpose of transferring to them the supreme authority, and that these two princes would then have no mercy on any of the persons who had contributed to their father's death, they resolved on putting them to death. Yazîd, the son of Khâlid al-Kasri, was charged to execute this decision, and Abû 'l-Asad, one of his father's mawlas, went, with some others, to the prison and beat the two youths to death with clubs. Yûsuf Ibn Omar was taken by them out of the same prison and beheaded, to avenge the death of Khâlid, the father of Yazîd. This occurred in the year 127 (A. D. 745). Yûsuf was then upwards of sixty years of age. When his head was separated from the body, a rope was tied to his legs, and the little boys began to drag the corpse through the streets of Damascus. A woman who passed by and saw how small the body was, exclaimed : " Why did they kill that unfortunate " boy?" A person (of Damascus) related as follows : "I saw Yûsuf Ibn Omar dragged through Damascus by means of a cord which had been tied to his testicles, " and I afterwards saw his murderer, Yazîd, the son of Khâlid al-Kasri, dragged " over the same ground by means of a cord tied to his testicles." According to another account, he (Yûsuf) was put to death towards the middle of the month of Zû 'l-Hijja, 126 (Sept.-Oct. A. D. 744).

(1) See vol. I, p. 556, and read *Ibn Abi Akil* in place of Ibn Okail.

(2) Literally : May God treat you and do with you! A common imprecation of old times and equivalent to : May God's curse be upon you !

(3) Literally : What is behind you ? In English we would say : What is going on below there ?

(4) The cloth of Yemana was probably at that time highly prized; but here, a Yemanian cloak means a governor from that place.

(5) At that time, one hundred millions of dirhems were equal to at least two millions five hundred thousand pounds sterling.

(6) To the indications given in vol. I, p. 436, I may add that al-Baladuri's history of the conquests effected by the early Musulmans has been published, in Arabic, at Leyden by M' de Goeje. It is a highly valuable work, full of original matter and most remarkable as a precise and conscientious treatise.

(7) According to the Arabian genealogists, the tribe of Thakif descended from Mudar through Kais Ailân.

(8) Al-Hamma is the name given to every place where there is a spring of hot water.

(9) This name, written in Arabic letters, is كُهور, but it is probably pointed incorrectly. The person who bore it was apparently one of the princes of India who were warring against the Musulmans established in Sind.

(10) Zaid, the son of Ali Zain al-Aâbidîn (vol. II, p. 209) revolted against the Omaiyide khalif Hishâm Ibn Abd al-Malik, A. H. 121 (A. D. 739), and fell on the field of battle, the following year.

(11) The life of Yûnus the grammarian will be found in this volume.

(12) The Arabic equivalent means : Fear God !

(13) I read كرمي.

(14) Sowwâr Ibn Abd Allah al-Anbar was appointed governor and kadi of Basra by the Abbaside khalif al-Mansûr, A. H. 136 (A. D. 773-4). He died in the following year.—(*Nujûm*.)

(15) The Traditionist Shomh Ibn Harb died A. H. 193 (A. D. 748-9).—(*Nujûm*.)

(16) The Arabic text inserts here : " who was also the mother of al-Hajjâj;" but this indication is in contradiction with what follows.

(17) Abû Mihnaf Lût Ibn Yahya, one of the earliest Arabic historians, composed a short work extending from the death of the khalif Ali to that of his son al-Husain. He wrote probably in the second century of the Hejira. A copy of this treatise is in the library of the Leyden university, under the n° 791.

(18) According to the indications furnished by the author of the *Merâsid*, the place called al-Bahbri was situated on the northern frontier of Hijâz.

YUSUF IBN TASHIFIN (1).

Abû Yakûb Yûsuf Ibn Tâshifîn (2), the Lamtûnide (3) and king of the *el-Mulath-thimûn* (4), bore the title of *Emir el-Muslimîn* (*Commander of the Moslims*) (5).   It

was he who founded the city of Morocco. In our articles on the two Spanish sovereigns al-Motamid Muhammad Ibn Abbád (*vol. III*, p. 182) and al-Motasim Muhammad Ibn Sumádih (*vol. III*, p. 200) we have mentioned some things concerning him
and related how he took possession of their states, reduced al-Motamid into captivity
and imprisoned him in Aghmát. As I have there given a full relation of these proceedings, to it I refer the reader, so that he may perceive the identity of the king
there mentioned with the great and powerful sovereign of whom we are now giving an
account. Historians relate many things concerning him, and one of their works,
which bears the title of *Kitáb al-Moghrib an Sírat Malik al-Maghreb* (*the Expositor,
setting forth the proceedings of the king of the West*), is that from which we have
extracted the following information. I preferred it because it was more comprehensive than the others, but I am unable to indicate the name of the author. All I
know of him is that, towards the beginning of the volume which I made use of, he
states that he commenced the work in the year 579 (A. D. 1183-4) (6) and finished
it at Mosul on the 1st of Zú 'l-Kaada of the same year. Out of this volume, which is a
middle-sized one, I have selected the following passages. — The southern part of
the country inhabited by the Maghrebins belonged to a Berber race called the Zenáta.
Against this people marched another which was designated by the name of *al-Mu-
laththimún* and which dwelt in the region that lies contiguous to the land of the
Negroes (7). The leader of the invaders bore the name of Abú Bakr Ibn Omar. He
was a man accustomed to a simple life, virtuous in his conduct, preferring his own
country to that of Maghreb and having no inclination for the luxuries of life. The
chiefs of the Zenáta had little power and, as they were unable to resist the *Mulaththimún*, the latter took possession of all their country, from the gates of Tilimsán
to the shore of the Surrounding ocean (*the Atlantic*). When Abú Bakr Ibn Omar
got this country into his power, he was informed that an old woman in his own
country had a female camel stolen from her in a foray and begun to weep, exclaiming : " Abú Bakr Ibn Omar has ruined us by entering into the land of Maghreb!"
This induced him to return to the South and leave as his lieutenant in Maghreb a
man called Yúsuf Ibn Táshifín. This Yúsuf was brave, just and enterprising. The
city of Morocco, in Maghreb, was founded by him on a spot where robbers used to
lie in ambush and which belonged to an old Masmúda woman. When his authority
was established throughout the country (*of Maghreb*), he conceived the wish of passing into Spain (*Andalus*), which peninsula was (*bounded and*) fortified by the sea.

He therefore constructed galleys and other vessels for the purpose of going across to that country. When the kings of Andalus (Moslim Spain) discovered his intention, they equipped a number of vessels and warriors for the purpose of resisting him, so much did they fear his approach towards their peninsula. The fact was that they stood in dread of his army which, as they well knew, would be for them most difficult to resist, and they shuddered at the idea of having enemies at both sides of them, namely, the Franks on the north, and the *Mulaththimún* on the south. Whenever they felt the Franks bear too heavily upon them, they kept them in check by manifesting their intention of contracting an alliance with Yúsuf Ibn Táshifín. That sovereign had acquired great renown by his effecting so speedily the conquest of the Zenatian empire and of Maghreb. It was reported that the bravest of the *Mulaththimún* warriors, when in battle, would cut a horseman in two with a single stroke of a sword and pierce through the bodies (of several adversaries) with a single stroke of a lance. Such was the practise of these (kings) and such the fear which filled the hearts of those who were summoned to war against the *Mulaththimún*. Thus did the kings of Andalus take refuge under the shelter of Yúsuf Ibn Táshifín's name; and yet they dreaded his crossing over to them, lest, on seeing their kingdoms, he might be tempted to seize on them. When they discovered that his intention of passing into Spain was already formed, they sent, one to the other, messengers and letters, requesting advice concerning him (Yúsuf). In that conjuncture, their main resource was the aid of al-Motamid Ibn Abbád, because he was the bravest of them all and the sovereign of the greatest kingdom. They therefore agreed on writing to him (to Yúsuf Ibn Táshifín), whose intention of going over to them they were now well aware of, requesting him to leave them as they were and assuring him of their perfect obedience. A kátib (writer, secretary), who was a native of Spain, drew up, in their name, the following letter : " If you let " us alone, your conduct will be attributed, not to weakness but to generosity, and " if we obey your orders, our conduct will be attributed, not to helplessness but to " prudence. We therefore prefer the attribution which is the more honorable for " ourselves, hoping that you will prefer the attribution which is the more honoura- " ble for you. The place which you hold is one in which you should not let your- " self be surpassed in noble acts ; by sparing (us who are) members of distinguished " families, you will obtain for the duration and the stability of your power all that " you can wish for. Salutation ! " The letter arrived, accompanied with gifts

and presents. Yúsuf Ibn Táshifín did not know Arabic, but he understood perfectly
well the drift (of such applications). His secretary, who knew the two languages,
that of the Arabs and that of the Almoravides (the Berber), then said to him :
" Emir ! this letter is from the kings of Andalus ; in it they offer you their profound
" respect, declare that they are partisans of your cause and acknowledge your autho-
" rity ; they request of you not to consider them as enemies and they say : ' We are
" ' musulmans, come of a noble race ; let us not therefore incur your displeasure (8).
" ' It is for us a sufficient misfortune to have close behind us a people of infidels.
" ' Our country is much straitened and cannot support numerous armies. Spare
" ' us therefore, as you have spared the people of Maghreb who acknowledged your
" ' authority. ' " Yúsuf then asked his secretary what he thought of the matter,
and received this answer : " The crown of royalty and its beauty have a testimony
" in their favour which cannot be repelled, provided that he (9) into whose hands
" the kingdom has fallen prove himself worthy of it by pardoning when pardon is
" asked and by granting favours when favours are requested. Every time that he
" bestows an ample gift, he increases his influence ; increase of influence consoli-
" dates his dominion, and when his dominion is consolidated, people think it an
" honour to obey him ; when obedience is felt to be an honour, the people come
" unto him, and he is not obliged to encounter fatigues for the purpose of reaching
" them, and he thus inherits the kingdom without ruining his (happiness in the)
" next life. Know that it was said by a great king, who was a sage well acquainted
" with the means by which royalty is to be attained : ' He who bestows may com-
" ' mand ; he who commands may lead, and he who leads (an army) becomes
" ' master of the land (10). ' " Yúsuf Ibn Táshifín, to whom this discourse was
addressed in his own language by the secretary, understood its import and felt its
truth. He therefore said to him : " Let those people have an answer ; draw up a
" fitting one and then read it over to me. " The secretary wrote as follows : " In
" the name of God, the Merciful, the Clement ! From Yúsuf Ibn Táshifín, greeting,
" with the mercy of God and his benedictions ! Such is the good wish of one who
" is in peace with you and salutes you. May God's decree respecting you be that
" of aid and assistance ! You have full power to enjoy as you please the royalty
" which is in your hands, being specially honoured with our favour and our bene-
" volence. As long as you hold to your engagements towards us, we shall hold to
" ours towards you ; that we may live in good brotherhood with you, you must live

" in good brotherhood with us.   May God dispense his grace to us and to you! Sa-
" lutation!"   When the secretary had finished writing, he translated the letter verbally to Yúsuf Ibn Táshifín, who approved of it and sent it off with a present of
Lamtian shields, things not to be procured except in his country. — I may here
mention that the adjective *Lamtian* is derived from *Lamta*, which is the name of a
small town in Ulterior Sûs, at a twenty days' journey from Sijilmassa.   So says Ibn
Haukal in his work entitled *Roads and Realms*.   That country is the only place
which furnishes Lamtian shields; it is said that they are not to be found any where
else. — When the kings of Andalus received this letter, they were filled with love
for Yúsuf and extolled him highly; they rejoiced at the offer of his friendship, were
pleased at his obtaining the sovereignty of Maghreb, and their hearts were fortified
in the hope of repelling the Franks.   It was therefore resolved on between them that,
if they remarked in the conduct of the king of the Franks anything to disquiet them,
they would inform Yúsuf Ibn Táshifín of the circumstance and become his
auxiliaries.   It was thus that Yúsuf, by the good management of his secretary (11), obtained that which he wished for, namely, the good-will of the people
of Andalus; all that he wanted was an opportunity of making war in their defense.   Alphonso, the son of Ferdinand (*Adhfonsh Ibn Ferdeland*), the sovereign of Toledo, which was the capital of the kingdom of the Franks, had (*again*)
begun to harry the (*Moslim*) territory, to take by force the towns of Andalus and
to make exorbitant demands from the kings of that country, exacting from them
the towns of which they were masters.   It was particularly towards al-Motamid Ibn
Abbád that he acted in this manner, because the latter was more exposed to his attacks.   In our article on al-Motamid (*vol. III. p. 189*), we have mentioned the date
of the taking of Toledo by Alphonso and inserted verses which had been composed on
that occasion.   Al-Motamid, having considered what was passing, perceived that
Alphonso had hopes of seizing on those parts of the country which were contiguous
to his own; so, he at length resolved on inviting Yúsuf Ibn Táshifín to come over to
Spain, notwithstanding the danger (*of his presence*) and his conviction that the
proximity of a people belonging to another race (*the Berbers*) would lead to the ruin
(*of the Arabs*).   He felt that the *Mulaththimún* (or *Almoravides*) would be for him
adversaries quite as formidable as the Franks.   " If we succumb," said he, " un-
" der the attacks of an adversary, it will be less painful for us to fall before the *Mu-*
" laththamún ; better that our children should tend the camels of the *Mulaththimún*

" than herd the swine of the Franks!" On this project he kept his eyes always fixed, (meaning to adopt it) whenever be should be forced to do so. On a certain year, Alphonso sallied forth with a great multitude of Franks and overran the provinces of Andalus. The (Moslim) kings feared for their states; the inhabitants of the villages and cantons fled before the invader and took refuge in the fortresses. Al-Motamid Ibn Abbâd then wrote to Yûsuf Ibn Tâshifîn, saying: "If you wish to en-" gage in the holy war, now is your time: Alphonso has invaded the country. Has-" ten therefore to come over to us and encounter him. We, the people of An-" dalus, will lead the march." Yûsuf, having already terminated his preparations, hastened to send his troops across the strait. When the kings of Andalus learned that the people of Maghreb were coming over for the purpose of engaging in holy war, they had already promised to themselves that they would assist them, and made preparations for marching. Alphonso, perceiving that they were all unanimous in the resolution of resisting him, felt that the year in which he was would be a year of conflict, and therefore called on the Franks to take the field. That people came forward in such numbers that God alone would have been able to count them. The troops continued to assemble and to join successively with others till the Spanish peninsula was filled with the cavalry and infantry of both parties; the troops of each kingdom being assembled around their respective sovereigns. When all the army of Yûsuf Ibn Tâshifîn had crossed over, to the last man, he sent after them so many camels that the peninsula was choked up with their multitude, whilst their cries reached to the vault of heaven. The people of Spain had never seen camels, and the Spanish horses, not being accustomed to the strangeness of their shape and the singularity of their cries, were filled with trouble and affright. Yûsuf had therefore a good idea in sending them over, so that they might form a line all round his army and be the first to enter into battle; he knew that the horses of the Franks would be scarred at the sight of them and start away. When all the troops were in readiness, they advanced against Alphonso, who was posted in a wide plain called az-Zallâka and situated near Badajoz. According to al-Daiyâsi (12), there is a distance of four parasangs between the two places. He says also (13): Before commencing hostilities, Yûsuf sent forward a letter by which, in accordance with the obligation imposed by the Sunna (or practise of Muhammad), he gave to Alphonso the choice of Islamism, or of war, or of tribute. One passage of this document ran as follows: "I have been " informed, o Alphonso! that you prayed for an encounter with us (لقاء) and wished to

"have ships in which you might cross over the sea to meet us. We have now cros-
"sed it to meet you; God has brought us both together in the same territory, and
"you will therefore see the result of your prayer. *But the prayer of the unbelievers*
"*serves only to lead them into error* (Koran, sur. 13, verse 15)." When Alphonso
heard the contents of this letter, the ocean of his choler boiled up, his arrogance increased still more, and he declared by a solemn oath that he would not stir from the
place where he was till he (Yúsuf) came to meet him. Ibn Táshifín and those who
were with him then advanced in the direction of az-Zallâka. When the Moslims arrived
there, they halted opposite the Franks. Al-Motamid Ibn Abbád had preferred being
the first to attack the enemy and agreed with Yúsuf Ibn Táshifín that, if his own
troops were repulsed and pursued, the African army would make a conversion so as
to encounter the Franks and operate its junction with the troops of Andalus. When
this movement was executed, the Franks were frustrated in their expectations; the
Moslim troops got in among them and direful was the slaughter. None of the Franks
escaped except Alphonso who, accompanied by less than thirty of his partisans, fled
to his capital, where he arrived in a miserable state. His arms, his horses and his
baggage fell into the hands of the Moslims, who thus obtained a rich booty. — I
must here observe that the battle took place on Friday, the 15th of Rajab, 479
(26th October, A. D. 1086). According to another statement, it occurred on one of
the last ten days of Ramadân (beginning of Jan. 1087). God knows best! — Al-
Baiyási states that the Moslim army (that of Yúsuf) landed at Algeziras in the month
of Muharram, 479 (April-May, A. D. 1086). — It is related that, on the field of
battle, wide as it was, not a spot was to be found where a man could set his foot
without treading on a dead body or in a plash of blood. The (Moslim) troops remained there four days, until the spoil was collected. When all was gathered in,
Yúsuf abstained from taking it and bestowed the whole on the Spanish kings, declaring, at the same time, that his purpose had been, not to gain booty but to make
war. These princes, seeing how he favoured them in preference to himself, were
profuse in testifying their respect, their love and their gratitude. Yúsuf then decided on returning to his own kingdom. When he was advancing to encounter Alphonso, he marched purposely through the open country, without passing
through any town or canton, and so he continued till he halted at az-Zallâka, over-
against Alphonso. There it was that he effected his junction with the troops of Andalus. — Abû 'l-Hajjâj Yúsuf Ibn Muhammad al-Baiyási says, in his *Tazkîr al-*

Adhil wa Tanbih al-Ghâfil (remembrancer for the intelligent and warner for the inattentive) : " Ibn Tâshifîn halted at the distance of less than a parasang from the
" enemy. This was on a Wednesday. The two parties agreed that the day of enga-
" ging battle should be the following Saturday, but Alphonso used deceit and perfidy.
" Early in the morning of Friday, the 15th of Rajab of the above-mentioned year,
" the scouts sent forward by Ibn Abbâd returned (to the camp), closely pursued by
" the Rûm (the Christians), and that happened when the Moslims thought them-
" selves secure from an attack. Ibn Abbâd hastened to get on horseback and order-
" ed the news to be spread throughout the army. All fell then into confusion; the
" surprise was successful, the earth shook (with the bustle), the soldiers were in di-
" sarray, unprepared, and not in order of battle. The enemy's cavalry came down
" upon them, overwhelmed Ibn Abbâd, crushed all opposition and left the ground
" behind them like a field just mown. Ibn Abbâd was borne to the ground, with a
" wound in one of his limbs. The Spanish (Moslim) chiefs fled and abandoned
" their camp, imagining that an irreparable catastrophy had arrived. Alphonso
" thought that the Emir of the Moslims (Yûsuf) was amongst those who were put to
" flight, but he did not know that final success is always reserved for those who fear
" God (Koran, sur. 11, verse 51). The Emir of the Moslims then rode forward in
" the midst of his bravest Sanhajian warriors, horse and foot, and surrounded by
" the chiefs of tribes. They directed their march towards Alphonso's camp, at-
" tacked it, entered and slew those who guarded it. The drums beat so that the
" earth trembled and every part of the horizon re-echoed the sound. The Chris-
" tians (Rûm) resolved to retake their camp on being informed that the Emir of the
" Moslims was there, and their assault was so vigorous that he was forced to retire.
" He then renewed the attack and expelled the enemy, but they marched against
" him again and obliged him to quit the place. This series of attacks and defeats
" did not terminate till the Emir of the Moslims ordered the negroes who formed
" his domestic troops to dismount. Four thousand of them got off their horses and
" penetrated into the midst of the fight. Bearing Lamtian shields, Indian swords
" and Zâhian (15) javelins, they stabbed the enemy's horses and made them rear
" under the riders, so that each steed separated from its fellow. Alphonso over-
" took a negro whose stock of javelins had been spent by his darting them
" off, and meant to cut him down with his sword. The negro closed with him,
" seized on the bridle of his horse, drew a dagger from his belt and struck it into

" his thigh. The weapon pierced through the rings of Alphonso's coat of mail,
" entered into the thigh and reached the padding of the saddle. On that day, at
" the hour of the sun's declining (towards the West), the gale of victory began to
" blow; God sent down his calm (sekina) to the Moslims and rendered his religion
" victorious. The true-believers charged upon Alphonso and his partisans with the
" greatest resolution and drove them from the camp. The enemies turned their
" backs, exposing their necks to the sword, and fled to a hill where they took refuge
" and fortified themselves, whilst the (Moslim) cavalry surrounded them on all sides.
" When the night got dark, Alphonso and his companions slipped off and left the
" hill at the moment that death had grasped them in its clutches. The Moslims got
" possession of everything that was in the camp; furniture, plate, tents and arms,
" all fell into their hands. Ibn Abbâd caused the heads of the Christians who had
" been slain to be collected and laid before him, and they formed a heap like a large
" hill. He then wrote a letter to his son ar-Rashîd, announcing the victory and
" dispatched it by a carrier-pigeon. This was on Saturday, the 16th of Muharram
" (read Rajab)." — It is related also that the Emir of the Moslims required from the
inhabitants of the country a subvention in aid of some undertaking in which he was
engaged (10). In the letter addressed by him on this subject to the people of Almeria
he stated that a number of doctors had declared the demand lawful, because it was
conformable to what (the khalif) Omar Ibn al-Khattâb had done under similar circumstances. The inhabitants of the town requested their kâdi Abû Abd Allah Ibn al-
Farrâ, who was as pious and as devout a man as could be, to draw up an answer to
Yûsuf's letter. He therefore wrote as follows: " The Emir of the Moslims, having
" exacted a subvention and remarked my delay (in obeying), states that Abû 'l-Walîd
" al-Bâji (vol. I. p. 593) and all the kâdis and legists, both in Africa and in Spain,
" have formally declared that such a requisition is legal, because a similar subvention
" was demanded by the blessed Omar Ibn al-Khattâb, who was the companion of
" the apostle of God, and who now lies beside him in the tomb and whose justice
" was never called into question. (Now, I say) that the Emir of the Moslims is not
" a companion of the apostle of God, neither does he lie beside him in the tomb,
" neither is he one whose justice can never be called into question. Therefore, if
" those legists and kâdis have placed you on a line with him for justice, God will
" take them to an account for what they have asserted respecting you. Omar, be-
" fore asking for a subvention, entered into the mosque of God's apostle and made

" oath that he possessed not a single dirhem in the public treasury, to spend
" upon the Moslims. Do you therefore enter into the great mosque of the place in
" which you are, and there, in the presence of the learned (the doctors of the law),
" make oath that you possess not a single dirhem and that the public treasury of
" the Moslims does not contain one either. The subvention must then be granted
" to you by right. Salutation!" — When the Emir of the Moslims had achieved
this victory, he ordered his army to keep its position and dispatch pillaging
parties into the territory of the Franks. The direction of these troops he confided to Sir Ibn Abi Bakr. Yûsuf meant to return by the same road which he had
followed in coming, but al-Motamid, desirous of doing himself honour, prevailed
on him to turn aside (from that line of march) and visit his kingdom. He induced
him also to accept the hospitality of his palace. Seville, the capital of al-Motamid's
states, was one of the handsomest cities that could be seen. When Yûsuf reached it,
he saw that it was situated on the border of a vast navigable river, by which vessels
were bringing cargoes of goods from Maghreb. To the west of the city lay an extensive district, twenty parasangs in length and filled with thousands of hamlets,
each of them (abounding in) figs, grapes and olives. This place is called the as-
Sharaf (Azarafe) of Seville. All Maghreb draws from thence its provision of these
kinds of fruit. At one side of the city stood the palaces (or castles, kusûr) erected by
al-Motamid and by his father al-Motadid. They were extremely beautiful and magnificent. In it (Seville) were to be found eatables, liquors, clothing, house-furni-
ture, etc., of all sorts. Al-Motamid lodged Yûsuf Ibn Tâshifin in one of these palaces and treated him with such honour and respect as procured him the warmest
thanks from his guest. Ibn Tâshifin's companions never ceased directing his attention towards the state of enjoyment and pleasure in which he was, and inciting
him to get up something of the same kind for himself. " Royalty," said they, " has
" for its main advantage that its possessor may pass his life in enjoyment and in
" pleasure, like al-Motamid and his companions." Yûsuf Ibn Tâshifin was very
moderate in his way of living; addicted neither to ostentation nor to prodigality, and
by no means nice in respect to food or any thing else: the early part of his life was
passed in his own country and had been full of hardships. He therefore disapproved
of the profusion to which they tried to lead him and said : " Respecting that man,"
— meaning al-Motamid, — " what appears to me is that he is ruining the kingdom
" of which he has possession. The money by means of which he has procured for

" himself all those things must have once belonged to others, and, from them,
" such sums could never have been possibly taken by just means; he must have
" procured them by iniquitous measures and here he spends them on mere vani-
" ties. Of all futilities, that is the most detestable. A man whose mind is set on
" spending money to such a degree and for no other purpose than the satisfaction
" of his sensual propensities, how can he have sufficient courage to defend his
" states, protect his subjects and augment the prosperity of the country?" Yûsuf
then asked if there was any relaxation in the pleasures which al-Motamid enjoyed,
and was answered that there never was : " His whole life," said they, " has been
" passed as you see."—" His companions," said Yûsuf, " and those who assisted
" him against his enemies and aided to establish his power, do all of them partake
" of those delights?" The answer was that they did not.—Do you then think,"
" said he, " that they can be pleased with him?" They replied that they were not
at all pleased with him. Yûsuf then began to reflect with downcast eyes and remained silent. — He passed some days with al-Motamid and, whilst he was stopping there, a man of a shabby exterior, but of great discernment, asked to see the
Spanish sovereign. On being admitted, he spoke as follows : " O king, may God
" direct you! One of the most essential obligations to fulfil is, to show gratitude
" for favours, and a manner of showing gratitude is, to give good advice. I am one
" of your subjects; in your empire I hold a poor rather than a middle station; and
" yet I feel obliged to give you a piece of advice, such as a subject owes to his king.
" One of the persons who accompany Yûsuf Ibn Tâshifîn, this guest of yours, ut-
" tered something which has reached my ears and which indicates that these people
" think themselves and their king better entitled to the enjoyments in which
" you indulge than you are. I have a counsel to give and, if you be pleased to
" hear it, I shall speak." — Being told by al-Motamid to continue, he said : " This
" man, to whom you have shown your kingdom, has always acted like a tyrant, in
" his conduct towards other kings. He overthrew the Zenata of Maghreb, deprived
" them of their empire and to none of them did he shew mercy. It is therefore to
" be feared that he may aspire, not only to the possession of your kingdom but of
" all the Spanish peninsula; now, particularly, that he has seen the pleasant life
" which you enjoy; and he certainly imagines that the other Spanish kings live in
" the same way as you. He has sons and relations whose secret advice he follows;
" persons who render agreeable to him the idea of settling in the fertile region

" which is now yours. He has destroyed Alphonso and that prince's army; he has
" overthrown their power and thus deprived you of a powerful auxiliary who would
" have been for you a right arm and an excellent shield. But now, that you have
" lost your chance of Alphonso, fail not to take a prudent decision, such a one as
" can be still executed." —" What decision," said al-Motamid, " is it possible for
" us to take at present?" —The man replied : " Take the resolution of seizing on
" this guest of yours and imprisoning him in your palace; declare positively that
" you will not set him at liberty till he give orders that all his troops evacuate the
" Spanish peninsula and return to the place from which they came, and that not
" even a boy of them be left behind. You will then make arrangements with the
" sovereigns of the Peninsula for the purpose of guarding that sea and preventing
" vessels containing troops of his from navigating therein. After that, make him
" swear by the most solemn oath possible that he will never conceive the thought
" of returning to this country, except there be an accord between you and him on
" that subject. That you may be assured of his keeping his promise, require hos-
" tages from him; he will give you as many as you wish, for he will set more value
" on his life than on any thing which you can exact from him. That man will then
" remain satisfied with a country which is really of no good for any one but him
" Thus will you be delivered from him as you have been delivered from Alphonso;
" you can then hold your position under the best circumstances; your renown will
" be yet more exalted among the sovereigns of the Peninsula and your kingdom will
" be enlarged. This proceeding will ensure you a reputation for good fortune and
" resolution; and the other kings will stand in awe of you. After that, take your
" necessary measures for the conduct which you have to hold as a neighbour of the
" man whom you have thus treated. Be assured that a heavenly order has prepared
" for you this opportunity; generations will pass away and torrents of blood be shed
" before the like of it comes again." Al-Motamid listened to the discourse of this
man and, feeling that the advice was good, began to consider how he should avail
himself of the opportunity. He had then with him some companions engaged in
convivial pleasures, and one of them said to this giver of advice : " Al-Motamid ala
" 'Llah is the paragon of the honourable and generous; he is not a man to act un-
" justly or betray a guest." To this the man replied : " Perfidy consists in depriving
" another of that to which he has just right; it is not perfidy in a man to defend himself against a danger, if it bring him into straits." The boon companion answered :

"Better to suffer wrong and act honestly than show energy in committing an ou-
"trage." The adviser then resumed and recapitulated his discourse, after which
he retired with a present given to him by al-Motamid. Yûsuf Ibn Tâshifîn, being
informed of what had passed, rose early, the next morning, for the purpose of departing, and accepted a quantity of magnificent presents which were offered to him by
his host. He then set out on his journey and crossed over from Algeziras to Ceuta
(Sibta). — I may here remark that Ceuta is a well-known place, on the strait of the
same name. It is one of the points of passage between the two continents, namely,
Spain and Maghreb. We have already mentioned it (vol. II. p. 419). — Yûsuf, on
crossing over to Maghreb, left his troops in Spain, so that they might take repose. (This
army) then followed in the trace of Alphonso and advanced into the heart of his
country. Alphonso, on returning to his former place, asked what had become of
his companions, his brave warriors and the heroes of his army. He was informed
that most of them were slain, and nothing was to be heard but the lamentations of
their widows and children. From that moment he neither ate nor drank, and died of
grief and chagrin (17). His daughter, the only child which he left, obtained the
sovereignty and fortified herself in the city of Toledo. — In this expedition, the Moslims made an immense booty, which they sent over to Maghreb. Their emir, Sîr
Ibn Abi Bakr, asked of Yûsuf Ibn Tâshifîn the permission of remaining in the
Spanish peninsula, and informed him that he had taken a number of fortresses situated on the enemy's frontiers. He stated also that he had established permanent
garrisons in these places, for the purpose of holding them, but, that it would not be
easy for those troops to continue there, as they were suffering from penury and con-
tinually exposed to the attacks of the enemy, whilst the kings of Andalus were enjoying all the pleasures of life in their rich and fertile territories. Yûsuf Ibn
Tâshifîn answered by a letter in which he ordered him to expel these kings from
their states and send them to Maghreb. He added that, if any of them resisted, he
should attack them and give them no respite till he dispossessed them. "Begin,"
said he, "by those who are in the neighbourhood of the (Christian) frontiers, and
"make no attempt against al-Motamid Ibn Abbâd till you have got the other king-
"doms into your power. Confide the government of these countries to the prin-
"cipal officers of your army." Sîr Ibn Abî Bakr began by the Bani Hûd and tried
to expel them from Rota (Rûda), their (principal) fortress. — I must remark that
Rûda, as here written, is the name of a fortress situated in a very strong position,

on the summit of a mountain. A well, at the very top of the mountain, furnishes the place with water. This fortress was filled with provisions and supplies of every sort and in sufficient quantity to last for a very long time. — Sir, not being able to take it, retired (to some distance) and, having then equipped some of his soldiers in the attire of Franks, he ordered them to march against the fortress as if they meant to surprise it, whilst he and his companions would lie in ambush near the place. This they did, and the garrison seeing that the invaders were but a feeble band, went out to pursue them. Sir Ibn Abi Bakr then sallied from his place of conceal-ment, seized on the lord of the fortress and took possession of the place. He then attacked the Bani Sumādih in Almeria. This fortress was of great strength, but the sovereign had neither good troops nor valiant warriors. They (the troops of Sir) attacked and defeated them. When al-Motasim Ibn Sumādih perceived that he was vanquished, he retired into his palace (or citadel) and died of grief that very night. The people, being preoccupied about him alone, surrendered the city. They then besieged al-Mutawakkil Omar Ibn al-Aftas in Badajoz. He was a man of great bravery and of a noble family. His father, Abù Bakr Muhammad Ibn Abd Allah Ibn Maslama at-Tujibi, surnamed al-Mozaffar Billah (victorious through God) was one of the most learned men of the time. Some works were composed by him, the greatest and most celebrated of which treats of history and is called, after him, the Muzaffari. He was king of Badajoz, a very handsome city. (Al-Mutawakkil) rejected (Sir's) proposals and took the alternative of resistance and war; but his troops revolted against him, seized on him and two of his sons and put them all to death. His youngest children were taken to Morocco. The other kings of the peninsula surrendered and passed into Maghreb; none remained except al-Motamid Ibn Abbād. Sir, having finished with these princes, wrote to Yûsuf Ibn Tâshifîn, informing him that the only one of them who remained in the country was al-Motamid, and requesting instructions how to act towards him. Yûsuf ordered him to march against that prince and invite him to retire into Maghreb with his family. " If he accept," said he, " it is well and good; if he refuse, attack " him." Al-Motamid, having received Sir's proposal, returned no answer. Sir then besieged him during three months, took the city by storm, expelled al-Motamid from his palace by main force, and sent him, in chains, to Maghreb. Al-Motamid went to reside at Aghmât and there he remained till his death. He was the only one of the kings of Andalus who was placed in confinement. Sir thus obtained posses-

sion of the peninsula. Yùsuf Ibn Tàshifìn died in the year mentioned lower down,
and the sovereignty passed to his son, Abù 'l-Hasan Ali Ibn Yùsuf. This was a
mild, grave, virtuous and just prince, submissive to the truth (the divine law) and to
its doctors. The imposts of his states were paid in regularly; no contrariety ever
happened to him; no untoward event ever troubled him on his throne. — I mentioned, in the article on Abù Nasr al-Fath Ibn Muhammad Ibn Abd Allah Ibn Khà-
kàn al-Kaisi (vol. II. p. 455), that the Kaldid al-Ikiyàn was composed by that author
for Ibrâhim, one of Yùsuf Ibn Tàshifìn's sons, and that the person who caused
him to be put to death was Ali, the son of Yùsuf Ibn Tàshifìn. After the death
of Ali, his son Tàshifìn obtained the sovereignty. It was under the reign of this
prince that the dynasty of the Almoravides was overthrown. We shall give the particulars of that event. Towards the commencement of the present biographical notice, we said that it was Yùsuf Ibn Tàshifìn who founded the city of Morocco. The
author of the work from which I extracted (the materials of) this article says, towards
the end of the volume : " Marràkush (vulgarly : Merràkoh), a very large city, was
" built by Yùsuf Ibn Tàshifìn on a spot which bore the name of Marràkomb. This
" word, in the Masmùda (Berber) language, signifies : pass quickly (18). The
" place here mentioned had been a resort for robbers and got this name because
" the persons who passed near it used to say these words to their companions." —
" Ibn Tàshifìn built the city of Morocco in the year 465 (A. D. 1072-3)." So says
Abù 'l-Khattàb Ibn Dihya (vol. II. p. 584) in the work to which he gave the title of
an-Nibràs (the candle) (19), and in (that chapter of it which treats of) the khalifat of
al-Kàim bi-Amr Illah. He adds : " It was one of the places where the inhabitants
" of Naffis (20) sowed their corn. Yùsuf bought it from them with money which
" he had brought with him from the desert (Sahrá). Naffis is the name of a moun-
" tain which overlooks Morocco." — I may add that it is in the territory of Aghmàt,
in ulterior Maghreb. — " His (Yùsuf's) motive for doing so (for building it) was
" that, having become accustomed to reign, after subduing the Berber tribes and
" getting delivered from the adversaries whom he had to contend with in the tribe
" of Lamtùna, he aspired to the honour of founding a city. On the spot which it
" occupies was a small village surrounded by a thicket of trees and inhabited by
" some Berbers. He built the city and erected in it palaces (or castles) and magni-
" ficent dwellings. It lies in the midst of a vast meadow (or swamp) and is sur-
" rounded by mountains, at the distance of some parasangs. One of these moun-

" tains is always capped with snow (21); it is the same which is noted for the
" mildness of its temperature and (the goodness of) its air." — In the year 464
(A. D. 1071-2) Yúsuf laid siege to the city of Fez which was at that time the capital
of Maghreb, and, having reduced the inhabitants to great straits, he got it
into his possession. The ordinary population he allowed to remain there, but the
Berbers and the troops (of the garrison) he expelled; he began, however, by imprisoning some of them and putting others to death. This augmentation of his power
contributed to fortify his authority in ulterior and exterior Maghreb. To those countries he added (later) the provinces which he conquered in the Spanish peninsula.
He was a man of resolution, skilled in the management of affairs, vigilant in main-
taining the prosperity of his kingdom, favorable to the learned and to religious men,
whose advise also he often had recourse to. It came to my knowledge that the
imám Hujja tal-Islâm Abú Hâmid al-Ghazzâli (vol. II. p. 621), having heard of
Yúsuf Ibn Táshifín's noble qualities and his predilection for men of learning, resolved on going to see him; but, when he arrived at Alexandria and was making the
necessary preparations (for his voyage), he received the news of his death. This
piece of information I found in some book or other, but, at present, I have totally
forgotten where. — Yúsuf was of a middle size, a tawney complexion and a lean
body; his cheeks were beardless and his voice feeble. He acknowledged the supremacy of the Abbasides and was the first who ever intitled himself Emir of the Moslims. His prosperous fortune, his grandeur and his power never ceased till his
death. That event took place on Monday, the 3rd of Muharram, 500 (4th Sept.
A. D. 1106). He was then aged ninety years, fifty of which he had passed on the
throne. Our shaikh (professor) Izz ad-Din Ibn al-Athîr (vol. II. p. 288) says, in his
greater historical work (the Annals) : " The Emir of the Moslims, Yúsuf Ibn Tá-
" shifín, was virtuous in his conduct, upright and just; he liked learned and pious
" men, treated them with honour and appointed them to act as magistrates in his
" states; he always let himself be guided by their counsels. In acts of clemency
" and the forgiveness of offenses he took great pleasure. As an example of that, we
" may relate the following anecdote. Three men met together; one of them ex-
" pressed the wish to obtain a thousand pieces of gold, so that he might trade with
" them; the other wished for an appointment under the Emir of the Moslims; the
" third wished to possess Yúsuf's wife, who was the handsomest of women and had
" great political influence. Yúsuf, being informed of what they said, sent for the

" men, bestowed one thousand dinars on him who wished for that sum, gave an
" appointment to the other and said to him who wished to possess the lady : ' Foo-
" ' lish man! what induced you to wish for that which you can never obtain.'
" He then sent him to her and she placed him in a tent where he remained three
" days, receiving, each day, one and the same kind of food. She had him then
" brought to her and said : ' What did you eat these days past.' He replied :
" ' Always the same thing.' — ' Well,' said she, ' all women are the same thing.'
" She then ordered some money and a dress to be given him, after which, she dis-
" missed him."—Ali, the son of Yùsuf Ibn Tàshifin, died on the 7th of Rajab, 537
(26th Jan. A. D. 1143); he was born on the 11th of Rajab, 470 (24th Nov. A. D.
1083). We have said something of him in our article on Muhammad Ibn Tûmart
(vol. III, p. 205), and to it we refer the reader. When Abd al-Mûmin set out on his expedition against the provinces of Maghreb, which he intended to take from Ali, the son of
Yùsuf Ibn Tàshifin, he directed his march along the mountains (the chain of the Atlas),
and Tàshifin, the son of Ali Ibn Yùsuf, being placed by his father at the head of an
army and sent to oppose him, marched in a parallel direction to that of his adversary, but without quitting the plain. These operations were still going on when
Ali Ibn Yùsuf died. Ali's officers then appointed his son Ishak to act, at Morocco,
as lieutenant of (the new sovereign, his brother) Tàshifin Ibn Ali. Ishak was then
a mere boy. Abd al-Mûmin's success was now becoming evident, the inhabitants of
the mountains, forming all together an immense population and amongst whom
were the Ghomàra, the (people of) Tadla (22) and the Masmûda, having submitted to this authority. Tàshifin Ibn Ali was quite dismayed; he felt that he
would be overcome and that the downfal of the Almoravide dynasty was at hand.
He therefore went to Oran, a maritime city, with the intention of making it his place
of residence and then, of embarking, if the empire was taken from him, and passing into Spain. There he meant to settle as the Omaiyides had done after the ruin of
their power in Syria and the countries (of the East). Outside of Oran, and on the
seaside was a hill called Sulb al-Kalb (the dog's backbone), on the top of which stood
a ribât (chapel) much frequented by devotees. The 27th of the month of Ramadàn,
539 (22nd March, A. D. 1145), Tàshifin went up to that ribât for the purpose of
being present at a sitting during which the whole of the Koran was to be read over,
and he took with him a few of the persons who were attached to his service. Abd
al-Mûmin was then at Tàjira (23) which, as we have mentioned in his life, was his

native place, and had happened to send a small troop of horse in the direction of
Oran. This detachment, which had for its commander the Shaikh Abù Hafs Omar
Ibn Yahya, one of the first companions of al-Mahdi, arrived near the city on the
26th of the month of Ramadán, and lay concealed during the following night. Having then discovered that Táshifín was (nearly) alone in the ribát, they went up to
the edifice, surrounded it and set fire to the gate. Those who were within now felt
that death was inevitable. Táshifín got on his horse, and galloped forward with the
intention of clearing the fire at a bound and thus effecting his escape, but the animal sprang wildly about, through terror, and, heedless of the rein, plunged with its
rider down a precipice on the sea-side. They fell upon a heap of stones, the horse's
limbs were broken, and Táshifín died on the spot. All the officers who accompanied him were slain. His army, being in another quarter, was not aware of what
passed that night. The news of this event was carried to Abd al-Mûmin, who immediately proceeded to Oran and gave to the place where the ribát is situated the name
of Sulb al-Fath (the force of victory). From that time he ceased to remain in the
mountainous country and descended into the plain. After that, he directed his
march towards Tilimsán (Tlemcen), which place is composed of two towns, the old
and the new, situated at the distance of a short gallop one from the other. He then
went and laid siege to Fez, which city he took in the year 540 (A. D. 1145-6). In
the following year he marched against Morocco and blockaded it during eleven
months. Ishák, the son of Ali (Ibn Yúsuf), was in the city with a number of the
principal officers of the empire. On the death of his father, he had been appointed
by them to act there as the lieutenant of his brother Táshifín. Abd al-Mûmin took
the city, having reduced the inhabitants to the utmost misery by famine. Ishák
was brought out to him with Sír Ibn al-Hájj (24) who was one of the bravest and
most eminent officers of the empire. They were led forward with their hands tied
behind their backs. As Ishák had not yet attained the age of puberty, Abd al-Mûmin
wished to spare the life of so young a boy, but, as his officers disapproved of his intention, he made no opposition to their wishes and let them do with the prisoners
what they pleased. Ishák and Sír Ibn al-Hájj were, in consequence, put to death.
Abd al-Mûmin then took up his residence in the palace (or citadel). This happened
in the year 542 (A. D. 1147-8), and thus fell the empire of the Bani Táshifín. —
In our article on al-Motamid Ibn Abbád we stated that Yúsuf returned to Spain the
year after the battle of az-Zallàka, yet I have indicated here that he did not

(then) go back to that country and that it was his lieutenants who conquered for him
the provinces of Andalus. This must necessarily induce the reader to suppose that
I am in contradiction with myself, but my excuse is that, in (my *materials for*) the
life of Ibn Abbâd, I found the first statement and, in (those for) the present article, I
found the second under the precise form in which I have given it. God knows
which is right! (25). — I have since found in Abû 'l-Hajjâj al-Baiyâsi's *Takhîr al-
Adkil* that Ibn Tâshifîn, on crossing the sea (*for the first time*), proceeded to Seville
and that Ibn Abbâd went forth to meet him with the (usual) repast of hospitality and
provisions (*for the army*). He then (*says our author*) left Seville with all his people,
from the highest to the lowest, directed his march towards Badajos and fought the
battle of which we have spoken. After that, he returned to his own country and, in
the year 481, Ibn Abbâd crossed the sea and asked his aid against those (dangerous)
neighbours whom he had in the enemy's country. Ibn Tâshifîn received him honourably and promised to assist him. Ibn Abbâd then returned to his kingdom and had
prepared to meet the foe when, in the month of Rajab, 481 (Sept.-Oct. A. D. 1088),
Yûsuf joined him. Alphonso took the field at the head of a numerous army, whilst
the kings of Andalus had already united their forces to those of Ibn Tâshifîn. He
(*Yûsuf*), seeing how great an army he (*Alphonso*) had collected, decamped from
his position; he had also lent his ear to the insinuations of his courtiers, who had told
him that the kings of Andalus intended to abandon him and leave him alone to contend with Alphonso. This information made so deep an impression on his mind
that he began a movement (*of retreat*) towards his own country, and all his troops
accompanied him, marching and halting as he did. When he crossed the sea and
reached his own kingdom, his heart was filled with indignation against the kings of
Andalus. They soon learned that his feelings towards them were changed and, fearing the consequences of his displeasure, they began to put their cities into a state of
defense and collect provisions. One of them (al-*Motamid*) was in such dread of Ibn
Tâshifîn that he applied to Alphonso for help and obtained the promise of aid and assistance. Alphonso, to whom he sent a great quantity of precious gifts, received
them willingly and declared by oath, that he would grant whatever the donor might
ask. Ibn Tâshifîn, being informed of this, flew into a violent rage, crossed the sea
for the third time and directed his march towards Cordova, a city which belonged to
Ibn Abbâd. He reached it in the month of the first Jumâda, 483 (July, A. D. 1090),
and found that Ibn Abbâd had arrived there before him. Ibn Abbâd went forth to

meet him and, having presented the repast of hospitality, was treated by him in the same manner as usual. Ibn Táshifín then took Granada from its sovereign, Abd Allah the son of Bolokkin Ibn Bádis Ibn Habbús, whom he cast into prison. Ibn Abbád hoped that Ibn Táshifín would bestow on him the conquered city and gave him a hint to that effect, but the other did not seem to mind it. He then began to fear Ibn Táshifín's intentions and imagined a plan by which he might be enabled to depart. Having represented to him that he had received letters from Seville informing him that the inhabitants were apprehensive of being attacked by the enemy (*the Christians*), who were in their neighbourhood, he asked and obtained permission to return there. *(* Ibn Táshifín then set out for his own country, crossed over to it in the month of Ramadán, 483 (Oct.-Nov. A. D. 1090), and remained there till the beginning of the year 484. He then resolved on going over to Andalus and besieging Ibn Abbád (*in Seville*). The latter, being informed of his project, began to make every preparation for resistance. Ibn Táshifín, having arrived at Ceuta, assembled a numerous army which he sent over (*to Spain*) under the orders of Sir Ibn Abi Bakr. Ibn Abbád, seeing his cities closely invested by these troops, called on Alphonso for assistance, but no attention was paid to his request. Then happened what we have already related. God knows best! — As we have mentioned the *al-Mulathlhimún* in this article, it is necessary that we should say something of them here. The information which I found concerning them is that they are a branch of (*the Arabian tribe of*) Himyar Ibn Sabá (26), that they possess horses, camels and sheep, that they inhabit the deserts of the South, that, like the Arabs, they keep moving from one (*source of*) water to another and that they dwell in tents made of hair, that of camels and other animals. The first person who formed them into a body, pushed them to war and encouraged them to conquer the provinces (*of Maghreb*) was the legist Abd Allah Ibn Yásín, who was afterwards slain in the war with the Bereghwáta (27). He was replaced by Abú Bakr Ibn Omar the Sanhájian, a chief who generally remained in the desert and of whom mention has been made in this article. Abú Bakr lost his life in a war with the Negroes. We have already mentioned by what means Yúsuf Ibn Táshifín obtained the supreme command. It was he who gave to his partisans the name of al-Murábitún (*Almoravides, dwellers* in ribáts) (28). This people always wear the *lithám* (*a dark blue veil or mask*) and never remove it from their faces; it was for that reason that they were called *al-Mulaththamún* (*the wearers of* lithams *or veils*). The custom of wearing the *lithám* is general among them and has passed down from one generation to another. Their motive for wearing it is thus accounted for : the tribe of Himyar used veils in order to protect their faces against the effects of heat and cold. It was only men of high rank among them who did so, but the practise became, at length, so general that even the common people wore the *lithám*. — According to another account, a hostile tribe intended to take them unawares, attack their camp whilst they were absent, and carry off their riches (*flocks*) and their women. One of their elders then advised them to dress the women in men's clothes and send them to a short distance, whilst the men remained in the camp, with their faces veiled and dressed like women. "Then," said he, "as the enemy, on coming, will take you for women, "you must sally out against them." They did so, attacked the enemy, sword in hand, and slew them. From that time they continued to wear the *lithám*, thinking that it would always bring them good luck, since it had then rendered them victorious. — Our *shaikh* Izz ad-Dîn Ibn al-Athîr says in his greater historical work [29] : "It is said that their motive for wearing the *lithám* was this : A troop of Lamtû-"nides sallied forth with the intention of taking by surprise a tribe which was their "enemy. That tribe took advantage of their departure and went to attack their "camp. There was no person remaining there except the old men, the boys and "the women. When the old men were certain that it was the enemy, they told "the women to dress in men's clothes, put on *lithám*s and draw them closely (about "*their faces*), so that they might not be recognised, and then to arm themselves. "They did so, and the old men went forth with the boys (*and stationed*) before the "women who had placed themselves around the camp. The enemy, on approa-"ching, saw a multitude of people and took them to be men. 'These fellows,' said "they, 'are keeping close to their women and will fight for them till they die. "' The best thing we can do is to drive off the flocks and go away; if they follow "' us, we will attack them, when they are separated from their women.' Whilst "they were collecting the flocks from the pasture-grounds, the men belonging to "the camp came up and, as the invaders were thus placed between them and the "women, a great number of them were slain; the women killed even more of them "than the men. From that time, they continued to wear the *lithám*, so that the "old men should not to be distinguished from the boys and the women, and they "never took it off, night or day. A poet said of the (*people who wear*) the li-"thám :

" They held the highest rank in (*the tribe of*) Himyar, and, when the descendants of San-
" hâja are asked for, they are the more. As they bore away the palm in every noble deed,
" they were overcome by their modesty and hid their faces with the *lithâm*. "

— In the year 454 (A. D. 1062), when Yûsuf Ibn Tâshifîn commanded the army of
Abû Bakr Ibn Omar the Sanhajian, he departed from Sijilmâssa. The year before
that, Abû Bakr Ibn Omar had gone to besiege Sijilmâssa, and he took it after much
hard fighting. Yûsuf Ibn Tâshifîn then seized on it [*for himself*] and subsequently
occurred the events (*which have been related*).

(1) This article is a mere collection of materials drawn from various sources and thrown together without
discrimination. The *Kitâb al-Morib*, which is our author's main authority, appears to me of little value.
I entirely concur with Mr Dozy in his appreciation of that work. (See *Histoire des musulmans d'Espagne*,
tome IV, page 191.) For the history of Yûsuf Ibn Tâshifîn see the work of Mr Dozy just mentioned, his
History of the Abbasides, the *Histoire des Berbers* d'Ibn Khaldûn and the Abû Zerâ's *Kartâs*.

(2) *Tâshifîn*, or *Teshfen* is by its form a Berber name, but the root does not, I think, belong to that language. It is the plural feminine of the word *Tashefa* which appears to be the Arabic word *shefa* (remedy)
under a Berber form.

(3) For the history of the tribe of Lamtûna see Ibn Khaldûn's *Hist. des Berbers*, tome II, p. 67.

(4) See vol. III, page 199, note (12). — It might perhaps have been well to replace, in this translation,
the word *al-Melathkhemdn* by *Almoravides*.

(5) As Yûsuf acknowledged the supremacy of the Abbaside khalîf, he could not take the title of *Emir al-
Mûmnîn* (*commander of the faithful*), which was exclusively reserved for the khalîfs. The Almohade and
Hafide sovereigns adopted the latter title, as chiefs of that Shîïte sect which formed the Almohade commu-
nity.

(6) The imperfection of the Arabic writing character is such that, in our manuscripts, the same group of
letters is pointed so as to give, in one, the date of 877, in another, that of 897, and in a third, that of 899.

(7) See *Hist. des Berb.*, t. II, p. 67.

(8) The text is corrupt here, but the meaning is sufficiently clear.

(9) I read ڡاڡى with two manuscripts.

(10) This discourse is evidently a mere fabrication. It is in the sententious style of those political testa-
ments which Arab writers were fond of attributing to the old Persian and Indian kings. It is, besides, difficult to imagine how the rude Berber language could have acquired, in few years, sufficient flexibility to
express such a series of abstract ideas.

(11) Or, according to another reading : by the prudent counsel of his vizir.

(12) The life of al-Baiyâsi is given in this volume.

(13) It is doubtful whether it be al-Baiyâsi or the author of the *Morib* whose words are cited here. To
judge from the style, it seems to be the latter.

(14) The true date of the battle of az-Zallâka is the 12th Rajab, 479 (23rd October, 1086). — (Dozy's
Hist. des musulmans Esp., t. IV, p. 299.)

(15) According to another reading: *Edaien. Yâk* is a province of North Africa, to the south of Constantine; *Yân* is the name given to a species of oak.

(16) This evidently happened at a much later period, after the complete overthrow of the Spanish Moslim kings.

(17) Alphonso VI, king of Leon, Castille and Galicia, died A. D. 1109, twenty-three years after his defeat at az-Zallâka.

(18) *Marr* (to pass) is Arabic, but is employed in Berber. I cannot find the word *Amr* in my Berber texts and vocabularies. It may, perhaps, belong to the Sheilûh, or Shelha, dialect.

(19) According to Hajji Khalîfa, this work is a history of the Abbasides.

(20) The name of this town should be pronounced *Niffis*. The geographer, Abû Obaid al-Bakri, speaks of it frequently in his *Description de l'Afrique septentrionale*. In the geographical table prefixed to the *Histoire des Berbers*, the name is written *Nefis* and its position indicated.

(21) Not only one but the greater part of them.

(22) The text has the false reading *Taïda*.

(23) Tâjira, or *Tîyra* as now pronounced, is a mountain in the khalifate of the Troro Sbarags. Its extremity advances into the sea and forms a cape to which the maps give the name of cap Noé (in Arabic *Roucra*). It lies at about eight miles to the N. E. of Nemours (*Jâmâ 'r-Arnûlâf*).

(24) See *Hist. des Berb.*, t. II, p. 578.

(25) The movements of Yûsuf Ibn Tâshfîn are explained by Mr Dozy in his *Hist. des musulmans d'Esp.*

(26) The *Almoravidides* were Berbers in race and language, not Arabs.

(27) For the history of these events consult Abû Obaid al-Bakri's *Description de l'Afrique septentrionale*, Ibn Khaldûn's *Hist. des Berb.*, t. II, and the *Kartâs*.

(28) See vol. I, p. 119. The word *ribât* is now pronounced *rabât*.

(29) See professor Thornberg's edition of the *Kâmil*, Arabic text, vol. IX, page 415.

YUSUF IBN ABD AL-MUMIN.

Abû Yakûb Yûsuf al-Kaisi al-Kûmi, the son of Abd al-Mûmin Ibn Ali, was one of the sovereigns of Maghrib. We have already noticed his father Abd al-Mûmin (vol. II. p. 182) and his son Yakûb (p. 335 of this vol.). On the death of his father and the deposition of his brother Muhammad Ibn Abd Al-Mûmin, he obtained the supreme command. Muhammad had been declared successor to the throne; his name was even inscribed on the gold coinage, his father having designated him to reign and obliged the troops to swear that they would serve him with fidelity. He manifested

however such a love of idleness and such a propensity for vain amusements, that
Yûsuf dethroned him. There was a third brother named Abû Hafs Omar; and to
him Yûsuf confided the government of the Spanish peninsula. Yûsuf was learned
in the law, the traditions and a number of other sciences; having been brought up
under the eyes of his father who, wishing to give a good education to the (three)
brothers, had placed about them the ablest preceptors that could be found amongst
the military men and the men of learning. Yûsuf passed his youth in constant occupation, now on horseback, amongst the bravest warriors, and then in study, under
the most eminent doctors. He was fonder of metaphysics and philosophy than
of literature and the other branches of knowledge. He was a hoarder and a sparer
(of money), gathering in carefully the imposts of his empire; and he showed great ability
in the government of his subjects. He would sometimes remain a long time in the
same city, as if he meant never to quit it, and sometimes he would go abroad and
stay there till people thought that he would never return. During his absence, the
kingdom was governed by deputies, agents and lieutenants whose talents he had been
able to appreciate, and to them he confided the administration of the empire. The
Magbribian dinars, called Yurûfians, were thus denominated after him. When he
had brought the affairs of the empire into order and established his authority on a
solid basis, he passed into Spain for the purpose of examining into the state of that
country and taking measures to advance its prosperity. This was in the year 566
(A. D. 1170-1). He departed with an army of one hundred thousand horsemen (1),
part of them Arabs and the rest Almohades (Berbers). When he arrived at Seville,
Abû Abd Allah Muhammad Ibn Saad, generally called Ibn Mardanish, who was at
that time the sovereign of Eastern Andalus, that is, of Murcia and its dependencies,
felt much alarmed, and the news weighed so greatly upon his heart, that he fell sick
and died. Some say that he was poisoned by his mother, because he treated very
badly the members of his family, his courtiers and the grandees of the empire. She
was giving him good advice, but in so harsh a tone that he threatened to punish
her; so she plotted against him and took away his life by poison. He died at
Seville (2) on the 28th of Rajab, 567 (27th March, A. D. 1172); he was born in
the year 518 (A. D. 1124-5), in a strong fortress situated in the province of Tortosa
and called Bunushkula (Peñiscola). On his death, his sons — or, by another
account, his brothers (3) — went to the emir Yûsuf Ibn Abd al-Mûmin, who was
then at Seville and surrendered to him all the provinces of Eastern Andalus which

had belonged to their father — or, to their brother (*according to the second statement*). He treated them kindly, took to wife their sister and gave them a high place
in his favour. He then began to retake the Moslim provinces which had fallen into
the hands of the Franks, and augmented his possessions in Spain to such a degree
that his foraging parties sometimes pushed forward to the gates of Toledo, the capital
of the enemy's states and the largest of their cities. He then laid siege to it, and all
the Franks assembled to attack him. Seeing his army reduced to great distress for
want of provisions, he raised the siege and returned to Morocco. In the year 575
(A. D. 1179-80), he went to Ifrikiya and took the town of Cafsa. In the year 580
(A. D. 1184-5), he passed into Spain with a numerous army and directed his march
towards the Western provinces of Andalus. He then besieged Shantarin (*Santarem*)
during a month, but, being taken ill, he died in the month of the first Rabi 580
(June—July, A. D. 1184). His body was placed in a coffin and carried to Seville.
He had nominated as successor to the throne his son Abû Yûsuf Yakûb, him whose
life we have already given. — Our professor, Ibn al-Athir (*vol.* II. p. 288), states, in
his *Annals*, that Yusûf died without designating his successor, and that the chiefs of
the Almohade troops agreed with the descendants of Abd al-Mûmin to take Yakûb,
the son of Yûsuf, for their king. This they did immediately after Yûsuf's death,
because they were close to the enemy's country and required the presence of a sovereign around whom all parties might rally. — Abû Abd-Allah Muhammad Ibn Abd
al-Mûmin, Yûsuf's brother, was deposed in the month of Shabân, 558 (July,
A. D. 1163). The emir Yûsuf then assumed the supreme power, his partisans having
agreed on nominating him and dethroning Abû Abd Allah. — Some verses of his
composition have been handed down, but, as they are not good, I abstain from inserting them. — As for Muhammad Ibn Mardanish, he composed, it is said, the
following piece :

In good truth, hers are eyes whose glances scatter death around. I cannot do without her,
neither can I live with her ; it would be better (*for me*) to meet death rather than her. But
yet I shall let my passion bear me towards her, come of it what may !

I have since found these verses in Ibn al-Katila's *Lamah al-Mulah* (*vol.* II. p. 286),
where they are attributed to Abû Jaafar Ahmad Ibn Sumâdih al-Binni. God knows
best ! Al-Bayâsi (4) says, in his *Hamdsa*, that the names of this author were Abû
Jaafar Ahmad Ibn al-Hussain Ibn Khalaf al-Binni al-Ubbadi al-Yamori (5); he does

not give these verses, but, farther on, he attributes the following piece to this Abû
Jaafar :

My abstaining from the pleasure of accompanying to some distance a friend who leaves me
proceeds from my wish to avoid the bitterness of the parting farewell. The consolation arising
from the one does not counterbalance the sadness resulting from the other; so I think it best to
abstain from both.

By the same author, on a lamp :

It points at the darkness with a serpent's tongue; it (*the darkness*) trusses up its robe (*in
order to depart*); it (*the flame*) rises up, and it (*the darkness*) retires.

When Abû Yakûb Yûsuf had breathed his last, Abû Bakr Yahya Ibn Mujîr, the
poet and literary scholar of whom we have spoken in the life of Yakûb Ibn Yûsuf
(*page* 344 *of this vol.*) composed on his death a long elegy in which he displayed great
talent and which began thus :

Sadness is great; shed therefore tears of blood; eyes are now of no other use but that.

— *Mardanîsh* is a frankish name and signifies *excrement* (6).— The name *Bunushkula* (Pehiscola) takes the vowels here given. — It is not necessary to mark the orthography of the other proper names, because they are sufficiently known. — *Bînsi*, the ethnic name of the poet above-mentioned, is to be pronounced as here indicated. — *Ubbadi* means *belonging to* (*Ubeda*,) an Andalusian town in the province of Jaen. It was built by Abd ar-Rahmân, the son of al-Hakam (7), and repaired by his son Muhammad. — After finishing this article, I found a collection of pieces in the handwriting of Imâd ad-Dîn Ibn Jibrîl Akhi 'l-Ilm (8) al-Misri, the intendant of the treasury in Egypt, and the same of whom we spoke towards the beginning of this work, in our article on Abû Ishâk al-Irâki (*vol. I. p.* 12). Imâd ad-Dîn's miscellany contains useful information respecting the people of Maghrib and other countries. I have made from it an extract which I subjoin to this biographical notice : Abd al-Mûmin designated as his successor Muhammad, the eldest of his sons. The oath of fidelity towards him being administered to the people, dispatches were written to all the provinces, announcing the inauguration. On the death of Abd al-Mûmin, his son Muhammad did not succeed in establishing his authority.

because he was noted for things which were incompatible with the sovereign power: he was addicted to wine, feeble in mind, very capricious and cowardly; besides which, he suffered, it is said, from a sort of leprosy. This turned the people against him and brought on his deposition, in the month of Shabân, 558 (July-August, A. D. 1163), after a reign of forty-five days. The persons who dethroned him were his brothers Yûsuf and Omar, the sons of Abd al-Mûmin. The sovereignty was then held jointly by these two brothers, who were the cleverest and most sagacious of Abd al-Mûmin's sons. Abû Hafs Omar abdicated soon after, leaving all the power to his brother Yûsuf. The people then took the oath of fidelity to the latter, and this nomination was universally approved of. Yûsuf was of a fair complexion, inclined to red; his hair was very dark, his visage round, his mouth wide, his eyes large, his stature somewhat above the ordinary size, his voice clear and mild, and his language elegant. He conversed well and was highly agreeable in company. No one knew better than he how the (ancient) Arabs expressed their thoughts, and none surpassed him in the knowledge of the battle-days of the Arab tribes, both before and after the promulgation of Islamism. He applied attentively to these studies and had frequent conferences with the learned men of Seville whilst he acted as governor of that city. It is stated that he knew by heart the Sahih of al-Bukhari (vol. II. p. 594). He possessed in a high degree the sentiments of a king, being noble-minded, beneficent and generous. Under his reign, the people acquired great wealth. He knew by heart the noble Koran and possessed some knowledge of jurisprudence. Having then formed the wish of studying philosophy, he began by the science of medicine and collected a great quantity of works on philosophy. Abû Bakr Muhammad Ibn Tufail (9), a man learned in these matters, was his frequent companion. Ibn Tufail possessed a solid acquaintance with all the branches of philosophy and had studied under a number of persons versed in that science, Abû Bakr Ibn as-Sáigh, surnamed Ibn Bâjja (Avempace) (vol. III, p. 130), for instance, and others. He composed a great number of works and endeavoured seriously to reconcile the (revealed) law with philosophy. He was a man of varied information. Persons learned in every branch of knowledge came from all countries to see him (Yûsuf), and amongst them was Abû 'l-Walîd Muhammad Ibn Ahmad Ibn Muhammad Ibn Rushd (Averroes) (10), who was a native of Spain. When Yûsuf had consolidated his authority and obtained possession of the provinces which Ibn Mardanish possessed in Spain, he set out from Seville with the intention of invading the states of Alphonso, which also were in Spain. He halted before a city called Webda (*Huete*) and blockaded it during some months, so that the garrison were reduced to great extremities. As they suffered very much from want of water, they sent to him and offered to surrender the place provided that he spared their lives. This proposal he rejected. The besieged were still suffering from thirst when, one night, a great noise and loud cries were heard proceeding from their quarter: they had all assembled to pray God (*for rain*), and then so heavy a shower fell that all their cisterns were filled (11). Their thirst being thus allayed, they were enabled to resist the Moslims. Yûsuf then left them and returned to Seville after making with them a truce of seven years. The annual taxes of Seville, amounting to one hundred and fifty mule-loads of money, were paid in to him regularly, over and above those which he received from the other provinces of Spain and from Maghrib. In the year 579 (A. D. 1183-4) he set out against the enemy with an immense army and, having crossed over to Spain, he stopped at Seville, according to his usual custom, and completed the equipment of his troops. He then departed for Santarem, a town in Western Andalus, small, but of great strength and well fortified. He blockaded it closely, but was unable to take it. The rainy season then set in, and the Moslims began to suffer from cold and to fear that the river would swell so as to become impassable, and prevent them from receiving provisions. Yûsuf, being advised to return to Seville and come back to Santarem when the weather got fine, accepted this counsel and said : " To-morrow, please " God! we shall decamp." These words were not made public because the conference had taken place in his privy council. The first who struck his tents and departed was the *khatîb* (*preacher*) Abû 'l-Hasan Ali Ibn Abd Allah Ibn Abd ar-Rahmân al-Mâlaki (*a native of Malaga*), who was a man of learning and talent. When the army saw that he was decamping, they did the same, being convinced that a person holding so high a place in the empire as he, knew all the secrets of government. The greater part of the army crossed the river during the night, in order to avoid the press and reach good quarters. None of the troops remained except those which were near the tents of the emir Yûsuf Ibn Abd al-Mûmin, and he had no idea of what had taken place. When the Christians (*Rûm*) saw that the army had passed the river and learned from their spies what was the intention of the emir Yûsuf and his companions, they took the opportunity of sallying out and reaching the place where he was. They slew, at the entrance of his tent, a great

number of officers holding a high rank in the army and reached Yûsuf, on whom
they inflicted a mortal wound, under the navel. The Moslims then rallied and
bet off the enemy. The emir Yûsuf was placed in a litter and carried across the
river; during two nights he was transported thus, but, on the third, he died. When
the corpse arrived at Seville, it was embalmed, placed in a coffin and carried to
Tin-Mall. It was there buried, near the tombs of Abd al-Mûmin and the Mahdi,
Muhammad Ibn Tûmart. Yûsuf died on Saturday, the 7th of Rajab, 580 (14th Oct.
A. D. 1184). Some months before his death he often repeated the following verse :

The succession of days and nights has rolled up that which I unfolded (*the tissue of my life*),
and the fair large-eyed maids know me no longer.

His son Abû Yûsuf Yakûb took the supreme command, having been solemnly
proclaimed, in the lifetime of his father, as successor to the throne. Some say,
however, that the great chiefs of the empire agreed on placing him at their head,
subsequently to his father's death. God knows best! —There was a literary scholar
named Abû 'l-Abbâs Ahmad Ibn Abd as-Salâm al-Gûrâwi (12) ; — Gârâya is the
name of a Berber tribe, the camp-stations of which were in the neighbourhood of Fez.
Some say that the name of this tribe was Jardâwa and that the letter J was replaced
by a G, so that it became Gardâwa; they add that the relative adjective derived from
it takes the forms of Jardâwi and Gârdâwi. — This learned man knew by heart an
immense quantity of poetry, both ancient and modern; in that kind of knowledge
he held the highest rank and was therefore admitted into the society, not only of
Abd al-Mûmin, but of Yûsuf, that prince's son, and of Yakûb, his grandson. He
drew up on the plan of Abû Tammâm's *Hamâsa* (vol. I. p. 348) a compilation of
pieces in verse on every subject; to this work he gave the title of *Safwa tal-Adab
wa Dîwân al-Arab* (*the quintessence of literature and the Archives of the Arabs*).
This work has obtained general circulation and is, for the people of the West
(*Maghrib*), what the *Hamâsa* is for those of the East. My object in speaking of this
accomplished scholar is to mention that he uttered many amusing and witty sayings
which were much admired by literary men, and that one of the anecdotes told of
him was the following : He went one day to the door of the emir Yûsuf and there
met the physician Saîd al-Ghomâri. — *Ghomdri* means *belonging to the Ghomâra*,
who are a Berber tribe. — Yûsuf then said to one of his servants : " See if any of

" my society are at the door. " The man went out and, on coming back, answered :
" Ahmad al-Gûrâwi is there and Saïd al-Ghomâri. " — " There, " exclaimed the
emir Yûsuf, " is one of the wonders of the world : a poet belonging to the tribe of
" Gûrâwa and a physician belonging to that of Ghomâra ! " When this was told to
al-Gûrâwi, he said : " The emir cites us as extraordinary examples, but has forgotten
" his own origin ; by Allah ! a khalif from the tribe of Kûmiya, is still more
" extraordinary ! " When this was related to the emir Yûsuf, he said : " I will punish
" him by shewing him indulgence and forgiveness ; that will suffice to prove that
" his (unfavorable) opinion respecting me is ill-founded. " — One of the poems
composed by al-Gûrâwi in praise of the emir Yûsuf contains a very original thought ;
here is the passage :

> The imâm (khalif) is the physician who has cared the ailments, both exterior and interior,
> of all mankind. He sustains the world and the world sustains him ; thus the soul sustains (the
> body) and is sustained (by it).

In the following lines he satirized the people of Fez, a city in Maghrib, which lies
between Ceuta and Morocco :

> Ignominy roamed over the world like an outcast, and wandered through all the countries of
> God's earth, both in the East and in the West. But, when it arrived at Fez and met with the
> inhabitants, they said to it : " Welcome ! heartily welcome ! "

A quantity of excellent poetry of all kinds was composed by him. He died at an
advanced age, having passed his eightieth year. His death took place towards the
end of the emir Yakûb Ibn Yûsuf's reign. For the year in which that
sovereign died, see his biographical notice in this work. The poet al-Gûrâwi persevered till the last in composing eulogies on the emir Abd al-Mûmin Ibn Ali and
on that prince's sons. — Shantarîn (Santarem) is a town in Western Andalus. Ibn
Haukal (13) says, in his Kitâb al-Masâlik wa 'l-Mamâlik : " Ambergris is cast on
" shore there, a circumstance not known to take place in any other European
" country on the borders of that sea. Some ambergris is thrown up on the shores
" of Syria. At a certain time of the year they find at Santarem an animal (the
" pinna marina) which rubs itself on the rocks in the sea and lets fall from its body
" a sort of wool (byssus) as soft as silk and of a gold colour. They collect enough
" of this substance to be spun into threads and woven into a kind of versicolor cloth.

" The Omaiyide sovereigns of Spain engross it all for themselves, so that it is neither
" exported nor offered for sale.   A garment made of it is worth more than one thou-
" sand pieces of gold, it is so rare and so beautiful. "—A native of Andalus, who was
a man of merit, told me that he saw a piece of this stuff, and he endeavoured to
describe it but could not find words to do so; he concluded by saying : " It is finer
" and more delicate than a cobweb; glory be to God whose power is so great, whose
" wisdom so subtile and whose works so good!   See how he favours specially each
" place with some marvellous thing!   Glory be to him!   How well Abû Nawâs (14)
" expressed himself when he said :

" Every object is a sign of his glory and indicates that he is the only (God). "

(1) According to al-Makkari, Târaf had with him ten thousand horse when he landed in Spain.

(2) This is a mistake ; Muhammad Ibn Mardanish died in Murcia, during the siege of that city by the
Almohades. — (Ibn Khaldûn's Histoire des Berbers, t. II, p. 200.)

(3) It was Hilâl, the son of Ibn Mardanish, who, with his brothers and relatives, surrendered to the Almohades.— (Ibn Khaldûn.)

(4) The life of al-Fayûmi will be found in this volume.

(5) Abû Jaafar al-Bisri was highly distinguished as a poet. His impiety, debauchery and satirical disposition gave such scandal that he was expelled from Majorca by Nâsir ad-Daula Mubashshar, who reigned
over the Balearic Islands after the death of Majâhid, king of Denia.   It is well known that Majâhid died
A. H. 436 (A. A. 1044).

(6) Ibn Khallikân derives Mardanish from morels; an absurd supposition, but worthy of remark as it shows
that the vowel-sign fat'ha was pronounced e.   Mardanish is the exact Arabic transcription of the Latin name
Martinez.   This family was of Christian descent.

(7) This Abd ar-Rahmân was the fourth omaiyide sovereign of Spain.

(8) The edition of Bûlâk reads al-Moallim in place of al-ilm. — All that follows is a later addition made
by the author.   The information which it contains respecting the emir Târaf is much more correct and satisfactory than that which he has just given.   None of our manuscripts contains this long extract, but it is to
be found in the edition of Bûlâk and that of Mr Wüstenfeld.   The text in both editions is not always
correct.

(9) Abû Bakr Muhammad Ibn Abd al-Malik Ibn at-Tufail al-Kaisi, a celebrated Spanish philosopher, was
of Arabic descent, as the progenitor of his family belonged to the tribe of Kais.   He was born at Gaudix, acquired great reputation as a mathematician, a physician and a philosopher.   He entered into the service of
the Almohade sultan Abû Yakûb Yûsuf, the son of Abd al-Mûmin, and died in the city of Morocco, A. D.
1185 (A. H. 581-2).   His philosophical romance Hai Ibn Yokdân was published at Oxford in 1671, by the
learned orientalist Edward Pocock, under the title of Philosophus autodidactus, sive epistola Ebn Tofail de
Hai ebn Yokdhan.   For a excellent article on Ibn Tufail and his works see Mr Munk's Mélanges de philoso-
phie arabe et juive.

(10) The celebrated philosopher, Abû 'l-Walîd Muhammad Ibn Roshd (Averroes) was born at Cordova A. H. 510 (A. D. 1126). He acted for some as chief Kâdi of all Moslim Spain. Towards the year 548 (A. D. 1153-75) he was nominated kâdi of Seville. He went to the city of Morocco a number of times and there met with the Almohade sultan Abû Yakûb Yûsef. Yakûb al-Mansûr, the son and successor of that sovereign, treated him with high favour. Ibn Roshd died in the city of Morocco, in the month of Safar, 595 (December, A. D. 1198); his corpse was transported to Cordova and there interred. See Mr Munk's *Mélanges*, etc., and Mr Renan's work entitled *Averroès et l'averroïsme* (in-8°, Paris, 1861).

(11) This event is mentioned also by the Christian historians.

(12) Various readings : *Al-Kârdai*, Bûlâk; *al-Kârdi*, Wüstenfeld. In Hajji Khalîfa's bibliographical dictionary, the name is written *al-Kurdai*.

(13) Abû 'l-Kâsim Muhammad Ibn Haukal, the author of one of those numerous geographical works which are designated by the title of *al-Masâlik wa 'l-Mamâlik* (routes and realms), belonged to a Baghdad family. He left his native place, A. H. 331 (A. D. 942-3), travelled over the greater part of the countries occupied by the Moslims; returned home in the year 356 (A. D. 968-9); was in Mauritania the following year and terminated the narrative of his travels towards the close of the year 366 (A. D. 977). Some chapters of this instructive work have been published in Europe. Professor Dozy says in his *Histoire des musulmans d'Espagne*, tome III, pages 17, 151, that Ibn Haukal was one of those spies who were employed by the Fatimide government to explore the state of the neighbouring countries. The date of this traveller's death is not known. For other information see the preface to Uylenbroek's *Iracae Persiae Descriptio*; an article of Mr de Slane in the *Journal asiatique* of 1842, and Mr Reinaud's introduction to his translation of Abû 'l-Fedâ's Geography, page LXXXII.

(14) See vol. I, p. 391. According to a marginal note in the Bûlâk edition, we should read *Abû 'l-Edheja*; see vol. I, p. 398.

THE SULTAN SALAH AD-DIN (SALADIN).

Abû 'l-Muzaffar Yûsuf, the son of Aiyûb, the son of Shâdi, bore the titles of Al-Malik an-Nâsir Salâh ad-Dîn (the helping prince, welfare of religion) and reigned over Egypt, the provinces of Syria, those of Irâk and those of Yemen. In this work we have noticed his father Aiyûb (vol. I. p. 243), a number of his sons, his uncle Asad ad-Dîn Shirkûh (vol. I. p. 626), his brother al-Malik al-Aâdil Abû Bakr Muhammad (vol. III. p. 235) and other members of the family. Salâh ad-Dîn was the central (and finest) pearl of that (brilliant) necklace, and his renown is so great that we need not descant upon it. Historians agree in stating that his father and family belonged to Duwîn (Tovin, in Armenia), which is a small town, situated at the farther extremity of Adarbaijân, in the direction of Arrân, and of the country of the Kurj (*the Georgians*). They (*Salâh ad-Dîn's family*) were Kurds and belonged to the tribe of *Rawâdiya*, which is a branch of the great tribe called *al-Haddâniya*. I was informed by a legist who was a native of Duwin and who never said any thing of which he was not certain, that, near the gate of that town lies a village called *Ajdânakân*, all the inhabitants of which are Rawâdiya Kurds, and that Aiyûb, the father of Salâh ad-Dîn, was born there. Shâdi (said he), went to Baghdad with his two sons, Asad ad-Dîn Shirkûh and Najm ad-Dîn Aiyûb, and from thence proceeded to Tikrît, where they settled. Shâdi died there, and his tomb with a cupola over it, is within the city. — I often endeavoured to trace up their genealogy, but could find no person able to tell me the names of any of their ancestors anterior to Shâdi. I read over a great number of title-deeds and instruments establishing pious foundations, which had been drawn up in the names of Shirkûh and of Aiyûb, but, in those documents, I found no other indication than Shirkûh, the son of Shâdi, and Aiyûb, the son of Shâdi. An eminent member of the (*Aiyûbide*) family informed me that Shâdi was the son of Marwân, and so it is stated by me in the lives of Aiyûb and Shirkûh. I saw (*however*) a roll which had been drawn up by al-Hasan Ibn Gharib Ibn Imrân al-Harasi (*a native of Haras in Egypt*), and which contained the following genealogy (1) : " Aiyûb, the " son of Shâdi, the son of Marwân, the son of Abû Ali, the son of Antara, the son " of al-Hasan, the son of Ali, the son of Ahmad, the son of Abû Ali, the son of " Abd al-Aziz, the son of Hudba, the son of al-Hassin, the son of al-Harith, the " son of Sinân, the son of Amr, the son of Murra, the son of Aûf, the son of Osâma, " the son of Nabhesh, the son of al-Harith Sâhib al-Hamâla, the son of Aûf, the " son of Ibn Abi Hâritha, the son of Murra, the son of Nushba, the son of Ghaiz, the " son of Murra, the son of Aûf, the son of Saad, the son of Dubyân, the son of Daghîd, " the son of Baith, the son of Ghatafân, the son of Saad, the son of Kais, the son of " Ailân, the son of al-Yâs, the son of Modar, the son of Nizâr, the son of Maadd, the " son of Adnân. " — From Adnân the writer traces the genealogy up to Adam. He then adds : " The Ali here mentioned as being the son of Ahmad Ibn Abi Ali Ibn Abd " al-Aziz, bore the surname of al-Khorâsâni and was one of those persons in whose " honour verses were composed by al-Mutanabbi (vol. I. p. 102). It is of him that " the poet speaks in the following verse, taken from one of his *kasidas* :

     " The sky is choked with dust when the powerful chief, Ali Ibn Ahmad, takes the field.

" As for al-Harith, the son of Aûf Ibn Abi Hâritha and surnamed *Sâhib al-Ha-*
" *mâla (the payer of the price of blood).* it was he who took upon himself the pay-
" ment of all the blood which had been shed in the feud between the tribes of Abs
" and Dubyân (2). Khârija Ibn Sinân, the brother of Harem Ibn Sinân (3), shared
" with him in doing this act of generosity. It was of them that Zuhair Ibn Abi
" Sulma al-Mazini (*the author of the Moallaka),* said, in one of his *kasîdas :*

" The rich among them feel bound to oblige those who apply to them (*for aid*), and even
" their poor are generous and prodigal. Can any other plant but the Indian cane produce fit
" shafts for spears? Do date-trees ever flourish except in a proper soil?

" This document was presented by the author to al-Malik al-Muazzam Sharaf ad-
" Dîn Isa (*vol. II.* p. 428), the son of al-Malik al-Aâdil (*vol. III.* p. 235) and sove-
" reign of Damascus. That prince and his son, al-Malik an-Nâsir Salâh ad-Dîn
" Abû 'l-Muzaffar Dâwûd, read it aloud (*and learned it by heart)* under the direction
" of him who drew it up, after which, they received from him certificates to that
" effect. This was towards the end of the month of Rajab, 619 (beginning of Sep-
" tember, A. D. 1222)." End of the extract made by me from that roll.— In the
History of Aleppo composed by the *kâdi* Kamâl ad-Dîn Abû 'l-Kâsim Omar Ibn
Ahmad, a native of Aleppo and generally known by the surname of Ibn al-Adîm
(p. 334 *of this vol.*), mention is made of the differences which occur in the genealogies
of the Aiyûbide family, after which, the author says : " Al-Moizz Ismaîl, the son of
" Saif al-Islâm Ibn Aiyûb and king of Yemen, pretended to draw his descent from
" the Omaiyides and, on that, he founded claims to the khalifate." (4) — I heard
our professor the *kâdi* Bahâ ad-Dîn, surnamed Ibn Shaddâd (*page 417 of this vol.*),
relate that the sultan Salâh ad-Dîn rejected that (*genealogy*) and declared that it had
not the least foundation. — Our professor Izz ad-Dîn Ibn al-Athîr's lesser historical
work, that which treats of the *Atâbek* sovereigns of Mosul, contains a chapter in
which is given an account of Asad ad-Dîn Shîrkûh and his journey to Egypt. We
there read as follows : " Asad ad Dîn Shîrkûh and Najm ad-Dîn Aiyûb, who was the
" eldest of Shâdi's sons, were natives of the town of Duwîn and drew their origin
" from the Kurdish tribe called ar-Rawâdiya. Having gone to Irâk, they entered
" into the service of Mujâhid ad-Dîn Bihrûz Ibn Abd Allah al-Ghiâthi, who was then
" *shîhna* (or *governor)* of that country." — I may here observe that this Mujâhid
ad-Dîn was a Greek slave and of a fair complexion ; he acted as *shîhna* of Irâk in the

name of the Seljúkide sultan Masûd Ibn Muhammad Ghiâth ad-Dîn, the same of
whom we have given an account (vol. *III.* p. 355); we have spoken also of his father (vol. *III.* p. 232) and other members of the same family. Bihrûz was a high-
minded man, fond of constructing great edifices and zealous in promoting the welfare of the country. He was noble-hearted, patient under every change and
vicissitude of fortune, aspiring after greatness and renewing his endeavours as often
as they failed. Tikrit had been granted to him as an appanage. He had been in
the service of the sultan Muhammad, the father of the Masûd just-mentioned. A
ribât (a *caravanseral*, or perhaps a *convent of dervishes*) was founded by him at Baghdad and richly endowed. His death took place on Wednesday, the 23rd of Rajab,
540 (9th Jaunary, A. D. 1146). *Bihrûz* is a Persian name and signifies *dies bonus*,
the terms being inverted conformably to the genius of the Persian tongue. —
" Mujáhid ad-Din," says Ibn al-Athír, " having remarked the intelligence, sound
" judgment and good conduct of Aiyûb, nominated him *dizdár* of Tikrit (*which he*
" *could well do*) as that city belonged to him."— I must here observe that *dizdár* (5)
is a persian title and means *keeper of the castle*, that is to say, its governor. *Diz* in
Persian means *castle* and *dár* signifies *keeper.*—(*Ibn al-Athír continues thus*) : " He
" (Aiyûb) went there (*to Tikrit*) with his brother Asad ad-Dín. When the *atábek*
" and martyr (6) Imâd ad-Dín Zinki was defeated in Irâk by Karâja ; "— I shall
give here a summary account of that celebrated battle : Masûd Ibn Muhammad Ibn
Malak Shâh, the Seljûkide, marched against Baghdad with Imâd ad-Dín Zinki, lord
of Mosul; their intention being to lay siege to that city. The *imâm* (*khalif*)
al-Mustarshid, who was reigning there, called to his assistance Karâja as-Sâki, whose
real name was Bers and who was then governor of Fars and Khûsistân. Karâja set
out to help him, attacked unawares and routed the army of the two princes, who had
to seek for safety in flight. He (*Ibn al-Athír*) says, in his History of the Seljûkides,
that the battle was fought near Tikrit, on Thursday the 12th of the latter Rabî, 526 (2nd
March, A. D. 1132). Osâma Ibn Munkid, a chief of whom we have given an account
(vol. *I.* p. 177), says, in the work wherein he treats of different countries and of the
princes who were his contemporaries, that he was present at that battle with Zinki
and that it took place on the date just indicated. This he mentions in two places:
first, in his article on Arbela, and then in the article on Tikrit. Let us return to
our subject : " Zinki," says Ibn al-Athír, " arrived at Tikrit, and Najm ad-Dín
" Aiyûb rendered him a good service by letting him have boats, in order to pass the

" river. He succeeded in crossing and was followed by his companions, to whom
" Najm ad-Din had shown great kindness and furnished provisions. Dihrûz, being
" informed of his conduct, sent to him a letter of blame, in which he said : ' You
" ' had our enemy in your power; why then did you treat him so well and let him
" ' escape? ' Some time after, Asad ad-Din Shirkûh had a dispute with a man in
" Tikrit and killed him. On this, Mujâhid ad-Din (Dihrûz) sent a person to expel
" them both from that city. They then went to join Imâd ad-Din (Zinki);"—who
was at that time sovereign of Mosul. — " Imâd ad-Din received them both in the
" kindest manner and, to acknowledge the service which they had rendered him,
" he settled on them a large appanage and admitted them into his army. When
" he took Baalbek, he appointed Najm ad-Din to act as dizdâr of that place. After
" the murder of Zinki, " — we have spoken of that event in his biographical notice
(vol. 1. p. 539) — " he (Najm ad-Din) was besieged by the army of Damascus; " —
the sovereign of that city was Mujîr ad-Din Abek (vol. 1. p. 275), the son of Muhammad Ibn Bûri and the grandson of the atâbek Zahir ad-Din Toghtikin.
It was he from whom Nûr ad-Din Mahmûd, the son of Zinki, took the city of Damascus after a siege. Our professor Ibn al-Athir continues thus : " Najm ad-Din
" Aiyûb then sent to Saif ad-Din Ghâzi, the son of Zinki, who had succeeded to his
" father in the government of Mosul, and, in this dispatch, he represented to him
" the state of affairs and requested that a body of troops might be sent to assist him
" in forcing the sovereign of Damascus to retire. Saif ad-Din, being then in the
" commencement of his reign, was endeavouring to live on good terms with the
" neighbouring princes and had not sufficient leisure to mind this application. The
" garrison of Baalbek being at length reduced to great distress, Najm ad-Din, ob-
" serving how matters stood and fearing that the place might be taken by storm,
" offered to surrender provided that a certain appanage which he pointed out were
" granted to him. The sovereign of Damascus accepted the condition and swore
" to fulfil it. (Najm ad-Din) Aiyûb then gave up the fortress, received the grants
" and privileges which he had stipulated and became one of the greatest emirs at
" the court of Damascus. His brother, Asad ad-Din Shirkûh entered into the ser-
" vice of Nûr ad-Din Mahmûd, after the death of Zinki, that prince's father. " — I
may here observe that Nûr ad-Din Mahmûd, the son of Zinki, was then sovereign of
Aleppo.— " As he (Nûr ad-Din) had already Shirkûh in his service before the death
" of Zinki, he took him into favour and settled on him an appanage. The bravery

" displayed by this officer in war and the acts of courage by which he made himself
" remarked and of which no other man was capable, fixed his sovereign's attention
" and obtained for him the gift of Emessa, ar-Rahaba and other cities, with his no-
" mination to the command of all the army." — I must here state that our professor, Ibn al-Athir, now passes to another subject and gives an account of Asad ad-
Din's expedition to Egypt and of the manner in which the authority was established
in that country. As this is not the fit place for such details, I shall relate the career
of Salih ad-Din, from the time of his entering into active life till he reached the
term of his existence. In this account, I shall include the history of the empire
which he founded and notice the height of power to which his family attained. In
our article on Asad ad-Din Shirkuh we gave some notions on that subject, but did not
enter into particulars, as it was our intention to treat that matter fully in the present
notice. — All historians agree in stating that the birth of Salah ad-Din took place in
the year 532 (A. D. 1137-8) and in the fortress of Tikrit, where his father and his
uncle were residing. It is evident that (the three) remained there only a short time
after that event, for we have already stated that, when Najm ad-Din and Asad ad-
Din left Tikrit, they went to Imad ad-Din Zinki, who received them honorably, took
them into favour, then made an unsuccessful attempt to take Damascus and proceeded to Baalbek of which he obtained possession on the 14th of Safar, 534 (10th October, A. D. 1139), after a siege of some months. We here admit the date given
by Osama Ibn Munkid in the work which treats of the provinces and their kings.
Abù Yala Hamza Ibn Asad, a native of Damascus and generally known by the surname of Ibn al-Kalanisi, says, in the historical work which he drew up as
a continuation of the chronicle composed by Abù 'l-Hasan Hilal Ibn as-Sabi (7), that
Imad ad-Din laid siege to Baalbek on Thursday, the 20th of Zù 'l-Hijja, 532 (29th
August, A. D. 1138); he then mentions, under the year 534, and towards the beginning of the chapter, that news was brought of Imad ad-Din's having succeeded in
putting the town and the citadel of Baalbek in a good state (of defense) and that he
had repaired the breaches which had been made in the fortifications. If (all) that
be exact, they (Aiyûb and Shirkûh) must have left Tikrit either before the close of the
year 532, that in which Salah ad-Din was born, or else in the year 533, for we
know that Zinki kept them with him at Mosul for some time, after which he besieged
Damascus and then took Baalbek, where he established Najm ad-Din Aiyûb as his
lieutenant. This appointment took place in the beginning of the year 534, as we

have already stated. It must therefore be concluded that they departed from
Tikrit on or about the epoch just mentioned. Since (writing what precedes) I met
with a member of their family and asked him if he knew at what time they left
Tikrit. His answer was: "I heard some of our people say that they left it on the
" night of Salâh ad-Dîn's birth, and that they augured ill of that circumstance, think-
" ing it a bad omen; but one of them said: ' Good may come of it, when you
" least expect it.' And such was really the case." Salâh ad-Dîn remained under
his father's care till he grew up. When Nûr ad-Dîn Mahmûd, the son of Imâd ad-
Dîn Zinki, obtained possession of Damascus, — for the date of this event, see his
life, — Najm ad-Dîn Aiyûb and his son Salâh ad-Dîn were attached to his service.
As every sign of good fortune was manifest in that youth's career, rising, as he did, by
his talent from one station to another, Nûr ad-Dîn took that into account and treated
him with great favour. It was from this sovereign that Salâh ad-Dîn learned to
walk in the path of righteousness, to act virtuously and to be zealous in waging war
against the infidels. (He remained with him) till he had to make preparations for
accompanying his uncle Shirkûh to Egypt. Of this expedition we shall speak farther on. — I read in a historical work composed by a native of Egypt that Shâwar
(vol. I. p. 608) was constrained to fly from that country by al-Malik al-Mansûr Abû
'l-Ashbâl ad-Dirghâm Ibn Aâmir Ibn Siwâr al-Lakhmi al-Mundiri, surnamed Fâris
al-Muslimîn (vol. I. p. 609) who, having become master of Egypt, took his place as
visir, according to the custom followed in such cases, and had killed Tai, Shâwar's
eldest son. The fugitive proceeded to Syria with the intention of asking assistance
from al-Malik al-Aâdil Nûr ad-Dîn Mahmûd, the son of Zinki. This occurred in the month of Ramadân, 558 (August, A. D. 1163). He arrived at Damascus
on the 23rd of Zû 'l-Kaada (23rd Oct. A. D. 1163). Nûr ad-Dîn sent him back
with a body of troops which he had placed under the orders of Asad ad-Dîn Shirkûh,
the son of Shâdi. Salâh ad-Dîn accompanied them, having been placed in the service of his uncle (Shirkûh), but he departed much against his will. Nûr ad-Dîn
sent off this expedition because he had two objects in view; in the first place, he
wished to oblige Shâwar for having applied to him and for coming to implore his
assistance; in the second, he was anxious to learn what was the state of affairs in
Egypt, having been informed that the armed force of the country was very weak
and that the utmost confusion prevailed there. He desired to know what was really
the case. Shirkûh, in whom he had great confidence from what he had remarked

of his bravery, his fidelity and his knowledge (of affairs), was charged to direct that expedition, and it was from him that his nephew, Salâh ad-Dîn, received the command of the vanguard.   They left Damascus with Shâwar in the month of the first Jumâda, 559 (March-April, A. D. 1164) and, in the month of Rajab (May-June), the same year, they arrived in Egypt and reduced it under their authority.—Our professor, the kâdi Behâ ad-Dîn Ibn Shaddâd (page 417 of this vol.) says, in the work to which he gave the title of Sîra Salâh ad-Dîn (8), that they entered into Egypt on the 2nd of the latter Jumâda, 558 (8th May, A. D. 1163); the date previously indicated is, however, more correct, for the hâfiz Abû Tâhir as-Silafi (vol. I, p. 86) states, in his Mojam (9), that ad-Dirghâm Ibn Siwâr lost his life in the year 559.   Another author informs us, moreover, that he was killed on Friday, the 28th of the latter Jumâda.   Ad-Dirghâm met with his death near the mausoleum of as-Saiyida Nafîsa (col. III. p. 574), which edifice is situated between Old and New Cairo.   His head was cut off, placed on a pike and borne through the streets of the city; his body remained lying on the ground during three days and was (partly) eaten by dogs, but it was afterwards buried near the Birka tal-Fîl (the pond of the elephant), and a dome was erected over the tomb.   I may here add that the dome still exists and that it is situated below al-Kabsh (10), which edifice has been lately rebuilt.   I saw in that funeral chapel a company of Juwâliki dervishes, who were residing there.   Ad-Dirghâm's death is placed by some in Rajab, 559, but all agree in stating that it occurred immediately after the entry (of Nûr ad-Dîn's) troops into Egypt.   It is therefore impossible that they could have arrived there in the year 558, because ad-Dirghâm's death occurred, by all accounts, in the year 559 and immediately after the arrival of Asad ad-Dîn's army.   The hâfiz as-Silafi was well informed on that point; he was in Egypt when they arrived and was more careful than any other man in marking with precision facts of that kind; such was, indeed, the branch of science which he specially cultivated, and his information was always better grounded than that of any one else. — Asad ad-Dîn Shîrkûh became master of Egypt as soon as he arrived there, and ad-Dirghâm then lost his life.   Shâwar, having thus attained his object, resumed his former post, established his power on a solid basis and took again the direction of public affairs.   He then acted perfidiously towards Asad ad-Dîn and, at his request, the Franks gave him their assistance and besieged that chief in Bilbais. Asad ad-Dîn, having now studied the state of the country, perceived that it was a kingdom without (fit) men and that the whole administration was directed by mere caprice and folly. He therefore conceived hopes of getting it into his possession and, on the 24th of Zû 'l-Hijja, 559 (12th November, A. D. 1164), he returned to Syria. Our professor, Ibn Shaddâd (Bahâ ad-Dîn, the historian of Salâh ad-Dîn), indicates the 27th of Zû 'l-Hijja, 558, as the date of that event, because he founded his opinion on what he had previously advanced in assigning the date of 558 to their entry into Egypt. — Asad ad-Dîn Shirkûh remained for some time in Syria, reflecting on the means of obtaining another mission into Egypt and flattering his hopes with the prospect of founding there an empire for himself. He thus continued, till the year 562 (A. D. 1166), laying the basis of his plan (and concerting) with Nûr ad-Dîn. Shâwar got notice of his proceedings and was filled with apprehension on learning that he aspired to the possession of the country. Being at length convinced that Asad ad-Dîn meant to invade it, he wrote to the Franks and consented to give them a solid footing in Egypt, provided that they came to his assistance and helped to exterminate his foes. Nûr ad-Dîn and Asad ad-Dîn, being informed of this correspondence and of the engagements taken by the two parties, feared that the Franks might obtain possession of Egypt and be thus enabled to subdue the (neighbouring) countries. An army was therefore placed by Nûr ad-Dîn under the orders of Asad ad-Dîn (Shirkâh) and sent off to Egypt. Salâh ad-Dîn, being attached to the service of his uncle Asad ad-Dîn, accompanied the troops. Their departure from Syria took place in the month of the first Rabî, 562 (Dec.-Jan. A. D. 1166-7), and their arrival in Egypt coincided with that of the Franks. Shâwar and all the Egyptians united with the Franks against Asad ad-Dîn, and a great number of encounters and fierce conflicts took place before the evacuation of the country by the Franks. Asad ad-Dîn then returned to Syria. The cause which brought about the retreat of the Franks was the invasion of their territory by the troops of Nûr ad-Dîn and the loss of al-Munaidhera (11), which that prince took from them in the month of Rajab, 562 (April-May, A. D. 1167). Asad ad-Dîn returned to Syria because his army had been much weakened in its encounters with the Franks and the Egyptians; the misery to which it was reduced and the dangers which it had incurred contributed greatly to his retreat. He did not, however, depart till had he concluded a peace with the Franks and obtained from them the engagement that they would evacuate Egypt and return to their own territory (in Syria) before the end of the year. To his great desire of getting possession of Egypt was now joined the extreme apprehension of seeing it fall into the hands of the Franks. He knew that they had examined into the state

of the country just as he had done and that they were now as well acquainted with it
as he himself.   He remained in Syria, ruminating over these matters with a troubled heart, whilst fate was leading him, without his knowledge, to a thing (*a throne*)
which was destined for another.   It was in the month of Zù 'l-Kaada of the year just
mentioned (August-Sept. A. D. 1167) that he returned to Syria, or, by another account, on the 15th of Shauwâl (4th August); God knows best! — I found, amongst
some rough notes in my own handwriting, a piece of information which I here give
without knowing from what source I derived it : " Asad ad-Din, being ambitious of
" getting Egypt into his possession, set out for that country in the year 562 (A. D.
" 1166) and followed the road which passes through Ouâdi 'l-Ghizlân (*gazelle valley*).
" He then appeared before [*the town of*] Ilfih and fought, in the neighbourhood
" of Ushmûnain, the battle of al-Bâbain.   Salâh ad-Dîn went to Alexandria
" and there fortified himself.   In the month of the latter Jumâda, 562 (March-
" April, A. D. 1167) he had to sustain a siege against Shâwar.   Asad ad-Dîn then
" left [*the province of*] Saîd and proceeded to Bilbais, where he struck up a peace
" with the Egyptians.   On this, they escorted to him Salâh ad-Dîn, who returned
" with him to Syria.   After that, Asad ad-Dîn invaded Egypt for the third time."
— Our professor, Ibn Shaddâd, says : " The cause of that was the conduct of the
" Franks who had assembled all their troops, horse and foot, and were marching
" towards Egypt.   The hope of getting it into their possession had induced them to
" break the engagements which they had taken with the Egyptians and Asad ad-
" Dîn.   When the latter and Nûr ad-Dîn heard of this proceeding, they were unable
" to support with patience such perfidy, and hastened to invade that country.
" Nûr ad-Dîn, being unable to accompany the expedition, furnished money and
" men, so great was his apprehension of seeing Egypt fall into the hands of the
" Franks.   (*He was prevented from going there*) because his attention had been un-
" expectedly drawn towards Mosul, in consequence of the death of Ali Ibn Bek-
" tikîn." — I may here observe that this prince is the same who bore title of Zain
ad-Dîn and who was the father of the sultan Musaffar ad-Dîn Kôkubûri, lord of Arbela, and that we have spoken of him in the life of his son (*vol. II. p. 535*). —
" Here," says Ibn Shaddâd, " is what happened : He (*Ali Ibn Bektikîn*) died in the
" month of Zù 'l-Hijja (12), 563 (Sept.-Oct. A. D. 1168).   He (*had*) delivered all
" his fortresses to Kutb ad-Dîn (*Maudûd*) the atâbek (*vol. III. p. 458*), with the ex-
" ception of Arbela, because that place had been given to him by the atâbek Zinki

" (vol. I. p. 539). As for Asad ad-Dîn (Shîrkûh, he contributed to this expedition
" by paying the rest of the expense) out of his own fortune and by accompanying it
" in person, with his brothers, his relations and his own men (13). The sultan
" Salâh ad-Dîn, may God rest his soul! said to me : ' I was the most unwilling of
" ' men to make a campaign at that time, and it was not by my own choice that I
" ' set out with my uncle. Therein was exemplified the truth of God's saying : You
" ' may perhaps dislike a thing which is for your good. (Koran, sur. 2, verse 213).'
" When Shâwar was informed that the Franks were invading Egypt with the inten-
" tion which has been mentioned, he sent to Asad ad-Dîn Shîrkûh a dispatch in
" which he begged of him aid and assistance. He (Shîrkûh) set out immediately
" and reached Egypt in the month of the first Rabî, 564 (December, A. D. 1168).
" When the Franks were informed that his arrival was a thing concerted between
" him and the Egyptians, they retraced their steps and effected their retreat. Asad
" ad-Dîn remained in Egypt, and Shâwar went to visit him from time to time. He
" (Shâwar) had promised to indemnify him for all the sums spent on the
" troops, but he had not yet sent him any thing. Asad ad-Dîn had now laid his
" clutches upon Egypt ; he well knew that the Franks would seize on it if they found
" the opportunity and that Shâwar was trying to delude him and the Franks alter-
" nately; (besides which) the masters (14) of that country professed heretical doctrines,
" as was well known. Being convinced that there was no means of getting Egypt
" into his power as long as Shâwar was there, he at length decided on arresting him
" at one of the visits which he received from him. The emirs who had accompanied
" Asad ad-Dîn to Egypt used often to go and present their respects to Shâwar who,
" on his side, went sometimes to visit Asad ad-Dîn. On these occasions he rode
" out in state, drums beating, trumpets sounding and colours flying, according to the
" custom followed by Egyptian vizirs. As none of Asad ad-Dîn's party dared to
" lay their hands on him, it was the sultan Salâh ad-Dîn himself who did so. The
" manner in which things passed was this : when he (Shâwar) was coming to visit
" him, he (Salâh ad-Dîn) went forth on horseback to meet him, and then, as he was
" riding by his side, he seized him by the collar and ordered his own soldiers to fall
" on those of the vizir. The escort was put to flight and plundered, whilst Shâwar
" was led off to an isolated tent. Immediately after, a note from the Egyptians,
" demanding the prisoner's head, was brought by a servant attached to the private
" service (of their sovereign) (15). Such was the custom followed by that people

" with regard to their vizirs. Shawar's head was cut off and sent to them, and, in
" return, the pelisse of the vizirat was sent to Asad ad-Din. He put it on, set out
" and entered into the citadel (al-Kasr), where he was installed in the office of vizir.
" This took place on the 17th of the first Rabi, 564 (19th Dec. A. D. 1168). From
" that time he continued to rule with absolute sway, and Salah ad-Din obtained the
" direction of public affairs, so highly was he esteemed for his talents, his informa-
" tion, his sound judgment and his ability in governing. This continued till the
" 22nd of the latter Jumada, the same year (23rd March A. D. 1169), when Asad ad-
" Din ceased to live."—As I have already spoken of what befel him and of the manner of his death, I need repeat that account here; I may also say the same for the death
of Shawar. All that precedes here was extracted by me from what is related by our
professor Baha ed-Din Ibn Shaddad in his *Life of Salah ad-Din*. I took there what
was requisite for my purpose and passed over the rest. — I found among my rough
notes one which is in my own handwriting and which contains these indications :
" Asad ad-Din made his entry into Cairo on Wednesday, the 7th of the latter Rabi,
" 564 (8th Jan. A. D. 1169); al-Aadid Abd Allah the Obaidite, who was the last
" (*Fatimide*) sovereign of Egypt, went forth to meet him and arrayed him in a dress
" of honour. On Friday, the 9th of the same month, he (*Asad ad-Din*) went to
" the hall of state (*diwan*), took his seat at the side of al-Aadid, who (*again*) arrayed
" him in a dress of honour. (*Asad ad-Din*,) seeing that Shawar made to him great
" demonstrations of friendship, asked him for money in order to pay his troops, but
" was put off till another time. He then sent to Shawar the following message :
" ' In my army all hearts are turned against you because they are without pay ; so,
" ' when you go out, be on your guard against them.' Shawar attached no impor-
" tance to these words, but resolved on inviting Asad ad-Din and (*the officers of*) the
" Syrian army to a great feast, at which he intended to take them all prisoners.
" Asad ad-Din discovered his project, and Salah ad-Din made an agreement with
" Jurdik an-Nuri (*a client of Nur ad-Din's*) and with some other officers that they
" should kill Shawar. Asad ad-Din, to whom they mentioned their design, for-
" bade them to execute it. (*Soon after*), Shawar went to visit Asad ad-Din at the
" Syrian camp, which had been established on the bank of the Nile, near al-Maks,
" and, being informed that he (*Asad ad-Din*) had gone on a pious visit to the
" tomb of the imam as-Shafi, in the Karafa (*cemetery*), he said that he would go
" and meet him. They (*Salah ad-Din and his party*) joined him on the way and,

" as they were all riding together, Saláh ad-Dín and Júrdík (with the other conspi-
" rators) got around him, forced him off his horse and tied his hands behind his
" back. Those who were with the vizir took to flight. Shawar was now their pri-
" soner and, as they dared not take his life without Núr ad-Dín's authoriza-
" tion, they shut him up in a tent, under a strong guard. Al-Aádid then sent them
" the order to put him to death. They obeyed and, having placed his head on the
" point of a spear, they sent it to the Egyptian sovereign. This took place on Sa-
" turday, the 17th of the latter Rabí of the above-mentioned year (18th Jan.,
" A. D. 1169)."—According to another statement, Asad ad-Dín was not present at
this deed (16); on the contrary, when Shawar went to visit him, it was Saláh ad-
Dín and Júrdík, having with them some soldiers, who met him on the way. Each
of the two parties saluted the other and then, as they were riding together, the deed
was committed by these two (officers). God knows best! (17) Immediately after
the death of Shawar, al-Aádid sent for Asad ad-Dín, who was then in the camp.
That chief, on entering into Cairo, saw such a crowd of common people that he felt
afraid; so, he said to them : " Our lord al-Aádid permits you to go and pillage
" the palace of Shawar." They immediately dispersed for that purpose and Asad
ad-Dín went in to al-Aádid, who received him politely, invested him with the robes
of the vizirship and conferred on him the titles of al-Malik al-Mansúr (the victorious
prince), Amír al-Juyúsh (commander in chief of the troops). Asad ad-Dín died soon
after, on Sunday the 22nd of the latter Jumáda of that year (23rd March, A. D. 1169).
His disorder was a suffocation (or quinsy). Some say that he died of a poisoned shirt
which they put on him whilst they were dressing him in the vizirial robes. He died
at Cairo and was buried in the palace of the vizirate, but the body was afterwards removed to the city of the Prophet (Medina). He held the place of vizir during two
months and five days. It is stated also that he went to visit al-Aádid for the first
time on Monday, the 19th of the latter Rabí of that year (20th January, A. D. 1169).
— In our article on Shawar and in that on Asad ad-Dín, some of the facts here related have been noticed ; if there be repetitions in this place, the cause is that we
have given a fuller account of things than before. In all that, our object was to
follow up the history of Saláh ad-Dín, indicate the degrees of rank through which he
passed and mark what happened to him from the beginning to the end of his career.
I preferred giving (here) that information in one continuous narrative, so that our discourse might not be interrupted by digressions. I shall now continue : Historians

state that the death of Asad ad-Dîn Shîrkûh consolidated the sultan Salâh ad-Dîn in his position at the head of affairs and completed the foundations of his future greatness. For him the state of things prospered gradually and assumed the fairest aspect; he was able to spend treasures, gain the hearts of men and, as a fit acknowledgment for the favours which God had granted him, he renounced the use of wine, and avoided all incitations to pleasure; putting on the tunic of energy and fortitude, he took a solid footing in the path of righteousness and continued, till his last day, in the practise of such works as brought him nearer and nearer unto God. Our professor, Ibn Shaddâd (*Bahâ ad-Dîn*) says: " I heard the following words from his own lips : " ' When God enabled me to acquire Egypt so easily, I knew that he meant (to " ' *help me to*) the conquest of Palestine; such was the thought which was impressed " ' upon my mind.' " As soon as he obtained the supreme command, he began to direct expeditions against the Franks and never ceased to launch plundering parties into the territories of al-Karak, Shaubek and elsewhere. The clouds of generosity and beneficence with which he overshadowed the people were such that their like had never been recorded in the annals of any other reign. All this he did, and yet he was only a visir in the service of the Fatemides; but he himself was a professor of the orthodox faith, a planter (*who established*) in that country doctors learned in the law, *sûfis* and religious men. People hastened to him from all quarters and came to him from every side (18). Never did he frustrate the hopes of those who applied to him and never was he without a visitor. This continued till the year 565 (1169). Nûr ad-Dîn, being informed that Salâh ad-Dîn had obtained the government of Egypt, took the city of Emessa from the lieutenants of Asad ad-Dîn. This was in the year 564. When the Franks learned what the Musulmans (*of Syria*) were doing (*in Egypt*) and heard that the authority of Salâh ad-Dîn had been fully established in that country, they felt that he, after acquiring such a force and such an empire, would come to conquer their own territory, ruin their abodes and tear up their establishments by the roots. They in consequence joined with the Greeks (*ar-Rûm*) and proceeded towards Egypt. As they meant to attack Damietta, they took with them the instruments of siege and all such provisions as might be required. The Franks of Syria, having learned this, took courage, seized by a stratagem on the castle of Akkâr which was occupied by the Musulmans, and got the governor into their power. This officer was one of Nûr ad-Dîn's mamlûks; he bore the name of Khotlokh and held the rank of *alam-dâr* (*standard-bearer of the sultan*). It was in the month of the latter Rabí, 565 (A. D. 1169-70), that this took place. When Núr ad-Dín learned that the Franks had appeared and were encamped before Damietta he resolved on giving them something else to occupy their attention and, in the month of Shabán (April-May) of the same year (A. D. 1170), he laid siege to al-Karak. The Franks of the Sáhil (Phœnicia) marched against him but, when he advanced to meet them, they did not await his arrival. News was then brought to him that Majd ad-Dín Ibn ad-Dáya was dead, — he died at Aleppo in the month of Ramadán, 565 (May-June, A. D. 1170). — His attention was in consequence turned towards that quarter because Ibn ad-Dáya acted there as executor of his orders. He therefore left the place where he was and returned to Syria. Being then informed that Aleppo and a great number of other cities had been ruined by an earthquake, on the 12th of Shauwál of that year (29th June A. D. 1170), he set out for Aleppo but, when he had got as far as Tell Dásher, news reached him that his brother Kutb ad-Dín had died at Mosul. On receiving this intelligence, he departed, the same night, for that city. This we have noticed in our article on that prince, whose name was Maudûd (vol. III. p. 459). When Saláh ad-Dín was informed that the Franks meant to attack Damietta, he equipped troops, filled that city with implements of war and promised to the inhabitants a reinforcement in case the enemy came to besiege them. Gifts and donations were distributed by him to a great amount, because he was now a vizir, acting with absolute power, whilst no one dared to control his orders. The Franks, having taken position before Damietta, directed against it a number of violent assaults, but he, may God have mercy on his soul! attacked them from without by means of flying parties, whilst the garrison fought against them from within. It was through his means and by his skilful measures that the Musulmans remained victorious. The besiegers, frustrated in their expectations, were obliged to decamp; their mangonels were burned, their (military) engines taken and a great number of their men slain. Saláh ad-Dín, having thus consolidated his power, sent to request of Núr ad-Dín that his father Najm ad-Dín Aiyûb should be allowed to join him: "My happiness" said he, "will thus be complete and "my adventure be similar to that of Yûsuf (Joseph) the faithful." In the month of the latter Jumáda, 565 (Feb.-March, A. D. 1170) he was joined by his father. — Such is the date assigned by Ibn Shaddád to the arrival of Aiyûb in Egypt, but the true one is that which we have mentioned in our article on that chief (vol. I. p. 245). — He (Saláh ad-Dín) received him with all due honour and respect, and offered to

resign to him the supreme command; but Aiyûb refused to accept it, saying : " My
" soul! God would not have chosen you to fill this place of authority, had you not
" been equal to the task. It is not right to change the object of fortune's favour."
He was then appointed by his son to the intendance of the treasury-stores and continued to hold the rank of a vizir till the death of al-Aâdid. — I must here observe
that the greater part of the foregoing information is extracted from Ibn Shaddâd's
History of Salâh ad-Dîn; the rest is derived from other sources. — Our professor,
the *hâfiz* Izz ad-Dîn Ibn al-Athîr, the same of whom we have made mention above,
gives, in his *History of the Atâbeks* the following account of the manner in which
Salâh ad-Dîn obtained the supreme command : " Some of the emirs whom Nûr
" ad-Dîn had sent to Egypt aspired to the command of the whole army and the
" possession of the vizirship." — This was subsequently to the death of Asad ad-
Dîn. — " One of them was the emir Aîn ad-Dawla al-Yârûki; another was Kutb ad-
" Dîn Khosrû Ibn Tallî, a nephew of Abû 'l-Haîja al-Hadbâni who, at one time,
" had been lord of Arbela." — The college at Cairo which is called *al-Madrasa tal-*
" *Kutbiya* was founded by this Kutb ad-Dîn. — " The third was Saif ad-Dîn Ali Ibn
" Ahmad al-Hakkâri, the same whose grandfather possessed the castles in the
" country of the Hakkâra Kurds." — He was generally known by the appellation of
al-Mashtûb (the scarred) and was the father of the same Imâd ad-Dîn Ahmad Ibn al-
Mashtûb whose life we have given in a separate article (vol. *I*. p. 162). — " The
" fourth was Shihâb ad-Dîn Mahmûd al-Hârimi, one of Salah ad-Dîn's maternal
" uncles. Each of these chiefs aimed at the supreme power and had prepared to
" seize on it by force. Al-Aâdid, the sovereign of Egypt, then sent to Salâh ad-
" Dîn, inviting him to come to the palace in order to receive his investiture as vizir
" and thus replace his uncle. What induced al-Aâdid to take this step, was his
" idea that Salâh ad-Dîn, being ill supported and having neither troops nor men
" to rely on, would have but little power in the exercise of his authority and would
" let himself be governed by the will of the sovereign, without daring to resist. He
" intended also to send an agent to the Syrian army for the purpose of gaining over
" a part of it and then sending the rest out of the country. He hoped, by this
" means to regain the mastery throughout all Egypt, which country he might then
" be able to protect against the Franks and against Nûr ad-Dîn, with the aid of the
" Syrian troops which had entered into his service. But here again was exempli-
" fied the fact indicated by the well-known saying : *I meant Amr, but God meant*

" *Khârija* (19)." — Of this proverbial expression, with which the learned are not
unacquainted, I shall give an account, if God so please, when I have terminated the
present article. Let us resume Ibn al-Athîr's recital : " Salâh ad-Dîn refused the
" offer, thinking himself unable to fill so elevated a place, but, yielding, at length,
" to the remonstrances of his father, he accepted it, much against his will : *Cer-*
" *tainly God will make (men) wonder at (seeing) people led to Paradise in chains (20).*
" On arriving at the palace, he was arrayed in the vizirial dress, which consisted in
" the *jubba* (robe), the turban and other objects; he then received the title of al-
" Malik an-Nâsir (*the helpful prince*), after which he retired to the palace of Asad
" ad-Dîn. There he remained for some time, without receiving the slightest mark
" of attention or any offer of service from the other emirs, who were hoping to ob-
" tain the power for themselves. The legist Dîâ ad-Dîn Isa al-Hakkâri, who staid
" with him, " — we have given a separate article (vol. *II.* p. 430) to this doctor, —
" then made advances to Saif ad-Dîn Ali Ibn Ahmad, and succeeded in gaining
" him over, by making him observe that the authority could not pass to him as
" long as Ain ad-Dawla, al-Hârimi and Ibn Tailî were living. He then went to
" Shibâb ad-Dîn al-Hârimi and said : ' There is Salâh ad-Dîn, your sister's son;
" ' what he possesses is yours, and now, as he has got the authority into his hands,
" ' be not the first to try and deprive him of it; never, in any case, will it come to
" ' you.' He did not discontinue his efforts till he induced him to appear before
" Salâh ad-Dîn and take the oath of fidelity. He then went to Kutb ad-Dîn and
" said : ' All the people now obey Salâh ad-Dîn; you and al-Yârûki are the only
" ' exceptions. In every case, that which should unite you to him is the reflexion
" ' that he (*like you*,) is a Kurd by origine and that the power should not be allowed
" ' to pass into the hands of the Turks.' At length, by magnificent promises and
" the offer of a larger appanage, he decided him on submitting to Salâh ad-Dîn.
" He then applied to Ain ad-Dawla tal-Yârûki, who was the principal chief among
" them and who possessed more troops than the others; but, on him he vainly em-
" ployed the charms of his (*discourse*) and the magic of his language. That chief
" declared positively that he would never serve under Salâh ad-Dîn, and then
" returned to Nûr ad-Dîn with some others. That sultan blamed him for leaving
" Egypt, but the fault was committed *in order that God might accomplish a thing*
" *which was (designed) to be done* (*Koran*, sur. 8, v. 43). Salah ad-Dîn's power
" was now established on a solid footing and his authority well consolidated.

" Acting as the lieutenant of al-Malik al-Aädil Nûr ad-Dîn, be had the *khotba* said in
" that prince's name throughout all the cities of Egypt; it was also in Nûr ad-Dîn's
" name that the agents of government fulfilled the duties of their office.   Nûr ad-
" Dîn, when writing to Salâh ad-Dîn, addressed him by the title *al-Amîr al-Isfah-
" salâr (the emir commander of the cavalry)* and signed his letters with the *aláma* (21)
" so as to avoid compromising the dignify of his name (*by subscribing it to missives*
" *of that kind).   His letters were never addressed to Salâh ad-Dîn himself but ran
" thus : ' The Amir Isfahsalar Salah ad-Dîn and all the other emirs in the Egyp-
" ' tian territory are hereby enjoined to do so and so.'   Salâh ad-Dîn gained the
" affection and the hearts of all men by lavishing on them the treasures heaped up
" by Asad ad-Dîn.   When al-Aädid was asked by him for money, he dare not re-
" fuse; having now become like the animal which dug up with its hoof the instru -
" ment of its death (22)." — Ibn al-Athîr says, in his greater historical work (23) :
" On examining the annals of the Moslim people, I perceived that, with regard to
" many of those chiefs who founded dynasties, the authority did not pass to their
" sons but to their collaterals.   Thus, in the early times of Islamism, Moawia Ibn
" Abi Sofyân was the first of his family who reigned, and the sovereignty passed
" from his posterity to his cousins of the Marwân family.   Some time after, ap-
" peared as-Saffâh, the first of the Abbasides who came to the throne; after him, the
" empire passed, not to his descendants but to those of his brother al-Mansûr.   At a
" later period, Nasr Ibn Ahmad, the first of the Samanides, founded an empire
" which passed to his brother Ismaïl Ibn Ahmad, in whose posterity it remained.
" Yakûb as-Saffâr was the first of his family who came to the throne, and the sove-
" reignty passed from him to his brother Amr, in whose posterity it continued.
" Such also was the case with Imâd ad-Dawla Ibn Buwaih: the authority passed
" from him to his brothers Rukn ad-Dawla and Moizz ad-Dawla.   After that came
" the Seljûkides, of whom the first sovereign was Toghrul Bek and who had for suc-
" cessors the descendants of his brother Dâwûd.   In the present case, we see
" that the supreme authority passed directly from Shirkûh to the son of his
" brother Najm ad-Dîn Aiyûb.   Were I not apprehensive of being led too far, I
" should mention a great number of other cases, similar to these.   The cause of
" that must be, I think, that when a man begins to found an empire, multitudes of
" lives are lost.   He then seizes on the (*conquered*) kingdom, but the hearts of those
" who were in it (*and had been dispossessed*) still remain attached to it.   God therefore

" excludes, for their sake, that conqueror's posterity from the throne and thus chastises
" him.—Salâh ad-Din then sent to Nûr ad-Din, requesting permission for his brothers
" to come and join him, but met with a refusal. ' No,' said the sultan, " I am afraid that
" ' one or other of them may oppose your measures and thus bring the state into con-
" ' fusion.' Learning, however, that the Franks had assembled with the intention of
" invading Egypt, he dispatched to that country a body of troops and, with them,
" the brothers of Salâh ad-Din. Amongst them was his elder brother, Shams ad-
" Dawla Tûrân Shâh Ibn Aiyûb, — the same to whom we have given a separate ar-
" ticle (vol. I. p. 284).—When he was on the point of setting out, Nûr ad-Din said
" to him : ' If, on going to Egypt, you mean to look upon your brother Yûsuf with
" ' the same eyes as when he was in your service, waiting on you whilst you re-
" ' mained seated, I advise you not to depart, for you would bring ruin on the
" ' country and I should be obliged to recal you and punish you as you deserved.
" ' But, if you go there to look upon him as the lord of Egypt and as my lieutenant,
" ' and to serve him as devotedly as you serve me, you may depart. Go then and
" ' be for him a firm support, an assistant in all his undertakings.' The other re-
" plied : ' I shall serve him and obey him, please God! in a manner which you will
" ' hear of (with satisfaction) ; ' and he behaved towards Salâh ad-Din as he said. "
— Some leaves farther on, Ibn al-Athir has a chapter on the fall of the Egyptian
dynasty and its replacement by the authority of the Abbasides, an event which took
place in the month of Muharram, 567 (Sept.-Oct. A. D. 1171). He there says :
" The name of al-Aâdid, sovereign of Egypt, then ceased to be mentioned in the
" khotba and was replaced by that of the imâm (khalif) al-Mustadi bi-Amr Illah, com-
" mander of the faithful. That change was effected in the following manner :
" when Salâh ad-Din had established his authority on a firm basis in Egypt and met
" no longer with any (chiefs) inclined to disobey him, al-Aâdid's influence was
" greatly diminished and not a man remained of all the Egyptian army. Nûr ad-
" Din then wrote to Salâh ad-Din, ordering him to suppress the khotba made for al-
" Aâdid and replace it by the khotba of the Abbasides. Salâh ad-Din hesitated to
" comply and excused his conduct by stating his fears lest that proceeding should
" excite a revolt among the people of Egypt who, being favorably inclined towards
" their old dynasty, would not consent to such a change. The sultan paid no atten-
" tion to this remonstrance and sent back such positive orders that Salâh ad-Din
" had no means of avoiding the task. Knowing that al-Aâdid was unwell, he con-

" sulted the emirs on the propriety of introducing the Abbaside *khotba*. Some of
" them approved and engaged to second him; others declared it dangerous, but the
" order of Nûr ad-Dîn was not to be disobeyed. A Persian named al-Amîr al-
" Aâlim, whom I often saw at Mosul, had just then arrived in Egypt. When he
" perceived their hesitation, he declared that he himself would be the first to say the
" (*Abbaside*) *khotba* and, on the first Friday of the month of Muharram, he got into
" the pulpit before the preacher, and offered up a prayer for al-Mustadi bi-Amr Illah.
" As no disapprobation was shown, Salâh ad-Dîn gave orders that, on the Friday
" following, the preachers (*attached to the mosques*) of Old and New Cairo should re-
" place the *khotba* for al-Aâdid by a *khotba* for al-Mustadi. This was done without
" provoking even the slightest opposition (24). He then sent to all the provinces of
" Egypt written orders to the same effect. As al-Aâdid was very ill, none of his fa-
" mily told him what had happened; ' If he recover, ' said they, ' he will learn it
" ' (*time enough*), and, if he is to die, let us not trouble the last days he has to live.'
" He died on the 10th of Muharram, without being aware of what was passing.
" Salâh ad-Dîn then held a sitting in order to receive (*as the defunct sovereign's
" vizir and lieutenant*) the addresses of condolence, after which he took possession
" of the palace (*or citadel, al-Kasr*) and of all that it contained. Previously to the
" death of al-Aâdid, he had placed there as its guardian the eunuch Bahâ ad-Dîn
" Karakûsh. " — We have given his life (*vol. II. p.* 520). — " This officer, being
" installed there as al-Aâdid's *ustad-dar* (*intendant of the household*), kept all things
" safe and delivered them up to Salâh ad-Dîn. Al-Aâdid's family were taken to an
" insulated mansion and placed under guard; his sons, his uncles and their chil-
" dren were lodged in one of the halls of the palace (*citadel*) and guards set over
" them. All the male and female slaves were removed from the palace; to some
" of them Salâh ad-Dîn granted their liberty ; others he gave away and others he
" sold. Thus did he empty the palace of its inhabitants; Glory be to Him whose
" reign shall never pass away and on whom no change can be effected by the suc-
" cession of ages! Al-Aâdid, in the height of his illness, sent for Salâh ad-Dîn, but
" he, being apprehensive of some treachery, abstained from going. After al-
" Aâdid's death, Salâh ad-Dîn discovered that his intentions had been friendly and
" regretted to have staid away. The Obaidite (*Fatimide*) dynasty had its commen-
" cement in Ifrîkiya and Maghreb; it began in the month of Zû 'l-Hijja, 299 (July,
" A. D. 912) (25). The first of these sovereigns was al-Mahdi Abû Muhammad

" Obaid Allah. He founded the city of al-Mahdiya and became master of all Ifri-
" kiya."—Such is the date assigned by our professor Ibn al-Athir to the conquest
of Ifrikiya by al-Mahdi, but the true one is that which we have given in our account
of his life (vol. II. p. 79), to which we refer the reader.—Ibn al-Athir then says :
" On the death of al-Mahdi, the sovereignty passed to his son al-Káim Abû 'l-
" Kásim Muhammad."—He then speaks of these princes, one after another, till
he comes to al-Aâdid, and there he says : " His death marked the downfal of their
" empire. They reigned two hundred and sixty-six years, two hundred and eight
" of which they passed in Egypt (26). Fourteen members of this family reigned,
" namely : al-Mahdi, al-Káim, al-Mansûr, al-Moizz, al-Aziz, al-Hákim, az-Zâhir,
" al-Mustansir, al-Mustali, al-Aâmir, al-Háfiz, az-Zâfir, al-Fáiz and al-Aâdid, who was
" the last of them."—As I have given, in this work, a separate article on each of
these princes, whoever wishes to know something of their history, will find what he
wants under their respective names. We need not therefore repeat that information here. Ibn al-Athir continues thus : " A summary account of the (princes)
" whose names we have collected here is given in our greater historical work;"—
he means the chronicle which he entitled the Kâmil; it is a work of great repute and
one of the best of its class. After that, he says : " Salâh ad-Din, having taken pos-
" session of the palace with what it contained, distributed part of the money and the
" treasures to the members of his family and his emirs. A considerable portion of
" the property which remained he sold. Amongst these treasures were precious
" stones and jewels in such a quantity as was never possessed by any other king.
" They had been collected during a long series of years and the lapse of ages.
" One of these objects was the (famous) rod of emerald which was one span and a
" half in length ; another was the (celebrated) string of rubies. There also were
" found one hundred thousand books, selected with great care and very fairly writ-
" ten ; some of them were in the mansûb (or eastern neskhi) character (27). When
" the khotba was said in Cairo for al-Mostadi, Nûr ad-Din took to him the good
" news. It gave the highest satisfaction to the khalif who, in return, caused a com-
" plete dress of honour to be borne to him by Imâd ad-Din Sandal al-Muktafawi
" (who was one of the khalif al-Muktafi's freedmen). This was a high mark of ho-
" nour, because Imâd ad-Din occupied an eminent position at the Abbaside court.
" He sent also a state-dress to Salâh ad-Din, but it was of a kind inferior to that
" which Nûr ad-Din had received. He dispatched also to Egypt a quantity of black

" standards, that they might be set up on the pulpits. These were the first emblems
" of Abbáside pomp which appeared in Egypt since the conquest of that country by
" the Obaidites. " End of the extract from Ibn al-Athir.—When news was brought
to the *imám (khalif)* al-Mustadi bi-Amr Illah Abû Muhammad al-Hasan, who was
the son of the *imám* al-Mustanjid and the father of the *imám* an-Nâsir li-Din Illah,
that his *(family's)* authority had been reestablished in Egypt and that his name was
not only pronounced in the *khotba* but inscribed on the coinage, after so long an
interval, Abû 'l-Fath Muhammad Sibt Ibn at-Taáwizi *(vol. III. p.* 162) composed
on the subject a magnificent *kasída* in which he celebrated the praises of that khalif.
In it he notices also the recovery of Egypt, the conquest of Yemen and the death of
the heretic who there took up arms and assumed the title of al-Mahdi. This occurred
in the year 571 (A. D. 1175-6 (27). Salâh ad-Din had just sent to him *(to the khalif)*
a large quantity of the treasures of Egypt and the spoils of the Egyptians. Here is
the beginning of the poem :

Say to the cloud which leans towards the earth whilst the southern gales are exciting the
flow of its waters : " Turn towards the valley in the sands *(where my beloved used to reside)*,
" and shed your drops profusely upon the spots which we frequented and upon the traces of
" the camp." Station where all our friends halted! noisy playground of the tribe! a few
lone corner-stones are now thy only occupiers, since friends and inhabitants are gone. Whither did the camel which bore off my beloved direct its steps? When did it depart? Ardent
is my passion to enjoy again the time which I passed in the tribe's reserved grounds! Blessings (28) upon a time such as that! Mine is the passion of a man who, forced away by the
hand of departure, is cast into a distant land. How well I recollect thee *(dearest spot!)*, where
I and my beloved met so often without being perceived by *(jealous)* fortune; at that time, thy
extensive pasture-grounds were never dusty; thy waters were never tainted. *(To see)* thy friendly
gazelles was for me, a necessity; for me thy soil was a bed (29). A censor blamed my conduct, but
without knowing who caused my passion and the agitation of my heart. My passion was for one
whose waist put to shame the pliant wand and *(whose sweet voice)* humbled the pride of the bleating
gazelle. She who was my torment could not have given me pain, had she taken pity on the person thus tormented. Through love for her, my tears have been set at liberty and my heart remains
a captive. O thou who art my torment! Thy disdain hath deprived of life a lover by thee afflicted.
On thy departure, thou didst devote him for ever to tears and to affliction. My heart has been
obliged to suffer the unremitting pain of travelling and sojourning. Have pity on those eyelids
now chafed by weeping and long deprived of sleep. Be not parsimonious *(of your kindness)*:
parsimony deprives the fairest face of its beauty. How many were the nights which I passed
till overcome by the wine-cup and the amphora! Then, in my wantonness, I strutted proudly,
sweeping the ground with my train and my long sleeves; my companion was slender-waisted,
pliant in stature, bending gracefully as she turned around, delicate in body. But the sin of
such nocturnal visit that I made to her is now expiated by the praises which I address to al-
Mostadi Abû Muhammad al-Hasan, a sovereign established on the highest pinnacle of the kha-

hlate, Prince! thou who hast trod for years in the path traced by the Prophet! thou who hast united in the same hands the aspect of the Prophet and the (*dignity of the*) khalifate! Kingdoms, fortresses and cities have humbly submitted to the awe which you inspire; subdued as they were by the sharp sword and the pliant spear. To thee have come the kingly spoils of Said (*Upper Egypt*) and of Aden. The pretended khalif is the lord of Egypt and the raised insurgent in Yemen have been despoiled of the treasures heaped up, since olden times, by Zû Roaín and by Zû Yazan (30). The hate and animosity with which they inspired you has now been quenched (*in the blood spilt*) by the points of your lances. Struck with terror (*by your anger*), they found that shields and castles were of no avail. One evening saw them led off as captives, humble and submissive as the victims which the pilgrims lead to sacrifice; and you gave up their extensive countries as an offering to calamities and disasters. Every day, a band of your troops made a hostile inroad, and thus you disclosed the secret of the minted Moslim warriors (*in former times*). You have washed away the stains of the filth left by heretic princes; and now, it is as if prayers had never been offered up for them from those pulpits.

The quantity of verses just given is quite sufficient, and, to it I shall limit the extract which I make from this long *kasîda*. Another piece composed by the same poet in honour of the khalif contains also allusions to these events. I cannot recollect any part of it except the passage in which the charms of the beloved are extolled, and, as it full of grace and beauty, I am induced to insert it here :

Welcome to the aspect of a (*fair*) visitor whose brilliant countenance puts darkness to shame! time has at length permitted us to meet. Despite all obstacles, she approached, and then passed the night in handing around the wine-cup. I was one those who could cope with her, but, inebriated by her glances, I did not require her wine. The maiden is fair and her canteen is to slay me, both by her departure and by her saying. (*I die*,) whether she casts her eyes upon me or retires with disdain. Never do her promises find the day of their fulfilment. The sun is her rival and the moon her (*admiring*) observer; morning appears over her *lithám* and night lies under her bowl (31). She belongs to the tribe of Modar and can trace back her origin to the (*corner of the*) red (*tent*) (32). Whilst she passed the night in her pavilion, shining spears circled around it. I feel the stroke of death when she is on the point of her departure, and again I feel it when we are about to meet. After a long absence, I passed by her verbal abode and by its open courts; my eyes then wept for those fawns (*maidens*). I stopped to look towards the orient tracts in which her beauty used to rise; hoping to discover the moons (*the handsome maids, who formerly shone*) in these heavens. There I wept till I nearly excited the compassion of the two *bán*-tree (groves) which grew in that valley. O thou who afflictest those eyes accustomed to shed tears (33), thou hast yet left within my bosom a spark of life, but it is dying out from the malady of weeping. My eyes long to see thee, but (*they cannot, because*) thou art (*carefully preserved*) within their pupils (34). By refusing to cast a look on me, thou greatest to my eyes time to collect fresh tears, which then flow as copiously as gifts fall from the khalif's hand.

After this passage, the poet commences the eulogium which, like the rest of the piece, contains ideas of great originality. Towards the end of this article, we shall insert some of the verses composed by him in honour of Salâh ad-Dîn. He used to send his *kasîdas* from Baghdad to that prince and, with each of them, another piece of verse containing the praises of al-Kâdi al-Fâdil; the latter received the packets and presented the *kasîdas* to Salâh ad-Dîn. — After the passages inserted above, our professor Ibn al-Athîr has a chapter on the origin of the coolness which arose between Nûr ad-Dîn and Salâh ad-Dîn, and which they both kept secret. He there says : "In the year 567 (A. D. 1171-2) something occurred which led Nûr ad-Dîn to dis- "trust Salâh ad-Dîn. Here is what passed : The former sent a dispatch to Salâh "ad-Dîn, ordering him to assemble the troops of Egypt, lead them into the terri- "tory of the Franks and blockade al-Karak, whilst he, on his side, would call to- "gether his army and join him there, so that they might both wage war against the "Franks and conquer their provinces. Salâh ad-Dîn left Cairo on the 20th of "Muharram and informed Nûr ad-Dîn by a dispatch that he would not loiter "on the way. Nûr ad-Dîn had already assembled his troops and made every "preparation for his departure. He did not intend to commence his march till he "was assured that Salâh ad-Dîn had begun his; so, when he received that intelli- "gence, he set out from Damascus with the intention of going to al-Karak. On "reaching that place, he received from him a letter of excuses in which he stated "that he was unable to depart in consequence of the agitation which prevailed in "the cities of Egypt and which was excited, as far as he could learn, by a partisan "of the Alides (*the Fatimides*). He added that the disaffected intended to surprise "and occupy these cities, and that he feared to lose them if he absented. This ex- "cuse was not accepted by Nûr ad-Dîn. The real cause of Salâh ad-Dîn's immobi- "lity was that his companions and intimate friends had excited his apprehensions "and deterred him from going to meet Nûr ad-Dîn. This disobedience to orders "highly displeased the latter who immediately resolved on entering into Egypt and "expelling his refractory servant from that country. Salâh ad-Dîn, being informed "of his intention, assembled the members of his family, amongst whom was his fa- "ther, Najm ad-Dîn Aiyûb, and his maternal uncle, Shihab ed-Dîn al-Hârimi. He "called also to that meeting all the other emirs. Having then informed them that "Nûr ad-Dîn had the intention of coming to attack him and deprive him of the "possession of Egypt, he asked their advice on the subject. All of them kept silent, "till at length his nephew Taki ad-Dîn Omar," — we have given his life in a sepa-

rate article (col. II. p. 891), — " said : ' If he come, we shall fight him and keep
" ' him out of the country.' Some other members of the family concurred with him,
" but Najm ad-Dîn Aiyûb, who was a man of foresight, prudence and sagacity, re-
" primanded them severely and declared that what had been just said was an
" enormity. Having then ordered Taki ad-Dîn to sit down, he scolded him and
" said to Salâh ad-Dîn : ' I am your father, and there is Shihâb ad-Dîn, your ma-
" ' ternal uncle ; do you think that, in all this assembly, there are persons who love
" ' you as much as we do and who are as anxious as we for your welfare?' — ' No,
" ' by Allah!' exclaimed Salâh ad-Dîn. ' Know then, ' continued Najm ad-Dîn,
" ' that, if I and your uncle Shihâb ad-Dîn met Nûr ad-Dîn, we could not possibly
" ' avoid dismounting and kissing the ground before him. Did he even order us
" ' to behead you with the sword, we should obey. From that you may judge of the
" ' other emirs. All the chiefs whom you see here and all the troops could not
" ' avoid dismounting and kissing the ground before Nûr ad-Dîn, were they to meet
" ' him. This country is his, and, if he wish to depose you, we shall obey him
" ' without hesitation. My advice is therefore that you write to him and say : ' I
" ' have been informed that you intend making an expedition for the purpose of
" ' (occupying) this country; but, what necessity is there for your doing so? Let
" ' your lordship send here a courier mounted on a dromedary, with orders to put a
" ' turban-sash about my neck and lead me off to you; no one here will offer to re-
" ' sist your will.' He then said to the persons present : ' Retire and leave us!
" ' we are Nûr ad-Dîn's mamlûks and slaves, he may do with us what he
" ' pleases. ' The meeting then broke up, and the greater number of those who
" had been there wrote to Nûr ad-Dîn, informing him of what had passed. Najm
" ad-Dîn, being left alone with his son Salâh ad-Dîn, said to him : ' You are very
" ' imprudent and know little of the men who formed that numerous assembly; you
" ' let them perceive your secret feelings and what you had upon your mind. If
" ' Nûr ad-Dîn heard that you meant to prevent him from entering into this country,
" ' he would leave aside all other affairs and direct his whole attention towards you :
" ' and, were he to come against you, not a single man of this army would help you;
" ' on the contrary, they would deliver you up to him. Now, that the sitting is over,
" ' these emirs will write to him and mention what I said. So, you must also write
" ' to the same purport and say to him : ' What necessity is there for your coming
" ' against me? Send one of your dromedary-couriers and let him cast a rope about

" ' my neck.' When he reads this, he will give up his project and turn his atten-
" ' tion to such affairs as he may consider more serious. Time runs on and God
" ' is doing something at every instant. By Allah! if Nûr ad-Dîn attempted to take
" ' from us a single sugar-cane of ours, I myself should fight against him and hinder
" ' him from doing so, were I even to lose my life in the struggle.' Salâh ad-Dîn
" followed his father's advice, and Nûr ad-Dîn, seeing how things stood, gave up his
" project, as Najm ad-Dîn had foretold, and did not resume it as long as he lived.
" The counsel given to Salâh ad-Dîn was really excellent." End of Ibn al-Athîr's
relation. — Our professor Ibn Shaddâd says in the historical work mentioned above:
" Salâh ad-Dîn then placed himself on the footing of ruling with justice, of practi-
" sing beneficence and of bestowing favours on all men. This continued till the
" year 508 (A. D. 1172-3), when he set out with his army for the purpose of inva-
" ding the territory of al-Karak and Shaubek. He began by these places be-
" cause they were the nearest to him and lay so close to the road that they inter-
" cepted the communications with Egypt and rendered impossible the passage of
" caravans, unless he himself went out (with troops) in order to help them through.
" He intended to widen that road and clear it of obstructions. That same year, he
" laid siege to the place (al-Karak) and had a number of encounters with the Franks,
" after which he retreated without obtaining any success. On his return, he lear-
" ned that his father Najm ad-Dîn Aiyûb had died some time before his arrival." —
I have given the date of that prince's death in his biographical notice (vol. I. p. 246).
— " In the year 569 (A. D. 1173-4), he saw (with satisfaction) the strength of his
" army and the number of his troops. Being then informed that a man called Abd
" an-Nabi Ibn Mahdi had become master of Yemen and gotten possession of its for-
" tresses, he sent his brother Tûrân Shâh against the usurper." — As we have given
an account of that event in the life of Tûrân Shâh (vol. I. p. 284), we need not repeat
it here. — In the year 569, Nûr ad-Dîn died, as we have stated in his life (vol. III.
p. 338). " Salâh ad-Dîn then learned that an individual called al-Kans had assem-
" bled a great multitude of negroes at Syene under the pretext of restoring the
" former Egyptian dynasty (the Fatimides), and that numbers of the people of Cairo,
" being desirous of reestablishing that family on the throne, had gone to join the
" rebel. He therefore placed his brother al-Malik al-Aâdil at the head of a nume-
" rous army and sent him against the insurgents. On the 7th of Safar, 570 (7th
" September, A. D. 1174), al-Aâdil encountered the enemy and routed them com-

" pletely. (By this victory) the authority of Salâh ad-Dîn was fully established."—
" Nûr ad-Dîn (in dying,) left a son called al-Malik as-Sâlih Ismail,"—we have
spoken of him in our article on Nûr ad-Din and mentioned that he was at Damascus when his father died. — " The citadel of Aleppo was then occupied by
" Shams ad-Dîn Ali Ibn ad-Dâya and by Shadbakht, the former of whom was
" meditating great projects. Al-Malik as-Sâlih left Damascus and, in the month
" of Muharram, 570 (August, A. D. 1174), he halted outside of Aleppo, having
" with him Sâbik ad-Dîn. Badr ad-Dîn Hasan (, the brother of Ali) Ibn ad-Dâya
" went out to him and then arrested Sâbik ad-Dîn. When al-Malik as-Sâlih en-
" tered into the citadel, the two brothers, Shams ad-Dîn and Hasan Ibn ad-Dâya
" were arrested and cast into prison along with Sâbik ad-Dîn. .That same day,
" Abû 'l-Fadl Ibn al-Khashshâb (35) lost his life in a riot which took place at
" Aleppo; another account says that he was killed on the day which preceded the ar-
" restation of the sons of ad-Dâya and that these chiefs were the authors of his death.
" After the death of Nûr ad-Dîn, it became evident to Salâh ad-Dîn that the son of
" the deceased prince was not old enough to undertake the direction of affairs or
" support the weight of the sovereignty, and that, in Syria, things would fall into
" the greatest confusion. A letter which he then received from Shams ad-Dîn Ibn
" al-Mukaddam (35*) decided him on taking the field with a large body of troops.
" He set out from Old Cairo, leaving there a sufficient garrison, and proceeded to Da-
" mascus, under the pretext that he was going to take charge of al-Malik as-Sâlih's
" interests. On Tuesday, the last day of the latter Rabî, 570 (27 November, A. D.
" 1174), Damascus was delivered up to him and its citadel also. The first house
" into which he entered was that of his father," — This residence is now called the
house of as-Sharîf al-Akhi and has opposite to it the Addiliya College, which is an
establishment well known in the city.— " The inhabitants gathered round him and
" expressed great joy at his arrival. .That same day, he distributed large sums of
" money, to the extreme delight of the Damascans. Having then left a garrison in
" the citadel, he set out for Aleppo. (On his way,) he besieged the city of Hems
" (Emessa) and took it in the month of the first Jumâda (December), but did not lose
" his time in attempting to reduce the citadel. He then proceeded to Aleppo and,
" on Friday, the last day of the first Jumâda (27th December), he attacked that city
" for the first time. Saif ad-Dîn Ghazi, the son of Kutb ad-Dîn Maudûd and the
" grandson of Imâd ad-Dîn Zinki, who was then reigning at Mosul, perceived from

" what was going on how redoubtable that man (Salâh ad-Dîn) had become and how
" great was the influence which he had acquired. Fearing that, if he neglected to
" take proper measures, Salâh ad-Dîn would obtain possession of the whole country,
" acquire a firm footing in the sovereignty and usurp the supreme authority, he
" sent against him an immense army, which he placed under the orders of his bro-
" ther Izz ad-Dîn Masûd. These troops were to expel Salâh ad-Dîn from the coun-
" try. The latter, being informed of their approach, decamped from before Aleppo,
" on the 1st of Rajab, the same year (20th January, A. D. 1175) and returned to
" Hamât whence he went again to Hems, the citadel of which place he then got into
" his possession. Izz ad-Dîn Masûd, having arrived at Aleppo, took off with him
" the troops of his cousin al-Malik as-Sâlih, who was then the sovereign of that city,
" and set out with an immense army. Salâh ad-Dîn, being informed of
" their march, advanced to meet them and joined them at Kurûn Hamât (30).
" As he was desirous of obtaining peace, he opened negotiations with them,
" but peace they refused to make; thinking to attain their object more rea-
" dily by risking a battle. Destiny leads, however, to things of which
" men are not aware : the two armies encountered and, with God's per-
" mission, Salâh ad-Dîn's adversaries were routed and fled most disgrace-
" fully. A number of prisoners fell into his hands and received from him their
" liberty. The battle was fought at Kurûn Hamât, on the 19th of Ramadân
" the same year (13 April, A. D. 1175). After gaining this victory, be returned
" to Aleppo and encamped before it, for the second time, but the chiefs of the
" city obtained peace by ceding to him Maarra, Kafertâb and Bârin. At the time
" in which the battle above-mentioned took place, Saif ad-Dîn Ghâzi was besieging
" his brother, Imâd ad-Dîn Zinki, in Sinjâr, of which city the latter was the sove-
" reign. He intended to deprive him of it because he saw that he had come to a
" good understanding with Salâh ad-Dîn; but, when on the point of taking it, he
" learned that his (other) army had been defeated. Fearing that the news might
" reach his brother, Imâd ad-Dîn, and encourage him to make a prolonged resis-
" tance, he entered into negotiations with him and concluded a peace. Immedia-
" tely after, he proceeded to Nasibin, where all his attention was directed to levying
" troops and providing for the necessary expenses. He then went to al-Bîra, cros-
" sed the Euphrates and encamped on the Syrian side of the river. From that place
" he sent to his cousin, Al-Malik as-Sâlih, the son of Nûr ad-Dîn and sovereign of

" Aleppo, for the purpose of settling the basis of an alliance which he wished to
" contract. He then proceeded to Aleppo, and al-Malik as-Sâlih went out to receive
" him. During the short stay which he made there, he went with an escort of his
" own troops to the citadel and, on going down from it, he set out for Tall as-
" Sultân," — a station between Hamât and Aleppo, — " taking with him a nume-
" rous army. Salâh ad-Dîn, having drawn from Egypt the troops which were quar-
" tered there, led them to Tall as-Sultân and there he halted. On the morning of
" Thursday, the 10th of Shauwâl, 571 (22nd April, A. D. 1176), the two armies drew
" up in line and had a terrible conflict. Salâh ad-Dîn's right wing was broken by
" Muzaffar ad-Dîn Ibn Zain ad-Dîn " — the lord of Arbela whom we have spoken of
elsewhere, and who' commanded Saif ad-Dîn's left wing.—" Salâh ad-Dîn then
" charged at the head of his troops, bore down all before him and took a number of
" prisoners. Amongst them were some of the great emirs, and these he set at li-
" berty. Saif ad-Dîn returned to Aleppo, carried off the treasures which were kept
" there and crossed the Euphrates in order to reach his own country. Salâh ad-
" Dîn prevented his troops from pursuing the fugitives, and, during the rest of that
" day, they occupied the tents of their adversaries who, in their flight, had left all
" their baggage behind them. The horses in the stables were distributed by him to
" his soldiers; all the treasures he gave away, and the tent of Saif ad-Dîn was be-
" stowed by him on his cousin Izz ad-Dîn Farrukh Shâh. " — This prince was the
son of Shâhin Shâh Ibn Aiyûb and the brother of Taki ad-Dîn Omar, sovereign of
Harât. Farrukh Shâh was lord of Baalbek; his son, al-Malik al-Amjad Bahrâm Shâh
became lord of that city. — " Salâh ad-Dîn then marched to Manbej, which place
" was delivered up to him. He then proceeded to the fortress of Azâz and com-
" menced to besiege it on the 4th of Zû 'l-Kaada, 571 (15th May, A. D. 1176).
" There he was traitorously assailed by some Ismaïlians, but God saved his life and
" the assassins were taken. He remained there till the 14th of Zû'l-Hijja (22nd
" June), when he got possession of the place. From that he went to Aleppo, where
" he arrived on the 16th of the same month, and remained some time before the
" city, after which he departed. Azâz was given up by him to a young girl, the
" daughter of Nûr ad-Dîn, who had been sent out (of the city) to request of him the
" restitution of that place. Salâh ad-Dîn then returned to Egypt for the purpose
" of examining into the state of the country. His journey thither took place in the
" month of the first Rabî, 572 (Sept-Oct., A. D. 1176). He had already nominated

" as his lieutenant in Damascus his brother Shams ad-Dawlat Tûrân Shâh, who had
" come from Yemen to see him. Having then made preparations for an expedi-
" tion into the *Sâhil* (*the littoral provinces of Syria occupied by the Franks*), he set
" out and had an encounter with the Franks at ar-Ramla, on one of the first (*ten*)
" days of the latter Jumâda, 573 (Nov.-Dec., A. D. 1177). In this battle the Mo-
" sulmans were defeated,"—in consequence of a circumstance too long to be related here (37).—" As they had no fortress in the neighbourhood to which they
" might have retreated after their defeat, they directed their march towards Egypt
" but, having lost their way, they were scattered and dispersed, so that a number of
" them fell into the hands of the enemy. Amongst these was the legist Isa al-
" Hakkâri, whose captivity was a great loss. God repaired this disaster by the fa-
" mous battle which was gained at al-Hittîn. With al-Malik as-Sâlih, the sove-
" reign of Aleppo, affairs were going on badly; he arrested the chief of his
" administration, Kumushtukîn, and put him to death because he could not obtain
" from him the cession of (*the fortress and territory of*) Hârim. The Franks,
" being informed of this event, laid siege to Hârim with the hope of get-
" ting it into their possession. This was in the month of the latter Jumâda (Nov.-
" Dec.) of that year (A. D. 1177). The garrison, knowing how much they had to
" fear from the Franks, delived up the place to al-Malik as-Sâlih, on one of the
" last (*ten*) days of Ramadân (Feb. March, A. D. 1178), the same year. This
" obliged the Franks to retire. Salâh ad-Dîn remained in Egypt till he had brought
" all things into order and repaired the losses which his partisans had suffered at
" ar-Ramla. Being then informed that affairs were in a bad posture in Syria, he
" resolved on invading that country again and turned his thoughts to the underta-
" king of a holy war. An ambassador then arrived from Killj Arslân, the sove-
" reign of Asia Minor (ar-Rûm) for the purpose of making a treaty of peace and of
" relating (*to Salâh ad-Dîn*) how much they had to suffer from the Armenians.
" Salâh ad-Dîn then decided on invading the son of Leon's country (38),"—that
is to say, the territory of as-Sis, which is the maritime region that lies between
Aleppo and ar-Rûm (*Asia Minor*),—" in order to assist Killj Arslân against him.
" He therefore set out and summoned the troops of Aleppo to come and join him.
" This they were bound to do by one of the conditions mentioned in the treaty of
" peace (*which had been made with al-Malik as-Sâlih*). Having then penetrated
" into the son of Leon's country, he took, on his way, and ruined a fortress, after

" which he granted peace to the enemy, at their humble request and returned back.
" Being then asked by Killj Arslán to make peace with all the people of the East, he
" gave his consent and, on the 10th of the first Jumáda, 576 (3rd Oct., A. D.
" 1180) he swore (to observe the treaty). In this peace were included Killj Arslán
" and the people of Mosul. He then returned to Damascus and from that to Egypt.
" After that took place the death of al-Málik as-Sálih, the son of Núr ad-Dín. " —
" For the date, see our article on his father (vol. III. p. 342). — Before dying,
" he made the emirs and the troops of Aleppo swear fidelity to his cousin, Izz ad-
" Dín Masúd, the lord of Mosul." — We have already spoken of this prince, who
was the son of Kutb ad-Dín Maudúd (vol. III. p. 356). — " On the death of Saif
" ad-Dín, " — the date is mentioned in our article concerning him (vol. II. p. 442),
— " his brother, Izz ad-Dín Masúd, succeeded to the throne. When the latter was
" informed of al-Málik as-Sálih's death and learned that he had bequeathed to him
" Aleppo, he hastened to that city, lest Saláh ad-Dín should get there before him.
" The first (of his partisans) who arrived at Aleppo was Musaffar ad-Dín, the son of
" Zain ad-Dín and the sovereign of Arbela (vol. II. p. 535). " — At that time he
was sovereign of Harrán only and in the dependance of (the sovereign of) Mosul,
to whom all that country belonged. — " Musaffar ad-Dín reached Aleppo on
" the 3rd of Shábán, 577 (12th Dec. A. D. 1181). Seventeen days later,
" Masúd arrived, went up to the citadel and took possession of all the treasures
" deposited there. On the 5th of Shauwál (11th Feb.) of the same year (1182),
" he married al-Málik as-Sálih's mother. " — Our professor Ibn Shaddád then
relates a number of events which have been already noticed in our articles on Izz
ad-Dín Masúd, on Imád ad-Dín Zinki, that prince's brother, and on Táj al-Malúk
Búri (vol. I. p. 272), the brother of Saláh ad-Dín. Whoever wishes to know them
may recur to these articles. I may now state, in a summary manner, that Izz ad-
Dín Masúd made an exchange with his brother Imád ad-Dín Zinki, giving him Aleppo
and receiving from him Sinjár. Zinki entered into Aleppo after the departure of Izz
ad-Dín but, when Saláh ad-Dín came to besiege him, he felt himself unable to keep
the city. Saláh ad-Dín encamped before it on the 26th of Muharram, 579 (21st
May, 1183), or on the 18th of that month, if we admit the statement of Ibn Shaddád.
The emir Imád ad-Dín Zinki had then a private conference with the emir Husám
ad-Dín Tumán Ibn Ghási and consulted him on what was to be done. The advice
of Tumán was to surrender Aleppo provided that some other cities were given to him

in exchange and that all the treasures in the citadel were left in his possession.
' That,' said Imâd ad-Din, ' is precisely what I thought of doing.' Usâm ad-Din
had then a secret conference with Salâh ad-Din and obtained his consent to the pro-
posed arrangement. Imâd ad-Din received Sinjâr, al-Khâbûr, Nasîbîn and Sarûj;
Tumân got ar-Rakka as a recompense for his mediation, and Salâh ad-Din swore to
observe the treaty. This took place on the 17th of Safar (11th June), the same year.
Salâh ad-Din had laid siege to Sinjâr and taken it on the 2nd of Ramadân, 578
(30th December, A. D. 1182), after which, he gave it to his nephew Taki ad-Din
Omar. When the peace was concluded in the form just mentioned, he remitted
Sinjâr to Imâd ad-Din and was put in possession of Aleppo. On Monday, the 7th
of Safar (21st May), he went up to the citadel and remained there till he terminated all his arrangements. On the 22nd of the latter Rabi, the same year (15th
August), he departed from the city, after establishing there his son al-Malik az-Zâhir,
who was then a boy. We have given to him a separate article. The government of
the citadel was assigned to Saif ad-Din Yâzkûj al-Asadi (one of Asad ad-Din Shîrkûh's mawlas), to whom also the sultan confided the interests of his son. On the
date just mentioned, Salâh ad-Din set out for Damascus. Ibn Shaddâd says : " On
" the 3rd of Rajab, the same year (22nd Oct. 1183), he left Damascus with the inten-
" tion of besieging al-Karak, and sent to his brother, al-Malik al-Aâdil, the order
" to join him there. He (al-Aâdil) left Egypt with a numerous army, and, on the
" 4th of Shâbân (22nd Nov.) he effected his junction with Salâh ad-Din in the
" neighbourhood of al-Karak. When this news reached the Franks, they assem-
" bled a great quantity of troops and set out for al-Karak, with the intention of taking
" a position opposite to the Moslim army. Salâh ad-Din, having then conceived
" fears for the safety of Egypt, sent there his nephew Taki ad-Din Omar. On the
" 16th of Shâbân (4th Dec.), the same year, he departed from al-Karak and, on the
" 24 of that month, he arrived at Damascus. His brother, al-Malik al-Aâdil, whom
" he had taken with him, then received from him the government of Aleppo,
" which city he entered on Friday, the 22nd of Ramadân, the same year (8th Ja-
" nuary, A. D. 1184). Al-Malik az-Zâhir then left Aleppo with Yâzkûj and arrived
" at Damascus on Monday, the 26th of Shauwâl (13 Jan. 1184). Salâh ad-Din loved
" him better than any of his other sons, because he remarked in him the most praise-
" worthy qualities, and it was only to effect a necessary arrangement that he depri-
" ved him of Aleppo. It is said that al-Aâdil obtained Aleppo from Salâh ad-Din by

" giving him a sum of three hundred thousand dinars to aid in carrying on the holy
" war; God knows best! Salâh ad-Dîn perceived afterwards that it would be more
" advantageous to send al-Malik al-Aâdil back to Egypt and restore Aleppo to al-
" Malik az-Zâhir." — It is said that his motive for doing so was what we are going
to relate : The emir Alam ad-Dîn Sulaimân Ibn Haidar [left al-Aâdil's service because that prince had acted unjustly towards him by giving the promotion which
he expected to another officer. He] was one of Salâh ad-Dîn's intimate acquaintances, even previously to the time in which that prince became master of so many
countries. Salâh ad-Dîn having fallen dangerously ill whilst besieging Mosul, was
carried to Harrân, where he recovered, after bequeathing to each of his sons a portion of his states. On his way to Syria, Alam ad-Dîn, who travelled at his side, addressed him in these terms : " You suppose that these bequests will be fulfilled as
" exactly as the orders which you give on going out to hunt with the intention of
" soon returning! How can you think so? Are you not ashamed to see that birds
" have more foresight than you?" — " How is that?" said Salâh ad-Dîn, laughing.
The other replied : " When a bird intends to make a nest for its young, it chooses
" the top of a tree, so as to preserve them from danger. But you have left the
" (lofty) fortresses to your relatives and placed your children on the ground. Aleppo,
" the capital of a large state, is in the hands of your brother; Hamât is held by
" your cousin, Taki ad-Dîn; Hems by the son of Asad ad-Dîn (Shîrkûh), whilst your
" son al-Afdal is in Egypt with Taki ad-Dîn, who can expel him from that country
" whenever he pleases. Another of your sons is under the same tent with a brother
" of yours, who may do with him what he likes." — " You are right;" replied
Salâh ad-Dîn, " but let what you have said remain a secret." He then took Aleppo
from his brother and gave it to al-Malik az-Zâhir; after that, he bestowed Harrân,
ar-Roha (Edessa) and Maiyâfârikîn on al-Malik al-Aâdil, in order to get him out of
Syria and to find, in that country, wherewithal to provide abundantly for his own
children. Then happened (what we have seen). Our article on Izz ad-Dîn Masûd,
the son of Kutb ad-Dîn Maudûd and sovereign of Mosul, contains a paragraph concerning the three unsuccessful sieges of Mosul by Salâh ad-Dîn. — Our professor
Ibn al-Athîr says, in his History : " The third time that he laid siege to it, the rainy
" season had set in; but he resolved on staying and cutting up all the province of
" Mosul into fiefs. It was in the month of Shabân, 581 [Oct. Nov. A. D. 1185) that
" he arrived; he remained there during the rest of that month and during the month of

" Ramadân. Frequent messages passed between him and the sovereign of the city,
" and this correspondence was still going on when he was taken seriously ill and
" obliged to return to Harrân. It was there that messengers brought to him the
" acceptance of the proposals which he had made. Peace was then concluded on
" these conditions : that the sovereign of Mosul should deliver up to him the city of
" Shahrozûr and its dependances, the government of al-Karayelli (39) and of the
" provinces on the other side of the (river) Zâb, that his name should be inserted in
" the khotba pronounced from the pulpits, and that it should be inscribed
" on the coinage. When the two contracting parties had ratified the treaty
" by their respective oaths, Salâh ad-Dîn sent lieutenant-governors to all the pro-
" vinces which, according to agreement, were to be delivered up to him, and he
" thus got them into his possession. He was still at Harrân and his indisposition
" increased to such a degree that his life was dispaired of. He then made all his
" people (his troops) swear fidelity to his sons. His son al-Malik al-Aziz Imâd ad-
" Dîn Othmân and his brother al-Malik al-Aâdil, who had arrived from his sove-
" reignty at Aleppo, were then with him. To each of his sons he assigned a portion
" of his states and appointed al-Aâdil to act as their guardian. After that, he reco-
" vered his health and, in the month of Muharram, 582 (March-April, A. D. 1186),
" he returned to Damascus. During his illness at Harrân he had with him his cousin
" Nâsir ad-Dîn Muhammad and to him he granted as fiefs (the cities of) Hems and ar-
" Rahaba. This prince then set out for Hems and, in passing by Aleppo, he sent for
" some of the militia and gave them money after making them (magnificent)
" promises. On arriving at Hems, he wrote to some natives of Damascus, engaging
" them to deliver their city up to him in the case of Salâh ad-Dîn's death. The
" latter recovered and, very soon after, Nâsir ad-Dîn died. That event took place
" on the night preceding the festival of the Sacrifice, the same year (20th Feb. A.
" D. 1187). He had drunk a great deal of wine and, the next morning, was found
" lifeless. Some people said that a man suborned by Salâh ad-Dîn went to visit
" him and then, at a convivial party, put poison into his drink. The next morning,
" this person was not to be found. His name was an-Nâsih Ibn al-Amîd. Enqui-
" ries were made about him, and the answer was that he had departed the same
" night. This circumstance contributed to fortify the suspicions which were enter-
" tained; God knows best! After his death, the fief held by him was given to his
" son Shirkûh, who was at that time twelve years old. He left great deal of

" money, with horses, mules and furniture in abundance. Salâh ad-Dîn, having
" then gone to Hems, examined into the fortune of the deceased prince, and took
" the greater part of it, leaving only what was of no value." Our professor then
adds : " I was told that Shirkûh, a year after his father's death, went to see Salâh ad-
" Dîn and was asked by him how far he had advanced in learning the Koran by heart.
" To this he replied : ' As far as : *Surely they who swallow up the wealth of orphans*
" ' *unjustly shall swallow fire into their bellies and shall burn in flames* (Sur. IV,
" ' vers. 11).' All the assembly and Salâh ad-Dîn himself marvelled at his sharpness.
" — " When Salâh ad-Dîn," says Ibn Shaddâd, " arrived at Damascus, after recover-
" ing from his sickness, he sent for his brother al-Malik al-Aâdil who, in conse-
" quence of that order, left Aleppo on the eve of Saturday, the 25th of the first
" Rabî, 582 (14th June, A. D. 1186) and proceeded to Damascus with an escort
" of light cavalry. He remained there, at the court of Salâh ad-Dîn, and had
" with him a number of conferences and discussions relative to the arrangements
" which they had to make. It was decided, at length, in the month of the latter
" Jumâda (Aug.-Sept.), the same year, that al-Aâdil should return to Egypt and give
" up Aleppo." — Al-Malik az-Zâhir was then sent to that city and made his entry
into the citadel on a Saturday, in the year 582. I have mentioned in his life, that
he died on the same day of the year as that on which he entered into Aleppo as sovereign (*vol. II.* p. 443). I have there indicated the date and the day but know not
from what source I drew that piece of information. The sultan (*Salâh ad-Dîn*) then
confided his son al-Malik al-Azîz to al-Aâdil, whom he appointed to act as *atâbek* (or
guardian) of that prince. Ibn Shaddâd states that al-Malik al-Aâdil related to him as
follows : " When that arrangement was made, I went to pay my respects to al-Malik
" al-Azîz and al-Malik az-Zâhir. Having sat down between them, I said to the for-
" mer : ' My Lord! I am ordered by the sultan to hold myself ready at your ser-
" ' vice and accompany you to Egypt; but I know that there are a number of auda-
" ' cious fellows who will say things of me which should not be suffered and
" ' who will endeavour to make you mistrust me. Now, if you be disposed to
" ' hearken to such people, let me know it immediately, so that I may not go
" ' there.' The prince answered me thus : ' How can you think it possible that I
" ' could hearken to their words or follow their advice?' I then turned towards
" al-Malik az-Zâhir and said : ' I know that your brother has sometimes listened to
" ' the calumnies said of me by insolent fellows and that I have no other friend but

" ' you. So, if I feel my bosom oppressed by any act on his part, I shall be quite
" ' satisfied to obtain from you the government of Manbej.' — He replied : ' May
" ' all turn out fortunately !' — and then said to me every thing kind. — The sultan al-Malik az-Zâhir took to wife Ghâzia Khâtûn, the daughter of his uncle (40),
al-Malik al-Aâdil, and consummated his marriage on Wednesday, the 26th of Ramadân (10th Dec.) the same year (A. D. 1186). After that took place the battle of
Hittîn, which was such a blessing for the Musulmans. (The historian) says that it
was fought on Saturday, the 14th of the latter Rabî, 583 (23rd June, A. D. 1187)
and (had begun) towards the middle of Friday. He (Salâh ad-Dîn) often wished
to encounter the enemy on a Friday, hoping to profit by the blessed effects of
the prayers offered up on that day by the Moslims and of the invocations then pronounced from the pulpits by the preachers. Having collected all the Moslim troops,
he set out with an army numerous beyond count or reckoning. They marched in
order of battle and in the fairest array. He had been informed that a great multitude of the enemy, on receiving intelligence that the Moslim troops were assembling, had met at a place called Saffûriya and situated in the territory of Acre. He
advanced towards the lake of Tiberias and halted on the top of the hill which
overlooks the town. There he waited, thinking that the Franks would advance to
attack him when they heard that he was encamped on that spot. This demonstra-
tion did not, however, induce them to move or to quit their posts. It was on Wednesday, the 21st of the latter Rabî, that they (the Moslims) took up that position.
When he saw that the Franks did not stir nor leave their ground, he set out with a
troop of cavalry to attack Tiberias, leaving his squadrons where they were, facing the
enemy. Having attacked the town, he stormed it in an hour's time and let it be
plundered by his troops, who had begun to slay, to make prisoners and to set the
houses on fire. The citadel, being defended by the garrison, held out. The enemy
were so greatly concerned for the loss of Tiberias that they set out to deliver that town,
and Salâh ad-Dîn, being informed of their approach, left a sufficient number of troops
to blockade the place and joined his army. On Thursday, the 22nd of the latter Rabî,
he met with the enemy on the western side of the (plain which forms the) summit of
the hill of Tiberias ; but night intervened and separated the two armies. The soldiers
of both parties slept on the ground, without quitting their ranks and, the next
morning, which was that of Friday, the 23rd, they got on horseback, charged and
engaged in a furious battle. It was fought on the territory of a village called Lûbya.

The enemy felt a compression in the throat and, like a flock driven forward, they advanced towards death which they saw (*right before them*). Certain that they were falling into misfortune and ruin, they felt that, on the following day, they would be visitors of the tombs. The flames of war raged; each horseman charged upon his adversary, and no safety was to be found except in victory. Evil fortune then befel the people of infidelity, but night intervened with its darkness. Both parties remained under arms till the next morning, Saturday, without leaving their stations. The Moslims knew that they had the Jordan behind them, the enemy's country before them and that nothing could save them but strenuous fighting in that holy war. The Moslim squadrons dashed forward from every quarter; the center advanced to the charge, and all shouted aloud as if with one single voice. God then cast terror into the hearts of the infidels, for he judged it right to help the true believers against their enemies. The *Comes* (*Raimond, count of Tripoli*), perceiving that no hopes remained, fled soon after the commencement of the action, and took the road of Tyre, closely pursued by a troop of Moslims, but he effected his escape. God thus delivered the true believers from his malice. The Moslims surrounded the infidels on every side, shooting at them with their arrows, striking them down with their swords, and making them drink out of the goblet of death. A part of the enemy fled but, being pursued by the bravest of the Musulmans, not one of them escaped. Another band took refuge on the top of Hittîn, a hill thus called after a village near which is the tomb of the prophet Shoaib (*Jethro*). Being closely pressed by the Musulmans, who had lighted fires all around them, they suffered greatly from thirst and were reduced to such straits that, through fear of death, they surrendered themselves prisoners. Their chiefs were taken alive but the others were put to death. Amongst these chiefs were the king Jofri (41) and his brother, the Brins Arnât (*prince Renaud de Châtillon*), lord of al-Karak and ash-Shaubek, the son of al-Honferi (*Humphrey of Thoron*), the son of the lord of Tiberias, the (*grand-*) master of the Templars, the lord of Jubail and the (*grand-*) master of the Hospitallers. " It was " related to me," says Ibn Shaddâd by a person in whose veracity I could confide, " that he saw a man in Haurân leading off upwards of thirty captives whom he had " tied together with the cords of his tent; such was the consternation into which they " had fallen. When the *Comes* who fled at the beginning of the action arrived at " Tripoli, he was attacked by a pleurisy which carried him off. The masters " of the Hospitallers and the Templars, with the prisoners who belonged to these

" orders were put to death by [the command of] the sultan. As for prince Renaud,
" the sultan had made a vow that, if he ever got hold of him, he would take his
" life. What induced him to do so was this : A caravan of Egyptian merchants
" passed by ash-Shaubek when the prince was there, and, notwithstanding a truce
" which had been concluded, he attacked them traiterously and slew them. When
" they implored him to respect the truce which existed between him and the Mos-
" lims, he answered in terms which denoted his contempt for the Prophet. Salâh
" ad-Dîn, being informed of this, was impelled by his honorable pride and his zeal
" for religion to vow that he would shed the blood of him who said so. When
" God had granted to him this signal victory, he held a sitting in the court before
" his tent, which had not yet been pitched, and ordered the prisoners to be brought
" before him. Whilst [his soldiers] were pressing forward to him with their cap-
" tives, he felt the liveliest joy at the victory which, through his means, God had
" granted to the Moslims, and, having taken his seat in the tent, which had now
" been set up, he thanked the Almighty for that signal favour. The king Jofri
" was brought forward with his brother and prince Renaud. — Jofri, to whom
" the sultan presented an iced sherbet (julâb) and who was suffering greatly from
" thirst, drank some of it and handed the cup to the prince; on which the sultan
" said to the interpreter : ' Repeat these words to the king : It is from you and not
" ' from the sultan that he has received the drink. ' By these words he alluded to
" one of the good customs which prevailed amongst the Arabs of the desert and
" which formed a noble trait in their character, namely, that the person who eat
" or drank of what belonged to his captor had no longer any thing to fear. He then
" ordered them (the king and his brother,) to be taken to a place which he indicated
" and where they got something to eat. When brought back, they found him
" there, with only a few servants in attendance. — He made the king sit down in
" the vestibule of the tent and, having ordered the prince to be brought in, he said
" to him : ' Here am I who shall take Muhammad's part against you; to save your
" ' life you must become a Moslim. ' On the prisoner's refusal, he drew his cutlass
" and, with one stroke it, dislocated his shoulder. The attendants put an end to
" the Christian's life and cast the body outside the door of the tent. The king, ha-
" ving seen what passed, was convinced that he would be killed also and dispatched
" after the other, but the sultan told him to draw near and allayed his apprehen-
" sions, saying : ' It is not the custom that one king should kill another. As for

" ' that man, he passed all bounds and audaciously insulted the Prophets of God.'
" — The Moslims passed the night in jubilation, exclaiming, as with one voice :
" Praise and thanks be to God ! There no god but God ! God is the greatest of all !
" This continued till daybreak.   On Sunday, the 25th of the latter Rabi (4 July),
" the sultan went down to Tiberias and, on that same day, he obliged the citadel to
" capitulate.   On Tuesday, he left that place and took the road of Acre, where he
" arrived on Wednesday, the last day of the latter Rabi.   On the morning of Thurs-
" day, the 1st of the first Jumáda, he commenced the attack of that fortress and,
" having taken it, he delivered from captivity upwards of four thousand Moslims who
" were confined there.   All the wealth and treasures contained in the place fell
" into his power, as also an immense quantity of merchandise, Acre being a great
" resort for traders.   Detachments of the army being then sent into all parts of the
" Sáhil (Palestine), took a great number of castles, fortresses and strong-holds.   Na-
" blos (Napluse), Haifa (Caipha), Kaisariya (Cæsarea), Saffúriya (Sephouri) and an-
" Násira (Nazareth) fell into their power because they had no garrisons; death and
" captivity having taken off the greater part of their defensors.   When order was
" re-established in Acre, the sultan distributed to his troops the treasures and the
" prisoners, after which he set out for Tibnín and, on Sunday, the 11th of the first
" Jumáda, he halted before that place, which was a strong castle.   Having then
" planted his mangonels against it and assaulted it repeatedly, he reduced the gar-
" rison to the last extremity.   As it was defended by troops of noted courage and
" zealously attached to their religion, it made a vigourous resistance, but God lent
" his aid against them and, on Sunday, the 18th (of the same month) it was taken
" by storm.   Those of the garrison who survived were led into captivity.   From
" that he went to Saida (Sidon) and halted before its walls.   On the following day,
" which was Wednesday, the 20th of the first Jumáda, he obliged it to capitulate.
" After establishing his authority in that place, he departed for Bairût, before which
" town he encamped on the eve of Thursday, the 22nd of the first Jumáda.   His
" mangonels were then mounted and directed against the walls; assaults were gi-
" ven, and hostilities continued without intermission till Thursday, the 29th of the
" same month, when he obtained possession of the place.   Juhail, which is beyond
" Bairût, was taken by (a detachment of) his troops.   As nothing more remai-
" ned in that quarter to occupy his mind, he resolved to march against Ascalon.
" On passing before Tyre (Súr), he halted, but then felt unwilling to lose his time

" in carrying on a long siege; more particularly as he saw how his troops were dis-
" persed throughout the Sáhil, where each detachment was operating for its own
" profit, and how his men were fatigued and harassed (42) with continual warfare
" and daily combats. All the Franks of the Sáhil had, besides, assembled in Tyre.
",Thinking therefore that it would be more difficult to take than Ascalon, he resu-
" med his march towards that city. On Sunday, the 16th of the latter Jumáda, the
" same year (23rd August, A. D. 1187), he arrived under its walls, after taking on
" his way a number of places such as ar-Ramla and ad-Dárûm. On halting before
" Ascalon, he set up his mangonels and attacked the place so vigourously that he
" forced it to surrender. This was on Saturday, the last of the latter Jumáda.
" During the siege, some of his troops took Ghazza, Bait Jibril and an-Nátrûn, with-
" out meeting with any resistance. Thirty-five years had elapsed from the con-
" quest of Ascalon by the Franks 'till its recovery by the Moslims; as it was taken
" from the Moslims on the 27th of the latter Jumáda, 548 (19th Sept. A. D. 1153)."
So says our shaikh Ibn Shaddád in his History (of Saláh ad-Dín), but Shiháb ad-
Din Yákût al-Hamawi (page 9 of this vol.) states, in the work to which he gave the
title of al-Mushtarik, etc., that they (the Franks) took it from the Moslims on the
24th of the latter Jumáda. — Ibn Shaddád says : " When Saláh ad-Dín got pomes-
" sion of Ascalon and the places which are situated around Jerusalem (al-Cods), he
" 'made active preparations for going to that holy city. Having collected the troops
" which were dispersed throughout the Sáhil, he began his march, referring his
" enterprise to the will of God in whom he placed all his confidence, and anxious to
" profit by the opportunity of finding the door of righteousness opened, a duty to
" which the blessed Prophet exhorted the people by these words : ' He for whom the
" ' door of righteousness is opened, should take advantage of the opportunity; for he
" ' knows not when it may be shut against him. ' On Sunday, 15th Rajab, 583
" (20th Sept. 1187), he halted at the western side of the city, which was filled with
" troops, both horse and foot. Their number, according to an estimation made by
" men of experience who were with him, amounted to upwards of sixty thousand (43),
" without taking into count the women and the children. On Friday, the 20th of Ra-
" jab, he removed to the northern side of the city, having found some advantage in
" that change of position, and then set up his mangonels. By continual attacks, he
" invested the place closer and closer till the miners were enabled to make a breach
" in that part of the wall which overlooks the valley of Jehannam (Gehenna). The

" enemies of God, perceiving the misfortune which was impending and which they
" had no means of avoiding, saw therein manifest signs of the taking of the city and
" of their defeat by the Moslims. They were besides in consternation at being de-
" prived of their bravest warriors by death and captivity, and at seeing their for-
" tresses given up to devastation and ruin. Convinced that the same fate which
" befel their comrades awaited them, they felt discouraged and asked for quarter.
" Messengers then passed between the two parties for the purpose of settling the
" bases of the treaty, and the city was delivered up to Salâh ad-Dîn on Friday, the
" 27th of Rajab (1st October, A. D. 1187). The eve of that day was the anniver-
" sary of the Prophet's miraculous ascension to heaven, a fact positively enounced
" in the sacred Koran. See what an extraordinary coincidence! See how God
" permitted the Moslims to regain the city at the same time of the year in which
" his blessed Prophet made the nocturnal journey to heaven! Therein was an evi-
" dent sign by which God denoted his acceptance of the obedience shown him (by
" the sultan). At this important conquest were present a great number of docteurs
" learned in the law and a multitude of dervishes and devotees. The fact was that,
" when they learned how God had facilitated the conquests made in the Sâhil, and
" were informed that the sultan was about to march against Jerusalem, the Ulemâ
" of Egypt and Syria hastened to join him, not one of them remaining behind.
" All voices were then raised in shouts of triumph, pious invocations, declarations
" of God's unity and of his greatness. On Friday, the very day of the conquest, di-
" vine service was said (in the mosque) and the khotba recited by a preacher." —
In the life of the kâdi Muhî ad-Dîn Muhammad Ibn Ali, generally known by the
appellation of Ibn az-Zaki (vol. II. p. 634), I inserted the khotba as it was pronounced by him, and to that article I refer the reader. In an epistle composed by al-
Kâdi 'l-Fâdil (vol. II. p. 111) and entitled by him ar-Risâla 'l-Kodsiya (the Jerusalem
epistle), I read that the fourth of Shâbân was the day on which the recitation of the
khotba took place. God knows best! As we have spoken of the conquest of Jerusalem and given the text of that khotba in a preceding part of this work, it is fit that I
insert here the letter in which al-Kâdi 'l-Fâdil announced these victories to the imâm
(khalif) an-Nâsir li-Dîn Illah Abû 'l-Abbâs Ahmad, the son of the imâm al-Mustadi
bi-Amr Illah. I do so the more readily as it is one of the most eloquent and most
original pieces of the kind. I do not give the whole of it (44), but only the finest passages; having omitted the rest because the document is rather long. It runs thus :

" May God prolong the days of the August Divan (45), the relative of the Pro-
" phet! May the efforts of that prince be always triumphant over the contuma-
" cious! May the divine favour enrich him (with wisdom) so that he can do without
" the counsels of skilful investigators. His efforts are consecrated to the acquisition
" of unreserved praise for his noble deeds; (the sword of) his assistance is always awake
" though its point be sleeping in the scabbard; his beneficence is present when
" (the fertilising rains of) the cloud are absent from the earth. The works of his
" generosity will always abound, even were there no one to give him thanks. The
" decisions of his justice are executed by a firm resolve which operates not like the
" bolt shot at random (46), but like the well-feathered arrow. His ample chari-
" ties to holy men are like showers for pasture-grounds and lamps for mosques.
" The bands of terror which he sends against the foe appear in the shape of horse-
" men watching from the heights, or in the form of spectres going to haunt their
" places of repose. Your servant has indited this token of profound respect, sub-
" sequently to a communication which emanated from him in the shape of good ti-
" dings respecting the first dawn of that resolute enterprise, and in the form of a
" preface to a treatise descriptive of a signal favour which, for us, is an ocean in
" which our pens long to swim and, in the bearing of which, gratitude is op-
" pressed by the burden. It is a joyful news, of which all minds require the ex-
" planation, and a felicity, for the publishing of which, disclosure has an ample
" field (maṣdrib). In the renewal of our thanks, God will feel satisfaction; the
" grace attached to that (favour) will have a duration of which the words : ' It has
" ' ceased ' shall never be said. The affairs of Islamism have taken an excellent
" turn, and the faith of its followers is now fixed by the most evident of proofs. The
" far-spreading shade cast by the hopes of the infidels is now reduced to a narrow
" compass, and God has been true unto those of his religion ; when the condition is
" not fulfilled, the stipulation is void (47). — In this country, the true faith was
" like a stranger in a foreign land, but now, it finds itself at home. Success
" was put up for sale, and lives were profusely bestowed to purchase it. The cause
" of truth, lately thought to be very weak, has gained the superiority, and the re-
" gion where it flourished is again peopled; that region which, when ruined and
" desolate, was an object of horror. The order of God has been executed in des-
" pite of the infidels, and at nightfall, the swords went to rouse from slumber the
" terms of men's lives. God's promise of making his religion triumph over all the

"others received its fulfilment and then flashed forth lights by which was clearly
"seen that, on the next day, there would be burying of corpses (*jandn al-janin*).
"The Moslims recovered an inheritance which had been for them as a runaway
"slave. The lover, in his dreams, sees the image of his mistress coming from afar to
"visit him; but they, whilst awake, obtained the view of that (*happiness*) which they
"did not expect. Their feet were set firmly upon the heights and their banners
"floated far and wide; their kisses were impressed on the *sakhra* (48) and, by it,
"though a stone (*sakhra*), their wounded hearts were cured, as thirst is cured by
"water. When these pious men approached it, the inmost feelings of their hearts
"were made known, and they congratulated its fellow, the black stone (of *Mekka*),
"on being in a temple which protected it against the infidel and his warfare. Your
"servant (*Saláh ad-Dín*) would not have acted as he did, had he not been anxious to
"obtain that supreme felicity; neither would he have undergone those sufferings,
"had he not the hope of gaining that favour. He would not have encountered in
"battle those who fatigued him by their tyranny, neither would he have replied
"with the point of the lance to those who devoted themselves to death by insulting
"him, had his wish not been to make the Moslim people of one mind, so that the
"word of God might acquire the superiority, and to obtain, not the transitory en-
"joyments of this life, but that precious jewel, happiness in the next. Sometimes
"insulted by the evil-tongued, he wounded them to the heart by the contempt he
"showed them; sometimes the cauldrons (*of their thoughts*) would boil over,
"but he allayed that ebullition by his patience and his endurance. He who seeks
"for greatness must encounter perils; he who tries to make a profitable speculation
"must have courage; he who undertakes to disperse a crowd of foes must fight.
"Treaties of peace are soft under the teeth of foreign infidels; therefore (, *since*
"*they tear them*,) he also must bite (*and lacerate*) them; the hilts of the swords
"are so weak in the hands of those (*infidels*) who brandish them, that he is
"induced to break them completely (49). Besides, it was not by means of treaties
"that the obligation of holy war could be fulfilled, and that he could maintain the
"rights which he has over the people; neither could he accomplish by treaties the
"duties of that submission which was placed as a collar around his neck by *imáms*
"(*khalifs*) who, in their equity, always decided rightly, and by khalifs who often
"asked when this glorious day would arrive. It was easy to be seen that (*their an-
"cestors*) left their happiness and their throne as an inheritance to descendants born

" of the purest race, to illustrious sons, to a noble progeny, to an offspring of exalted
" merit. The title to be inscribed on the page of their excellence will never be
" without finding (what it requires :) the black (ink) of the pen and the white-
" ness of the leaf. They have never been absent there where he (Saláh ad-Dín)
" was present; their eyes were never closed when he was waking. He has passed
" to them the recompense which he obtained for himself, and they have shared
" with him in the works which were accepted of him (by God). He has become
" their companion on the couches (of glory), between the sides of which he now
" takes repose, and (he has met them) in the pages (of history) with (noble deeds)
" the odour of which is retained within the folds of the leaves (30). Through these
" deeds he (the khalif) has gained renown such as never ceases to be the subject of
" conversation by night and of contemplation by day. The East is directed by his
" (guiding) lights; nay, when the light of his person appears, the West exclaims :
" ' Cover it! (it is too bright).' It is really a light which the deepest shades of dark-
" ness cannot hide, and a renown which the leaves of (numerous) volumes would be
" unable to contain. This letter from your servant announces what follows : God
" has given (us) a victory over the enemy whose spears are now broken to pieces
" (tashattatat kandsuhu shukakán), whose sword is now blunted to a staff, whose army,
" though greater in number and stronger in hands (than ours) has been routed,
" whose troops are scattered (tárat firakuhu firakán) and whose impetuous attacks
" are paralysed. That was by stroke which put a bridle on the sight (i. e. quicker
" than sight) by a chastisement such that he who had a hand in it must have been
" without hands (i. e. a superior being, God). The feet slipped from under the foe,
" even on the ground which they had worn bare (halīka), and his eyes were cast down
" (in fear) whilst the eyes of the swords opposed to him were numerous. The eyelid
" (the scabbard) of his sword was asleep, but a flash of lightning which removed slum-
" ber from all eyelids awakened it. The noses (points) of his spears were cut off,
" they which had been so long cocked up in vain hopes or bloody with (inflicting)
" deaths. The holy land has become the pure one, after being in a state of impurity;
" there the only God is now one, he who, according to them, was the third (of the
" trinity). The temples of infidelity have been overturned and the fangs of polytheism
" are now plucked out. Its hands, once so brave, have agreed on surrendering their
" strong castles, and its champions fully equipped have humbly given up their ample
" fiefs. For they discovered that the water (the temper) of their swords would no

" longer be for them a defense and that the fire (warmth) of confraternity would
" no longer stand them in aid.   Disgrace and humiliation have fallen upon them ;
" God has replaced bad by good and transferred the house of his worship from
" people predestined to be placed on his left hand to people predestined to stand
" at his right. Your servant (Salâh ad-Dîn) had already encountered them and, as
" God came to his assistance with the angels, he inflicted on them such a defeat as
" could never be retrieved, and prostrated them so low that, please God ! infidelity
" will never get upon its feet again.   The prisoners were taken in such numbers
" that all our chains were filled, and so many were the slain that our swords also
" were killed (put out of service).   The conflict, on ceasing, disclosed to view horses,
" arms and infidels lying on the ground, offering thus an example of fitting retri-
" bution (inadf mukhtî), for they (who cut and destroyed) were slain with cutting
" swords and destroying spears.   Whilst our weapons retaliated on them, they re-
" taliated on our weapons (by causing them to be worn out and spoiled).   How many
" were our crescent (-shaped) swords which inflicted strokes till they became (as
" blunt) as the spathes of the date-tree ! how many the star (-bright) lances which
" inflicted wounds till the y were rendered (curved) like aged men ! how many the
" Persian horses which galloped forward with their valiant riders towards the fate by
" which they were immediately seized !   The bow opened its mouth (emitted a
" twanging sound) and bit (struck) the adversary, far off as he was, making him
" thus its prey.   On that day, multitudes were assembled and the angels were there
" as witnesses.   Infidelity then cried out (like a woman in labour), but Islamism
" was the child (which it brought into the world).   The ribs of the unbelievers be-
" came fuel for Gehenna.   Their despot was taken prisoner, bearing in his hand
" the object in which he placed his utmost confidence, the strongest bond by which
" he held to his religion, namely, the cross of the Crucifixion, by which were led to
" battle the people of arrogance.   In every serious affair, he would stand in the
" midst of the assembly and stretch forth his arm (with that cross), but on this oc-
" casion, he stretched forth his arms to bid it farewell.   These moths of his did not
" fail to cast themselves into the flame which he lighted up, and his reptiles never
" missed to congregate under the shade of his misguidance.   Under that cross,
" they would fight the crossest and the most resolute of battles ; they considered it
" as the best guarantee of the stipulations which they contracted, and they thought
" it to be a wall (of protection), round which the trench was dug by the continual

" treading of their horses' hoofs. On that day, their chiefs were made prisoners
" and their crafty men disappeared (*from the world*); no one of any consequence es-
" caped with the exception of the *Count* who, may God curse him! had, that same
" day, plenty of fighting and, on that day of frustration, plenty of disappointment.
" He got off, but how? flying lest he should be struck by the beak of the lance or by
" the wing of the sword; and then, soon after, the hand of God fell upon him, took
" his life (*and sent him*) to his appointed place. Such is, in truth, their promised
" retribution. Thus was he delivered up to the angel (*Malek*) of the kingdom of
" death. Your servant (*Salâh ad-Dîn*) then went through the country and extended
" over it the Abbaside standards, so black (*in colour*) and so white (*fortunate*) in their
" effects. — It was they that fluttered and shook, but the hearts of the foe flutter-
" ed still more. These (*standards*) were rendered victorious, as also the resolutions
" of their partisans, by the light which they spread around when the zephyr opened
" their eyes, and when their fringes pointed towards the face of victory. He took this
" place and that, which were really towns and cities, though designated by the names
" of countries, because they possessed corn-fields and tillage-grounds, strong-holds
" and good lands, lakes and islands, mosques and pulpits, troops and soldiers.
" Your servant placed garrisons in them and passed on, leaving them behind after
" seizing on the opportunity (*of taking them*). Out of them he mowed away infi-
" delity and in them he sowed Islamism; from their places of prayer he cast down
" the cross and set up the *adân* (*the Moslim call to prayer*). The altars were repla-
" ced by pulpits and the churches converted into mosques; the people of the Koran
" succeeded to the people of the cross and formed there settlements whence they
" might carry on war for the religion of God. His (*Salâh ad-Dîn's*) eyes and those
" of the Moslims were rejoiced to find that, for him and for his troops, victory was
" always attached to a proposition and its complement (51). They were delighted
" at his getting possession of every rampart the fall of which could not have been ex-
" pected till the day on which the trumpet (*of the resurrection*) is to be sounded, and
" (*were much pleased to find*) that nothing remained (*to be taken*) except Jerusalem,
" in which all the scattered bands and fugitives had taken refuge. From far and
" near all fled to it as an asylum, imagining that it would protect them against
" God and that its church would be with Him their intercessor. Your servant, on
" halting before the place, saw that it was a town as large as a city and (*that it con-*
" *tained*) a multitude equal to that of the day of mutual interpellation (*the day of judg-*

" ment). In it (he perceived also) resolutions firmly concerted and combined to
" (encounter) death. He took position on a spot before it, whilst the garrison
" thought light of (drinking at) the pond where the sword allays its thirst, even were
" they to die, choked with that draught. On the side of the city where he had
" encamped, he saw a deep valley, a precipice rugged and profound, with a wall
" which encircled the city like a bracelet, and towers which represented the larger
" pearls of the necklace worn by that place of residence. He therefore removed to
" another side which was more accessible and to which cavalry could approach.
" There he took his stand and invested the place, pitching his tent so near (the walls)
" that its sides could be reached by the missiles (of the besieged). He pushed the
" walls with his shoulders (i. e. he advanced close to them), faced the city and attacked
" it, assailed it and pressed it so closely that its capture was expected. The people
" collected in it fell into disunion and behold, rather than fall by the edge of the
" sword, they preferred captivity (52). They sent a message to him with the offer of
" paying tribute for a certain time; hoping thus to obtain some respite from their
" sufferings and to await the arrival of succour. Your servant, perceiving their in-
" tentions through the equivocal meaning of their words, replied in a tone of supe-
" riority and brought forward those engines, the mangonels, which are charged to
" inflict chastisement on rebellious and contumacious (?) fortresses. He strung
" against the enemy the bows of these arbalets which shoot off without being depri-
" ved of arrows (being always well provided with them), and these arrows were
" not deprived of points. They reached the wall, and, behold! the arrows ser-
" ved as toothpicks to the teeth (the embrasures) of the battlements. Victory sent
" to announce its arrival a mangonel which like it, was to have its basis upon the
" earth whilst its apex touched the stars (53). It wounded the heads of those towers
" which served to repel attacks and made a noise which the deafest of the infidels
" must have heard. It struck up a cloud of dust like a beacon, depriving the wall
" of its defenders and the fight of its spectators. The miner thus got an opportunity
" of removing the veil from the face of war (54) and of converting stone into its
" pristine form, that of earth. He approached the rock (the wall), gnawed its tissue
" with the tooth of the crowbar and undid its knots with heavy strokes, showing
" thus the dexterity of his fingers. He made the holy Sakhra hear his sighs and in-
" vocations, so that it almost had compassion on his eyes (which were inflamed with
" weeping). Some of the stones renounced their attachment to others and then

" took with ruin the engagement never quit the ground again.   A breach was made in
" the wall, and that opening closed the doors against their escape.   Whilst the pas-
" sage was making through these stones, the infidel exclaimed : ' O that I were dust!'
" (Koran, s. 78, v. 41).   Then the infidels despaired of the (safety of) the occupiers
" of the houses, as the infidels despair of (the resurrection of) the occupiers of the
" tombs (Koran, s. 60, v. 13).   The order of God came to pass (Koran, s. 40, v. 78),
" and the deceiver deceived them concerning God (Koran, s. 57, v. 13).   At that in-
" stant, the chief of their infidelity, the director of their affairs (whose name was) Ibn
" Barisân (Barizan or Baléan d'Ibelin), came out to request that the city might be
" taken by capitulation, not by force, by a treaty of security, not by storm.   Thus
" did he expose himself to receive death or to be covered with the humiliation of
" captivity after enjoying the grandeurs of sovereignty; he cast his side upon the
" ground, that side which no adversary was ever able to cast down.   He offered
" tribute to an amount such as the most covetous could not have hoped for and he
" said : ' We have there some thousands of Moslim prisoners, and the Franks
" ' are resolved that, in case their city is stormed and their shoulders are to feel all
" ' the burden of war, they will commence by speeding them (out of the world)
" ' and redouble (the slaughter) by killing their own women and children.   After that,
" ' they will advance to meet the foe ; not a combatant shall die without being reven-
" ' ged, and not a sword shall be laid down till it is shattered and broken.' — The
" emirs were of advice that the mildest measures should be taken against a city des-
" tined to be captured.   For, said they, if it be taken by assault, their bravest war-
" riors will certainly rush to the fight and there will be a great loss of lives in an
" enterprize of which the commencement has so well answered our expectations.
" The wounds already inflicted on our soldiers are sufficient to shackle every
" assault (al-fatakát) and impede every movement. — The offer made by the be-
" sieged, gratuitously and humbly, was accepted, and the partisans of fighting,
" though victorious, abstained from what they had the power to execute.   The Mos-
" lims then regained possession of a place which, when they last saw it, contained
" only the vestiges of inhabitants, but which had been so well attended to by infi-
" delity that it had become a paradise.   Assuredly it was God who turned the (Franks)
" out of it and expelled them, and who, in his anger against them, favoured the
" true believers.   The infidels, may God frustrate their projects! had defended it
" with the lance and the sword, and had rebuilt it with columns and slabs of mar-

" ble. It was there that they had established their churches and the dwellings of
" the Templars and Hospitallers; (*there they had erected*) all those curious (*foun-*
" *tains*) of marble which poured forth water in abundance and of which the flow
" never ceased. (*For them,*) iron was easy to be cut and let itself be twisted into a
" variety of forms; so that the metal which is so stubborn became (*as ductile*) as the
" gold which is subservient to our pleasures. Nothing is seen there but sitting-
" places that resemble gardens and are coated with shining marble; there are co-
" lumns to which sprouting leaves give the appearance of trees. Your servant then
" ordered that the Aksa should be restored to its former state and appointed to it
" *imâms*, charged to celebrate the usual divine service. — On Friday, the 4th of
" Shâbân (8th Oct. A. D. 1187), the *khotba* was recited in it with such effect
" that the heavens had nearly split, not with indignation (55) but to shed tears (of
" joy), and the stars left their places, not to lapidate (56) but to make rejoicing.
" The profession of the divine unity, to make which the road had been closed, was
" then raised up to God, and the tombs of the prophets were brought to light after
" having been covered with filth and trodden under foot. The five daily prayers
" which Trinitarianism had suppressed were established again, and the tongues
" which had been tied by the enchantments of infidelity proclaimed aloud that God
" was great. The name of the Commander of the faithful was announced from the
" pulpit, from that noblest of stations which a khalif can hold, and it received such
" welcome as is given by those who have already made the pilgrimage to those who
" have just fulfilled that duty. The doctors of the law kept flitting about in both
" sides of the mosque which, had it been capable of flying, would have done so.
" Your servant writes (*to you*) whilst occupied in reducing the remainder of the for-
" tresses and in giving relief to those hearts which had been oppressed by the con-
" tinuance of war; for the sources which furnished strength to his soldiers had been
" drained out and the fountains of suffering had been often visited. The conquer-
" ed country, that which has been already indicated, is overrun by troops, its
" stores have been plundered, its crops eaten up; it is now a country which asks for
" aid and from which none should be required; it must repose in order to recover
" its strength, and therefore, it should not be exhausted; it stands in need of pecu-
" niary assistance and cannot furnish any, ships must be sent to its sea and
" posts established to guard its coasts (57). He (*Salâh ad-Dîn*) is actively engaged
" in arming the walls and repairing the ruins of the fortresses, but the greatest toil

" is easily borne when counterbalanced by this conquest. Since it has been effec-
" ted, the hopes entertained by the Franks have been deferred, but are not aban-
" doned; if they offer up prayers, your servant hopes that God will not listen to them,
" and that their hands will be withheld from this country till they are totally cut
" off. The particulars of this fortunate event can hardly be furnished without the
" assistance of the tongue nor can their recital be completed except by oral com-
" munication. For that reason, your servant has sent to you a tongue which will
" relate them all, set fort clearly and in regular order the details of this good news and
" pass in review all these subjects of joy, from the first to the last. His name is so
" and so. God is he who grants true favour. " — Here ends al-Kâdi 'l-Fâdil's
dispatch. I intended to abridge it, in retaining its beauties, but, on commencing
the task, I said to myself: It may happen that one of my readers, on perusing
these fragments, may be desirous of reading the whole document; I therefore gave
up my former idea and inserted it all; besides, it is rarely to be met with. As the
copy of it which I followed was inexact (lit. *was sickly*), I endeavoured to correct it,
as far as I was able, and thus brought it into its present form. — The *kâtib* Imâd
ad-Dîn al-Ispahâni also wrote an epistle on the conquest of Jerusalem, but, not to be
prolix, I abstain from inserting it The same author composed, on that subject,
a book in two volumes (or *sections*) which he entitled *al-Fath al-Kussi* (see *vol. III*,
p. 303, etc.). Some time ago I saw an elegant epistle relating to the conquest
of that city and drawn up by Diâ ad-Dîn Nasr Allah Ibn al-Athîr al-Jazari (*vol. III*.
p. 541). Every writer wished to try his hand on the subject, but the Kâdi 'l-Fâdil was
the great master in that branch of composition and, when he undertook any thing
of the kind, no one was capable of being his rival or of surpassing him. I therefore
have given his production and omitted the others, lest I should extend this article
too much. — Rashîd ad-Dîn Abû Muhammad Abd ar-Rahmân Ibn Nasr Ibn al-Hasan
Ibn Mufarrej an-Nâblusi, a poet of some celebrity, who was present at the taking of
the city, recited to the sultan Salâh ad-Dîn a *kasîda* of his own composing which
began thus :

This is what every day expected; let people then fulfil towards God what they have vowed.

It is a long poem, containing upwards of one hundred verses. In it the author
praises Salâh ad-Dîn and congratulates him on that conquest. Having terminated
what we had to say on this subject (58), we shall now resume the narration made

by Ibn Shaddâd in the History of Salâh ad-Dîn: " Then," says he, " was thrown " down the cross which stood on the dome of the Sakhra and was of an im- " mense size; thus, God furnished to Islamism, through him, a powerful assistance." — In our article on Ortuk (vol. *I.* p. 171) we have spoken of Jerusalem and mention- ed that it was taken from Sokmân and Il-Ghâzi, the sons of that prince, by al- Afdal Amîr al-Juyûsh (col. *I.* p. 612). It was afterwards taken by the Franks, on Friday, the 23rd of Shaabân, 492 (15 July, 1099); or, according to another account, on the second of that month; some say that Friday, the 26th of Ramadân (16th August), is the date of that event. It remained in their hands till it was taken from them by the sultan Salâh ad-Dîn on the day of which we have already indicated the date. Let us return to Ibn Shaddâd's recital : " The main " condition of the peace was that every man (of the city) should pay twenty pieces " of gold, every woman five Tyrian dinars, and the children, male and female, each " one dinar. Those who paid this tax were to obtain their liberty, and those who " did not were to be made captives. All the Muslim prisoners detained in the city " recovered their liberty, and their number was very great. He (Salâh ad-Dîn) re- " mained there till he had collected the money and distributed it to his emirs and sol- " diers. He gave part of it also to the doctors of divinity, the legists, the ascetics " and the persons who had come to see him. Orders were issued by him that those " Franks who had paid the tax imposed on them should be safely escorted to Tyre, " their place of refuge. He did not leave the city till he had given away all the " sums which had been collected for him and which amounted to nearly two hun- " dred and twenty thousand dinars (£. 132,000). His departure took place on Fri- " day, the 25th of Shaabân, the same year (30th Oct. 1187). After conquering Jeru- " salem, he thought it would be right to march against Tyre, being well aware that if " he delayed doing so, he would probably have great difficulty in reducing such a " fortress. On his way, he passed through Acre and halted in order to examine the " state of that place, after which, he set out for Tyre. This was on Friday, the 5th " of Ramadân (8th Nov.). Having halted near the city, he dispatched messengers " with orders to send him the machines of war and, when all were brought, he took " position and attacked the place with great vigour. This was on the 12th of the " same month. The Egyptian fleet, which he had called to this assistance, having " then arrived, he attacked Tyre by sea and by land, whilst some of his troops went to " reduce Hûnain, which place surrendered on the 23rd of Shauwâl (26th December,

" 1187). Some time afterwards, the fleet of Tyre sallied out by night, surprised
" the Moslim fleet, of which they took five vessels with the *mokaddam* (*the military*
" *chief*) and the *raïs* (*the naval commander*). In this combat a great number of
" Moslims lost their lives. It took place on the 27th of the month just mentioned
" (30th Dec.). Saláh ad-Din was vexed to the heart by this contrariety and,
" as the rainy season had set in with extraordinary violence, he consulted his offi-
" cers as to what should be done. Their advice being that he ought to raise the
" siege, so as to repose his army and have time to collect more troops, he decamped
" and took with him as many of the engines of war as he could carry off. The re-
" mainder he burned, being unable to remove them on account of the mud and the
" rain. It was on Sunday, the 2nd of Zû 'l-Kaada (3rd January, 1188) that he
" commenced his retreat. The army then separated, and each of its divisions ha-
" ving received permission to depart, returned to the country from which it came.
" He remained at Acre with his own private troops and staid there till the beginning
" of the year 584 (March, A. D. 1188). In the begining of the month of Muharram
" (March), he laid siege to Kaukab with the small body of men which had not left him.
" As Kaukab was a strong fortress, full of men and stores, he perceived that it could
" not be taken without hard fighting, and therefore proceeded to Damascus, where he
" arrived on the 6th of the first Rabî (5th May)."—The same author says : " When
" he was posted near Kaukab, I went to offer him my services, but soon left him
" for the purpose of making a pilgrimage to Jerusalem and Hebron, and then I re-
" turned to Damascus, where I arrived on the same day as he did." — Of this we have
spoken in our article on Ibn Shaddâd (page 420 *of this volume*). — " He remained
" five days in Damascus," said Ibn Shaddâd, " and, being informed that the Franks
" were in march with the intention of taking (*the fortress of*) Jubail (*Jebeil*) by surprise,
" he set out in all haste and dispatched messengers to every quarter for the purpose
" of calling his troops together. When the Franks heard that he was in march
" for Jubail, they gave up their attempt. Saláh ad-Din having then learned that
" Imâd ad-Din (*Zinki II*), the sovereign of Sinjâr, and Musaffar ad-Din Ibn Zain ad-
" Din had arrived at Aleppo with the troops of Mosul and that they intended to place
" themselves under his orders and make a campaign with him, proceeded to Hisn
" al-Akrâd (*the castle of the Kurds*)." — He says in the same work : " On the 1st of
" the first Jumâda, 584 (28th June, A. D. 1188), I entered into the sultan's ser-
" vice. All that I have already related is given on the authority of persons in whose

" veracity I confide, and from this out, I inscribe nothing (in my work) except what
" I have witnessed or what I learned from persons whose statements were (for me)
" almost as worthy of belief as the actual sight (of the occurrences)." — " On Friday,
" the 4th of the first Jumáda, the sultan penetrated into the enemy's country in
" full military array, each division of the troops being drawn up in proper order;
" that which formed the right wing took the lead, under the commandment of
" Imád ad-Dín Zinki; that of the left wing, under the orders of Muzaffar ad-Dín,
" brought up the rear, and that of the center was between them both. The sul-
" tan arrived before Antartús on Sunday, the 6th of the first Jumáda, after day-break
" and halted so that he might examine the aspect of the place. He was then in
" march for Jabala, but as it (Antartús) did not appear to him very formidable, he
" resolved on attacking it and called back the right wing. He retained the position
" which he had taken, whilst the left wing was posted, by his orders, on the sea-
" coast (at one side of the city) and the right wing on (the coast at) the other side.
" — The army thus invested the city from the sea (on one side of it) to the sea (on
" the other). Antartús was of great strength, being situated on the sea and defen-
" ded by two towers as large as castles. The troops mounted (on horseback)
" and advanced towards the place; the assault was then given and, by a vigo-
" rous attack, they carried it when hostilities were least expected. Their tents
" had not been all pitched when the ramparts were scaled and the place was taken
" by storm. Every thing contained in it became the prey of the Moslims. He (Sa-
" láh ad-Dín) caused the city to be burnt down and remained outside of it
" till the 14th of the first Jumáda. Muzaffar ad-Dín was charged to take one of the
" towers and directed his attacks against it till he laid it in ruins. Al-Malik az-
" Záhir then came to join his father, in pursuance to that sultan's orders, and brought
" with him a large body of troops. He (the sultan) then marched against Jabala,
" reached it on the 18th of the first Jumáda, the same year (15th July, A. D. 1188)
" and took it before the rest of the army had come up and taken position. This
" place contained a Moslim population, and the people had a kádi charged to settle
" their differences. The citadel being vigourously attacked, capitulated on Satur-
" day, the 19th of the first Jumáda. The sultan remained there till the 23rd of the
" month and then set out for al-Ládakiya. He halted before that place on Thurs-
" day, the 24th of the same month. It was an agreeable town, without walls, and
" possessed a harbour of great renown. (For its defense) it had two castles, one

" touching the other and both situated on a hill by which it was commanded. The
" town was taken after a severe struggle which lasted till the end of the day, but the
" castles held out. The victors found in it an immense booty, as it was a place of
" commerce. The castles were then attacked by assaults and by a mine which finally
" attained the length of sixty cubits and was four cubits in width. When the troops
" in these forts perceived that the next assault would be successful, they asked for
" quarter. This was on the evening of Friday, the 25th of the same month. They
" offered to capitulate on condition that they, their women and their children should
" retire in safety and be allowed to retain their personal property; consenting, at
" the same time, to deliver up the grain and other provisions which were in their
" stores, and, moreover, their arms and their machines of war. This proposal
" being accepted, the Moslim standard was set up there, on Saturday. Salâh ad-
" Dìn remained outside the place till Sunday, the 27th of the month and then de-
" parted for Sahyûn. On Tuesday, the 29th of the month, he arrived there, and
" his troops, after some hard fighting, took the town. This was on Friday, the 2nd
" of the latter Jumâda (29th July, A. D. 1188). After that, they advanced against
" the citadel and attacked it vigorously. The garrison, perceiving (that farther re-
" sistance would be their) perdition, asked to be taken into safeguard, which favour
" was granted on condition that each man should pay ten dinars, each woman five,
" and each child, whether male or female, one dinar. The sultan remained in that
" part of the country till he took Platanus and a number of other fortresses in the
" dependencies of Sahyûn. He then went to Bakâs, which is a strong castle situa-
" ted on the Orontes and from beneath which flows out a stream of water. He ar-
" rived there on Tuesday, the 6th of the latter Jumâda and attacked it vigorously
" till Friday, the 9th of that month, when God enabled him to take it by assault.
" The greater part of the garrison was slain and the survivors were reduced to bon-
" dage. The Moslims plundered the place and took all it contained. To it (Bakâs)
" belonged another castle called ash-Shughr, which was very strong and with
" which it communicated by means of a bridge; there being no other road to
" it. He directed his mangonels against the fortress, from every side, till the gar-
" rison, seeing that no one was coming to their relief, asked to capitulate, provided
" that a respite of three days were given to them. This was on Tuesday, the 13th
" of that month. The condition was accepted and, on Friday the 16th, the place
" surrendered and the Moslim standard was planted upon its walls. He then pro-

" ceeded towards a group of castles called Burzaih, the strength of which was prover-
" bial throughout the territory of the Franks. This fortress was surrounded on all
" sides by deep valleys and stood on a hill upwards of five hundred and seventy cu-
" bits high. He arrived before it on Saturday, the 24th of the month and, on Tuesday,
" the 27th, he took it by assault. The strong castle of Darbessak, against which he
" then turned and which he reached on Friday, the 8th of Rajab (2nd Sept. 1118),
" was vigorously attacked by him and, on Friday, the 22nd, the Moslim standard was
" planted on its walls. Having given this place as a present to the emir Alam ad-
" Dîn Ibn Haidar(59), he departed on Saturday morning, the 23rd, and halted before
" Baghrâs, a strong castle in the neighbourhood of Antioch. On the 2nd of Shaabân
" (26th Sept.), after some hard fighting, he planted the Moslim standard on its walls.
" The people of Antioch having then sent to ask for a truce, he acceded to their
" prayer because his army was heartily tired of this (continual) warfare. The truce
" was to last seven months and no longer, and the conditions imposed on them were
" that they should set at liberty all their captives and surrender the city if no one
" came to their assistance. On his departure from that place, he accepted the invi-
" tation of al-Malik az-Zâhir, prince of Aleppo, who requested of him to pass through
" that city. He arrived there on the 11th of Shaabân, stopped three days in the
" citadel and was treated by az-Zâhir with great hospitality. After leaving Aleppo
" he was met by his nephew Taki ad-Dîn Omar, who took him up to the for-
" tress of Hamât where he partook of a repast and heard a concert of music, such as
" is performed by the Sûfis (dervishes). He passed one night there and bestowed on
" his nephew the towns of Jabala and al-Lâdakiya. He then took the road which
" passes through Baalbek and arrived at Damascus, a few days before the commen-
" cement of Ramadân. — On one of the first ten days of that month, he set out for
" Safad, which place he attacked unremittingly till the 14th of Shauwâl, when the
" garrison capitulated to save their lives. In the month of Ramadân (Oct.-Nov.,
" A. D. 1188), al-Karak was surrendered (to al-Malik al-Addil), and the officers who
" commanded there obtained, on giving up the place, that their master, who had
" remained in captivity since the battle of Hittîn, should be set at liberty." — Such
are the words of Ibn Shaddâd, but they are in disaccord with what has been already
mentioned respecting (Arndt), prince of al-Karak and ash-Shaubek, who had been
taken prisoner at Hittîn and whom the sultan slew with his own hand: To clear up
this difficulty, it would be requisite to examine elsewhere. — " The sultan then pro-

" ceeded to al-Kaukab, which place ho invested and attacked with great vigour.
" The rain fell incessantly, the muddiness of the ground augmented, the storms
" were continual and the besieged had the advantage of an elevated position; yet
" they were soon convinced that they should be taken prisoners unless they surrende-
" red. It was on the 15th of Zù 'l-Kaada, the same year (5th Jan. 1189), that the sul-
" tan granted them a capitulation and obtained possession of the fortress. He then
" went down into (the territory of) al-Ghaur and encamped there, after dismissing
" the greater part of his troops. Towards the end of the month he set out again,
" with the intention of visiting Jerusalem and of accompanying so far his brother
" al-Aàdil, who was proceeding to Egypt. On the 8th of Zù 'l-Hijja he arrived in
" that city, (on the 10th) he presided at the prayer of the Festival and, on the 11th,
" he set out for the purpose of examining the state of Ascalon, which place he then
" took from his brother al-Aàdil, giving him al-Karak in exchange. After that he
" visited and inspected the towns of the Sàhil; then he went to Acre and remained
" there during the greater part of Muharram, 585 (Feb.-March, A. D. 1189). Ha-
" ving put all things there into proper order, he appointed the emir Bahà ad-Dln
" Karàkûsh (vol. II. p. 520) to the government of the place and ordered him to get
" the walls into a good state of defense. He then departed for Damascus, where he
" arrived on the 1st of Safar (21st March). He remained there till the month of
" the first Rabi (April-May) and then set out for Shakîf Arnûn, which was a place
" of great strength. On the 17th of that month, he encamped in Marj Ayûn, a
" low plain in the neighbourhood of as-Shakîf. For some time he directed in
" person the attacks made upon that fortress, whilst troops came every day to join
" him. — The lord of as-Shakîf, perceiving his inability to resist, went out to see Sa-
" làh ad-Dln so secretly that no one was aware of his presence till was seen standing
" at the entrance of the sultan's tent. Salàh ad-Dln ordered him to be introduced
" and received him with every mark of honour and respect. This chief was one of
" the greatest among the Franks and one of most intelligent: he knew Arabic and
" had some acquaintance with historical facts and narratives. — When presented to
" the sultan, he behaved with becoming deference and, after dining with him, he
" said to him in private: I am your mamlûk (slave) and your servant. This for-
" tress I shall deliver to you without giving you the trouble (of besieging it); but I
" must obtain from you a dwelling in Damascus, because it would be impossible for
" me to live among the Franks after doing so. I must have also an appanage suffi-

" cient for my own maintenance and that of my family. The sultan agreed to these
" conditions and to some others which were proposed. In the month of the first
" Rabi, news reached him of the surrender of ash-Shaubek, which place he had kept
" blockaded for the space of a year, till the garrison, having consumed all its provi-
" sions, asked to capitulate. Having then discovered that the sovereign of Shakif's
" proposals were a mere deception, he caused him to be arrested. Soon after, he
" was informed that the Franks had marched against Acre and laid siege to it on
" Monday, the 13th of Rajab, 585 (27th August, A. D. 1189). That same day, he
" sent the lord of Shakif to Damascus after covering him with humiliation. — He
" then visited Acre unexpectedly, with the intention of giving heart to those who
" were in the town, and dispatched messengers to all parts, with orders to send up
" troops. When these reinforcements arrived, the enemy had about two thousand
" horse and thirty thousand foot under arms; but the Franks continued to arrive in
" such numbers and became so formidable that, on Thursday, the last day of Rajab
" (13th Sept.), they were able to invest Acre completely and prevent people from en-
" tering into it and from leaving it. The sultan took this greatly to heart and set
" his mind on opening by main force a passage into the town, so that convoys might
" furnish it with provisions and supplies. The emirs, being consulted by him on
" the subject, were all of opinion that they should close with the enemy and force a
" passage. This being executed, the Moslims were enabled to enter into the place
" with the sultan, who went in to examine the state of affairs. During some days,
" frequent conflicts took place between the two parties and (our) people then retired
" to Tall al-Ghaiâdiya (60), a hill overlooking the town. It was at this place of
" station that Husâm ad-Din Tumân, the emir of whom we have spoken (p. 509)
" breathed his last. This chief, who was noted for his bravery, died on the night
" preceding the 15th of Shabân, 585 (28th Sept. A. D. 1189)." — Our shaikh Ibn
" Shaddâd now proceeds to narrate a number of conflicts which we have no motive
" for indicating here; a full account of them would lengthen this article too much,
" and our object is to notice main points only and nothing else. If I have mention-
" ed the taking of these fortresses, it was merely because the reader might wish to
" know the dates, and I spoke of those only which (by their importance) might draw
" his attention; as for the others, I passed them over in silence. — The sultan,
" being informed that a great sickness prevailed in the plain of Acre and was
" spreading through both armies, recited in my hearing the following verse :

" My two friends ! kill me with Mâlik ; kill Mâlik with me.

" By that he gave us to understand that he was willing to die provided that God
" destroyed His enemies. " — The origin of this verse requires to be explained :
Mâlik Ibn al-Hârith, surnamed al-Ashtar an-Nakhâi, bore a high reputation for courage and bravery; he was one of Ali Ibn Abi Tâlib's chief partisans. At the battle
of the Camel, he and Abd Allah, the son of az-Zubair, seized on each other. This
Abd Allah also was renowned for bravery and was then (*fighting*) on the side of his
maternal aunt Aâisha, the mother of the faithful (*and Muhammad's widow*). —
Talha and az-Zubair were on the same side, fighting against Ali. — When the two
champions seized one on the other, he that was the strongest would get his adversary under him and weigh upon his breast; this they did alternately, a number
times, and Abd Allah, the son of az-Zubair, kept exclaiming : *Kill me with Mâlik !*
kill Mâlik with me ! By *Mâlik* he meant al-Ashtar an-Nakhâi. Such is the substance of the long narration which is given in the books of annals. Abd Allah Ibn
az-Zubair said, in speaking of this affair : " I encountered al-Ashtar an-Nakhâi
" at the battle of the Camel and, for every blow I gave him, he returned me six or
" seven. Then he caught me by the foot, threw me into the ditch and said :
" ' By Allah ! were you not related to the Prophet of God, not a single member
" ' of your body should remain joined to another.' Abû Bakr Ibn Abi Shaiba
said : " When Aâisha learned that Ibn az-Zubair had escaped with his life after en-
" countering al-Ashtar, she gave ten thousand dirhems to the man who brought her
" the news." It is related that, subsequently to the battle of the Camel, Aâisha
received a visit from al-Ashtar and said to him : " It was you, Ashtar ! who meant to
" kill my sisters's son on the day of the battle?" To this he replied by reciting
these verses :

" O Aâisha ! had I not been without food for three (*days*), you would have found your sis-
" ter's son among the slain, on the morning of the day in which he exclaimed with a feeble
voice, whilst spears were directed against him : ' Kill me with Mâlik. ' When saved him from
" me was his breakfast, his youth and the emptiness of (my) stomach which could not support
" (*long fasting*). "

Zahr Ibn Kais related as follows : " I went to the bath with Abd Allah Ibn az-
" Zubair and I remarked on his head a scar so deep that it would have held the contents

" of an oil-flask. He asked me if I knew who gave him that blow and, on my re-
" plying that I did not, he said : ' It was your uncle's son, al-Ashtar an-Nakhâi.'
" —Let us return to our subject : "The Franks," says Ibn Shaddâd, "then received
" reinforcements from beyond the sea and prevailed, at Acre, over the assembled
" Musulmans. Amongst the latter were the emirs Saif ad-Din Ali Ibn Ahmad al-
" Mashtûb al-Hakkâri (vol. I. p. 164) and Bahâ ad-Din Karâkûsh, one of Salâh ad-
" Din's domestics. The enemy pressed the Moslims so closely that they put it out of
" their power to keep the town any longer; so, on Friday, the 17th of the latter Ju-
" mâda, 587 (12th July, 1191), a man swam from Acre with letters in which the
" besieged described the state to which they were reduced, and declared that all was
" certainly lost and that the besiegers would strike off their heads in case the place
" was taken by storm; they had therefore consented to capitulate on the following
" conditions : the town was to be delivered up with all it contained, such as en-
" gines of war, military stores, arms and ships; a contribution of two hundred thou-
" sand dinars was to be paid; five hundred prisoners, not otherwise designated, and
" one hundred whose names were mentioned, should be delivered up and the cross
" of the Crucifixion should be restored. The besieged would then be allowed to
" retire in safety, carry off their personal property, such as money and clothing,
" and take with them their women and children. By another article they engaged
" to pay four thousand dinars to the Marquis (Conrad of Montferrat) who had been
" the chief director in this negotiation. When the sultan heard the contents of these
" letters, he disapproved in the most formal manner of the arrangement which had
" been made and took the matter greatly to heart. He assembled those grandees of
" his empire who were capable of giving good advice and asked them what was to
" be done. After wavering in his resolutions and hesitating between conflicting
" thoughts, he remained greatly troubled in mind, but at length decided on sen-
" ding,. that very night, the same swimmer to the besieged garrison, with
" a letter in which he blamed the arrangement concluded between the parties.
" He was still hesitating when behold ! the standards of the enemy, their
" crosses, their fires and their distinctive emblems appeared on the walls of the
" town. This was on the noon of Friday, the 17th of the latter Jumâda of the
" same year. The Franks uttered simultaneously a loud cry which fell like a
" heavy stroke upon the Moslims who, in their deep affliction, began to wail, to
" groan, to weep and to lament." — Farther on Ibn Shaddâd says : The Franks

"set out from Aere with the intention of taking Ascalon, and followed the
"shore-road whilst the sultan kept opposite to them with his army. On reaching
"Arsûf they fought a battle by which the strength of the Moslims was greatly
"broken. Advancing in the same order as before, they reached a halting-place,
"and there was terminated the tenth day of their march from Aere. The sultan
"then went to ar-Ramla, where news was brought to him that the enemy intended
"to rebuild Jaffa and establish in it a garrison with provisions and instruments of
"war (62). He therefore called in his ordinary counsellors and asked their advice
"respecting Ascalon, whether that place should be demolished or preserved.   They
"were all of opinion that al-Malik al-Aâdil should remain and face the enemy whilst
"the sultan himself went to destroy Ascalon; for it was to be feared that the Franks,
"if they occupied it whilst it was still inhabited, would be enabled, from that posi-
"tion, to take Jerusalem and cut off all communication with Egypt. The troops
"were, besides, unwilling to enter into a place where they might meet with the
"same fate as had befallen the Moslims of Acre.   It was therefore decided that As-
"calon should be destroyed and that the conservation of Jerusalem should be pre-
"ferred to every thing else.   The demolition was to begin by ruining simultaneously
"different parts of the city which were indicated before-hand.   This assembly was
"held on Tuesday the 17th of Shâbân, 587 (0th September, A. D. 1191). On the
"morning of the next day, they set out for Ascalon." — In another place, Ibn
Shaddâd says: " He (Salâh ad-Dîn) spoke to me respecting the destruction of the
"town, after having conversed with his son al-Malik al-Afdal on the same subject,
"and he finished by saying : ' I should rather lose all my sons than throw down a
" ' single stone of that place; but since God has decided that it must be done and
" ' since it will be advantageous for the Moslims, by what means can it be avoided?'
The same author says elsewhere : " When the resolution of destroying Ascalon was
"formed, God made him feel the necessity of that (sacrifice) and perceive its utility;
"especially as the Moslims would be unable to keep the place. — The work of des-
"truction was begun on Thursday morning, the 19th of Shâbân. The task of de-
"molishing the walls was shared among the troops, each emir and his men having
"one of the curtains and one of the towers assigned to them.   When these troops
"entered into the town, the inhabitants uttered loud cries and lamentations; for it
"was a very agreeable town, protected by strong walls, possessing lofty buildings
"and much liked as a residence. The destruction of Ascalon was a great affliction

" for the people (*the Musulmans*), and loud were the lamentations of the inhabitants,
" then forced to quit their homes. They sold whatever they could not carry away,
" giving for one dirhem an object which was worth ten. A dozen of hens were sold for
" one dirhem; all was confusion in the town; the inhabitants went to the camp,
" whence some set out for Egypt and others for Syria, and all underwent the greatest
" hardships (*on the way*). The sultan and his sons did their utmost to ruin the
" town before the Franks were aware; he feared that the enemy might hasten up and
" render the destruction of the place impossible. The people (*soldiers*) passed a
" very uncomfortable night, fatigued as they were in toiling at the demolition of the
" place. That same night a courier arrived with a dispatch from al-Malik al-Aädil
" in which was mentioned that the Franks had parleyed with him for a peace and
" that they asked to retain for themselves all the towns of the sea-coast (63). He felt
" that there was an advantange in such an arrangement; knowing, as he did, that
" his troops were harassed with warfare and burdened with debts. He therefore
" authorised his brother to treat (*with the Franks*) and make such arrangements as
" he thought fit. At an early hour on Friday, the 27th of Shàbàn, he was seen pres-
" sing the work of destruction and hastening the efforts of his men. He gave them
" permission to take as much grain as they pleased out of the granary in which the
" produce of the mîra (*land-tax paid in kind*) was hoarded up; for he feared that the
" Franks might burst into the town before he could carry it off. He then gave or-
" ders that the town should be burned, and the soldiers set fire to the houses. The
" demolitions continued till the end of Shàbàn and, on Monday, the 1st of Rama-
" dàn, the sultan ordered his son al-Malik al-Afdal to take charge of that work and
" finish it with the assistance of his own people; and I saw that prince carrying wood
" for the purpose of keeping up the fires. On Wednesday, the 3rd of Ramadàn, he
" arrived at ar-Ramla and then visited Ludd, which place he ordered to be demolished
" after inspecting it. The castle of ar-Ramla was demolished at the same time. On
" Saturday, the 13th of Ramadàn, he retired with his troops towards the high lands,
" in order that the soldiers might be able to send off their beasts of burden for the
" things of which they stood in need (64). The sultan then made the circuit of an-
" Natrûn and, by his order, the demolition of this strong castle was commenced. "
— Ibn Shaddàd then relates that al-Ankeïdr (*Richard, roi d'Angleterre*), who was
one of the greatest of the Frankish kings, sent to al-Malik al-Aädil, requesting an
interview. Al-Aädil consented and, on Friday, the 18th of Shauwàl, the same year,

they had a conversation which lasted for the greater part of the day and they separated on terms of sincere friendship. *Al-Anketâr* requested of al-Aâdil to procure for him an interview with the sultan, and the latter, to whom al-Aâdil spoke on the subject, consulted the grandees of the empire. They were all of opinion that the answer should be : "Let there be peace between us; the interview may take place "after." A messenger then arrived from al-Anketâr and said (in *that king's name*) : "Your friendship and good will are what I desire. You say that you have given "to your brother these countries here, in the Sâhil. Now, I wish you to judge "between him and me and divide that region between us. As for Jerusalem, it "must, of course, be included in my share." The envoy spoke to a great length on the subject and the sultan replied by fair words. The messenger, on whom this (*reception*) made a deep impression, was then authorised to retire. "After the en-"voy's departure," says Ibn Shaddâd, "the sultan said to me : 'Were we to make "'peace with them, we should never be secure from their perfidy. Were I to "'die, such an army as this could never again be assembled and the Franks would "'become powerful. What I had best do is to continue the war against the infi-"'dels till I expel them from the Sâhil or till I meet with my death.' Such was "his real opinion, but he was obliged to make peace." — "Then," says the same historian, "envoys passed back and forward for the purpose of establishing the "peace." — He gives a long account of these (*proceedings*), but that, I omit, because we have no necessity for it. Then took place a number of events which I abstain from noticing, the account given of them by the author extending to so great a length; the abstract of it is that peace was concluded and ratified by oath on Wednesday, the 22nd of Shâbân, 588 (2nd Sept., A. D. 1192). A proclamation was then made, announcing that peace was established and declaring that the Moslim territory and that of the Christians should equally enjoy repose and security; so that persons of either nation might go into the territory of the other and return again, without fear and without apprehension. That day, crowds were assembled, and the joy felt on both sides was such as God alone could conceive; but the Almighty knew well that he (*Salâh ad-Dîn*) had not made peace through choice and freewill but for a certain advantage : his troops were tired of war and manifested openly their unwillingness to obey orders. God alone knew what that advantage was to be : Salâh ad-Dîn died subsequently to the peace; had he died when the (*previous*) events were taking place, Islamism would have been in danger. The troops which were

arriving from distant countries for the purpose of reinforcing the army, received permission to return home and departed. The sultan, having no longer any cause of uneasiness from that quarter, resolved on making the pilgrimage (to Mekka). The Moslims now frequented the territory of the Franks who, on their side, visited that of the Moslims; goods and merchandise were carried to the towns, and a great number of the Christians went to visit Jerusalem. The sultan also set out for the purpose of inspecting that place; his brother, al-Malik al-Aádil, went to al-Karak; his son, al-Malik az-Zâhir, proceeded to Aleppo, and al-Afdal, his other son, departed for Damascus. The sultan, during his stay in Jerusalem, distributed fiefs to his people (his officers) and authorised them to return home; he made also preparations for a journey to Egypt. Having no longer any desire of making the pilgrimage, he continued to mind what he was engaged in till he at length learned positively that al-Anketâr had sailed for his own country on the 1st of Shauwâl (10th October, 1192). He then decided on entering into the Sâhil with an escort of cavalry; his intention being to examine the state of his maritime fortresses, advance to Bauyâs, go from that to Damascus, pass a few days there, return to Jerusalem and then set out for Egypt. Ibn Shaddâd says: "He ordered me to remain in Jerusalem till his return,
" so that I might direct the instalment of an hospital and the completing of a college
" which he had founded there. He departed on the morning of Thursday, the 6th
" of Shauwâl, 588 (15th Oct., A. D. 1192) and, after inspecting his fortresses and
" remedying their defects, he arrived in Damascus on Wednesday, the 26th of
" Shauwâl. There he found his sons, al-Malik al-Afdal, al-Malik az-Zâhir, al-Malik
" az-Zâfir Muzaffar ad-Dîn al-Khidr, surnamed al-Mushammer, and his younger
" children. He liked that city and preferred it as a residence to all others. On
" Thursday morning, the 27th of the same month, he held a public audience so
" that the people, who longed to see him, were enabled to gratify their de-
" sire. Pieces of verse were then recited to him by the poets, not one of
" whom, from the highest to the lowest, staid away. He remained in the city,
" spreading out the wings of his justice, pouring forth the showers of his liberality
" and beneficence, and putting a stop to the acts of oppression which his subjects
" had to complain of. On Tuesday, the 1st of Zû 'l-Kaada, al-Malik al-Afdal gave
" a great dinner to al-Malik az-Zâhir who, on arriving at Damascus and learning that
" (his father) the sultan was on his way (to that city), had stopped there in order to
" have the pleasure of seeing him again. He seemed to have felt in his mind that

"the sultan's life was drawing to its end, for, on this occasion, he repeated again
"and again the parting farewell. At this repast al-Afdal displayed magnificence
"worthy of his noble heart; it was as if he intended to render an equivalent for the
"hospitable reception which he found at his brother's, on arriving that prince's city.
"All those, who held a high rank in the world and those (who were entitled to one)
"in the next shared in that repast. The sultan also was invited and, to give
"his son satisfaction, he went there. I have been told that immense crowds had
"assembled to witness the splendors of that day.—Al-Malik al-Aadil, having in-
"spected al-Karak and terminated all the ameliorations which he intended to make
"there, took the road of his provinces (east of) the Euphrates and reached Da-
"mascus on Wednesday, the 17th of Zu 'l-Kaada. The sultan went out to meet
"him and, whilst he awaited his arrival, he hunted over the country around Gha-
"baghib and from that to al-Kcawa. When they met, the hunting recommenced
"and it was at a late hour on Sunday evening, the 11th of Zu 'l-Hijja, 588 (18th
"Dec., A. D. 1192), that they entered into Damascus. The sultan continued to
"hunt with his sons and his brother, going over the grounds about Damascus and
"visiting the places inhabited by gazelles. He seemed to have found in the chase
"some relief from his continual fatigues, his toils and his lengthened vigils. This
"might be considered as his last farewell to his children and to the spots where he
"used to take his pleasure. He thought no more of his projected journey to Egypt,
"other affairs having turned up and other projects being formed." The same historian says : " I received from him, at Jerusalem, a letter by which he called me to
"his court. Heavy rains were then falling and the mud was very deep, yet I set
"out from Jerusalem. My departure took place on Friday, the 23rd of Muharram,
"589 (29th Jan. A. D. 1193), and I arrived at Damascus on Tuesday, the 12th of Safar
"(17 Feb.). The 15th of that month, which was a Friday, the sultan rode out to
"meet the pilgrim-caravan, and that was the last time he got on horseback. On
"the eve of Saturday he felt a great lassitude and, a little before midnight he had
"an attack of bilious fever. This indisposition was more in the interior of the body
"than in the exterior. On Saturday morning, he felt greatly exhausted in conse-
"quence of the fever, but did not let his sufferings appear. I and al-Kadi al-Fadil
"went to see him; his son al-Malik al-Afdal came in also, and we remained sitting
"with him for a considerable time. He complained of the agitated night which he
"had passed and felt some relief in conversing with us. A little before noon, we

" retired, but our hearts remained with him. We then received from him the order
" to partake of a repast at which al-Malik al-Afdal presided ; al-Fâdil, not being ac-
" customed (to such things) went away, but I went in and found the tables laid out in
" the Southern Hall, and al-Afdal sitting in his father's place. Being greatly af-
" fected at the sight, I had not the courage to sit down, and withdrew. His occu-
" pying that place was considered as a bad omen and caused many tears to be
" shed on that day. From that time the sultan's illness continued to increase :
" we went to visit him regularly, morning and evening, and al-Kâdi 'l-Fâdil enter-
" ed with me into the sick-chamber several times every day. His disorder was in
" the head, and the absence of the physician who was well acquainted with his consti-
" tution and who attended him constantly whilst journeying and sojourning, led peo—
" ple to think that he had not long to live. The (other) physicians were of advice that
" blood should be drawn, and, on the fourth day, he was bled. The illness then
" became more intense ; the moisture of the body diminished, exsiccation prevailed,
" and the state of the patient became worse and worse, so that he was rendered ex-
" tremely weak. On the sixth day, and the seventh and the eighth the disorder in-
" creased gradually and reached such a height that the intellect became deranged.
" On the ninth day, he had fainting fits and refused the draught which was offered
" to him. The city was filled with apprehension and the people (the merchands)
" were so much alarmed that they removed their goods from the bazars. All the
" inhabitants were overcome with grief and affliction such as could not be described.
" On the 10th day of the illness, two injections were administered and procured
" him some relief. This excited great joy among the people, but the malady still
" increased and the doctors at length despaired of the patient's recovery. Al-Malik
" al-Afdal then began to make the people (and the troops) swear allegiance to
" himself. On Wednesday, the 27th of Safar, 589 (4th March, 1193), after the hour
" of morning prayer, the sultan breathed his last. The day of his death was, for
" Islamism and the Musulmans, a misfortune such as they never before suffered
" since they were deprived of the four first khalifs. The palace, the empire and the
" world were overwhelmed with grief such as God only could conceive. I often
" heard of persons saying that they would willingly die in order to save the life of
" one whom they loved dearly; but, till that day, I considered such declarations as
" mere hyperboles and lax expressions; now, however, I solemnly declare, after my
" own feelings and those of others, that, if the life of one man could be redeemed

" by the life of another, many lives would have been offered to save his. Al-Malik
" al-Afdal held a sitting after his father's death, in order to receive the condolences
" of the people. The corpse was washed by ad-Daulái." — The person thus denominated bore the title of Diá ad-Dln and his names were Abù 'l-Kásim Abd
al-Malik, the son of Zaid, the son of Yàsin, the son of Zaid, the son of Kàid, the son
of Jamll. He belonged to the tribe of Thaleb (ath-Thalabi) and drew his descent
from al-Arkam (al-Arkami). He was a doctor of the Shafite sect and filled
the place of preacher (khatlb) at Damascus. His death took on the 12th
of the first Rabi, 598 (10th Dec. A. D. 1201). — Being asked respecting the
year of his birth, he replied : " The year 507 " (A. D. 1113-4), but afterwards mentioned other dates; God knows best! He was buried in the cemetery of the martyrs
(Makábir ash-Shuhadá), outside (the gate called) Dáb as-Saghlr. — Ibn Shaddád continues thus : When the afternoon prayer was said, the body was brought out in a
coffin over which a sheet was spread as a pall. At this sight a loud outcry was raised
and the people began to weep, to lament and to pray over the corpse in successive
bands. It was then carried back to the garden-house in which the sultan had resided during his last illness, and was buried under the estrade at the western side of
it. The asr (vol. I. p. 584) prayer was on the point of being said when the body was
lowered into the grave. — Ibn Shaddád then expatiates on the subject, but I omit
his discourse lest I should fatigue the reader. He concludes his work with a verse
composed by Abù Tammám at-Tài (vol. I, p. 348) and which we give here :

> Those years and the people who lived therein have passed away ; years and people have disap-
> peared like dreams.

May the Almighty have mercy on him (Saláh ad-Dln) and sanctify his soul! for
he was the ornament and the admiration of the world. — Sibt Ibn al-Jausi (vol. I.
p. 439) says, in his chronicle, under the year 578 (A. D. 1182-3) : " On the 5th of
" Muharram, Saláh ad-Dln set out from Old Cairo, on his way to Syria and halted
" at al-Birka (65). The great officers of the empire went out to bid him farewell
" and the poets recited to him valedictory poems. He then heard a voice, outside
" the tent, pronounce these words :

> " Enjoy now the odour of the ox-eyes which grow in Najd ; after this evening, you will find
> " them no more.

" The person who spoke was sought for, but could not be found. These words
" saddened the sultan's mind and were considered by those who were present as a
" bad omen. Indeed, they turned out to be true, for the sultan was kept so much
" occupied by the affairs of the Eastern provinces and by the Franks, that he was ne-
" ver able to revisit Egypt." — I may here observe that the line just mentioned was
taken from a piece of verse that may be found in that section of the *Hamása* which
contains the amatory poems. Our professor, Izz ad-Din Ibn al-Athir (vol. *II.* p. 288)
relates the same anecdote under another form in his greater historical work. He
there says: " An extraordinary example of an evil omen's being fulfilled is the follow-
" ing: When the sultan left Cairo, he stopped where his tent was pitched, till the
" troops were collected into one body. He had with him the principal officers of
" the empire, the doctors of the law and the eminent literary scholars, some of whom
" were there to take leave of him, and others to accompany him on his journey.
" Each of them was saying his word on the subject of adieus and separation from
" friends, when a tutor of one of the sultan's children thrust forward his head, over
" the shoulders of the company, and pronounced that verse. Saláh ad-Din who, a
" moment before, was very gay, shuddered at the bad omen and all the persons in
" the assembly felt ill at ease. He never again returned to Cairo." — Ibn Shaddád
says in the first part of his historical work: " He (*Saláh ad Din*) left, on dying, nei-
" ther gold nor silver in his treasury, with the exception of forty-seven Nasirian
" dirhems (66) and one gold piece coined at Tyre. He possessed neither estates, nor
" houses, nor lands, nor gardens, nor villages, nor tillage-grounds. Imme-
" diately after his death, al-Kádi 'l-Fádil wrote to al-Malik az-Záhir, the sovereign
" of Aleppo and one of the sultan's sons, a letter of which we here give the contents:
" —'You have in the apostle of God an excellent example. (Koran, s. 33, v. 21); verily
" the earthquake of the (last) hour (will be) a terrible thing. (Koran, s. 22, v. 1). —
" I have written this to al-Malik az-Záhir; may God grant him good consolation, alle-
" viate his affliction and give him a compensation for it on that hour.—The Moslims
" have received a violent shock; tears have furrowed every cheek, hearts have come
" even to the throats. (Koran, s. 23, v. 10), and I have said to your father, who
" was my master, a farewell never to be followed by another meeting. I kissed
" his face for myself and you; to almighty God I delivered him now vanquished
" in dexterity, weakened in strength and resigned to the will of God. There is
" no might nor force but through God. At his door troops were marshalled up

" and arms were (ready) in their scabbards, but they were unable to repel this af-
" fliction; no king can resist the decrees of fate. All eyes are shedding tears, all
" hearts are humbled and our only words are : ' Let God's will be done! for thy
" ' sake, o Yûsuf! are we in sorrow!' As for counsels, you need them not, and as
" for my opinion, the stroke I have received prevents me from forming one by dis-
" tracting my attention. But, to judge from the aspect of affairs, (*I shall say that,*)
" if concord reign, you will suffer no other loss than that of his noble presence. If
" otherwise, his death will be a less misfortune than the evils which may happen.
" That is the main subject of apprehension. Receive my salutations!' — How ad-
" mirably well said! In this short epistle he has displayed great novelty (*of expres-*
" *sion*) even when inserting in it sound advice, suitable to a state of things which
" would make a man forget his own interests." — I have given a separate article to
all the sons of Salâh ad-Dîn whose names occur in the present notice, and have
indicated the dates of their birth and their death.—Those whom I mean are al-Afdal,
az-Zâhir and al-Azîz. The only one of them whom I have passed over is al-Malik
az-Zâfir, surnamed al-Mushammer and, as I have mentioned his name in this article, it is necessary for me to say something concerning him. He bore the title of
Muzaffar ad-Dîn and the names of Abû 'd-Dawâm and Abû 'l-Abhâs al-Khidr. He
was designated by the appellation of al-Mushammer because he exclaimed, when
his father shared his states between the elder brothers : I also am ready (*mu-
shammer*).— This became a nickname by which he was generally known. He
was born in Cairo on the 5th of Shâbân, 568 [22nd March, A. D. 1173], and
had for mother the same woman who gave birth to al-Malik al-Afdal. He died
at Harrân, in the month of the first Jumâda, 627 [March-April, A. D. 1230];
being then with his cousin, al-Malik al-Ashraf, the son of al-Malik al-Aädil. Al-
Ashraf did not then possess Harrân; he was only passing through it on his way to the
country of ar-Rûm (Asia Minor), where he was going on account of the Khowa-
rezmites (67). — Another author says : The (*body of the*) sultan Salâh ad-Dîn remained interred within the citadel of Damascus till a tomb was built for its reception,
on the northern side of the Kallâsa, which edifice lies to the north of the great
mosque of Damascus. This (*mausoleum*) has two doors, one opening on the Kallâsa,
and the other on a street in which there is no thoroughfare and which is contiguous to the Aaläiya college. — I entered into this *kubba* (*chapel with a dome*) by the
door which gives on the Kallâsa and, after reciting a portion of the Koran over the

grave, I invoked God's mercy on its occupier. The warden, who was also the intendant of the *kubba*, then produced to me a packet containing Salâh ad-Dîn's
body-clothes, among which I remarked a short, yellow vest (*kubâ*) with black
cuffs (68), and I prayed that their sight might be a blessing to me. — The same narrator says : " The body was removed from the citadel to this *kubba* on Thursday, the
" 10th of Muharram, 592 (15 Dec. A. D. 1195), and Koran-readers were attached
" to the establishment, with servants to keep it in good order. Some time after,
" his son, al-Malik al-Aziz Imâd ad-Dîn Othmân, the same of whom we have spoken
" (*vol. II*. p. 195), took Damascus from his brother, al-Malik al-Afdal, and erected
" at the side of this mausoleum the college which bears the name of *al-Madrasa 'l-*
" *Azîziya* and endowed it richly. — A grated window of the *kubba* looks towards
" the college, which is one of the most noted in Damascus. " — On the first Friday
of the month of Ramadân, 680 (April, 1281), I visited this tomb and saw on the
chest which it supports, the date of the sultan's death followed by these words : " Al-
" mighty God! let his soul be acceptable to thee and open to him the gates of Para-
" dise; that being the last conquest (*lit.* opening) for which he hoped. " The warden of the place told me that this prayer was of al-Kâdi 'l-Fâdil's composition. —
When the sultan Salâh ad-Dîn became the master of Egypt, there was not a single
(*orthodox*) college in that country, because the dynasty which had reigned there
followed the doctrine of the Imamians (*the Shîites*) and did not admit the utility of
such establishments. He therefore founded, in the Lesser Karâfa, near the tomb of
the *imâm* as-Shâfi, a college of which we have spoken in our article on Najm ad-Din
al-Khubûshâni (*v. II*, p. 645). — He built also another college in Cairo near the
mausoleum which is dedicated to al-Husain, the son of Ali, and settled on it a
large endowment. He converted into a college for the Hanifites and endowed richly
the house which had belonged to Abbâs, the same person of whom we have spoken
in our articles on az-Zâfir al-Obaidi (*vol. I.* p. 222) and al-Aâdil Ibn Sallâr (*vol. II.*
p. 351). — He endowed also very richly, for the Shafites, a college in Cairo which
goes under the name of Zain at-Tujjâr (69). Inside the citadel (*kasr*) of Cairo he built
an hospital, on which he settled considerable property. Another hospital, richly
endowed, and a *khângâh* (*convent for dervishes*) were founded by him in Jerusalem.
In Old Cairo he founded a college (*madrasa*) for the Malikites. — I have often thought
of that man's acts and said to myself : " He was fortunate in this world and must be
" so in the next; here he wrought those famous deeds, such as his numerous con-

" quests, and founded so many establishments richly endowed and of which not one
" is publicly known by his name.   The college founded by him in the Karáfa is cal-
" led by the people *the Shafite college*; that which is near (*al-Husain's*) mosque is de-
" signated by them as the *Mash-hed*; the *khánqáh* is named after Saïd as-Suwadá (71);
" the Hanifite college is called the *Madrasa* of Saïf ad-Din; that which is in Old
" Cairo bears the name of Zain at-Tujjár and the other college in the same place is
" called the *Malikite*.   Here is really an example of good works done secretly.   It
" is remarkable that the college founded by him in Damascus, near the hospital of
" Núr ad-Din, is called the *Saláhian* after him, though it is without an endowment,
" and that his Malikite college, in the same city, does not bear his name.   For
" this favour (, *that of escaping from vain-glory*,) he was indebted to the grace of
" God."   Though he possessed so extensive a kingdom and such vast dominions,
he was extremely kind and condescending; being affable to all men, tender-hearted,
full of patience and indulgence.   He befriended the learned and the virtuous, admitted them into his society and treated them with beneficence.   Towards talents of
all kinds he was favorably inclined and, being a great admirer of good poetry, he
would repeat pieces of verse before the company at his assemblies.   Often, say they,
did he recite the following lines, attributed by some to Abù Mansúr Muhammad Ibn
al-Husain Ibn Ahmad Ibn al-Husain Ibn Ishak al-Himyari, and, by others, to Abù
Muhammad Ahmad Ibn Ali Ibn Khairán, who was governor of Almeria in Spain
and who bore the surname of al-Aámiri because his grandfather, Khairán, was one
of the captives made by al-Mansúr Ibn Abi Aámir :

> The harbinger of spring let its voice be heard, and the image of my beloved visited me in a
> dream, taking every precaution against jealous spies.   I had nearly awakened those around
> me by the joy which that visit gave me, and she, through desire, had nearly torn asunder the
> veil which concealed her love.   I awoke when my hopes had led me to imagine that I would
> obtain my utmost wish; but then, my happiness was changed into sorrow.

It is related that he admired greatly the following verses composed by Nashú 'l-
Mulk Abù 'l-Hasan Ali Ibn Mufarraj, surnamed Ibn al-Munajjim, who was a native
of Maarra tan-Nomán (*al-Maarri*), but had settled and died in Cairo.   They were
composed on the custom of giving a black die to gray hair :

> It is not for the uncomeliness of gray hair that they are dyed; for, certainly, hair, when it

loses its colour, is still more accursedly. But they do so because, when youth is dead, its dwelling-place is blackened in order to denote how greatly the loss is regretted.

It was related that (the sultan), on pronouncing the words : youth is dead, would take hold of his mistress, look at her and say : Yes, by Allah ! youth is dead. — The kátib Imâd ad-Dîn al-Ispahâni states, in his Kharída, that the sultan Salâh ad-Dîn had just commenced to reign when he wrote to one of his friends in Damascus these two verses :

O you who are absent (and far) from us, though our recollections have rendered you my neighbours (, present) in my heart ! Ever since I have been deprived of you, I see you visibly, with the eyes of my imagination.

As for the two kasídas which, as I said, were sent from Baghdad by Síbt Ibn at-Taáwízi, the poet imitates, in one of them, a poem composed by Surr Durr (c. II, p. 321), of which I have given some verses in the life of the vizir al-Kunduri (vol. III, p. 292) and which begins thus :

Is this the requital which my fellow men receive for their love ?

Here is Ibn at-Taáwízi's kasída :

If thy custom, when in love, resembles mine, stop thy camels at the two sand-hills of Yabrin, and kiss a soil which my very eyelids would kiss, were my camels to bear me up to the tops of its hills. Seek there for my heart, under the pretext of discovering its gazelles; but my folly is caused by other gazelles than those of the sandy desert ! My poem (was recited) between the tents, but, to turn away suspicion, I spoke only of large-eyed gazelles. Were it not through dread of foes, I should have designated the glances of these maidens and their graceful bearing by other emblems than tender fawns and pliant branches. What admirable pearls were concealed, on the day of their departure, within the vaulted palanquins ! each of them surpassing in beauty its companions and requiring no ornament to set it off; maidens who, when they appear, display the moon of heaven in (the brightness of) their cheeks and (of) their foreheads. In the morning, their (abiding) teeth had scarcely flashed forth their lightnings when my eyelids poured forth floods of tears. If they perceive not the breath of the zephyr, it is because they have just passed near the sighs proceeding from my afflicted heart. When the camels looked back, as they ascended the mountains, I also turned my head, and that gesture excited a tender sadness in her heart and mine. O Salma ! if you break your engagements with me, the person in whom I placed my trust is no longer worthy of confidence. Your promises were made to a dupe, but, in affairs of tender passion, I am not the first lover who has been duped. (Act with) mildness ! the moment of separation has cruelly oppressed one whose tears flow without control and who remains as a pledge in the bonds of love. But what have

I to do with the affection of fair maidens, so parcimonious of that (love) which, for me, was all I needed? Yet, why should I complain, if they defer the payment of what they owe me, whilst their glances shed with impunity my heart's blood? Let me give up three follies! what have fair maids to do with a man who has now passed his fiftieth year? Asking gifts from a miser or expecting good-faith from a deceiver is, for me, the greatest of afflictions. O that she who is so sparing of favours to her lover had learned liberality from Salāh ad-Din!

Here is the second *kasida*:

How long must I be pleased with loving you, and you be displeased? How long will you afflict me with false imputations and then upbraid me? My only failing is to have incurred your disdain; and every time that your disdain was manifested, you said that the fault was mine. Testify your dislike in every manner; I have a heart not to be cast down by affliction. Do you think that I can ever feel consolation if deprived of you? sooner will you show kindness than I receive consolation. On your account, my bosom burns, through sadness, with a fire not to be extinguished, and the sources of my tears are never dried up. Have you forgotten those days and nights which we passed in sport, giving free career to wanton folly? those days in which there was no detractor ready to count my passion for you as a crime, no censor ready to blame me. You formerly rendered justice to my love and, in fondness for me, you faced the same perils which I boldly encountered. But now I am satisfied if, during my slumbers, your image passes near my couch and appears to me at night, during my dreams. I did not think that the days of love would pass away, just as a new garment is worn out; neither did I imagine that I should ever be divested of the raiment of youth. But, at length, the clouds of delusion were dissipated, the guide which led darkness on its way took the right path and the shades of night withdrew. Maidens, fair and handsome, now shun (*me*): Soád herds me not, and Zainab pretends not to know me. She whom I loved, being shocked at the whiteness of my hair and the thinness of my body, exclaimed: "The best part of you has disappeared." (*I replied*:) "If you find fault with my body, your waist also is thin; disdain not the whiteness of my hair; your teeth also are white (*ashnab*)."

That is admirably said! He has enounced the idea as perfectly as possible, though he imagined that the root *shonab* signified the whiteness of the teeth. He employed it as having that meaning and thus completed the expression of his thought, which was this: when she whom he loved reproached him with his infirmities (*and emaciation*), he twitted her with the thinness of her waist and, when she expressed her dislike of white hair, he retorted by saying that her teeth also were white. It was if he said that the whiteness of his hair was counterbalanced by the whiteness of her teeth. But, he was mistaken in supposing that *shanab* had that signification: this word, as employed in the language, does not mean the *whiteness* of the teeth but their *sharpness*. Some say, however, that it designates their *coolness and sweetness*, but the other meaning is the right one. The sharpness of teeth indicates *youth*,

for they are sharp when they first appear and, after serving for some years, they are
ground down and lose their acuity. The thought itself is borrowed from a well
known *kasîda*, in which the author, an-Nâbigha ad-Dubyâni, says :

> No defect can be found in them except the state of their swords, which are notched with
> striking upon hostile squadrons.

Mention has been made of this verse in our article on Orwa Ibn az-Zubair (vol. II.
p. 200), where the reader may find it. The *kâtib* Bahâ ad-Dîn Zuhair Ibn Muhammad (vol. I. p. 512), recited to me, as being of his own composition, a piece of verse
in which one of the lines, offering a similar thought, is as follows :

> There is no defect in her except the languor (*lit.* the weakness) of her eyes.

Let us resume and finish the text of the *kasîda* composed by Sibt Ibn at-Taâwîzi :

> You who seek for the pleasures of life when your hair has turned gray ! (*know that*) time
> which maketh all things pass away, has also passed away (*for you*). Do you think, after count-
> ing up your forty years, that you can still obtain the favours of the fair? That, alas! would
> be highly difficult (73). Dwelling of my beloved! were it not for my Ozrite love (73), never
> should I have rejoiced at the aspect of glimmering lightnings, deceptive (*of our hopes that rain
> would fall upon the country in which you are situated*). Never should that have been; never
> also shall I commence degrading my self-respect (*by soliciting gifts*) ! never shall I do so as
> long as the beneficence of Salâh ad-Dîn flows by, copious as a torrent.

All the poets of the age celebrated the praises of Salâh ad-Dîn and came from every
quarter to partake of his beneficence. One of them was Alam ad-Din as-Shâtâni,
the same whose article we have given amongst those of the Hasans (vol. I. p. 403),
and who made that sultan's eulogy in a *kasîda* rhyming in R and beginning thus :

> I see victory attached to your yellow standard ; proceed therefore and conquer the world, for
> you are worthy of its possession.

Another poem was composed in his praise by Muhaddab ad-Din Abû Hafs Omar
Ibn Muhammad Ibn Ali Ibn Abi Nasr generally known by the surname of Ibn as-
Shihna 'l-Mausili (*the son of the governor of Mosul*). It begins thus :

> Let the salutation of a lover, emaciated by his passion, be borne to the females of the tribe
> which has now separated.

This kasîda contains one hundred and thirteen verses, two of which are currently known. One of them is the following:

> I love you for the noble qualities which I am told that you possess; the ear can be smitten with love as well as the eye.

This thought he borrowed from Bashshâr Ibn Burd, who said:

> Know, good people! that my ear is enamoured of a person in that tribe; for the ear is sometimes enamoured sooner than the eye.

The second of these verses in the following:

> My lover said to me: "If you meet the sons of Aiyûb, you will prosper."

Eulogies were composed on Salâh ad-Dîn by Ibn Kalâkis (vol. III. p. 537), Ibn az-Zarawa, Ibn al-Munajjim (Nasku 'l-Mulk), Ibn Sanâ 'l-Mulk (vol. III. p. 589), Ibn as-Sâati (vol. II. p. 328), an-Najrâni al-Irbili, Ibn Duhn al-Hass al-Mausili Muhammad Ibn Ismail Ibn Hamdân al-Khairâni and other poets, most of whom we have noticed in this historical work. If I have given a great extent to this biographical notice, I shall excuse myself in the words of the poet al-Mutanabbi:

> The nobleness of him whose merits I extol gives nobleness to my verses; the eulogy of a base fellow (timbil) is itself abased.

The word timbil signifies a man of stature. — In the present article, where we related that (the Fatimide khalif) al-Adid sent for Salâh ad-Dîn in order to invest him with the vizirship, mention is made of the proverbial expression: I meant Amr, but God meant Khdrija. — As some of my readers may not be acquainted with its origin and signification, I will explain it, so that they may not be obliged to search for its meaning elsewhere. The Amr here spoken of was the son of al-Aâsi and belonged to the Sahmide branch of the Koraish family. His father was the son of Wâil, the son of Hâshim, the son of Soaid, the son of Saad, the son of Sahm, the son of Amr, the son of Husais, the son of Kaab, the son of Luwai. Amr's surname was Abû Abd Allah, or, as some say, Abû Muhammad. He was one of the Prophet's companions, having embraced Islamism in the eighth year of the Hijra, anteriorly to the conquest of Mekka. That city was taken by the Prophet in the month of Ramadân, A. H. 8 (Dec.-Jan. 629-630). This statement is rejected by some (traditionists), who say that he became a Moslim in the interval between the expedition of al-Hudaibiya and that of Khaibar; but it is nevertheless the true one. He and Khâlid Ibn al-Walîd al-Makhzûmi set out with Othmân Ibn Talha Ibn Abi Talha, a member of the Koraishide family called the Bani Abd ad-Dâr (al-Abdari), and went to the Prophet, who was then at Medina and before whom they appeared as Moslims. On seeing them, the Prophet said (to his companions): "Mekka has cast out to you the most pre-"cious of its treasures." (74)—Al-Wâkidi (vol. III. p. 61) says: "Amr Ibn al-Aâsi was "already a Moslim when he went to join the Prophet. He had become a convert "at the court of an-Najâshi, the king of Abyssinia. With him came Othmân Ibn "Talha and Khâlid Ibn al-Walîd. They arrived at Medina in the month of Safar "(A. H. 8). Some say that he did not leave Abyssinia till he became a believer in "Islamism and that his conversion was brought about in the following manner: "An-Najâshi said to him: 'Tell me, Amr! how it happens that you take no con-"' cern about the affairs of your cousin (Muhammad). By Allah! he is really "' God's apostle.' Amr replied: 'Are you sure of that?' An-Najâshi answered: "' Yes, by Allah! so follow my counsel.' On this, Amr left him with the inten-"tion of going to join the Prophet. He was then sent off to Syria by the Prophet "with an armed troop, for the purpose of calling his father's maternal uncles to the "Moslim faith, and he arrived with three hundred men at as-Salâsil, which is a wa-"tering-place in the territority of the Judhâm tribe, in the country possessed by the "Kodâa. That was the reason why this expedition was called the Inroad of Zât as-"Salâsil. Being afraid that his troop was too small, he wrote to the Prophet "for assistance and received from him a reinforcement of two hundred horsemen, "part of them emigrants from Mekka, the rest natives of Medina, and all of them "belonging to noble families. Amongst them were Abû Bakr and Omar. The "command of this detachment was given by the Prophet to Abû Obaida Ibn al-"Jarrâh. When they came up, Amr Ibn al-Aâsi said: 'I am your chief and you "are only my auxiliaries.' To this, Abû Obaida replied: 'By no means! you are "the chief of those whom you have with you, but I shall be the chief of those who "are with me!' As Amr rejected this proposal, Abû Obaida said: The apostle of "God made me this recommendation: When you reach Amr, give, both of you, "examples of obedience and let there be no dissentions between you; so, if you re-

" fuse to obey me, I must obey you. Amr replied : I refuse to obey you.—Abû Obaida,
" on hearing this, saluted Lim and stood behind him at the public prayer, with all
" the troops, the number of which amounted to five hundred men." — Amr Ibn
al-Aâsi was appointed by the Prophet to the government of Omân and held that place
till the latter's death. In the twelfth year of the Hijra, Abû Bakr sent him to Syria
with Yazîd Ibn Abi Sofyân the Omaiyide, Abû Obaida and Shurahbîl Ibn Hasana.
Khalid Ibn al-Walid then came from Irak and joined them. The first conquest
effected by them in Syria was that of Bosra, which they took by capitulation.
Omar Ibn al-Khattâb, who succeeded to the khalifate on the death of Abû Bakr, gave
the command of the troops to Abû Obaida, and by this chief was effected the conquest of Syria. He gave also to Yazîd Ibn Abi Sofyân the government of Palestine
(Filistîn), a province of which the capital was ar-Ramla. When Abû Obaida died,
Moâd Ibn Jabal succeeded in the command, and, on Moâd's death, Yazîd Ibn Abi
Sofyân took his place. Yazîd died also and was succeeded by his brother
Moawia Ibn Abi Sofyân, and Omar sent to the latter a diploma investing him
with the authority which had been exercised by Yazîd. All these governors died in
the eighteenth year of the Hijra ; being carried off by the plague which then raged
at Amawâs, a town of Syria, situated between Naplûs and ar-Ramla. Some say that
Yazîd died at Damascus in the month of Zû 'l-Hijja, A. H. 19 (Nov.-Dec., 641),
subsequently to the conquest of Cæsaria (Kaisariya). After the death of Yazîd,
Omar gave to Amr Ibn al-Aâsi the governments of Palestine and the Jordan (Urdunn);
to Moawia he confided those of Damascus, Baalbek and al-Balkâ, and to Said Ibn
Aâmir Ibn Hi lhyem he gave the government of Emessa. After that, all the provinces
of Syria were united under the command of Moawia, and Amr, having received from
him a written order, set out for Egypt in the twentieth year of the Hijra (A. D. 641),
took that country and governed it till the death of Omar. During four years,
Othmân allowed him to retain that command and then replaced him by his own
foster-brother, Abd Allah Ibn Saad Ibn Abi Sarh al-Aâmiri. Amr Ibn el-Aâsi then
retired to Palestine and made an occasional visit to Medina. When Othmân was
murdered, he accepted an invitation from Moawia and, having gone to join him, he
fought on his side at the battle of Siffîn. It was there that he managed the arbitration which those who are conversant with this branch of science (history) are well
acquainted with. When Moawia obtained the supreme authority, Amr asked from
him the government of Egypt and adressed to him, one day, a request drawn up

in this form :

Moawia ! I shall not sacrifice to you my religion (i. e. *my happiness in the next life*) unless I obtain from you (*the good things of*) this world; see therefore what you have to do! If you give me Egypt, consider yourself to have made an excellent bargain; for I am an old (*experienced*) man who can be hurtful (*to his foes*) and useful (*to his friends*) (73).

He then obtained from Moawia the government of Egypt and continued to hold it till he died, being at that time ninety years of age.—His death took place on the day of the breaking of the Fast (1st *Shawwâl*) A. H. 43 (6th Jan., 664). Other accounts indicate the years 42, 48 and 51 as the dates of that event, but the true one is what we have just given. He was interred at the foot of Mount Mokattam.—His son Abd Allah recited over him the funeral service and, on his return, presided (as *governor*) at the public prayer which is said on the festival of the fast-breaking. Moawia replaced this Abd Allah by his own brother, Otba Ibn Abi Sofyân. About a year afterwards, Otba died, and Moawia appointed Maslama Ibn Mukhallad to the vacant place.—Amr Ibn al-Aâsi was one of the bravest horsemen among the Koraishides and, in the time of paganism, he was one of their heroes. By his shrewdness in worldly matters and by the soundness of his judgment, he stood pre-eminent. When Omar wished to tell a man that he was a shallow fellow, he would say to him : "I declare that the same Being who created you created Amr!" meaning (*God, who created things by*) contraries.—Abû 'l-Abbâs al-Mubarrad (vol. *III.* p. 31) relates as follows, in his *Kâmil :* "When Amr was on his death-bed, Ibn Abbâs "(col. *I.* p. 89) went in to him and said : Abû Abd Allah! I heard you "often say that you would like to meet with an intelligent man who was on the "point of death, in order to ask him what were his feelings. Now, I address that "question to you. Amr replied : I feel as if the sky was applied closely to the "earth and that I was between the two, breathing as if through the eye of a needle. "After these words, he exclaimed : ' Almighty God! take away from me what you "' please!' His son having then come in to him, he addressed him thus: ' My son! "' take that chest!' The other replied : ' I have no need of it.'—' Take it;' said "Amr, ' it is full of money.' — ' I have no need of it; ' said the son, ' I had ra- "' ther it were filled with dung (76).' After that, he (*Amr*) raised up his hands "and said : ' Almighty God! you ordered and I disobeyed; you forbade and I trans- "' gressed; I am not innocent enough to deserve pardon neither am I so strong

" ' that I can prevail (*over your will*).' He then breathed his last (قَضَى). — The verb (قَضَى) which is also written (قَضَى) means *to die;* a poet has said in employing the word (قَضَى) : " They do not bury those among them who are dead. '— As for the Khárija whose name occurs in the proverb, he was the son of Hudháfa Ibn Ghánim Ibn Abd Allah Ibn Aûf Ibn Obaid Ibn Owaij Ibn Adï Ibn Kaab, and was one of the Adî family, which is a branch of the Kuraish tribe. " He assisted at " the conquest of Egypt and, having obtained a lot of ground at Old Cairo, he took " up his residence there. — He commanded the fourth part of the auxiliary troops " which Omar Ibn al-Khattâb sent to assist Amr Ibn al-Aâsi in conquering Egypt. " When Amr governed that country in the name of Moawïa Ibn Abi Sofyân, Khá- " rija commanded the *shurta* (*the police-cavalry*) of Old Cairo. — He was assassi- " nated in the fortieth year of the Hijra by a Khárijite who had mistaken him " for Amr. " — So says Ibn Yûnus (*col. I. p.* 93) in his history of Old Cairo, and the same statement is made in Ibn Abd al-Barr's *Istíâb,* where the genealogy is set out in the form which it bears in our statement. The same author adds : " It was said that he alone counted for one thousand horsemen." According to some persons versed in genealogy and history, Amr Ibn al-Aâsi wrote to Omar Ibn al-Khattâb for a reinforcement of three thousand horse, and Omar sent him (*only three men*) Khárija Ibn Hudháfa, az-Zubair Ibn al-Awwâm (*vol. II. p.* 109) and al-Mikdâd Ibn al-Aswad (77), Khárija was at the taking of Old Cairo, and it is said that he acted there as a *kádi* when Amr Ibn al-Aâsi was governor ; others state that he was the commander of Amr's *shurta.* He continued to reside there till he was murdered by one of those Kharijites who had conspired to kill Ali Ibn Abi Tâlib, Moawïa Ibn Abi Sofyân and Amr Ibn al-Aâsi. Khárija had been sent, that day, by Amr, to preside as his deputy, at the morning prayer. The assassin, being taken and brought before Amr Ibn al-Aâsi, said : " Who is this man before whom " you have brought me?" They answered : " Amr Ibn al-Aâsi. " — " Who was " it, " said he, " that I killed?" They replied : " Khárija." On hearing this, he said : " I meant Amr but God meant Khárija." Some say that the words were : " You meant Amr, etc. " and attribute them to Amr, but God knows best (78). The murderer belonged to the tribe of al-Anbar Ibn Amr Ibn Tamîm and bore the name of Dâdawaih or Zâdawaih; according to others, he was only a *mawla* of that tribe. " It has been stated that Khárija, he who was " mistaken for Amr Ibn al-Aâsi and killed by the Khárijite in Old Cairo, was a

" member of the Sahm family, the same to which Amr belonged." — End of what
the author of the *Isâba* says on the subject. Another historian relates that
Amr Ibn al-Aâsi was obliged by a derangement in his stomach to remain at
home that night, and that Khârija was presiding (in his stead) at the evening prayer
when the Khârijite killed him. (*They add that*) Amr said afterwards : " My belly
" never rendered me any service except on that night." — Such is the origin of
the proverb. An allusion to this event is made by Abû Mohammad Abd al-Majîd
Ibn Abdûn al-Andalusi (79) in the elegy (*kasîda*) composed by him on the downfal
of the Aftasides who reigned at Badajoz and beginning thus :

Misfortune afflicts (us, *first*) by its aspect and then by the traces (*which it leaves*).

Here is the verse containing the allusion :

Since fortune scrapped the life of Khârija for that of Amr, she might have obtained the lives
of as many as she wished in exchange for that of Ali.

It is a splendid *kasîda* and contains a great quantity of historical allusions. A
full commentary was composed on it by the eminent literary scholar Abû Marwân
Abd al-Malik Ibn Abd Allah Ibn Badrûn al-Hadrami (a *descendant from the Arabs of
Hadramaut and*) a native of Silves (in *Portugal, ash-Shilbi*) (80). We terminate
here our discourse on the proverb, but, as the verse requires to be explained, I shall
give here the commentary, in abridging it, for it is rather long. — Historians tell us
that Ali Ibn Abi Tâlib was proclaimed khalif the same day on which Othmân Ibn Affân was murdered. Then began the revolt of those people who fought
against him at the battle of the Camel. In our article on Yamûl Ibn al-Muzarra
(p. 392 of this vol.), we have spoken of that conflict in a continued narration and
noticed the main facts of it. After that was fought the battle of Siffin, when Moawîa Ibn Abi Sofyân the Omaiyide and Amr Ibn al-Aâsi revolted against Ali Ibn
Abi Tâlib. (*This khalif*) marched from Irak to attack them and they advanced from
Syria to meet him. The encounter took place at Siffin, on the border of the Euphrates and in the vicinity of ar-Rahaba. This famous battle was fought in the
thirty-seventh year of the Hijra (A. D. 657). The Syrians, being overpowered, requested Ali to let matters be settled by arbitration; messengers went to and fro several times, and Ali at length consented to the proposal. On this, a number of his

partisans abandoned him, saying : " You have submitted a question of religion to
" the judgment of men and not to that of God. " They departed for an-Nahrawân,
and Ali went there, fought with them and exterminated nearly all of them.   This
conflict is generally designated as the *Battle of the Kharijites.* — Things continued
in a troubled state for some time and they *(the surviving Kharijites)* assembled and
said : " Ali, Moawia and Amr Ibn al-Aâsi have ruined the cause of the nation;
" could we kill them, things would be all set to rights." Abd ar-Rahmân Ibn
Muljam al-Murâdi then offered to kill Ali.   " How will you manage?" said they.
He replied : " I shall take him unawares." Al-Hajjâj Ibn Abd Allah as-Sarîmi (81),
surnamed al-Durak *(the sluggard)*, offered to kill Moawia, and another individual,
called Dâdâwaih, or Zâdâwaih, the same of whom we have made mention in
speaking of Khârija Ibn Hudhâfa, declared that he would slay Amr.   It was agreed
upon that these murders should be accomplished on the same day.   Ibn Muljam
went to Kûfa where Ali was and, having purchased a sword for one thousand dirhems (82), he steeped it in poison till it could absorb no more.   When Ali went to
say the morning prayer, Ibn Muljam rushed out from a place of concealment and
wounded him on the head, exclaiming : " It is for God to judge, not for you!"
Some say that he struck him whilst celebrating the prayer.   This happened on Friday morning, the 17th of Ramadân, A. H. 40 (24th Jan. 661), but other dates
have been given. — Al-Durak as-Sarîmi went to Damascus, where Moawia was, attacked him whilst he was in prayer and wounded him in the sitting-part.   Some
say the nerve of generation was cut through, so that he was never afterwards
capable of begetting children. — Of Amr we have spoken in our account of
Khârija. — There is a abridged explanation of the proverb and the verse;
God know best!

(1) This genealogy is evidently an impudent forgery.

(2) See Mr Caussin de Perceval's *Essai sur l'histoire des Arabes*, tome II, pp. 197 et suiv.

(3) See *Essai*, etc., t. II, pp. 408, 409.

(4) In Johannsen's *Historia Yemanæ* will be found some account of al-Moizz, Salâh ad-Din's nephew.

(5) Our author says that this word should be pronounced *dundâr*, but he is mistaken.

(6) Ziaki was murdered whilst besieging a Moslim chief who was holding out in Kaàki Jaahar.   The title
of martyr *(shahîd)* was given to him by persons who wished to gain the favour of his son Nûr ad-Din.

(7) See vol. I, p. 119 and vol. III, p. 622.

(8) This is the work of which the text, with a latin translation, was published at Leyden, in 1748 by Albert Schultens. Further on, Ibn Khallikan gives numerous extracts from it.

(9) This work is not noticed by Hajji Khalifa. From its title, *Mojam es-Safer*, which means *Dictionary of the journey*, we may suppose that it contained an account, arranged in alphabetical order, of the learned and eminent men whom the author met with in his travels and of the information which he received from them.

(10) This was the name of a large belvedere or pavilion which was erected on a hill, in the neighbourhood of the mosque of Tûlûn, by al-Malik as-Sâlih, the son of al-Malik al-Kâmil, between the years 640 and 647 of the Hijra (A. D. 1242-1249). Al-Makrizi gives an historical account of this edifice in his *khitat*; see the Bulak edition, vol. II, p. 133.

(11) According to the author of the *Marasid al-Ittilâ*, there was a castle in the neighbourhood of Tripoli which bore the name of al-Munaidhara; that is, the little watch-tower. This castle, situated on one of the tops of mount Lebanon, gives its name to a tract of country, 20 miles S. of Tripoli.

(12) Ibn Khallikân (vol. II, p. 616) places Ibn Bektikin's death in Zû 'l-Kaada, a month sooner than the date given by Ibn Shaddâd.

(13) These extracts from Bahâ ad-Din's work do not always agree with the text given in the printed edition; they are often fuller.

(14) I read *mollâkaho*.

(15) This passage has been already inserted in the life of Shâwar (vol. I, p. 640). The expression *ais yed Khaddâm Hadm*, rendered here by *a servant attached to the private service*, is translated differently and perhaps, less exactly, in the first volume. A. Schultens renders it by *per eunuchum*, which is certainly a mistake.

(16) Apparently, the crreption of Shâwar.

(17) There is no difference between the servants unless it be that, according to the letter, the two parties met by accident.

(18) This is also extracted from the work of Bahâ ad-Din.

(19) For the explanation of this proverbial expression, see towards the end of the present article. Abû 'l-Fedâ gives it in his *Annals*, under the year 10 of the Hijra, and so does Ibn Bedrûn, in his commentary on the *kasida* of Ibn Abdûn, page 197 of professor Dozy's edition.

(20) This appears to be one of the sayings attributed to Muhammad.

(21) See vol. II, p. 211, and my translation of Ibn Khaldûn's *Prolegomena*, vol. I, p. XXX and vol. II, p. 61.

(22) A well known proverb of which the origin is thus related: an Arab caught a gazelle but had no instrument to kill it. The animal, in struggling to escape, pawed up the sand and laid bare a knife which had been concealed there.

(23) The passage which here follows is evidently out of its place; and, as some of the manuscripts do not give it, we may consider it as an addition made by the Khatîb on the margin of his copy, without his indicating where it was to be inserted.

(24) Literally: and two goats did not fight for it with their horns.

(25) Al-Mahdi, the first Fatimide sovereign was placed on the throne A. H. 297.

(26) The Fatimides reigned two hundred and seventy years; they possessed Egypt during two hundred and five years.

(27) In the second volume, page 581, is a note on the sort of handwriting called *maarik*. To the observations contained in it, the following remarks may be subjoined. The *maarik* handwriting got into use

before the middle of the first century of the hijra. It was nothing else than the stiff and clumsy *kûfic*, reduced to a running hand. It spread throughout all Moslim countries, and has continued unchanged till this day in Mauritania. In the East, a slight alteration was made in this character by Ibn al-Bawwâb, and from it is derived that *neskhî* which prevails there and which was most probably what was called the *mansûb* character. The *mansûb* is therefore a simple modification of the old *neskhî*, and by no means, as had been supposed, the *neskhî* itself; it is the oriental hand, as the old *neskhî* is the occidental.

(28) Literally : may the morning-rains water it !

(29) Lit. : a residence.

(30) For the history of these ancient Yemenite princes, Mr Caussin de Perceval's *Essai* may be consulted.

(31) The word rendered here by *hood* is *ridâ*, which word designates a curtain, a sheet or any large piece of stuff serving to cover the body. The *lithâm* is a veil covering the lower part of the face.

(32) For the reason of Moâur's being denominated *the owner of the red tent* (hamrâ), see Mr Caussin de Perceval's *Essai*, tome I, page 100.

(33) Literally : O thou who rendered *wild* an eye which was *tamed* by long weeping.

(34) In English, this idea might be expressed by the words : She is as dear to me as the pupil of my eye; but Arabian lovers preserved their mistresses in their eyes or in their hearts.

(35) Al-Malik as-Sâlih was only eleven years of age on the death of his father Nûr ad-Dîn. The emirs of the deceased sultan, thinking that the young prince would be safer at Aleppo than at Damascus, sent him off to the former city under the protection and guidance of Kumushtikîn, emir of Mosul. It was this latter who arrested Ibn ad-Dâya at Aleppo, which city was then torn by factions. Part of the population was Shiite and devoted to the Fatimides; the rest professed the orthodox faith. Shams ad-Dîn Ibn ad-Dâya, one of Nûr ad-Dîn's principal emirs, had obtained from him the government of Aleppo but was obliged to keep within the citadel, as another emir, Emir ed-Dîn, commanded in the city. Abû 'l-Fadl Ibn al-Khashshâb was âddî of the place and, according to Ibn al-Athîr, he was also chief of the militia (*shiddah*) and of the Shiite party. All these emirs were jealous one of the other; each of them endeavoured to become sole master at Aleppo and obtain the guardianship of the young prince, so as to govern under his name. One plotted against the other's life and every sort of treachery was practised by them against their rivals, till Kumushtikîn arrived in Aleppo and imprisoned them all. — (Kamâl ed-Dîn's *Zubda tal-Halab*.)

(35 bis) Shams ad-Dîn Ibn al-Mukaddem had been named guardian of the young prince, Al-Malik as-Sâlih. Alarmed by the conduct of Saad ad-Dîn Kumushtikîn (*Gumishtikîn* i. e. *silver worker*), he sided with Salâh ad-Dîn and put that prince in possession of Damascus.

(36) Zurîn Hamât (*the peaks of Hamât*) is the name of a hill situated at about ten miles from that city, in a north-western direction.

(37) The defeat of the Moslims at Ramla resulted from a false manœuvre on the field of battle. Their commander ordered the troops of the left wing and those of the right to change places when the action had already commenced. The operation failed and brought on the defeat of the army.

(38) Moslim historians designate the sovereigns of Lesser Armenia by the title of *Ibn Lâwûn* (the son of Leon).

(39) *Karnpelli*, a Turkish word signifying *subject to streams*, (literally, *to the black wind*), designates a mountain-pass in the province of Kerkûr, on the eastern bank of the Tigris. A road leading from Mosul to Baghdad passed through it. The true orthography of the name is given in Abû 'l-Fedâ's own copy of his *Annals*.

(40) The text has اِبنة أخيه (*the daughter of his brother*); but marriage between uncle and niece is forbidden by the Moslim law. Besides, al-Adil, the lady's father, was az-Zâhir's uncle, not his brother.

(41) The author should have said : the king and his brother Jofri (*Geoffroi de Lusignan*). Farther on, he falls into the same mistake.

(42) Literally : how their teeth were set on edge.

(43) Some manuscripts read : thirty thousand.

(44) Our author inserts the whole letter and then states his reasons for doing so. The document itself is written in a most pretentious and affected style, full of enigmatical expressions, verbal quibbles and obscure allusions. Some of the passages are so turned that they seem to express the very contrary of the writer's meaning. This extravagant style was highly fashionable at that period. The text of this epistle being very difficult to understand, has varied greatly under the hands of the copyists. Some passages of it are here rendered by conjecture.

(45) *The Augent Dîwân* (ad-Dîwân al-Azîz) was the title by which the khalif himself was then designated and which was prescribed by the court etiquette of the time. Other examples of it occur in the works of contemporary historians.

(46) Here, the meaning of the original text is very doubtful.

(47) This appears to be a maxim of Moslim law. The writer cites it with reference to the violation of treaties by the Christians.

(48) The *Sakhra* is an enormous stone in the very center of the mosque of Omar, at Jerusalem. It is supposed to be the same upon which the Jews set up the tabernacle.

(49) This is another of the passages in which the meaning of the text is doubtful.

(50) Here again the meaning of the text is very doubtful.

(51) The writer meant to say that God would always grant victory to the Moslims. The preposition and its complement are those which occur in the Moslim war-cry : *Help from God and a speedy victory.* Such grammatical allusions were greatly admired.

(52) The translator has here endeavoured to find a meaning for a passage the text of which is evidently corrupt. By the substitution of ... for ... and ... for ... a phrase is obtained which might be rendered thus : They would not patiently endure the servitude of the edge in order to avoid the enfranchisement of the flat. That seems to mean : they would not submit to the edge of the sword and die in order to avoid being wantonly struck, when prisoners, with the flat side of it.

(53) Literally : reached the *Simâk*; i. e. the star which we call *Spica virginis*.

(54) The text may also signify : of unveiling himself for war. In either case, its true meaning is difficult to be discovered.

(55) This is an allusion to the 92nd verse of the 19th surat of the Koran, which Sale renders thus : " They " say : the Merciful hath begotten issue. Now you have uttered an impious thing; it wanteth little but on " occasion thereof, *the heavens be rent* and the earth cleave in sunder."

(56) According to Moslim doctors, the shooting stars are fire-brands cast by the angels against the demons who go to listen at the gates of heaven.

(57) The khalif must have expected that this conquest would have brought him in money; Salâh ad-Dîn, being aware of that, gives him to understand that there was none for him.

(58) Most of the manuscripts omit this passage.

(59) Some manuscripts read *Jandor*.

(60) Some of the manuscripts have *Fall al-Jadîya*.

(62) In many of these extracts, and here particularly, Ibn Khallikan has abridged the narrative made by Ibn Shaddád. — The note (61) has been suppressed.

(63) Or : all this p scrt of the Sáhil.

(64) Our author r at very inattentively the text of Balá ad-Din, who says that the sultan returned to the hills so that his men might send their beasts for forage.

(65) Al-Birka (the pond) is probably the same which is situated at eleven miles north of Cairo and is usually called Birka lal-Háeg (The pond of the pilgrims).

(66) The Naurien diehems were probably inscribed with the names of al-Malik an-Násir Saláh ad-Din.

(67) Jalál ad-Dín Khowaresm-Sháh had laid siege to Akhlat, in Armenia, which fortress was then governed by one of al-Malik al-Ashraf's lieutenants.

(68) Such appears to be the meaning of the Arabic words, which, if rendered literally, signify : and the best of the two sheens with black.

(69) Abú 'l-Abbás Ahmad Ibn al-Mozaffar Ibn al-Husein, surnamed Zaín al-Tujjár, was a native of Damascus and a doctor of the Sháfite rite. He professed in Saláh ad-Din's college and died in the month of Zú 'l-Kaada, 591 (Oct. — Nov. A. D. 1195). — (Makrizi's Khitat, vol. II, p. 563.)

(70) This note has been suppressed.

(71) Said as-Seoudda was one of the eunuchs (nafádin) employed in the East, or palace, of the Fatimides at Cairo. He was entrenchment by the khalif al-Mostansir and put to death in the month of Shaabán, 544 (A. D. 1149). — (Kitlat, vol. II, p. 413.)

(72) Here follows a verse which is given in two manuscripts, but the text of it is corrupt. The meaning of it seems to be that, to c urt a young girl (Lin) when one's hair has turned gray, is nothing more or less than an act of folly.

(73) The young men of the tribe of Ozra were noted as ardent, passionate and devoted lovers. See the commentary on Hariri's Makamât, page 176 of de Sacy's edition.

(74) Literally : the fragments of its liver ; a well known expression.

(75) To be hurtful and useful was one of the talents which, according to the Arabs, were required to form the character of a perfect man.

(76) Abd Allah Ibn al Amr was extremely pious and devout. Some of the Traditions handed down by him have been adopted as genuine by al-Bokhári. For the date of his death see vol. II, p. 400.

(77) Mikdád Ibn Amr Ibn Thaálabi, a member of the tribe of Kinda and the adopted son of al-Aswad Ibn Abd Yaghth, was one of the earliest of Muhammad's companions and assisted him in all his battles. At that of Badr he was the only mussulman who fought on horseback and, for that reason, he obtained the title of Fáris al Islám (the cavalier of Islamism). He was present at the conquest of Egypt. His death occurred at al-Jurf, a place ten miles distant from Medina, A. H. 33 (A. D. 653-4), being then aged nearly seventy years. He transmitted down a number of Traditions, some of which were accepted as authentic by al-Bokhári. — (Tabakát Nojám ; Tabakát al-Fukahá.)

(78) The text merely says : God knows which of the two said so. The translator has rendered the phrase more intelligible by adding the words : Some say that the words were.

(79) Ibn Abdún, a native of Evora, in Spain, was highly distinguished as a poet and composed a celebrated elegy on the downfal of the Aftaside dynasty which reigned at Badajoz. He had been patronised by these princes, but afterwards, he entered into the service of the Almoravide chief who had overturned their throne.

He died at his native place, A. H. 519 (A. D. 1134-5). In the year 1818, professor Dozy published at Leyden the text of this poem with Ibn Badrûn's commentary. See the next note.

(80) Ibn Badrûn, the commentator of Ibn Abdûn's poem, was an accomplished literary scholar. He composed his work in the last half of the sixth century of the Hijra, between A. D. 1163 and A. D. 1184. Little is known of his history, but he appears to have inhabited Seville. His commentary on the elegiac, lamberting *kasîda* of Ibn Abdûn is a learned, instructive and very interesting work.

(81) Or, *ar-Nuroïmî*. The names and surnames of this individual are not well ascertained. They vary in each historical work and even in manuscripts of the same work.

(82) One thousand dirhems would be equivalent to twenty-five pounds sterling; rather a large sum for a sword.

AL-MUWAFFAK IBN AL-KHALLAL.

Abû 'l-Hajjâj Yûsuf, the son of Muhammad al-Khallâl (*the vinegar-maker*), bore the title of al-Muwaffak (*favoured by God*). He was president of the Board of Correspondence, in Old Cairo, under the reign of al-Hâfiz Abû 'l-Maimûn Abd al-Majîd al-Obaidi (*, the Fatimide khalif*) whose life we have already given (*vol. II. p. 179*), and of that prince's successors. Imâd ad-Dîn al-Ispahâni (*vol. III. p. 300*) says of him, in the *Kharîda*: "He was the superintendent of Egypt and the pupil of its eye; com-"bining (*in himself*) all the noble qualities of which that country can justly boast. "He was charged with the correspondence and had a great talent for inditing epis-"tles, writing them in whatever (*style*) he pleased. He lived to an advanced age "but, having lost his sight in the latter part of his life, he remained unemployed "and never left his house till he exchanged it for a tomb. He died three or four "years after the conquest of Egypt by al-Malik an-Nâsir (*Salâh ad-Dîn*)." This au-thor then gives a number of pieces composed by him in verse, and some of these we shall reproduce farther on. Diâ ad-Dîn Abû 'l-Fath Nasr Allah Ibn al-Athîr (*vol. III. p. 541*), surnamed al-Jaziri(*the native of Jesîrat Ibn Omar*), and afterwards al-Mausili (*the native of Mosul*), mentions him in the first chapter of the work entitled *Al-Wathi 'l-Markûm*, and says: "In the year 588 (A. D. 1192), al-Kâdi 'l-Fâdil Abd "ar-Rahim Ibn Ali al-Baisâni (*vol. II. p. 111*), being then at Damascus and em-"ployed as scribe in the service of Salâh ad-Dîn's government, spoke to me in these

" terms: ' The art of epistolary writing flourished and prospered under the dynasty
" ' of the Alides (Fatimides), and the Board of Correspondence was never without a
" ' chief holding the first rank, not only by his place but by his style, and maintai-
" ' ning, with his pen, the authority of the sultan. It was then customary for the
" ' directors of public offices, when any of their children grew up and had acquired
" ' some knowledge of literature, to present them at the Board of Correspondence
" ' in order that they might be instructed and exercised in epistolary writing, and
" ' that they might see and hear (how things were done there). My father, who was
" ' then kádi in the frontier town of Ascalon (1), sent me to Egypt, under the reign
" ' of al-Háfiz, one of their khalifs, and told me to go to the Board of Correspon-
" ' dence. The person who was then at the head of that establishment was called
" ' Ibn al-Khallál. When I entered into his office, I stood respectfully before him
" ' and told him who I was and what I came for. He received me in the most obli-
" ' ging manner and said : ' What means have you procured for yourself in order
" ' to acquire the art of epistolary writing?' I answered : ' None at all, unless it
" ' be that I know by heart the noble Koran and the Hamdsa.'—' That, said he,
" ' will do.' He then told me to attend him regularly. After going often to see
" ' him and exercising my talent in his presence, he bade me turn the verses of the
" ' Hamdsa into prose. This I did, from the beginning to the end of the book.
" ' He then told me begin again and I obeyed.'' End of Ibn al-Athîr's relation.
—After borrowing it from him and giving it under this form, I met a person who
had assiduously cultivated polite literature, and particularly that branch of it
(biography); no man was better acquainted than he with the particulars of al-
Kádi 'l-Fádil's life. From him I learned that the truth of Ibn al-Athîr's relation could not possibly be established and that he must have made some mistake in
it. Al-Kádi 'l-Fádil, said he, did not go to Egypt till az-Záfir, the son of al-Háfiz,
was on the throne; he arrived there with his father for an affair which concerned
them personally. I then found in a note written by myself and taken from
some source which I cannot now discover, that al-Kádi 'l-Ashraf, the father of
al-Kádi 'l-Fádil, was a native of Ascalon and acted as deputy-kádi and superintendant (názir) in the town of Baisán. He went to Egypt in the reign of az-Záfir,
the son of al-Háfiz, in consequence of a discussion which he had with the governor
(wáli) of the place respecting a large and very valuable estate which they (his family)
held in their possession. The governor, through complaisance, allowed him to

retire without arresting him, and, for that reason, was called up to Old Cairo and ordered to justify himself. A fine to a considerable amount was then required of him, but he obtained protection from one of the grandees of the empire. This gave rise to much talk respecting the *kâdi's* conduct; he was ordered up (*to the capital*) and forced to pay so much money that nothing was left to him. None of his sons were with him except al-Kâdi 'l-Fâdil. The treatment he underwent weighed so greatly upon his mind that he died at Old Cairo on the eve of Sunday, the 11th of the first Rabî, 546 (28th June, A. D. 1151). He was interred at the foot of Mount Mokattam. Al-Kâdi 'l-Fâdil then went to the frontier city of Alexandria and presented himself to Ibn Hadid, the *kâdi* and superintendant (*ndzir*) of the place. That functionary, having known him by reputation and been acquainted with his father, took him for secretary. When the Franks got possession of Ascalon (A. H. 548), his brothers came to him for refuge. The dispatches which Ibn Hadid sent to Old Cairo were drawn up with such extreme elegance that the clerks in the Correspondence office were filled with jealousy and, as they feared that the writer might be placed over them, they intrigued against him and gave az-Zâfir to understand that the secretary in Alexandria was inadequate to the task of writing official communications. It is related that the *kâdi* al-Athîr Ibn Bayân, who was then director of that board, having gone to see az-Zâfir, that sovereign said to him : " Write to Ibn " Hadid and order him to cut off the hand of his secretary." On hearing these words, he took the secretary's defence and said : " My lord! that man is by no means incom- " petent, but the clerks, being jealous of his talent, have calumniated him in order " that he may be ill-treated by your Majesty." Az-Zâfir replied : " Write to Ibn " ' Hadid and tell him to send us the man; he shall be our secretary." Ibn Bayân " related as follows : ' Some time after, I was at Zâfir's levee and saw there al-Kâdi " ' 'l-Fâdil, who had just arrived and was standing before the sovereign, having been " ' taken into his service." — The *kâtib* Imâd ad-Dîn says, in his *Kharîda* : " The " following verses were recited to me by Murhaf Ibn Osâma (*vol. I. p.* 146), who sta- " ted that they were communicated to him orally by al-Muwaffak Ibn al-Khallâl, " who gave them as a part of a *kasîda* composed by himself:

Delightful were the nights (*which I*) passed at al-Ozaib, and sweet the meetings which were embellished by the meeting (*with my beloved*). But passed (*are*) those nights and lost the re- remembrance (*of those delights*), which would have captivated the man whose heart was till then free (*from love*), and deprived of reason him who (, *after suffering from unrequited love,*) had been conceded. Bright are those rosy cheeks which, by means of their beauty-spot, enchain even the indifferent in the bonds of love. They tell me that she is descended from chieftains of the tribe of Hilâl; that must be true, for the full-moon also (, *that emblem of perfect beauty,*) proceeds from a crescent (*hilâl*).

Imâd ad-Dîn says also in the *Kharîda*: " From the work entitled *Jinân al-Janân* " *wa Riâd al-Adhân (gardens for the heart and meadows for the mind),*" — this work was composed by ar-Rashîd Ibn az-Zubair (vol. *I. p.* 113 — " I extracted " the following verses of which Ibn al-Khallâl was the author :

" (*I think*) of that gazelle (*maiden*) the sword of whose glances could cut through sabres " with its edge. By her tenderness and her sharpness she put to shame lances and scimitars. " People wonder how I can still be alive after having been afflicted by her disdain; but my " body, though emaciated and exposed to the fire of her aversion, still resists, like the amber " of her beauty-spot which is placed on the furnace of her cheek.

" Here is another piece of his :

The tongue sometimes manifests and sometimes conceals (*our thoughts*); O that our eyelids could hold in their flowing tears! By the arrow of your glances you have struck him (*your lover*) to the heart; why then should he be blamed for shedding tears of blood? The sickness caused by the torture you inflicted has made him (*as it were*) a signal-post (*alem*), yet he never revealed what he knew (*alem*) of your cruelty. Why should the silent (*lover*) be blamed when his sickness creates in each member of his body a man (to *utter his complaints*).

Imâd ad-Dîn gives the following (*enigma*) composed by the same author on a candle :

Sound (*in constitution*) and white, it causes light to shine through darkness and (, *whilst consuming*) by its malady, it heals the eyes (*which were unable to see*). In the time of its youth, its crest is grey, but, as it wears away, its top is black. Like the eye, it has its covering (*the lantern*), and its tears (*drops*), and its blackness, and its whiteness and its brightness.

The same author devotes an article of the *Kharîda* to the *kâdi* Abû 'l-Maâli Ab l al-Azîz Ibn al-Husain Ibn al-Hubâb, and, in it, he gives some verses which that person addressed to ar-Rashîd Ibn az-Zubair relatively to a misfortune which had befallen al-Muwaffak Ibn al-Khallâl. Here are his words : " He was his maternal " uncle," — without indicating which of them was uncle to the other, — " and a

" misfortune which happened to Ibn al-Khallâl gave him a headache. "—The verses which he speaks of are these :

> Hearken to my words, Ibn az-Zobair! for you are worthy of hearing them.   We are afflicted with a kinsman, a doubtful one, who is of little use to us even when he enjoys an easy life.   If any thing good happens to him, we never hope (to partake of) it; but, if he receives a box on the ear, we also are sure to receive one.

This idea is borrowed from the following verse in which the Kharijite, Hossin Ibn Hafsa as-Saadi, addressed Kotari Ibn al-Fujâa (vol II. p.522), the chief of that party :

> Thou art he from we cannot separate; your life brings us no advantage, but your death would be our ruin.

I then endeavoured to clear up what Imâd ad-Dîn meant by the words : *he was his maternal uncle*, without indicating which of them, and I discovered that Ibn al-Khallâl was uncle by the mother's side to Ibn al-Hubâb. — *The Sail wa az-Zail*, a work composed by Imâd ad-Dîn as a supplement to the *Kharîda*, contains an article on Ibn al-Khallâl in which are given as his the following verses :

> (*I am thinking*) of a gazelle (*a maiden*) the fire of whose cheek has lighted up a flame in my bosom.   She possesses eyes of which the glances assist my passion against my patience. I shot glances at her cheeks and she hid them under the protection of the coat of mail (*the gauze veil?*)

This last verse is borrowed from a famous poet of Baghdad called Abû Muhammad al-Hasan Ibn Muhammad Ibn Jaklina (2), but some say that it was taken from another author.   I have since discovered the following piece in Imâd ad-Dîn's *Kharîda tal-Kasr*, where it is attributed to Abd as-Salam Ibn al-Hakam as-Souwâl, who was a native of Wâil :

> Had it depended upon me, I should have made for my use a provision before your departure.   Your eyes shoot their arrows at my heart ; why then has your cheek put on its coat of mail ?   Your lips are a honey comb, and the proof of it is that we see an ant (*the downy spot*) creeping up your cheek.

Abû 'l-Hasan Ali Ibn Zâfir al-Azdi al-Masri (*of the tribe of Azd and of the city of Cairo*) (3) relates, in his work entitled *Badât al-Badâya*, that Abû 'l-Kâsim Ibn Hâni, a poet of later times, composed a satire on Ibn al-Khallâl, who, having heard the piece, conceived for the author a deep hatred which he carefully concealed. It happened that, during one of the festivals at which it was customary for the sovereigns of Egypt to be present in order to hear the (poetical) elogiums composed in their honour, (the Fatimide khalif) al-Hâfiz Abû 'l-Maimûn Abd al-Majîd, who was then reigning, took his seat and listened to the poems which were recited. When Ibn Hâni's turn came, he read a piece in which he displayed great talent. Muwaffak (Ibn al-Khallâl), being then asked by al-Hâfiz what he thought of it, praised the poem highly and expatiated on its beauties; after which, he said : " Did the author claim for himself no other merit than his descent from Abû 'l-" Kâsim Ibn Hâni (vol. III. p. 123), the poet of your majesty's family, the extoller " of its glory and the versifier of its noble deeds, (that would have been quite suffi-" cient for his reputation); but there is a verse of his which the ill-humour felt by " him on entering into this country induced him to compose." Al-Hâfiz asked to hear it; Ibn al-Khallâl made difficulties about repeating it and, whilst the prince was insisting on hearing it, he composed and recited the following verse :

> Curse upon Egypt ! its khalifate is now become a bone which passes from one dog to another.

Al-Hâfiz was greatly incensed on hearing it and deprived the author of the custo-mary gift; he even had thoughts of punishing him more severely. God knows best! — Ibn al-Khallâl continued to direct the Board of Correspondence till he was far advanced in age and hardly able to move about. He therefore retired to his house and never left it. It is stated that al-Kâdi 'l-Fâdil was not unmindful of his obligations towards Ibn al-Khallâl, with whom he had resided and under whom he had studied, and that, during the remainder of his former master's life, he furnished him with every thing that he might require. Ibn al-Khallâl died on the 23rd of the latter Jumâda, 566 (2nd March, A. D. 1171).

---

(1) Ascalon belonged, at that time, to the Fatimides of Egypt. The Crusaders took it from az-Zâfir, the son of al-Hâfiz, A. H. 544 (A. D. 1133-4).

(2) See vol. I, p. 174 and vol. II, p. 498. In some of the manuscripts this name is written with an H instead of a J. Its true pronunciation is not yet determined.

(3) According to Hajji Khalîfa, this Ibn Zâfir, who must not be confounded with the author of the Solwân al-Mutâa, died A. H. 452 (A. D. 1060).

YUSUF IBN HARUN AR-RAMADI.

Abû Omar Yûsuf Ibn Harûn al-Kindi (*a member of the tribe of Kinda*), surnamed ar-Ramâdi (1) was a poet of great celebrity. Abû Abd Allah al-Humaidi (*vol. III. p. 1*) says of him, in the *Judwa* : " I believe that one of his ancestors was " a native of ar-Ramâda, a place situated in Maghrib. He was a poet of Cordova, " remarkable for the quantity of his productions and for the promptitude with which " he enounced his ideas, noted in that place, by people high and low, for following " those paths in the various sorts of poetry which lead to general approbation (2). " (*So great was his talent*) that the most eminent teachers of the *belles lettres* at that " time used to say : ' The art of poetry began in (*the tribe of*) Kinda and has been " ' perfected in (*the tribe of*) Kinda ;" indicating by these words Amr 'l-Kais and " al-Mutanabbi (*vol. I. p. 102*), and then his own contemporary Yûsuf Ibn Harûn " ar-Ramâdi. I might adduce to confirm that opinion the eulogium addressed by " the latter, in the form of a *kasîda*, to Abû Ali Ismaîl Ibn al-Kâsim al-Kâli (*vol. I.* " *p. 210*), who had just arrived in Spain. The piece to which we allude begins " thus :

" Who is to be the judge between me and my censurers ? My pains are really pains ; my " complaints are really complaints. "

Abû Ali 'l-Kâli's arrival in Spain took place in the year 330 (A. D. 942), as we have already stated in his life. Al-Humaidi then relates some of the poet's adventures and cites a quantity of verses composed by him. He adds that he drew up a treatise on falconry and had been imprisoned for some time. Abû Mansûr at-Thaâlibi (*vol. II. p. 129*) has inserted in his *Yatîma tad-Dahr* the piece in which Yûsuf Ibn Harûn extolled the merits of Abû Ali 'l-Kâli and, after the verse which we have just mentioned, he introduces those which follow here :

To preserve my tormentor (, *I should enclose her within my body*); but is there a single member of it unscathed by the torture and sufferings (*which she inflicted*)? If I say : " (*I* " *shall treasure her*) in my eye, " there my tears have their source ; and if I say : " In my " heart, " there is the thirst which consumes me. Three dishonours have settled on my hend (3), and their settling there is a sign of my (approaching) departure. For three misfortunes which came down upon me, three others have arisen against me: a delator, the face of a spy and that of an importunate (adviser). Then hast dismissed me from (the field of) love; judge of my humiliation by that which a man feels who is dismissed from office.

The poet then passes to the eulogium, after giving a description of the chase and of meadows, and says:

A meadow often visited by the rain-cloud and (so verdant) that one would think it had received the visit of Isauli's (al-Âdh'r's) presence. Compare with him (thou elegant speakers), the Arabs of the desert, and you will acknowledge that he deserves the preference. Each of their tribes has its distinct dialect, but he possesses the dialects of them all. The East seems empty after his departure from it, and appears as if ruin had settled in its abodes once so populous. He has appeared like a sun in one (country, the) West, after disappearing, by his setting, from the countries of the East. Here, sir! is my encomium on you; it is not feigned neither is it offered in exchange for a gift. If it expected a gift, know that I am a man who expects no other gift than your friendship.

The following verses were taken from a piece composed by him on a girl who lisped in pronouncing the letter r:

The letter r cannot hope for thy favour neither can I; your repulsion includes us both and renders us equal (in misfortune). When I was alone, I inscribed that letter on the palm of my hand and I then lamented and wept, I and the r (h).

He said also of the same person:

Repeat again the lisping of the r; had Wâsil heard you, he would have abstained from suppressing the r.

The Wâsil here mentioned is the Wâsil Ibn Atâ of whom we have spoken (vol. III. p. 642). In our article on him we made mention of the poet (ar-Ramâdi) and inserted some of his verses. Ibn Bashkuwâl (vol. I. p. 491) speaks of him in the Silat and says: "Yûsuf Ibn Harûn ar-Ramâdi, a native of Cordova, bore the surname of "Abû Amr and was one of the most celebrated poets whom the people of Andalus "(Moslim Spain) ever possessed; holding (, as he did,) a place far above the others. "He taught orally the contents of the Kitâb an-Nawâdir (5) which he had learned "from the lips of the author, Abû Ali 'l-Baghdâdi,"—the historian means al-Kâli. —"Abû Omar Ibn Abd al-Barr (p. 398 of this vol.) learned from him some pieces

" of his poetry and inserted them, under the name of their author, in one of his
" works."— Ibn Haiyân (vol. I. p. 479) says : " He died, poor and destitute, on
" Whitsunday, (al-Ansara) A. H. 403 (25th June, A. D. 1013), and was buried in
" the Kald cemetery." The day of al-Ansara is well known in Spain; it is a festi
val for the Christians, like the Nativity (al-Miláddd), and falls on the 24th of Hazirân
(June). It is the anniversary of Yahya Ibn Zakariya's (John the Baptist, the son of
Zacharias) birth. It was on a Whitsunday that God stopped the sun for Joshua
(Yûshá), the son of Nûn, who had been sent to Jericho (Artha) by Moses, his maternal uncle, for the purpose of fighting against the mighty ones. He slew part of
them and, fearing that the night might intervene and hinder him from extermi-
nating the rest, he prayed Almighty God to stay the sun over him, till he had
dispatched the whole. God stopped the sun at his prayer. Poets have often alluded
to that event in their verses; Abû Tammâm at-Tai (vol. I. p. 348), for instance, who
says, in one of his longer kasîdas :

> The sun has been restored to us, against the will of the night, by the presence of one of their
> sons (breasties) which appeared from behind the curtain (of the palanquin). Its light effaced
> the dark tint of the night, and its brightness caused the noble raiment of the sky to be folded
> up. By Allah! I knew not whether it was a vision, appearing in a dream, which approached
> me, or if Joshua was in the caravan.

Abû 'l-Alâ al-Maarri (vol. I. p. 94) says also, in one of his longer kasîdas :

> Joshua brought back Bâh for a part of a day, and you, when you unveil yourself, bring us
> back Bâh.

Bâh is one of the names given to the sun. — Yâh is also a name of the sun. — Ari-
ha is a town of Syria, situated between al-Cods (Jerusalem) and as-Sharîh (the Jordan.) It was one of Lot's cities. — Ramâdi means belonging to ar-Ramâda. — Yakût
al-Hamawi (p. 9 of this vol.) says, in his dictionary of geographical synonyms, the
Mushtarik, under the word ar-Hamada, that there are ten places which bear this
name; he then begins to enumerate them and says : The third is the Ramâda of
Maghrib, and from it Yusûf Ibn Hârûn derived his surname. — Kuld (ـلد) is the
name of the cemetery at Cordova; but God knows best! Ibn Saîd (6) says, in his
Kitâb al-Maghrib fi Akhbâr Ahl il-Maghrib , that ar-Ramâdi acquired his philological knowledge from the professor Abû Bakr Yahya Ibn Hudail al-Kafif (the blind),

who was the ablest literary scholar of Spain and the author of these verses :

> Blame me not for stopping near the dwelling (*of my beloved*), the inhabitant of which gave me sickness for a bed-fellow. They opened to me the way which led me to love them, and when I entered, they closed that door and hindered my retreat.

The same author says : " Yahya Ibn Hudail died A. H. 386 (A. D. 996-7), or " 385, at the age of eighty-six years. "

(1) Er-Remmâda, with a double m, is the name of a town situated on the border of the sea and traversed by the road which leads from Alexandria to Barka, in Cyrenaica. Its name is still borne by the gulf situated immediately to the east of the Akaba tas-Sollum (*the declivity of the ladder*), called also the greater Akaba, anciently *Catabathmus Magnus*.

(2) Literally : for which there was a good market; an expression in general use.

(3) It may be supposed that the poet meant grey hair, loss of teeth and weakness of sight.

(4) What the poet meant by this verse, the translator is unable to indicate.

(5) *Nawâdir* signifies *anecdotes, literary curiosities, indications little known*.

(6) Abû 'l-Hasan Ali Ibn Mûsa, surnamed Ibn Said, a member of an illustrious Spanish family, the Beni Said, was born at Granada in the month of Shaawâl, 610 (Feb.-March, A. D. 1214). After finishing his preliminary studies in Cordova, he went to the Levant, visited the principal cities in that country and then returned to Spain. He died at Tunis in the year 673 of the Hijra, according to Hajji Khalifa, in his bibliographical dictionary, but an author who must have been much better informed, the celebrated vizir of Granada, Lisân ad-Din, places his death in the year 685 (A. D. 1286-7). Ibn Said composed some works, one of which is a compendium of geography (see the *supplément arabe* of the Bibliothèque Impériale, no 1983). Another and much more important work of his was that of which Ibn Khallikan has here given the title and which formed fifteen volumes. This interesting compilation is known to us only by extracts given by other authors. M. de Gayangos has inserted a notice on Ibn Said in his translation of al-Makkari, vol. I, p. 389.

IBN AD-DARRA.

Yûsuf Ibn Durra, a poet of great reputation and generally known by the surname of Ibn ad-Darrâ, belonged to a family of Mosul. From his youth he displayed great intelligence. Abû Shujâa Muhammad Ibn Ali Ibn ad-Dahhân (*vol. III. p. 175*) says of him in his History (1) : " He died in accompanying the pilgrim-caravan, A. " II. 545 (A. D. 1150-1), when it was captured by the Zieb. (ذئب)." Imâd ad-Dîn al-Ispahâni (vol. III. p. 300) mentions him in the Kharîda tal-Kasr, and Abû'l Maâli Saad Ibn Ali al-Hizlri (vol. I. p. 563) speaks of him in the Zîna tad-Dahr. The best known of his poetical productions is the following (epigram) on a man who had large feet; it is certainly well turned :

> That man with the heel so (flat and) round, him you might employ to (tread over and)
> destroy a young plantation or to break down (thalli) a throne. If his eye glanced at the
> Pleiades, it would drive them out of Ursa Major's company (2).

He composed also other good things. Our professor, the hâfiz Izz ad-Dîn Ibn al-Athîr al-Jazari (vol. II. p. 288), says, in the abridgment which he made of Abû Saad Ibn as-Samâni's (vol. II. p. 156) work on patronymics : " I say that this name " should be written Ziêbi ذئبي ; it means descended from Zieb, who was the son of " Malik Ibn Khulâf Ibn Amro'l-Kais Ibn Buhtha Ibn Sulaim (3). The Zieb formed " a notable branch of the Sulaim tribe. It was they who captured the pilgrim- " caravan in the year 545 ; an immense number of the pilgrims were killed or died " of hunger and thirst. From that time till now God has afflicted the Zieb with " a great diminution of their numbers and with degradation." — Durra is to be pronounced with an u after the D and a double r. — Darra has an a after the D, a double r and a short a (4).

---

(1) In the article on Ibn ad-Dabbán no mention is made of this work.

(2) What the wit of this may be, the translator is unable to discover.

(3) Ibn al-Athîr must have probably read in as-Samâni's work that the name of this tribe was Zophha ذئج, and this he considered to be a mistake. But the mistake is his : Ibn Khaldûn, in his Histoire des Berbers, tome I, pages 121, 168, says that the name is Zoghba. He must have known it well, because he lived among them for some time. The greater part of this tribe had been sent into North Africa, A. H. 443 (A. D. 1051-2).

(4) So say all our manuscripts, but etymology would require a long á.

AS-SHIHAB ASH-SHAUWA.

Abû 'l-Mehâsin Yûsuf Ibn Ismail Ibn Ali Ibn Ahmad Ibn al-Husain Ibn Ibrahim, surnamed ash-Shauwâ (*the roaster*) (1), and entitled Shihâb ad-Dîn (*the flambeau of religion*), belonged to a family of Kûfa, but was born and bred in Aleppo, where also he died. — As a literary scholar he displayed great abilities; in prosody and versification he was well skilled, and in poetry he composed pieces of two or three lines, containing singulary original ideas. The *diwân* (or *collection*) of his poems fills four volumes. He wore the dress of the old-fashioned people in Aleppo, with a two-peaked turban (1). He was a constant attendant at the lessons (lit. *the circle*) of the shaikh Tâj ad-Dîn Abû 'l-Kasim Ahmad Ibn Hibat Allah Ibn Saad Ibn Said Ibn Saad Ibn Mukallad , generally known by the surname of Ibn al-Jibrâni, who was an eminent grammarian and philologer, and a native of Aleppo. Under this master he studied principally philology and profited greatly by his tuition. Another teacher whose lessons he attended for some time was at-Tâj (*Tâj ad-Dîn*) Masûd Ibn Abi 'l-Fadl an-Nakkâsh, who was also a native of Aleppo and a poet of some reputation. Under him he learned the art of poetical composition. A close intimacy and a sincere friendship were formed between me and ash-Shihâb ash-Shauwâ; we frequently met at conferences where we discussed points of literature. He often recited to me verses of his own composing, and he was my inseparable companion from the latter part of the year 633 (A. D. 1236) till the time of his death. Before we became acquainted, I often saw him sitting on the sofa, beside Ibn al-Jibrâni, in that part of the mosque at Aleppo where the latter delivered his lectures. He used to walk about in the mosque, as was the custom of the people there and as we see them do in the mosque of Damascus; at that time we did not know each other. His conversation was agreeable, his delivery pleasing and his demeanour grave and modest. The first verses of his own composing which he recited to me were the following :

Behold, my friend ! the hills of Lâlâ; I implore you in Allah's name to turn aside and follow me. Let us there dismount between the tents erected on the sands; for those vernal pastures-grounds have again received their population. There we may pass the day in contemplating the inhabitants or in expressing our tender feelings for that beloved spot.

Here is another of his pieces which he recited to me :

(*I think*) of that graceful youth on whose cheek time has been working till it clothed it with a double raiment, one of night (*dark hair*) and one of day (*a clear complexion*). The charms of his face would be an excuse for my admiring him, even did his flourishing *izâr* (2) excite my dislike.

One day, whilst we were conversing on literary subjects, he recited to me the following verses which Sharaf ad-Dîn Abû 'l-Mahâsin Muhammad, generally known by the appellation of Ibn Onain (*vol. III. p. 176*), had composed upon a native of Bokhara, or of Saraklis, as some say, whose name was Sadr Jihân and who bore the surname of Ibn Mari :

It would be easier for needy solicitors to strip the bark off the thorny acacia-tree (3) or to take hold of the polar star, than to obtain any of Ibn Mâra's money. His constancy in hoarding that money prevents it from passing into other hands and makes it resemble a singular noun in the vocative case (4).

"That verse, said he, is not good." I asked him why, and he answered : " It is " not absolutely necessary that the singular noun, in the vocative case, should " receive the *domma* ; if it be indefinite and have nothing to determine " it, there is no need of its taking the *domma*; *ex. : Ya rajulân* (5). But I am " composing things on the same subject. " —Shortly afterwards, he met me in the mosque and told me that he had accomplished the task. I asked to hear the verses, and he recited to me these :

We have a friend whose qualities denote clearly the meanness of his origin. They are in him (*as invariable*) as the word *hnitâ*; were it not better that they should be like *amsi* (i. e. *past and gone*).

On this, I said to him, that his piece also might incur objections. He asked me of what kind and I replied : " The particle *haith* admits of various forms : some of " the desert Arabs make it indeclinable with a final *u*, others, with a final *a* and " others with a final *i*; besides which it can assume other forms (as *hîth*, etc.). As " for *amsi*, some of the Arabs make it invariable with a final *i*, whilst others say that

" it is declinable but does not take a particular inflexion for each case ; an example
" of what I state is offered by this verse :

> " I have seen a strange thing since yesterday evening (amsan, for amsin) ; five old women
> " like ogresses.

" Here amsan (امسل) is definite (marks a particular time), but when it is inde-
" finite, it retains always one and the same inflexion (amsi)." My friend (, on hearing this,) did not utter another word. — He frequently introduced terms of Arabic
grammar into his pieces, one of which I shall cite ; I do not know if it was he who
repeated it to me or not, for he communicated to me orally a great quantity of his
own poetry and I neglected writing all of it down. This remark applies equally to
the other pieces of his which I am about to give ; and, as I am unable to say from
whom I learned them, I insert them at a venture. — Here is the piece of which I
am speaking :

> We were fifteen years in accordance and, despite the envious, there was nothing to rule it.
> I thus became a tanwin (6) and the beloved was always in the state of annexion (7).

He said also of a girl who let one of her ringlets hang down and kept the other
tied up :

> My sweetmeat let one ringlet hang down and kept the other twisted up ; giving thus a deal of
> pain to him who tried to describe her charms. That which was on her cheek I took for a ser-
> pent running about, and the other appeared to be a scorpion (8). One was (as straight) as (the
> letter) alif, but it was not the alif of union ; the other was (curved) like the wāw (و), but
> it was not the wāw of conjunction.

The kátib Bahá ad-Dín Zubair Ibn Muhammad (vol. I. p. 542) recited to me a
piece of the same cast, containing a verse which I give here :

> O wāw of her cheek ! perhaps (you will have) pity on me by effecting my union (with the
> beloved) ; for I know that the wāw is a connecter.

The following piece is by Abú 'l-Mahásin ash-Shauwá :

> I said to her who, in complexion, was like the sun, whilst my body, in occultness, was

like a shadow : " O thou splendid one who art more *definite* (i. e. *evident*) than a pronoun ! be " kind to a feeble being who is the most *indefinite* (i. e. *obscure*) of beings. "

He said of a person who could not keep a secret :

I had a friend who never came (to me) without repeating calumnies and scandals. No man resembled the echo more than he : if you say a word, he immediately repeats it.

By the same :

They told me that my beloved exhaled such fragrance as perfumed the country all around, and I replied, on observing a beauty-spot upon her cheek : " See you not that the fire (*the red- " ness of her cheek*) is consuming ambergris ? "

Our article on Yahya Ibn Nizâr al-Manbeji (p. 134 *of this vol.*) contains some verses composed by Imâd ad-Din al-Muhalli and others, in which the thought comes near to what is expressed here. — The following piece is by Abû 'l-Mahâsin ash-Shauwâ :

O thou who art so full of pride ! I have no wile by means of which I can gain thy love. Du- ring all my time thy *revis* (i. e. *arts*) were divided into three which never varied. Your pro- mising was always in the *future*, my endurance was in the *preterite*, and my passion for thee is always in the *present*.

By the same :

I should sacrifice my life for Râs-Ain, for those who dwell there and for the white (*limpid*) streamlets which circulate around its blue (*dark*) palm-trees (9). Whilst its flowing waters were charming my sight, the eyes of its maidens caused my blood to flow.

By the same :

If they conceal her from me through jealousy, I shall remain contented with her (*simple*) re- collection. She is like musk ; its odour we perceive though the place where it is escapes disco- very ; its emanations suffice to reveal its presence.

By the same :

With joy I congratulated my young friend on his circumcision, and I said, when he was overcome by apprehension : " To deliver you from pain a person has approached you whose

" tender solicitude is excited even when the zephyr obliges your body to bend before it. O
" you who cause my earnalmen I how have you been able to support the pain with firmness ? is
" not the young gazelle the most timorous of beings? Were this purification not a rite al-
" ready instituted by Abraham, I should have vigorously attacked the operator (10) when he
" came forward with Moses (11) in his hand though you were Moses (*to be wounded*) (12). "

Most of his poetry is of the same cast, but the specimens here given may suffice.
He was one of those sectaries who held the most extravagant doctrines of the Shiite
sect (13). The greater part of the people, at Aleppo, knew him by the appellation
of *Mahâsin ash-Shauwâ*, but his real names were what we have mentioned in this article, that is to say, *Yûsuf*, surnamed *Abû 'l-Mahâsin*. Since writing what precedes (14), I met with the *Okûd al-Jumân* (*strings of pearls*), a work composed by
my friend al-Kamâl (*Kamâl ad-Dîn*) Ibn ash-Shiâr al-Mausili (*of Mosul*), (see p. 426
of this vol.) and, in it I found the biographical notice of this poet ranged amongst
those of the persons who bore the name of *Yûsuf* and the surname of *Abû 'l-Mahâsin*.
Now, al-Kamâl was a friend of his, had learned from him a quantity of his poems
and was better acquainted with his history than any other person. — The birth of
ash-Shauwâ may be placed approximately in the year 562 (A. D. 1166-7), for the
date has not been well ascertained; he died at Aleppo on Friday, the 19th of Muharram, 635 (11th Sept. 1237), and was buried in the cemetery which lies to the west
of the city, outside the gate of Antioch. A circumstance happened which prevented
me from attending his funeral. May God have mercy on him, for he was an excellent friend! His professor, Ibn al-Jibrâni, belonged to the Bohtor family, which is
a branch of the tribe of Tâi. He came from a village situated in the government of
Azâs and called Jibrin Kûrestayâ (15) and, from it he drew his surname (al-Jibrâni).
This we give after his own declaration. He had an extensive acquaintance with general literature and particularly with philology, which had been his predominant
study. He taught as a professor in the mosque of Aleppo and held his sittings in
the eastern *maksûra* (vol. I. p. 228), that which is raised above the floor of the mosque and lies opposite to the *maksûra* in which the *kâdi* of Aleppo says the prayer on
Fridays. — I was one day sitting in that pew, near the grating which faces the court
of the mosque, when I saw al-Jibrâni come in with a number of his pupils, and
amongst them Abû 'l-Mahâsin Ibn ash-Shauwâ. He took his seat in the small
mihrâb (vol. I. p. 37) which is in the other *maksûra* and in which he gave his
lessons as professor. I directed my attention to what he said, as I was then en-

gaged in literary studies, and I heard him treat of the rule which applies to such tri-
literal verbs as have a w for their first radical and an i after the second radical; for
instance wajila. He observed that the aorist of such verbs had four forms, ex. yaw-
jalu, yaijalu, yajalu and yijalu. The exceptions (, said he,) are eight in number :
warima, waritha, warid, warida, wamika, wathika, wafika and walia which, in the
aorist, take an i (after the second radical and change the first syllable). Having
indicated this exactly, he observed that the exceptions were wasid, yasad, and walid,
yalad, each of which, in the aorist, takes an a after the second radical, through the
influence of the guttural letter. — On this subject he made a long discourse which I
was unable to commit to memory, the paragraph just given being all that I heard
distinctly. He (al-Jiordni) was born on Friday, the 22nd of Shauwál, 561 (21st
August, A. D. 1166), and he died at Aleppo on Tuesday, the 7th of Rajab, 628 (11th
May, A. D. 1231). He was buried at the foot of Mount Jaushen (16).

(1) Literally : with a split turban (mashkúka); another reading is mashkúfa (a roofed turban).

(2) See vol. I, Introduction, p. XXXVI.

(3) The word haldd, here rendered by orario tree, designates the troyoconthus.

(4) The singular noun in the vocative receives for final vowel the u or damma, when the noun is definite.
The noun is then said to be madmûm, which word signifies accompanied with a damma, and also held
fast.

(5) The words, I say, man! may be rendered in Arabic by ya rajulu, with the sign of the definite nominative, or ya rajulin, which is the sign of indefinition. See de Sacy's Grammaire Arabe, 2me éd. t. I,
p. 89.

(6) The tawrid is indicated by two vowel signs of the same kind; it is therefore a couple of signs, a pair.
The poet meant that he and his mistress formed a pair. Such, at least, appears to be his meaning.

(7) To explain the technical terms of Arabic grammar which follow would lead us too far.

(8) See vol. I, introduction, page XLVI.

(9) The second manzil appears to be a plural formed from mida, which is also a plural. Plurals of plurals
are frequent in Arabic. All the places inscribed here are full of double meanings and verbal quibbles.

(10) The word mansyia, here rendered by operator, signifies literally eduuur, and is one of the terms employed to designate a barber. In Moslim countries, the barbers are also surgeons.

(11) Músa in Arabic, is the name of the prophet Moses and signifies also a clasp-knife or a razor.

(12) The word Kelim, here rendered by Moses, has two significations, wounded and spoken to. Moses was
called the Kelim Allah because God spoke to him on Mount Sinai.

(13) That is, in believing that Ali and the imams, his descendants, were incarnations of the Divinity.

(14) This passage is given in the printed editions but is not to be found in our manuscripts.

(15) This place, whatever may be its name, lay at about thirty miles NNW of Aleppo.

(16) Mount Jaushen lies on the west side of Aleppo.

ABU 'L-HAJJAJ AL-BAIYASI.

Abû 'l-Hajjâj Yûsuf Ibn Muhammad Ibn Ibrâhîm al-Ansâri al-Baiyâsi (descended from a Medina family and native of Baeza, in Spain) was one of those accomplished scholars and exact traditionists who were an honour to Spain, Versed in
philology, learned and gifted with preeminent talents, he possessed a perfect knowledge of the language spoken by the desert Arabs and was acquainted with it in all its
divisions, both in poetry and prose. He was a professional narrator of the occurrences which marked the history of that people, their wars, and their battle-days.
I have been informed that he knew by heart the Hamâsa of Abû Tammâm at-Tai
(vol. I. p. 348), the works of the six poets (1), the collected poetical works of the
same Abû Tammâm, the Diwân of al-Mutanabbi (vol. I. p. 102), the Sikt az-Zand by
Abû 'l-Alâ 'l-Maarri (vol. I. p. 94) and a great quantity of pieces composed by the
poets who flourished in the days of paganism and by those who lived in Moslim
times. He visited the different provinces of Spain, travelled over the greater part
of them and proceeded to the city of Tunis where he compiled for the sovereign of
Ifrîkiya, the emir Abû Zakaria Yahya, the son of Abû Muhammad Abd al-Wâhid
and the grandson of Abû Hafs Omar (2), a work which he entitled Kitâb al-Ilâm
b-il-Hurûb il-Wâkia fi Sadr il-Islâm (the book of information respecting the wars
which took place during the first period of Islamism.) — In it he commenced by relating the assassination of the khalif Omar and terminated by an account al-Walîd Ibn
Tarîf ash-Shâri's revolt in Mesopotamia against the authority of Hârûn ar-Rashîd.
In our article on this Walîd (vol. III. p. 668) we have narrated his history and adventures and mentioned that he fell by the hand of Yazîd Ibn Mazyad Ibn Zâida ash-
Shaibâni. To this Yazîd we have given a separate article (page 218 of this vol.); so,
by means of both, the history of al-Walîd can be fully made out. Al-Baiyâsi's work
forms two volumes, which I met with and read. It is well drawn up and evinces, by
its contents, that the author was master of his subject. I also met with a copy of
his Hamâsa in two volumes; which copy had been read over to the author; it bore

his signature dated in the last third of the month of the latter Rabî 650 (commencement of July, A. D. 1252). In concluding the work he says: " The compilation " and arrangement of this book were terminated in the month of Shauwâl, 646 (Jan.-" Feb., A. D. 1249), at Tunis, which city may God protect!" — I extracted from it that part of the preface which follows the doxology, and shall insert it here : " In " the time of my boyhood and the days of my youth I had a strong passion for lite-" rature and a great fondness for the language of the Arabs. I persevered unremit-" tingly in searching out the meaning of its terms, examining into its fundamental " principles and grammatical forms, till I acquired a mass of such knowledge as no " serious student should be unacquainted with and which every person who directs " his attention to this branch of science should possess. My fondness for that study " and the passion which I felt for it impelled me to collect all the. poetical pieces " which I had admired and which were selected by me from the works of the Arabs, " not only of those who lived in the days of paganism and those who flourished both " in pagan and in Islamic times, but also of those who figured after the promulgation " of Islamism. (I collected also) such pieces of later authors, inhabitants of the East, " Spain and other countries, as might serve to embellish conversation and furnish " matter for discussion. Having then perceived that any attempt to preserve this " collection, unless it were reduced into a regular form and put into the shape of a " dîwân, would only serve to proclaim its speedy disparition and bring on its destruc-" tion, I thought it advisable to collect those chosen extracts, assemble those beau-" tiful passages and arrange them in classes, in order to retain what might go astray " and preserve what was rare. After reflecting on this matter, I could find no classifi-" cation more simple, no arrangement better than that which Abû Tammâm Habîb " Ibn Aûs had adopted for his Hamâsa. (I resolved) on imitating it with care and " on following its plan, more particularly as the author held the first place in " that art and stood alone in it by his abundant share (of erudition) and by the " value of his information. I therefore adopted his system, pursued the same " course as he, and joined (each piece) to those which resembled it by their subject, " uniting it to those of a similar character. I sifted them well; choosing them " with all the care of which I was capable and with the utmost attention, doing " to the best of my power." — The author continues in a long discourse which we need not reproduce. From that work I made some extracts, such as the following, taken from the section of elegies : " Abû Ali 'l-Kâli (vol. I. p. 210) stated that Abû

" Bakr Ibn Duraid (*vol. III. p. 37*) had recited to him the following piece, declaring
" that he had learned it from the lips of Abù Hàtim as-Sijistàni (*vol. I. p. 603*) :

> " How many (*of those who fought*) in the cause of God are now enclosed in the bosom of
> " the earth or confided to the soil of the desert ! (*They were brilliant*) moons enlightening
> " the world when darkness covered it, and their heads, in times of drought, poured forth
> " showers (*of beneficence*). O, thou who rejoicest at their death, exult not at their fall !
> " Their life procured them glory, and their death a wide renown. Their life kept the enemy
> " in dejection (*gheiza*); their death was an honour for those who could claim them as relations.
> " Whilst they remained upon the surface of the earth, all its groves were verdant; and
> " now, that they are in its interior, that surface remains forlorn. "

The section of amatory pieces furnishes us with the following lines, composed by
al-Abbas Ibn al-Ahnaf (*vol. II. p. 7*) :

> Bear with the greatest injustice done to you by her whom you love; if you are the injured
> man, say that you were the transgressor. If you do not pardon the faults of the beloved, she
> will abandon you, in despite of your wishes.

" The following piece," says our author, " was composed by al-Wàwà ad-Dimishki
" (*vol. II. p. 340*) ; " but I am greatly inclined to believe that it was composed by
Abù-Faràs Ibn Hamdùn (*vol. I. p. 366*) :

> My two friends ! I beg of you in the name of Allah, your Lord, to turn (*from the road and
> go*) to her whom I love. Then reproach her; a reprimand may, perhaps, induce her to re-
> lent. Allude to me and say, whilst discoursing with her : " What has your servant done that
> " you are killing him with your disdain ? " If she smile, say to her in a coaxing way :
> " What harm would it do, were you to take him into favour ? " If she then testifies anger,
> deceive her by saying : " We know not the person. "

(*The same work contains*) the following piece of which the author is al-Majnùn (3) :

> I got attached (*taalakta*) to Laila whilst she was still a girl without experience, and before
> the time that her companions perceived the swelling of her bosom. We were then both young
> and tended flocks; O, that we and our lambs (*baham*) had never grown up!

The word *baham* means *a young sheep* and is the plural of *bahma.* — These two
verses are cited by grammarians in order to prove that the term which indicates the
state (*of a thing or person already mentioned*) and which is put in the accusative case
may, though a single word, refer at the same time to the agent and the object of the

action. Here, the word *saghírain* (*both being young*) is 'put in the accusatif as a term indicating the state, and yet it refers to the pronoun *t* in the verb *taallaktu* (4) and to the noun *Laila*, which is in the accusative case. Another example of this (*construction*) is offered by the following verse, of which Antara 'l-Absi (5) is the author:

If ever you meet me (*talkani*) and we be both alone (*faradain*), the hinder parts (6) of your breech will quiver with fear.

The word *faradain*, being employed here to express a state, is in the accusative and refers not only to the agent but to the object of the action in the verb *talkani*. This verse is cited by Ibn al-Anbári (*vol. II. p. 95*), in his *Asrár al-Arabiya*, chapter on the (*terms which indicate a*) state. —The following piece by Wáwá ed-Dimishki is given by al-Daiyási in his *Hamdsa*:

(*I think*) of a visitor whose aspect charmed all men and was more grateful than an economy granted to him who is in fear of death. She cast upon the night a deeper shade by the darkness of her locks, and the morning, abashed (*by the brightness*), dreaded her appearance. She tried to kill me by her disdain, but, when I appealed to her (*clemency*), she took me into favour and drew my soul out of the hands of death. Thus, through her (*kindness*), I became the prince of lovers; that principality existed before my time.

(*We read in the same work*): "'Ali Ibn Atiya Ibn ar-Rakkák, a native of Valencia, said:

" (*I think*) of her whose movements were so graceful, whose waist was so pliant and whose
" haunches were so large. She drew near, and the night, unable to contend with her, took
" to flight, though it had no other wings than (*our mutual*) joy (7). She visited me on the
" sweetest of nights and held me embraced till the morning was morning. Her arms were
" passed around my neck, like a shoulder-belt, and mine were passed around her waist,
" like a girdle."

" Ahmad Ibn al-Hussin Ibn Khalaf, generally known by the surname of Ibn al-
" Binni al-Yamori," — a person of whom we have spoken in our article on Yúsuf
Ibd Abd al-Múmin (*p. 479 of this vol.*), the sovereign of Maghrib, — " was expelled
" from Majorca by the governor of that island and sent across the sea. After the
" first day of the voyage a wind arose and forced them to return. To this he
" alluded in the following piece:

O my friends! you whom people blamed on my account, whilst they banished me ; the moment of farewells soon drew near. Separated from you, who were such gay and amusing companions, shall I ever again find pleasure in life? After sailing for a day, I said : " Is it desire " that impels our ship (to go back) or is it violence? As it flew along with us, it hovered " round you, as if our hearts had been its sails. "

" (The khalif) al-Wáthik Billah said, in a piece which alone would suffice to " evince his talent :

I did not know what the pains of separation were till the people cried out : " Here come the " ships!" My beloved, drowned in tears, leaned forward to bid me farewell and uttered some words so indistinctly that their meaning could not be seized. She bent towards me, kissing me and saying that she would willingly give her life for mine ; like her the pliant branches in the garden bend before the zephyr. She then turned away, and exclaimed, in weeping: O that I had never known you !

In the section which contains the passages on hospitality, guests, vaingloriousness and eulogy, the author inserts the following verses, which were pronounced by Abú 'l-Hasan Jaafar Ibn Ibráhím Ibn al-Hajjáj al-Lúrki :

Admire (in me) a man who seeks for praise, though he avoids giving away any thing of his own, and who directs (lit. who opens) his hopes towards return, though he does not open his hand. Why should I act like the (presence of a) guest, and hasten with joy to receive him, if he eats of his own provisions, and praises me for my hospitality?

" Amongst the verses attributed to Abd Allah Ibn Abbás (vol. I. p. 89) are the following, which he pronounced after losing his sight :

" Though God has deprived my eyes of their light, a portion of that light remains in my " tongue and in my heart. My heart is acute, my intelligence unimpaired and, in my mouth, " is something as sharp and as cutting as a sword. "

In the section which contains the satires, reproaches and pieces connected with such subjects, he gives the following piece as the production of Abú 'l-Aálla Ahmad Ibn Malik ash-Shámi :

I speak in dispraise of Baghdad as a residence, after having gained information and experience. No gifts can be expected from its princes; no alleviation for the grief of the afflicted. These princes have left to others the path of honour and given themselves up to debauchery and crime. He who wishes to succeed with them must first be introduced and then possess three things : the wealth of Kárún (6), the years of Noah (9) and the patience of Job.

(*Here the author says* :) " Abû Bakr Muhammad Ibn Yahya as-Sûli mentioned that
" the following piece was composed by Abû 'l-Attâf al-Kûfi and directed against
" Sâlih Ibn Abd ar-Rahmân Nashîi :

> " Son of al-Walîd! explain to us, and let your explanation remain within bounds : Why do
> " we see you at liberty? What has become of your chains and fetters ? is iron now dear in your
> " country or is it incapable of holding you ?"

Here finish our extracts from al-Baiyâsi's *Hamdsa*. They are sufficient for our
purpose, which was, to select out of the pieces chosen by him a certain number
which might indicate his (*extensive*) acquaintance with poetry. He was born on
Thursday, the 14th of the first Rabî, 573 (11th Sept. A. D. 1177), and he died at
Tunis, on Sunday, the 4th of Zû 'l-Kaada, 653 (5th Dec. A. D. 1255). — " *Bai-*
" *ydsi* means *belonging to Baydsa* (Baeza), which is a large town of Moslim Spain
" and now included in the province of Jaen." So says Yakût al-Hamawi (*page 9*
of this vol.) in his dictionary of geographical synonyms.

---

(1) The six poets whose works are inserted in this collection were Amro 'l-Kais, an-Nâbigha ad-Dubyâni,
Alkama, Zuhair, Tarafa and Antara. For further information see the translator's edition of the *Dîwân* of
Amro 'l-Kais, preface, page x.

(2) For the history of Abû Zakariya Yahya, the founder of the Hafsida dynasty, see Ibn Khaldûn's *Histoire
des Berbers*, tome II, p. 107 et seq.

(3) See Mr de Sacy's remarks relatively to Majnûn in the *Anthologie grammaticale arabe*, page 150.

(4) It is the second *t* in that word which represents the pronoun of the first person singular.

(5) For the history of Antara, the author of one of the *Moallakas*, see Mr Caussin de Perceval's *Essai sur
l'histoire des Arabes*, tome II, pp. 514 et suiv.

(6) Read روائي with the manuscripts. For the signification of this word see the *Hamdsa*, p. 565, l. 15
and az-Zauzal's commentary on the sixteenth verse of Amr Ibn Kulthûm's *Moallaka*.

(7) This translation is merely conjectural.

(8) For the Moslim legend respecting Kârûn, the Corah of the Bible, *Numbers*, xvi, see Sale's note on the
twenty-eighth sûrat of the Koran.

(9) According to the Koran, sûrat xxix, verse 13, Noah tarried among his people one thousand years, save
fifty years.

YUNUS IBN HABIB.

Abû Abd ar-Rahmân Yûnus Ibn Habib the grammarian.   Abû Abd Allah al-Marzubâni (vol. III, p. 67) says, in his work entitled Kitâb al-Muktabis (Book for him who desires information) and containing the history of the grammarians : " He " was attached to the tribe of Dabba by the bonds of enfranchisement, or, by ano- " ther account, to the family of Laith Ibn Bakr Ibn Abd Manât Ibn Kinâna.   Others " say that he was a client, by enfranchisement, of Dilâl Ibn Harmi, a member of the " family called the Dubaiya Ibn Dajâla and that he was a native of Jabbul.   His " birth took place in the year 90 (A. D. 708-9) and his death in the year 182 (A. D. " 798-9).   He sometimes said that he recollected the death of al-Hajjâj (1). " Some place his birth in the year 80.   According to others, he saw al-Hajjâj and " lived to the age of one hundred and two years; another account says, ninety-eight " years. " — The following indications are furnished, not by al-Marzubâni, but by another author : " Yûnus learned philology from Abû Amr Ibn al-Alâ (vol. II. p. 399) " and Hammâd Ibn Salama (vol. I. p. 261), but the study of grammar became his " predominant occupation.   He obtained, by audition (much philological informa- " tion) from the Arabs (of the desert); Sibawaih handed down much (information of " that kind) on his authority, and lessons were given by him to al-Kisâi (vol. II. " p. 237) and al-Farrâ (page 63 of this vol.).   In grammar he followed a system of " analogical deduction and of rules which was peculiar to himself.   As a philologer, " he belonged to the fifth class (2). — It was at Basra that held his school (lit. his " circle), which was much frequented by literary men and (even) by the most elegant " speakers among the Arabs and the inhabitants of the desert. " — Abû Obaida Ma- mar Ibn al-Muthanna (vol. III. p. 388) said : " I frequented (the school of) Yûnus " during forty years and, every day, I filled my tablets with notes which he dictated " from memory." — The grammarian Abû Zaid al-Ansâri (vol. I. p. 570) said : " I " sat (as a student) by the side of Yûnus Ibn Habib during ten years, and Khalaf al- " Ahmar (vol. I. p. 572) before me did the same during twenty years. " — Yûnus himself said : " Rûba Ibn al-Ajjâj (vol. I. p. 527) addressed me, one day, in these " terms : ' How long will you be asking me questions about those (philological) futi-

" ' lities, and how long must I be adorning them for your (*pleasure*)? Do you not
" " perceive that the greater part of your beard has turned gray?' — Amongst the
works which Yûnus drew up (*and published*), we may notice the *Kitâb Madni 'l-Korân*
(*on the rhetorical figures employed in the Koran*), the *Kitâb al-Loghât*, the *Kitâb al-
Amthâl* (*book of Proverbs*) and the lesser collection of Anecdotes (*Nawâdir*) (3). Ishak
Ibn Ibrâhîm al-Mausili (*vol. I, p. 183*) said : " Yûnus lived eighty-eight years; he was
" never married, never kept a concubine and never thought of any thing but acqui-
" ring knowledge and conversing with distinguished (*literary men.*)" —Yûnus said :
" If I formed the wish of being able to compose in verse, I should not desire to
" utter any thing better than the verse in which Adi Ibn Zaid (4) said :

" O you who rejoice at other's woes and deride the fickleness of Fortune! are you then
" safe from danger and perfectly secure?"

This verse belongs to a piece which is currently known among literary men and
contains moral exhortations with examples. The next lines we here give :

Do you know the history of ancient times (5)? No! you are ignorant and misled. Whom
think you that destiny will render immortal? Who has always a guardian, so that he may not
be harmed? What has become of Chosroes, the Chosroes of kings, Andshrewân? What has
become of Sâpûr before him? The noble race of Asfar (6), kings of the Romans,
have left no recollection worthy of being recalled. (*Think of*) the founder (7) of al-Hadr (8),
when he built it and when tribute was paid to him by (*the countries situated on*) the Tigris and
the Khabûr. He lined it with marble, coated it with plaster, and, on its pinnacles, the birds
built their nests. The vicissitudes of time alarmed him not, but his kingdom departed from him
and the door of his palace was abandoned. Think of the lord of al-Khawarnak (9), when he
looked, one day, from the top of his castle, — and reflection leads to wisdom; — he rejoiced
in his kingdom and his ample possessions; (*he contemplated with pleasure*) the river flowing
before him and (*the palace of*) as-Sadîr. Then his heart was troubled and he said : " What
is the felicity of living beings who are always journeying towards their death? After enjoying
prosperity, ruling over a kingdom and a people, they fall as an inheritance to the grave, and
become like the dry leaves which are blown about by the east wind and by the west.

These verses would require a long commentary; if I undertook to give one, I
should be led into prolixity and digress from my subject; more particularly as many of
them have a historical, and the rest a philological, import. I therefore keep within
bounds, giving what is necessary for my purpose and nothing more. As a full explanation of the verses would fill four or five quires (*of twenty pages each*), it could
not find a place here. — Muhammad Ibn Sallâm al-Jumahi (10) relates that Yûnus

said : " The Arabs (of the desert) never expressed grief with more energy than in
" lamenting (the loss of) youth, and yet they did not do full justice to its value."
Mansûr an-Namari (page 131 of this vol.) took hold of this expression and said, in a
kasîda of some length which he composed in praise of Hârûn ar-Rashîd :

> Whilst my youth was in its prime, I did not appreciate its value, and, when it passed away,
> (I perceived that) the world also was passing away (for me).

It was mentioned by Yûnus that the (desert) Arabs said : " Separation from friends
" is sickness for the heart." He then recited these lines :

> Were my eyes to shed tears of blood, forebulling loss of sight, they could not do justice even
> to the tenth part of two things; departure of youth and separation from friends.

He related also that Labîd (the author of the Moallaka), after the introduction of
Islamism, never uttered a line of poetry except the following :

> Praise be to God for not bringing me to the term of my life till I had put on the robe of
> Islamism.

Abû Obaida Mamer Ibn al-Muthanna related as follows : " Djaafar Ibn Sulai-
" mân the Abbaside (vol. II. p. 347) was visiting the khalif al-Mahdi. On retur-
" ning home, he sent for Yûnus Ibn Habîb and said to him : ' I and the Commander
" of the faithful have differed in opinion respecting the meaning of this verse :

> " ' The blackness (of the hair) being invaded by grayness, is like the night (lail), at the
> " ' beginning and the end of which, day (nahâr) utters its cry (is on the alert),

" ' What do the words lail and nahâr mean ?' Yûnus replied : ' Lail has here the
" ' meaning with which you are familiar and so also has nahâr.' Djaafar then
" ' said : ' Al-Mahdi maintains that lail means a young partridge and nahâr a young
" ' bustard.' Ibn Habîb was in the right with regard to the signification of these
" words; the meanings assigned to them by al-Mahdi are no where recognised ex-
" cept in treatises on the unusual terms of the language." — Yûnus related the following anecdote : Jabala Ibn Abd ar-Rahmân (11) used, in ordering his dinner,
to write out a list of the dishes which he wished to have served, and send it to the
cook. In this list he always employed such uncommon and agrestic expressions that

the cook never knew what was wanted till he consulted Ibn Abi Ishak (12), Yahya Ibn Yamar (see p. 59 of this vol.) and other well-informed men.—When he obtained from them the explanation of the difficult words, he would bring to his master what was required.—One day Jabala said to him : " Woe betide you! I am dying of hun-" ger." The cook answered : " Make easy phrases and your dinner will be easy (to " get ready)." — Jabala replied : " You son of a slut! must I lay aside my pure " Arabic on account of your doltishness! " — Yûnus was a native of Jabbul, a town situated on the Tigris, between Baghdad and Wâsit. He did not like to be considered as having come from that place (or to hear it named). A man belonging to the Bani Abi Omair family met him one day and said : " Tell me, Abu Abd ar-Rahmân ! " Jabbul is it of the first declension or the second?" — The other answered by abusive language, and the Omairide looked round for some one whom he might take as a witness of the insult, and, not seeing any person, he went away. The next morning, when Yûnus was sitting with his pupils around him, the same man came to him and said : " Tell me, Abû Abd ar-Rahmân ! Jabbul is it of the first declension " or of the second?" To this Yûnus replied : " The answer is the same as that " which you received yesterday." — As-Samâni (vol. II. p. 156) says, in his Ansâb, that Jahbul (J,b,l,) is to be pronounced with an a after the J and a double b followed by the vowel u. This (13) was the native place of Abû 'l-Khattâb al-Jabbuli, a poet of some celebrity and the author of these lines :

> To reach you, how many deserts did I not cross which, had I been unsupported by my passion, I should never have been able to pass through. To get near you I faced the greatest dangers, but, to encounter perils for the pleasure of seeing you is a welcome task.

" Abû 'l-Khattâb, says as-Samâni, died in the month of Zù 'l-Kaada, 439 (April-" May 1048).—A poetical rivalry existed between him and Abû 'l-Alâ al-Maarri (vol. I. " p. 94) and it was to him that the latter addressed the kasîda which begins thus :

> " My religion and my creed declare improbable (lamentations over the dead and the song " of the camel-driver) (14)."

Here as-Samâni is mistaken : the poem was written by Abû 'l-Alâ and sent to Abû Hamza al-Hasan Ibn Abd ar-Rahmân, a native of Maarra tan-Nomân and a hanifite doctor, who was then acting as a kâdi at Manbej. The same remark has been made by the kâdi Kamâl ad-Din, in his history of Aleppo.— Habîb was the name of his

(*Yûnus's*) mother, and, as it is therefore of the feminine gender (*and a proper name*), it belongs to the second declension. The name of his father is not known. Some say that Yûnus was born after the divorce of his mother, who had been legally separated from her husband in consequence of a mutual anathema (15). According to others, *Halîb* was his father's name; if so, it is of the first declension. The same observations apply equally to the name of Muhammad Ibn Habib (16), the genealogist. — Yûnus entered, one day, into the mosque, tottering in his gait and supported by two men, one on each side of him, because he was very old. A man of whose friendship he had doubts then addressed him and said : " Abû Abd ar-Rahmân! may " I attain the state in which I see you!" Yûnus replied : " That which you see may " you never attain!" (17). A number of poets took hold of this idea and put it into verse.—Abû 'l-Khattâb Ziâd Ibn Yahya said : " Yûnus is like a bottle with a narrow " neck : to put any thing into it is difficult and, to get it out is impossible." By " these words he meant that Yûnus (*learned slowly and*) forgot nothing. The dates of his birth and of his death are given at the commencement of this article, but some say that he died in the year 183 (A. D. 799). — Abd al-Bâki Ibn Kâni (*vol.* 1, *p.* 374) states that his death took place in the year 184. It is said that he lived to the age of ninety-eight years.

(1) Al-Hajjâj died A. H. 95. See vol. I , p. 363.

(2) The word *elass* means here *generation* of oral teachers.

(3) It there be not an omission in the Arabic text, there must have been then in circulation a greater *Na-raddir* composed by some other author, perhaps Ibn al-Anbâri.

(4) See vol. I, p. 189. A fuller and more satisfactory account of this celebrated poet is given in M. Caussin de Perceval's *Essai sur l'histoire des Arabes*, tome II, page 118 et seq.

(5) The text may also signify : have you the old covenant (or *testament*) of days? that is, the Bible, containing the history of ancient times. Adi Ibn Zeid was a Christian.

(a) The Arabs designated the Romans and their emperors by the title of *Benâ 'l-Asfar*. They were probably aware that Vespasian and his successors bore the surname of *Flavius*; and this word, being confounded by them with *Flavus*, was rendered by *Asfar*.

(7) Literally : the brother.

(8) See vol. III, p. 318. In M. Caussin's *Essai*, vol. II, p. 40, will be found an historical account of al-Hadr, called *Atra* by the historians of the Roman emperors.

(9) The castles of al-Khawarnak and as-Sadîr were built in the neighbourhood of Hira by an-Nomân al-Awar. See M. Caussin's *Essai* vol. II, p. 33, and the sources there indicated.

(10) As-Soyûti says, in his *Dictionary of Grammarians*, ms. of the Bibl. imp., no 633 : " Abû Abd Allah ' Muhammad Ibn Salîm Ibn Obaid Allah Ibn Sâlim al-Jumahi, a *maula* of Muhammad Ibn Kâb, who, him-

self was a mawla of Kināna Ibn Maʿādd, a member of the Jumaḥ family, which was a branch of the Ku-
"raish tribe, is placed by az-Zubaidi (vol. III, p. 59) in the fifth class (or generation) of the philologers who
"belonged to the school of Basra. He died in that city, A. H. 231 (A. D. 845)."— We read in the Fihrist:
"Abû Abd Allah Mohammed Ibn Sallâm al-Jumaḥi was one of those who transmitted down orally
"historical relations and pieces of poetry. He composed many works, such as the Fazl, treating of the
"beauties of historical narratives and of poetry, an account of the noble houses (or families) among the
"Arabs, a classified account of the poets who lived in pagan times, another of the poets who lived in the
"times of Islamism, and a work containing anecdotes of horse-racing."

(11) This Jabala was evidently a man of high rank, perhaps one of the generals who commanded in Khorásán, under the orders of al-Hajjáj.

(12) Abû Bahr Abd Allah Ibn Abi Isḥak Zaid Ibn al-Hârith al-Hadrami, was a native, or an inhabitant, of
Basra. He acquired a high reputation by his learning as a grammarian and by his profound acquaintance
with the Koran-readings. He lived to the age of eighty-eight years and died A. H. 127 (A. D. 744-5). (Abû
'l-Fadl's Annals, Flügel's Grammatische Schulen der Araber, 1st part, page 29).

(13) This passage is given in the printed editions but is not to be found in our manuscripts.

(14) The rest of the verse, omitted here, in the Arabic text, and inserted in the translation, runs as follows:

نوح ياك ولا تزنم شدى   The song of the camel-driver alludes to the journeys undertaken by lovers for
purpose of visiting the spot inhabited by the beloved.

(15) If a husband accuses his wife of infidelity, and persists in declaring that the accusation is true whilst
the wife asserts that it is false, both parties must affirm their declarations by oath and invoke God's curse
upon themselves if they are perjured. This double anathema dissolves the marriage.

(16) Abû Jaafar Muhammad Ibn Habib, a mawla of the Hâshim family, was versed in the science of genealogies, skilled in grammar and well acquainted with the accounts of the battle-days of the Arabs. He
was considered as an exact and trustworthy authority. He died at Samarra in the month of Zû 'l-Hijja, 245
(A. D. 860). — (Nujûm, Flügel's Grammatische Schulen, 1st part, page 67.)

(17) This answer, if taken as a complement, means: may you never be so decrepit as I; but it has another
meaning: may you not live as long as I.

YUNUS IBN ABD AL-AALA.

Abû Mûsa Yûnus Ibn Abd al-Aala Ibn Mûsa Ibn Maisara Ibn Hafs Ibn Haiyân
as-Sadafi, a native of Egypt and a doctor of the Shafite sect, was one of as-Shâfi's
(vol. II. p. 569) most assiduous pupils and one of the most active in transmitting
down what that imâm taught. To his profound piety and his firm religious convic-

tions he joined so extensive an acquaintance with the history (*of the learned*) and with the Traditions that no person of that age could equal him. We have spoken in this work (vol. *II.* p. 93) of his grandson, Abû Saîd Abd ar-Rahmân Ibn Ahmad Ibn Yûnus, the author of the History of Misr (*Old-Cairo*), and of this Abû Saîd's son (vol. *II.* p. 305), Abû 'l-Hasan Ali Ibn Abî Saîd Abd ar-Rahmân Ibn Yûnus, a famous astronomer and the author of the (*Hakemite*) tables. Each of them was a master in the science which he cultivated. Yûnus learned the koran-readings (vol. *I.* p. 152) by reciting that book aloud under the direction of Warsh (vol. *III,* p. 434), Soklâb Ibn Shunaina (1) and Moalla Ibn Dihya (2). The systems (*of reading*) with which he thus became acquainted were that of Nâfê (vol. *III,* p. 522) and that which Ali Ibn Kîsa (3) had learned from Sulaim (4) and which Sulaim had learned from Hamza Ibn Habîb az-Zaiyât (vol. *I.* p. 478). He heard traditions delivered by Sofyân Ibn Oyaina and Abd Allah Ibn Wahb (vol. *II.* p. 15), the Egyptian. Koran-reading was taught on his authority by his pupils Nawâs Ibn Saîd (5), Muhammad Ibn ar-Rabî (6), Oshma Ibn Ahmad (*at-Tujîbi*), Muhammad Ibn Ishak Ibn Khuzaima (7), Muhammad Ibn Jarîr at-Tabari and others. He held a high rank as a Traditionist. Abu Abd Allah al-Kudâi (vol. *II.* p. 616) speaks of him in his topographical description of Misr (*Old Cairo*) and says : " He was one of the most eminent men of that time and ranked " with the most intelligent. It has been handed down that as-Shâfi said : ' I never " ' saw in Misr a more intelligent man than Yûnus Ibn Abd al-Aala.' From as-" Shâfi he learned Traditions and jurisprudence, which information he taught to " others in his master's name. He received a pension out of a mortmain (*habs*) held " by the board of government (*diwân al-hukm*), and left posterity. His house is si-" tuated in the district of as-Sadif and bears an inscription containing his name and " dated in the year 215 (A. D. 830-1). He was one of those inhabitants of Misr " who were authorised to act as witnesses (*to bonds*), and he filled that office during " sixty years." Another author states that Traditions, received from Yûnus Ibn Abd al-Aala, were taught on his authority by the *imâm* Muslim Ibn al-Hajjâj al-Kushairi (vol. *III,* p. 348), Abû Abd ar-Rahmân an-Nasâi (vol. *I.* p. 58), Abû Abd Allah Ibn Maja (vol. *II.* p. 680) and others. Abû Muhammad al-Hasan Ibn Zûlâk (vol. *I.* p. 388) relates the following anecdote in his History of Misr : Bakkâr Ibn Kutaiba being nominated *kâdi* of Misr, set out for that city from Baghdad and, on reaching al-Jifâr (8), he met Muhammad Ibn Laith, the former *kâdi* of Misr who, after his deposition, was returning to Irak. In a conversation which he had with him, he

said : " I am a stranger to Misr and you know the place well; indicate to me the per-
" sons whom I may take as advisers and on whom I may place reliance." Ibn al-
Laith replied : " I recommend to you two persons, one of them very clever and na-
" med Yûnus Ibn Abd al-Aala; I know well that he is clever, because I endeavoured
" to have him condemned to death and he found means of getting me outlawed.
" The other is Abû Hârûn Mûsa Ibn Abd ar-Rahmân Ibn al-Kâsim; (*I indicate him*)
" because he is a very devout man." Bakkâr expressed the wish to know what was
their personal appearance and Ibn al-Laith said : " Yûnus is a tall man, of a clear
" complexion," describing him fully, after which, he gave the description of Mûsa.
When Bakkâr arrived at Misr, the people came to see him, and amongst the
visitors was a man whose appearance answered the description given of Yûnus.
Bakkâr made him sit down in the place of honour, and began to converse with him,
calling him Abû Mûsa every time he addressed him. They were still talking, when
Yûnus himself came in. Bakkâr then turned towards the other, and said to him :
" You Sir! who are you? why did you keep silent! I might have confided to you
" some of my secrets!" Yûnus then advanced and was installed in the place of honour. After that, Mûsa came in, and Bakkâr took them both for friends and advisers. — It is related that the *kâdi* Bakkâr admitted Mûsa into his intimacy because
he considered the acquaintance of so pious a man to be a blessing, and said to him
one day : "Tell me, Abû Hârûn! how do gain your livelihood?" The other answered. " Out of a mortmain (*wakf*) founded by my father in my favour." — " Is it
" sufficient for you maintenance?" said Bakkâr. — "It is quite sufficient," replied the
other, " and now, since the *kâdi* has addressed me questions, I wish to address some
" to him." — " Begin ; " said Bakkâr. — " Did the *kâdi*, when at Basra, get so deeply
" into debt that he consented to accept this kadiship?" - The other answered : " No."
— " Was he obliged," said Mûsa, " to accept it because God had granted him a num-
" ber of children?" — "No," replied Bakkâr, " I was never married." — " Have you a
" number of relatives to support?"—" No."—" Did the sultan force you to accept
" this office and threaten you with tortures if you refused?" — " No." — " So
" then, you kept whipping the flanks of camels, from Basra to Misr, without being
" under the necessity or the obligation of doing so? I take God to witness that I
" shall never come to see you again!" — "Pray, forgive me ; " said Bakkâr. — "No,"
replied Mûsa, " you began the asking of questions; had you remained silent, I
" should not have spoken." He then departed and never returned again. — Yûnus

related that he had a dream in which he heard a voice say to him : " The name of
" the Almighty God is : There is no god but God (9)." — The work entitled *Kitáb*
al-Muntazem fi akhbár man sakan al-Mukattam (the digest, being an account of the
persons who inhabited Mount Mokattam) contains an article on Yúnus, from which
I extract this passage : " One of the anecdotes which he related, saying that he had
" learned it from another person, was the following : A man went to a coppersmith
" and asked for the loan of one thousand dinars, to be repaid at a fixed time.   Who
" will answer to me for the payment? said the coppersmith. — The other replied :
" Almighty God. — The smith gave the money, and the man set out on a trading
" voyage.   When the time of payment arrived, the debtor wished to go to his cre-
" ditor, but, being prevented by the calm weather, he took a chest, placed in it one
" thousand dinars, locked it up, nailed it and cast it into the sea, saying : ' Almighty
" ' God! here is what you were engaged to pay for me. '   The creditor having gone
" out to see if his debtor was coming with the money, perceived a dark object float-
" ting on the sea and had it brought to him by his servants.   It was that very chest
" of which we have spoken and, on opening it, he found one thousand dinars.
" The other man, having afterwards collected a sum to the same amount, took ad-
" vantage of a favorable wind and set out with the intention of seeing the copper-
" smith.   On arriving, he saluted him and, being asked who he was, he replied I
" am the person who got from you the thousand, and here they are."   The coppersmith replied : " I will not accept them till you tell me what you did with your
" money. "   The man related to him what had passed and mentioned that the wind
had been unfavorable to his return. " Almighty God, " said the coppersmith, " took
" charge of bearing to me that thousand in your name, and I have received it. " —
A great number of anecdotes related of Yúnus and by him have been preserved.   He
stated that the following verses were composed by as-Sháfi :

> Scratch yourself with your own nails; always do your own business, and, when you intend
> asking for a service, go to a person who can appreciate your merit.

Yúnus related that as-Sháfi said to him : " Tell me, Yúnus! did you ever go to
" Baghdad? "   He answered that he had never been there, and as-Sháfi then
said : " In that case, you have not seen the world or its inhabitants. " — He related
also that he heard as-Sháfi make an observation which could be uttered only by one
like him; it was this: " To please every body is an impossible task; seek there-

" fore what may be advantageous for your spiritual and temporal welfare, and stick
" to that. " — Ali Ibn Kadid said : " Yûnus Ibn Abd al-Aala knew the Traditions
" by heart and acted by them. " Abû Abd ar-Rahmân Ahmad Ibn Shoaib an-
Nasawi (10) declared that Yûnus was a trustworthy authority. Another author states
that Yûnus was born in the month of Zû 'l-Hijja, 170 (May-June, A. D. 787) and
that he died on Tuesday, the 27th of the latter Rabî, 264 (6th Jan. A. D. 878);
the same year in which took place the death of al-Muzani (vol. I. p. 200). He
died in Misr (Old Cairo) and was interred in the cemetery of the Sadif tribe. His
tomb is a well-known object in the lesser Karâfa. — His father, Abd al-Aala, was a
man of holy life and bore the surname of Abû Salama. One of his sayings was :
" Buying what one does not require is selling what one requires." "I know by ex-
" perience the truth of that, " said his son Yûnus. Abd al-Aala died in the month
of Muharram, 201 (August, A. D. 816); he was born in the year 121 (A. D. 738-9).
— Abû 'l-Hasan Ahmad, the son of Yûnus, was the father of Abû Said Abd ar-Rahmân Ibn Ahmad, the author of the History of Misr. The latter says, in that work :
" My father (Ahmad Ibn Yûnus) was born in the month of Zû 'l-Kaada, 240 (March-
" April, A. D. 855), and died on Friday, the 1st of Rajab, 302 (20th Jan. A. D.
" 915). He was counted as one of the Sadif family, but did not belong to it either
" by birth or by enfranchisement." — Sadaf, with an a after the S and another
after the d, is the adjective derived from Sadif with an i after the d. According to
as-Suhaili (vol. II. p. 99), this name may be pronounced Sadif or Sadaf; but, in the
adjective derived from it, the a is employed after the d in order that there may not
be two i (kesras) before the double (final) i (11). It is thus that Namari is formed
from Namir. — There exists a difference of opinion respecting the person who bore
the surname of as-Sadif. Some say that it was Malik, the son of Sahl, the son of
Amr, the son of Kais; and such is also the statement made by al-Kudâi in his Topography. As-Samâni (vol. II. p. 156) continues that genealogy in his Ansâb : " As-
" Sadaf, " says he, " was the son of Sabl Ibn Amr Ibn Kais Ibn Moâwia Ibn Ju-
" sham Ibn Abd Shams Ibn Wâil Ibn al-Ghauth Ibn Haidân Ibn Katan Ibn Arîb Ibn
" Zuhair Ibn Aiman Ibn Humaisa Ibn Himyar Ibn Sabâ." According to ad-Dârakutni (vol. II. p. 239;, the true name of as-Sadif was Sahl al Ibn Domi Ibn Ziâd Ibn
Hadramaut. Al-Hâzimi (vol. III. p. 11) says, in his Kitâb al-Ojâla, which is a treatise on patronymics, that as-Sadif's name was Amr, the son of Malik. God knows
best! Al-Kudâi states that the family of Sadif was counted among those of the tribe

of Kinda. He was called as-Sadif because he turned (*sadafa*) his face away from his
people when the torrent of Arim (12) came down upon them; they assembled for the
purpose of stopping up the breach, but he turned his face from them (*and went*) towards Hadramaut. — Some relate thus the circumstance which procured him this
name : He was so brave that not one of the Arabs was able to overcome him. A certain Ghassanite king sent a man with orders to bring him before him, but he attacked the messenger, slew him and took to flight. A numerous body of horse was sent
after him by the king and, every time that they came up to an Arab tribe and asked
for him, the answer was : " He turned (*sadaf*) away from us and we did not get a
" sight of him." From that time, he was called as-Sadaf. Having then reached
the tribe of Kinda, he settled among them. — Genealogists say that the greater part
of the Sadaf tribe is in Misr and in Maghrib. God knows best ! — We have here digressed from our subject, but what we have said is not devoid of useful information (13).

(1) Abû Said Sahlab Ibn Rhumaima, a native of Old Cairo, studied Koran-reading under Nâb. He died
A. H. 191 (A. D. 806-7). — (*Tabakât al-Kurrâ*, ms. of the Bib. imp. ancien fonds, no 748, fol. 18 verso.)

(2) Abû Dih-ya Moalla Ibn Dihya, a native of Old Cairo, was well acquainted with the Koran-readings, having studied them under Nâfi. — (*Kurrâ*.)

(3) I adopt the reading given by the *Tabakât al-Kurrâ*, fol. 88, and one of the manuscripts of Ibn Khallikân's work.

(4) Abû Im Solaim Ibn Isa Ibn Solaim, a native of Kûfa and a teacher of Koran-reading, was Hamza's
principal disciple and replaced him as a teacher. He learned Traditions from Hamza and Sofyân ath-Thaori.
— (*Kurrâ*, fol. 38.)

(5) Mawâs Ibn Sahl is mentioned in the *Kurrâ*, fol. 88, as a disciple of Yûnus Ibn Abd al-Aala.

(6) In the *Kurrâ*, fol. 88, is a simple mention of this name.

(7) Abû Bakr Mohammed Ibn Ishak Ibn Khuzaima, a native of Naisâpûr, was so highly distinguished for
his knowledge of the Traditions and the Koran-readings that he became the Shaikh al-Islam of Khorâsân. He
left a work on the *Hief* or *defects* which may impair the validity of Traditions. He died A. H. 841 (A. D.
818-930), aged upwards of ninety years. — (*Tabakât al-Huffâz*.)

(8) Al-Jifâr was the name given to that part of the desert which lies between Syria and Egypt.

(9) See vol. I, page 88, note (7).

(10) Narawî and Nadî both mean, o *native of the town of Nadî*, in Khorâsân. The person here indicated
is the celebrated Adfû an-Nadhî, of whom our author has spoken, vol. I, p. 88.

(11) This was to avoid the awkward pronunciation of the word *Sadhfif*.

(12) See vol. II, page 588, and M. Cassain de Perceval's *Essai*, vol. I, page 83.

(13) Our author was probably not aware that Arabic historians knew very imperfectly the ancient history
of their nation ; that many of the genealogies given by them were altered or forged under the first Khalifs,
and that their explanations of the origin of proper names are, most of them, fanciful inventions.

YUNUS IBN MANA.

Abù 'l-Fadl Yûnus Ibn Muhammad Ibn Manà Ibn Mâlik Ibn Muhammad Ibn Saad Ibn Said Ibn Aàsim Ibn Aàid Ibn Kaab Ibn Kais, bore the title of Rida ad-Din (acceptable for piety) and was a native of Arbela. We have spoken of his two sons, Imâd ad-Din Abû Hâmid Muhammad (vol. II. p. 656) and Kamâl ad-Din Abù 'l-Fath Mùsa (vol. III. p. 466). The genealogy given here was found by me in the handwriting of one of our literary men, but I cannot say where he discovered the links which he added to it; all that I knew of it was given in the articles on the two sons. The shaikh Yùnus belonged to a family of Arbela and was born in that city. Having gone to Mosul, he studied jurisprudence there under Abù Abd Allah al-Husain Ibn Nasr al-Kaabi al-Juhani, surnamed Tâj ad-Din and generally known by the appellation of Ibn Khamis (vol. I. p. 442). After hearing that professor dictate the text of most of his works and of the traditional information which he had received, he embarked on the river and went down to Baghdad, where he studied jurisprudence under the shaikh Abù Mansùr Said Ibn Muhammad Ibn Omar, surnamed Ibn al-Bazzâz, who was then chief professor in the Nizâmiya college. After that, he went up by land to Mosul, settled in a neighbouring village and was perfectly well received by the governor of Mosul, Zain ad-Din Abù 'l-Hasan Ali Ibn Bektikin, the father of al-Malik al-Moazzam Muzaffar ad-Din, the sovereign of Arbela (vol. II. p. 535). That emir confided to him the professorship and the administration of the mosque founded by himself and bearing his name. Yûnus, having begun to teach, to act as a mufti (casuist, consulting lawyer) and to hold conferences, drew to his lessons a great number of persons desirous of studying under him and of discussing points of doctrine with his two sons, those of whom we have spoken. He continued to act as a mufti, as a professor and as a chief of conferences till he died. His death took place at Mosul, on Monday, the 6th of Muharram, 576 (2nd June 1180). I heard from a friend of that family, that he died in the year 575, but the shaikh Kamâl ad-Din, that doctor's son, declared that he ceased to live in the year 570, and he must have been better informed on the subject than any one else. Yûnus Ibn Manà was buried in a tomb which he had erected for himself in

the vicinity of Zain ad-Din's mosque. He died in his sixty-eighth year. — We have
spoken of his grandson Sharaf ad-Din Ahmad (vol. I, p. 90), the son of the shaikh
Kamâl ad-Din Mûsa Ibn Yûnus. In a word, that family produced a number of
eminent men who, by their talents, contributed greatly to the instruction of those
who inhabited Arbela and distant countries. Students came to them from Irâk,
Persia and other provinces. May God have mercy on them all! (1) [Yûnus composed
some good poetry of which we give here a passage :

> She visits me once a year, but sometimes the months of the year pass by without our meet-
> ing. Favour and disdain (are shown by her) for no motive whatever; except that her humour
> is like that of Fortune which (sometimes) grants and (often) refuses.]

(1) Here ends the last biographical article in the manuscripts A, B, C, D and E.

IBN MUSAED.

Yûnus Ibn Yûsuf Ibn Musâêd (1), a member of the Mukbarik family (al-Mukha-
riki), which is a branch of the tribe of Shaibân, was the superior (shaikh) of that order of dervishes which is denominated after him the Yûnusiya. He was a man of
great sanctity. I asked a number of his followers the name of his superior and they
replied : " He never had a superior; he was a majdûb." By this word they designate a person (who entered into the devout life) without a master (to guide him);
they call him majdûb (attracted), because he was drawn (by divine grace) into the
path of virtue and righteousness. They often speak of the miraculous manifesta-
tions operated in his favour. The shaikh Muhammad Ibn Ahmad Ibn Obaid told me
that, when he a was a boy, he saw his father Ahmad in company with this holy
man : " We were travelling," said he, " and the shaikh Yûnus was with us. We
" halted, on our journey, at Ain al-Bawâr, the place from which the Bawâr salt is
" brought and which is situated between Sinjâr and Adna. As the road was dan-

"gerous (on account of robbers), none of us could sleep, that night, through fear,
"with the exception of the shaikh Yûnus. When he awoke, I said to him : ' How
"' was it possible for you to sleep?' and he answered : ' By Allah!   I should not
"' have slept had not Ismail, the son of Abraham, come to me and undertaken to
"' lock the door.'   When morning came, we departed, without harm, thanks to
"the merits of the shaikh Yûnus."   Another time, he related as follows : " I was
"with the shaikh Yûnus, in his village, when I resolved on making a journey to
"Nasibîn, and he said to me : ' When you arrive there, buy a shroud for Omm Mu-
"' sâêd.'   She was the mother of his son and then enjoyed good health; so, I asked
"him if there was any thing the matter with her that could render such a purchase
"necessary.   He answered : ' There can be no harm in doing so.'   On my return, I
"found her dead." — Other anecdotes respecting his miraculous gifts and his ec-
stasies were related to me by the same person, from whom also I learned a mawalia
(vol. I. p. 42) which I give here :

> It was I who protected the reserved grounds and who dwelt therein. It was I who cast the
> creatures into the ocean of perplexity. He who wished for a gift from me, it was I who gave
> it; I am a hero not to be injured by the person in whom is assimilation (2).

The same shaikh Muhammad informed me that Yûnus died, A. H. 619 (A. D.
1222-3), in his village, which place bears the name of al-Kunaiya and is situated in
the province of Dârâ.   Kunaiya is the diminutive of kanâ (lance).   His tomb is
a well-known object there and attracts numerous pilgrims.   He was upwards of
ninety years old when he died.

(1) This biographical notice is not to be found in any of our manuscripts.   According to al-Makrizi, in his
Khitat, vol. II, p. 488, Yûnus Ibn Mushid died in the year 719 the Hijra.   If his statement be true, the Khallikân, who died in the year 681, could not have drawn up this notice.   The editor of the Bûlâk edition of
this Biographical dictionary declares in a marginal note that the date given by al-Makrizi is false, and his
assertion is confirmed by the author of the Ghirbâl ex-Zemân, ms. ar. suppl. 786, who places the death of Yûnus
in the year 619.

(2) These verses have no meaning, unless their import be mystical.   In that case, it is God who speaks,
and the reserved grounds are the gardens of Paradise.   Assimilation may perhaps mean being attached to the
world and making one's God of it.

Here ends the work to which I gave the title of *Wafaydt al-Aiydn wa Anbâ Abnâ ez-Zamân*, (*Book of the Deaths of eminent men and history of the sons of the epoch*); praise be to God for his bounty! It was terminated on the 22nd of the latter Jumâda, 672 (3rd Jan. A.D. 1274) in Cairo the well-guarded.—The humble servant, who stands in need of the mercy of God and who is named Ahmad Ibn Muhammad Ibn Ibrahîm Ibn Abi Bakr Ibn Khallikân, he who is the author of the present work, says : I began to compose this book at the epoch mentioned in the preface, and (*I drew it up*) in the form which is there indicated, though my hours were passed in judging lawsuits, in Cairo, and pronouncing sentences in conformity with the divine law. When I came to the article on Yahya Ibn Khâlid Ibn Barmek (*page 113 of this volume*), I was obliged to set out for Syria in the train of his high Lordship and imperial Majesty, the support of the world and of the faith, the sultan of Islamism and of the Moslims, al-Malik ez-Zâbir Abû 'l-Fath Baibars, the colleague of the Commander of the faithful; may God perpetuate his sovereignty and consolidate, by the duration of his reign, the foundations and the pillars of the empire! Our departure from Cairo took place on Sunday, the 7th of Shauwâl, 659 (4th Sept. 1261) and, on Monday, the 7th of Zû 'l-Kaada, the same year (3rd October), we arrived at Damascus. That prince then appointed me to act as chief *kadi* over all the provinces of Syria. My nomination took place on Thursday, the 8th of Zû 'l-Hijja (3rd november) of the same year. Being therefore overwhelmed with business and surrounded by obstacles which hindered the completion of this work, I abstained from continuing and, having left it in the state to which I had brought it, I concluded it by requesting that my numerous occupations might serve me as an excuse for not completing it. I said also that if God granted me time and helped me in my undertaking, I should commence another work containing every requisite information on this branch of science. — At length took place my departure from Syria and my return to Egypt, after residing in Damascus the well-guarded during ten whole years, neither a day more nor a day less : I entered into Damascus on the date just mentioned and I left it on the morning of Thursday, the 8th of Zù 'l-Kaada, 669 (18th June, 1271). On my arrival in Cairo, I met with a number of works which I was desirous of seeing and which, before that, I had not time enough to consult. So, having, at last, *more leisure than the surgeon-barber of Sâbât*, after being *more occupied than the woman with the two bags* (1), I perused those books and extracted from them what I required. Having then undertaken to finish the present work, I terminated it in the form which it now bears; but my intention is still to begin the work which I promised to draw up, in case that God allow me and that he come to my assistance by smoothing the way to its accomplishment. If any well-informed person remark, in examining this book, that it contains faults, he should not hasten to blame me, for I always aimed at being exact, as far as I could judge; and, besides, God has allowed no book to be faultless except his noble Koran. This production of mine is the fruit of efforts made by one whose information is very limited, but who has done all in his power (*to render it correct*). Moreover, no man is obliged to accomplish what exceeds his force, and « far above the « possessors of science is the Being who is all-knowing (*Coran;* sur. XII

verse 76)." As the preface of this book contains my excuses and exposes
my motives for engaging in such an undertaking, I need not repeat these
considerations here.   May the Almighty God spread over our faults the
veil of his indulgence, so ample in its shade, and may he not trouble the
pure source of the favours which he has allowed us to enjoy!   In him do
we place our trust, for he is the excellent guardian (*Coran*; sur. III,
verse 167).

(1) The explanation of these two expressions will be found in Freytag's translation of the *Proverbs of al-
Meidani*, vol. II, p. 797 and vol. I, p. 447.

ADDITIONS AND CORRECTIONS

Page 59, line 14. For *Adwan* read *Adwin*.

P. 110, *line 99*. In some copies the Arabic word is inverted.

P. 161, *line 21*. For *merchand* read *merchant*.

P. 113, *line 19*. Insert the article *a* before *prayer*.

P. 115, *line 10*. Suppress the word *Irak*.

P. 101, *line 15*. For *Qohe* read *Qihhe*.

P. 171, *line 11*. For *Mutarraf* read *Mutarrif*.

P. 191, *lines 10 and 27*. For *wemmen* read *women*.

P. 170, *line 7*. For *misspellet* read *misspelled*.

P. 313, *line 20*. The words *A. H. 262* should have been included within the parentheses

P. 384, *line 15*. Read *Bismillah* here and in the note (2), page 350.

P. 397, *line 8*. For *Ridchi* read *Ridchi*.

P. 466, *line 29*. After the words " God knows best ! " insert the reference to note (16).

P. 591, *line penult.* For *Laith* read *al-Laith*. ,

INDEX TO THE FOURTH AND LAST VOLUME

PART. L — PROPER NAMES.

The names preceded by an asterisk are those of persons or places particularly noticed in this volume. In consulting this list, search for the name or surname by which the person was usually known, and neglect all prefixes, such as Abd, Ibn, etc.

PART. II. — NOTES.

END OF THE FOURTH AND LAST VOLUME.

PARIS — PRINTED BY EDWARD BLOT, RUE BLEUE, 7.

www.ingramcontent.com/pod-product-compliance
Lightning Source LLC
Chambersburg PA
CBHW021931110726
47901CB00003B/794